THE EVOLUTION OF
DIALECTICAL MATERIALISM

THE EVOLUTION OF
DIALECTICAL MATERIALISM

A PHILOSOPHICAL AND
SOCIOLOGICAL ANALYSIS

Z. A. JORDAN

MACMILLAN
London · Melbourne · Toronto

ST MARTIN'S PRESS
New York
1967

MACMILLAN AND COMPANY LIMITED
Little Essex Street London WC 2
also Bombay Calcutta Madras Melbourne

THE MACMILLAN COMPANY OF CANADA LIMITED
70 Bond Street Toronto 2

ST MARTIN'S PRESS INC
175 Fifth Avenue New York NY 10010

Library of Congress catalog card no. 67–19737

PRINTED IN GREAT BRITAIN

Contents

Preface

IT is not the purpose of this study to add another historical account of dialectical materialism to those already available in English and other European languages. Its main task is to trace the origin and development of dialectical materialism from its inception to the present day and to examine critically a certain conception, or rather misconception, as this study intends to show, concerning its nature and content. This misconception was originated in the Soviet Union but has also been accepted by Western exponents of dialectical materialism, as well as by the majority of students of the 'Marxist theory' who concentrate their attention on its economic, social, and political aspects and are only marginally interested in its philosophical foundations.

The common misconception consists in considering dialectical materialism as a single, continuous, and uniform doctrine, conforming to one set of fundamental principles and methodological rules. It is supposed to be based upon the unvarying assumptions first formulated by Marx and Engels, the joint founders of the doctrine, which later were only explained, amplified, and defended by their followers. 'Marxism' is the name customarily given to the tradition of orthodoxy allegedly first established by Marx and Engels, preserved and protected from distortions by Plekhanov and Kautsky, and held to have been codified in its pristine purity by Lenin and Stalin.

'Marxism' is not a name with proper credentials. It is an ambiguous term, having several closely related and interlocking meanings. It is also a vague term, since it is impossible to say to which views it is applicable. Vagueness is different from ambiguity. Each meaning of an ambiguous expression may have a sharply defined extension, a set of objects which it denotes. When a term is vague, its field of application is blurred or undefined. But an expression may be both ambiguous and vague, and 'Marxism' is an instance of this. What it is presumed to designate is merely a figment of the imagination and what it does denote is a wide and vaguely circumscribed collection of views, often incompatible with each other.

ix

'Marxism' can be used to refer to practically anything you choose and is thus a confusing or meaningless term.

That dialectical materialism was formulated once and for all in its final and perfect form by Marx and Engels is an idea deeply embedded in Soviet philosophy. While Lenin and Stalin are duly credited with having enriched many parts of the 'Marxist theory', no such merits are ascribed to them in matters concerning dialectical materialism. They are praised only for having safeguarded the 'theoretical foundations of Marxism', that is, dialectical and historical materialism, from the motley crowd of revisionists, for having restored the true doctrine of Marx and Engels and preserved it for posterity. Their reputation as theorists is based upon the fact that having mastered these 'theoretical foundations' they were able to apply the basic principles of dialectical materialism to the new problems arising in 'the epoch of imperialism and proletarian revolution', and advance the 'Marxist theory' in certain respects, such as the economic and social doctrines, the competition for world markets, class struggle, socialist construction, or the strategy and tactics of the proletariat.

The Western exponents accept, implicitly or explicitly, the assumption of Soviet philosophy that dialectical materialism is a single doctrine, coherent and fixed in its content. Unlike Benedetto Croce or Georges Sorel, who emphasized the multiplicity of interpretations to which Marx's works lend themselves, they feel that it is right to recognize the existence of Marxism as a uniform philosophic tradition. If they discern any differences of opinion among its supporters, they regard these as unimportant and insubstantial. Consequently, what they examine as dialectical materialism is a synthetic creation of their own invention, compounded of the views of Marx, Engels, Lenin, and Stalin in various more or less arbitrary combinations. The doctrine of dialectical materialism constructed from fragments extracted from different authors is supposed to reflect faithfully the original beliefs of those credited with its formulation as well as the views of those classified as dialectical materialists in general.

The assumption common to the Soviet and Western exponents of dialectical materialism is clearly untenable. First of all, the traditional and practically universally accepted view that Marx and Engels were the joint founders of dialectical materialism is not supported by the available evidence; it is to Engels alone that its authorship should be credited (this fact is recognized by some leading historians and analysts of dialectical materialism, for instance by J. M. Bocheński, who, however, seems to ignore its implications). Furthermore, there are numerous and important differences between Engels on the one hand, and Lenin and Stalin on the other, in their respective interpretations of dialectical materialism which, consequently, cannot be treated as a single doctrine. It is almost a commonplace to observe that to expound the views of an influential and controversial thinker is to develop them in some definite direction, and the views of Marx are no exception to this rule. For instance, *Capital* has been described at one time or another as an economic treatise, a critique of capitalism, a book of sociology and social history, or a study concerned with the philosophy of history. The difficulty of deciding the dispute among these incompatible claims is child's play compared with tracking down Marx's views concerning the nature of reality and the significant traits of the universe. To maintain, under these circumstances, that there is an apostolic succession, to use H. B. Acton's expression, leading from Marx and Engels through Lenin and Stalin to some of their successors today, is to recognize certain political and ideological realities, not a distinctive trend of philosophical thought. Rather than being a fixed doctrine, dialectical materialism has varied in the form and content of its successive formulations and it has its own history of development. To follow this process, to analyse the changes in the conceptual framework of dialectical materialism, and to inquire into the causes responsible for them, is the main task of this study.

Marx and Engels held an instrumentalist conception of knowledge; they valued theoretical thinking as a means of social reconstruction rather than for its consistency and truth. Their followers went even further and showed little inclination to theorize unless their inquiry had historical, social, or political significance. The 'Marxists', commented Georges Sorel, have indulged in so many plays of fantasy that serious people have been disinclined to consider them authoritative interpreters of Marx. What Sorel described as fantasy is the product of instrumental, goal-oriented, and ideological thinking decked out in theoretical terms. If the successive formulations of dialectical materialism from Engels to Stalin are carefully differentiated, it becomes possible to explain its changes and to discover the ideological roots and purposes of its revisions. This should become increasingly clear as the study proceeds and the thread of transformations is gradually unravelled.

The synthetic doctrine of dialectical materialism known from its Soviet and Western expositions, the doctrine compounded from the bits and pieces of different provenances, not only obliterates certain stages of its development but also tends to underestimate the ideological significance of the whole construction or of the particular beliefs included in it. Moreover, the way in which the different elements of dialectical materialism are combined into a single whole is itself determined, at least in some cases and in some respects, by the ideological idiosyncrasy of the mind which makes the selection and carries out the construction. Everybody familiar with the works of Marx is probably aware of the fact that it is not always easy to understand him dispassionately. Much of what has been written about Marx reveals the writer's ideological or philosophical affiliation and the conformity to the laws of selective perception. These laws are operative in the reduction to a smallest common denominator of the views supposedly held by all dialectical materialists and in the selection of the component parts regarded as essential for a complete statement of dialectical materialism.

Finally, the analytic approach to dialectical materialism as opposed to the synthetic procedure, followed by a logical analysis of historically ascertained facts, enables us to deal effectively with certain stereotypes which are bound to accumulate when the views of a thinker or group of thinkers are much discussed, for one reason or another, for a long time, and are more often reproduced from second-hand sources than studied in the original. There are many fixed views about Marx, which have been transformed into self-evident truths by frequent repetitions. These require re-examination and revision.

The most baleful is the firmly held and long-established belief that the views of Marx and Engels are identical. To say that Marx and Engels had, as it were, a twin mind is to assume something extremely improbable and incompatible with the evidence available. The presupposition of identity is fateful for the interpretation of the philosophy of Marx, for the correct understanding of Engels's account of what Marx's and his own views were, and for the placing of the further stages of development of dialectical materialism in their proper perspective.

According to another stereotype, Marx 'converted dialectical idealism into dialectical materialism' or, as it is more often put, the philosophy of Marx is Hegelianism inverted. The first of these interpretations is clearly unsound, for it presupposes what should first be proved, namely, that Marx was a dialectical materialist in Engels's sense. But also the second statement surprises rather than enlightens. One cannot really invert a philosophical doctrine. Therefore, to speak of the inversion of the Hegelian philosophy allegedly accomplished by Marx is to make use of a metaphor which no one up to now has tried to translate into plain language. The metaphoric description of the philosophy of Marx as Hegelianism inverted conceals more than it reveals, because it prevents us from discovering the distinctive characteristics of the Marxian view of the world.

To give the final example, Marx is often described as a thinker who never emancipated himself from the influence of Hegel, while Engels is presented as an empirically-minded philosophical writer sympathetic to positivism and scientifically oriented philosophy. In fact, as the study will show on the basis of the re-examined source material, the two friends should be described exactly the other way round.

Before proceeding *in medias res* and presenting in detail what the Preface has touched upon, one more explanation is necessary. Dialectical materialism is usually understood to include a theory of knowledge, a methodology which embraces both logic and methodology of science, and a metaphysics or rather a cosmology, for the metaphysics of materialism cannot really be differentiated from its cosmology. The present study deals with the second and third parts of dialectical materialism and leaves the first out of account. The theory of knowledge of dialectical materialism is Lenin's specific contribution to this doctrine. Moreover, it has exercised little if any influence upon the main body of beliefs of which it is supposed to be a part, being an adventitious appendage of a deductive metaphysics rather than its epistemological foundation. The inclusion of the theory of knowledge would extend the scope of this study without yielding any significant gains in the achievement of its main objective. What the author wished to say on this subject, he has said elsewhere.*

Z. A. J.

University of Reading,
March 1966

* See Jordan, *PHI*, chaps. 16 and 17.

Acknowledgements

MUCH of the work involved in writing this book was accomplished during the period of a fellowship awarded me, for 1962-3 and the first half of 1963-4, by the Russian Institute, Columbia University. I am deeply grateful to the Institute for the leisure to study and write, and to its Director and members for help and encouragement. My work on this book was greatly aided by the stimulating discussions which I have enjoyed during my stay at Columbia University.

The first six sections of Chapter VII were published in *Slavic Review*, Columbia University. I wish to thank its Editor for his permission to make further use of this material in this book.

Z. A. J.

Abbreviations*

AD	Engels, *Anti-Dühring (Herrn Eugen Dührings Umwälzung der Wissenschaft)*.
Cours	Comte, *Cours de philosophie positive.*
CPE	Marx, *A Contribution to the Critique of Political Economy.*
CSF	Marx, *The Class Struggles in France, 1848 to 1850.*
CW	Lenin, *Collected Works.*
CWC	Engels, *The Condition of the Working Class in England.*
CWF	Marx, *The Civil War in France.*
DHM	Stalin, *Dialectical and Historical Materialism.*
DM	Wetter, *Dialectical Materialism.*
DMH	Plekhanov, *The Development of the Monist View of History.*
DN	Engels, *Dialectics of Nature.*
EBLB	Marx, *The Eighteenth Brumaire of Louis Bonaparte.*
EHM	Plekhanov, *Essays in the History of Materialism.*
EL	Lenin, *The Essentials of Lenin.*
EPHS	Hegel, *The Encyclopaedia of the Philosophical Sciences.*
EPS	Stalin, *Economic Problems of Socialism in the USSR.*
FML	Kuusinen *et al., Fundamentals of Marxism–Leninism.*
FNLF	Plekhanov, Foreword to the first edition (from the translator) and Plekhanov's *Notes* to Engels's book *Ludwig Feuerbach and the End of Classical German Philosophy.*
FPM	Plekhanov, *Fundamental Problems of Marxism.*
GI	Marx–Engels, *The German Ideology.*
GMPH	Konstantinov *et al., Grundlagen der marxistischen Philosophie.*
GPHZ	Feuerbach, *Grundsätze der Philosophie der Zukunft.*
HCL	Engels, *On the History of the Communist League.*
HF	Marx–Engels, *The Holy Family.*
HQ	Engels, *The Housing Question.*
KHR	Marx, *Zur Kritik der hegelschen Rechtsphilosophie. Einleitung.*
KM	Engels, *Karl Marx.*
KMX	Lenin, *Karl Marx.*
KSF	Rozental' and Yudin, *Krótki słownik filozoficzny (Short Philosophical Dictionary).*
LF	Engels, *Ludwig Feuerbach and the End of Classical German Philosophy.*
MCP	Marx–Engels, *Manifesto of the Communist Party.*
MCPE	Engels, *Karl Marx: A Contribution to the Critique of Political Economy.*
MEC	Lenin, *Materialism and Empirio-Criticism.*

* For a fuller description of the abbreviated book titles see Bibliography, p. 459.

xv

MEGA	Marx–Engels, *Gesamtausgabe.*
MEM	Lenin, *Marx–Engels–Marxism.*
MPL	Stalin, *Marxism and Problems of Linguistics.*
OD	Plekhanov, *Our Differences.*
OS	Popper, *The Open Society and Its Enemies.*
PHH	Hegel, *The Philosophy of History.*
PHI	Jordan, *Philosophy and Ideology.*
PHM	Hegel, *The Phenomenology of Mind.*
PHN	Lenin, *Philosophical Notebooks.*
PHR	Hegel, *The Philosophy of Right.*
PPH	Marx, *The Poverty of Philosophy.*
PWG	Engels, *The Peasant War in Germany.*
SAHD	Plekhanov, *For the Sixtieth Anniversary of Hegel's Death.*
SDM	Bocheński, *Der sowjetrussische dialektische Materialismus.*
SGM	Engels, *Speech at the Graveside of Karl Marx.*
SL	Hegel, *Science of Logic.*
SPP	Comte, *Système de politique positive* (1822).
SPS	Plekhanov, *Socialism and the Political Struggle.*
SPW	Plekhanov, *Selected Philosophical Works.*
SUS	Engels, *Socialism: Utopian and Scientific.*
SW	Marx–Engels, *Selected Works.*
TF	Marx, *Theses on Feuerbach.*
VTRPH	Feuerbach, *Vorläufige Thesen zur Reform der Philosophie.*
WDLS	Feuerbach, *Wider dem Dualismus von Leib und Seele, Fleisch und Geist.*
WFPA	Lenin, *What the 'Friends of the People' Are.*
WIBD	Lenin, *What Is To Be Done?*
WLC	Marx, *Wage Labour and Capital.*
WPP	Marx, *Wages, Price and Profit.*

PART ONE

THE PHILOSOPHICAL SOURCES

OF

DIALECTICAL MATERIALISM

I

The Origins of Dialectical Materialism

In the history of Marxian thought the publication of *Anti-Dühring* (*Herrn Eugen Dührings Umwälzung der Wissenschaft*) turned out to be an epoch-making event. Originally planned as a polemical tract with a narrowly defined objective of no more than transitory importance,[1] *Anti-Dühring* gained the distinction of being the canonical statement of the doctrine which came to be known as dialectical materialism and acquired great renown all over the world. Engels is the founder of dialectical materialism but he never used its now familiar name, calling it simply 'modern materialism'. While he saw its modernity in being dialectical,[2] that is, in the application of dialectics to the phenomena of nature, he left it to Plekhanov and Lenin to coin the new term 'dialectical materialism'.[3]

Although the term 'dialectical materialism' is of later origin, there is no doubt that the oldest and most authoritative exposition of the doctrine itself is to be found in *Anti-Dühring*. *Dialectics of Nature*, published posthumously only in 1925, is another important source of our knowledge about dialectical materialism. But while *Anti-Dühring* gives a text fully approved and twice revised by Engels himself, *Dialectics of Nature* is only a collection of fragments, notes, and other materials for private use, accumulated by Engels in the years 1873–83 in preparation for a book which he never managed to complete.[4] Therefore, it is *Anti-Dühring* rather than *Dialectics of Nature* that should be regarded as Engels's fully considered formulation of dialectical materialism. The commonly accepted view that Engels wrote *Anti-Dühring* in close collaboration with Marx has considerably enhanced its authority and reputation.

I. THE SIGNIFICANCE OF ANTI-DÜHRING

In the spring of 1876, in response to the pressing demands of his political friends in Germany,[5] Engels finally decided to settle

3

accounts with Eugen Dühring (1833–1921), Marx's detractor and short-lived rival for the intellectual leadership within the German Social Democratic Party. While feeling duty-bound to face Dühring's challenge, Engels was also disgruntled and in private complained to Marx of having to 'go after the scalp of the boring Eugen Dühring'.[6]

In the Preface to the first edition of *Anti-Dühring* Engels emphasized that his book was by no means the fruit of any 'inner urge'. He undertook the task of refuting Dühring's 'new socialist theory' only because it was imperative to prevent sectarian quarrels and splits from developing within the Party. The popularity of Dühring was symptomatic of the revival of utopian socialism which replaced the 'materialistic basis' of socialism 'by modern mythology with its goddesses of Justice, Liberty, Equality, and Fraternity'.[7] Since Marx and he had tried to emancipate the German workers from sentimentality and socialistic day-dreams for decades, they could not allow some 'muddleheads' to influence the leaders of German socialism with their 'silly, stale, and reactionary' utopianism. However, he undertook the polemical task reluctantly, for Dühring was not a serious opponent and on his account he was forced to neglect more important work. Although Engels thought that his exposure of Herr Dühring's 'banalities' and 'sublime nonsense', necessary as it appeared at that time, would soon become useless and fall into oblivion, two more editions of *Anti-Dühring* were published before Engels died in 1895 and many more after that date.[8]

Engels clearly had no inkling that his polemical examination of Dühring's views would make history. The opponents of Engels in his dispute with Dühring were no more perspicacious. When *Anti-Dühring* first began appearing in *Vorwärts* by instalments, some of its readers described it as 'completely without interest' and the annual congress of the German Social Democratic Party, held in Gotha in May 1877, nearly decided to suppress it altogether. *Anti-Dühring* was saved from being withdrawn from further publication by the transfer from the main columns to a theoretical supplement of *Vorwärts*.[9]

From its first publication *Anti-Dühring* gained the reputation of being, next to *The Communist Manifesto*, the most successful work that came — as it has been believed — from the pen of Marx and Engels. Moreover, it is widely accepted that no book except *Capital* has done as much as *Anti-Dühring* for the dissemination of Marxian thought. Antonio Labriola called it 'the most accomplished' and 'the un-excelled book in the literature of socialism'.[10] According to Lenin, *Anti-Dühring* 'is a wonderfully rich and instructive book'.[11] For Plekhanov the first part of *Anti-Dühring* was the main and the most authoritative source from which the philosophical views of Marx and Engels could be learnt.[12] Karl Kautsky conceded that *Capital* was an altogether more powerful book but added that 'only owing to *Anti-Dühring* did we learn to read and understand *Capital* the right way'.[13] As Engels himself observed, *Anti-Dühring* provided the most detailed account of historical materialism;[14] it has remained, ever since, one of the most authoritative. Few people, if any, who are interested in the views of Marx and Engels would disagree with Bertrand Russell's opinion that the clearest statements of the materialist conception of history are to be found in *Anti-Dühring*.

The passage of time has confirmed these impressions and views about *Anti-Dühring*. As his biographer Gustav Mayer observed, what Engels considered as a thankless task turned out to be 'the decisive blow for the conversion of Continental social democracy to Marxism'. In *Anti-Dühring* the original views of Marx and Engels were revealed for the first time in simple and lucid language to a whole generation of social democratic leaders, writers, and thinkers, to men like Bebel, Bernstein, and Kautsky in Germany, Plekhanov and P. B. Axelrod in Russia, Victor Adler in Austria, Labriola and Turati in Italy. Only upon the publication of *Anti-Dühring* 'were a real Marxian school and a real Marxian tradition created on the Continent of Europe'.[15] Furthermore, at the suggestion of Paul Lafargue, Marx's son-in-law, Engels extracted three chapters, the most relevant and free from polemics, from *Anti-Dühring*, which Lafargue translated into French and published in *La Revue Socialiste* and under separate cover in 1880. This pamphlet, known in its English version under the title *Socialism: Utopian and Scientific*, caused, to Engels's delight, a 'real revolution in the heads of the French'.[16] It was translated during its author's lifetime into ten languages and became as famous and widely read as *The Communist Manifesto*. While the circumstances to which *Anti-Dühring* owes its existence have long been forgotten, the book has not lost its signifi-cance many years after its publication, but continues to be read and, rightly or wrongly, is a recognized source of knowledge of Marxian theories.

2. THE PREVAILING VIEW ON THE INTELLECTUAL
PARTNERSHIP OF MARX AND ENGELS

Dialectical materialism as formulated in *Anti-Dühring* has been traditionally regarded as the common product and property of Marx and Engels.[17]   Some contemporary writers go even further and attribute dialectical materialism to Marx exclusively.   According to G. A. Wetter, Marx may 'be considered as the founder of dialectical materialism'.[18]   In the opinion of Henri Lefebvre, the extension of *la dialectique concrète à la nature* was accomplished by Marx and only followed by Engels under Marx's close supervision and approval.[19] While eschewing this extreme point of view, others firmly dismissed as groundless the idea that Marx and Engels could differ in their views concerning the problems of the philosophy of nature.[20]

The only justification of the traditional belief that *Anti-Dühring* represents not only Engels's but also Marx's *Naturphilosophie* comes from Engels himself.

> I must note in passing that inasmuch as the mode of outlook expounded in this book was founded and developed in far greater measure by Marx, and only in an insignificant degree by myself, it was understood between us that this exposition of mine should not be issued without his knowledge.   I read the whole manuscript to him before it was printed and the tenth chapter of the part of economics (*From the Critical History*) was written by Marx. . . . As a matter of fact, we had always been accustomed to helping each other out in special subjects.[21]

It is easy to understand why Engels's account has been accepted uncritically by practically everybody.   Engels's statement in *Anti-Dühring* merely brought out with explicit reference to a particular issue what people have always felt to have been the case in general, namely, that the views of Marx and Engels were without exception absolutely the same.

Franz Mehring emphasized the identity of thought and intellectual development of Marx and Engels and Gustav Mayer followed in his footsteps.[22]   Heinrich Cunow was confident that Engels wrote nothing without the approval of Marx, who was even in the habit of seeing the proof sheets of what Engels was about to publish.[23] M. M. Bober, an American scholar, wrote that 'the two friends thought and worked together and it would be impossible to dissever the thoughts of one from those of the other. Even if the task were possible, it is doubtful whether it would yield fruitful results.'[24] Both friends and foes, and among the former, persons as different as Karl Kautsky, Plekhanov, Lenin, Karl Vorländer, or Sir Isaiah Berlin are in full agreement that, as Kautsky put it, 'the totality of Marx's and Engels' literary production constitutes a spiritual union (*eine geistige Einheit*)'.[25] According to Vorländer, from 1845 [26] Engels's philosophical development was interlinked in every respect with that of Marx and they could no longer be differentiated. Marx's philosophical views may be inferred from those of Engels and what Engels said about his friend's contribution and assistance behind the scene is inherently reliable.[27] This must also have been the belief of Lenin, who in his essay *Karl Marx* drew almost exclusively upon the works of Engels to outline Marx's conception of materialism and dialectics. R. N. Carew Hunt described *Anti-Dühring* in Lenin's manner as 'the best general exposition' of Marx's philosophical views,[28] and Sir Isaiah Berlin went even further, for he claimed that Engels 'understood his friend's new, only half articulated ideas sometimes better than he understood them himself'.[29] It is clear from this wide range of opinions that according to the common implicitly or explicitly accepted assumptions one cannot and should not differentiate the views of Marx from those of Engels, for those views were perfectly identical. The two friends were intellectually twin brothers whose achievements constitute a living unity.

There is no reason to dispute the fact that during Marx's lifetime Engels, with his knack of writing quickly and clearly and with his talent for popular exposition, often interpreted Marx's main doctrines. It is right to emphasize that frequently it was owing to Engels that others first came to understand how Marx viewed the course of history and what inferences he drew from his interpretations. After Marx's death the authority of Engels, Marx's lifelong friend and editor of his manuscripts, increased enormously. Engels's likeable character, his admirable modesty and humanity, his unswerving loyalty to Marx, his intellectual honesty and common sense, implicitly induced trust and confidence in his testimony. He considered himself and was recognized by others as the faithful and rightful guardian of Marx's original thought. This does not necessarily provide the guarantee that Marx's thought is to be found authentically in Engels's writings. The fact that Engels was the recognized interpreter of Marx's system and that he was also a writer in his own right prompts the re-examination of the whole question concerning Engels's intellectual relationship to Marx.

3. ENGELS'S TRADITION IN THE INTERPRETATION OF MARX

It was Sidney Hook who in the early thirties challenged the accepted opinion that from the beginning of their personal, intellectual, and literary friendship the views of Marx and Engels were identical. Considering the indisputable fact that they were minds of a different order, the alleged identity of views is highly implausible. In a letter to J. P. Becker, Engels frankly confessed that 'in Marx's lifetime I played second fiddle'.[30] He wrote to Franz Mehring with his unfailing and also self-revealing modesty that Marx was a man with a 'more rapid *coup d'œil* and wider vision' than himself. If after Marx's death he was given more credit than he deserved, 'history will set all this right in the end'. Engels felt sure that:

> What Marx accomplished, I would not have achieved. Marx stood higher, saw further, and took a wider and quicker view than all the rest of us. Marx was a genius, we others were at best talented.[31]

Engels never tired of emphasizing that it was owing to Marx alone that 'socialism became a science'. Marx made the two great discoveries, namely, he revealed the secrets of capitalist production in his theory of surplus-value and formulated the materialist conception of history. Although the second of these discoveries was attributed to both Marx and Engels, Engels claimed for himself 'only a very insignificant share' and publicly and consistently discounted any suggestions to the contrary. The greater part of its leading basic principles in the realm of economics and history and their final trenchant formulations belonged to Marx; he limited his own share to their elaboration and application. Similarly, *The Condition of the Working Class in England* represented only one phase of the embryonic evolution of modern socialism which was 'since [then] fully developed as a science, chiefly and almost exclusively through the efforts of Marx'. Notwithstanding Marx's appreciative references to *The Condition of the Working Class in England* and *Outlines of a Critique of Political Economy* Engels held unflinchingly to the position that 'what I contributed . . . Marx could very well have done without me'.[32]

Engels's self-effacement may have been exaggerated and was actually excessive. That Engels was Marx's intellectual inferior is a fact, however, of which not only Engels himself was aware but which was also recognized by others, including some of the greatest admirers of Engels.[33] On the other hand, there is no reason to believe that because Engels had neither the inventive genius nor the deep historical and social insight of Marx, they were divided by a gulf of important differences of opinion. On the whole, it is enough to assume, as Hook did, that Engels gave a characteristic twist to the doctrine of Marx.[34]

The emphasis given by Engels to Marxian thought consists in viewing it as a monistic system concerned with the ultimate constituents and laws of the universe rather than as an application of a unified method. Thus, for instance, Engels gave final currency to the belief that *Capital* was an exposition of a system of political economy, and not a critical, sociological, and historical analysis of a particular socio-economic formation, undertaken from the standpoint of the class-conscious proletariat of Western Europe and, above all, *eine Streitschrift*, as Eduard Bernstein put it. In philosophy, a similar shift was accomplished, for Marx, who, after his break with Hegel, was uninterested in academic metaphysics and the theory of knowledge, was presented by Engels as a supporter of dialectical materialism and naïve realism. But Marx did not embrace Engels's modern materialism; neither did he accept Engels's theory about sensations being images or copies of the objects of the external world. These doctrines are incompatible with the views to be found in Marx's works, with his 'naturalistic activism' and the conception of sensations as 'forms of practical, sensory activity'.[35]

If Engels had never published *Anti-Dühring*, and this might easily have happened considering the circumstances of its publication, nobody would have regarded Marx as a dialectical materialist in Engels's sense. Marx's own works do not contain the basic assumptions of dialectical materialism and do not justify the application of this label to their author. As has been mentioned earlier, apart from Engels's account in the Preface to the second edition of *Anti-Dühring*, which was written and published after Marx's death, there is no other evidence that Marx dissociated 'history' from 'nature' or differentiated between 'dialectical' and 'historical' materialism and regarded the former as logically prior to the latter.

Marx did not disavow the responsibility for the views expounded by Engels, but he need not have seen any necessity for doing so ; he might have felt that there was no danger of a work of Engels being construed as an exposition of his own philosophical beliefs.   In the Preface to the first edition of *Anti-Dühring*, published in Marx's life-time, Engels said that the criticism of Dühring's philosophy gave him the opportunity to set forth 'my views on controversial issues which are today of a quite general scientific and practical interest'.[36] He suggested nowhere that what he wrote committed Marx in any way.   Quite a different problem is the question as to what was Marx's opinion about Engels's peculiar combination of science and speculative philosophy, and the most plausible answer is that Marx did not trouble to make up his mind about it.   At that time Marx was entirely engrossed in his own work, above all in the completion of the remaining volumes of *Capital*, which increasingly prevented him from becoming interested in matters unrelated to his main task.

In 1873 Marx's health began deteriorating seriously and there was constant fear that he might suffer a stroke.   Although Marx tem-porarily rallied his ebbing strength, thanks to an extended medical treatment, annual visits to the seaside and Karlsbad, a complete recovery was never achieved.   Having completed the second edition of the first volume of *Capital* (1872) and the editing of its French translation (1875), he kept up his vast correspondence but wrote practically nothing apart from short articles.   In 1878, that is, the year of the first publication of *Anti-Dühring*, Marx suffered a relapse of bad health and was able to do no more work, even on *Capital* (the last revisions and additions incorporated in the second volume of *Capital* date from 1878).   About the same time the anxiety con-cerning his wife, who was suffering from cancer, began in earnest. Frau Marx died in December 1881 and, as Engels said, on the day of her death 'the Moor also died'.[37]   One year later (January 1883) Marx suffered the second painful blow, the sudden death of his eldest daughter Jenny Longuet.

There were, therefore, ample reasons why Marx should have showed little interest in what Engels was doing, especially since at first they both regarded a reply to Dühring as a task too unimportant to be bothered about. There is really no need to explain why Marx allegedly acquiesced in the attribution of Engels's doctrine to him, for no such attribution was actually made during his lifetime. Marx was probably entirely unaware, and he had every right to be so, of the implications which were to be drawn from *Anti-Dühring* with respect to his own philosophical beliefs.

The fully developed division of the 'theory of Marxism' into dialectical materialism (providing the most general assumptions and procedures) and historical materialism (based on dialectical materialism and applying its laws to the study of society and history) can be found only in Marxism–Leninism, that is, in Lenin's interpretation of the doctrine attributed by him to Marx and Engels. But many basic Leninist ideas are contained in their rudimentary form in *Anti-Dühring* or are based upon the views of Engels expounded in this work. In particular, contrary to the views of some exponents, Engels tried to deduce dialectics of society from dialectics of nature and to provide the communist world outlook with a *Naturphilosophie*.[38] In the Preface to the second edition of *Anti-Dühring* Engels confessed that his work contained more than he originally intended to say. He realized *post factum* that in his examination and refutation of Dühring's doctrine his 'negative criticism became positive' and that 'the polemic was transformed into a more or less connected exposition of . . . the communist world outlook'. This comprehensive system which, in his opinion, was the common property of Marx and himself, comprised the views presented to the world in *The Poverty of Philosophy*, *The Communist Manifesto*, and *Capital* as well as some 'positive conceptions' developed alongside the polemic against the philosophy of Dühring.[39] The latter ranged over a vast area of subjects, both practical and scientific, and dealt, to use Engels's own words, 'with everything under the sun and with some others as well'. As he frankly conceded, he followed Dühring into realms where at best he could only 'claim to be a dilettante' and had 'to exercise great caution'.[40] Engels was aware that he went further than he originally planned. He knew that he overreached himself and was uneasy about it, although later his self-criticism gave way to the pleasure which the success of *Anti-Dühring* aroused in the author's breast.

Notwithstanding Engels's original uneasiness, *Anti-Dühring* became the main source of knowledge about 'the philosophy of Marx and Engels'. Unintentionally and somewhat unknowingly Engels established the tradition which ascribed to Marx a coherent monistic system of materialistic metaphysics in the accepted sense of this term, comprising a philosophy of nature, a theory of society, and a view of history, all three derived from a common set of first principles and logically supporting each other. *Anti-Dühring* is the original and most important source of this tradition and, in particular, of the false belief that the materialist conception of history is closely connected with or deducible from philosophic materialism.

It was in this way that at the turn of the century *Anti-Dühring* was read by the first generation of students and followers of Marx. 'As its name already shows,' wrote Bernstein, 'the materialistic conception of history closely hangs together with a materialist world outlook.' [41] The same view was voiced by Ludwig Woltmann, who claimed that 'historical materialism is only a special application of dialectical materialism to the history of mankind, for history itself should be conceived as a segment of the universal natural process (*Naturprozess*)'.[42] Plekhanov conceded that the 'general public' often used the term 'Marxism' to refer to historical materialism, but he asserted that this was not correct and that historical materialism cannot be separated from 'philosophical materialism' to be found 'fairly fully set forth, although in a polemical form, in the first part of Engels's book *Herrn Eugen Dührings Umwälzung der Wissenschaft*'.[43] It has rightly been said that the doctrine of Marxism, as understood by Plekhanov, came into being in the period separating the death of Marx from that of Engels.[44] Engels's philosophy was taken to be a faithful presentation of Marx's original views and acquired the status of Marxian orthodoxy.

Engels's interpretation of Marx, later codified by Lenin and Stalin into the canonical doctrine of so-called Marxism or Marxism–Leninism, was, however, subject to some important revisions. In the early twenties Georg Lukács maintained that when Engels extended Marxian dialectics outside the realm of history and society, he misunderstood Marx entirely.[45] About the same time Karl Korsch argued that Marx's historical materialism did not need the support of philosophical materialism or even of the materialism expounded by Engels in *Anti-Dühring*.[46] Similarly, a few years later Sidney Hook claimed that Marx did not conceive of dialectical materialism as a doctrine of nature, distinct from a theory of society and history, for the attempt to apply the dialectics to nature was incompatible with his basic position.[47] Sidney Hook was supported by

Bertrand Russell and, more recently, by a number of other scholars and historians.[48] If the view of these writers is essentially correct and *Anti-Dühring* does not provide a substantially true account of Marx's philosophy, the question arises as to how Marx's philosophic position should be described.

4. THE NATURALISM OF MARX AND THE DIALECTICAL MATERIALISM OF ENGELS

Marx believed that man is an object of nature ; that his mind or soul is not a supernatural entity ; that there is an essential unity of mind and body ; and that human behaviour can be explained by means of empirical hypotheses to be tested by the procedure accepted in natural science. But these beliefs do not make of Marx a dialectical materialist, nor even a materialist in the usual sense of the word unless naturalism and materialism are considered identical.

Naturalism is usually defined as the view which regards mind as part of nature and demands that it should be investigated by the same method as that applied to other parts of nature. This brief statement is not incorrect but it does not do justice to all essential beliefs of naturalism and might lead to the confusion of materialism and naturalism.

Naturalism comprises a cosmological and methodological component.[49] As a cosmological doctrine, naturalism claims the self-sufficiency of nature, rejects the primacy of mind, accepts ontological pluralism, and emphasizes the basic significance of the categories of time, space, and causality for the knowledge of the world. As a methodological conception, naturalism asserts that we can have reliable knowledge only of such objects as can be investigated by scientific method. Scientific method is not identified with the procedures applied in physics or biology, but with certain accredited ways or standard procedures of acquiring knowledge, such as observation, experiment, and inference, of which different sciences make use in different ways, determined by the subject-matter and technical means available. As a rule, a naturalist combines the methodological conception of naturalism with some naturalistic cosmological principles which expose him to the objection of being a concealed materialist. Marx has constantly been described as a materialist, a name which he himself did not renounce and did not wish to disclaim, and contemporary naturalism is often criticized for disguising its true nature by using a misleading name.[50]

The methodological premises of naturalism imply that human behaviour can be adequately explained in terms of causal laws of the same sort as those which govern the conjunction and sequence of natural phenomena, without resorting to the teleological order of events, to ideals, values, spirit, or normative standards. To accept the existence of only such objects as can be studied by scientific method does not necessarily imply metaphysical materialism. It is important to realize this distinction although it was not clearly made and applied in the times of Marx; Marx himself used 'materialism' and 'naturalism' synonymously, perhaps because he defined materialism as the opposite of Hegelian spiritualism, that is, as the view which denies the independent existence of mind without matter.

While materialism, in some sense of the term, may be a true doctrine, it can never be known to be true. On the other hand, while materialism may be false, it can never be disproved. Since naturalism is compatible with both the truth and falsehood of materialism, naturalism cannot imply materialism and still less be identical with it, as some philosophers seem to believe. Naturalism is not a metaphysical but rather an epistemological and methodological doctrine. It is a systematic reflection upon the procedures applied in the acquisition of knowledge about the world and not a system of beliefs concerning the ultimate constituents of the world.

If the naturalism of Marx should be differentiated from the dialectical materialism of Engels, the problem arises as to how the latter emerged from the former. To answer this question, the problem has first to be extended. Naturalism is closely related to positivism and clearly opposed to metaphysics or speculative philosophy. To regard Marx as a naturalist philosopher seems to militate, therefore, against the accepted view of Marx being deeply affected by Hegel and sharply critical of Comte and positivism. On the other hand, dialectical materialism is hostile to positivism and favourably disposed to speculative philosophy. This particular combination of intellectual attitudes appears in turn to be incompatible with the view that Engels is the founder of dialectical materialism, for he is, or is widely considered to be, a positivist rather than a Hegelian.

In order to disentangle this intricate cluster of conflicting influences and intellectual loyalties, the impact of Hegelianism and

French positivism upon Marx and Engels has to be re-examined. There is much evidence that in their formative years both Marx and Engels were affected by these two schools of thought, which at that time were the major centres of philosophical attraction. While the examination of the relation of Marx and Engels to Hegelianism and positivism has an inherent interest of its own, it also affords an occasion for defining and explaining the important differences in their respective philosophical positions. It may also help towards an understanding of how dialectical materialism, a conception essentially alien to the philosophy of Marx, emerged from and replaced the naturalism of Marx.

Historically, the incompatibility of naturalism and positivism on the one hand and Hegelianism on the other is not as unquestionable as it might appear. F. A. Hayek introduced the term 'Hegelian positivism' to denote a trend among those thinkers — Ernest Renan and Hippolyte Taine in France, Marx and Engels in Germany, Benedetto Croce in Italy, John Dewey in the United States — who succeeded in combining the ideas derived from Hegel and Comte.[51] 'Hegelian positivism' is an apt expression to designate Engels's dialectical materialism. As presented in *Anti-Dühring*, dialectical materialism combines the elements of three different trends of thought, namely, the naturalism of Marx, Hegelian philosophy, and French positivism. The contribution of each of these trends to the final outcome has to be examined before the historical development and logical analysis of dialectical materialism are undertaken.

II

Marxian Naturalism

EXCEPT during his youth Marx was not actively interested in metaphysics (though his pronouncements sometimes appear to entail definite metaphysical commitments). This suggests, if in a roundabout way, the conclusion that Marx was not a materialist, for all materialists are metaphysicians.

The writings of Marx are free from metaphysical speculations, if by metaphysics is meant the claim to knowledge about what is behind appearances or the nature of the world as it exists independently of us and on its own account. There cannot be the slightest doubt that Marx rejected the view according to which the world is dependent for its existence on being perceived or known. Although absolute materialism implies epistemological realism, one can support epistemological realism without embracing absolute materialism.

Marx would not dissent from some of the beliefs of materialism, but it is doubtful whether he would attach as much importance to them as the eighteenth- and nineteenth-century materialists did or as contemporary dialectical materialists do. For it is right to say, as Marx emphasized in *Economic and Philosophic Manuscripts of 1844*, that 'consistent naturalism or humanism' should be distinguished not only from idealism but also from materialism.[1] Marx's basic philosophic attitude differed from absolute and reductive materialism, the only form of materialism known at that time, and could best be described as naturalism, a classificatory name which he chose himself. In this respect Marx is a Feuerbachian, for it was Feuerbach who declared his indifference to all previous philosophical schools and claimed that his own philosophy, being concerned with man, was neither materialist nor idealist.[2] Nature is a more comprehensive concept than matter. It includes matter and life, body and mind, the motions of inanimate objects and the flights of passion and imagination. 'Nature', wrote Santayana, 'is material but not materialistic',[3] a comment that might have come from Feuerbach or from Marx.

I. THE SOLE REALITY OF NATURE

The peculiar brand of 'naturalism or humanism' which is characteristic for Marx's approach to the problems of philosophy is already apparent in his doctoral dissertation *Differenz der demokritischen und epikureischen Naturphilosophie.* In this short but impressive study Marx did not conceal the fact that in spite of the inconsistencies of Epicurus he placed him above Democritus and sympathized with the former rather than with the latter. In the *Critique of Pure Reason* Kant described Epicurus as the outstanding and perfectly consistent sensationalist philosopher; unlike Aristotle or Locke, he never sought to pass by inference beyond the limits of experience. Although Marx admired Epicurus because he never raised a claim to absolute knowledge, he admired him still more for other reasons. While Democritus was exclusively concerned with the atom as a 'pure and abstract category' and with atomism as a hypothesis intended to explain the phenomena of physical nature, Epicurus was anxious to understand nature in order to help man get rid of fear and spiritual bondage. Philosophers who construct a cosmology to teach their fellow men the way of life they should follow cannot be judged by the standards of logical consistency alone. Epicurus, Marx wrote, was 'the greatest Greek enlightener (*Aufklärer*)', the founder of the 'natural science of man's self-consciousness', whose philosophy, unlike that of Democritus, contained 'an invigorating principle'.[4] This invigorating principle was the naturalistic quality of Epicurus's thought, his conception of the world formulated in terms appropriate to the description of man's experience and activities in the world. Since in Epicurus's philosophy nature and man could be described and explained in the same terms, there was no gulf dividing the world of nature and that of human affairs.

Marx's 'new materialism' is closer to the definition of it given by Engels in *Ludwig Feuerbach* than to the dialectical materialism of *Anti-Dühring.* This is comprehensible if one remembers that *Ludwig Feuerbach* was meant to be an account of Marx's and Engels's philosophical development in relation to the system of Hegel and

E.D.M.—C

Feuerbach, of the influence these philosophers exercised upon them, and of how they overcame their attraction. Engels's recollections and retrospective observations should not be accepted, however, at their face value, since they are misleading and in some respects wrong.

In his account Engels spoke of Feuerbach's *The Essence of Christianity* (1841) which 'without circumlocution placed materialism on the throne again' and suggested that it was this work that exercised a decisive influence upon Marx's philosophical development. Engels's dramatically and vividly presented account is only partly confirmed by Marx's own statements on the subject. Marx recognized that in *The Essence of Christianity* Feuerbach had discovered the anthropological roots of Hegel's theological and philosophical speculations. But the formulation of Feuerbach's 'true materialism and real science', based on the premiss that philosophy arises from and reflects 'the social relations " of man to man " ', is to be found in Feuerbach's smaller and lesser known writings, *Vorläufige Thesen zur Reform der Philosophie* (1842) and *Grundsätze der Philosophie der Zukunft* (1843). Marx described these works as having a profound and enduring significance. They carried out a thorough critical settling of accounts with the philosophy of Hegel, they displaced the old philosophy from its position of dominance, and accomplished 'a real theoretical revolution'. Feuerbach became 'the true conqueror' of Hegelianism by subjecting it to an analysis from Hegel's own point of view and by formulating the theoretical basis of philosophical anthropology from which every speculative philosophy could be effectively criticized.[5] Notwithstanding his later objections to Feuerbach's philosophical position in *The German Ideology* and the *Theses* of 1845-6, Feuerbach's role with respect to Marx could be compared to that of Hume's to Kant.

The exclusive and excessive significance attached by Engels to *The Essence of Christianity* at the expense of Feuerbach's other writings, has led to a misinterpretation of Marx's own philosophy.[6] If the role of *Vorläufige Thesen zur Reform der Philosophie* and *Grundsätze der Philosophie der Zukunft* in Marx's philosophical evolution towards naturalism is ignored, the philosophical premisses of Marx's thinking are bound to be misunderstood or misconstrued.[7]

Feuerbach's materialism was neither the mechanistic reductive materialism of the eighteenth century nor could it be equated with Engels's dialectical materialism. It is a philosophical position which is best described as anthropological materialism or naturalism.[8] It is *anthropological* naturalism because it makes man the chief object of philosophy, and it is anthropological *naturalism* because it declares that consciousness and personality without nature is an empty abstraction. 'As man belongs to the essence of nature, in opposition to common materialism,' wrote Feuerbach, 'so nature belongs to the essence of man, in opposition to subjective idealism.' Nature is that which is not dependent upon man's mental activity and by which man is involuntarily affected, which is when man is not, when he does not think of it or feel it.

> Nature, matter, cannot be explained as a result of intelligence; on the contrary, it is the basis of intelligence, the basis of personality, without itself having any basis; spirit without nature is an unreal abstraction; consciousness develops itself only out of nature.[9]

Personality without a body is inconceivable. 'Take away from thy personality its body, and you take away that which holds it. . . . Only by the body is a real personality distinguished from the imaginary one of a spectre.' That which has no basis in nature has no reality at all.[10]

All sciences should found themselves upon nature, Feuerbach declared, for all knowledge remains hypothetical as long as it has not found its natural basis. This applies also to philosophy.

> Philosophy must again unite with natural science and natural science with philosophy. This union, based upon a reciprocal need, an inner necessity, will be more fruitful than the *mésalliance* existing up to now between philosophy and theology.[11]

All manner of investigations about law, art, philosophy, freedom, or personality which leave man out of account and proceed over and above him are speculations devoid of significance, sense, and substance. Truth is not to be found either in materialism or idealism, either in psychology or physiology. Truth reveals itself in anthropology and can be discovered from the viewpoint of sensibility (*der Standpunkt der Sinnlichkeit*), for only where sensibility begins does all doubt and controversy cease.[12]

Feuerbach wrote about himself 'I am nothing but a natural philosopher in the domain of mind'.[13] He followed in the footsteps of Locke, who, as an empirical philosopher, knew nothing of the transcendent individuality of man and defined the self as a 'conscious thinking thing', which is sensible of pleasure or pain, capable of happiness or misery and, generally, is concerned for itself so far as its consciousness extends.[14]   Feuerbach adopted and defended this naturalistic and empirical interpretation of the ego against Hegelian transcendentalism.   The philosopher's starting-point is 'the man who is and knows himself as the self-conscious being of nature, as the being of history, as the being of the state, as the being of religion', whose essential characteristics cannot be determined when he is separated and isolated from others but only 'in the community of man with man'.[15]

> While the old philosophy has taken as its starting-point the statement 'I am an abstract, an exclusively thinking being, and my body does not belong to my essence', the new philosophy starts with the statement 'I am a real, a sensuous being, my body belongs to my being and, indeed, my body in its totality is myself, is itself my essence'.[16]

The soul and the brain are mere hypostatizations of certain functions of the human individual and they disrupt what in fact is an inseparable totality; the separation of the soul from the body or of the sensuous from the non-sensuous essence of man is a purely theoretical act which we constantly refute in our everyday life and to which nothing corresponds in reality.   Man is a 'soul invested brain' (*das beseelte Gehirn*) and an 'embodied soul' (*die eingekörperte Seele*).[17]   Feuerbach regarded man as a mind in a body and as a part of nature.

Engels presented Feuerbach's basic position in a similar way. According to Engels Feuerbach believed that 'nature exists independently of all philosophy' and that 'nothing exists outside nature and man', man himself being a 'product of nature' which, as Engels said elsewhere, 'has developed in and along with its environment'.[18]

To assume that everything exists within the all-embracing and self-sufficient system of nature, that is, that neither nature should be set over against the transcendental, nor man against nature, is to adopt the attitude called 'naturalism'.   It was this attitude with which Engels identified Marx's 'new materialism'.   Materialism in the new sense, which Marx adopted under Feuerbach's influence, assumed that

the material sensuously perceptible world to which we ourselves belong is the only reality; and that our consciousness and
thinking, however supra-sensuous they may seem, are the product of mind but mind itself is merely the highest product of
matter.[19]

To adopt the materialist standpoint is to conceive things and events
in their own and not in imaginary connections and 'to comprehend
the real world — nature and history — just as it presents itself to
everyone who approaches it free from preconceived idealist crotchets'.[20]

Expressed in contemporary terms, the 'new materialism' is based
upon the assumption of the causal primacy of the material world,
viz. of things accessible to sensory perception or of the constituents
of such things, whose qualities, relations, functions, or modes of
behaviour may be real aspects or parts of nature but cannot be
independent causes, since they are not material objects. The basic
premiss of naturalism leaves no place for spirit or mind as a disembodied force; it does not imply the denial of spirit or mind but only
the existence of mind without material substance.

The second characteristic of the 'new materialism' is its claim to
universality, by virtue of consistent application of its basic premiss
to all domains of experience, both to nature and to history. Engels
maintained that Feuerbach failed to live up to this obligation for
he did not apply the naturalistic approach to history and can,
therefore, be described as 'a materialist below and an idealist
above'.[21] For his part Marx pointed out that 'as far as Feuerbach is
a materialist he does not deal with history, and as far as he considers
history he is not a materialist. With him materialism and history
diverge completely'.[22]

'History', as used by Marx and Engels in the quoted contexts,
does not mean *res gestae* recorded by the historian. It means the
social world in which men involved in making history live and by
which they are determined, 'the action and interaction of man in
society' or 'the social world conceived as the totality of activities
performed by the individuals who compose it'. It also means the
historicity of human nature, human activity, and human affairs in
general.[23]

Engels asserted that for Feuerbach the various experiences and
actions constituting the warp and woof of history were not natural
processes; they combined the characteristics ascribed to two totally

different realms, namely, to the realm of nature and to the realm of spirit. It was only Marx who brought 'the science of society, that is, the sum total of the so-called historical and philosophical sciences into harmony with the materialist foundation' by reconstructing the science of society on a naturalistic basis.[24]

While Engels gave a somewhat exaggerated account of the differences between Feuerbach and Marx, it is basically true to say that Feuerbach's naturalism lacked the sociological dimension which so markedly differentiated Marx from the preceding philosophers of naturalism. Engels's evaluation is in agreement with Marx's criticism in the *Theses*, where Feuerbach's narrow and inadequate understanding of the basic relationship between the individual and society and between society and nature is cited in an ever recurring objection to Feuerbachian naturalism. Marx's development beyond Feuerbach's standpoint began in *The Holy Family* but it attained a clear formulation only in *The German Ideology*.[25]

2. THE OLD AND THE NEW MATERIALISM

In *The Holy Family* Marx described the historical origin of his 'new materialism', from which, in the course of time, was to emerge his materialist conception of history and which he called 'the materialistic basis of my method (*die materialistische Grundlage meiner Methode*)'.[26] There were two trends in French materialism of the eighteenth century; one traced its origin to Descartes, the other to Bacon, Hobbes, and Locke. Descartes was one of the founders of the mathematical natural philosophy. He originated the mechanistic view of nature and prepared the ground for conceiving life, consciousness, and all the intellectual functions of man as the products of mechanical changes. Descartes completely separated his physics from his metaphysics, but within his physics matter is the only substance endowed with mechanical motion and self-creative power. French materialists followed Descartes's physics and opposed his metaphysics by rejecting his metaphysical distinction between *res cogitans* and *res extensa*. This school reached its zenith with the physicians Cabanis and Lamettrie, who applied to man Cartesian ideas about animal organism and affirmed that the 'soul is a *modus* of the body and ideas are mechanical motions'. Thus, Cartesian physics gave rise to mechanistic materialism and merged with natural science. Marx never concealed his intellectual hostility to the idea of *la bête machine* of Descartes, which in his opinion only showed that Descartes saw the world with the eyes of the manufacturing period,[27] and of *l'homme machine* of Lamettrie, which was a simplification stultifying the development of materialism.[28]

The other branch of French materialism led directly to socialism and communism. Its ancestor was Bacon and its immediate protagonist was Locke, after his views were civilized, given wit, flesh and blood by Condillac, his French admirer and follower.[29] Condillac expounded Locke's views about the origin of ideas and 'proved that not only the soul but the senses too, not only the art of creating ideas, but also the art of sensuous perception are matters of experience and habit. The whole development of men therefore depends on education and environment.' Helvétius conceived these ideas immediately in their application to social life and it was thus that French and English socialism and communism were born. Babeuf, Fourier, Cabet, and Robert Owen were direct successors of Helvétius.[30]

The close connection between the second branch of French materialism and socialism and communism is apparent. Materialism emphasized the omnipotence of experience, of habit and education, and, generally, the influence of the environment on man. Therefore, progress and virtue require not to be preached, but to be prepared by an appropriate arrangement of social relations.

> If man draws all his knowledge, sensation, etc., from the world of the senses and the experiences gained in it, the empirical world must be arranged so that in it man experiences and gets used to what is really human and that he becomes aware of himself as man. . . . If man is shaped by his surroundings, his surroundings must be made human. If man is social by nature, he will develop his true nature only in society, and the power of his nature must be measured not by the power of separate individuals but by the power of society.[31]

In the writings of his youthful period Marx stated repeatedly and emphatically his conviction that the materialism or naturalism — he used these terms synonymously — which is the philosophical basis of communism, is real humanism; it promotes a full development of man's power and potentialities. This conviction implied the repudiation of the traditional mechanistic materialism symbolized by the name of Lamettrie and the adherence to the materialism of Helvétius. It also prompted a determined opposition to all kinds of idealism. Marx wrote that the naturalistic humanism of Helvétius had 'no more dangerous enemy in Germany than spiritualism or speculative idealism which substitutes "self-consciousness" or the "spirit" for the real individual man'. The Young Hegelians provided a clear demonstration of the fact that idealist philosophy replaced an authentic revolution intended to change the social conditions of life by an illusory revolution, restricted to the realm of speculative thought. They thus reversed the true sequence of events and in spite of their world-shattering pronouncements became the staunchest conservatives.[32]

Feuerbach went back to Helvétius over the heads of the Young Hegelians, for he rejected their Hegelian substitution of self-consciousness for the 'real man on the basis of nature'. Man is not a mere accident of the eternal substance. Marx contrasted Feuerbach's position with that of the Young Hegelians and emphasized that for Feuerbach the real man lives and suffers in society, shares in its pains and pleasures, and is a manifestation of its life.[33] But Feuerbach failed to go beyond the point reached by Helvétius. He too conceived of man as a purely passive recipient of stimuli supplied by nature and as the product of education, circumstances, and influences of nature acting upon him; he forgot that 'it is men that change circumstances and that the educator himself needs educating'.[34] Man changes not only in response to the influence of nature upon him, but also in reacting upon nature in his struggle for existence. Changing nature, he changes the environment and changing the conditions of life, he changes himself.

Moreover, Marx came to regard Feuerbach's anthropological materialism as a failure for reasons essentially the same as those for which he broke his connections with the Young Hegelians. According to Marx, communism was materialism expressed in terms of practical action. Feuerbach, however, was content to show the errors of the Hegelian philosophy; he only interpreted the world, never abandoned the contemplative attitude of a theorist, and thus failed to formulate the conclusions that would attack, revolutionize, and change the existing world.[35] Marx's criticism of Feuerbach was based on the assumption that there was a revolutionary dynamic in materialism as applied to social life and historical development and that it was enough to discover the material conditions of human existence to reveal both the inevitability and the desirability of their change. If men come to understand the circumstances of their lives and see that they are wanting the power to realize the aspirations of human spirit, they rise up against their circumstances and spontaneously exert themselves to overthrow them. The materialist philosophers who were anxious only to interpret the world were in no position to discover a true view of it.

Engels's retrospective evaluation of Feuerbach and his failure to improve upon Helvétius was derived from altogether different premisses. He considered it to be self-evident that once the inadequacy of mechanistic materialism was clearly realized, dialectical materialism was bound to replace it, for only the latter remedied the defects and dealt successfully with the difficulties left unsolved by the former.[36] Feuerbach recognized the truth of the antecedent but not the truth of the consequent of the above statement; on this account his materialism remained inconsistent and vacillating. The natural-scientific materialism of Büchner, Moleschott, and Vogt provided no alternative to mechanistic materialism. Feuerbach too was aware of the fact that natural-scientific materialism supplied the groundwork of the edifice of human knowledge but not the edifice itself. We live not only in nature but also in human society and the question, therefore, was how to 'bring the science of society . . . into harmony with the materialist foundation and to reconstruct it thereupon'.[37] Engels was convinced that the only right solution to this problem was to discover the 'laws of motion' which govern both natural phenomena and historical events and which, in his opinion, were to be found in the laws first formulated and developed by Hegel.[38] Unlike Marx, Feuerbach did not rise, however, to the realization of this fact and because he did not know dialectical materialism he was bound to fail. Engels believed that it was actually Marx and not himself who formulated the foundations of dialectical materialism and who maintained that it was the one and only one objectively valid and fruitful alternative to mechanistic materialism. While Marx supplied the ideas and the principles, Engels only elaborated upon them, systematized Marx's thinking and provided its detailed validation.[39] Engels decried his own share in the formulation of dialectical materialism as much as he belittled his role in the development of other genuinely Marxian ideas.

Neither in *The Holy Family* nor in *The German Ideology* nor in other publications of this and later periods can a single piece of evidence be found to substantiate and confirm Engels's view. While Marx firmly rejected mechanistic materialism early in his life and never wavered in his decision, his efforts to establish an alternative theoretical foundation to the abandoned position of mechanistic materialism moved in a direction quite different from that which Engels would lead us to expect. Marx did not view the problem in the way Engels did in *Anti-Dühring* and *Ludwig Feuerbach*, nor did he accept what Engels took for granted, namely, that a materialist conception of nature and history which was to succeed mechanistic materialism could not be anything but dialectical materialism.

Marx had a more or less coherent and organized system of beliefs as to the nature of reality and the nature of man. The materialist presuppositions which were shared by Marx might have included the principle of the sole reality of matter ('matter' being the term used to denote the totality of material objects, and not the substratum of all the changes which occur in the world), the denial of the independent existence of mind without matter, the rule of the laws of nature, the independent existence of the external world, and other similar assumptions traditionally associated with materialism. But while materialism in the indicated sense might have constituted Marx's general frame of reference, it did not provide the premisses from which Marxian historical materialism was inferred. Marx did not accept some of the materialist metaphysical principles or some of the physical and biological factors, extra-social and extra-historical, such as geographical conditions or the struggle for existence (to mention those actually discussed by Marx), as the explanation of social processes and historical development. Marx's new materialist conception of nature and history is not based, as Engels suggested, on a single set of laws, discovered by Hegel, which apply both to the physical universe and the human world ; nor are his views on society and history either definitionally or inferentially dependent upon or reducible to an absolute materialism, whether mechanical or dialectical. Since the general assumptions of the Marxian conception of nature, man, and society make exclusive use of social and historical terms, they should not be regarded, as will be shown later, as materialism in the accepted sense of the word.

The 'new materialism' of Marx is actually naturalism, rediscovered and extended by Marx to apply both to man's biological and spiritual existence and to account for social and historical phenomena. This revision and extension required the establishing of a common principle or a common method which would take into

account the fact that man is not only a natural entity
social being, which would enable him to establish the
society on 'the materialist foundation', and which co
for the purpose of describing both the world of nature and ...
world.

By rejecting mechanistic materialism Marx did not adopt a
dialectical but an anthropological conception of nature.[40] By the
anthropological conception of nature should be understood the
view which, in Marx's words, leaves 'the priority of external nature
unassailed' but abolished the distinction between man and nature,
for man's 'unceasing sensuous labour and creation' is 'the basis of
the whole world as it now exists'.[41] If the concept of nature became
for Marx a social and historical concept, he cannot be called a
dialectical materialist, for the dialectical and the anthropological
conception of nature are clearly mutually exclusive.

3. THE ANTHROPOLOGICAL CONCEPTION OF NATURE

Nature *an und für sich*, the external world of Engels and Lenin that
exists without and independently of us and yet is completely knowable, was for Marx a 'nullity', a 'nothing . . . devoid of sense' or
mere 'externality'.[42] Its existence is not problematic, but the
question as to the mode of its existence has no meaning. To reject
this assertion and to maintain that we are able to discover what the
universe itself is like, is to assume that man can attain an omniscient
being's view of the world.

In *Economic and Philosophic Manuscripts of 1844* and *The German
Ideology* Marx rejected as entirely wrong the theory of knowledge of
the British empiricists, the French materialists, and Feuerbach, who
conceived men as products of circumstances and upbringing, the
human mind as a passive recipient of sensation, and perception as a
mere effect wrought in the senses by outside causes. The causal
theory of perception fails to explain the simplest act of cognition
and applied to the whole range of human experience does not
account for social change and the evolution of man. Marx was
convinced that the idealists, and this meant Hegel and the Hegelians,
were right in emphasizing the contribution and the role of the subject
in the process of knowledge, and he put this conviction on record
in the first and third of his *Theses on Feuerbach*.

Although 'only abstractedly', since idealism does not know 'real, sensuous activity as such', it was idealism that developed the 'active side' of cognition. Hegel was wrong when he conceived the mind as an autonomous entity, independent of and undetermined by its material and social environment which he regarded as posited by the mind's creative activity. Although Hegel's identification of reality with thought should be rejected, Hegel was right when he insisted upon the constitutive function of consciousness in the process of knowledge. His discovery becomes of considerable importance if the constitutive role of consciousness is conceived as 'human sensuous activity', that is, perception combined with action, instead of being, as in Hegel, an act of abstract thought.

Marx refused to follow the path of mechanistic materialism which severed the natural connection between man and his environment and maintained that the relation of cognition to the external world may be reduced to the relationship of cause and effect. For Marx man is not a *tabula rasa*, a mere receiver of impressions from the outside world, passively registering and reproducing the external stimuli, but an actively responding cognizing subject, endowed with a selective perceptive faculty, contributing to cognition his memory and anticipations, his norms and values, his social and historical heritage. Instead of being the mere effect of external causes, sensation, cognition, and action are the results of interaction between the environment and an active and sensitive individual, responding with intelligence to the pressure and challenge of the external world. No account of experience can be adequate unless the contributing activities of the knower are recognized and the knower himself is considered as a product of his time, culture, and social system. The knower is not, as it were, the sum total of the Kantian categorical forms ; nor should he be conceived as an individual of the traditional theory of knowledge who rises above history and time. From the naturalistic viewpoint society is prior to the individual, and the knower is a social individual, situationally and socially determined. Consequently, objects of knowledge are always socially mediated objects and nature as the totality of things and their relations articulated by man's social action is a man-made nature.

An external world the knowledge of which is independent of the perceiving subject is a fiction beyond our comprehension, for all our concepts as well as our language are inevitably related to the

socially subjective world. To form an idea of the external world
as it exists independently of our knowledge of it is as impossible as to
distinguish the socially determined characteristics of man from those
of his traits which the individual would possess if he had always lived
in isolation. Marx did not only reject the idea that Rousseau's
'man in the state of nature' could ever exist but also refused to see
in it an empirically significant concept. Similarly, the concept of
nature that preceded all human history is devoid of cognitive
meaning. It would have to differ entirely from the nature in which
we live or which does or could exist anywhere for anyone today.[43]
We cannot, as it were, remove from nature the traces left behind
by the evolution of the human species which constantly shapes and
reshapes the world and which is responsible for the fact that the
world appears to the cognizing subject in one manner rather than
another. This is the point of view which Feuerbach described as
the 'anthropological truth' and Marx called 'consistent naturalism'.[44] Within a consistent naturalism there is no more room for
the concept of material substance than for that of disembodied
spirit or mind. Marx rightly argued that naturalism thus understood 'distinguishes itself both from idealism and materialism,
constituting at the same time the unifying truth of both'. Although
what men see, touch, or grasp are responses to external stimuli, the
external objects are determined by the selective activity of the senses
and the senses in turn are constantly modified by the biological,
social, and cultural evolution of the human species. In a certain
sense, then, there are no natural data, no God-given external facts
of nature, but only socially mediated objects.[45]

The world as known to man is a man-made world; it is the totality
of 'things for us' and not of 'things-in-themselves'. The only knowable is the world that appears in man's experience, that is causally
transformed by human action, divided into species and particulars,
class members and classes, articulated into objects and their relations, into things with a definite form, arrangement, and structure,
and cut out from the chaotic mass of the pre-existing world as it
persists by itself. This humanized world is knowable because it is
a world determined by man, the outcome, as Marx said in the first
Thesis on Feuerbach, of 'human sensuous activity'. As a natural being
man shapes the environment according to his needs, and the needs
determine the articulation of the world into separate things and
their connections. External objects are, as it were, the objectified

centres of resistance in the environment encountered by the human drives striving for the satisfaction of needs. If the needs were different, the world would look differently too, as it does to other animal species.

Although sensuous objects are different from thought objects, they do not exist in the form of objects unless they are made such by human activity. Cognition is not simply a matter of discovering or disclosing some entities which exist independently of us. The cognizing subject participates in the determination of the objective nature and order of things and, in a certain sense, creates it in the act of continuous world-objectification (*Vergegenständlichung*). While according to Marx, man's practical activity creates an objective world in the indicated sense, objectification should not be conceived as a spiritual but as a natural act and, therefore, as an act of production rather than that of creation in the proper sense, that is, of bringing something into being *ex nihilo*. Consequently, man's capacity of objectifying what gratifies his needs and provides him with enjoyment presupposes the 'sensuous external world'. This external world is the material on which man's labour becomes manifest, from which and by means of which external objects are produced.[46]

The subjective world, articulated and determined in its structure by man's needs, tendencies, and impulses, is not a forever changing, transient, and ephemeral world. For man is a natural being, that is, a member of an animal species, and a social being destined to act together with others. Since, in his relation to the external world, man is not an isolated but a social subject, his cognitive capacities and organizing forms or categories of thought are socially determined too. Marx accepted Condillac's theory of knowledge, according to which general knowledge is impossible without language and thus is bound to be a product of social life as much as language itself. Having accepted Condillac's theory of knowledge Marx also reached the conclusion established by Rousseau that in the state of nature, that is, without the abilities which men acquire by communicating with each other, man would be reduced exclusively to sensations.[47] As Feuerbach put it, only through his fellow men does man become self-conscious. Without this bond of community man would lose his individuality in the ocean of nature. 'That he is, he has to thank nature; that he is man, he has to thank man; spiritually as well as physically he can achieve nothing without his fellow-man.'[48] The same applies to distinctively human powers and achievements. They are products of human society and not of man as an individual. The intellectual and moral development of man, the acquisition and advance of arts and science, are a consequence of social life.

> Language, like consciousness, only arises from the need, the necessity, of intercourse with other men. . . . Consciousness is therefore from the very beginning a social product and remains as long as men exist at all.[49]

The subjective world of man is, therefore, socially subjective and could not be subjective in any other sense. Being socially subjective it displays certain persisting traits, corresponding to the durable characteristics of the human species.[50]

'Nature' always meant for Marx 'man-made nature', that is, nature articulated, conditioned, and modified by man's cognitive and social activity. Marx's favourite terms for this object-constituting activity, regarded by him as the primary datum of philosophy, were 'practice' (*Praxis*) and 'practical activity' (*praktische Tätigkeit*), which appear over and over again in *Theses on Feuerbach*. While by making use of these expressions Marx wished to emphasize the active attitude of the new as compared with the contemplative attitude of the old materialism and appealed to the meaning in which 'practice' is opposed to 'mere theory' or 'speculation', the main sense of 'practical' is clearly 'being biologically relevant' or 'significant', that is, important for the life of the human organism and for the survival of the species. From this biological point of view, nature may be conceived, as it is by Marx, as 'man's inorganic body with which he must remain in continuous intercourse if he is not to die'.[51] Nature is considered by Marx only in so far as man, the primary object of his interest, is part of nature and man's physical and spiritual life is linked to and reflected by nature which, in turn, is transformed by man's practical activity into an objective world.

Marx's approach to the problem of the relation between nature and man reversed the order of inquiry accepted in the materialist tradition. Instead of the inquiry of nature paving the way for the inquiry into the nature of man, it was the inquiry into the nature of man that was to guide the inquiry into the problems of nature. While the revolution in natural science of the sixteenth and seventeenth centuries destroyed the idea of man and social order established in the Middle Ages, now it was the revolution in the 'science of man' that was to lead to a complete philosophical reassessment of our knowledge of nature.

The external world, as it exists *an und für sich*, never enters Marx's social and historical investigations. The Marxian theory of knowledge is based on the assumptions that the sensuous world around is not a thing given directly from all eternity, but is constantly moulded by man's theoretical and practical, cognitive and productive activity; that reality is of historical nature in the sense that it is the outcome of specifically human actions of a whole succession of generations; and that each generation stands on the shoulders of the preceding one, continues the traditional activity in completely changed circumstances and modifies the old circumstances with a completely changed activity. Marx's theory of knowledge upholds Hegel against Feuerbach's belief in the certainty and finality of sense experience and its historic character. On the other hand, while emphasizing the contribution to cognition made by man's perceptive faculty, conditioned historically and socially, Marx preserves the realistic component of the materialist theory of knowledge. He combines the principles of naturalism and realism with the Hegelian idea that reason is historically determined and that it is involved in impressing upon man's physical and social environment its shape and form. Therefore, it is history, the record of human actions in society, which provides the starting-point for considering nature as the totality of physical objects. Man always has before him a 'historical nature' and it is a 'natural history' that provides the key to its secrets.

> The sensuous world . . . is not a thing given direct from all eternity, ever the same, but the product of industry and the state of society; and, indeed, in the sense that it is a historical product, the result of the activity of a whole succession of generations, each standing on the shoulders of the preceding one, developing its industry and its intercourse, modifying its social organization according to the changed needs.[52]

Unlike other animal species, man is not only a successor but also an heir to a cumulative tradition which, whether for good or bad, affects his powers, way of life, and activity.

Thus, the old materialism, including Feuerbach's materialism, with its claim that man is a creature of nature, determined by and depending on his environment, is only a half-truth; it leaves out the fact that the physical and social environment is the outcome of man's sensuous and social activity. What Feuerbach emphasized in his criticism of Hegel's speculative philosophy, namely that we take cognizance of objects by coming under their action and that sensation precedes thinking, was for Marx an indubitable fact. Marx went beyond Feuerbach's view by insisting that man is induced to think 'chiefly by the sensations he experiences in the process of his acting upon the outer world', as Plekhanov suggestively reformulated the first *Thesis on Feuerbach*.[53] There is a constant action and reaction of the natural and social environment on man and of man on his natural and social environment, both being determined by and determining each other. As Marx put it, 'circumstances make men as much as men make circumstances'.[54] Since in the course of the struggle for existence man acts upon the outer world, from which he derives his knowledge of it, Marx's theory of knowledge is closely linked with his views on man's advancement, that is, with his view of history and the history of civilization.

In the third *Thesis on Feuerbach* Marx drew attention to the paradoxical consequences of the idea expounded by Helvétius and Robert Owen according to which the character of men is entirely determined by circumstances and environment. If this assumption were true, Marx argued, nothing could be changed by the free and deliberate action of educators and reformers, for their ideas and conduct would also be strictly determined by the circumstances of their life. Nobody would be able to accomplish any social improvement and change men by education; everything would occur as it does and could not occur otherwise. On the other hand, if men are not only determined by circumstances but also circumstances by the action of men, not everything is fixed by natural necessity. The paradox of materialism may be solved and social change rationally explained provided that human activity is considered as 'revolutionary practice', that is, conceived in terms of the challenge of environment and man's social response.

It should be observed that Marxian anthropological realism found no favour with Marx's Hegelizing followers. Engels must have been familiar with Marx's realism and, as a matter of fact, he seems to refer occasionally to some of its implications.[55] But Engels's epistemological observations were more confusing than enlightening. Engels combined some fragments of the Marxian approach with his own theory of knowledge, a variety of representative realism, into an incongruous and incoherent whole. Engels's epistemological views reveal a clear inclination towards naïve realism and the conception of perception as images produced entirely by external stimuli. Thus, the importance of what the cognizing subject contributes to what is perceived and thought, emphasized by Marx, is lost in Engels.

Lenin moved still further away from the Marxian epistemology than did Engels, for Lenin's copy theory of perception is incompatible with Marx's anthropological realism. Anthropological realism concedes that knowledge of the external world is relative to the mind, and this view, according to Lenin, ultimately entails epistemological idealism, that is, the proposition that the external world is completely dependent upon the mind. In *Materialism and Empirio-Criticism* Lenin argued over and over again that no consistent materialism could deviate in the slightest way from the copy theory of perception, for only this theory unqualifyingly denies the dependence of knowledge of the external world upon the mind and is, therefore, in no way tarred with the idealist brush. Thus, without knowing it Lenin also put Marx's anthropological realism out of court as a materialist theory.[56] Lenin made of Engels a protagonist of the copy theory of perception and established it as an integral part of orthodoxy.

4. SACRED AND PROFANE HISTORY [57]

Some aspects of the Marxian theory of knowledge have reappeared in a developed form in contemporary philosophical trends. Thus, Bertrand Russell suggested that the identification of knowledge with the process of knowledge in the course of which both subject and object are transformed may be described as an anticipation of Dewey's instrumentalism.[58] The Existentialists claim their affinity with the Marxian way of viewing the world by referring to Marx's reduction of nature to the 'social reality of nature' and to his conception of man as a 'being-within-the-world', both conditioned by and responding to the circumstances of life.

For the understanding of Marx a different point is, however, important. The Marxian conception of nature, of man, and man's relation to nature disposes of many traditional epistemological problems. Marx neither needs to prove existence of the external world, nor disprove its existence. From his point of view both these endeavours are prompted by false assumptions concerning the relation of man to nature, by considering man as a detached observer, setting him against the world or placing him, as it were, on a totally different level. For man, who is part of nature, to doubt the existence of the external world or to consider it as in need of proof is to doubt his own existence, and even Descartes and Berkeley refused to go to such a length.

This conclusion is of considerable significance for the interpretation of Marxian philosophy. As Marx refused to dissociate nature from man and man from nature and conceived man not only as part of nature but also nature in a certain sense as a product of man's activity and, thus, part of man, Marx's naturalism has no need of a metaphysical foundation. Moreover, since man knows only socially mediated nature, 'man', and not natural reality, 'is the immediate object of natural science'. To use Marx's terminology, the natural science of man is logically prior to all other knowledge.[59] What Feuerbach said about his anthropological materialism applies even more fittingly to Marx's naturalism. 'The new philosophy', wrote Feuerbach, 'makes man, including nature as the basis of man, the sole, universal and highest object of philosophy, makes, therefore, of anthropology, including physiology, the universal science.'[60]

The natural science of man that unveils the genesis and development of human society is a natural historical science. In the preface to the first edition of *Capital* Marx observed that in this work 'the evolution of the economic formation of society is viewed as a process of natural history'. This natural history must be differentiated from history which is conceived in the Hegelian manner as a development of Mind and Spirit.[61] The latter takes an abstract definition of man as its starting-point, substitutes consciousness for the living individual (Hegel regarded self-consciousness as the essence of spirit and, consequently, also of man), rises far above space and time and, being incapable of following the real progressive movement of events, produces phantasmagorias of the historian's mind. The spiritualistic conception of history is selective and restrictive; it reduces history to 'main political, literary and theological acts'. Just as it separates itself from the world and society from nature, it also 'separates history from natural science and industry, and sees the origin of history not in the coarse material production on the earth but in vaporous clouds in the heavens'.[62] From this viewpoint society is the result or emanation of transcendent ideas, which also provide men with their explanatory and normative principles, and history consists in the unfolding and transformation of one idea into another. This is not history, Marx wrote, referring first of all to the brothers Bauer, 'but old Hegelian junk, it is not profane history — a history of man — but sacred history, a history of ideas. From this point of view man is only the instrument of which the idea of the eternal reason makes use in order to unfold itself.' [63] This imaginary world of *Geist* was overthrown by Feuerbach, who substituted the investigations of men in their interaction and social relations for the Hegelian grand fantasy of self-developing thought. 'Man is not an abstract being, existing outside of the world', Marx concluded his reflections upon Hegel's view of man. 'Man is the world of men, the state, society.' [64]

In sacred history, religion makes man, in profane history, man makes religion; in sacred history social, political, and economic institutions are the manifestations of Spirit; in profane history they are the historical product of human activity and interaction pursued by a whole succession of generations. Being produced by ourselves, these institutions may, however, crystallize into an 'objective power above us' that grows out of control, thwarts our expectations and brings to naught our calculations.[65] They do not deprive history of its profane nature, though they reveal the truth that man is not only the maker of society but also its victim.

It is the 'real life-process' — the way by which men produce the means of subsistence and the forms of social relations restricting their interaction for the purpose of production — that is the primary datum of profane history; it constitutes the basis which is itself not subject to questioning and with reference to which problems of history are formulated and examined. On the other hand, the various manifestations of spirit are an outcome and reflection of this 'real life-process'. Thus, the history that may rightly claim the name of the natural science of man starts from the actual conditions of social life and tries, by virtue of these, to account for the ideas and conceptions flowing from the life-process of individuals. 'After the disappearance of the other-worldliness of truth (*das Jenseits der Wahrheit*) the task of history is to establish the truth of the this-worldliness (*die Wahrheit des Diesseits*).' [66] It is a fateful error to set society and culture over against nature. For society and culture which grows within it are a part of nature rather than a state of human existence opposed to nature, and culture originates not only in but also through society.

5. THE IDEALIST AND THE MATERIALIST CONCEPTION OF HISTORY

The antithesis of sacred and profane history, of the shadows of reality and of the real life-process, of the imaginary man and of real individuals, was defined fifteen years later in the familiar terms of the materialist and the idealist conception of history.[67] The idealist conception of history which, as Marx asserted, was common to all historians up to that time, rests on the assumption that history is always under the sway of ideas. This assumption clearly substitutes interconnections manufactured by and emanating from the mind of the philosopher for the real interconnections to be discovered in the events themselves. For in every epoch the ruling ideas are the ideas of the ruling class, and the class wielding the dominating economic power in society is thereby its ruling intellectual force. The class which controls the means of material production has control at the same time over the intellectual production ; those who rule as a class rule also as thinkers, as producers and distributors of the ideas of their age. These ideas are 'neither pure nor external'. The ruling ideas express the dominant material relationships grasped as ideas, that is, they reflect the relationships which make a given class the ruling one and secure its domination. Consequently, to say that a system of ideas was dominant in a certain epoch without inquiring about the conditions of production and the producers of the ruling ideas is to fall victim to the illusion of the epoch.[68]

Taking advantage of the fact that the protagonists of history act with deliberation, behave purposefully, and consciously set themselves definite aims, the idealist theories of history explain the sequence of events in terms of human design, divine providence, or an absolute idea. They see in history the political actions of princes and great historical individuals, religious and other conflicts of all sorts, which the Idea or Truth, or some other abstraction, uses in its striving towards consciousness of itself. Human action may be prompted by passion or deliberation, motivated by ambition, personal hatred or whim, love of truth or justice. The error of the exponents of the idealist conception of history is not in recognizing these various motives but in failing to search for the real causes behind the alleged ones. They do not question the motives given by the protagonists themselves but accept them as if they were the determinants of action. While in ordinary life people are able, as a rule, to distinguish between what somebody professes to be and what he really is, the idealist historians fail to give evidence of such common sense. 'They take every epoch at its word and believe that everything it says and imagines about itself is true.' [69]

The materialist conception of history does not search for the ideas of the epoch, forms of self-consciousness or motives prompting the actors on the stage of history, but tries to discover what in fact sets men in motion. Its starting-point is 'real men' and 'individuals as they really are', and 'not as they may appear in their own or other people's imagination', that is, 'as they produce materially and are active under definite material limits, presuppositions and conditions independent of their will'.[70] Marx claimed that labour is the primary factor in social development because labour must be recognized as a necessary condition for the existence of the human race; without labour there is no 'material exchange between man and nature', that is, no production of commodities for the satisfaction of human wants.[71] With this 'eternal nature-imposed necessity' independent of all forms of society, is associated another, the necessity arising from man's inability to produce what he requires without the assistance of other men. Since needs cannot be met on an adequate level without tools and tools are manufactured and used in social co-operation, 'production by isolated individuals outside of society . . . is as great an absurdity as the idea of the development of language without individuals living together and talking to one another'.[72] In order to live, men have to enter into relations with their fellow men and, since they can never escape productive labour, they must constantly reproduce these relations. Thus every society is the 'product of men's reciprocal action' which expresses the primary condition of the life of the human species and maintains its biological existence. Social interaction is conditioned by the productive forces already won and by the social organization in existence, for they are handed down to each generation by its predecessors. History is nothing but the succession of separate generations, each of which makes use of the productive forces and social relations inherited from all preceding generations. The materialist interpretation of history can be defined in Marx's own terms as the view according to which 'the life process of society is based on the process of material production', and the formation of ideas is explained in terms of this 'material practice' instead of the practice being accounted for in terms of ideas.[73]

In the Preface to *A Contribution to the Critique of Political Economy* Marx referred to the doubts as to the justness of Hegel's *Rechts-philosophie* which had assailed him more than fifteen years earlier and which led to his critical studies of the Hegelian philosophy. He recounted that these studies persuaded him that the ideological forms of social life, of state and legal relations in particular, have their roots in the 'material conditions of life', the sum total of which, following Hegel, he called 'civil society'. Civil society is not an aggregate of human atoms unrelated to each other, as the British economists and utilitarians imagined it to be. Civil society is the state of mutual dependence of all upon each other or the totality of various social bonds which connect men with one another for the satisfaction of their primary needs and which have to be differentiated from the political constitutions under which they live.

> It is natural necessity, essential human properties, however alienated they may seem to be, and interest that hold the members of civil society together ; civil, not political life is their real tie. . . . Only political superstition today imagines that social life must be held together by the state whereas in reality the state is held together by civil life.[74]

The conclusion concerning the relation of the forms of state and legal systems to civil society produced in turn the conjecture that the 'anatomy of civil society is to be sought in political economy', or, as the French historians of the Restoration put it, in the state of property. Thus, while civil society, which is reflected in the juridical superstructure of property relations or, more plainly, the laws of property in force, constitutes the basic foundation of the entire social order, civil society results from and rises over the economy and the way society produces its means of subsistence. The particular form that civil society assumes is determined by the mode of production, the mode of production being the combination of the existing productive forces together with the knowledge and skills necessary for their operation.[75]

The mode of production is what Marx assumed to be 'the natural', 'the real', 'the material basis of all history'.[76]

> Assume a particular state of development in the productive faculties of man and you will get a particular form of commerce and consumption. Assume a particular stage of development in production, commerce and consumption and you will have a corresponding social structure, a corresponding organization of the family, of orders or of classes, in a word, a corresponding civil society. Assume a particular civil society and you will get particular political conditions, which are only the official expression of civil society.[77]

While men establish their social relations in conformity with their material production, they produce ideas, principles, and categories in conformity with their social relations. To the continual movement of growth in the productive forces, there corresponds the transformation of social relations and the formation of new ideas.[78]

Starting with the material basis, the materialist conception of history tries to show how civil society determines the forms of political power, morality, religion, metaphysics, and all the rest of ideology, together with their corresponding forms of the social consciousness. In general, the materialist conception of history reveals how men in developing their material production and their relations of production alter their ways of thinking and ideas along with their material existence. Man's nature is the result of his own labour and man is what his activity makes him to be. 'Life is not determined by consciousness but consciousness by life (*nicht das Bewusstsein bestimmt das Leben, sondern das Leben bestimmt das Bewusstsein*).'[79]

6. THE SOCIAL ORIGIN OF MAN'S DISTINCTIVE CHARACTERISTICS

In the first of his *Theses on Feuerbach* Marx recognized the fact that the conceptual framework of 'all hitherto existing materialism', including Feuerbach's anthropological materialism, was inadequate to the complexity and variety of man's actual life experience and left some of its essential aspects untouched. This was partly due to the failure to observe that there is no knowledge without activity, no apprehension of environment without its alteration, no perception without action in relation to the object perceived. What was

neglected by 'contemplative materialism', was developed by idealism, by which Marx meant, above all, Hegel's philosophy of the
spirit.

Unlike Engels, who seems to have attached the greatest significance to Hegel's *Naturphilosophie* and *Philosophy of History*, Marx
emphasized above all the importance of Hegel's investigations on
the phenomenology of mind, that is, his study of consciousness. 'It
goes without saying', wrote Marx in *The Holy Family*, 'that Hegel's
Phenomenology, in spite of its speculative original sin, gives in many
instances the elements of a true description of human relations.' [80]
Marx could not have had in mind Hegel's central conception of
transcendental idealism, the idea that a universal mind or consciousness determines all being, including the mind of the individual man.
Neither could he have been thinking of Hegel's assertion that the world
is established by the cognitive activity of universal consciousness,
this assumption being an important step towards the reduction of
external reality to mind and of nature to spirit. Marx must have
had in mind Hegel's conception of man's active and creative role
in knowing and shaping the world of experience. While Hegel
was entirely wrong in conceiving of human thought and activity
as a manifestation of the world spirit, the Hegelian conception of
cognition, expressed in sensationalist and naturalistic terms, cor-
rected the errors and eliminated the defects of the traditional materialist world outlook.

Interpreted naturalistically, *the Phenomenology of Mind* was to be
read as an account of the evolutionary development of human nature.
The creative spontaneity of the individual, which Hegel took for
granted as a primary characteristic of spirit, became in the Marxian
system a capacity acquired by individuals in society and by social
intercourse with other men. Man develops his potentialities and
extends his self-knowledge in the process of transforming nature.
He unfolds his powers in an evolutionary process of self-genesis
through labour, that is, in the course of acting upon and responding
to an environment in which he seeks the satisfaction of his needs.[81]
The Hegelian concept of the expanding and advancing spirit is
transformed by Marx into the concept of social evolution, based on
the fact that men are unable to satisfy their needs in isolation and
have to combine and co-operate with other men to survive and
achieve their purpose.[82]

The concept of social evolution constituted an important development beyond the world outlook of eighteenth-century materialism and allowed naturalism to extend to the whole sphere of man's spiritual activities. In this respect the 'old materialism' was inadequate. The theories of mechanistic materialism concerning the appearance of mind, consciousness, values, and all distinctively human characteristics and achievements had no explanatory significance. The apparent unsatisfactoriness of these theories only played into the hands and indirectly supported the claims of the idealists who maintained that the 'essence of man' could not, demonstrably, be explained in terms of natural science and that man was thus clearly shown to be a spiritual and not a material being. Marx fully agreed with the view that mechanistic materialism did not contribute to the understanding of man's action, of his cultural attainments and social development. Nothing can be accomplished if man is assumed to be merely the highest species in the animal evolution and if his behaviour is to be explained by the laws of biology and, ultimately, of physics and chemistry. This is the kind of materialism which Marx called 'one-sided' and of which he maliciously said that in order to overcome the incorporeal spirit it 'was obliged to mortify its flesh and become ascetic'.[83]

The failure of mechanistic materialism was due to the fact that from its point of view the world was an external object to be observed and described. But men are not primarily observers. Men must be in a position to live in order to be able to search for knowledge, and in order to live they have to act to satisfy their primary needs.[84] Human nature has to conform to biological determination. There are certain sequences of activities, determined by human physiology and the physical characteristics of environment, which constitute the ultimate basis of all human motivation and which are indispensable for the survival of the individual and the species. Since they are incorporated in each system of organized behaviour, their vital importance was overlooked by most philosophers.

It is in his active life, above all, that man comes into contact with the external world, that is, with the natural and social environment into which he is born. The environment acts upon him through his sense organs and is acted upon and changed by his exertions. But if the environment which determines man's behaviour is in turn constantly made and remade by man's labour, each generation is a progeny of its ancestors both biologically and socially. The determination of man by prior circumstances is in fact the determination by the activity of preceding generations.

The social evolution of the human species is the necessary outcome of its dependence upon environment and of its precarious situation in the world. In response to the challenge and under the pressure of circumstances men, in their active life, constantly expand their powers, above all, their faculty of thinking, produce material tools and create science and technology. Their activity influences their thought. As Engels observed, 'In the measure that man has learned to change nature his intelligence has increased.' [85] As men become increasingly interdependent, social relations bind them more and more closely together, their minds become open to new ideas, and their distinctive qualities slowly emerge. By working with others, man 'develops his slumbering powers and compels them to act in obedience to his sway'. While society is the product of man's reciprocal and collective activity, of which labour is the most fundamental, it is 'the fully constituted society that produces man in all the plenitude of his being, the wealthy man endowed with all the senses, as an enduring reality'.[86]

Marx stated his basic position in the hypothesis that man 'develops his true nature only in society' and that only as a social individual, 'the species man' in the Marxian terminology,[87] does he 'become aware of himself as man' and able to bring out all his latent powers. 'Man is in the most literal sense of the word a *zoon politicon*, not only a social animal, but an animal which can develop into an individual only in society'.[88] It is in community with others that men acquire the means of cultivating their gifts in all directions and of becoming ultimately free individuals.[89]

This was in fact the position already reached by Feuerbach, but with an important distinction. Feuerbach showed his superiority over the materialists who had preceded him in realizing that man is an irreducible natural entity, that his powers are products of human society, and that only 'community constitutes humanity'. Feuerbach failed, however, to make the decisive step and to draw the important conclusion from his premiss, which Marx then did. Feuerbach, Marx pointed out repeatedly, remained in the realm of theory and did not consider men in their actual conditions of social life, for he would then have realized that these conditions not only produce the abstraction *man* but also make real and active men what they are — some healthy and strong, others overworked and consumptive wretches (*schwindsüchtiger Hungerleider*) —

thus separating them into distinct, stratified classes.[90]

There is no such thing as man or human nature independent of the social and historical context in which men live and act. The non-biological characteristics of individuals are generated by the social framework into which individuals are born, and these non-biological characteristics are socially produced. As Marx expressed it in his own language, still strongly reminiscent of the Hegelian terminology, 'consciousness is from the very beginning a social product, and remains so as long as men exist at all'.[91] Thus, there are no intrinsic and permanent non-biological components of human nature; they are all social components and 'historical fact'. They vary from one particular form of society to another and, as the structural differentiation increases, within the same society in time as well. There is an observable correlation between human nature, viz. the characteristics of the individuals who compose a given society, and the structure and complexity of this society. The individual is determined by the structural and cultural conditions of the society to which he belongs and is entirely dependent upon his position in the society and in its class structure. As Marx put it, the conditions of his existence are thus predetermined, his personal development is assigned to him, and he becomes subjected to all kinds of ideas.[92]

Man is made self-conscious through his fellow men and not because man's finite mind is spiritual and spirit necessarily involves self-consciousness. The distinctive human traits are not a manifestation of man's supernatural origin and substance; they are as natural as man's animal characteristics. They derive and evolve from the association and interaction of individuals and, generally, from life in society. The individuality of man should not be placed at the beginning of society but must be regarded as a late development in and outcome of social evolution; to use Marx's own way of speaking, the individual is a product of history and not of nature. An isolated hunter or fisherman of Adam Smith or Ricardo was for Marx 'an insipid illusion of the eighteenth century', unrelated to the reality of social life. The further back we go into history, the more dependence on a larger social whole and the less individuality we encounter.[93] If the state of nature ever existed, it would have been a state where in Hobbes's famous words the life of the savage man was 'solitary, poor, nasty, brutish, and short'. Marx's epigram, 'It is not the consciousness of man that determines his existence, it is his social existence that determines his consciousness', which of course was directed, above all, against idealism in its Hegelian form, may be understood to imply that the 'human mind, the needs, the hopes, fears and expectations, the motives and aspirations of human individuals, are, if anything, the product of life in society rather than its creators'.[94]

Man is transformed from a pure creature of nature into a social being because he must work. Labour is a permanent natural condition of human existence, common to every stage of production. But 'productive life is the life of the species', that is, production of the means of subsistence is always a collective, social activity. As Marx wrote elsewhere, 'In production men not only act on nature but also on one another. They produce only by co-operating in a certain way and mutually exchanging their activities.' [95] The individual's capacities increase through the division of labour and the ensuing structural differentiation of society. 'The entire so-called history of the world', Marx wrote in 1844, 'is nothing but the begetting of man through human labour.' [96] The spiritual life of man, his social and cultural advance, grow out of his involvement in social life and result from the evolutionary laws of human society. Only in community with others can the individual extend the range of his mental and social activities and attain the free development of personality.[97]

Unlike mechanistic materialism, which is anxious to explain how ideas and systems of thought are produced by physical and chemical processes in the brain, historical materialism tries to show how ideas and systems of thought emerge from and are determined by social conditions, which both shape and mould man's behaviour and are shaped and moulded by man. But historical materialism also goes beyond what mechanistic materialism was ever able to consider, namely, it tries to explain how man as a natural entity, analogous to other natural entities, acquires his human characteristics through social existence and social evolution. While many thinkers were of the opinion that the increasing complexity and structural differentiation of society constitutes the road to serfdom, Marx believed that it emancipates individuals from various restrictions, enriches their personality and, in the true community of the future, also secures their personal freedom.[98]

Marx conceived of society in a way exactly opposite to that of John Locke, Adam Smith, John Stuart Mill, and Spencer. Granted the fact that all men share certain wants or needs, Mill believed that society can be constructed out of an aggregate of individuals and that the 'laws of society' are nothing but 'the laws of the actions and passions of human beings united in the social state', viz. the laws of psychology. 'Human beings in society', Mill declared, 'have no properties but those which are derived from, and may be resolved into, the laws of the nature of individual man.' [99] For Marx, however, society was no mere product of human art nor simply an abstraction which should be set against the real existence of individuals. Social facts are the result of human acts and situations, but contrary to the views of John Stuart Mill this does not imply that a positive social science must be established by deduction from the general laws of human nature.[100]

In the opinion of Marx, it is an error to assume that the primary psychological constitution of the individual can be distinguished from his socially acquired characteristics and that the latter, being a product of social existence, are in a sense artificial and secondary, since they are derivable from the former. The differentiation between what man owes to society and to his primary, true, and unchanging nature, can be disregarded as a pseudo-problem or a mere figment of speculation. The 'normal man', ever the same in each historical epoch, who provided Jeremy Bentham with his yardstick of utility in the past, present, and future, existed only in Bentham's own mind. With an incomparable naïveté, Bentham took the English shopkeeper for his model and regarded what was useful to this queer normal man and to his world as absolutely useful.[101] Engels may have praised Rousseau as a forerunner of dialectics, admiring his dialectical ingenuity which enabled him to show how man in the state of nature, free from any social bonds and inclinations, was constrained to enter into social life, and thus came to form society and to establish law and government. But Marx ignored Rousseau's dialectics as spurious, firmly holding to the view that men have always lived in society and believing that the individual is 'a social being' or 'an *ensemble* of the social relations'. Consequently, society is as real as the interacting individuals of which it is composed are real.[102] The social laws are not an artificial human product, established by convention or imposed by the will of a powerful lawgiver who can change or discard them as he thinks fit. 'Marx considers social evolution to be a natural process governed by laws which do not depend upon the will, consciousness, or the intention of men,' wrote the Russian reviewer of *Capital*, whom

Marx praised for the accuracy of his evaluation in the preface to the second edition of this work. Marx's own view on society is aptly reflected by Émile Durkheim's observations made some fifty years later, that it is no easier to modify the type of society than the species of an animal. The more man emancipates himself from the original dependence on nature by social co-operation and becomes an individual by social action, the more he falls under the influence of his social environment and, more specifically, of the mode of existence of his society.[103]

It does not follow from the fact that 'society is the product of men's reciprocal action' that society is governed by laws that are made arbitrarily or are deducible from unchangeable human nature and applicable to the behaviour of individual men, always and everywhere. Since social life results from, or is based upon, human interaction, the study of the behaviour of individual men taken separately of their motives and aspirations, hopes and expectations, is irrelevant to social investigations. Society is not an aggregate of individuals but a totality of interacting individuals. Therefore, society changes and develops according to its own laws which are not psychological but specifically social laws. They help towards understanding social phenomena and the social behaviour of individuals. As Marx put it, just as society is produced by men, so society itself produces man as man.[104]

Having included man within nature and recognized all human experience and activity as processes of interaction between different parts of nature and thus as natural events, Marx, like Hegel, considered all experiences and activities of man amenable to a single method. While for Hegel spirit was history's only motive and formative power, Marx accepted the self-sufficiency of nature. Consequently, what Hegel regarded as manifestations of spirit, Marx recognized as natural processes and replaced Hegel's spiritualization of man and of the world by their 'naturalization'. Hegel's method was either teleological or dialectical and described human activity in terms of final causes, of values, ends, and norms of conduct. Marx's method, however, was to be scientific, in that its task was to discover what is the case and not what ought to be, to make exclusive use of observation and inference, and to reveal causal or functional relationships among the various objects and processes of nature. Apart from its formal advantages, the universality of scientific method reflected Marx's assumption that neither the external world nor society nor man can be conceived of and explained separately but only in their interaction, as they determine each other and change through reciprocal impact and natural influences.

As applied to social phenomena the method of science disposed of the long-established belief that society is the outcome of human design and calculation, and introduced the new conception according to which society is brought about by natural causes that produce their effects irrespective of what men intend or fail to do, without their knowledge or deliberate action. Marx held that human action conforms to laws in the same sense as the phenomena of nature do. Man's social and spiritual life constitutes a stratified and interconnected whole, the parts of which exercise a reciprocal influence on one another.[105] His spiritual power and cultural achievements — language, government, social organization, law, art, science, and religion — are not created by or effects of supernatural forces; they are a product of society. The naturalistic interpretation of social phenomena does not preclude the belief in the existence and action of spiritual factors; it only precludes those views which on the one hand are based on or inferred from the recognition of this fact and on the other, which ascribe to spirit an independent causal efficacy in the realization of anything else.[106] That human nature and all its manifestations should be explained on the basis of social life, conceived as an ever-changing network of interacting individuals who produce together what transcends the powers of each of them acting separately, was a principle bound to affect deeply the whole 'science of man'.

Durkheim observed that nothing has so retarded the establishment of social science as what Comte described as the belief in the unrestricted and creative power of legislators over civilization (*la puissance indéfinie et créatrice des législateurs sur la civilisation*).[107] The legend of the lawgiver refers to the assumption that social phenomena depend on human will and that a lawgiver endowed with a limitless power is able to devise, modify, and discard laws as he pleases (Rousseau still dreamed of playing the role of a Lycurgus and the utopian socialists cherished the same ambition). If this assumption were true, everything in human societies would be utterly fortuitous, and if any determinate order in them were found it would be a matter of pure accident.

Durkheim maintained that for the establishment of social science two premises were necessary. First, societies must be assumed to have a certain structure of their own which results from the nature, arrangement, and connection of the elements composing them, and which governs the coexistence and succession of social phenomena. Second, social science would not have any definite subject-matter to explore unless it is clearly realized that social phenomena of different categories are interrelated and constitute parts of a whole.

From this point of view, Montesquieu, Comte, and Marx have paved the way for sociology and may be regarded as its founders. Comte himself paid high tribute to Montesquieu who, he claimed, rose above the metaphysical mode of thinking of his contemporaries, including Rousseau, regarded social phenomena 'as no less subject than all other phenomena to invariable laws', and tried to establish politics (*la politique*) as a science about facts and not about dogmas.[108] But Montesquieu did not succeed in raising politics to the level of the sciences of observation (*des sciences d'observation*), that is, the positive sciences, and an element of ambiguity still persisted in his concept of social law. Only Comte and, we should add, Marx, clearly saw that social laws are descriptive laws, not different from those applying to the rest of nature.

While both Comte and Marx are the unquestionable founders of sociology, they were perhaps more interested in it as an indispensable element in the completion of a more comprehensive scheme than in taking advantage of the established sociological groundwork for the expansion of social knowledge. Comte noted in his *Cours de philosophie positive* that the study of man and the study of the physical world seemed entirely irreconcilable until he managed to formulate his positive philosophy which required the establishment of sociology as a positive science.[109] In the case of Marx, too, it was the establishment of sociology, the 'new natural science of man', that enabled Marx to go beyond Feuerbach's anthropological materialism, to remove or to reduce the chasm dividing the world of nature and the world of spirit, and to comprise all the natural and historical phenomena in one coherent and organized system. Sociology provided a fulcrum and a leverage by means of which Marx could extend the principle of naturalism, to apply it uniformly to the whole range of man's life experience, and to reveal the unity of knowledge.

The idea that man acquires his distinctive characteristics by participating in social life turned out to be extremely fruitful and provided sociology with one of its lines of development. It established the philosophy of social realism in sociology and inspired the socio-logical conception of personality which conceives personality as the point of intersection of innumerable social influences derived from participation in group activities. 'The group with which the in-dividual is affiliated', Georg Simmel wrote, 'constitutes a system of co-ordinates, as it were, such that each new group with which he becomes affiliated circumscribes him more exactly and more un-ambiguously.' [110] On this assumption, all culture-producing acti-vities of man arise from and are interwoven with his social existence and activity. The number and variety of social groups to which the individual belongs becomes one of the earmarks of culture.

7. IS MARX A MATERIALIST?

Marx was fully justified in saying that his 'new materialism' was essentially different from the old, viz. from the French materialism of the eighteenth century, Feuerbach's anthropological materialism, or the natural-scientific materialism of Marx's contemporaries. Plekhanov rightly observed that when Marx ceased being a follower of Feuerbach, he did not cease sharing many of his philosophical views. But while Marx retained some assumptions of Feuerbach's anthropological materialism or naturalism, he also extended it to include both the physical universe and the entirety of the human world. Based as it is on a sociological foundation, the Marxian view on the relation of man to the physical universe goes beyond Feuerbach's naturalism.

As far as the natural-scientific materialism of his contemporaries was concerned, Marx felt only scorn for it. The realization that we are both mind and body, spirit and flesh, is a basic assumption of Marxian naturalism. While Marx did not differ from the materialists in their belief that body is more fundamental than mind, he also clearly put the spirit high above the flesh. Marx cherished the spiritual aspirations and the spiritual world of man as much as the most determined idealist and showed little appreciation for the material in the everyday use of this term. Although he was close to materialists, Marx was so emphatic about the worth of man's spiritual life that he was rightly described — in the sense in which a paradox might state an important truth — as a thinker who leaned, so to speak, towards a practical dualism of body and mind and wished to liberate men from the bondage of their material nature.[111]

At the turn of the century the objection against describing the Marxian conception of history as historical materialism was widely voiced by numerous writers, including Engels himself. In the Special Introduction to the English edition of *Socialism: Utopian and Scientific* (1892), Engels was both ironic and embarrassed in explaining how it came about that the expression 'historical materialism' had been adopted to denote the view that the economic development of society provides the moving power and constitutes the ultimate cause of historical events. He indicated that the term might be inappropriate, but it was the best he could think of.[112] In 1890 Engels complained to one of his correspondents that 'materialist' as used in reference to the Marxian approach to the study of history had lost every definite connotation because nobody knew what meaning it had in the first place. 'In general, the word "materialist" serves many of the younger writers in Germany as a mere phrase with which anything and everything is labelled without further study, that is, they stick on this label and then think the question disposed of.'[113]

After Engels, Eduard Bernstein was the first to say that the designation 'the materialist conception of history' 'does not completely fit the thing'. He recommended that it be replaced by the expression 'the economic interpretation of history', for in spite of all that could be said against it, it was the most appropriate description of the Marxian theory of history. ('An economic interpretation of history does not necessarily mean that only economic forces, only economic motives, are recognized; but only that economics forms an ever recurring decisive force, the cardinal point of the great movements in history.'[114]) Heinrich Cunow agreed with Bernstein as to the appropriateness of the name 'the economic interpretation of history', which, he thought, was more suitable than the traditional one, 'the materialist conception'.[115]

Plekhanov and Lenin wrote hundreds of pages of polemics against N. K. Mikhailovsky, a prominent Russian critic of Marx in the fourth quarter of the last century, in which they were greatly concerned with the question in what sense the Marxian view of history could justly be classified as materialism. While for Lenin *Capital* provided a 'model of scientific materialist analysis' and both *The Poverty of Philosophy* and *The Communist Manifesto* were clearly 'based on the principles of materialism',[116] Mikhailovsky suggested that the Marxian conception of history was only an economic materialism. Both Lenin and Plekhanov refused to accept this new name; while Lenin dismissed it with a shrug of the shoulders, together with Mikhailovsky's 'empty and pretentious babbling', Plekhanov rightly argued that it was inept and misleading. The expression 'economic materialism', used by Mikhailovsky and other Russian critics of Marx to designate his theories, was 'extremely inappropriate', for it suggested a reductive materialism and a monistic economic doctrine of historical causation, and thus completely misrepresented the Marxian ideas. Plekhanov himself was not entirely certain which designation was the best and he used several of them — 'the materialist conception' or 'explanation', 'historical materialism', 'dialectical materialism' or 'the historical theory of Marx' — when he wished to refer to the views of Marx by a single name.[117]

A considerable number of writers objected less to the use of this or that qualifying term in the expression 'historical materialism' than to 'materialism' itself. Antonio Labriola, Benedetto Croce, Edwin R. A. Seligman, Eduard Bernstein, Max Adler, Karl Vorländer, and Bertrand Russell deplored the use of the term 'materialism' to denote the Marxian theory and suggested the expression 'the realistic view of history' as its alternative and more appropriate name.[118] They recognized that Marx's materialism was not a metaphysical transcendent doctrine. When historical materialism is discussed, we should forget the meaning of the term 'matter' in so far as it implies a hypothetical ultimate substratum of experience or denotes something that it is opposed to another ultimate factor called 'spirit'. In their view, Marx's materialism was, as it were, a method of thinking which tried to explain social and historical phenomena in terms of real objects, that is, those existing in time and space and subject to causal laws, in contradistinction to ideal or imaginary objects of the Hegelian philosophy. The real world of Marx may be coextensive with the material world of the metaphysician, but it should not be identified with it. The real world of Marx is rather the sensed natural and social environment into which man is born and where his consciousness and ideas have their origin.

These terminological and conceptual objections were of no avail, and the practice, originated by Engels, of qualifying the Marxian view of history as materialist has been followed until today. The dispute about the term which would appropriately denote the Marxian view actually concerned the concept, the meaning to be attached to the expression 'the Marxian conception of history'. Engels's terminological victory was of considerable importance, for it contributed to the belief that Marx was not a naturalist but a materialist and, in particular, a dialectical materialist.

F. A. Lange and also Bertrand Russell observed that in modern times 'materialism' is often used almost synonymously with 'scientific outlook', to denote a theory of nature which is believed to be simply an outcome of science, an exclusive result of experience, as opposed to speculations. They argued that for this very reason modern materialism should not be compared with similar views of the more distant past.[119] Marx was familiar with this linguistic usage. To establish 'true materialism' in the investigations of social relations was to establish a 'real science' (*die reelle Wissenschaft*) of these relations.[120] The method that starts with the actual relations of life in the explanations of historical events, Marx wrote, 'is the only materialistic and, therefore, the only scientific one'.[121] Materialism which is supposed to be just the sum total of views about the world established by scientific method was called 'natural-scientific materialism' by Engels and 'spontaneous materialism' by Lenin. This use of the term 'materialism' may, however, give rise to numerous misunderstandings, for it deviates too much from its traditional usage. Natural-scientific materialism is often a methodological rather than a metaphysical doctrine.

When Engels introduced the expression 'the materialist conception of history', he was not prompted by the semantical consideration that the terms 'materialist' and 'scientific' are synonymous in certain contexts. Engels was most likely to have thought of materialist metaphysics which supplied some of the elements of Marx's views of history and appeared to have achieved in this view its confirmation and extension.[122] Engels seemed to have been unaware of the fact that the connection between materialist metaphysics and Marx's view of history is extrinsic and not intrinsic, of historical and not of logical nature. To call Marx's conception of history 'materialist' did not indicate its own distinctive characteristics but only the philosophical tradition to which it belonged and was, thus, to use Croce's expression, merely a way of speaking.

To justify this assertion, the concept of primary historical factors must first be introduced. When we analyse a sequence of historical distinguish a number of causes or causal factors, such ...hical conditions, economic organization, political and ...stitutions, the character of leaders or the psychology of the people, which in some combination are supposed to be responsible for producing a given sequence. These factors may be evaluated as to their degree of importance and considered to be causally dependent on, or interacting with, each other. A factor is primary if it accounts for the occurrence of other factors, that is, strictly speaking, if it is their sufficient and necessary condition. A factor is relatively primary if it is primary with respect to some factors and not to others; otherwise, it is an absolutely primary factor. An absolutely primary factor would be the unique cause of any historical event and, thus, the unique cause of the historical process as a whole, which the traditional philosophies of history tried to discover

A theory of history is materialistic if it identifies the absolutely primary factor of history with some extraneous physical factor, that is, with some observable characteristics of physical environment. Such are, for instance, the geographical interpretation of history, first formulated by Montesquieu and expanded by Buckle and Taine, Marx's contemporaries, or the biological and racial theories put forward in the wake of the Darwinian revolution. These theories are reductive for they reduce all variations and changes in society to the ultimate action of the physical world. They are reductive also in the sense that they presuppose mechanistic materialism. This particular kind of materialism was based on the assumption that man is nothing but a mechanism and that his behaviour is ultimately subject to laws of physics and chemistry. As applied to social phenomena, reductive materialism is based on the assumption that every sociological statement is logically reducible to a conjunction of psychological statements which themselves are logically reducible to statements about physiological or chemico-physical states of the human organism.

There can be no doubt that Marx repudiated mechanistic materialism. This assertion is not only justified by Engels's consistent criticism of mechanistic materialism but also by what Marx himself said in *The Holy Family* about the philosophical sources of socialism and communism. These sources were not to be sought in the materialistic trend which culminated in the materialism of the French physicians and their discovery of *l'homme machine*, but in the mat-

erialism of the French supporters of Locke who were trying to overcome the dualism of man and nature by a naturalistic approach to
the relation of man to his physical and social environment. Reductive mechanistic materialism is incompatible with Marx's conception
of man as being both determined by and responding to the circumstances, including the physical factors, of his environment, which he
moulds and transforms by his action.

Marx also repudiated the materialist theories of history which
reduced primary historical factors to some physical characteristics
of man's natural environment. This can be seen from his discussion in
Capital of the role to be assigned to geographical conditions, such
as the fertility of the soil and the bounty of nature in general. Marx's
conclusion to this discussion was that natural conditions set limits to,
but do not strictly determine, the human or social response. Moreover, in proportion as industry advances, these natural limits
recede. More generally, in the course of historical development, the
significance of social bonds takes increasing precedence over dependence upon nature. Nature, Marx maintained, does not impose
upon man any necessity to improve himself and his conditions. A
natural force must be brought under the control of society to become
a socially significant fact and, generally, social and cultural factors
mediate and co-determine the role which natural resources, climate,
or topography, may play in history.[123] Marx did not earn the tag
with which he is labelled and which others, e.g. Montesquieu,
deserved more than he. For Montesquieu believed that such factors
as population, the geographical character of the territory, the nature
of the soil or the type of climate directly condition the general
structure of society and even the substance of its laws.[124]

In general, Marx could not have accepted an observable part of
physical reality as the absolute primary factor of social action and
relations, because in his view nature cannot function as a condition
determining human consciousness unless it is first defined in socio-
cultural terms, that is, unless it is a socially and culturally mediated
entity. Consequently, Marx could not and actually did not accept
any explanation of social activity in any other but social terms.
'Everything which sets men in motion', wrote Engels, 'must go
through their minds.'[125] Marx emphasized this fact in *The German
Ideology* to justify the view that not only circumstances make men,
as the 'old materialism' maintained, but men also make circumstances, as the 'new materialism' asserted.

The Marxian conception of history is clearly an anti-reductive theory, irrespective of whether it can justifiably be called materialistic or not. When Marx surveyed social or historical events, he introduced numerous factors whose interaction was to explain them. These factors were things familiar from everyday life, such as tools, machines, buildings, soil, natural resources, animals, and men, in whom soul and body, physical needs, and spiritual aspirations were inextricably merged. Marx never intended to examine the question whether these various factors could be reduced to one another and, indeed, such an undertaking would not be feasible. On the other hand, if historical factors are not concrete objects but categories of social phenomena or of social relations (such as the means of production, productive relations, ideologies, and so forth), the question whether these phenomena or relations are reducible to one another could arise and was actually raised. While Marx always admitted the existence of various historical factors, regarded them as parts of a single whole and investigated their interaction, occasionally he appeared to favour a reductive economic monism. For instance, the formulation of the materialist conception of history in the Preface to *A Contribution to the Critique of Political Economy* lends itself easily to the interpretation in which the economic factor becomes 'the only determining one'. But in the same Preface Marx refers the reader to *The German Ideology*, *The Poverty of Philosophy*, *Wage Labour and Capital* and *The Communist Manifesto* for a fuller exposition of his conception of history. To the works mentioned by Marx himself *The Eighteenth Brumaire of Louis Bonaparte* and *Capital* should be added. When all these publications are considered, it is impossible to see a reductive economic theory of history in the Marxian conception.

The problem was finally cleared up after Marx's death and the verdict was against reductive monism and for a multi-factorial and functional approach to the analysis of social and historical phenomena. Engels's letters on historical materialism (1890–94) are a firm rejection in his own and Marx's name of an interpretation of historical materialism which would make of it a reductive economic theory of history. Writers and thinkers as different as Bernstein, Croce, Labriola, and Plekhanov opposed the transformation of historical materialism, conceived as a method of investigating social and historical phenomena, into an economic theory of history, and they often did it with trenchant arguments, wit, and perspicacity.

But even if it were true that Marx wished all history to be (plained in economic terms alone and to assert that history is nothing but economic history and the rest futility and appearances, the economic interpretation could not be called 'materialistic', for neither the social relations of production nor the mode of production are concepts definable in terms of physical objects alone.[126] It is an elementary error to say that economic materialism is materialism and 'can hardly be described in other terms'.[127] Nor is the Marxian view justifiably described as materialism, because Marx explains the social activity of man and man's history 'by his needs and by the means and methods of satisfying these needs'.[128] No historian can avoid resorting to this kind of explanation and, consequently, all historians would be materialists. The Marxian conception of history, whether conceived as a reductive or a non-reductive theory, is not a materialistic theory in the sense in which theories introducing physical conditions as primary factors in history may be justifiably called materialistic.[129]

What can be said about the Marxian conception with certainty concerns its naturalistic character. As Marx saw it, within an all-inclusive and self-sufficing nature there was no place for the operation of disembodied forces, of a mind, a soul, a spirit. Consequently, in Marx's view of the physical world, man, society, and history, not the slightest trace of the supernatural was left. Man is a natural entity among others and does not hold a privileged position in the universe. Even when man struggles with and tries to secure his control over nature, he remains part of it.

This does not mean that the knowledge of man can be reduced to a natural science and his activity accounted for by the mechanical laws of inanimate nature. Furthermore, the general assumptions of naturalism do not imply that only what is material exists; for instance, neither the social relations which bind people together nor society itself are material entities whose mode of existence and structure are subject to the laws of material bodies. But the assumptions of naturalism may be conceived as implying materialism. In this case, the difference between naturalism and materialism disappears, and Marx's naturalistic conception of history is reduced to a materialistic theory. Engels did make materialist inferences from Marx's naturalism and passed them on to posterity as Marx's own metaphysical doctrine.

8. MARX'S CONTRIBUTION TO NATURALISM

When Marx maintains that his method of investigating history has a materialistic basis, he does not proclaim thereby his adherence to an absolute materialism; there is no warrant for such an interpretation. The philosophical principle on which the application of his method depends is not materialism but naturalism, the belief that nature is a self-contained and self-regulating system comprising everything that exists. Marxian naturalism was to surmount the Hegelian dualism of nature and spirit, concealed by the subordination of the former to the latter, and Feuerbach's residual dualism of man and nature. While Hegel's speculative philosophy is clearly anti- or supra-naturalistic, the remnants of supra-naturalism in Feuerbach's anthropological materialism are less conspicuous.

Feuerbach's case is really representative for the whole materialistic tradition, which obviously was unable to account for the variety of human experience. As long as materialism regarded man as a complicated machine, it had to remain unhistorical and to recognize its limitations and the impossibility of describing the whole range of man's life-experience in materialistic terms. This was inevitable, for even the simplest cognitive act cannot be explained as an effect of a mechanical cause; external mechanical stimuli do not engender meaningful responses. As Sidney Hook pointed out, Marx objected to every previous doctrine of materialism because it made perception, thought, cognition, and creative act, whether in art or science, social and political life or morality, 'appear to be either unnecessary or miraculous'.[130] Consequently, materialism exposed itself to a not unjustifiable charge of ignoring, or failing to consider in its system, a wide area of human experience and essential human values, thus becoming one-sided, soulless and, as Marx put it, 'hostile to humanity (*menschenfeindlich*)'.[131]

On the other hand, if materialism wished to acknowledge the whole scale and richness of man's experience, it had to become untrue to itself and to accept in some form or other idealistic or spiritualistic conceptions. Materialists themselves were doubtful whether particles of matter in motion could possibly account for the varied content and the distinctive qualities of man's moral, religious, artistic, or intellectual experience. Recognizing the strength of the Cartesian argument that the effect cannot exceed its cause in perfection, such materialists, and Feuerbach was one of them, made concessions to the traditional prejudices about the unworthiness of the physical aspect of human nature and regarded its higher aspirations as the only genuinely human qualities.[132] Marx maintained that the widespread confusion about the lower and higher moral worth to be attached to different human activities — reflected in the ethical implications commonly associated with materialism and idealism and with the distinction between nature and culture — was responsible for the fact that history was written according to extraneous standards. That which had no connection with ordinary life was presented as supremely historical, and that which reflected the 'real production of life' was beneath history.[133]

Feuerbach refused to recognize the simple fact that man is what he is and not something else, for his own inadequate system provided arguments for the view ascribing an irreducible spiritual factor to the human person. As Engels repeatedly emphasized in *Ludwig Feuerbach*, Feuerbach displayed a defective discrimination and appreciation of the variety inherent in human life in all its complexity and intricacy. This was not always Feuerbach's fault, for the deficiencies of his ways of viewing man and society were due to the materialistic doctrine current at that time, against which he fought, but of which he was unable to shake himself free. The old materialism was of real benefit as a corrective to the metaphysical imagination and its pretensions of penetrating by pure thought into the world of things. But the old materialism was inadequate and barren for the understanding of art and culture and inappropriate for the examination of the highest functions of the human spirit.[134]

In Engels's opinion, which developed in full a point of view succinctly stated by Marx a few years earlier,[135] mechanistic materialism in general and Feuerbach's materialism in particular showed an 'astonishing poverty', imaginative blindness and shallowness when compared with Hegel's wealth and profundity of thought, his sense of the historical, of the complexity, richness, and variety of factors involved in the historical process. This feeling was shared by Plekhanov, who constantly emphasized Hegel's superiority over metaphysical materialism and pointed out that pre-Marxian materialism did not know how 'to give a materialist explanation to all sides of human life'.[136] Lenin, too, supported this assessment indirectly when he wrote that 'intelligent (sc. dialectical) idealism' is closer to 'intelligent (sc. dialectical) materialism' than any other kind of materialism.[137]

The criticism of Feuerbach's materialism can be reduced to the assertion that Feuerbach was unable to explain human activity in terms of his own materialistic philosophy. This criticism could have been directed against the whole materialistic tradition. 'Materialism', wrote F. A. Lange, its historian, 'can hardly close the circle of its system without borrowing from idealism.' What the idealists lack in scientific knowledge and habits of mind, they make up for by their insight into various forms of human experience which do not lend themselves easily to examination in terms of scientific categories.[138]

The conclusion was inescapable that neither the French materialists nor Feuerbach managed to provide an adequate materialist foundation on which a comprehensive science of man could be established. The French materialists were so anxious to show that the materialist conception of nature could be universally applied and give all the explanation required from it that they were satisfied with the idea of considering man as a member of the animal kingdom and as an organization of material bodies subject to the laws of mechanics. But to consider man merely as *matière sensible*, as Holbach did, or merely as 'an object of the senses' in the manner of Feuerbach, was to bar the approach to the understanding of human activity, social life, and historical development. On the basis of mechanistic materialism there could be no history of man, and without change and development it was impossible to explain how man, being a natural entity, could acquire his distinctively human characteristics. The only history that mechanistic materialism would allow for was a record of how the blind forces of nature operate and determine man's behaviour.

In this respect, Feuerbach's anthropological materialism was no improvement upon French materialism. It is true that Feuerbach regarded man as an irreducible natural entity, but he continued to regard him only as a passive object, and never as an active subject, of history. Consequently, since he did not wish to confine himself to the examination of man as a member of the animal kingdom and tried, though unsuccessfully, to do justice to the complexity and richness of human nature, he could not avoid making concessions to idealism or spiritualism.

Feuerbach managed to overcome the Hegelian conception of man in philosophy, but sociologically man remained what he was for Hegel, namely, an abstract being, a concept and a metaphysical entity whose existence was outside of historical development and social and economic evolution. Feuerbach's anthropological materialism still left room for differentiating various realms of reality. Moreover, it was methodologically inadequate to provide a unified approach to the investigations of man and other natural objects, of which, according to the thesis of anthropological materialism, he was one.

This objective was achieved by Marx's naturalism. His naturalistic theory replaced Hegel's idealistic conception in which mind, as a manifestation of the Idea or Spirit, was endowed with an original power, autonomous activity, and inherent energy. The successful attempt to widen the scope of natural phenomena is perhaps Marx's most important contribution to philosophy.[139] According to Marx's 'consistent naturalism or humanism', the emergence of the human spirit takes place at a late stage in the evolution of man. It is a product of the power of development immanent in the 'species life', generated and impelled by man's life in society, the development which accounts for constant human growth and ever new achievements. All events are equally natural; in particular, social, moral, and spiritual life, all that is truly creative and powerful in man, belongs to the natural order of things, as much as man's biological life.[140] The power, activity, and energy of spirit are the 'fantastic reflection of our own essence', that is, spirit is man's objectified and reified capacity for creative self-expression. 'Activity', wrote Feuerbach, 'is the positive sense of one's personality . . . the happiest, the most blissful activity is that which is productive.' To paraphrase Feuerbach's famous statement, to view the idea or spirit of transcendental idealism as the projected personality of man is to discover that the secret of metaphysics is nothing but anthropology.[141]

Since the whole range of human experience and activity has the quality of natural events, all man's differential ways of action can be accepted as distinctively human traits. Marx explicitly recognized such distinctive human characteristics and made no effort to explain them away as a combination of other characteristics to be found in the whole animal kingdom.[142] Marx was not one of those naturalistic philosophers of whom George Santayana said that they have but cursory and wretched notions of the inner life of mind, hate poetry and fancy and passion and even philosophy itself, and are despised by the academic and cultivated world harking back to Plato or Aristotle or Hegel, since these thinkers at least were conversant with the spirit of man.[143]   Marx looked for the kind of naturalistic philosophy which would make full allowance for 'human self-consciousness' and would not yield precedence to idealism in explaining man's creative achievements.

It was the establishment of the 'science of man' that provided Marx with intellectual tools for advancing beyond 'all the hitherto existing materialism' and for the solution of his problem.   Without the assistance of sociology Marx would have been helpless against the claim of idealism that man's spiritual experience, his autonomous social, moral, artistic, religious, and intellectual life, gives a better key to the understanding of the universe than materialism, based on natural science, would ever be able to provide.   Marx's solution of the problem set by idealism consisted essentially in widening the scope of natural phenomena, in recognizing in society a natural entity, subject to laws of its own, and in regarding man's nature as the changing product of social evolution and historical progress.

Unlike his predecessors, with the exception of Comte, Marx did not hold society to be an artificial creation, added to or superimposed upon nature, but a natural entity.   Hobbes was mistaken when he said that the social order was generated and maintained by an act of will of the ruler; Rousseau misinterpreted facts when he contrasted natural man as he came from the hands of nature with artificial man as made by society; and the French *philosophes* were equally wrong when they saw in the decisions of the lawmaker the source of social laws and the efficient cause of social processes. There is a determinate order inherent in social existence itself.   The laws which govern social phenomena are as much laws of nature as the laws of physics and biology are.   These social laws determine the evolution of society and with it the evolution of man's nature.   The social being is rooted in nature and human nature is rooted in society.

Man is not an entity of a higher order, an immortal spirit in a carnal tomb, confronting nature as its judge and arbiter, and trying to reach perfection against the opposition of the blind and elemental forces of nature.   The concept of a merciless struggle against nature or of a romantic unity with nature are, according to Marx, entirely inappropriate for the description of the actual relationship between nature and man.[144]   There is no human nature independent of society and there is no man distinct from social men whose ever-changing characteristics are determined by the entire structure of society. Man acquires novel characteristics, for he is not only shaped by his natural and social environment but also changes and transforms this environment through his responsive action. To maintain his existence man acts on the external world and by his action changes his own nature. Since man's action is not individual but social, all human action is to be explained in terms of the social conditions in which it takes place. The distinctive characteristics of individuals, acquired in the course of social evolution, should be conceived as moulded by a particular form of social organization and related to its structural differentiation at any given time.

These assumptions allowed Marx to consider man entirely within nature, within the totality of objects all of which belong to the same realm of being and thus lend themselves to treatment by one single method. There are no ontological differences of level within human experience and activity, although there is an order of succession in time in their appearance. Just as the same method applies to all events and to all areas of human experience, so all human experience, from the 'lowest' to the 'highest', is equally amenable to a non-reductive analysis and, in principle, to the same method of investigation as that used with respect to any ordinary object or aspect of nature. Since reality is entirely uniform, the various sciences, whether natural or social, can use one and the same method in dealing with each of its parts.

All culture-producing activities of man, all his creative acts and strivings towards perfection grow out of human work and social activity concerned with the ordinary process of living, with the production and reproduction of life. Their growth is determined by social relations and interaction, processes in which individuals participate, and not by 'human essences' or 'human nature' conceived as a spiritual substance that is autonomous in its being and spontaneous in its development. Recognizing by implication the principle of the continuity of causal influences,[145] Marx can accept the appearance in man of characteristics which are novel as compared with those of other species, that is, irreducible to any combination of their characteristics, and which continue to be dependent on circumstances, not necessarily distinctively human. They illustrate the emergence of a 'higher' activity from a 'lower', the different types of activity being causally related to, but not identical with, each other.

Marx recognized the process of cumulative development, social advance or progress. The emergence of a 'higher' activity from a 'lower' or of a superior form of social organization from an inferior one is a manifestation of an increase in complexity and differentiation of social processes. However, the principle of evolution and progressive advance does not imply the ontological doctrine of emergence, which does not seem to be compatible with an anthropological naturalism and of which no trace can be found in Marx.

III

The Influence of Hegel's Philosophy

In his study *From Hegel to Marx* Sidney Hook observed that to juxtapose the names of Hegel and Marx is to raise a challenging problem in the history of philosophical thought, and not simply to state a recognized relationship or a logical connection. This opinion is confirmed by the fact that there is a striking lack of consensus in the evaluation of Marx's relation to Hegel.

At one extreme there are those who see a pervasive and overwhelming influence of Hegel's thought upon Marx's philosophical development and beliefs. Their point of view has recently been expressed in the neat formula 'Marx is unthinkable without Hegel'; since Marx never escaped from the domination of Hegelian philosophy, in a certain sense he remained a Hegelian throughout his life.[1] Marx remained a Hegelian in spite of the fact that he was a materialist and Hegel an idealist. Ever since Engels made this point, dialectics provided the latent bond uniting Hegel and Marx over and beyond their manifest differences. Engels, Plekhanov, and Lenin are the most prominent representatives of the *Verhegelung*, of the Hegelizing interpretation of the philosophy of Marx. This view is also supported by some Western historians of philosophy. To give two recent examples, Gustav A. Wetter and Robert C. Tucker maintain that Marx's doctrine is Hegel's 'metaphysics of identity' turned upside down or that 'Marxism may be seen as Hegelianism inverted'.[2]

At the other extreme there are the adherents of the opinion that there is a complete break of philosophical continuity between Hegel and Marx. According to Karl Löwith, Marx and Kierkegaard were Hegel's most prominent opponents; together they succeeded in destroying his entire intellectual world.[3] After Hegel's death, wrote Herbert Marcuse, 'the history of Hegelianism became the history of a struggle against Hegel in which he was used as a symbol for all that the new intellectual efforts opposed'. The true content of Hegelian philosophy was taken over by Marx but its historical heritage consisted solely in its critical tendencies which Marx applied to social theory and practice. Marx accepted Hegel's demonstration that the material and spiritual powers of mankind achieved a stage of maturity; this made it possible to reorganize social and political reality in accordance with the requirements of reason. It is not possible, however, to show the transformation of the Hegelian categories into those to be found in Marx. The framework and particular concepts of the Marxian doctrine cannot be derived from the theories either of Hegel or of Feuerbach.[4]

The Hegelizing approach to the philosophy of Marx has been rejected by an array of distinguished thinkers and writers. While recognizing the fact that during a relatively short period in his youth Marx was indeed a Hegelian, they deny that his surrender to the intellectual fashion of the day left any permanent traces in his mind or inspired his mature views. No philosophical relationship, as distinct from a historical connection, links Hegel and Marx.

Finally, there is the third group of the exponents of Marx's doctrine who believe that in his development — from the acceptance of Hegelian philosophy to the formulation of his own point of view — both the continuity and the break with Hegel can be discovered. Marx was a Hegelian for a time but then ceased to be one. He did not remain unaffected by his study of Hegelian philosophy but his views are not a simple *Umkehrung* of those of Hegel. In order to discover what Marx had borrowed from Hegel a historical and logical analysis is necessary, because Marx expressed Hegel's ideas in terms of a different philosophical framework before introducing them into his own system. Sidney Hook's *From Hegel to Marx* is an outstanding instance of this approach.

I. THE VARIOUS INTERPRETATIONS OF THE RELATION OF MARX TO HEGEL

Engels, Plekhanov, and Lenin, who shared the view of the importance of Hegel for the philosophy of Marx, were all staunch and enthusiastic admirers of Hegel. Each of them left a comprehensive testimony to his high esteem of the Hegelian system, to his respectful appreciation of Hegel's insight and vision, encyclopaedic knowledge, and breadth of view.[5] Within the Marxian tradition, the combined impact of the opinions of Engels, Plekhanov, and Lenin has played a decisive role in the evaluation of Hegelian philosophy and of its part in the formation of the Marxian doctrine. Consequently, Hegel came to be regarded the most important thinker before Marx, equalled only by Aristotle and surpassed only by Marx himself.

According to Engels, these three thinkers alone closely investigated dialectics and the evolutionary processes occurring in nature and society, thereby establishing a dynamic world-view that replaced the familiar static outlook.[6] However, only Hegel gave to Aristotle's masterly conception of nature its distinctive and consistent form. Once Hegel's idealist starting-point and his partiality to a fact-defying system are set aside, there remains Hegelian dialectics, both a system of the most general laws of the universe and a set of the rules of procedure on which modern materialism is based.[7]

It was Engels's opinion, endorsed by Lenin, that without German idealist philosophy, particularly that of Hegel, 'German scientific socialism . . . would never have come into being'.[8] The Hegelian system had epoch-making merits and achievements to its credit; it was 'the last and most consummate form of philosophy' after which 'all philosophy collapsed', bequeathing the conception that 'the natural, historical and intellectual world moves and transforms itself endlessly in a constant process of becoming and passing away'. The legacy bequeathed by Hegelian philosophy to its successors required a search for the laws of motion of this process of transformation, a task taken up and successfully accomplished by Marx.[9]

Without knowledge of Hegelian philosophy, wrote Plekhanov, it is difficult to grasp the method of Marx, who is a true successor of Hegel. In Hegel's hands dialectics became 'the most powerful scientific weapon', making Hegel 'the founder of the most progressive ideas of today'. 'This idealist of genius,' wrote Plekhanov, 'this greatest of idealists seems to have set himself the task of clearing the road for materialism.'[10]

Lenin shared the views of Engels and Plekhanov. He felt that Hegel excelled in profundity many scientists and scholars of his time, and described his own work as 'the continuation of the work of Hegel and Marx'. He was convinced that the study of the former was a difficult but necessary approach to the understanding of the latter. The seeds of historical materialism existed in embryo in Hegel.[11] More generally, Engels was right when he said that 'Hegel's system was materialism turned upside down'.[12] According to Lenin, the inversion of materialism attributed to Hegel applies not only to the content but also to the method of Hegel's philosophy, for Hegel detected the dialectics of things in the dialectics of concepts.[13]   The basis of Marx's method was Hegelian dialectics materialistically conceived.   'It is impossible to understand *Capital*', Lenin observed, 'without having thoroughly studied and understood the whole of Hegel's logic. . . . Consequently, half a century later none of the Marxists understood Marx.' [14]

The fact that Engels, Plekhanov, and Lenin had a tremendous admiration for Hegel, had and continues to have, important implications for the interpretation of Marxian philosophy by its supporters. The feeling is widespread among them that Marxian philosophy is bound to lose its distinctive features if it is torn away from its Hegelian background.   This view is also shared by some historians of social and political ideas.   They feel that the framework of Marx's historical and sociological theories is 'undeviatingly Hegelian', even though the turn he gave 'to the master's doctrine was one which the latter would doubtless have been the first to repudiate'.[15]   In both cases the firm conviction that the Hegelian categories constitute an essential part of Marx's philosophy leads to some strange consequences.   Since the influence of Hegel upon Marx, which the exponents under discussion believe to have been decisive, is apparent above all, on the linguistic level, the hidden Hegelian significance of Marxian beliefs has to be revealed by some sort of depth analysis.

Robert C. Tucker tried to demonstrate that the true meaning of what Marx wrote is quite different from what he actually said. Marx's basic sociological, economic, and political doctrines have a speculative and not an empirical origin ; they were based on the development of German philosophy and theology from Immanuel Kant to Ludwig Feuerbach, were derived from the philosophy and theology of Hegel, and remained, essentially, an eschatology and a theology.   'Marx founded Marxism in an outburst of Hegelizing' and 'created his own system on the basis of a misreading of Hegel'.[16] Feuerbach showed that Hegel's conception of history as a process of self-realization of God in the self-consciousness of mankind was an inverted representation of man alienated from himself in religion. Marx believed that Feuerbach erred by confining himself to theology, since Hegel really tried to express the self-estrangement of man in all his productive activity, including the process of labour.

Marx reached his political economy by 'the mental process of turning Hegel upside down in accordance with Feuerbach's prescription'; even *Capital*, ostensibly a book about economics and the capitalist system, has perhaps more in common with *The Phenomenology of Mind* than with *The Wealth of Nations*.[17] Marx wished to create 'a Hegelianism of the market place, in which not the spirit but man strives for self-realization through the struggle of a divided self to resolve its inner conflict and recover its lost unity'.[18]

To say that the Marxian doctrines are but an inversion of the Hegelian theological and mystical idea of the absolute spirit which, divided against itself, strives for self-realization and, finally, having completed its succession of inner transformations through history, attains redemption, is a conclusion apparently supported by its own inherent logic. Any view which contains its own confirmation is always suspect, and this rule applies to the exegesis in question. It is possible to give a theological interpretation of a naturalistic system, such as that of Marx, and find suitable quotations in its support. But such illustrations are methodologically unsatisfactory and they do not assure interpretative adequacy. An interpretation is adequate if it does justice to all the main theses of the interpreted systems without resorting to the device of conferring upon them a latent, esoteric meaning in substitution for their manifest, exoteric meaning, that is, for what they in fact state. The interpretation of Marxian theories as inverted Hegelianism does not seem to pass this crucial test of adequacy.

It seems, for instance, utterly erroneous to argue that the alienation of man from himself, as described by Marx, is a quasi-religious experience resulting from the dissociation of the self from the double life, metaphysically or theologically conceived, of a divided human being, and not a social phenomenon produced by the division of labour, technical progress, and the class structure of society.[19] In Marx's times some perceptive minds were fully aware of the fact that the increasing specialization and division of labour were breaking up society into innumerable small fractions and were responsible for much social, moral, and intellectual hardship which, unless remedied, would be a serious abatement from the benefits of the advance of civilization.[20] Marx fully agreed with this view. Similarly, he had no patience with the thinkers who believed that theology rather than sociology provided the key to the understanding of history and society. In a reference to the brothers Bauer and

Hegel in *The Holy Family*, Marx said that men are neither gods nor potential gods; on the contrary, men are determined in what they are and do by the social conditions of their life.[21] In *The German Ideology* Marx spoke scornfully of the dominance of religious ideas in German philosophical criticism from David Strauss to Max Stirner and of the futility of reducing metaphysical, moral, political, and other problems to religious or theological conceptions in whose terms they were to be discussed and solved.[22] It is difficult to reconcile Marx's attack on theology in its mystical or secular form, represented by Hegel and the Young Hegelians respectively, with Marx as theologian or philosopher obsessed by a religious and moral vision of reality. Finally, *Capital* is clearly what it claims to be, an empirical rather than a speculative work, a social history and a sociological and economic analysis of the capitalist system. To describe it as a chapter in the history of the self-creation or self-realization of man in the process of productive labour is to use an irrelevant and confusing mode of expression.

At the other extreme of the spectrum of opinions concerning the relation of Marx to Hegel are those who regard the Hegelizing interpretation of Marx's doctrines either as grossly exaggerated or even as entirely wrong. According to Benedetto Croce, Marx took from Hegel only his phraseology. Moreover, he adopted it 'with a freedom that at times seems not to lack an element of mockery'.[23] Karl Löwith objected to the Young Hegelians in general for having reduced Hegel's conceptual dialectics to a stylistic device. Georges Gurvitch went even further by describing the Hegelianism of the Left as a *saint-simonisme hégélianisé*, that is, Saint-Simonism expressed in Hegelian terms.[24] That Hegel's influence upon Marx was terminological rather than conceptual is a view more or less common to all the writers of the anti-Hegelian orientation. Marx's predilection for the obscure language of Hegel and his pseudo-technical vocabulary, rich in oracular and mystical intimations, is plain and clear; it makes some of his early writings hardly readable and some later works more involved and difficult to understand than was necessary. That the common vocabulary of Hegel and Marx should be distinguished from their alleged conceptual affinity is a view which can be supported by what Marx himself said on the matter in the Preface to the second German edition of *Capital*. Marx confessed that having been angered by the Young Hegelians' contemptuous silence over Hegel, 'I openly avowed myself the pupil of that mighty thinker and even here and there . . . coquetted with the modes of expression peculiar to him'.

Werner Sombart believed that Marx never took anything from Hegel without having first expurgated it from the 'conceptual mythology' (*Begriffsmythologie*) characteristic of Hegel. But Sombart was certain that after this expurgation had been accomplished nothing essentially Hegelian remained in what Marx borrowed from Hegel (in this respect Sombart differed, for instance, from Georg Lukács). Consequently, Sombart had no doubt whatsoever that Marx had nothing in common with the spirit of Hegelian philosophy. 'Marx often made use of Hegel's jargon and took over from him very many particular, isolated ideas. But basically he is not in the least related to Hegel. Metaphysically, ontologically, historiosophically, in brief, in all decisive respects, Marx stands in the sharpest opposition to Hegel.' [25]

Benedetto Croce's impressionistic observations on the relation of Marx to Hegel were further elaborated by Karl Vorländer. He did not entirely deny Hegel's influence upon Marx but reduced it to what Engels called Hegel's 'tremendous sense of the historical' which left a lasting impact upon Marx's thought. The tacit distinction between the works of the beginner, the young Marx infected by Hegelianism, and those of the mature thinker, the author of *Capital*, helped Vorländer to disregard other evidence of Hegel's influence upon Marx.[26] Vorländer calculated that Marx quoted Hegel eleven times in the first volume of *Capital* (and only once in the remaining two volumes). All these references could really be dispensed with, for they were merely meant to indicate either some analogies between Hegel's and Marx's views or to testify to his respect for certain aspects of the Hegelian system which replaced the derisive scorn for Hegel so conspicuous in some of Marx's earlier writings. They should be treated, to use Marx's own explanation, as a flirtation with Hegel's peculiar phraseology, as a homage to the 'mighty thinker' at that time reviled by his 'arrogant and mediocre' detractors, and thus as a testimony to Marx's utter contempt for them, this contempt being disguised as a respectful tribute paid to the old master by his former follower.[27]

To regard Hegelianism in Marx as merely apparent or to say that his thought shows no influence of Hegel's speculative philosophy is a view which has repeatedly been challenged for a number of relevant and irrelevant reasons. Engels's opinion on this matter was accepted by German Marxist orthodoxy at the turn of the last century and later also by Marxism–Leninism. In the course of time it has become 'common knowledge' that Marx formulated rigorously and scientifically, as Plekhanov put it, 'what in Hegel is accidental, a guess of greater or lesser genius'.[28] The acceptance of the Hegelizing interpretation was due, above all, to the enormous prestige which Engels enjoyed in the socialist movement as the guardian of Marx's authentic thought. Another accidental reason was the fact that the first attempt to dissociate Marxian philosophy from its Hegelian ancestry, particularly from Hegelian dialectics, was made by Eduard Bernstein. This implied, at least until Stalin's anti-Hegel pronouncement, that to free Marxian philosophy from its connection with Hegel was to indulge in revisionism.

> It is the greatest misfortune in the history of Marxian theory that Bernstein combined his drift toward reformism with an attack on the Hegelian Marxian philosophy. That philosophy was already dying a natural death among all sorts of Marxists, revolutionary and reformist alike; but Bernstein's overt attack upon it in the name of reformism automatically revived it in the minds of all genuine revolutionists.[29]

Bernstein felt that the Marxian doctrine could do without the 'treacherous' Hegelian dialectics which set snares upon Marx's thought and handicapped any consistent analysis of things. Whatever Marx and Engels accomplished, Bernstein wrote, they did not achieve by means of the dialectical method but in spite of it.[30]

Karl Kautsky and Plekhanov rejected Bernstein's conclusion. According to Plekhanov, the dialectical method was the most powerful instrument bequeathed by German idealism to its successor, modern materialism.[31] 'What remains of Marxism', asked Kautsky, 'if it is deprived of dialectics, its "best working tool" and its "sharpest weapon"? Was not Marx's and Engels's thinking dialectical through and through?'[32] Although Kautsky only repeated certain well-established opinions, above all, those of Engels, without examining their validity, his views prevailed in the dispute and were later endorsed by Max Adler and Heinrich Cunow on the one hand and by Lenin on the other. Cunow regarded dialectics as the most important procedure of Marx's method without which *Capital* could not have been written. He was altogether convinced that 'he who knows Hegel sees his influence in practically every sentence of Marx'.[33]   Similarly Lenin felt that dialectics provides the central point of convergence for the entire body of Marx's and Engels's ideas ; to eliminate it from their system was to deprive them of the 'thing that constituted the masterly advance they made in the history of revolutionary thought'.[34]   As Lenin pointed out in *The Three Sources and Three Component Parts of Marxism*, the Marxian doctrine was the legitimate successor to the best that was created by mankind in the nineteenth century, of which the one essential part was German classical philosophy, the other two, English political economy and French socialism.   In contradistinction to Kautsky, Lenin's verdict was based on some acquaintance with the philosophy of Hegel and was prompted by his tremendous admiration of it, repeatedly expressed in his *Philosophical Notebooks*.   After Engels, it was Lenin who contributed most to establishing the view among Marx's followers that Marx shared some basic presuppositions and concepts with Hegel.

This opinion is also supported by numerous philosophers and historians of philosophy, although they may differ as to which particular elements of Hegel's philosophy they consider most important for an understanding of Marx.   That Marx was indebted to Hegel for some of his ideas and categories is as plain as is his firm rejection of other Hegelian conceptions.   This simple fact provides the starting-point for Sidney Hook's important study *From Hegel to Marx*.

Hook was impressed by the fact that in Marxian philosophy we are faced by the 'persistence not merely of Hegelian terminology but of basic Hegelian categories'.   Consequently, Hook contended, there are reasons to believe that the 'Hegelian elements in Marx are integral to his system'.   The fact that Hegel and Marx share some doctrines is as conspicuous as that they entirely disagree in others.   It is important to emphasize both the similarities and dissimilarities in order to invalidate past, and to forestall future, attempts at Hegelizing the Marxian teaching in a one-sided way.[35]

Nobody can deny that in his youth Marx's mind was steeped in Hegel's doctrine and that at that time he shared the illusions about the efficacy of critical philosophy, the war cry and the weapon of the Hegelian Left, by means of which social consciousness was to be freed from its limitations and social reality reorganized on a rational basis.   Marx was a Hegelian because he assumed that

'Reason is the Sovereign of the World' and that man is a thinking being. He was a Young Hegelian of the Left because he believed that thinking can bring reality into line with reason and re-establish their unity. As Marx put it in his own words at the time, 'you cannot transcend philosophy without realizing it'. But Marx soon discovered that to realize philosophy the weapon of criticism was not enough. A struggle that used as its weapon ideas alone was doomed to failure, for 'ideas cannot carry anything out at all'. In order to make ideas effective, men who dispose of actual power are needed.[36] As Marx wrote elsewhere, 'material force can only be overthrown by material force'. No theory becomes a material force unless it has seized the masses and moved them 'to overthrow all those conditions in which man is an abased, enslaved, abandoned, contemptible being'.[37] Critical philosophy was not such a theory; instead of producing real changes it merely indulged in phrase-making and combined the intellectual attitude of critical rationalism with an unqualified willingness to be reconciled to intolerable social and political conditions. Marx began searching for an explanation of how it was possible that a deep involvement in ideas could be combined with a disdainful ignorance of the true state of reality. The source of this divergence, he maintained, should be sought in the nature of theory itself, in its failure to find a material weapon to support its weapon of criticism.

The basic defect of the Young Hegelians was their belief that they could realize philosophy without transcending it in actual life. More generally, they shared Hegel's failure to understand that no philosophy is realized in a people unless it fulfils the needs of the people.[38] Having made this discovery, Marx passed on from the criticism of the illusory achievements of the Young Hegelians to the critique of Hegel's philosophy. The defects of the Young Hegelians only reflected the more fundamental defects of their master, Hegel.

This critique comprised the Hegelian notion of the state whose sovereignty over civil society, rent by conflicts and strife, and over the people (*das Volk*), given to action 'irrational, barbarous frightful',[39] was supposed to establish the rule of reason; the conception of history as a movement of logical categories which generate and turn into each other; the conception of man's self-creation through spiritual activity and the conception of dialectics as the source of change and the *modus operandi* of the Spirit.

This critique of the Hegelian intellectual world made Marx a consistent opponent of Hegel and prompted some exponents to adopt the conclusion that the *Economic and Philosophic Manuscripts of 1844* and *The Holy Family* marked Marx's final and complete emancipation from the influence of Hegelian philosophy.[40]   In fact, the disdainful hostility towards Hegel was an indication of Marx's abandonment of speculative philosophy and his transition into an empirically oriented 'science of man', into the study of history and political economy as domains of positive knowledge.   In a letter to his father written in Berlin towards the end of 1837, Marx had referred to the grotesque, luring, and yet repelling melody (*groteske Felsen-melodie*) of Hegelian philosophy which had made him feel ill at ease ; he had fallen under the spell of this 'world philosophy', although he described this fact with a touch of self-irony.[41]   Now the spell was broken.

The new orientation of Marx's thought became increasingly apparent not only in the content but also in the language of his contributions posterior to *The Holy Family*, with the possible exception of *The Poverty of Philosophy*, for he abandoned the ambiguous idealist terminology and replaced it by a more precise and clear mode of expression.   However, as Marx himself indicated in his Preface to *A Contribution to the Critique of Political Economy*, his criticism of Hegel was not exclusively destructive.   It was in the course of his critique of Hegel's idealist cosmology, philosophy of history, and political and social theory that Marx arrived at the formulation of his own views on these matters, in which some of Hegel's conceptions were bound to survive.   Although they underwent a metamorphosis in the process of adaptation to the naturalistic world-view of Marx, they do bear the marks of their intellectual origin.

2. MARX'S ATTITUDE TOWARDS HEGEL

Before the impact of Hegel's speculative philosophy upon Marx is examined more closely, another problem has to be considered.   In the Foreword to *Ludwig Feuerbach*, Engels suggested that the evolution of Marx's and his own attitude to Hegelian philosophy was identical.[42]   Engels's statement has been tacitly accepted by practically every student of Marx.   Merely by stating explicitly the implicit admission, one can see at once that it is untenable.

As far as philosophical training and qualifications were concerned, Marx and Engels were not on a par. Hegel's influence on Marx was modified by Marx's wide philosophical knowledge and familiarity with the pre-Socratic philosophers, Plato, Aristotle, Epicurus, the Stoics; Bacon, Locke, Hobbes, Berkeley, Hume, Descartes, Spinoza, Condillac; the French materialists and *philosophes* of the French Enlightenment, Kant and Fichte.[43] When Marx wrote his doctoral dissertation, Hegel was for him an intellectual giant and the creator of great new departments of knowledge. For instance, as Marx emphasized in his dissertation, prior to Hegel there was no history of philosophy worthy of note. But however high his regard for Hegel might have been, the young Marx viewed Hegel as standing on the shoulders, building on the foundations, of his predecessors; he could excel their achievements not by the force of his own mind, but only because of the intellectual inheritance which they had bequeathed to posterity. Hegel was for Marx a philosopher of genius and yet his system did not veil the whole world from Marx's eyes. His admiration for Hegel was not the kind that makes the follower blind or uncritical to the master's intellectual defects.

If Hegel was an intellectual giant for the young Marx, his reputation went to pieces under the blows of Feuerbach's criticism, never to rise again to its previous Olympian heights. In his *Kritik der Hegelschen Staatsphilosophie* Marx treated Hegel with bitter contempt. He referred to him as a 'sophist' who 'throws trivialities around' and indulges in arguments that are 'pure tautologies'. 'Confused thoughts' (*verworrene Gedanken*) and 'wild conceptions' (*wüste Vorstellungen*) of which Hegel accused others existed in fact in his own mind.[44] In Hegel's mode of thinking,

> The right approach is turned upside down. The simplest becomes the most intricate and the most intricate becomes the simplest. What should provide the point of departure, turns out to be a mystical conclusion, and what should be a rational conclusion is a mystical point of departure.[45]

When Marx left Germany to live in Paris and Brussels, a highly critical or even scornful attitude to Hegel became manifest in practically all his works.[46] In *Economic and Philosophic Manuscripts of 1844*, Marx gently proceeded to point out 'Hegel's one-sidedness and limitations', but in *The Holy Family* and *The German Ideology* his voice grew sharper and in *The Poverty of Philosophy* Hegel was treated as a laughing stock. Marx found in Hegel 'inconsistencies' and 'drunken speculations', and he likened his dialectics of concepts to the 'war of gods known to the philosophers alone'. Marx spoke with malice of 'the Hegelian miracle apparatus', by which metaphysical categories 'break out of logic' and assume a familiar form of physical or human existence. Since Hegel reduced everything to a logical category, everything that happened was just what was going on in Hegel's own mind, and history became the history of his own philosophy. It was by a mere trick that Hegel proved the hegemony or spirit in history; he first drowned the whole of reality in a world of abstractions and fictions of the mind and then proceeded to demonstrate that 'all that exists, all that lives on land and under water can be reduced to a logical category'. The sacred history of the Young Hegelians was just the 'old Hegelian junk' which, in turn, was 'nothing but the speculative expression of the Christian-Germanic dogma of the opposition between God and the world'. When Marx derided Proudhon for having misunderstood Hegel, he ridiculed him both for his ignorance of Hegel and for having believed that Hegel might provide the key to the real history. Even the object of Marx's former admiration — Hegel's *The Philosophy of History* — was derided because in it, as in *Philosophy of Nature* (which is the second part of *The Encyclopaedia of the Philosophical Sciences*), 'the son engenders the mother, the Spirit nature, the Christian religion paganism, the result beginning'.[47] Summing up his basic attitude towards Hegel at that time, Marx observed that Hegel

> must transpose all questions from the form of human common sense to the form of speculative reason and change the real question into a speculative one to be able to answer it.[48]

Hegel's answers remained obscure for he replied to ordinary questions in the incomprehensible language of speculative philosophy. Nothing is explained if familiar, better known and intelligible terms are replaced by unfamiliar, less known, and unintelligible ones.

In the *Contribution to the Critique of Hegel's Philosophy of Right* Marx's denunciation of the German world did not rise above a diatribe, however brilliant theoretically and vigorous intellectually it was. Although he observed marginally that there was a definite relationship between the abstractedness and presumptuousness of German philosophy, on the one hand, and the degenerate state of German social and political reality, on the other, he emphasized at the same time that the Germans were trying to achieve, at least in thought, what other nations had accomplished in fact.[49]   In *The German Ideology* he felt that he could account for the appearance of Hegel's speculative philosophy and of the Young Hegelians in sociological terms.   Their doctrines were the illusions and distortions of ideologists, to be explained by their 'material surroundings' and 'position in life'.   Philosophers do not grow like mushrooms straight from the soil; they are the fruit of their times and nation.   Philosophical systems, evolved in the philosopher's brain, are constructed by the same spirit (*Geist*) which builds railroads with the hands of the workers.[50]   The confused nationalism and ponderous rhetoric of the Germans reflected the fact of their being the most anachronistic of Western peoples.   If the German situation of 1843 were suddenly done away with, Germany would still not have reached the pre-1789 era in terms of French chronology.   There was a clear connection between German philosophy and German reality; Hegel and post-Hegelian developments were the price which Germany had to pay in the domain of the mind for her economic, social, and political backwardness.   The speculative philosophy of Hegel left the real man entirely out of account, because for the German state the individual did not count at all.   Although the 'dreamy and muddled German nation' took pleasure in watching its philosophers struggle with the shadows of reality, this spectacle — the exploitation of the absolute spirit, as Marx described it — testified to the fact that 'across the Rhine . . . history stopped happening'.[51]

The outcome of this settling of accounts with Hegel was a complete break with his speculative philosophy.   This did not preclude the assimilation and adaptation of some of Hegel's assumptions into Marx's own view of social and historical reality.   A few Hegelian ideas, redefined and transformed, remain embedded in the thought of Marx and this may account for the view of him as a lifelong Hegelian.

It is fairly certain that in later years Marx did not look up Hegel, until one day in 1858 the German poet and revolutionary, Ferdinand Freiligrath (1810–76), found some volumes of Hegel which originally belonged to Bakunin and sent them to Marx as a present.   While informing Engels about this event, Marx made the often-quoted statement that he 'would greatly like to make accessible to the ordinary human intelligence, in two or three printer's sheets, what is rational in the method which Hegel discovered but at the same time enveloped in mysticism'.[52] He never carried out this intention, for lack of time, as is usually claimed, or for lack of interest, as is more probable.

Freiligrath's present turned out to be a more important event in Engels's life than in Marx's. The works of Hegel left behind by Bakunin may account for the eleven references to Hegel in *Capital*, according to Vorländer's count, but, contrary to what Georg Lukács suggested,[53] they did not revive Marx's interest in Hegelian philosophy. It is true that in later life Marx spoke of Hegel with a greater respect than he did in his youth, but he referred to him only when others raised the subject of his own alleged connections with, or dependence on, Hegel. These occasions were few. They concerned one single point, namely, the dialectical method of Hegel and Marx, and dealt exclusively with the differences between Hegelian and Marxian dialectics.

Thus, there were three distinct stages in Marx's relation to Hegel. First, in his youth, he was an ambiguous admirer of Hegel, only to become very shortly his disenchanted and disdainful philosophical opponent. At a mature age, Marx forgot both his admiration and hostility and was able to discuss Hegel's merits and demerits dispassionately. For various reasons, he no longer paid any attention to the philosophy of Hegel. The philosophy that had once dominated Marx's mind receded more and more into the background and slowly fell into oblivion. The more sober mood in German philosophy in the second half of the nineteenth century encouraged this attitude of indifference towards Hegel.

3. ENGELS'S ATTITUDE TOWARDS HEGEL

Unlike Marx, Engels never lost interest in Hegel. The longer he lived the greater an admirer of Hegel he became, and his intellectual history explains why he differed in this respect from Marx.

Engels left the Gymnasium at Elberfeld before he passed the *Abitur* (the school-leaving examination qualifying for admission to a university) and, consequently, he never received an academic education. Having left school prematurely he decided, like his father, to make business his career. He thus outwardly complied with the standards accepted in his native Barmen, which he himself described in his *Briefe aus dem Wuppertal*.[54] The merchants of Barmen who could play whist and billiards, discuss politics and pay compliments to ladies, enjoyed the reputation of being well-educated persons. The young men were brought up carefully by their elders and they offered every hope of being perfect replicas of their fathers. This was not, however, to be the case with the old Engels's son, for whom Barmen with its drowsy life, sanctimonious piety, and philistine outlook soon became 'too horrible' for words.[55]

Engels followed in his father's footsteps, but during his business training in his father's firm in Barmen and later in Bremen he also began to cherish the ambition of becoming a writer. He wrote poetry, came under the influence of Young Germany, and tried his hand at literary journalism, in which he gained a fair reputation under the pen-name Friedrich Oswald.[56] D. F. Strauss's *Life of Jesus* (1835) seemed to have influenced Engels considerably and awakened his philosophical interests. Although he continued to write poetry and to think of literary laurels for a few years more, he soon disowned his previous artistic connections. He came to the conclusion that the writers of Young Germany were precious aesthetes, ignorant of and unconcerned with the 'political movement' and 'the striving for emancipation' originated by the 'great man' Hegel and carried on by Strauss, Feuerbach, Bruno Bauer, and the *Deutsche Jahrbücher*.[57]

Engels was neither a born philosopher nor did he become one through education and hard thinking. Gustav Mayer, his biographer, has emphasized that although Engels's inexhaustible appetite for work and his unusually versatile mind enabled him to read widely and to profit from his reading, his education was not systematic and this accounts for his dilettante traits. He had neither the time nor the opportunity to study philosophy. But even if he had had, he would not have excelled in the realm of abstract thought. His nature betrayed a constant craving for action and he was at his best when he could exercise his practical capabilities. While his capacity for logical and philosophical analysis was not conspicuous — as Franz Mehring put it, he lacked 'in speculative depth' — his talent for disseminating and popularizing ideas was outstanding.

Engels's first knowledge of philosophy came from reading and discussing Hegel during his year-long stay in Berlin, where he went from Bremen for his military service in 1841. His earlier literary achievements secured him easy admission to a group of radical philosophical writers and literary pundits in the Prussian capital. The group, dominated by Bruno Bauer and Max Stirner, was known as the 'Freemen' (*Die Freien*), a new name given to the former club of the Young Hegelians. Engels joined the Freemen and followed their discussions among themselves and with their opponents.[58] Thus it was the members of this group who introduced Engels to philosophy, that is, to Hegelian philosophy, and supplied him with his philosophical bearings for the rest of his life. For Engels philosophy meant always, and above all, the philosophy of Hegel. Beyond this, 'his philosophical equipment was light indeed'.[59]

Moreover, Engels's attitude to Hegel was strongly coloured emotionally. Engels saw in German idealist philosophy, of which the Hegelian system was the culmination, the 'glory of Germany in the days of its deepest political humiliation'.[60] He also believed that Hegel inspired progressive tendencies in the German bourgeoisie and particularly in the German educated classes, who, as soon as Hegel was put aside and forgotten, transferred their temple from the philosopher's study to the stock exchange, came to be philistine, took to money-making, and became self-complacent in their outlook.[61] Engels also felt duty-bound to defend Hegelian philosophy against the 'vulgarizing peddlers and dabblers in materialism', that is, against Ludwig Büchner, Jacob Moleschott, and Karl Vogt, who ministered to the intellectual comfort of the bourgeoisie, converted to materialism, and derided the 'colossal chap', i.e. Hegel. It was in this patriotic spirit that Engels pronounced the German working-class movement to be the inheritor of German classical philosophy,[62] a statement otherwise to be dismissed as empty rhetoric or philosophical vagary.[63] In this respect, too, Engels's attitude to Hegel differed greatly from that of Marx to Hegel. Marx spoke with derision of the 'glow of national pride' in the breast of the Germans, awakened by their idealist philosophers, for the object of this pride merely reflected, in his opinion, the anachronism and parochialism of life in Germany.[64]

Engels himself confessed that he had 'a great feeling of piety and devotion' towards Hegel. This feeling was prompted, above all, by Engels's conviction that Hegel made a real and considerable

E.D.M.—G

contribution both to philosophy and natural science.[65] He said in an article written in his youth (1843) that never, since men had learnt to think, had there been a philosophical system as comprehensive as that of Hegel, and he did not change this view throughout his life.[66] Engels sometimes attributed to Hegel ideas which by no stretch of imagination could be found in him.[67] Hegel's involved, ponderous, and pompous style persuaded Engels that Hegel's ideas contained an extraordinary depth and richness of insight incomparable with anything to be found in any other philosopher. Unlike Marx, who saw through Hegel's deceptions, Engels mistook Hegel's plain abuse of language, elementary errors of reasoning, and pretentious trivialities for originality, audacity, and profundity of thought. His philosophically untrained mind was impressed by Hegel's oracular pronouncements and deceived into believing that Hegel's intractable speculations were a paradigm of philosophical analysis and the product of an infallible philosophical method. Engels was utterly insensible to the poverty and shoddiness of Hegel's argument, to the verbosity and arrogance of his style, and to the obscurity and confusion of his language. All these considerations perhaps explain the fact that 'Engels swallowed more of Hegel than, as a naturalist, he could properly digest'.[68] It can almost be said that Engels's materialism is a naturalized Hegelianism.

The works of Hegel, offered by Freiligrath to Marx, some of which, at least *Philosophy of Nature*, passed into Engels's hands, marked a recrudescence of Engels's interests in the philosophy of Hegel and an increasing assertion of Hegel's influence over Engels's thinking. As the time when Engels started reading Hegel again coincided with his studies of natural science, the outcome of which was *Anti-Dühring* and *Dialectics of Nature*, the consequences of this renewed interest in Hegelian philosophy were disastrous.

In his review of Marx's *A Contribution to the Critique of Political Economy*, written shortly after its publication, Engels noted that the revived interest in natural science, which was manifest in Germany after 1848, pushed the philosophy of Hegel aside and restored the 'Wolffian-metaphysical method' to its former prominence. The distinction between the two modes of thought, the Hegelian and the Wolffian, is exactly the same as that between metaphysics and dialectics, as elaborated in *Anti-Dühring*. Engels made no secret of the fact that he considered ignorance of Hegelian philosophy and the restored prestige of the 'old metaphysics' as a development highly disadvantageous to the advance of knowledge. Although he conceded that 'the Hegelian method was absolutely unusable in its available form', he was still absolutely certain that it was the only method that could be used fruitfully at all. In Engels's view, the Hegelian method was essentially sound; it had numerous critics, but not one of its opponents had been able to 'make a breach in its proud structure'. It fell into oblivion because the Hegelian school had not the slightest notion what to do with it, and brought it into disrepute by reducing it to a ludicrous and clumsy manipulation of the simplest tricks. The dialectical method required a 'thoroughgoing criticism' to reveal its fruitfulness but since this criticism was not an easy matter, all 'official philosophy' shirked from undertaking it. What others failed to do was accomplished by Marx.

Marx was, and is, the only man who could undertake the work of extracting from the Hegelian logic the kernel which comprises Hegel's real discoveries in this sphere, and to construct the dialectical method, divested of its idealistic trappings, in the simple shape in which it becomes the only true form of development of thought.[69]

While, in his review, Engels restricted the benefits to be derived from the Marxian revision of Hegelian dialectics to political economy, in his private notes and correspondence he went further and associated the unobstructed development of all scientific knowledge with the application of the reconstructed dialectical method. The future was to belong to a combination of Hegelian philosophy and natural science.

There is no doubt that Engels placed his full confidence in the inventive power of the dialectical method. 'Where it is a question of concepts', he wrote, 'dialectical thinking will carry us at least as far as mathematical calculation.' [70] In his periodic table of elements, Mendeleyev achieved a scientific feat which it is not too bold to put on a par with Leverrier's calculation of the orbit of the planet Neptune. But Mendeleyev made his discovery 'by means of the unconscious application of Hegel's law of the transformation of quantity into quality'. Similarly, Darwin's theory of evolution provides 'the practical proof of Hegel's account of the inner connection between necessity and chance'.[71] Engels failed to observe that Mendeleyev's classification of elements was based on a large collection of empirically established regularities concerning the properties of chemical substance. Nor did Engels touch the crucial point of the matter, namely, the question as to whether these alleged confirmations are actually deducible from the laws of dialectics; for instance, whether the periodic table could be logically deduced from Hegel's law or not. If it cannot be thus deduced, it is incorrect and futile to say that Mendeleyev arrived at his discovery by the conscious or unconscious application of the law of the transformation of quantity into quality.

Hegel, Engels argued, was accused of having twisted words because he was thinking dialectically. 'But if nature itself proceeds exactly like old Hegel, it is surely time to examine the matter more closely.' The fact is, Engels continued, that Hegel was capable of giving the most striking illustrations of the dialectical laws from nature and history and of anticipating, by means of these laws, later scientific discoveries.[72]

In his correspondence with Marx, Engels was inclined to credit 'the old man', that is, Hegel, with having 'scented', with the assistance of the dialectical method, many contemporary discoveries in physics, chemistry, or biology. The cell 'is Hegel's "Being-in-itself" and its development undergoes exactly the Hegelian process, resulting in the "idea", i.e. the particular completed organism'.[73] The molecule 'as the smallest part of matter capable of independent existence is a perfectly rational category, a "node", as Hegel put it, in the infinite series of divisions, which does not conclude them but establishes a qualitative difference'.[74] Comparative physiology provides very fine instances of 'the Hegelian qualitative leap in the quantitative series'.[75] Whatever doubts Engels might have felt as to the predictive power of Hegelian philosophy, allegedly revealed by these 'instances', he was certain that 'if Hegel had a philosophy of nature to write today, the facts would come flying to him from every side'.[76] As he wrote elsewhere, philosophy was taking its revenge posthumously on natural science for its desertion.

Engels made no secret of the fact that he regarded English empirical philosophy as greatly inferior to German idealist philosophy. English empiricism was a symptom of philosophical backwardness or an infantile disorder which English thinkers would eventually overcome with maturity, then to rise themselves to the heights of German idealism.[77] Herbert Marcuse's observation that

German idealism rescued philosophy from the destructive onslaught of British empiricism faithfully reflects Engels's thinking on the matter.[78]   British empiricism involved the abdication of reason, the abandonment of the unity and universality of knowledge which cannot be found in or based upon empirical reality. British empiricism surrendered the intellectual and material existence of men to the blind and fortuitous pressure of events and prevented them from ever becoming the masters of their historical fate. As Moses Hess put it, the cult of soulless facts deprives us of the ability to act freely and spontaneously. Engels vied with Hegel in making plain his scornful attitude towards empirical knowledge and his *Dialectics of Nature* swarms with abuse for 'mere experience' or 'shallow empiricism' and with contemptuous *obiter dicta* about the 'whole swindle of induction'. Engels became more and more convinced that natural science needed, above all, Hegelian philosophy and its dialectical method to make ever more discoveries of all kinds. As he saw it, German idealism was a necessary and constitutive element of all knowledge which gave a true view of the world and helped man to gain increasing mastery over nature and society.

Hand in hand with Engels's increasing confidence in the inventive power of the dialectical method went his increasing respect for Hegel himself. Engels's view on Hegel's importance for natural science resulted from his deep conviction that even in the scientist's own special sphere philosophers can acquire knowledge superior to scientific knowledge. For this reason he put Leibniz above Newton, Kant above Laplace, and Hegel above all the natural scientists of his time. Engels admired Hegel's profundity of thought which was unaffected by the 'absurdities of detail' and which was allegedly combined with a thorough knowledge of mathematics and natural science.[79]   Hegel was a man of the greatest genius, whose achievements as a dialectician could not be surpassed. It was Hegel who formulated for the first time the general laws of development of nature, society, and thought, which 'will always remain an act of historical importance'.[80]   Engels was firmly convinced that once Hegel's idealist point of departure and his arbitrary construction of the system were discarded, Hegel was nearly infallible. Not Hegel himself but his followers, above all the Young Hegelians and 'true socialists', were responsible for Hegelianism acquiring the reputation of being 'abstract and abstruse'.[81]   Engels was always ready to defend Hegel, tooth and nail, and he was confident that soon every-body would speak of Hegel with the reverence which he so amply deserved.[82]　For Engels, only Karl Marx rose above the heights reached by Hegel; otherwise Hegel was head and shoulders above everybody else, including Newton, 'the inductive ass', who man-aged to establish himself as the founder of modern mechanics, although this title should have been bestowed upon Kepler.[83] Hegel was the man most often referred to and quoted admiringly both in *Anti-Dühring* and *Dialectics of Nature* and in this respect no one else, neither Newton nor Darwin, came even close to Hegel. Engels presented Hegel as a thinker who foresaw the path which the advancement of knowledge would take.　His works were full of 'prophetic passages' which were confirmed by the development of science.

Engels never renounced his conviction that inexhaustible riches of ingenuity, perceptiveness, and truth were concealed in Hegel's philosophy.　Since they were hidden 'beneath the false form and within the artificial connections', the 'truth and genius' in Hegel-ian philosophy had to be discovered.　This was one of the great contributions of Marx and his own as well.　Engels's defence does not essentially differ from the argument of contemporary admirers of Hegel who claim that 'what Hegel says abstractly and obscurely can be put concretely and lucidly'.　Consequently, to bring to light Hegel's merits and greatness, no more is neces-sary than to translate what he said into plain English.[84]　The translation thus accomplished leaves, however, considerable doubt as to whether it reveals Hegel as a philosopher and a social theorist of genius or simply testifies to the inventive ability of the translator.

Engels's conviction that the Hegelian philosophy was, as he put it, 'only another expression' of what modern science continued to discover at every step of its advancement,[85] greatly influenced the way he presented the Marxian doctrine and his own philosophical contributions, above all, dialectical materialism.　Dialectical materialism acquired numerous idealistic features and became per-meated with speculative and irrationalistic elements.　In its context, terminology, and even particular formulations, it showed the birth-marks of its origin, that is, of the philosophy of Hegel, from which its main themes were derived.　For Engels, this was a legitimate pro-cedure in view of the fact that 'the Hegelian system represents merely a materialism idealistically turned upside down in method and content'. This view, endowed with the authority of Engels, had and continues to have fateful consequences for the development of Marxian naturalism.

4. MARX'S INDEBTEDNESS TO HEGEL

Hegel's influence upon Engels's philosophical views is very apparent, as Engels often simply rehashed or reproduced textually the opinions of the 'great dialectician'. The impact of Hegel's philosophy upon Marx was less conspicuous. It can be detected only in certain general attitudes and orientations which Marx shared with or adopted from Hegel.

This applies, for instance, to the basic Hegelian idea of universal movement and the interconnection between all things. Lenin regarded both the Marxian materialist conception of history and the Darwinian theory of evolution as an 'application to life and society' of Hegel's 'dialectic of negativity'; Hegel's development of the concept out of itself, in the course of which the concept engenders its determinations and establishes its connection with other concepts, became self-movement, self-generating change, and the spontaneous activity of materialist philosophy.[86] There is no reason to suppose that Darwin was inspired by Hegel, but there is much agreement about Lenin's claim that Marx was influenced by Hegel's view of history. For instance, it is often said that Marx made use of 'the dialectical negativity as the moving and generating principle' and that he transformed it into his conception of 'the self-genesis of man', that is, of social evolution.[87] Marx himself admitted that he conceived history as 'the process of development of man himself' under Hegel's influence. To comprehend 'objective man — true, because real man — as the outcome of man's own labour' is the outstanding and final conclusion of Hegel's *The Phenomenology of Mind*.[88]

Moreover, it is widely believed that not only the conception of the self-genesis of man but also, if not more so, the whole theoretical framework of the Marxian view of history is Hegelian. Engels and Plekhanov emphasized this aspect of Marx's dependence upon Hegel very strongly. Hegel, wrote Engels, was the first who 'attempted to show a development, an inner coherence, in history'.

On this account Marx, notwithstanding his complete repudiation of Hegelian philosophy, allegedly greatly admired Hegel for the 'grandeur of his fundamental outlook'. It was Hegel's 'epoch-making conception of history' which 'was the direct theoretical premiss for the new materialist outlook'.[89] According to Plekhanov, Marx owed to Hegel the conception of the history of humanity as a process regulated by law.

> Like Hegel, Marx saw human history as a process conforming to laws and independent of man's arbitrariness; like Hegel, he considered all phenomena in the process of their appearance and their disappearance; like Hegel, he was not satisfied with barren metaphysical explanations of historical phenomena, and lastly, like Hegel, he endeavoured to trace to a universal and single source all the acting and interacting forces of social life.[90]

To say that Hegel was the first to see development, coherence, and a process conforming to law in history is not entirely correct. He was preceded by an array of French writers of the Enlightenment, above all, by Voltaire, Turgot, and Condorcet, by Giambattista Vico (1668–1744), Adam Ferguson (1723–1816), Montesquieu (1689–1755), and Kant (1724–1804), all of whom were known to Marx.[91] Comte spoke of historical development as a universally known idea. 'Nobody can deny the reality of the movement [in history], which is deeply felt even by those who curse it.' [92] Comte's preliminary outline of an organic view of history, *Système de politique positive*, which was first published in Saint-Simon's *Catéchisme des Industriels* and was known to Marx, appeared in 1822. Hegel was not the first to discover development and coherence in history, but the first to make systematic use of them and to adopt 'the true historical view, the genuinely philosophical position' of 'always treating the part in its relation to the whole'.[93] This is one of the important reasons why in some philosophical circles in Germany and elsewhere the view has been held that Hegel had contributed greatly to the discovery of the concept of evolution and that his idea of evolution not only preceded but was also superior to that of Darwin.[94]

Engels's assertion that Hegel's conception of history provides the theoretical premiss of the materialist outlook is either false or misleading. Hegel regarded history as the unfolding of a single meta-

physical substance, of which human individuals were
bearers, and insisted that its transformations were not a
but a logical process making manifest the potentialities
in the notion; he thus denied the idea of evolutionary change, or
the development of the higher from the lower in time. To say that
concepts develop is to speak either metaphorically or nonsensically;
clearly, concepts do not develop into anything else or into each
other. For Marx history had no metaphysical substance; it was
not 'a person apart, using man as a means for its own particular
aims'. History was the action of men who being divided into
economically determined groups and classes represented conflicting
social interests and, hence, were the compelling force of change.
While development in the Hegelian sense was the transformation
of one concept into another, Marx was able to describe it in genuinely genetic or evolutionary terms and could show how each state
of society grew out of the preceding one and was parent to the subsequent state. Hegel presented us with a series of dramatic situations, ostensibly logically related to each other. Marx described a
process of social transformation.[95] The theories of Hegel and Marx
differ entirely in their universe of discourse and the relations obtaining among the individuals which make up their respective
universe. They also differ widely in their procedure of discovering
regularities and of testing their hypotheses. While Hegel made
oracular pronouncements, Marx applied what Hegel contemptuously called 'the abstract, non-philosophical method of the sciences',
that is, he tried to base his various theories on experience and provide
them with empirical significance. As Plekhanov emphasized, the
similarity of particular ideas and general orientations underlying
the Hegelian and the Marxian conception of history is undeniable,
but the latter cannot be derived from the former. Their respective
theoretical frameworks are entirely dissimilar; they are constructed
on the basis of mutually exclusive assumptions and by means of
utterly different rules of procedure.

The similitude of attitudes combined with antithetical basic
assumptions and contrasting procedures can also be found in the
Marxian principle of ontological holism, which Marx might have
adopted from Hegel.[96] For Hegel, ontological holism was a consequence of the metaphysical fact that the real is the universal. But
his holism emphasized, above all, the superior worth of wholeness
or totality, of such entities as the state, nation, or society which,

being the perfect embodiment of spirit, have a self-contained and self-sufficient existence. When contrasted with the interests of the totality, the interests of the individual are subordinate, for it is the individual who exists for the sake of the whole and not the whole for the sake of the individual. Hegel was not concerned with living and struggling men unless they incarnated abstract categories and the aspirations of spirit. As he stated over and over again in *The Philosophy of Right*, the 'individual counts as only one amongst many' and the individual's worth lies in 'aligning himself with the universal'.[97]

The ontological holism of Marx had no normative basis; it reflected an empirical state of affairs and did not express a value judgment. For Marx as for Feuerbach, men precede man and the human individual. 'Peter only establishes his own identity as a man by first comparing himself with Paul as being of the same kind' and 'man first sees and recognizes himself in other men'.[98] The principle of ontological holism in the Marxian sense was concerned with the fact that society and groups are prior to the individuals who compose them and it stated in an abstract way what sociological determinism expressed in empirical terms. Individuals, Marx explained, have their conditions of existence, their position in life, and their personal development predestined by their class.[99]

From the principle of ontological holism Marx deduced the methodological rule that man should never be dissociated from his environment nor be considered apart from his social setting, and that the behaviour of individuals should be explained by the laws of the social system as a whole. Individuals acting and reacting upon one another give rise to a new reality whose characteristics are impersonal in the sense that they are not determined by the particular characteristics of individuals. Since social facts, of which this new reality consists, result from the association and interaction of individuals, they cannot be reduced to the psychological laws which determine the activity of particular individuals.

That these ideas, constituting a component part of the materialist conception of history, might have been conceived under the influence of Hegelian philosophy cannot be denied, but this genetic relationship does not depreciate the originality of the Marxian view. To say that there is a conformity to law in history is one thing; to state this law explicitly and to explain how it operates is quite another. Apart from sharing the belief in the lawfulness of the historical process, Hegel and Marx went their own, entirely different ways. The materialist conception of history remains an independent creative effort to discover the regularities of the historical process and, as Engels put it, provides a solution to the problem that Hegel propounded but did not solve.

The Marxian anthropological realism and theory of knowledge — which were influenced by Hegel in the sense that Hegel persuaded Marx of the necessity to dissociate naturalism and materialism from the causal and representationist theory of perception — help us to understand the function of the dialectical method in Marx's way of conceiving the world.[100] There is a *consensus communis*, including Marx himself, that he derived his dialectics from Hegel's; that before he adopted the Hegelian method he changed it considerably or, to use his own words, he transformed Hegel's method into 'its direct opposite'; and that the Marxian dialectics no longer applies to the self-developing thought or spirit but to the 'material world', thus becoming the 'method of dealing with matter'.[101] But in spite of this wide measure of agreement, the crucial point about the dialectical method of Marx, namely, how it should be understood, remains unexplained. Marx and Engels repeatedly spoke of the mystifying side of Hegelian dialectics, by which they did not necessarily mean its idealistic presuppositions but simply the fact that one really does not know to what it applies, which elements it relates, and, consequently, how it operates. The same objection could easily be raised against the Marxian dialectical method.

Like Hegelian dialectics, the dialectical method of Marx includes both some specific metaphysical presuppositions and some rules of procedure. Marx referred to these presuppositions as 'a scandal and abomination to the bourgeoisie and doctrinaire professors', because it

> includes in its comprehension and affirmative recognition of the existing state of things, at the same time also, the recognition of the negation of that state, of its inevitable breaking up; because it regards every historically developed social form as in fluid movement, and therefore takes into account its transient nature not less than its momentary existence; because it lets nothing impose upon it, and is in its essence critical and revolutionary.[102]

Engels writing some thirty years later about the 'great fundamental thought' underlying the dialectical method felt, unlike
Marx, that it had become so widely accepted as to be virtually
uncontradicted. The basic assumption of the dialectical method
was that

> the world is not to be comprehended as a complex of ready-
> made things, but as a complex of processes, in which the things
> apparently stable no less than their mind images (*Gedanken-
> abbilder*) in our heads, the concepts (*die Begriffe*), go through
> an uninterrupted change of coming into being and passing
> away, in which in spite of all seeming accidentality and of all
> temporary retrogressions, a progressive development asserts
> itself in the end.[103]

The assumption concerning the constant action, change, transformation, and development of the whole world and everything in
it is so strongly emphasized in and so little differentiated from Marxian dialectics that it could and did lead to the identificaton of dialectics with its presupposition. 'The dialectic', wrote Benedetto
Croce, 'is the rhythm of the development of things, i.e. the inner
law of things in their development.' [104]   Max Adler saw in dialectics
a 'magnificent mode of thought' based on the idea that the world
constantly develops and obeys a force immanent and inherent in
itself.[105]   A similar point is made by Karl Vorländer for whom the
all-pervasive and relentless process of evolution provides the core
of dialectics.[106]   According to M. M. Bober, dialectics is 'the pervasive power instinct in all phenomena' which controls their flow
from one state to another and their development. 'The dialectics
is the law of evolution discernible in all domains; in nature,
society, and human thought.' [107]   According to Sidney Hook, Marx,
even more than Hegel, recognized the primary character of change
and development on every plane of existence. Everything which is
given, be it a system of morals or a style of art or the price of a
commodity, has been produced and is bound to disappear at some
time. 'That is what in the first instance the dialectical method of
Hegel meant for Marx.' [108]

But the basic assumptions of Hegelian dialectics involved not only
universal changeability but also some definite stages through which
every change had to pass. Moreover, change carried within itself
the dynamic principle which accounts for its occurrence and which

was perpetuated by the constant tension between conflicting, struggling, and incompatible forces. Without some rhythmic articulation of the flow of self-generating change, there could be no dialectics and no dialectical method. The inventive and predictive power of the method was supposed to reflect the fact that its rules reproduced, as it were, what in nature and history asserted itself unconsciously.[109] These rules were the correlates, or 'moments' in Hegelian language, of the patterns of change embodied in the dialectical process. For that reason Marx could have said of Hegel that he conceived all philosophy as method, and the Hegelizing exponents of Marx's philosophy could have inferred the plainly absurd conclusion that since motion can be understood only in terms of moving thought a special method, that is, the dialectical method, was necessary to understand change in nature and society.[110] For the same reason, though turned the other way round, Engels and later Lenin associated the dialectical method with the science of the 'general laws of motion, both of the external world and of human thought'. Without being based on external or objective dialectics, the dialectical method could not be regarded as a reflection of the most general regularities of nature and would lose its claim to universal validity.

Marx was not concerned with all these problems which attracted so much attention on the part of Engels, Plekhanov, and Lenin. Marx conceived nature in historical and social terms and the assumption of the 'identity of thought and being' could only have a sociological but never a metaphysical meaning for him. The anthropological realism of Marx precluded the adherence to absolute materialism of any sort, including dialectical materialism. As no dialectical materialism can be found in Marx, there is no room in his philosophy for any dialectics of nature nor for dialectics as a method of natural science. One has to agree with Werner Sombart that it is a monstrous idea to apply Hegelian dialectics to the world of experience. From an empirical point of view, Hegelian dialectics is utter nonsense.[111]

For Marx the dialectical method is not a universal procedure, applicable to any subject matter; dialectics is a purely historical and social concept and applies exclusively to social phenomena and historical events. That the dialectical method is a historical method was rightly seen and convincingly stated by Georg Lukács in his celebrated work *Geschichte und Klassenbewusstsein*, by Sidney Hook and, more recently, also by many others.[112] The dialectics of nature, irrespective of whether it is a constitutive principle in nature or not, provides no basis for the class struggle and social revolutions. It is not even suited to supplying the analytical means for the investigation of social action and social change.

It is the concept of reciprocal action or interaction that is central to Marxian dialectics. Marx's thought seems to be dominated by the idea that the interaction — conflict being a particular kind of interaction — between parts or elements of a given social or historical system is the ultimate source of its change, development, or progress.[113] Marx held this view implicitly and stated it in *The Poverty of Philosophy* explicitly. Civilization is based on conflict. 'No antagonism, no progress ; this is the law that civilization has followed up to our days.' [114] The most important aspect of social change, whose propulsive force is provided by interaction, antagonism, conflict, and strife, is the change in the relative position of major social groups, that is, of social and economic classes.

It is often said that Marx's views of society as the scene of constant conflict and unavoidable strife is a transposition of Hegel's conception of development as the unfolding of the contradiction inherent in all things. In Hegel's philosophy this assumption is closely connected with the belief that everything carries within itself the conditions of its own disappearance. This pattern of change lies, according to Hegel, at the root of every natural process, provides its dynamic, and 'forces nature out of itself'. The rhythm of the pendulum is even more apparent in the spiritual world where it tends, by force of immanent necessity, to bring about the transition of one state of affairs into its direct opposite.[115] To Engels's delight, before Hegel was born, Rousseau had played with this idea in his description of the transformation of free, equal, and happy societies of the past into ones riddled and disrupted by the distinction of class, wealth, and power. This approach, characterized by bold flights of imagination and supported by merely a handful of illustrations, has also been attributed to Marx and has allegedly put him yet deeper in Hegel's debt.[116] According to Marx's celebrated prophecy, the capitalist mode of production created by its own development the conditions from which it must perish. Expropriation of labour during primitive accumulation leads to the expropriation of the expropriators and the re-establishment of individual property on the basis of social ownership of land and of the industrial means of production. The Marxian way of viewing social and historical reality seems to presuppose his acceptance of the Hegelian conception concerning negativity as the manifest trait, and logical contradiction as the universal form, of reality.

There is not the slightest doubt that Engels embraced this Hegelian conception; but there is no evidence, apart from Engels's endorsement of Hegel's doctrine on contradiction, that Marx ever did. Again, the anti-metaphysical, anthropological conception of nature makes it extremely unlikely that after his youthful period of Hegelizing Marx took Hegel's dialectic of negativity seriously. Marx himself pointed out that in his view about the economic basis of class structure and class conflicts as an essential characteristic of capitalist society he was influenced by 'bourgeois historians' and 'bourgeois economists'. Among the bourgeois historians who were first to discover the existence of classes in modern society and to describe the struggle between them Marx mentioned Guizot and, above all, Thierry, 'the father of the "class struggle" in French historiography'. The bourgeois historians were supported in their views by 'the master-minds among the economists of Europe', by Malthus, Ricardo, Mill, Say, Torrens, Wakefield, McCulloch, Senior, Whately, R. Jones, and others. The economists showed that 'the economic basis of the different classes are bound to give rise to a necessary and ever growing antagonism among them'. Marx concluded that no credit was due to him and, by implication, to Hegel, for the discovery of the existence of classes and their struggle in modern society.[117] Contrary to the Hegelizing interpretation, Marx's social theory based on strife and conflict owed at least as much to historiography and economics as to the speculative philosophy of Hegel. Moreover, the reality of class antagonism and its role in history were clearly recognized by many utopian socialists, as Marx himself admitted in *The Communist Manifesto*.[118] If Marx's indebtedness to Hegel is to be accepted, Herbert Marcuse's interpretation seems to be more probable and convincing. According to Marcuse, Hegel's negativity of reality became a historical condition in Marx, a time-bound form of society, which should no longer be hypostatized into a metaphysical state of affairs. Each socio-economic formation produces in men the awareness of its defects and of the appropriate remedies to correct these defects.[119]

In the Marxian conception, social change resulting from interaction arises spontaneously and, as it were, inevitably in view of the fact that society is the 'product of men's reciprocal action'.[120] Thus, for Marx the necessary conditions of social change are also the necessary conditions of the very existence of society. Moreover, there is the dialectical nexus, that is, the reciprocal action between the natural and material conditions of production on the one hand and social organization on the other. Human evolution is the combined result of the determination of man by his natural conditions and of the alteration of nature by human activity.

Man changes and develops his nature by reacting upon his environment, by which he is determined. More specifically, men live and operate within a natural and social framework which is no creation of their own will. They are by no means free to choose the form of society for themselves, for this form exists before they do and is the product of former generations. Consequently, men experience these conditions as an alien and objective force; objective in the sense that it exists outside of us and reaches us from without. The objective conditions generate various needs and desires, set goals and purposes, stimulate men to action and, generally, produce the means by which they themselves may be changed. Every action arises from objective conditions and strives to change them by transcending the given state of society. The measure of its failure and success depends upon the circumstances in which action takes place. There was not the slightest doubt in Marx's mind that there might be a wide gap between what people desire and strive to achieve on the one hand and the objective possibilities in the given situation on the other. No society can surmount the barriers standing in the path of its development by a sort of *salto mortale*. It has to clear them in turn, one by one, and no bargains with history are possible on that score.[121]

This seems to be the rational element in the Hegelian method of which Marx wrote to Engels upon glancing again through Hegel's *Science of Logic* in 1858. Freed from its speculative embellishments it is too little to deserve the name of a method, for it is not a set of rules for the validation of scientific statements. Nor is it, as Engels claimed in *Anti-Dühring*, a set of rules intended to help us in scientific inquiry and discovery. It is at most a general directive based on the assumption that social systems change spontaneously, the change arising from the interaction of the parts of such systems and the interaction being conceived as wide as to include all forms of conflicts. The directive itself recommends the use of this assumption in the approach to, and the investigation of, social and historical facts. The general directive could only be developed into a method if some specific rules of procedure were added and the directive itself served as criterion for deciding as to whether a specific rule of procedure is or is not part of the method. We cannot discover, however, such specific rules in Marx.

It is misleading, therefore, to speak of the Marxian dialectical method, if the term *method* is used in its proper sense. The dialectical method of Marx is something that may merely be talked about, but not applied. The Hegelizing interpreters of Marx often speak of his masterly use of the dialectical method and of the inability of other people to grasp it, but they never state explicitly which of Marx's procedures they have in mind, how and to what particular problem Marx applied it. They seem to perform some kind of ceremonial ritual whose origin and meaning are forgotten but which is cherished by the worshippers. The Hegelizing interpreters are satisfied with repeating certain traditionally accepted utterances, although they would be hard put to explain what they mean and imply.

Engels defended Marx against Dühring's criticism according to which Marx justified the inevitable self-annihilation of the capitalist formation by means of the Hegelian negation of the negation. Every attentive reader of *Capital* will agree with Engels that Marx first established certain trends in contemporary capitalism on the basis of historical and economic facts and then in addition described these trends in terms of the Hegelian dialectical law. Engels then proceeded to point out the difference between a method of analysis or discovery and that of validation, between the method of inquiry and that of presentation, to re-state the same in Marxian terms,[122] and insisted that Marxian dialectics is a method of discovery and not of validation. We should infer from these distinctions which Engels, perhaps prompted by Marx himself, so strongly emphasized, that whatever is discovered by following the Marxian dialectical directive is not valid knowledge until it is established independently by the accepted rules of scientific procedure. As Labriola put it, Marxian dialectics is neither an instrument of research nor a method of proof 'but only a comprehensive formula, valid, indeed, but *post factum*'.[123]

This is, however, a conception of the relation between dialectics and scientific procedure *toto coelo* different from that adopted by

Engels himself and later firmly established in Marxism–Leninism. According to the Engelsian and Marxist–Leninist conceptions, it is not dialectics that is subordinated to scientific method but vice versa. While in the case of Marx, dialectics does not require the abandonment of scientific method, but on the contrary presupposes its validity and observance, the approach of Engels and Marxist–Leninists reduces scientific method to a subordinate role and imposes restrictions upon its application and validity.

5. THE HEGELIAN REVIVAL IN THE PHILOSOPHY OF ENGELS

Hegel's influence upon Engels was incomparably wider and more decisive than it was upon Marx. Marx approached Hegel critically, followed Hegel's conceptions selectively, and modified considerably the views adopted from Hegel in order to make them suit his theoretical purpose. Engels's attitude to Hegel was marked not by a critical spirit but by a feeling of devotion and piety.[124] He borrowed from Hegel without discrimination and what he took over he incorporated sometimes even in its original formulation. Numerous passages in *Anti-Dühring* and *Dialectics of Nature* are merely summaries of views to be found in Hegel.[125] It was Engels's boundless admiration for 'Hegel's discoveries in the sphere of dialectics' that produced the dialectics of nature as a constitutive principle of the universe. Engels was convinced that once the Hegelian logic is stated in a simple and clear language, the dialectical method becomes 'the only true form of development of thought'.[126] He not only adopted the Hegelian logic of dialectics but also borrowed practically all illustrations of it from Hegel's various works. Engels took over Hegel's theories lock, stock, and barrel, without questioning their validity and scientific character.

Among the numerous conceptions of Hegel to be found in Engels, Hegel's view on the relation of philosophy to science and his distinction between the metaphysical and dialectical modes of thought are most important. They opened the gates through which the Hegelian philosophy flooded Marxian philosophy or, to be more precise, what Engels presented as Marxian philosophy and what, on his authority, has been accepted as such ever since.

Engels's conception of the relation of natural science to philosophy is purely Hegelian. 'There is a fundamental delusion in all scientific empiricism,' wrote Hegel. It employs some definite metaphysical categories, such as matter, force, infinity, and so forth, but 'all the while it is unaware that it contains metaphysics'.[127] It is impossible to think and to escape metaphysics. Consequently, only animals are mere physicists, for they alone do not think; man, being a thinking being, is a born metaphysician. 'The real question', Hegel asserted, expressing a thought which Marxism–Leninism has taken hold of, 'is not whether we shall apply metaphysics, but whether our metaphysics is of the right kind.'[128] Empiricism and, generally, in Hegel's words, 'the abstract, non-philosophical method of the sciences', adopts 'one-sided forms of thought' and makes these rigidly fixed categories the basis of its theoretical examination. While priding itself on being free from speculation, it contains metaphysics of the worst kind and becomes 'the quintessence of shallow thinking'.[129] For this reason Hegel considered his own speculative philosophy, which was openly and uncritically metaphysical, superior to all philosophy of common sense. This was also the point made by Engels.

> Natural scientists may adopt whatever attitude they please, they are still under the domination of philosophy. It is only a question whether they want to be dominated by a bad, fashionable philosophy or by a form of theoretical thought which rests on acquaintance with the history of thought and its achievements.[130]

Hegelian philosophy became dominant in Engels's mind not only because it provided a basis of theoretical thought which, as Engels felt, was extremely fruitful for acquiring new knowledge, but also because Hegel alone was able to show conclusively the superiority of his own system over other philosophies. The decisiveness of this demonstration was based on Hegel's discovery of the temporality of philosophy. The true significance of Hegelian philosophy lay in the fact that it 'once for all dealt the death blow to the finality of all products of human thought and action'. Truth could be discovered only in the historical development of knowledge, which advances constantly but never reaches the ultimate goal. The philosophy of Hegel reveals that everything is transitory; the only enduring thing is the uninterrupted process of becoming and passing away, of gradually ascending from the lower to the higher stages of development, a process which is reflected in the progress of scientific knowledge and of philosophy as its crowning achievement.[131]

The support given to Hegel's criticism of empirical knowledge and to his 'philosophical science' based on speculative thought pushed Engels in the direction which ultimately led him to the subordination of scientific knowledge to metaphysical fancies. While he insisted that we should start with facts and not with preconceived ideas, his mind was dominated by *a priori* metaphysical conceptions concerning the reality underlying observed phenomena and concealed behind appearance. With Engels as with every metaphysician, the concealed reality was more real than any particular thing. Although Engels was genuinely convinced that he followed scientific procedures in discarding appearances for the sake of the concealed reality, the metaphysical element in Engels's thought played havoc with his positivistic leanings. Engels tried to base empirical science on the theoretical foundations of a philosophy which called in question the truth of empirical science and which was inspired by a distrust of empiricism. Engels's partiality to Hegel was destined to produce disastrous consequences for the school of philosophy which he helped to establish. To accept the view that a metaphysician or a *Naturphilosoph* is in possession of knowledge superior to scientific knowledge is to hold a belief both false and harmful, for it provides a convenient justification for imposing restrictions on scientific inquiry.[132]

The Hegelian distinction between metaphysics and dialectics was first introduced by Engels in his review of *A Contribution to the Critique of Political Economy*. He elaborated the distinction in the introductory chapter of *Anti-Dühring*, and commented upon it throughout the work. While in *Ludwig Feuerbach* it comes up again but only marginally, in *Dialectics of Nature* it provides the main vantage point from which the whole field of contemporary science and philosophy is critically reviewed. Most of the content of *Dialectics of Nature* was written after the publication of *Anti-Dühring* in the years 1878–82, which corroborates the opinion that Engels's allegiance to Hegel was unswerving and immune to the passage of time.

To establish conclusively the Hegelian origin not only of the distinction between the metaphysical and dialectical modes of thought but also of their various ramifications which brought along whole clusters of Hegelian ideas into the Engelsian, Leninist, and Stalinist interpretation of Marxian philosophy, it is necessary to describe the Hegelian distinction between the philosophy of understanding on the one hand, and the philosophy of dialectical and speculative reason on the other. Only on this basis can the extent and scope of the Hegelian infiltration be fully appreciated.

According to Hegel, there are three aspects or 'moments' (*Momente*) in logically real, that is, ontologically valid, thought; he described them as Understanding, Negative or Dialectical Reason, and Positive or Speculative Reason.[133] The distinction between Understanding (*Verstand*) and Reason (*Vernunft*) comes from Kant, but Hegel gave it a different meaning and endowed the two *modi* of thought — for Dialectical and Speculative Reason can be combined into one single *modus*, as was usually done by Hegel — with entirely different cognitive functions. According to Hegel, Kant, in his critique of Reason, never really went beyond the critique of Understanding, in the Hegelian sense of this term.

Understanding is thought acting in its analytical capacity, as it apprehends empirically given, isolated, and only externally related objects, in their specific differences, these differences being 'finite', that is fixed and independent of one another. Understanding adopts the maxim of the heterogeneity of real objects, 'Everything is essentially distinct', and follows the laws of identity, of non-contradiction and of the excluded middle. Although it is anxious to avoid contradiction, regarding it as 'an accident, a kind of abnormality, or paroxysm of sickness', it is bound to fail in this endeavour. In Hegel's opinion, which distorts and misrepresents Kant's real purpose, Kant demonstrated that philosophy based on the principles of formal logic unavoidably leads to antinomies, thereby dealing a mortal blow to the belief in the fitness of Understanding in philosophy.[134]

Since Understanding is based on 'immediate sense-perception and the play of fancy', it produces concepts adequate only to distinct, delimited entities, and fixed relations between them. It yields thinking which is shallow, abstract, and non-philosophical in making use of concepts unreflectingly accepted. This type of thinking prevails in everyday life, in science, and in common sense and empirical philosophy as represented by Locke or Hume. Hegel emphasized time and again that the philosophy of mere Understanding is not the path on which philosophical truth can be found for it is undisciplined, as he said, by 'proper philosophical reflection'.[135]

Thought at its dialectical stage comprehends that every 'finite characteristic' is self-contradictory and thus involves its own 'self-suppression'. Every characteristic ϕ, considered as fixed, is one-sided and requires its opposite $\sim\phi$, by which ϕ is defined and determined.

> By dialectics is meant the indwelling tendency outwards by which the one-sidedness and limitation of the predicates of Understanding is seen in its true light, and shown to be the negation of them. For anything to be finite is just to suppress itself and put itself aside.[136]

According to Hegel, everything contains its negation, owing to which it is linked with its opposite and must become what it is not. This negativity and contradictoriness are an essential characteristic of being, ignored by Understanding and apprehended only by Dialectical Reason.

While thought at its dialectical stage is able to see that 'finite characteristics' require their opposites, it does not grasp the unity of all opposites. Only thought as Positive and Speculative Reason comprehends the ground, i.e. the unity of identity and difference, and affirms the immanent connection of characteristics opposed to each other, their mutual relatedness and their transition into one another, which lie beyond the compass of Understanding. Speculative philosophy, Hegel explained elsewhere, consists in the comprehension of the unity of opposites and in the application of this knowledge in a systematic way.[137] Reason is the capacity of thought to transcend the 'either-or' mode of thinking and to recognize the unity, the difference, and the identity of opposites which, according to the Understanding, are incompatible with each other.

The philosophy of Speculative Reason endeavours to ascertain the 'inner unity of all existence' and, in the words of *The Phenomenology of Mind*, 'to recognize in what seems conflicting and inherently antagonistic the presence of mutually necessary moments'. This implies that 'the principle of identity' has to be rejected and replaced by the 'principle of contradiction'. Logic of Speculative Reason differs basically from 'logic in the ordinary sense', which is a product of Understanding; it is a mature and advanced form of logic that evolves through the criticism of 'the older' or 'former metaphysics' and takes its place as 'the scientific reconstruction of the world . . . to be built of thoughts alone'.[138] Reason pierces through the schematic conceptions of Understanding. It recognizes that everything is not only identical with but also different from itself; that it is and is not what it appears to be; and that everything is subject to the ontological law of contradiction. 'All things are contradictory in themselves.' [139]

Although the term 'Understanding' has in Hegel as depreciatory a meaning as 'Speculative Reason' an appreciatory one, Hegel did not deny that the 'merits and rights of the mere Understanding should unhesitatingly be admitted'. Neither common sense nor philosophy, neither theory nor practice, neither science nor art, can proceed without Understanding. But it is dialectics that is the 'soul of all knowledge which is truly scientific', and it is dialectics and not Understanding, that is 'an ultimate'.[140] While Understanding constitutes a stage in the development of thought, it is a stage at which philosophy should not stand still for ever.

This is, however, what happened in the philosophy which had prevailed in Germany prior to Kant and which Hegel called 'the former' or 'older metaphysics' (*die vormalige Metaphysik*), that is, 'metaphysics of Understanding' (*Verstandes-Metaphysik*). The old metaphysics can be said to belong to the past only in the sense that it preceded the critical philosophy of Kant and Hegel's philosophy of Speculative Reason historically. Otherwise, Hegel explained, 'the thing is always and at all places to be found, as the view which the abstract Understanding takes of the objects of Reason'.[141]

The old metaphysics is a philosophy of Understanding. This accounts for its limitations and defects, for Understanding is a philosophically inadequate mode of thinking. The old metaphysics, as described by Hegel, is based on the assumption that the determinations of abstract thought are the essential determinations of things and that knowledge is acquired by the assignment of predicates. Hegel maintained that the main problem of pre-Kantian metaphysics was to discover whether a given predicate should or should not be attributed to an object or a class of objects. Each of these predicates was believed 'valid by itself'; it was cut off from its 'connections and solidarity' with its opposite and everything was alleged to have one or the other of the mutually exclusive predicates. Categories 'separated from each other', 'absolutely firm', with their extension drawn by hard and fast lines and supposed to be 'permanently fixed', are merely 'finite' and inadequate predicates. As Hegel put it, instead of expressing the truth, they only impose a limit, that is, they differentiate the things in their immutability and identity by excluding contraries. This means, however, that the philosophy of Understanding does not rise above the immediate data of consciousness, is satisfied with its half-truths and fails to discover the way of access to reality.[142] To use Heinrich Rickert's simile, however small and fine may be the meshes of the conceptual network formed by the method of Understanding, reality which knows no sharp boundaries and is in constant flux is bound to flow between and through these meshes without being apprehended.

The philosophy of Understanding was to be found, above all, in metaphysics, in such systems as those of Descartes, Spinoza, or Wolff, which Hegel mentioned by name as instances of it. These systems were constructed by means of deductive, quasi-mathematical methods which 'however indispensable and brilliantly successful in their province', are as a matter of course 'unserviceable for philosophical cognition'. The unsuitability of the deductive method in philosophy is due to the fact that it cannot do without axioms, without uncritically accepted presuppositions, and, above all, that its procedure conforms to the 'canon of formal identity'.[143] The deductive method, held up as a model of perfection before philosophy, is based upon the distinctiveness and definiteness of concepts, the independence and consistency of axioms, the unambiguity and permanence of deductive rules, which are all instruments of Understanding and of its inadequate and unsatisfactory mode of philosophical thinking. Casual philosophical reflections and less systematic ways of deductive reasoning to be found in philosophical arguments, called by Hegel '*Räsonnierungen*',[144] shared with the deductive method its defects and limitations. Some contemporary exponents of Hegel's philosophy have voiced the opinion that Hegel's objections to the 'older metaphysics' would also apply to all kinds of positivism, to analytical and linguistic philosophy, and logical empiricism, for they too clearly exemplify a philosophy of Understanding.[145] The procedure peculiar to this kind of philosophy reveals the poverty of its purpose by accepting uncritically the knowledge provided by Understanding and by its failure to transcend the given reality. Speculative philosophy, philosophy *tout court* in Hegel's sense, must scorn these defective methods if it wishes to attain knowledge with any spiritual significance and truth in it.[146]

Hegel contrasted the analytic or deductive procedures used in the

philosophy of Understanding with the dialectical method of speculative philosophy.   This dialectical method is supposed to help the
thinker to discover the process by which categories of thought give
rise to each other.   It is the general principle of the dialectical
method that 'negation is just as much affirmation as negation' or
that each category contains its opposite and what it is not.[147]
Thus, for instance, we should recognize that the idea of pure being
contains the idea of nothing, that being and nothing are not only
different but also identical, and that the one passes into the other.
In Hegel's own words, 'In fact, being . . . is nothing, neither more
nor less. . . . Nothing is the same determination (or lack of determination), and thus altogether the same thing, as pure being.' [148]
This assertion is justified by the rejection of the law of non-contradiction and the acceptance of existent 'contradiction'.   That
everything contains 'both being and nothing' is a primary truth of
speculative philosophy, one that needs no elucidation or justification.[149]

The 'existent contradiction', being itself and something else in
the same respect and at the same time, compels us to search for
another category combining and reconciling the characteristics of
being and nothing.   Since a thing is and is not at the same time
when it is becoming, the third category which resolves the contradiction of being and nothing is becoming.   The mode of thought
characteristic of Positive Reason does not imply, therefore, that
'Reason is in contradiction with itself'.   But the recognition of the
existence of contradiction lifts Reason above the limitations of
Understanding and reveals a truth hidden from it.[150]

Hegelian dialectics is apparently not a method by which we
deduce categories from each other, but one by which categories
deduce themselves.   As Hegel put it in *Science of Logic*, he did not
really follow the method in his system, but rather his system followed
its own method.[151]   We always apply the triple rhythm, for we first
discover how an affirmative category produces its own contradiction
out of itself and then how the two categories jointly produce out of
themselves the third.   The third category contains and transcends
the first two contradictory ideas of the triad from which it has
arisen.[152]

Hegel claimed that a correct dialectical transition from one notion
to another is necessary, that is, that it could not be accomplished
otherwise, and that dialectics, being a method of discovery, is at the

same time one of infallible rigour. 'I know', Hegel wrote, 'that it is the only true method', the only one capable of 'securing scientific progress'. The dialectical development follows a 'resistless course, free from all foreign elements, admitting nothing from outside'.[153] Every dialectical step implies one and only one dialectically valid continuation which reveals the necessary interconnection of ideas.

The dialectical method is a reflection of objective or external dialectics, that is, the dialectical process (*die Dialektik*) as distinct from subjective thinking which applies the rules of dialectics to some subject-matter. 'I call dialectics', Hegel explained, 'the concept's moving principle', the development of the concept out of itself in the course of which the concept engenders its determinations. Thinking as something merely subjective looks on, as it were, at this development and does not add to it anything of its own. 'The sole task of philosophic science is to bring into consciousness this proper work of the Reason of the thing itself.' [154]

Objective dialectics is like an elemental force which is at work 'whenever there is movement, whenever there is life, whenever anything is carried into effect in the actual world'. Everything that surrounds us, Hegel wrote, may be regarded as 'an instance of dialectics', for everything finite 'instead of being stable and ultimate is rather changeable and transient'. We say, for instance, that man is mortal, which appears to imply that man's mortality is due to some outward circumstances. But the truth of the matter is that life involves the germ of death and that the finite involves its own suppression. Thus, we have a vision 'of dialectics as the universal and irresistible power before which nothing can stay, however secure and stable it may deem itself'.[155]

Objective dialectics has its origin in the negativity of being; the conversion of Spinoza's proposition, 'All negation is determination' or 'Negation is inherent in the essence of positive being', is Hegel's basic ontological axiom. The state of privation or deficiency generates tension and pressure and induces the tendency in all things to realize their potentialities and to overcome their imperfection. The negativity of being becomes manifest in the dialectical process as contradiction and contradiction turns out to be an essential and universal form of reality. The dialectical process is the unfolding of the contradiction inherent in every object and in the course of which things change into their opposites. Contradiction is the universal force impelling change and progress.

To silence any objection to his extraordinary discovery and any doubt as to its validity, Hegel curtly announced that 'with regard to the assertion that contradiction does not exist, we may disregard this statement'. Although it is commonly accepted that it is impossible to think anything contradictory, the very opposite is true. All things are contradictory objects, 'the contradiction being present in them and not merely in an external reflection'; contradiction is 'the root of all movement and life'; and all motion is nothing but 'existent contradiction itself'. To say all this is to express a profound and essential truth about things.[156] Hegel claimed that he understood what all these statements meant but his claim is, of course, open to doubt.

It is clear that Engels's distinction between the metaphysical and the dialectical mode of thought reproduces Hegel's differentiation between Understanding and Dialectical and Positive Reason. Not only the distinction, but also the description of the two modes of thinking is expressed in the Hegelian terminology. Finally, the conclusion which Engels draws from his differentiation and which provides him with his conceptual framework for the analysis of philosophical and scientific knowledge are purely Hegelian.

Plekhanov was the last follower of Marx who was fully aware that Engels's distinction between metaphysics and dialectics was a paraphrase of Hegel; that Engels's dialectics corresponds to Hegel's speculative philosophy, that is, to metaphysics in the traditional sense; and that 'the former metaphysics' of Hegel and metaphysics in Engels's sense included any philosophy, whether idealist or materialist, which adhered to the principle of non-contradiction and the principle of identity.[157] Plekhanov seemed also to have been aware of the fact that Engels's use of the term 'metaphysics' conformed to Hegel's and was at variance with Marx's, to be found, for instance, in *The Holy Family*.[158] Hegel's speculative philosophy and Engels's dialectics are clearly metaphysics in Marx's sense.

The metaphysician in Engels's sense, whom he identified historically with a supporter either of the Wolffian or of the 'old metaphysics',[159] is Hegel's 'philosopher of Understanding'. Just as his Hegelian model, he considers things in isolation, apart from each other and from their connection with the vast whole. He conceives them as objects 'fixed, rigid, given once for all'; as constant, not as essentially variable, 'in repose, not in motion . . . in their death not in their life'.

He thinks in absolutely irreconcilable antitheses. His communication is 'yea, yea; nay, nay'; for whatsoever is more than these cometh of evil. For him a thing either exists or does not exist; a thing cannot at the same time be itself and something else. Positive and negative absolutely exclude one another; cause and effect stand in a rigid antithesis one to the other.[160]

Engels's metaphysician follows in the footsteps of Hegel's philosopher of Understanding, adopts his maxim 'Everything is essentially distinct', recognizes the ordinary logic with its laws of identity, non-contradiction, and of the excluded middle, forgets that things change and move and are alive.[161]

Like Hegel, Engels conceded that the metaphysical mode of thought is 'justifiable and necessary' within certain limits, but beyond them 'becomes one-sided, restricted, abstract, lost in insoluble contradictions'. Reality with its wealth of continuous differentiation eludes every concept or system of concepts established by the metaphysical method of concept formation which is a manner of thinking that suits only sound common sense and is adequate for everyday purposes. It may, as Hegel would say, reach 'formal truth, bare correctness'. What Hegel called 'truth in the deeper sense' cannot, however, be discovered by means of Engels's metaphysical mode of thought. For this the methods of dialectics, the correlate of Hegel's speculative philosophy, are necessary.[162]

According to Engels, it is the dialectical mode of thought which, like the dialectical and speculative philosophy of Hegel, 'comprehends things and their representations, in their essential connections, concatenations, motion, origin, and ending'. Therefore, the methods of dialectics are indispensable in natural science, for 'nature works dialectically and not metaphysically', in the investigation of the universe as a whole and of its evolution, of the development of man and his conception about himself and the world in which he lives. The dialectical method of thinking is indispensable for apprehending any process of becoming and passing away, of change, transformation, and development.[163] This is exactly what Hegel said when he claimed that the dialectical method is required 'whenever there is movement, whenever there is life, whenever anything is carried into effect in the actual world'.

Engels followed Hegel in his insistence that the comprehension of motion, change, and life demands the rejection of the 'principle of identity' and its replacement by the 'principle of contradiction'. It was Hegel's opinion that formal logic obstructs the understanding of the dynamics of development, for these dynamics are provided by 'negativity in its essential determination . . . which consists of nothing else but an exhibition of contradiction'. Engels is in full agreement with this opinion; motion, change, life are a contradiction or involve a contradiction. It is the 'objective presence' of a contradiction in things and processes themselves that supplies them with an 'actual force' and makes them move, change, and live.[164] This is Hegel again with his all-pervading contradiction and the dialectics of negativity, the moving and generating principle of *The Phenomenology of Mind*, so much admired by Marx in his youth. The dialectics of negativity gives rise to the 'inherent pulsation of self-movement', and is the source of all change, development, and progress, including the progress of Speculative Reason.

Finally, there are the dialectical laws, which are the 'general laws of all motion . . . just as valid for motion in nature and human history as for the motion of thought'.[165] The dialectical principle, said Hegel, in its true and proper character, constitutes the 'life and soul of scientific progress, the dynamic which alone gives immanent connection and necessity to the body of science'. It is the dialectical principle that helps to discover the 'real and true' as opposed to the external and finite.[166] It is Engels's firmly established view that dialectics provides superior knowledge, unobtainable by any other means. Dialectics cannot be despised with impunity, without science being led into errors, superstitions, and barren speculations; it is an 'absolute necessity' for natural science, for it is the sole method of thought appropriate to the present outlook on nature; it is a 'method of arriving at new results', extending the 'narrow horizon' of metaphysical thought; it 'contains the germ of a more comprehensive view of the world'.[167]

Generally speaking, dialectics is the science of interconnections in contrast to metaphysics, which is the knowledge of things considered in isolation. The universal interconnection is expressed in three laws; the law of the transformation of quantity into quality and vice versa; the law of the interpenetration of opposites; and the law of the negation of the negation. All three, Engels emphasized, were discovered and developed by Hegel from whose works Engels also appropriated practically all their instances.[168] Hegel's error was in foisting these laws on nature and history as laws of thought instead of deducing them from nature and history. It was enough, however, to 'turn the thing around', which meant, if we are to judge from *Dialectics of Nature*, to present Hegel's laws as the most general laws of the universe and to illustrate them with some examples from physics, chemistry, and biology, to make everything 'become simple and clear as noonday'.[169]

Engels was clearly looking at the world through the eyes of the 'great dialectician'. This is not intended to imply that Engels wanted to take credit for the ideas of another or that he tried to appear in borrowed plumes. A much more plausible explanation is Engels's intellectual helplessness with respect to Hegel's ability to deceive himself and others and his exaggerated view of the significance of Hegel's philosophy. In his philosophical innocence Engels applied to Hegel's system one of Hegel's basic philosophical ideas, expounded in detail in Hegel's *Lectures on the History of Philosophy*, namely, that there is an immanent necessity in the historical sequence of philosophical systems. Philosophical systems are 'moments of an organic unity' and their diversity reflects the progressive evolution of philosophical truth.[170] In particular, Engels adopted the Hegelian idea that the last system of an epoch synthesizes or, to put it in Hegelian language, supersedes (*aufheben*), that is, overcomes and preserves, all previous stages of philosophical development and constitutes its crowning phase. With Hegel, Engels wrote, philosophy comes to an end. First, because in his own system Hegel summed up the whole development of philosophy and, second, because Hegel showed that the task of philosophy is no longer the construction of systems but the pursuance of truths supplied by the positive sciences and the 'summation of their results by means of dialectical thinking'.[171] Engels did not see the Hegelian philosophy for what it was, a monster of speculative metaphysics and the very height of extravagant abstraction, as Marx described it, but construed it as the final phase in the necessary line of philosophical development to be recognized by every philosopher worthy of his name. Incredible as it may seem, the Hegelian system meant for Engels the end of speculation and the beginning of scientific philosophy.

IV

French Positivism and the Philosophy
of Marx and Engels

THE relation of Marx and Engels to French positivism is distorted
by their political enmity to Comte. It is also obscured by the dispute
between the Saint-Simonists and the Comtists concerning the origin
of positivism. The political hostility of Marx and Engels to Comte
clearly coloured their views about positivism and influenced their
evaluation of the relative importance of Saint-Simon and Comte in
the history of philosophical, social, and political ideas. The poor
opinion that they held of Comte, both as a social reformer and
philosopher, greatly affected their followers, who frequently took
it for granted that Marx and Engels could not have been influenced
by a thinker whom they held in so little esteem.

While 'positivism' is a term closely associated with Comte's name
and his conception of knowledge, Comte neither coined the term
nor defined the concept. Madame de Staël introduced the expression 'the positive sciences' and 'the philosophy of the positive science'
in 1800, and Saint-Simon may have adopted them from her. Saint-
Simon used the terms 'positive philosophy' and 'positive science'
frequently and gave them the meaning derived from the views of
the *idéologues*.[1] The *idéologues* were anxious to be empirical in their
investigations, including their examinations of moral and political
problems; they believed that to achieve this goal they should
emancipate their investigation from religious and metaphysical
presuppositions and base them on anthropological or sociological
foundations. This is the meaning which Saint-Simon gave to the
expression 'positive science' and which it retained, with some
revisions and amplifications, in Comte.[2]

Comte was not the only founder of positivism as a conception of
knowledge or philosophical doctrine; he shared this distinction
with Saint-Simon. Although Comte failed to recognize Saint-
Simon as his forerunner, and later in his career spoke abusively of

him, Comte's claim to complete originality cannot be accepted. After Émile Durkheim's study of this controversial issue no doubt remains that whereas Comte developed the positivist philosophy and gave it its systematic form, Saint-Simon provided its first outline, even if he expressed it ineptly and confusedly.[3]

The dual authorship of the positive philosophy throws much light on the relation of Marx and Engels to this doctrine. Marx and Engels may have been exposed to the influence of positivism not only through Comte, of whom they spoke disparagingly, but also through Saint-Simon, whom they extolled. Moreover, their severe and contemptuous criticism of Comte has been understood to imply that they rejected positivism altogether. This inference is based on the premiss that one cannot have positivism without Comte and that one cannot be influenced by a thinker whom one dismisses as a political philosopher and reformer. This conclusion is incorrect. Simply because Marx and Engels did not wish to have anything to do with Comte does not mean that they remained in point of fact entirely unaffected by their encounter with positivism.

I. THE EVALUATION OF SAINT-SIMON AND COMTE BY MARX, ENGELS, AND THEIR FOLLOWERS

Marx and Engels expressed their views about Saint-Simon (1760–1825) and Comte (1798–1857) frequently and there is not the slightest doubt that they admired the former and abhorred the latter. To judge from his observation on 'savage communism' which degraded equality and crushed liberty, Comte seems to have reciprocated the hostility.

Marx and Engels despised Comte mainly because of his social and political views, formulated in the period to which Comte referred as his second career, and during which he accomplished the transfiguration from the philosopher and author of *Cours de philosophie positive* into the high priest of the religion of humanity, expounded in the *Système de politique positive* and other works.[4] Marx regarded Comte as a philosopher of reaction for a number of reasons. Comte defended the institution of private property and supported the rule of the rich over the poor and the rights of the bourgeoisie against the proletariat; he welcomed Louis Bonaparte's deliverance of the Republic from parliamentary government and subordinated the political and economic emancipation of the people to their moral regeneration; he urged the acceptance of religion, though religion without a god, as a motive to socially desirable conduct (sc. *vivre pour autrui*) and as a source of collective emotions that preserve social unity and stability from revolutionary upheavals.[5] Marx rejected all these views and ideas because he regarded them not only as sociologically erroneous but also as politically harmful. It is true that in the 1860s Marx came into contact with the French and English Comtists who took part in the organization and activities of the International Working Men's Association and that his association with the 'positivist' Edward Spencer Beesly was particularly close. Since Marx and the Comtists discovered a certain measure of agreement in their views on the urgent political tasks facing the working class at that time, Marx's hostility towards Comte's followers relented somewhat. This did not change, however, in the slightest, his opinion of Comte and positivism.[6]

Marx and Engels did not follow in the footsteps of Émile Littré in France and of John Stuart Mill in England, who differentiated between the first and second part of Comte's work, between his clear, original, and important exposition of positive philosophy, on the one hand, and his subsequent speculations on politics, morality, and religion, on the other. Marx, as well as Engels, refused to see in Comte's positivism any merit at all and held as poor an opinion of his philosophy as of his politics.

'As a Party man', Marx wrote to E. S. Beesly, 'I entertain a thoroughly hostile attitude toward Comtism, while as a scientific man I have a very poor opinion of it.'[7] He regarded *Cours de philosophie positive* as 'trashy', 'wretched', in every respect inferior to the philosophy of Hegel, and unworthy of the fuss that the British and French reading-public made over it at that time.[8] 'It seems to me', Marx said to Engels, 'that positive philosophy means as much as the ignorance of everything positive.' A Comtist is a man who indulges in writing 'recipes for the cook-shops of the future', that is, is a belated utopian, who is obliged to support 'all sorts of crotchets'.[9]

Engels discovered in Comte's system a 'series of brilliant thoughts', which were, however, practically always useless 'because of insufficient development', a 'narrow, philistine mode of outlook', and a thoroughly pedestrian 'hierarchically organised religious constitution', 'Catholicism without Christianity'. He was sure that Comte's partiality to religion provided the clue to the discrepancy between the brilliance of his mind and the philistinism of his outlook. Moreover, 'Comte took all his bright ideas from Saint-Simon but mutilated them' and 'dragged them down to a lower level, reshaping them in philistine fashion to the best of his ability'.[10] The Comtists were even worse than Comte himself. They were in danger of outdoing the Hegelians who, in the words of a Bonn professor, understood nothing about anything but wrote about everything.[11]

On the other hand, Saint-Simon was one of the 'three great utopians', the other two being Fourier and Owen, who 'in spite of all their fantastic notions and all their utopianism, have their place among the most eminent thinkers of all times'. They 'anticipated innumerable things', Engels wrote, 'the correctness of which is now being scientifically proved by us'.[12] Whatever their shortcomings and defects were, they attacked in the words of *The Communist Manifesto* 'every principle of existing society' and 'hence they are full of the most valuable materials for the enlightenment of the working class'.[13] It is true that in *Capital* Marx showed considerable reserve with respect to Saint-Simon, for the latter did not recognize the class antagonism between industrial capitalists and workers but lumped them together in a single class under the name of *travailleurs*, and failed to rise to the awareness of the historical role to be played by the proletariat. Consequently, practically all the writings of Saint-Simon were 'mere glorifications of modern bourgeois society against feudal society'. The single exception was Saint-Simon's last work *Le Nouveau Christianisme*, where he spoke 'directly for the working class' and declared 'their emancipation to be the end of his efforts'.[14] But Engels explained in an editorial footnote that this criticism of Saint-Simon did not represent Marx's balanced judgment, for as a rule, Marx 'spoke only with admiration of the genius and encyclopedic brain of Saint-Simon'.[15] Engels's testimony is corroborated by a comparison of Saint-Simon's and Marx's views, which reveals that Marx is in deep debt to Saint-Simon's philosophy of history.

In Engels's opinion, Saint-Simon was not simply one of the three great utopians but the greatest of them all, endowed as he was with a 'comprehensive breadth of view, by virtue of which almost all the ideas of later socialists that are not strictly economic are found in him in embryo'.[16] His encyclopaedic knowledge was second to none, including Hegel, and this praise, coming from Engels, a great admirer of Hegel's erudition, could not be exceeded.[17]   Saint-Simon was a 'genius and mystic in one', a writer and thinker who 'positively suffered from repleteness of thought', and whose reputation unjustly declined after his death because his followers 'developed certain aspects of the master's teaching to the detriment of the magnificent conception as a whole'.[18]   Engels's admiration for Saint-Simon did not clash with his contempt for Comte because the main significance of Saint-Simon was, according to Engels, his philosophy of history, his influence on the initial phases of the development of socialism, and his eagerness to introduce the 'new age', that is, to establish a system of social organization appropriate for the industrial stage of civilization.   Although Engels regarded Saint-Simon as a political thinker rather than a philosopher, he was at the same time inconsistently inclined to credit Saint-Simon with most, if not all, of the philosophical ideas usually ascribed to Comte.

Most of the followers of Marx and Engels, especially the Russian wing, shared the feelings of the founders about Comte and Saint-Simon.[19]   That Comte did not influence Marx and Engels is a view accepted by practically all exponents of their views.   Karl Popper speaks of ample circumstantial evidence against the conjecture that Marx was affected directly by Comte.[20]   The name of Comte is not even mentioned by Franx Mehring in his biography *Karl Marx* or by Auguste Cornu in his detailed biographic study *Karl Marx et Friedrich Engels*.   It is mentioned only once by Maximilien Rubel in his intellectual portrait *Karl Marx* and there merely to say that Marx condemned Comtean positivism.[21]   Gustav Mayer, the biographer of Engels, denied by implication any connection between Comtean positivism and Engels's philosophical views.   Engels, he wrote, did not know what to make of positive philosophy.[22]   Only a handful of Marx's followers and commentators, notably an Austrian — Max Adler, an Italian — Antonio Labriola, and a Pole — Kazimierz Kelles-Krauz thought otherwise and recognized the existence of some connection between Comte and Marx.

Labriola showed as fierce a dislike of Comte as Marx did ; it was Labriola who referred to Comte as 'that degenerate and reactionary disciple of the genial Saint-Simon'.[23]   He recognized, however, that Marx was influenced by positive philosophy.   'Positivism', wrote Labriola, 'has from its beginning walked at the heels of socialism. So far as the ideas are concerned the two things were born about

the same time in the vague mind of the genius Saint-Simon.' [24]
Ever since, Labriola observed elsewhere, the positivists were sometimes our 'embarrassing guests' and sometimes our 'most open
adversaries'. The methodological affinity between Comte and
Marx was undeniable. The materialist conception of history provides a verification of Comte's law of the three stages and 'marks
the culminating point of the new tendency in the investigations of
the historic-social laws'. It shows how human thought is gradually
purified of theological and metaphysical conceptions and finally
securely based on the prosaic assertion that 'in the interpretation
of history we must limit ourselves to the objective co-ordination of
the determining conditions and of the determined effects'. [25]

Kelles-Krauz and Adler reached the same conclusion. Although
Kelles-Krauz denied any actual connections between Comte's
positivism and Marx's naturalism, he was fully aware of the numerous and essential affinities, which he ascribed to Saint-Simon's
influence on Marx. He said that the Marxian doctrine could justifiably be called 'social positivism' and deplored the ignorance and
indifference of Marx's followers towards Comtean positivism. [26]
Adler disagreed with the view that the social theories of Marx were
'a variety of positivism' and asserted, quite erroneously, that the
development of positivism did not precede but coincided with the
development of Marx's thought (when Marx finished his doctoral
dissertation the six volumes of the *Cours* were already available in
print). He was ready, however, to give Comte his due for his 'great
idea of a positivistic conception of the spiritual life of humanity'
and for renouncing the search after essences, efficient and final
causes, which was to be replaced by a social science based on the
observation of facts and the discovery of their invariable laws.
Adler justly emphasized that Comte was satisfied with drawing up a
general programme only of how sociology could be made a positive
science and of how politics could become scientific by being supported by a social theory. It was Marx, however, who carried
Comte's idea into effect and thereby laid the foundations of modern
sociology. [27]

A different development appeared among the Russian followers of
Marx. Plekhanov fully accepted Engels's verdict on Saint-Simon
and Comte; his adverse attitude to positivist philosophy, coupled
with his Hegelizing interpretation of Marx, may have contributed
to the intense hostility to positivism in Soviet Marxism later.

Plekhanov's knowledge of Comte was limited and inaccurate and he completely misunderstood Comte on some important points. Consequently, Plekhanov saw in the Comtean doctrine 'only an endless movement round a vicious circle' with 'no trace of science in it'.[28]   At the same time, he spoke with considerable knowledge and sympathy of Saint-Simon, whose works, like those of Fourier and Owen, were remarkable for their 'profound thoughts'.   He ascribed to Saint-Simon the discoveries claimed by Comte as his exclusive possession, in particular the law of the three stages, and credited him with much insight and many new ground-breaking conceptions.   Plekhanov agreed with Bernstein, whom he fought ruthlessly on other issues, that Saint-Simon and the Saint-Simonists had left a definite impact upon Marx's mind.[29]

It was Lenin who turned the scales decisively in Soviet Marxism and initiated its virulent philosophical and ideological hostility to positivism, a hostility different in kind and more extreme than Marx's.   Lenin did not simply follow the pattern set up before him of piling high praise upon the genius of Saint-Simon and resounding denunciation upon the head of Comte.[30]   He hardly associated the name of Comte with the establishment of a distinctive philosophical trend and was unable to differentiate Comtean positivism from the philosophy of other thinkers who came a little later, such as Spencer, the Neo-Kantians, Renouvier and the French neocriticist movement. He was, however, familiar with, and interested in, the philosophy of Ernst Mach, Henri Poincaré, Pierre Duhem, and Abel Rey, called 'the second positivism' in the terminology of Soviet philosophy.   It was the second positivism on which Lenin concentrated his scornful and abusive attitude.   Lenin's condemnation of Mach's philosophy was based on its interpretation as a kind of subjective idealism.   According to him, Mach believed that the world consists of sensations or perceptions or sense-data.   Lenin deduced this assertion from the methodological demand, common to the first and second positivism, that statements in which constructs such as energy, force, or mass occur cannot be literally true unless they are translatable into statements about sense observations.[31]   If the philosophy of Mach was idealistic, then every kind of positivism was tarred with the same brush.   Lenin's militant hostility towards the second positivism was accepted by Marxist–Leninists and extended to the third positivism, i.e. to logical positivism and logical empiricism, with which British analytical philosophy and American philosophy of science is sometimes mentioned in one breath.[32] Since the second and third positivism are historically related to the positivism of Comte, Lenin and Marxist–Leninists refused to recognize any connections between Marx and French positivism.

An ideological critique reinforced the epistemological refutation of positivism. Marxist–Leninists look at the relation of Marx to Comte in the light of the present historical situation and believe that the sociology of the nineteenth and twentieth centuries has developed in anticipation of, and in opposition to, the theory and practice of modern revolutionary socialism. From this point of view, bourgeois sociology is mere ideology and a weapon in the class struggle raging throughout the world. This precludes *a priori* any link between the doctrines of Comte and Marx. It is self-evident that Marx could not have anything in common with the founder of sociology and his 'philosophy of acceptance' which expressed and supported the interests of the victorious bourgeoisie of the nineteenth century.[33]

While Marx and Engels, giving free vent to their ideological idiosyncrasy, minimized the philosophical significance of Comte and maximized the political importance of Saint-Simon, the role of positivism in the formation of their philosophy was disappearing from sight. Although in the first generation of the followers of Marx and Engels there were some writers who tried to evaluate the part played by positivism impartially, the repudiation of positivism became absolute with Lenin and its influence upon Marxian philosophy was denied altogether. A number of Western commentators tried to investigate the relation of Marx and Engels to positivism but they all failed to establish their case for one reason or another.[34]

Although it appears certain that Marx read *Cours de philosophie positive* only in his mature years, the view that there is no connection between the philosophy of Marx and Comtean positivism cannot be upheld. Marx did not need to study the *Cours*, the classical formulation of the first positivism, to be influenced by positivism, because the *Cours* was neither the first nor the only source from which its basic ideas could be learnt. As will be seen presently, Marx became acquainted with positive philosophy and other doctrines of Saint-Simon and Comte at an early age and before his own philosophy was formulated.

It should be borne in mind that the *Cours de philosophie positive*, 'very nearly the grandest work of the age', as John Stuart Mill described it,[35] was slow in gaining prominence in France and elsewhere. Upon its first publication, the *Cours* was received with more sympathy in England than in Comte's native land, and in both countries it was known and appreciated by only a handful of individuals.[36] No wide interest in Comte's work among the French and English reading-public was aroused until the publication of its second edition in 1864; the popularity of positivism in the wider meaning of this term reached its high-water mark only in the last two decades of the nineteenth century.[37]

Marx was not among the handful of people in France and elsewhere who read the *Cours* when it first came out. One of his letters to Engels seems to leave little doubt that Marx read it only in 1866, that is, when the publication of the second edition caused considerable stir in France and England and prompted him to study it.[38] Marx's first knowledge of positivism came from his reading of Saint-Simon and the Saint-Simonists, for which *The German Ideology* provides direct and ample evidence.[39] This work makes it clear that Marx's knowledge of the Saint-Simonist doctrine was based on the original works of Saint-Simon and his followers,[40] and not on second-hand sources.[41] Moreover, there is some evidence that Marx might have made his first acquaintance with the doctrine of Saint-Simon very early and at the most impressionable age of his life. He might have come across Saint-Simon's ideas when he was still at school in Trier through Ludwig Gall, a local celebrity, who greatly admired Saint-Simon and published a pamphlet about his teaching in 1834. He certainly heard of Saint-Simon from his paternal friend and future father-in-law, Ludwig von Westphalen, another admirer of Saint-Simon, and from Eduard Gans, the jurist, one of his teachers at the University of Berlin, who reputedly influenced his intellectual development. Finally, he most certainly became familiar with Saint-Simonism through Moses Hess whom he met first in 1841, and with whom he worked on the *Rheinische Zeitung* in the years 1842–3.[42] Besides, after France it was Germany where the Saint-Simonist doctrine gained the greatest foothold. In the early 1830s so many books, pamphlets, and articles about the Saint-Simonist doctrine appeared there that practically everything could be learnt about it from German sources.[43]

Among the Saint-Simonist writings which Marx was most likely to have studied at first hand, none was more important than Comte's early contribution to the positivist doctrine, *Système de politique positive*, known also under the cumbersome title *Plan des travaux scientifiques nécessaires pour réorganiser la société*, published during Saint-Simon's lifetime in his *Catéchisme des Industriels* in 1822.[44] Comte's long article contains a concise and clear exposition of his main philosophical and sociological ideas, later expounded in great detail in the *Cours*. F. A. Hayek suggested that it reached a much earlier and wider audience than the *Cours* did after its first publication and exercised, therefore, a greater influence than Comte's classical work did, at least at first. 'It seems to me to be one of the most pregnant tracts of the nineteenth century, infinitely more brilliant then the now better known ponderous volumes of the *Cours*.'[45] Since Comte described himself in his article, which appeared in Saint-Simon's publication, as 'a pupil of Saint-Simon' whose ideas he 'tried to systematize, to develop, and to improve',[46] his readers, including Marx, may have failed to differentiate Comte's views from the vaguely defined body of ideas known as the Saint-Simonist doctrine. It was possible, therefore, for Marx to borrow ideas from Comte's contribution without giving him credit for them, and to praise Saint-Simon for the ideas which were actually Comte's.

2. THE POSITIVISTIC BACKGROUND OF MARXIAN PHILOSOPHY

The relation of Marx and Engels to Comte closely resembles their relation to Hegel. While Comte's 'brilliant ideas' appear plainly and clearly in the philosophy of Engels, in Marx's case the Comtean influence can only be established indirectly. This influence is revealed by a considerable number of sociological and historical conceptions which Marx held in common with Saint-Simon and Comte, and which seem to preclude a mere chance similarity emanating from the prevailing climate of philosophical opinions. However, Marx not only absorbed but also elaborated upon these conceptions and, having looked deeper into the structure of society, and discovered in its texture some connections that escaped the notice of either Saint-Simon or Comte, he transcended the views which he adopted from them. The belief that French positivism exercised a lasting influence upon Marx does not entail the conclusion that the Marxian doctrine is nothing but a variant of positivism.

It is true that *l'esprit positif* never gained ground in Germany. 'In Germany, whose scholastic atmosphere was always inimical toward anything that could be called positivism, Lange tried, to a very modest extent, to propagate understanding of Comte and Mill, but the effect was quite unexpected; it caused a reaction which opposed the "undue prevalence of the ideas of natural science" and proclaimed an "autarchy of the humanities (*Geisteswissenschaften*)".'[47] However, in Germany it was not Comte, but Marx, who became the embodiment of *l'esprit positif* in the social and historical sciences. As the names of Ferdinand Tönnies, Rudolf Stammler, Werner Sombart, Max Weber, Ernst Troeltsch, Max Scheler, or Karl Mannheim testify, many developments in the theory and methodology of the historical and social sciences, which elsewhere would have been related to the positivism of Comte in one way or another, should be tracked back in Germany to the impact of the theories of Marx.

Although Marx appears to have performed the same function in Germany as Comte did in other European countries, the identity of function should not be confused with the identity of views. To-day, probably nobody would endorse the verdict of Paul Barth to the effect that Marx contributed nothing to the naturalistic or positivistic conception of history but merely systematized the ideas of Saint-Simon (and Louis Blanc), especially those concerned with the function of technology and the role of class struggle in social development, infusing them with a certain Hegelian speculative drive.[48] This is not only a greatly exaggerated but also an erroneous opinion, for Marx did incorporate certain views of Saint-Simon into his own system but not without first adapting them to his own way of perceiving social reality. For instance, both Saint-Simon and Marx emphasized the importance of economic change, but the former regarded it as a dependent and the latter as an independent variable. For Saint-Simon, the primary cause of progress was the accumulation and advancement of knowledge; economic change, its effect; for Marx, economic change was the source of all progress, including the accumulation and advancement of knowledge. In spite of their similarity in some respects, the doctrines of Saint-Simon and Marx remain essentially different. To establish the influence of one thinker upon another or to discover an affinity in their views does not entail the conclusion that only one of them should be credited with original and significant ideas.

Saint-Simon showed a lively interest in history and made a significant contribution to the philosophical study of this subject. He held a poor opinion of the historiography of his time, because it had not yet abandoned, as he put it, the language of infancy. It was the mere story of the founders of religion, sages, kings, or conquerors who could do with society whatever they pleased, a mere collection of facts which were not linked together by a theory. Since the historians failed to discover 'the cause of the order of events', they were unable to provide 'the means of judging what will happen from what has happened'. The fact that historiography was not in a position to predict the future was the best indication that it could not be classified among the positive sciences.[49]   Saint-Simon was anxious to remedy its defects, and produced a philosophy of history which was destined to play an important role in the further development of ideas. Comte adopted and amplified Saint-Simon's philosophy in his own view of universal history and Marx was also affected by it in many ways.

The number of ideas common to the Saint-Simonian and Marxian conception of history is considerable. Both Saint-Simon and Marx considered history as a succession of developmental phases which is subject to invariable laws and which the human species has to pass through in its advance. The very object of social science is to discover the laws of progress, that is, to investigate the necessary order of the successive stages of social evolution and the contribution of each of them to the determination of the following ones. The law of progress relates the different forms of civilization and explains how each of them was brought about by, or gave rise to, another, for a social system is always formed in the bosom of the preceding one, however antagonistic the two might be or actually are. One does not create or abolish a system of social organization; one simply discovers its formation or disappearance. 'A social system', Saint-Simon observed, and Marx reproduced his remarks in the Preface to *A Contribution to the Critique of Political Economy*, in almost identical words, 'can only disappear to the extent that another already exists entirely formed and ready to take its place immediately'. Since peoples move towards the same goal and follow the same necessary course of evolution, which no force can change or resist, the knowledge of the law of progress can merely 'explain a development which is inevitable', help to remove the obstacle barring its advance, and persuade people to 'do consciously, and with better directed and more useful efforts, what they have hitherto done unconsciously, slowly, indecisively and too ineffectively'. As Saint-Simon wrote elsewhere, the law of progress of the human spirit 'carries along and dominates everything; men are but its instruments. . . . All we can do is to obey this law by accounting for the course it directs, instead of being pushed by it.' The first intimation of the Marxian vision of social development as a lawful process which unfolds itself 'with iron necessity towards inevitable results', whose successive stages cannot be cleared by bold leaps, and whose pangs of birth and growth can be only lessened or shortened by conscious action, is to be found in Saint-Simon.[50]

Like many others, including Marx, Saint-Simon emphasized that the discovery of the laws of social evolution was important not only for the purpose of acquiring knowledge but also, and above all, for the perfection of civilization. The knowledge of laws enables us to grasp the causes of events and to predict what will happen in the future; it gives us, therefore, the power to influence events and provides the means of turning them to the advantage of man. 'The true intelligence, the positive intelligence, is revealed in the prediction of the march of events in which one is involved, in the knowledge of how to protect oneself from those which might be harmful and of how to profit by those which might be advantageous.'[51]

Finally, for Saint-Simon, historical inevitability was a beneficial force, and 'the march of the human spirit' was destined to produce the greatest happiness for the greatest number. The law of progress was bound to bring about what ought to be, another conception, or rather pre-conception, common to Marx and Saint-Simon. Both believed that social evolution leads, one way or another, to the progressive emancipation of men from all forms of degrading dependence upon each other, promotes the growth of co-operative association and social solidarity, allows men to make the most of their natural capacities, to expand their distinctively human potentialities, and to live a satisfying life. In disregard of what he said about historical inevitability, but in keeping with his earlier beliefs, Saint-Simon urged his fellow men to create a new society by conscious effort. The main theme of *Le Nouveau Christianisme* was that society should be organized in a manner most advantageous to the largest number, and that all human work should be directed to the amelioration — as prompt and complete as possible — of the moral and physical conditions of existence of the most numerous and most suffering class.[52]

In his lectures on the Saint-Simonist doctrine, Armand Bazard drew the consequences implicit in Saint-Simon's exhortations. Bazard condemned the anarchy of capitalist production, the disastrous effects of free competition, and the injustice of the monopoly of wealth. He compared the 'exploitation of man by man' to slavery in the ancient world and demanded that it be replaced by the 'exploitation of nature by man associated with man'. Each man should be placed 'according to his capability' and rewarded 'according to his work'. The rights of property which allow some to impose a levy on the labour of others and live in idleness must be changed. The human race is becoming more and more unified and humanity is gravitating to 'universal association'. These formulations strike familiar chords, for Marx incorporated them into his own view of society and social evolution. As a social and political philosopher, Marx owed more to Saint-Simon and the Saint-Simonists than to any other of his socialist forerunners.[53]

For Saint-Simon sociology and philosophy were so intimately connected that it was almost impossible to separate them from each other.[54] The bond between philosophy and sociology could be explained by the fact that they both were concerned with the same subject-matter, differing only in their respective approach and procedure. It was the very object of philosophy to systematize the whole of knowledge available at a given time, and of sociology to study the same body of knowledge 'in action' and as reflected in social life. Saint-Simon believed that what unites men in society was a common way of perceiving and reacting to the world and, consequently, that all human society was grounded on a system of collectively held, fundamental opinions. Religion, politics, morality, or education were simply 'applications of a system of ideas' prevailing at a given period.[55] But if every social order is the embodiment of a philosophical system, sociology is a branch of philosophy and philosophy has a social significance and practical implications. To speak in the language of the Young Hegelians used by Marx in his youth, philosophy is realized in the corresponding social order. We cannot abolish an old society and institute a new one without first establishing a new philosophical system, for the one is an application of the other.

Comte adopted the Saint-Simonist conception of the relation between philosophy and sociology, but with an important difference. He insisted that philosophy must be clearly separated from sociology, and social theory from applied social science. From the viewpoint of positive philosophy these distinctions were essential. In his first major work, *Système de politique positive* of 1822, Comte criticized Saint-Simon, without mentioning him, for his failure to differentiate between social theory and its application, to the disadvantage of both. As a qualifying term, 'positive' was to indicate the transformation of knowledge from the speculative to the scientific stage, when facts, instead of being explained *a priori* by means of personified abstractions, 'become connected by general ideas or laws of a completely positive kind, suggested or confirmed by the very facts'.[56] In every branch of knowledge that reaches the scientific or positive stage of development, a clear and sharp distinction between its theoretical and practical functions is of utmost importance. While objecting to Saint-Simon's haste in applying a science which did not yet exist, Comte did not repudiate Saint-Simon's ultimate objective which, however, was to be attained by the prior establishment of sociology as a positive theoretical science.

It was the Comtean conception of social physics rather than the Saint-Simonist social physiology as a kind of applied philosophy that influenced Marx. It is in his determination to apply scientific method to social life, to discover invariable laws to which social phenomena conform, and to establish a science of society, that Marx is most clearly indebted to the Comtean methodological and sociological conception. Since it was the sociological approach to intellectual and moral phenomena that enabled Marx to move beyond the old materialism and to formulate a consistent naturalistic outlook, the influence of French positivism is of crucial importance in the development of Marxian thought.

To say that Comte had 'the disdain for truth in itself'[57] seems to be an observation overreaching its evidence and, at best, misleading. Both Comte and Marx shared the conception of science known as 'instrumentalism'. They did not value knowledge for its own sake, but as a necessary condition of man's control over his natural and social environment. True knowledge is useful because it gives us the power of prediction, and prediction provides the basis for intelligent action. The instrumentalism of Marx and, especially, of Comte can be traced back to Francis Bacon whom the Encyclopaedists, Comte's direct intellectual predecessors, admired perhaps more than any other philosopher of the past. Bacon encouraged men to acquire knowledge, for knowledge gives power over nature, which in turn increases human happiness. 'Hostile to systems,' wrote d'Alembert of Bacon, 'he conceives of philosophy as being only that part of our knowledge which should contribute to making us better or happier, thus . . . confining it within the limits of the science of useful things.' [58]   One need not feel disdain for truth if one assumes that knowledge is practical power and urges men to use it for their own benefit.   Apart from Bacon or Comte, many philosophers have been more interested in human morality and happiness than in knowledge for its own sake.   It is perhaps unwise to be too unfavourably impressed by such attitudes.   As Bertrand Russell observed, a pure desire for knowledge, which only philosophy can give, is extremely rare.   Comte had to admit, however, that the possibility of exerting influence upon the forces of nature is very small, for they operate according to laws over which we have no control.   Our entire power lies in the discovery of these laws through observation, and in the prediction of what happens in conformity to the inevitable succession of events.   Comte emphasized that this applied to political action in the same way and for the same reason as to physical, chemical, or physiological phenomena.   'All political action is followed by a real and durable result, when it is exerted in the same direction as the force of civilization and aims at producing changes which the latter necessitates.'   Comte added that 'on every other hypothesis it exerts no influence or a merely ephemeral one'.[59]

That the function of knowledge, both in natural and social science, is to 'reveal the future' is a view which deeply impressed both Marx and Engels.   It impressed them because of its obvious relevance for natural theology and philosophical anthropology.   Comte insisted throughout the *Cours* that the principle of rational prediction was 'the most unchallengeable criterion of scientific positiveness' (*le plus irrécusable critérium de la positivité scientifique*).   Our power of foreseeing phenomena is closely connected with our power of controlling them and these two powers together do away with the belief that the external world is governed by a supernatural will.   When men learn how to predict and control the phenomena of nature, the theological mode of thought cannot last out much longer.   Although the principle of rational prediction is compatible with the belief in a supreme intelligence provided that this intelligence adheres to invariable laws, both Marx and Engels were inclined to think that it helped to get rid of it.

The predictive power of positive science also had important implications for man's views about himself and his place in nature. It inspired Engels with a boundless confidence in the efficacy of collective action and prompted his statement that men are in a position to exercise control, founded on knowledge of natural necessity, over their destiny and over the external world by making natural laws 'work towards definite ends'.[60]   Since man is powerless if he does not act in conformity to the laws of nature, Marx regarded as utopian any social science which, instead, of being supported by the law of social evolution, was based on moral considerations alone, or the principle of justice, or the ideals of an unchanging human nature.

The concept of prediction sharply differentiates the Comtean and the Hegelian views of progress, which otherwise evince a certain similarity.   Both Hegel and Comte take progress for granted, assume that it is a process determined by law, and believe that this law becomes manifest in the advance of the mind or spirit.[61]   But Hegel did not see any connection between prediction and progress or between prediction and effective action; this is the meaning frequently attached to the oracular saying about the owl of Minerva spreading its wings only with the fall of dusk.   While for Hegel progress represented an aspect of Spirit and disclosed an essential characteristic of the Absolute, for Comte, progress reflected the changes in man and society and revealed the fact that in each successive age the main social phenomena were different from what they were in the preceding age.   While Hegel could only point retrospectively to the unfolding of an ideal slowly embodying itself in the actual form of historical cultures, the Comtean law of progress provided a means of interpreting the past and predicting the future in order that man might increasingly improve the organization of society.   Leopold von Ranke's celebrated pronouncement that every epoch is directly related to God and that its value does not lie in what it engenders but in what it is, its own self, could well be fitted into the Hegelian conception of progress but not within that of Comte or Marx.   There can be no doubt that Comte, rather than Hegel, affected Marx's views about progress and the role of prediction in its realization.

The recognition of social laws, which dominate social life, imposes far-reaching limitations upon the effectiveness of human action. According to Comte, the progress of civilization is essentially unalterable ; man's interference can modify it only in certain respects and within certain limits. The modification brought about by man's intervention cannot, for instance, reverse the natural course of development, nor take a leap forward nor avoid any intermediate phases in the fixed succession of evolutionary stages. The natural progress of civilization determines for each epoch the improvements of which society is susceptible and only such improvements can in fact be attained by conscious effort. Human actions may accelerate or retard the speed of change but it cannot affect its nature and direction.[62]

To use John Stuart Mill's expression, Comte's principle of social determinism gives 'a scientific shape' to the view originally formulated by Saint-Simon and brings to focus the affinity between the Saint-Simonist and the Marxian conception of social change. By the same token, it throws doubt upon the statement often regarded as self-evident that it was Hegel alone who was responsible for the Marxian way of thinking of society in terms of change, evolution, and invariable laws. Comte's social dynamics, as the science of the continuous movement and lawful transformation of humanity from one state into another, could have influenced Marx as much as Hegel's conceptions.[63] Indeed, when Marx speaks of 'the successive phases of normal social development' or of 'the laws of motion of modern society' he speaks clearly in the language of Comte, not Hegel.

Comte's concept of social evolution is modelled on the process of biological development. Comte spoke of social evolution as a fixed course of change determined exclusively by the causes inherent in the nature of changing society. Social change is not induced from outside, but self-generated ; [64] it results from socially determined activities and is itself, therefore, socially determined, 'a spontaneous social movement ruled by natural laws' (*un mouvement social spontané et réglé par les lois naturelles*), as Comte insisted in the *Cours*. Society evolves in the same way as a plant develops from a seed or an animal from an embryo or a man from a child, an image that also underlies the seventeenth- and eighteenth-century conception of human progress.[65] Comte ignored the possibility that social evolution might be likened to a process of growth determined both by internal and external factors and thus modifiable by innumerable favourable or unfavourable circumstances, of which the socialization of children, the learning of skills, the improvement of tools, or the cultivation of abilities provide instances. Comte clearly thought in biological rather than in non-biological — cultural or sociological — terms.

When Marx spoke of society discovering 'the natural laws of its movement' or 'the successive phases of its normal development', he made use of the Comtean biological concept of evolution. His formulation suggests that the normal development of society is a process of change independent of any external factors and taking place in conformity to an invariable law. Marx explained that in *Capital* he used England as the chief illustration of the capitalist mode of production, because England was its 'classic ground' and thus permitted him to study the 'occurrence of the phenomena in its normality'. Marx pointed out that other nations could and should learn from England's example what the future holds in store for them. He denied, however, that by taking advantage of this knowledge other nations could spare themselves the experience. To those doubting the truth of this statement he answered, 'De te fabula narratur'.[66]

The instrumental conception of knowledge common to Comte and Marx accounts for yet another resemblance between their respective views. Comte did not deny that the search for knowledge is inherent in the human mind, but he emphasized the intimate relation between knowledge, forecast, and action, 'science, hence foresight; foresight, hence action' (*science, d'où prévoyance; prévoyance, d'où action*).[67] It becomes more evident every day, Comte wrote, how hopeless the task of reconstructing political institutions is without the prior remodelling of beliefs and of life. Philosophy was to secure the foundations for morality and religion, and these were to provide the basis for scientific politics and the reorganization of society. Thus, *philosophie positive* was not an autonomous but a heteronomous end, that is, a means for the attainment of an end.[68] 'Had Comte thought it possible to reorganize society without first reorganizing morals, and to reorganize morals without first reorganizing beliefs, he would not perhaps have written the six volumes of the *Cours de philosophie positive. . . .* He would have gone straight to what was of supreme interest.'[69]

Saint-Simon, the Saint-Simonists, and Comte were as much social reformers as they were social philosophers. They saw in knowledge a basis for action and a guide to social reconstruction. They felt that a comprehensive historical and sociological theory which provides a way of viewing the world and a code of life precepts was indispensable in their task. In both these respects, Marx shows an essential similarity to his positivist predecessors. There is a close parallel between Saint-Simon's demand for a new philosophy of which the society of the future would be an application, or Comte's insistence that only a comprehensive and coherent system of positive science could provide the foundation for the establishment of a stable social order, and Marx's statement that philosophy was the head of man's political and social emancipation and the proletariat its heart.[70] The last thesis on Feuerbach epitomizes Marx's overriding concern with social reconstruction, of which a philosophical *Weltanschauung* was an indispensable prerequisite.

Comte claimed that he founded social physics or sociology by extending the positive mode of thought to moral and social phenomena which had previously been studied according to the theologico-metaphysical mode. As Comte pointed out, prior to his own investigations, 'imagination was not subordinate to observation' in the study of social facts ; the facts themselves were considered to be modifiable, practically without restriction, by the action of the ruler or the legislator ; and social phenomena were explained by means of mental abstractions which, being conceived as real entities, could exert power and produce change. A science is positive if it does not ask the question why something happens but how it happens ; if it does not search for efficient or final causes but for natural laws.[71]

To become a positive science, sociology has to satisfy a number of conditions. First, its subject-matter must be properly defined. The task of sociology is to investigate the collective phenomena and the collective development of the human race. Being concerned with the study of man in all his aspects (*l'homme dans toute son extension*), social physics is, in a sense, a branch of physiology, a continuation and indispensable complement of the natural history of man.[72] Second, to become a positive science, sociology had to abandon the assumption that social life — the human race, as Comte put it — is entirely passive and can be changed at will by the temporal or spiritual legislator armed with appropriate authority.[73] Third, having rejected the assumption of the omnipotence of the legislator, sociology must conceive social life as endowed with a structure or organization of its own which is not only connected with but determined by the state of civilization. Fourth, sociology as a positive science recognizes that the progressive march of civilization follows a natural and irrevocable course ('la civilisation est assujettie à une marche naturelle et irrévocable') and that civilization develops according to a necessary law ('les progrès de la civilisation se développent suivant une loi nécessaire'). Since the state of social organization is the outcome of the state of civilization, the forces of social life and their progressive change are determined by the march of civilization, that is, by the laws of the evolution of human society.[74] Sociology as a positive science in Comte's sense is the 'science of society' to which Marx adhered when he recognized that there are no fundamental differences between different kinds of human experience, that they are natural events and can be investigated by scientific method.

Comte, like Saint-Simon before and Marx after him, rejected the view that social phenomena are reducible to biology or physiology. It was Saint-Simon who first broke with the eighteenth-century materialistic preconceptions that the 'science of man' should be established on the foundations of mechanics. Saint-Simon felt that physiology, which at that time was understood to provide a general theory of living bodies, would make a more important contribution to the new science of society than mechanics, for society was a living organism and not a machine.[75] Having established this new link between natural science and the postulated 'science of man', he insisted that 'social physiology' dealt with a reality *sui generis*, distinct from the physiology of human individuals. Consequently, although they were related to each other, social and individual physiology should never be confused or regarded as identical. Comte was more specific than Saint-Simon and amplified and elucidated his doctrine. In his opinion reductivism was a philosophical aberration; it led to materialistic metaphysics with which positivism had nothing to do; and it constituted the greatest single obstacle to the establishment of sociology as a positive science. What is true of phenomena is also true of their laws. The laws of biology are logically prior to the laws of sociology, but the latter cannot be deduced from the former. Moreover, the laws of human society are subject to change in the course of history and cannot, therefore, be particular cases of the laws of animal societies which display neither development nor progress.[76] Marx and all his followers accepted unconditionally the Comtean anti-reductivist principle, but neither Marx nor his supporters argued this principle as ably and persuasively as Comte did.

That society is an organized whole, prior to the individual, and in fact determining his role and action within it, is a view already clearly formulated by Saint-Simon.

> Society is not at all a simple agglomeration of living beings whose actions, independent of any finite goal, have no other cause than the arbitrary will of individuals and no other effects than chance events, ephemeral and unimportant accidents. On the contrary, society is, above all, a veritable organized machine, all of whose component parts contribute in a different way to the working of the whole.[77]

For Saint-Simon, Comte, and Marx alike, society is the true reality, and the individual the abstraction. From the viewpoint of *l'esprit positif*, nothing but humanity really exists, for human individuals owe all their development to society. If society is still regarded as an abstraction, then only because this view is a survival of the theological stage.[78] It is an essential characteristic of society *qua* society, which differentiates it from an animal herd, that is, from a mere plurality of individuals, that within it every action is a collective, general, and combined action, as Comte put it.[79] In a certain sense, we cannot even say that society is composed of individuals. The family is the basic social unit, for the family is homogeneous with society and gives rise to the various attitudes characteristic of individuals in society.[80] Sociability is spontaneous in the human species; individuals lean instinctively towards common life, often against their immediate interests.[81] It is social life, the cumulative experience and influence of past generations over the present which, in the opinion of both Comte and Marx, has made possible the extraordinary development of the intellectual and moral functions in man.[82]

According to Comte, it is the interaction between individuals (*l'action des individus les uns sur les autres*) and, above all, 'the gradual and continuous influence of human generations upon one another' that establishes sociology as a distinct science and is responsible for its irreducibility to psychology or, to use Comte's terminology, to physiology.[83] Moreover, social life manifests to the highest degree a universal interdependence between its diverse parts and a 'constant mutual action and reaction' which these parts exercise upon each other. This universal interdependence — the terms used by Comte are '*le consensus universel*' and '*la solidarité fondamentale*'[84] —

also applies to the relationships between various social institutions and the state of civilization, between political power and civil society.[85]

The peculiar nature of social phenomena accounts for some of the distinctive characteristics of the sociological method. In sociology, the various social elements cannot be studied in isolation; such studies are bound to be sterile.[86] Moreover, the method proper to sociology reverses the ordinary relation between deduction and induction. Both in the sciences concerned with 'inanimate objects' (natural science) and those dealing with 'organized bodies' (the biological and social sciences) we always have to proceed from the known to the unknown. In the first we rise from elements and parts to the class and the whole, because knowledge of details is more accessible to us than knowledge of the *ensemble*. In the second, however, we begin by descending from the general to the particular and from the whole to the parts, for we are more intimately acquainted with the former than with the latter. The sociological method reverses the procedure of natural science because in sociology 'the whole is surely much better known and more accessible to us than are the diverse parts which later on can be distinguished as its components'. Consequently, in sociology we first gain knowledge of the most inclusive laws and descend from them to the less inclusive ones.[87] This Comtean rule is also a basic methodological principle of the materialist interpretation of history. Social theory must start from knowledge of directly apprehended wholes and their distinctive 'laws', however complicated they may be — as indeed is the case in the Marxian theory concerned with the social wholes known as socio-economic formations — and proceed on this basis to the investigation of particular problems.

The laws of sociology are not the laws of human nature, psychological laws, as we would say today, for human beings are always modified by the accumulated influence of past generations, by human society, and, therefore, are always historically moulded human beings. Unlike John Stuart Mill, Comte and Marx believed that social laws are laws *sui generis*, irreducible to those of psychology, and that society determines the nature and behaviour of the individual rather than the other way round.[88] Very early in his life Comte announced his adherence to the irreducibility of the physiology of the species (*la physiologie de l'espèce*) to the physiology of the individual (*la physiologie de l'individu*) and maintained that the study of 'the social phenomena of the human species' must be separated from the study of the individual taken separately, outside society.[89] To ignore the fact that human nature is a product of social life, Comte observed in a Marxian manner, is to elevate a passing phase in human evolution to the status of a permanent and indestructible human nature or to regard essentially variable human characteristics as stable and fixed by a fanciful decree.[90]   The laws of sociology are holistic laws; [91] they are not concerned with individuals but with their organized groups, with the state and structure of any part of society as a whole, with the natural development of the human race, with the order and conformity to law exhibited by this development and with the successive phases through which society must pass. Consequently, in sociology observation and the comparative method play a subordinate role, and experiments are out of the question. The specific sociological method, which allows us to deal with the problems of both social statics and social dynamics, is the historical method. 'No history, no sociology', Lévy-Bruhl commented, was Comte's final word on the method most appropriate and effective in social studies. For Comte, sociology does not differ essentially from the history of civilization and the natural history of man considered in all his manifestations.[92]

Practically all the principles of Comte's sociological theory can be found in Marx, who, however, unlike Comte, did not expound them systematically. Marx is not a systematic thinker in the sense that he does not define the concepts of his theoretical framework before making use of it. But he lays the same emphasis upon the fact that at any time the state of every part of a social system is interdependent with the state of all the other parts; that no aspect of social life should be studied separately but always in *l'ensemble du sujet*; that change in one social sub-system is bound to be followed by change in the other; and that the development of society from one phase to another results from a fundamental transformation that is followed and reflected in all the parts or the sub-systems of the social whole. Marx shared Comte's belief that the historical method is the appropriate method for sociology; that human nature is not unchanging and universal but changeable and determined by the achievements of past generations; and that sociology has to start with the most general principles before it can deal with details. Both the Comtean social dynamics and the Marxian materialist conception of history are theories of social change and evolution based on the assumption that each state of society is the necessary effect of the preceding state and the whole cause of the succeeding one.

Within this common framework Comte and Marx agreed on some objectives of their respective undertakings and disagreed on others. They shared the ambition to establish a positive or naturalistic social science which could be applied to the reorganization of society as successfully as the natural sciences had been applied to the transformation of the natural environment. They also shared the conviction that once sociology were established, what Comte called the 'theologico-metaphysical mode of thought' and Marx the 'illusion of the epoch' or, more generally, 'ideologies', would lose their stronghold and the mind would be liberated from the phantoms of its own creation. The emancipation of politics from mythology, theology, and metaphysics, by which it has so long been dominated, will open a new era of human relations and a new chapter in history. The elevation of politics to the rank of positive science was, according to Comte, the most urgent task of his time.[93] They viewed history in a similar fashion, trying to analyze it into interdependent causal chains and to discover the filiation of the states of society on one another. They were in agreement that history should provide the material for the discovery of sociological laws and that conversely sociology could help in explaining the course of history in the past and in predicting its future.

They differed sharply, however, in their respective ways of perceiving and interpreting society. For Comte, society could exhibit intellectual and moral anarchy but was essentially based on 'an evident and spontaneous harmony' which always, even in times of revolution, 'tends to hold between the whole and the parts of a social system'. Social solidarity results from the division of labour and is itself the basic cause of the continued extension and growing perfection of the social organism.[94] For Marx, society was an arena of social conflicts; class antagonism and strife provided the driving force of change and development. Comte regarded ideas and ideals as important factors which determine the course of human evolution; he recognized the autonomy of the moral order and assigned to it the vital task of making social and altruistic sentiments predominate over selfish and individualistic impulses; and he considered the advancement of knowledge to be the main agent in the progress of mankind, conceived as the growth of distinctively human attributes and their increasing ascendancy over our animality. For Marx the

Comtean belief in the independence of reason and the autonomy of morals was pure fantasy, unrelated to the actual course of history and to the 'real life process'. For instance, Marx would recognize that a steady increase in man's knowledge and mastery over nature accelerates the rate of social change. In *The Communist Manifesto*, he emphasized the incessant disturbances of all social conditions, the disruption of all fixed relations, and the rejection of all opinions as soon as they were formed, which followed the rapid scientific advance and technological change during one hundred years of the rule of the bourgeoisie. But having recognized the dependence of the rate of social change upon the increase in man's knowledge, Marx considered the advance of science as a socially determined factor. He did not dismiss moral ideals altogether but believed that they reflected the vital requirements inherent in the social situation of those holding them, whose outlook and actions were in turn class-determined. Again, it is enough to remind oneself of Marx's description of the social disintegration which under the rule of the bourgeoisie, and in spite of its reverential tributes to high-sounding ideals, destroys important social and human values. Bourgeois interests, Marx concluded in *The Communist Manifesto*, lurk in ambush behind law, morality, and religion.

The sharp differences in the way in which Comte and Marx perceived and interpreted social reality were ultimately due to their mutually exclusive social values. Although they both demanded that the domain of social facts should be examined like any other field of natural phenomena, they failed to live up to their own precept. Their respective social theories are not free from an ideological critique based on evaluative criteria opposed to each other ; their theories not only seek to explain how society functions but also how it ought to function. On this account they were bound to clash on every practical issue, however agreed they may have been on matters of pure theory. The clash of opinions on events taking place under their eyes, their conflicting social and political commitments, their fundamental differences in the general mode of conceiving the human universe, and their persistent disagreement on the evaluative level tended to obscure the fact that in their non-evaluative parts their social theories reveal numerous striking similarities.

Émile Durkheim said of Comte that he declared social facts to be facts of nature, without, however, treating them as things.[95] The meaning of Durkheim's charge is not entirely clear. If he wished to say that Comte failed to establish sociology as a positive science, Durkheim was perfectly right. A subject of study becomes a science only if it is presented as a systematic, logically connected body of general propositions in which the relation between the more and less inclusive concepts and statements is clearly shown and the facts can be recognized as particular cases of a law or laws. Although Comte contributed a great deal to the discovery of the principles and methods that could be used to make a positive science of sociology, he failed to apply them and give to the social science the requisite logical and systematic form.

Mill challenged the opinion that Comte created sociology for another reason. Montesquieu and even Machiavelli, Turgot and Adam Smith, most of the political economists both in France and England, Bentham and all his followers, rejected the theological and metaphysical viewpoint in the social sciences and accepted the positive position as firmly as Comte himself. Although Comte went further than these thinkers, it was not reserved to him to initiate positive inquiries in sociology. Moreover, from the point of view of Mill's methodological psychologism, Comte was responsible for the grave error of having failed to see that 'the phenomena of man in society result from his nature as an individual being'. The conclusion was, therefore, inescapable that Comte 'has done nothing in sociology which does not require to be done over again, and better. Nevertheless, he has greatly advanced the study.' [96]

Durkheim's and Mill's observations converge towards a single conclusion that while Comte did not create sociology, he laid the foundations on which sociology could be constructed. While Comte was engaged in discovering the principles and methodological rules which would make of sociology a positive science, Marx was exploring new avenues to social and historical knowledge. To put it differently, Comte investigated the possibility of establishing sociology and Marx established a sociological theory. They are both founders of modern sociology, though their claim to this title is based on different credentials.

3. THE ELEMENTS OF POSITIVIST PHILOSOPHY IN ENGELS

As has been mentioned earlier, the influence of Comte upon Engels is direct and conspicuous. The elements of positivism in Engels are most apparent in his conception of philosophy and in his views on the relation of philosophy to science.

According to Comte, an essential characteristic of positive philosophy is that it considers all phenomena as subject to invariable natural laws whose discovery enables us to make predictions and whose gradual reduction to the smallest possible number is an important mark of scientific advance. On the other hand, positive philosophy regards the search for essences, efficient and final causes, that is, causes which are not themselves physical or observable phenomena, as absolutely impracticable and meaningless. *L'esprit positif*, Comte wrote, 'is generalized and systematized common sense'.[97]

Comte's distinction between positive and speculative philosophy corresponds to the distinction between the empirical and metaphysical attitude. While a metaphysician claims that he grasps the reality concealed behind appearances, an empirical philosopher makes no such claim and is satisfied if his knowledge is in agreement with experience. The difference between the empirical and metaphysical method may be illustrated by the contrast between Descartes's *Principia Philosophiae* and J. B. Fourier's *Théorie analytique de la chaleur*, to which Comte referred. Descartes believed that he knew the essence of matter and that he could deduce all its properties from this knowledge. He did not differentiate, therefore, between physics and metaphysics, between the study of phenomena and their laws and the examination of the essence of matter, which he regarded as the cause of physical phenomena and the source of their laws. On the other hand, Fourier declared at the very beginning of his treatise that he did not know the fundamental causes of heat, which, like gravity, fills every part of space, but that these causes are subject to simple and constant laws whose study is the object of natural philosophy. Fourier's objective was to construct a theory of heat, based on a few principles, to which he was led by common observation and which were confirmed by experiments.

That science is not concerned with essences, first causes or things-in-themselves, but with phenomena and the laws of their co-existence and succession, was a view fully endorsed by Engels. He subscribed to the positivistic belief that we know a thing if we know its qualities. There is no sense in going any further, for there is nothing left to know. As in Comtean philosophy, successful predictions, based on the knowledge of laws, provide the test of the correctness of our knowledge of these laws.[98]   Views similar to those of Engels were described by John Stuart Mill as the general property of the age, but they happened to be an important part of Comte's conception of knowledge.

Comte observed that the search for essences is bound to raise the claim to absolute truth.   On the other hand, a positive science gives up the pursuit of absolute knowledge by the very fact that it strives for the knowledge of laws.   A law, if true at all, is never true absolutely but always under some definite conditions.   The discovery of laws depends on the available means of observation which improve constantly and make the attainment of certainty, of absolute and perfect knowledge, recede ever further.   'The relative character of scientific conceptions is necessarily inseparable from the true notion of natural laws, in the same way as the chimerical tendency to absolute knowledge spontaneously accompanies whatever use we make of the theological fictions and metaphysical entities.'[99]   The doctrine of the relativity of knowledge implies that the search for absolute knowledge is futile and that the history of human conceptions of the world is the only positive theory of knowledge. The mind can examine ways of acquiring knowledge only by the investigation of the successive products of its own cognitive activity.[100]

The doctrine of the relativity of knowledge is an integral part of Engels's philosophy of science.[101]   Engels regarded Hegel's claim to having discovered absolute truth as one of the most serious objections to Hegelian philosophy.   A system of natural and historical knowledge, Engels wrote, can make giant strides from age to age.   No single philosopher is able to accomplish what can only be achieved by the entire human race in its progressive development.   Once this is realized,

> there is an end to all philosophy in the hitherto accepted sense
> of the word.   One leaves alone 'absolute truth', which is un-
> attainable along this path or by any single individual; instead
> one pursues attainable relative truths along the path of the
> positive sciences, and the summation of their results by means
> of dialectical thinking.[102]

It is true that Engels credited Hegel with having shown Marx and himself the 'way out of the labyrinth of systems to real positive knowledge of the world'.   Although in Engels's mind his emancipation from the cult of the system might have been associated psychologically with Hegel, actually there is no logical connection between Hegelian speculations and Engels's abandonment of philosophy as a system-constructing activity.   In spite of his admiration for Hegel, Engels did not accept Hegel's announcement that in his philosophy the reconciliation of ideas and reality had been effected, leaving nothing else for others to do.   Incredible as it may appear, there were German philosophers who took Hegel's verdict seriously. 'The deep surge of conviction that philosophy had come to an end coloured the first decades after Hegel's death.' [103]   But Engels was not among these philosophers.   He ignored the claim that in Hegel philosophy had reached its destination and that 'the negation of philosophy' having been accomplished there was no further room or need for philosophical thinking.   His definition of the new function of philosophy combined the Comtean criticism of speculative knowledge with the efforts to restore metaphysics to its previous position over and above positive science.

To discuss this problem more fully it should first be approached from another direction.   Comte thought that only the establishment of sociology as a positive or natural science (*une science naturelle*, as he sometimes used to say) could safeguard the positivist conception of knowledge and protect human intelligence from a relapse into the theologico-metaphysical mode of thought.   Two arguments might be used in support of this view.   First, the intellectual and moral life has always been the main source of theological and metaphysical conceptions, and a positive sociological study of these and other social phenomena should close the gap through which the metaphysical invasion of materialism or spiritualism usually took place.[104]   Second, with the establishment of sociology, positive philosophy acquires true universality.   In spite of their distinctiveness, the six fundamental sciences constitute only different branches of a single tree.   Between them they can deal with all the facts which ever occur, and apply in their examination one single procedure of investigation.   As Durkheim put it, from the moment when it is recognized that above the individual there is society, a system of active forces, a new manner of explaining men, neither materialistic nor supernaturalistic, becomes possible.[105]

These views are to be found again in Engels.   With the establishment of the materialistic conception of history, 'idealism was driven from its last refuge, the philosophy of history'.[106]   Marx's discovery of a method applicable to every realm of human life, explaining human knowledge and the whole range of man's activity, provided the key-stone of modern materialism, that is, naturalism, and made it possible to study all human phenomena, from the lowest to the highest, as natural events.

> Modern materialism . . . no longer needs any philosophy standing above the other sciences. As soon as each special science is bound to make clear its position in the great totality of things and of our knowledge of things, a special science dealing with this totality is superfluous. That which still survives, independently, of all earlier philosophy is the science of thought and its law — formal logic and dialectics. Everything else is subsumed in the positive science of nature and history.[107]

It was Engels's view that the establishment of Marxian sociology, which enables us to study the intellectual, moral and, generally, the spiritual life of man by the scientific method, provides modern materialism with the universality which it hitherto lacked. Since all the facts could be investigated by the same method, philosophy could no longer claim a separate realm of reality as its own exclusive preserve. But whereas in agreement with Comte Engels maintained that speculative philosophy as a pre-scientific mode of investigation of any subject-matter became superfluous with the establishment of the system of positive science, he also deviated from the Comtean conception, for he did not seem to hold this view about philosophy which was not speculative in the above sense.

It has been said of Comte that he did not leave any room in his system of positive science for philosophy, not even for a methodology or a logic of science. One of Comte's fundamental ideas, repeatedly emphasized in the *Cours,* is that methods cannot be studied apart from the investigation in which they are applied or that the problems of positive science cannot be neatly divided into substantive and methodological ones. The study of scientific method apart from its application is conceivable but neither necessary nor advisable. The logic of a science can best be seen in operation, through the science itself of which it is the logic. On the other hand, the study of the system of positive science as a whole belongs to social statics and social dynamics; science is a component part of civilization and the connection between various elements of civilization are the subject-matter of sociology.[108] The expansion of *l'esprit positif* and the establishment of sociology, which completes the system of positive science, culminate in philosophy making itself redundant.

That the advancement of knowledge leads to the gradual extinction of philosophy is a view which both Marx and Engels seem to have adopted, though the latter with some important qualifications; their endorsement of this view is sometimes considered as conclusive evidence of the influence which French positivism exercised upon them.[109] In *The German Ideology*, Marx described the progressive elimination of philosophy as an inevitable development in the advance of knowledge.

> Where speculation ends, in real life, there real, positive science, as the representation of the practical activity and the practical development of men, begins. Empty and irrelevant talk about consciousness ceases and real knowledge has to take its place. When reality is depicted, philosophy as an independent branch of activity loses its medium of existence. At the most its place can only be taken by a summary of the general results which are derived by abstraction from the historical development of men. Considered in themselves and detached from real history, these abstractions have no value whatsoever.[110]

Some of Engels's statements on this matter point in the same direction. They seem to imply that with the establishment of the materialist conception of history, modern materialism no longer requires philosophy conceived as the universal science and standing above the other sciences, which were its more or less distinctly separate parts.[111]

Marxist-Leninists in the Soviet Union and elsewhere have challenged the interpretation attributing to Engels the positivist view about the end of philosophy.[112] Although Engels did state that modern materialism no longer needed 'any philosophy standing above the other sciences', he added a proviso which conferred upon his statement a different meaning.

> It [sc. modern materialism] is no longer a philosophy at all, but simply a world outlook which has to establish its validity and be applied not in a science of sciences standing apart, but in the positive sciences. Philosophy is therefore 'sublated' here, that is, 'both overcome and preserved', overcome as regards its form, and preserved as regards its real content.[113]

Marxist–Leninists maintain that when Engels spoke of the end of 'all philosophy', he meant only 'all philosophy in the hitherto accepted sense of the word'. He supported positive knowledge against futile speculations but he also added that the positive sciences are not self-sufficient; they remain for ever provisional, and require 'the summation of their results by means of dialectical thinking'.[114] While acknowledging the increasing erosion of philosophy by the steady advance of positive knowledge, Engels left no doubt whatsoever that philosophy retained and would continue to hold its controlling position as a general theory of science which 'brings the individual spheres of knowledge into the correct connection with one another'. It is actually impossible to renounce philosophy altogether without falling under the domination of the worst philosophy possible.[115] When the 'positive science of nature and history' is established, much of 'all earlier philosophy' becomes extinct, but philosophy does not disappear altogether in positive science, for there remains 'the science of thought and its laws — formal logic and dialectics'.[116] There is no perfect analogy between the Comtean conception of philosophy and Engels's.

The Marxist–Leninist objection to attributing Comte's conception of philosophy to Engels seems to be justified. Engels did qualify the view of philosophy becoming unnecessary or superfluous. He saw not only a distinct function but also a distinct subject-matter for philosophy which, in contradistinction to the pre-Hegelian philosophy and in deference to Hegel, he called 'dialectics'. According to Engels's familiar definition, dialectics is 'the science of the general laws of motion and development of nature, human society and thought',[117] and thus attains a truly universal knowledge, surpassing in the generality and certainty of its conclusions anything that a positive science might provide. Like Hegel's reason at the speculative stage, philosophy in Engels's sense, that is, dialectics, stands over and above the particular sciences.

Engels's view differs, however, from Hegel's in that he saw a greater complexity in the relation of philosophy to the particular sciences. Engels recognized that philosophy was dependent upon the positive sciences because they determined the existing state of knowledge and thereby the subject-matter of philosophy. On the other hand, however, the task of philosophy was to grasp and generalize the knowledge provided by the particular sciences, and thus philosophy was in a position to dominate them and to legislate as to how they should proceed in their investigations. In later years Engels's semi-positivistic and semi-metaphysical conception of philosophy led to some baneful consequences, for Marxist–Leninists took advantage of it to justify the interference of politicians, ideologists and political philosophers into the methodological and substantive problems of science.[118]

Engels was not the first in assigning these incompatible functions to philosophy; the same idea can be found in Saint-Simon and in some revisions of the original positivist doctrine, both during Comte's lifetime and after his death. According to Saint-Simon, philosophy was the universal science (*science universelle*) of which the particular sciences were the elements. Therefore, as soon as the latter have become positive, the former would become wholly positive too.[119] This meant, however, that the only task of philosophy was to systematize the whole of knowledge and Saint-Simon was not prepared to accept this consequence. For in its application to social physiology philosophy became a study of man and society and acquired a second function, irreducible to the systematization of positive knowledge. This study involved the problems of politics, morality, and religion, dealt with values, value judgments, and norms and neither was nor could any longer be made positive, in the original meaning of the word. Hence the duality in Saint-Simon's attitude to philosophy, behind which was concealed the inescapable fact that if philosophy were reduced to a sort of encyclopaedia of positive knowledge, it could not supply a code of ethics. Saint-Simon wanted philosophy to perform two incompatible functions and hence reached the paradoxical position that 'positive philosophy remained speculative even though it had purportedly been disarmed of the poisonous fangs of speculation'.[120]

The same duality reappeared in some interpretations of Comtean positivism. On the one hand, there was John Stuart Mill who in his essay *Auguste Comte and Positivism* was inclined to define positivism as a mode of thought or a philosophy of science. Since Mill understood by philosophy 'the scientific knowledge of man, as an intellectual, moral and social being', this definition of philosophy disposed him to regard the logic of science, the investigation of the process by which knowledge is acquired and validated, as the core of positive philosophy.[121] Mill's view of positivism might be described as its minimalistic interpretation, for it emphasized the concern of positive philosophy with epistemological and methodological questions in the natural and social sciences. In the minimalistic interpretation there is no room for philosophy as a branch of knowledge with a subject-matter of its own, distinct from and independent of positive science.

On the other hand, Émile Littré in France, later seconded by Lucien Lévy-Bruhl, defined positivism as 'a view of the world that results from the systematized whole of positive knowledge'.[122] In this capacity positivism is a true *Weltanschauung*, capable of providing a faith, an ideal, a view of history, and a commitment in the destiny of humanity. In the maximalistic interpretation of positivism, the emphasis upon its conception of knowledge is strangely combined with the traditional view of philosophy as a comprehensive synthesis whose main function is to give us bearings and a sense of purpose in life.

The desertion of the strict positivist standpoint and the tendency to combine positivism with theories that are alien to it can be traced to Comte himself, at least during his 'second career'. The presence of non-positivist elements in Comte has usually been explained by his divided intellectual allegiance, by the tension and conflict which he did not manage to resolve between the requirements of science and of social reconstruction. But Comte was by no means alone in revising and complementing positivism by adding ethics, metaphysics, or religion to science.

In the mid-nineteenth century a number of French thinkers, who regarded themselves as supporters of positivism — with Ernest Renan and Hippolyte Taine at their head — were unwilling to accept strictly the implications and the specific conclusions of the positivist philosophy of science. Their reluctance to recognize the inherent limitations of human experience led to the misinterpretation of positivist philosophy to the point of distorting it into a quite different doctrine. The distortion arose from the substitution of scientism for positivist philosophy and from the merging of this redefined positivism with the Hegelian speculative philosophy.[123] On the supposition that scientism was the essence of positivism, it became possible to regard oneself as a positivist without recognizing its epistemological assumptions. In order to be a positivist it was sufficient to extol the concept and value of scientific knowledge, which was to gain in significance and comprehensiveness by its affiliation with speculative philosophy. Philosophy was defined as a universal science entirely different from the old metaphysics

E.D.M.—L

because it derived its conclusions by inference from scientific facts. While the fusion of the two inflexibly antagonistic philosophical attitudes or schools of thought produced in due time an anti-positivist reaction, it was first used or misused to establish the 'scientific' social, political, and ethical system of Comte, the 'scientific' religion of Renan, and the 'scientific' method for metaphysics of Taine.[124]

Engels was clearly affected by the intellectual tendency of the time. His conception of philosophy and its relation to science is based on the strange alliance of positivism with Hegelianism, that is, with the most extreme form of anti-positivism. Engels claimed that by using the methodology of positivism he could establish metaphysical conclusions comparable in scope and content with those of Hegel's speculative philosophy. But to maintain that metaphysical knowledge could be reached by the positivist method is not only to mix Comte and Hegel but also to renounce both of them at the same time.

For Comte empirical knowledge constituted the whole of science; for Hegel empirical knowledge served only as a medium in which the mind developed its self-consciousness and, therefore, it lay entirely outside of what he regarded as science, that is, speculative philosophy. For Hegel all knowledge based on factual evidence was uncertain and problematic; the knowledge of facts was reliable only as far as it was derived from the first principles which alone could be known with an absolute intuitive certainty. For Comte the knowledge of facts was primary and the knowledge of principles was secondary; whereas the knowledge of facts was as certain as anything could be, the reliability of every principle depended on the role which it played in ordering the variety of facts and in furthering our control over them.

Positivism is incompatible with idealism as well as with materialism, for they are both metaphysical doctrines in the positivist meaning of this expression. They go beyond the limits of observation and empirical verification and maintain that all phenomena derive from material or spiritual substance respectively. From the viewpoint of positivist epistemology, it is a great fallacy to claim universally valid knowledge which transcends the apparent limitations of human experience and is thus immune to doubt. On its part, Hegelian philosophy represents a complete refutation of positivism in its historically known form. It rejects the authority of experience and the certainty of facts as the negation of philosophical truth, because facts are not independent of, but 'posited' by, the subject. It sets the liberating knowledge of essences over against the submissive acceptance of observable facts and verifiable laws, and proclaims the predominance of the universal over the particular. To have any rationality, everything immediately 'given' has first to be justified before reason, which alone is capable of making final and irrevocable pronouncements.

'Hegelian positivism' is an apt denotation for Engels's view on the relation of philosophy to scientific knowledge.[125] He wished to construct, on the firm basis of the system of positive science, the superstructure of a speculative philosophy possessing legislative powers with respect to the realm of facts. Engels's invective against 'gross' or 'shallow' or 'one-sided empiricism', which can be found in many pages of *Dialectics of Nature*, seems to indicate that in his opinion the system of positive science stood in need of supervision by speculative philosophy. This supervision was to be established not only by the subordination of science to philosophy, but also by the reduction of the fundamental laws of particular sciences to a set of supreme universal laws, which would show that the former can be inferred from the latter. Such a reduction, which in Engels's view is the essence of the Hegelian conception of philosophy, is incompatible with positivism and cannot be accomplished without relapsing, to put it in the Comtean language, into the theological-metaphysical mode of thought. The irreducibility of the laws of particular sciences to the laws of the universe as a whole is a consequence of the positivist epistemology and philosophy of science. The assumptions derived from Hegel and Comte are irreconcilable; the discordant thoughts and divergent attitudes which they produce cannot be removed or adjusted without allowing one of the antagonists to overpower the other. They cannot be joined together in the expectation that they would achieve jointly what neither of them could accomplish separately.

Engels parted ways with Comte and chose a course which, according to Comte in his sober mood, is *une absurde utopie* and misuse of the deductive method for purposes for which it was not designed, a course based on a false evaluation of our mental powers as well as of the difficulties involved. Comte pointed out that our knowledge of the laws of the universe is fragmentary, that the number of distinct and independent, i.e. irreducible, laws which would have to be considered, is much larger than is usually imagined,[126] and that the way in which they work together in order to produce a given result is too intricate to be correctly traced by human reason. *Mathesis universalis* is beyond the reach of the human mind, and to try to construct a deductive system comprising the whole of knowledge is to chase a 'chimerical unity'. No progress of lasting value can be achieved by searching for the unity of knowledge in Engels's sense, that is, for a system in which all particular laws are deducible from a set of primordial laws dominating the universe as a whole.[127]

PART TWO

THE FOUNDATIONS
AND THE REVISIONS OF
DIALECTICAL MATERIALISM

V

The Foundations of Engels's
Dialectical Materialism

WHETHER Marx and Engels jointly or Engels alone originated dialectical materialism, there can be no doubt that only Engels should be credited with its codification. This was recognized implicitly by Lenin in *Materialism and Empirio-Criticism*, for he based his account on what he considered to be the Marxian philosophy on the works of Engels, above all, on *Anti-Dühring* and *Ludwig Feuerbach*.

Engels's system of dialectical materialism contains a definition of matter and materialism, a formulation of the dialectical laws, and a theory of the relativity of knowledge. These three main parts of Engels's dialectical materialism will be examined in the indicated order.

I. GENETIC AND ABSOLUTE MATERIALISM

Engels approached the problem of defining 'materialism' (which may have different senses, and has actually been understood in many different ways) from two complementary, rather than two different, viewpoints. In *Ludwig Feuerbach*, he argued that materialism rests upon a definite conception of the relation between nature or matter and spirit or mind. Materialists of various schools regard matter as primary and mind as secondary, and idealists assert the primacy of spirit to nature. According to the idealists, it is the development of mind that explains the development of nature, whereas the materialists derive mind from matter and explain the development of mind by natural causes. To differentiate materialism from idealism, Engels adopted as his vantage point the view put forward by Feuerbach against Hegel, 'Thinking arises out of being, but being does not arise out of thinking.' [1]

151

According to Engels, materialism and idealism, thus understood, presuppose different theological conceptions and entail different epistemological consequences. Thus to affirm the primacy of spirit to nature is to assert the creation of the world. On the other hand, to regard matter as primary is to conceive it as eternal. Moreover, the question of the relation of spirit to nature includes that of the relation of thinking to being or, as Engels put it, of 'our thoughts about the world' to 'this world itself'. Both idealism and materialism maintain that we are able to 'produce a correct reflection of reality'. But while idealism regards 'real things as images of this or that stage of the absolute concept', materialism comprehends 'concepts as images of real things'.[2] Ontological idealism presupposes theism and entails epistemological idealism, whereas materialism presupposes atheism and entails realism.[3]

'Materialism' as defined in *Ludwig Feuerbach* can be called 'genetic materialism', for it asserts that mind originates from and is the highest product of matter. The expression ' product of matter' is not intended to suggest that mind is nothing but matter. The concept of mind designates the phenomena of sense perception, thought, and consciousness, and these are regarded as emergent qualities of matter organized in a particular way.

Lenin explained that the materialist elimination of the 'dualism of spirit and body' consists in the assertion that spirit is a function of the brain and, through the brain, of the external world, in and along with which it develops, and that it does not exist independently of the body.[4] Lenin's explanations not only denied the autonomy of the mental, and of mind generally, but also implied that for Engels matter was involved as a primary factor in the constitution of the universe, but mind was not. Therefore, from Lenin's viewpoint, genetic materialism should be regarded as a metaphysical theory. For genetic materialism, as he understood it, does not claim merely that mental phenomena occur only if certain material conditions are found to exist, but maintains that these material conditions are ultimately the entire cause of mental phenomena and that mind is identical with the functioning of the organism, viz. an epiphenomenon. Without this bold step beyond what could be stated from the standpoint of science, a genetic materialist would have no grounds to affirm that mind is not a primary factor in the universe. It should perhaps be mentioned that to abolish the contrast of mind and nature, mental and physical, by a metaphysical pronouncement is not the same as to invalidate this distinction by means of empirical evidence which alone would carry conviction. This is the reason why scientists prefer to reserve judgment until the mind–body problem can be approached empirically instead of being decided metaphysically.[5]

Genetic materialism should be distinguished from absolute materialism, which asserts that only matter exists or is real, that matter is the ultimate constituent of the universe, and that there is nothing else in the world : to be is to be material. It is clear that absolute materialism involves genetic materialism as its special thesis, but one can support genetic materialism without endorsing absolute materialism. Absolute materialism is the conception expounded by Engels in *Anti-Dühring*. 'The real unity of the world consists in its materiality', Engels wrote, 'and this is proved not by a few juggled phrases, but by a long and wearisome development of philosophy and natural science.' [6] Engels was confident that the advance of natural science would increasingly demonstrate man's 'oneness with nature'. The greater this advance is, the more 'impossible will become the senseless and unnatural idea of a contrast between mind and matter, man and nature, soul and body', and in this way absolute materialism will be finally securely established.[7]

The assertion 'To be is to be material' is a metaphysical statement as much as Descartes's proposition, 'The essence of matter is extension'. Both formulae reach boldly into what is over and beyond all experience, asserting what is the very nature of matter and what is real. Marx believed that we can study the nature of reality but not its ultimate nature.[8] Engels was no longer inclined to make or accept this distinction.

Engels's absolute materialism appears to have arisen from Marx's naturalism, i.e. his belief in the sole reality of nature. Absolute materialism was to answer the question why it should be possible to extend the method, primarily devised for the study of natural bodies, to all phenomena, including those which reveal man's distinctively human traits. Engels's answer transformed Marx's naturalistic methodological monism into a metaphysical monism of absolute materialism, and replaced the Marxian unified frame of reference for the description and explanation of human action and experience by a metaphysical theory concerned with the innermost characteristics of nature.

These transformations, accomplished by Engels, turned out to be pregnant with far-reaching and fateful consequences, for they helped to establish dialectical materialism as a comprehensive theory of the world allegedly based upon, and confirmed by, natural science. Thus, the concern with the evolution of man in society, which had been Marx's chief theoretical interest, has been pushed into the background and the human, moral, and sociological aspect of Marxian philosophy has been subordinated to an abstruse metaphysics appearing in public under the guise of positive science.

While Engels's role in the further fortunes of the Marxian philosophy cannot be denied, he should not be blamed entirely for what happened many years after his death. Engels did go beyond Marx, who was a naturalist thinker and could never be described as a materialist in Engels's sense. But underlying Marx's naturalism was the belief that only material objects are real. Where Engels stated explicitly what was implicit in Marx, it was not a question of his misunderstanding the latter.[9] He erred when he failed to recognize the invalidity of all metaphysics, both materialistic and idealistic, as opposed to empiricism, and when with inadequate intellectual resources, as he himself admitted, he indulged in system-building activities.[10]

Engels did not postulate the existence of a corporeal substance, a primitive uniform matter, out of which the world of natural things is made. In this respect he differed from Leucippus and Democritus, or from Descartes or Hobbes in modern times. According to Aristotle, Leucippus and Democritus believed that atoms were like many distinct pieces of gold; they were distinguished from one another by their shape but 'their nature was one'. Descartes expressed himself with even greater clarity, 'there is but one and the same matter in the whole universe'.[11] Although Engels supported a monistic solution of the metaphysical problem and saw the unity of the world in its materiality, he did not thereby declare the existence of a unique material substance. To say that the universe is a unity is to assume that it has a nature as a whole. While materialist thinkers of the past identified the nature of the universe as a whole with the material substance underlying all phenomena, Engels seems to have departed from this tradition. To consider matter as the sole reality does not necessarily mean that the irreducible diversity of physical objects should be denied. Qualitative differentiation of physical objects is not incompatible with their having the property of corporeality in common.[12]

Engels argued that the resolution of the diversity of physical things and processes into differentiated forms of matter in motion, transformed into one another in accordance with definite laws, did not presuppose the homogeneity of matter and, consequently, did not imply that matter should be conceived as the substratum of all observable changes in the world. He suggested that this diversity 'was abolished from science by the proof of their interconnections and transitions', and not by their reduction to a common material substance. He also suggested that the natural unity of the world, established by the evidence of 'the interconnections and transitions' of one form of matter into another, opens the prospect of bridging the gulf between organic and inorganic nature, a gulf that otherwise remains impassable.[13]

There are good reasons for abandoning the Aristotelian, Thomist, and Cartesian way of thinking and its assumption that change presupposes an unchangeable substance. If in the search for this single kind of stuff, the Aristotelian *materia prima* is not reached, the task of constructing the material substance by a process of abstraction appears to remain incomplete. But to press the search to its logical conclusion is to cross the point of no return, for the reductive step cannot be reversed. Matter which is an absolutely constitutive ontological factor ceases to function as a principle of individuation. We are unable to deduce the world of nature with its richness of directly observable qualities from an indeterminate primordial matter and mechanical motion. The failure to discover the passage from the original uniform matter to the world of nature as known in experience, or to fill the wide gap separating observable qualities from shape and motion, has been regarded as a serious defect of mechanistic theories or even as conclusive evidence that cosmology cannot be built upon a materialistic foundation.[14] The weakness of the 'theory of the absolute qualitative identity of matter' was clearly seen not only by the adversaries of materialism, but by Engels as well.

Moreover, the assumption that 'all matter consists of identical smallest particles' is the basis of the Cartesian–Newtonian mechanistic conception of nature, in which everything is in a state of continuous change but nothing new emerges, for all change is really cyclical and produces the same results over and over again. In general, the category of substance appears to lead to the interpretation of nature in terms of the stability, constancy, and permanence of things. The physiologist or psychologist, wrote Mach about the same time (1885), can make nothing of the notion of a 'rigid matter', of which the only changes are changes of place.[15] Engels rejected the concept of primordial matter because it undermined the reality and reduced the significance of growth, evolutionary development, and the emergence of novelty. Ultimate reality is, by definition, fixed and immutable. For, if it were not, it could not be ultimate. Thus change is spurious, for it does not affect the 'identical smallest particles' or the material substance, and there is no coming into being and passing away in the Aristotelian sense, for there is no substantial change. The category of material substance reflects, as Engels put it, 'the anti-dialectical manner of philosophizing' and 'the unhistorical view of nature'. It suggests a static universe in which change is subordinated to substance and novelty to constancy.[16]

Thus, Engels was led to a conception of matter, first suggested by Helvétius and Holbach, in which matter is not regarded as a material substance, *un être unique*, but as *un genre d'être*,[17] 'the *summum genus* of the classification of bodies on the basis of their physical and chemical properties'.[18] Matter, wrote Helvétius, is not a substance but a concept, and in this sense, a creation of man. 'Matter is not a being, for in nature there are only individuals to which the same *body* has been given. . . . The word "matter" can only be understood to connote the collection of properties common to all these bodies.' [19] Engels followed in the footsteps of Helvétius and Holbach and conceived matter as a theoretical construct whose relation to reality had to be explained and established, as we would say today, by means of semantical definitions or operational rules of meaning. These rules or definitions would have to state the necessary and, preferably, the sufficient conditions, such as extension, impenetrability, solidity, and so forth, which an object would have to satisfy to be a material object, a body in Helvétius's sense of the term. Therefore, for Engels, the term 'matter' signified a metatheoretical concept rather than a concrete entity and was part of the metalanguage of science rather than of its object language.

> Matter as such is a pure creation of thought and an abstraction. We leave out of account the qualitative differences of things in lumping them together as corporeally existing things under the concept of matter. Hence matter as such, as distinct

from definite existing pieces of matter, is not anything sensuously existing. When natural science directs its efforts to seeking out uniform matter as such, to reducing qualitative differences to merely quantitative differences in combining identical smallest particles, it is doing the same thing as demanding to see fruit as such instead of cherries, pears, apples, or mammals as such instead of cats, dogs, sheep, etc., gas as such, metal, stone, chemical compound as such, motion as such.[20]

Engels's argument against 'matter as such' follows in the footsteps of Berkeley's criticism of material substance and, oddly enough, the philosophical tradition of phenomenalism which he originated. Berkeley argued that if no sensible qualities can be attributed to matter, matter becomes 'something in general' and has 'no more claim to existence than a golden mountain or a centaur'. Locke's 'unknowable somewhat' that underlies all known corporeal qualities is a mere play with words employed 'to no manner of purpose, without any design or signification whatsoever'.[21] In a similar manner Engels jokingly argued that first we make sensuous things into abstractions and then we want to know them through the senses, to see time and smell space. 'Matter as such and motion as such have not yet been seen or otherwise experienced by anyone . . . because they are creations of thought and not sensuous objects.' [22] Engels was unaware of Bishop Berkeley's view on the subject; though he explicitly referred to Hegel who had rejected the concept of indeterminate universal matter as an instance of 'bad metaphysics',[23] that is, of what Engels called the 'metaphysical mode of thought'.

Engels believed that the proposition 'Only matter exists' is meaningful and true if and only if the term 'matter' is taken in its distributive sense, if it refers to matter under some particular form, and denotes the class of material or physical objects, the 'totality of bodies', as Engels explained, of 'all material existences extending from stars to atoms'.[24]

> Matter is nothing but the totality of material things from which this concept is abstracted, and motion as such nothing but the totality of all sensuously perceptible forms of motion; words like 'matter' and 'motion' are nothing but abbreviations in which we comprehend many different sensuously perceptible things according to their common properties.[25]

Engels rejected the Aristotelian framework of substance and property in terms of which the objects of sense experience were to be described. In this respect he showed a striking understanding for the tendencies inherent in modern physical theories. Modern physical theories increasingly depart from the Aristotelian ontological frame of reference, for it is not applicable to the objects investigated by physics.

One of the necessary conditions of an object being material is that it exists independently of being perceived. Absolute materialism implies realism.[26] But the belief in independent physical objects is not equivalent to the belief in the sole reality of matter. To be a material object is to exist in time and space,[27] to be impenetrable and heavy, uncreatable and indestructible.[28] Above all, to be a material object is to be in motion ; a motionless state of matter is an absurdity. 'Never anywhere has there been matter without motion, nor can there be. . . . Matter without motion is just as inconceivable as motion without matter.'[29] The term 'motion' is used by Engels, and also by Marx, in the broad Aristotelian, not in the narrow modern, sense. It does not mean 'change of place' alone but 'all changes and processes occurring in the universe, from mere change of place right up to thinking'.[30]

While in classical physics the concept of motion implies matter — movement entails something that moves and kinetic energy presupposes the mass $(E = \frac{mv^2}{2})$ — matter does not imply motion. A motionless body is neither logically nor physically impossible. Engels could claim that matter and motion were in fact inseparable, but he clearly overreached himself by asserting that it could not be otherwise.[31] An empirical truth is not a truth of logic. Confusing the two is not made respectable by providing an argument against natural theology.

Motion is the mode of existence of matter ; it accounts for its individuation and the infinity of its forms. It is motion that breaks the continuity of matter, differentiates it into individual bodies, determines their properties, and establishes their irreducible qualitative diversity.[32] The motion of matter includes the 'possibility under favourable conditions of being transformed into heat, electricity, chemical action, life', to the list of which, in another context, Engels added consciousness. The capacity of producing these various forms out of itself is an inherent characteristic of moving matter. Consequently, in the eternal cosmic cycle of one universe developing from another — a cosmogonic doctrine highly favoured in the nineteenth century and supported by Engels — matter always reproduces the conditions favouring the appearance of organic life and of man, 'even if only after millions and millions of years, and more or less by chance, but with the necessity that is also inherent in chance'.[33] Engels combined the hypothesis of emergent evolution, about which more will be said later, with a cosmogonic doctrine of eternal return, to show that materialism offers an alternative to creationism.

Engels did not adhere consistently to the distributive conception of matter. But the fact that he was a qualified reist prevented him from falling into the error of which Lenin fell victim, namely, a purely epistemological definition of matter.

Although in *Materialism and Empirio-Criticism* Lenin went out of his way to emphasize that his epistemological and philosophical concept of matter did not deviate from the tradition established by Engels, their respective use of the terms 'matter' and 'materialism' is entirely different. Engels had a metaphysical concept of matter which was distinct from Lenin's epistemological concept and more general. Engels was a realist in the theory of knowledge which, in his opinion, was an obvious position to adopt once Hegel's perversion of the true relation of consciousness to being was exposed. While Plekhanov in his comments on *Ludwig Feuerbach* (1892) felt that the arguments against epistemological realism, produced from the viewpoint of Berkeley, Hume, and Kant, should not simply be dismissed with a shrug of the shoulders, Engels saw no need of refuting the 'agnostics' on the question of the objective reality of the external world. In his view, the untenability of the 'agnostic position' in the theory of knowledge did not admit even the shadow of doubt. Although materialism involves realism, its conception of the relation of mind to matter (genetic materialism) and its belief in the sole reality of matter (absolute materialism) is what makes it a distinctive theory of the world. It is the belief in the materiality of the objects of the external world, and not in their independent existence, which distinguishes materialism as a metaphysical doctrine.

Genetic and absolute materialism constitute what Engels called 'materialism as a general world outlook' as distinguished from other outlooks and from its own special form, that is, from a materialist doctrine formulated at a definite historical stage and dependent in its content on a given state of knowledge.[34]   Engels pointed out that with each 'epoch-making discovery' this special form of the materialist world outlook was bound to be changed, and Lenin emphasized that a revision of this kind did not constitute revisionism, i.e. the abandonment of Engels's materialism, but was 'demanded by Marxism'.[35]

The proposition attributing materiality to all real objects is a permanent component part of the materialist theory of the world, but the description of what this materiality consists in, being dependent on the knowledge available at a given time, constitutes a special form of the materialist world outlook.   In the past — and also in our present everyday language — the concept of matter was related by an appropriate semantical definition to something extended, heavy, and impenetrable.   For the twentieth-century physicist, matter consists of electrons, protons, positrons, and so forth.   The operational rules of meaning of the past do not apply universally any longer to matter in the sense of the twentieth century; we would not get very far if we tried to find out whether a sub-atomic particle is material in that sense and carried out the appropriate testing operations.   The operational rules of meaning which govern the use of the term 'matter' change with time.   On the other hand, we cannot liberate 'matter', as it were, from all operational rules and fix its meaning once and for all, if we wish to retain it as an empirically meaningful theoretical term.[36]

2. THE CRITICISM OF REDUCTIVE MATERIALISM AND THE DOCTRINE OF EMERGENCE

Engels's absolute materialism is as anti-reductivist as Comte's positivism.[37]   While the term 'reductivism' cannot be found in Engels, the concept of reductivism can, referred to by such expressions as 'mechanistic' or 'vulgar' materialism.

Engels did not wish to have anything to do either with mechanistic or with vulgar materialism.   The former belonged to long-past times when chemistry was in an infantile stage and biology lay in swaddling clothes; the latter, a 'shallow popularization of materialism', was a survival of the past and was capable of flourishing in Germany in the 1850s because it made up for the lack of science there.[38] These two schools of materialism were clearly attempts to establish a world outlook with data inadequate for this task. They were disowned both by philosophers and men of science.

It was the mechanistic conception of nature which at that time was the stronghold of reductivism. The mechanistic conception tried to establish a comprehensive theory which would unify all domains of natural science — physics, chemistry, and biology in particular — in terms of a set of common basic concepts and principles and, at the same time, provide a secure basis for the further advancement of knowledge, including the progressive integration of other sciences and the elaboration of more specific theories. Furthermore, the mechanistic conception of nature was regarded as final. 'As long as humanity attempts to develop science, mechanism will continue to be developed with it.' Only the explanation of phenomena in terms of motion is 'really eternal'.[39]

At the time under discussion, classical mechanics was considered the fundamental science of nature. It was hoped that mechanics would absorb other domains of physics and that this extension would make possible the reduction of chemistry and biology to mechanics. If the suggested reductions were actually successful, they would have affected our knowledge about the ultimate nature and constitution of things in general. Thus, for instance, the reduction of thermodynamics to statistical mechanics, successfully accomplished by a definitional assumption that temperature is the average kinetic energy of the constituent molecules, seemed to support the view that all change is a change of place. More generally, successful reductions of a less inclusive physical theory to a more inclusive one, ultimately based upon mechanics, appeared to justify the view that all qualitative differences, given in experience, are reducible to quantitative differences. Thus only the latter should be regarded as real.[40] The mechanical conception claimed real knowledge of the material universe obtained by, or rather over and above, the results of its reductions.

Engels's criticism of reductivism was prompted by epistemological and ontological considerations. The ontological reduction of one level of reality to another or the epistemological reduction of science S_1 to science S_2 were, in Engels's opinion, unacceptable. He felt that the material world was not as homogeneous and constant as reductivism requires it to be. Mechanistic theories cannot explain the origin and processes of life. Thought may be correlated with molecular and chemical motions in the brain, but thought is not identical with these motions. There is a gulf between animal and human activity and no common set of laws describes both of them adequately.[41]

It was inadmissible to define chemistry as a kind of mechanics. Mechanics knows only magnitudes ; it deals with masses and velocities. In physics and chemistry many qualitative changes have to be taken into account and it remains to be shown that all of these are quantitative changes in disguise. The laws of mechanics remain valid in chemistry and biology, but they are overshadowed by 'higher laws', characteristic of chemical and biological phenomena. There is both a connection and a distinction between chemistry and mechanics, a continuity and a discontinuity. As Engels explained elsewhere, 'in spite of all gradualness, the transition from one form of motion to another always remains a leap, a decisive change'. The fact that science moved in the direction of reductivism did not prove that this was the correct course or that it would 'exhaust the whole of physics and chemistry'.[42]

It is one thing to assume for certain purposes that heat is molecular motion, and another to assert that heat is nothing but a displacement of molecules. This is not merely a linguistic confusion, but also a logical and factual error. The fact that changes of temperature are correlated with the expansion and contraction of the mercury column does not imply that temperature is nothing but the height of the mercury column. Similarly, the statement that heat is correlated with molecular motion does not entail that heat is nothing but the physical conditions of its occurrence. If two phenomena are functionally related, this does not imply that the relation of identity between them has been established. Engels's views on reductivism were enlightened and advanced for the times.[43]

Engels's decisive arguments against reductivism are of a metaphysical nature. The mechanistic conception of nature is based on two fundamental conceptions : all change is change of place and all qualitative differences result from quantitative ones. If we accept these two assumptions, we inevitably arrive at the doctrine of primordial indeterminate matter ; everything is an aggregate of 'identical smallest particles', and the differences in their configuration and number account for the whole variety of physical objects. This conclusion, however, goes beyond available evidence. Empirically, this doctrine can neither be confirmed nor refuted [44] and, as has been mentioned earlier, lends to the mechanistic conception of nature an air of implausibility. No amount of theorizing can dispose of the fact that there are qualitative differences and qualitative changes in nature which are irreducible to the displacement of the ultimate identical particles. Although he was a materialist, Engels was closer to the Aristotelian view of nature than to the physics of Democritus.[45]

The implausibility of the view that all diversity is in reality quantitative difference becomes still more apparent owing to the clash of the mechanistic conception of nature with the idea of evolution. It is possible to describe a natural object, be it animate or inanimate, as if it were the product of purely mechanical causes. But it is not possible to describe it simultaneously as a machine and as a developing entity.[46] A machine cannot become what it is not, that is, it cannot develop; growth and advance is a process of progressive change which results in the emergence of new things or qualities. The mechanistic conception of nature was based on eighteenth-century natural science which, to use Engels's expression, 'accepted things as finished objects'. On the other hand, in the nineteenth century, natural science is essentially 'a science of the processes of the origin and development of these things and of the interconnection which binds all these natural processes into one great whole'. Biology concerned with the growth of the individual organism, evolutionary cosmogony and geology, the biological doctrine of evolution — all these were the offspring of the nineteenth century. The establishment of evolution as a pervading trait of physical and social reality clearly meant that the mechanistic conception had to be abandoned and replaced by what Engels called the 'dialectical conception of nature'.[47]

Its abandonment was necessary for yet another reason. It was Newton who clearly saw that a mechanical world would require a transcendent God as its designer, creator, and ruler. God prevents the heaven of fixed stars from collapsing into the middle of space and the mechanism of the world from running out of gear. The idea of nature as a machine is incompatible with materialistic monism, for it cannot be applied consistently without incurring absurd consequences. A machine presupposes the constructor who conceived and built it; as Gilson put it, 'there is no known example of a self-made machine spontaneously arising in virtue of the mechanical laws of matter'.[48] German materialists of the nineteenth century believed that they could remedy this defect of mechanistic materialism by producing new proofs against the existence of a creator of the world.[49]   Their efforts were irrelevant with respect to this basic flaw of mechanistic materialism.

Marx in *A Contribution to the Critique of Hegel's Philosophy of Right* and Engels in *Ludwig Feuerbach* both recognized that Feuerbach had made a step forward by explaining how men come to believe in God's existence.   But Feuerbach's anthropology could not and did not dispose of natural theology.   Laplace made a considerable contribution to the problem at issue when he showed in his *Traité de mécanique céleste* that the 'entire natural world is governed by law, and absolutely excludes the intervention of action from without'.[50] Laplace established what Newton had not succeeded in doing ; he demonstrated that the movements of the planets in our solar system were deducible from the law of gravitation.   The remaining discrepancies were so small that it was considered certain that they would be removed either by improved observation or by a correction of calculations.

Engels argued that while Laplace reduced the difficulty inherent in the mechanistic conception, he did not dispose of it altogether ; he showed that the universe was in no need of a ruler, but failed to demonstrate that it required no creator.   However, if we accept the new materialism and its dynamic theory of matter, then this difficulty disappears.   If matter were not in motion but could exist at rest ; if motion were not an essential property of matter ; and if matter without motion were not just as inconceivable as motion without matter — we would not be able to get from immobile matter to matter in motion without an impulse from outside, that is, we could not do without God.   But once the corpuscular theory of matter is replaced by the dynamic theory and the assumption of the invariability of natural forces by the idea of the transformation of energy, 'the last vestige of the extramundane creator is obliterated'.[51] The evolutionary conception of the universe achieves what even Laplace failed to accomplish ; it requires neither a ruler nor a creator.[52]

When Engels referred to the evolutionary conception of the universe, he meant not only the dynamic conception of matter, but also the hypothesis of emergent evolution.   This new doctrine, based on the convertibility of force and motion which were attributed to matter as its intrinsic primary characteristic, was to provide an alternative to the mechanistic view of nature.   Matter was no longer conceived as immutable, inherently passive, and entirely lacking in spontaneity. Physicists like John Tyndall discerned in it 'the promise and potency of every form and quality of life' and Engels might have recognized in their announcements a view similar to the idea of the young Marx, who had once attributed to matter not only mechanical motion but also 'impulse, vital life-force, tension' (*Trieb, Lebensgeist, Spannkraft*) as the first and most important of its inherent qualities.[53] Although people continued to regard the mechanistic conception of nature as applicable to the totality of natural phenomena and as unexcelled by its internal consistency and its empirical confirmation, they showed thereby, in Engels's opinion, a lack of acquaintance with any but the 'most mediocre vulgar philosophy'. Inert matter of the mechanistic theory which neither acts upon our senses nor upon other bodies must remain unknown to experience; whatever does not act does not exist. Moreover, apart from the fact that we are able to know matter only by its effects, matter is a principle of differentiation in space. As Marx said, matter includes the 'individualizing forces of being', which produce the distinction between the species, and the forms of life which evolve from matter by self-generated development. This dynamic property of matter is incompatible with its being absolutely inert. A 'motionless state of matter is therefore one of the most empty and nonsensical of ideas'.[54]

The doctrine of emergent evolution should be distinguished from a narrower conception which is concerned with emergent qualities or emergent laws. A quality or a law is emergent if it cannot be deduced from previously known qualities or laws before an instance of the quality or law in question is observed. Being unpredictable before the event, such qualities or laws are also called '*a priori* unpredictable'. For instance, the smell of a new chemical compound is an emergent quality, for it cannot be foretold from the knowledge of the properties which the separate elements of the compound are known to have.

The doctrine of emergent evolution is a hypothesis concerned with novelties which are not mere new combinations of their component elements and which are supposed to occur in the course of natural development, such as the emergence of life or of mind. The strict doctrine of causality is a theory of change without novelty; it may account for novelty in number and in quantity alone but it precludes the possibility of the emergence of qualitative novelty, of things with new properties and of objects new in kind, at least as a natural event.[55] The hypothesis of emergent evolution brings to light the fact that in a genuine evolution the resultant process is continuous with, but not reducible to, the phenomena from which it evolves, and that it contains more than its causes are supposed to produce. Consequently, the theory of change, in terms of which evolutionary processes could be adequately described, should impose some limitations upon causal determinism.

In contradistinction to the strict doctrine of causality, the hypothesis of emergent evolution starts with the assumption that the successive stages of evolutionary development are marked by increasingly complex and irreducible novel structures, in virtue of which natural entities or their systems acquire new intrinsic qualities and new properties in relation to other entities. When such processes take place, new levels of existence may appear and reveal the emergence of some specific and qualitatively new modes of being. The doctrine of emergent evolution assumes, therefore, that the present qualitative diversity of things in the world represents an advance from a less complex stage in the development of the universe and that this development will continue to give rise to novelty of increasing complexity.[56] It also assumes that 'real evolution' is as inconsistent with the uniform continuity as with the discontinuous emergence of novelty *ex nihilo* and, more generally, that both continuity and discontinuity are inherent traits of the world.

The wide use of the expression 'emergent evolution' is some forty years older than *Anti-Dühring*. But those who take Hegel seriously, and Engels was one such, firmly believed that the general scheme of life as emerging from matter and mind from life has become a commonplace since Hegel.[57] There is ample evidence to support the view that Engels's conception of emergent evolution was closely related to Hegel's dialectics conceived as an objective dynamic tendency that 'forces nature out of itself'.[58] Moreover, it should be noted that the concept of emergence in its present connotation is contemporaneous with *Anti-Dühring*, both concept and term appearing in G. H. Lewes's *Problems of Life and Mind*, published in 1875. But irrespective of the question as to where to look for Engels's forerunners and inspiration, the fact cannot be denied that the central idea of emergent evolution is to be found in *Anti-Dühring* and *Dialectics of Nature*.

The central idea of emergent evolution is the logical product of the three following assumptions : material reality has a multilevel structure ; each of these levels is characterized by a set of distinctive properties and irreducible laws ; and each level has emerged from temporally prior levels according to laws which are absolutely unpredictable with respect to those operating at the lower levels.[59] These levels can be considered either epistemologically as the levels of scientific knowledge, such as physics, chemistry, biology, sociology, and so forth, or ontologically as the corresponding objective structural levels of the external world.

In the case of Engels, the emphasis is clearly laid upon the ontological conception, upon the gradual emergence of the atomic, chemical, and biological level, the latter with its numerous emergent transitions to higher and higher forms of life. Engels made constant use of the metaphysical insight that the higher level of existence emerges from and has its roots in the lower ; that the higher level constitutes a new order of being with its own irreducible laws ; and that this process of evolutionary advance is governed by laws of development which reflect basic properties of 'matter in motion as a whole'. According to Engels, the capacity of differentiating the motion of matter and of transforming matter into various forms, those of 'heat and light, electric and magnetic tension, chemical combination and dissociation, life and, finally, consciousness', is 'inherent in moving matter'. The three great discoveries of natural science : the law of the transformation and conservation of energy, the discovery of the cell, and Darwin's theory of descent, which show the whole of nature as a system of interconnected bodies, reveal the fundamental fact that the emergence of novelty is an essential attribute of matter. 'It is in the nature of matter', Engels wrote, 'to advance to the evolution of thinking beings ; hence this always necessarily occurs when the conditions for it (not necessarily identical at all places and times) are present.' [60]

3. THE DOCTRINE OF DIALECTICS

Engels's doctrine of emergent evolution is part of his dialectical conception of nature. 'Dialectics', Engels repeatedly stated, 'is the science of interconnections' ; it deals with systems of physical bodies which exist in relations of mutual interdependence. What these relations of interdependence are is expressed in the dialectical laws. The laws of dialectics do not apply to particular material objects taken in isolation — 'for in nature nothing takes place in isolation' — but to parts of a functional whole whose characteristics are determined by the intrinsic nature of this whole. The dialectical laws are, therefore, holistic laws.

Engels knew three laws of dialectics : the law of the transformation of quantity into quality and vice versa, the law of the interpenetration of opposites, and the law of the negation of the negation. Although their first formulation by Hegel was, in Engels's opinion, an act of historical import, Hegel's achievement was not free from serious faults. First, instead of deducing these laws from natural phenomena and historical developments, Hegel produced them out of his head and then foisted the creation of his own mind upon nature, history, and society. Second, he conceived them as 'mere laws of thought'.[61] On his part, Engels was convinced, first, that the laws of dialectics are universally valid and empirically verifiable laws, and second, that these laws apply as much to the development of thought as to the development of nature and human society. 'The dialectical laws', Engels wrote, 'are real laws of development of nature, and therefore are valid also for theoretical natural science.' [62] Thus, dialectics, which as a 'law of thought' could serve as a tentative way of describing the development of intellectual conceptions about the world, becomes with Engels a general theory of the world established upon the basis of natural science. From the empirical viewpoint this is a fantastic idea, for Hegelian dialectics has no empirical significance. This has already been emphasized in the past. Werner Sombart thought that the dialectics of Hegel becomes absolutely meaningless when it is applied to the empirical world.[63] Jean-Paul Sartre said of Engels that he 'a tué la dialectique en prétendant la découvrir dans la nature'.[64]

The law of the transformation of quantity into quality includes two statements. The first of these says that the quality of a body cannot be altered without addition or substraction of matter or motion in a manner exactly fixed for each individual case, i.e. without quantitative alteration of the body concerned.[65] Since it was not Engels's intention to assert that every 'addition or subtraction of motion' produces qualitative change, the first part of the law formulates only the necessary condition of the emergence of a new quality. Without saying what its sufficient condition is, the second statement claims that at certain nodal points — such as the boiling- and freezing-points of liquids, the critical melting temperature of metals or the temperature of liquefaction of gases — the 'purely quantitative increase or decrease gives rise to a qualitative leap', that is, the mere quantitative change of a body brings about a qualitative change in it. To give the well-known example, water under normal atmospheric pressure changes at 0° C. from the liquid state into the solid state, and at 100° C. from the liquid into the gaseous state. The temperatures of water at 0° and 100° C. are the nodes at which the leaps to new states of aggregation take place and 'quantity is transformed into quality'.[66] Engels's other examples, together with his comments thereon, suggest that no new quality appears unless a new structure emerges with the quantitative change. 'As for example the fact that the cooperation of a number of people, the fusion of many forces into one single force, creates, to use Marx's phrase, a "new power", which is essentially different from the sum of its separate forces.'[67] In this case a new whole, with an intrinsic nature of its own, suddenly emerges upon the quantitative change and gives rise to a novel quality.

The first law of dialectics applies to alteration or qualitative transformation (*alloiosis*) but serves to account, above all, for substantial change (*genesis*) as defined by Aristotle. According to Aristotle, qualitative change involves only properties of a thing whose substance remains unaffected, for instance, the properties of water when it passes from one state into another. On the other hand, *genesis* is creative of a new substance and of new characteristics different from, and irreducible to, the properties to be found in the elements taken separately. Aristotle's *genesis* is the same kind of essential change which today is known as appearance of novelty and his analysis of substantial change deals with the same phenomena which the theory of emergent evolution tries to explain.

It is no accident that Engels placed the law of the transformation of quantity into quality and vice versa before the other two. The law in question clearly differentiates mechanistic and dialectical materialism. It expresses Engels's anti-reductivist attitude and his belief that there is no reason to accept Galileo's methodological decision to consider only primary qualities, the geometric and mechanical magnitudes, as real, and secondary qualities as merely apparent. Engels endorsed whole-heartedly Hegel's view that if quality is compared with quantity, the former is by nature prior to the latter. Qualities are as real as quantities, and among the former there are not only additive and subtractive properties but also emergent characteristics. Qualitative diversity and qualitative transformation belong to the nature of things and are not mere additions to experience dependent upon the constitution of the perceiving mind.

But the law of the transformation of quantity into quality is not merely a statement about the irreducibility of sensible qualities or the inadequacy of the purely quantitative approach to natural phenomena which paved the way for the mathematical and mechanistic conception of nature. The law is clearly meant to state an invariant connection between the increase and decrease in quantity and the change in quality, between the quantitative and qualitative definiteness of natural phenomena. Engels himself considered the law as firmly moored in direct observation and confirmed by 'hundred of facts' provided by the natural and social sciences.[68] It is in this capacity, as a 'general law of nature, society, and thought', that its claim to universal validity should be investigated.[69]

The role assigned by Engels to the law of the transformation of quantity into quality admits yet another interpretation. His instances of the law taken from physics, chemistry, economics, and Napoleon's military tactics, seem to suggest that what he had in mind was not merely a lawlike correlational statement but, above all, a doctrine of evolutionary advance.[70] Evolutionary advance is marked by the emergence of primary novelties and by the production of qualitatively different bodies, for instance, the first occasion on which a certain combination of oxygen and hydrogen took place on the surface of the Earth to form a new substance, water.[71] What Engels says about the transformation of quantity into quality at certain definite nodal points, namely, that the transformation combines a purely quantitative increase or decrease with a qualitative leap, suggests that he may have wished to formulate a law of evolutionary cosmology.[72]

Thus interpreted, the law of the transformation of quantity into quality would be a statement concerned with the necessary conditions of the emergence of novelty rather than with the irreducibility of qualities to quantities, or with the connection between the two. The hypothesis of emergent advance does not deal with sensible qualities, such as colours or heat, but with the distinctively different behaviour of various natural objects, above all, those which are alive and those which are not and, within the organic matrix, with the qualities of consciousness and reflective thought.

The law of the interpenetration of opposites and the law of the negation of the negation, neither of which was ever formulated by Engels in a general way, can be discussed together. The first law provides the presupposition on which the second is based, namely, it states that the world is full of contradictions 'in so to speak corporeal form'. The instances of contradictions present in things and phenomena of nature, which Engels gave, clearly indicate that he wished to make the statement: all changing objects and all objects in motion are contradictory. An object O is contradictory if and only if it has and has not an attribute B in the same respect and at the same time. But if there are contradictory objects, the principle of non-contradiction has to be abandoned or restricted. A conjunction of contradictory statements is no longer necessarily a falsehood.[73]

The law of the negation of the negation is the Hegelian triad (thesis, antithesis, and synthesis) in which thesis and antithesis are merged; for the first 'negation' stands for 'negation of the thesis', that is, for 'antithesis', and 'negation of the negation' for 'synthesis'. Since it is based upon the assumption that contradictions are objectively present in nature, Plekhanov was not entirely wrong when he said that the triad 'only follows from one of Hegel's principles: it does not in the least serve him as a main principle itself'.[74] Plekhanov had some doubts about the correspondence of the triadic course of development to reality, but Engels had none. He claimed that contradictions are the cause of all change and motion and that development which occurs by agency of the dialectical triad is, therefore, 'development through contradiction' and constitutes a 'spiral form' of evolutionary advance.

The law of the triad is universal. As Engels put it, it is 'an extremely general — and for this reason extremely far-reaching and important — law of the development of nature, history and thought'. The development through contradiction or the negation of the negation 'asserts itself everywhere in nature' and determines all change, motion, growth, and evolutionary advance.[75]

There is no doubt whatsoever that to admit, as Engels did, 'the objective presence in things and processes themselves of a contradiction which is moreover an actual force',[76] is to adopt a Hegelian doctrine. For Hegel, the power that impels change is the 'negativity' of things. Any self-movement or impulse, Hegel asserted, is nothing else than the fact that something is itself and is also deficiency or the negative of itself, in one and the same respect. Abstract self-identity has no life; but the fact that Positive in itself is negativity causes it to pass outside itself and to change. Something, therefore, has life only in so far as it contains Contradiction.[77]

Since everything that surrounds us is, according to Hegel, an 'instance of the dialectical process', of the universal and irresistible power before which nothing stays and by which everything becomes changeable and transient, 'there is absolutely nothing whatever in which we cannot and must not point to contradictions or opposite attributes'.[78]

> Contradiction is the very moving principle of the world; and it is ridiculous to say that contradiction is unthinkable. The only thing correct in that statement is that contradiction is not the end of the matter, but cancels itself.[79]

What Hegel had in mind was not only the 'motion of thought', but also actual change and movement in space. As he emphasized,

> Something moves, not because it is here at one point of time and there at another, but because at one and the same point of time it is here and not here, and in this here both is and is not. But we must grant the old dialecticians the contradictions which they proved in motion. What follows is not that there is no motion, but rather that motion is existent Contradiction itself.[80]

These views of Hegel were adopted by Engels almost verbally. So long as we consider things as being at rest and lifeless we do not run up against any contradictions in them.

> But the position is quite different as soon as we consider things in their motion, their change, their life, their reciprocal influence on one another. Then we immediately become involved in contradictions. Motion itself is a contradiction: even simple mechanical change of position can only come about through a body being at one and the same moment of time both in one place and in another place, being in one and the same place and also not in it. And the continuous organization and simultaneous solution of this contradiction is precisely what motion is.[81]

Scientific thinking which is abreast of the advancement of knowledge does not let 'the contradiction . . . block its path'. Contradictions are inherent in simple change of place, in the higher forms of motion, and especially in organic life; all development results from 'progressing contradictions'.

> Life is also a contradiction which is present in things and processes themselves, and which constantly originates and resolves itself; and as soon as the contradiction ceases, life, too, comes to an end, and death steps in.[82]

In his *Dialectics of Nature*, Engels stated generally that 'so-called objective dialectics prevails throughout nature'. He defined objective dialectics as the motion through opposites which clash and pass into one another or into higher forms. Engels objected strongly, however, to an interpretation which would reduce objective dialectics to the 'platitude' of forces moving in opposite directions, of antagonistic or conflicting tendencies and of opposing interests.[83] Mere 'antagonism of forces' is no contradiction. If two opposite pulls act upon a body, as often happens, there would be 'opposition', but no contradiction, between the two propositions which express this fact and which are both true. Engels does not quarrel with ordinary logic in such cases. But conflicts of tendencies and similar complex phenomena should be contrasted with objective contradictions, an instance of which would be provided by the two propositions asserting about the same body *B* with respect to the same frame of reference and at the same time that '*B* is moving to the South' and '*B* is moving to the North'. According to ordinary logic, these two propositions cannot be true together, but according to Engels they are both true. He insisted on the fact that things change or move because of such contradictions, of having contradictory attributes in the same respect and at the same time. Contradiction is only nonsense to a metaphysician who adheres to antiquated logic and science with their rigid categories and hard-and-fast lines of division in thought and nature.[84]

To penetrate into what Hegel called the 'inner unity of all existence', and Engels the 'dialectics in nature', the principles of identity and of the excluded middle have to be replaced by the principle of contradiction.

> It has been a fundamental prejudice of hitherto existing logic and of ordinary imagination that Contradiction is a determination having less essence and immanence than Identity; but

indeed, if there were any question of rank, and the two determinations had to be fixed as separate, Contradiction would have
to be taken as the profounder and more fully essential.   For as
opposed to it Identity is only the determination of the simple
immediate, or of dead Being, while Contradiction is the root
of all movement and life, and it is only in so far as it contains
a Contradiction that anything moves and has impulse and
activity.[85]

Speculative philosophy replaces the maxim of Understanding
'Everything is essentially distinct' by its own 'Everything is
opposite'.   Neither in the world of mind nor nature, Hegel wrote, is
there anywhere such an abstract 'either-or' as Understanding maintains.   'Whatever exists is concrete, with difference and opposition
in itself.' [86]

Engels endorsed these Hegelian views also with the full confidence
that he was paving the way for scientific progress.   Common sense
may protest against identifying things which are different, for
'abstract identity', like other metaphysical categories, suffices for
everyday use.   But the law of identity implies that nothing changes
and this consequence is 'refuted by natural science, bit by bit in
each separate case'.   Therefore, nothing is simply identical with
itself, but it both is identical with and becoming distinct from itself.
'Concrete identity', which replaces the abstract kind, 'includes
difference'.   That identity contains difference within itself is made
clear by the simplest sentence, 'The lily is a plant' or 'The rose is
red', in which the predicate is necessarily different from the subject.
Engels accepted Hegel's view that the connective 'is' in the proposition 'The rose is red' does not signify the relation of class
inclusion but that of identity.   Consequently, in Hegel's own words,
the proposition in question 'affirms that the individual, or subject, is after all not individual but universal'.   Everything is itself
and something else at the same time; it is, therefore, contradiction.[87]

Thus, however, the validity of the law of the excluded middle has
to be restricted.   Valid scientific thinking 'besides "either-or"
recognizes also in the right place "both this — and that" and recon-
ciles the opposites'.   To 'think in irreconcilable antitheses' is a
metaphysical, that is, an anti-dialectical, manner of philosophizing.
To the metaphysician a thing either exists or does not exist; it
cannot at the same time be itself and something else.   This may be

good enough for everyday but not for scientific purposes. For science reveals that 'nature works dialectically and not metaphysically'.[88]

The law of the negation of the negation is more closely associated with the Hegelian philosophy than either of the two previously considered laws and is often simply identified with the dialectical method. In this restricted sense dialectics is a theory and a schema. The schema is the dialectical triad : thesis, antithesis, and synthesis, the three inevitable stages in the development of ideas. The theory is a single statement to the effect that the development of social movements and human thought in art and science, religion and philosophy, always occurs by agency of the dialectical triad. This single statement expresses a belief about intellectual history which unrestricted does not appear to be valid.

Moreover, Hegel's and Engels's treatment of events to be fitted into the triadic schema gives the impression of considerable arbitrariness. The methodological vagueness and arbitrary character of the triadic interpretation are very apparent in Engels's example in which he intended to show how the antithetical triadic procedure is able to reveal the dialectical advance in philosophy. The philosophy of antiquity, Engels argued, was natural materialism, unable to solve the problem of the relation of mind to matter. It was negated by monotheism and idealism, which in turn became untenable, and were negated by modern materialism. Modern materialism, being the negation of the negation of old materialism, preserves the permanent foundation of the latter and enriches it with the achievements of philosophy and natural science over two thousand years of history.[89]

The extension of the law of the triad to the world of nature rests on the presupposition that there are contradictory objects. These are the objects which, to use Engels's expression, are both this and that, like square circles and round triangles or any changing or moving body. The assumption that contradictions are objectively present in nature is not sufficient, however, to apply the negation of the negation to natural phenomena. The assumption must also be made that these contradictions are an 'actual force' that makes things change, move, grow, develop, and create novelty. The Ionians, Plato, and Aristotle conceived nature as permeated by dynamic power; nature was for them a world of spontaneously, self-moving things. Engels's view of nature was in certain respects like that of the Greeks, but unlike the Greek thinkers Engels was a materialist. He was not free, therefore, to say with Thales that 'all things are full of gods', that natural bodies are the seat of the soul, which, as Empedocles taught, hates and loves. Thus Engels's theory of nature was bound to become anthropomorphic. For to describe natural processes in terms of dialectical negation or the negating force is to endow material objects with consciousness and purposefulness which only human beings display.[90] Contradiction becomes a mysterious entity that is enclosed in material objects and which animates them. This entity is able to negate the opposites within itself, to reconcile or raise them to a higher unity, in which the contradiction is sublated, that is, overcome and preserved. Thus it is able to impel change, motion, and development. This is worse than using a metaphorical language; this is a verbal jugglery, as Eugen Dühring justifiably argued.

The anthropomorphic implications of the law of the triad are not invalidated by the distinction, taken over from Hegel, between subjective or immanent dialectics and objective or external dialectics, the former being the reflection of dialectics prevailing throughout nature.[91] Engels argued that dialectics can be regarded as 'two sets of laws which are identical in substance but differ in their expression' and which 'we can separate from each other at most only in thought but not in reality'. First, the laws may be considered as methodological principles which the human mind applies in the investigations of physical, social, and mental phenomena. Second, they are statements about reality, reflecting regularities in nature and history.[92] For instance, there is the 'dialectically subjective' requirement that things should be considered in their 'essential connection' of mutual causal interdependence; at the same time, this methodological requirement holds as a 'dialectically objective', that is, metaphysical principle stating that the whole of nature forms an interconnected totality of bodies.

Dialectics may thus appear as a dual power whose two branches, the methodological rules and the statements about physical reality, support and verify each other. This fallacy rests upon the Hegelian assumption that to be is the same as to be known. If we assume the identity of reason and being, we can infer from the dialectical development of thought that reality develops dialectically too. Those, however, who reject this Hegelian assumption cannot make such an inference. In particular, one of the cardinal points in the

Marxist–Leninist theory of knowledge is that knowledge involves the prior existence of a world which is to be known and that if there were no world existing independently there could be no knowledge of it. Therefore, what dialectical materialists state as methodologists and metaphysicians is a tautology; they say twice what needs saying only once.

4. THE DOCTRINE OF THE RELATIVITY OF KNOWLEDGE

The assumption concerning the dialectical constitution of the world directly establishes the relativity of knowledge. John Stuart Mill used the phrase the 'doctrine of the relativity of knowledge' as a family name for various kinds of phenomenalism, that is, the belief that our knowledge about external objects consists of nothing but the sensations which they excite and, therefore, that objects are to us that which affects our senses in a certain manner.[93] This is the view to which Mach and his supporters, as well as Avenarius and his school, subscribed and which Lenin so vehemently opposed in *Materialism and Empirio-Criticism*.[94] Engels's doctrine of the relativity of knowledge had nothing to do with the phenomenalism of Mill, Mach, or Avenarius.

The relativity of knowledge in Engels's sense stands for the proposition that scientific knowledge is provisional, cumulative, evolutionary, and thus never exhaustive and final. Engels seems to have followed in the footsteps of Comte, whose epistemological and sociological considerations for the relativity of knowledge he fully endorsed. But in Engels's mind these considerations were associated with his dialectical outlook on nature. It is this outlook that provided the background against which Engels evaluated the metaphysician's vain dream of attaining absolute certainty and immutable truth.

If all the processes of nature are 'systematically connected', an adequate description of this interconnection and the formation of an 'exact mental image of the world system' is not possible for us.

> Because of the nature both of men and of the world system, this task can never be completely fulfilled. . . . Each mental image of the world system is and remains in actual fact limited, objectively by the historical conditions and subjectively by the physical and mental constitution of its originators.[95]

E.D.M.—N

The subjective limitations, from which the relativity of knowledge results, are determined by the fact that no single generation can attain perfect and complete knowledge; only an endless succession of generations can approximate this objective. At every stage of knowledge there is always more that can be improved upon than not. It includes a number of 'relative errors' and gaps due to inadequate information, the absence of relevant evidence, or the transitory nature of the subject-matter. Moreover, all knowledge is socially determined and, in this sense, is relative and never absolute, approximate and never ultimate. Consequently, the knowledge attained by every generation is never final or complete.[96]

Engels felt that the doctrine of the relativity of knowledge grew out of the Hegelian dialectical philosophy, of its insistence on the transitory character of everything and its refusal to consider anything as final and absolute.[97] He implied that the influence of Hegel's philosophical speculations in the acceptance of an evolutionary approach to knowledge was due to the fact that in Hegel's time a scientifically formulated concept of evolution could not be put forward at all. Kant's cosmological theory continued to be regarded as a mere curiosity, the evolutionary ideas in geology had not yet appeared, and the 'evolution of species' was a hypothesis still unheard of. It should be emphasized, however, that the idea of development was in the intellectual atmosphere, and Hegel's philosophy was only one of the trends in the advance towards an evolutionary world outlook which finally destroyed the view of the immutability of nature.[98] The doctrine of the relativity of knowledge must be considered against a wider historical background, an impressive description of which is to be found in the introductory chapter to *Dialectics of Nature* and in the so-called Old Preface to *Anti-Dühring*.

According to Engels, three periods and three conceptions of nature can be differentiated in the history of European thought: the cosmology of Greek antiquity, modern cosmology, and the evolutionary cosmological conception of today.[99] Modern research into nature began with the Renaissance and without its systematic, all-round development, the new evolutionary outlook would not have come about. But theoretically the middle stage in the history of cosmology was a period of regression, and the evolutionary cosmology of today is a return to the outlook initiated by the founders of Greek philosophy rather than a continuation of a more recent past.

The cosmological conception formulated by the founders of Greek philosophy was based on the premiss that the whole of nature, from grains of sand to suns, from *Protista* to man, 'has its existence in eternal coming into being and passing away, in ceaseless flux, in unrest and motion and change'. For the Greeks, the world was something that had emerged from chaos and had developed. They viewed nature as a whole and were aware of the universal connection of natural phenomena. Although the Greek conception of nature was the result of intuitive understanding and direct contemplation, and its knowledge of natural science was inferior to that of modern cosmology, Greek antiquity stood above modern cosmology in its general outlook on nature.[100]

The central point of the modern cosmological conception was the belief in the immutability of nature. All development and real change were denied. The planets and the stars, the Earth's surface and the species of plants and animals had remained the same since they had come into existence and would remain unchanged to the end of the world. Natural scientists of that period regarded the order of nature as fixed and 'created at one stroke'. The first breach in this outlook was accomplished by classical German philosophy from Kant to Hegel. When Kant formulated his nebular hypothesis, later endorsed and developed by Laplace, the solar system appeared as something that had come into being, and thus for the first time in the modern period a natural object was shown to possess a 'history in time'.[101] The new ideas, which Kant introduced in his *Allgemeine Naturgeschichte und Theorie des Himmels* (1775), were finally victorious with the publication of *The Origin of Species* in 1859. This was the beginning of the new evolutionary or historical outlook on nature.

The modern period witnesses an enormous advance in scientific knowledge, an advance that was achieved by the 'analysis of nature into its individual parts, the grouping of the different natural processes and objects in definite classes'. This method established the metaphysical mode of thought. Natural objects were observed in isolation instead of in their interrelation, in repose and not in motion, as unchanging and not as essentially variable.[102]

Although Kant paved the way for the historical conception of nature, the cosmology of immutability continued to dominate the minds of scientists and philosophers for another century. But this was the period of the growth of various seminal scientific ideas which finally destroyed the metaphysical conception of nature. Laplace and Herschel in astronomy, Lyell in geology, Mayer and Joule in physics, Lavoisier and Dalton in chemistry, Oken, Lamarck, Baer, and Darwin in biology, all helped to establish an entirely new historical, dialectical, or evolutionary outlook on nature. Classical German philosophy and, above all, the philosophy of Hegel, which also contributed to the dissolution of all rigidity and fixity and to the view of nature as moving in eternal flux, fall into this period.[103]

Thus, the historical or dialectical conception of nature has been based on the view that the world attained its present state not by an act of creation, but by a slow process extending over long periods. With the recognition that 'everything must have a history in time', that changeability is a pervading trait of reality, and that reality has a multi-level structure, the dialectical method becomes 'the most important form of thinking for present-day natural science'. For it is the dialectical method alone that is able to explain 'the evolutionary processes occurring in nature, interconnections in general, and transitions from one field of investigations to another'.[104]

As has been pointed out earlier, Engels's distinction between the metaphysical and dialectical modes of thought is based on Hegel's distinction between the philosophy of Understanding and that of Speculative Reason. Like Hegel's philosopher of Understanding, Engels's metaphysician adheres to the laws of identity, the excluded middle, and non-contradiction and, consequently, is unable to attain knowledge of nature as a whole. This can only be achieved by dialectical thought which rejects the laws of formal logic, follows its own rules, and is thus capable of grasping change, motion, and development, in which contradictions are present in corporeal form.

But Hegel's speculative distinctions between Understanding and Speculative Reason acquire, in Engels's conception, additional characteristics drawn from the contrast between modern cosmology and evolutionary cosmology. The assumption of the immutability of nature gave rise to the metaphysical mode of thought; once this mode of thought was established, it reinforced and perpetuated the view that 'nature had no history'. On the other hand, the Kantian hypothesis concerning the origin of the solar system, which turned out to be the point of departure for further advance towards the historical conception of nature, was an instance of dialectical thought.

The evolutionary conception of nature and the dialectical mode of thought are as closely associated with each other as are modern cosmology and the metaphysical mode of thought.

The main difference between the two conceptions of nature is that the latter considers every constituent of the world as fixed and unchanging, whereas the former shows everything as moving in 'eternal flux'. To emphasize this difference between the two outlooks on nature is not such an obvious commonplace as some critics maintain.[105] Modern cosmology did not deny change as long as the transformation from state A to state B was so related to its predecessors and successors that whatever changed from state A to state B always ultimately returned from this state B to that state A. 'It is true', Engels wrote, 'that nature was obviously in constant motion, but this motion appeared as an incessant repetition of the same processes.'[106] In other words, according to modern cosmology, there was change, but change was cyclical, and there was motion, but motion did not involve advance and development.[107] The flow of time had no significance and time itself was a mere co-ordinate. The concept of reversible natural processes contained no absurdity and implied the denial of real novelties in the universe.

On the other hand, the evolutionary outlook emphasized the irreversibility of time and the creative advance of nature which Whitehead was to describe as 'the perpetual transition of nature into novelty'.[108] The evolutionary outlook replaced the Democritean concept of motion by the Aristotelian concept of change, alteration, or transformation, and conceived the motion of a body as no mere displacement but as a manifestation of some inherent change within the moving body itself. Therefore, change was no longer repeatable and cyclical but involved an evolutionary development and the emergence of novelty.

The two outlooks are clearly differentiated by their conceptions of time and their attitudes to history. According to modern cosmology nature has known no passage of time and has had no history ; in the evolutionary view it has had a development in time and a history.[109] To put it differently, whereas modern man followed in the footsteps of his ancestors of archaic societies and depreciated concrete, historical time, the man of today who lives within history and recognizes its autonomy was born only in the very recent period which Engels identified with the post-Hegelian era.[110]

Engels's differentiation between the two conceptions of nature in modern times both amplified and restricted the distinction of the metaphysical and dialectical modes of thought. This was understood neither by his opponents nor by his supporters, Marxist–Leninists in particular. Engels did not hold the metaphysical mode of thought responsible for the denial of change which is repeatable and cyclical, but for the denial of change that is a process of growth, development, and advance. The point at issue between metaphysics and dialectics is not whether Parmenides or Heraclitus is right, but whether nature moves eternally in a recurring circle or goes through a 'real historical evolution'.

VI

Plekhanov's Revisions of Dialectical Materialism

THE importance of Plekhanov in the history of dialectical materialism is based primarily on the fact that he was a pioneer of Marxian
teaching in Russia and its first Russian theorist. Trotsky wrote of
Plekhanov that he was 'the profound and brilliant commentator of
Marx, the teacher of entire generations, the theorist, the politician,
publicist, and creator of European fame and European connections'.[1]
Prominent political writers and political leaders, including P. B.
Struve, Y. O. Martov, and Lenin, testified to the influence and
persuasiveness of Plekhanov's writings and to his decisive role in
their conversion to 'Marxism'. Plekhanov won over hundreds of
young Russian men and women to Marxian teaching, imbued the
Russian working-class movement with the ideas of Marx, and
supplied it with wide political horizons.[2]

Lenin was in intellectual debt to Plekhanov and paid high tribute
to his merits and to the excellence of his work. He recognized that
alongside Chernyshevsky Plekhanov was the chief architect of a
materialist tradition in the history of social thought in Russia.[3] He
praised Plekhanov for the determined struggle against political and
philosophical revisionism which he carried on 'from the point of
view of consistent dialectical materialism'.[4] In a letter to Gorky
(which coincided with the start of his work on *Materialism and
Empirio-Criticism*), Lenin confessed that it was Plekhanov who had
opened his eyes to the fallacy of the views of the Neo-Kantians, the
Machians, and their Russian supporters. In general, Plekhanov
made him realize the importance of philosophy for an 'ordinary
Marxist,' as Lenin described himself.[5] Lenin's high opinion of
Plekhanov probably accounts for the fact that he was not entirely
forgotten in the Stalinist period and that his merits in educating 'a
whole generation of Russian Marxists' were duly emphasized.[6] But

his reputation declined because of his firm resistance to 'revolutionary Marxism' and his restraint in the treatment of ideological opponents. Only now, in the post-Stalinist era, does he seem to be coming back into his own.

No less important than Plekhanov's political influence and activity was the part he played in the interpretation of the philosophical views of Marx and Engels. He brought to this task a versatile mind, philosophical knowledge, and a general erudition far superior to the scholarly equipment of his more famous successors, including Lenin. Russian and Western scholars alike found much to commend in him. Sidney Hook praised Plekhanov for his unprejudiced mind, his independence of judgment, and his willingness to follow the lead of evidence. V. V. Zenkovsky, the historian of Russian philosophy, credited Plekhanov with profundity, great literary talent, and a subtle critical sense. These qualities made him 'a lively and interesting writer, in whom loyalty to Marxism never smothered his genuine moral nobility or his interest in truth and progress'. S. H. Baron, Plekhanov's American biographer, attributed to Plekhanov a keen sensitivity, a lively imagination, and a scholarly approach notable for its wide scope and detachment. Particularly in his historical studies Plekhanov showed 'striking intuition, frequent flashes of brilliance, and no little originality'.[7]

It was Plekhanov who first used the expression 'dialectical materialism'. As has been mentioned earlier, Plekhanov considered the dissociation of Marx's historical and philosophical materialism a grave error and asserted that Marxian philosophy was to be found in the works of Engels, above all, in *Anti-Dühring* and *Ludwig Feuerbach*. Moreover, he regarded dialectical materialism as the central and most important part of, and even identified it with, Marxian philosophy as a whole. 'The philosophy of Marx and Engels is not only a materialist philosophy; it is dialectical materialism.'[8] While Plekhanov used the term 'dialectical materialism' in various meanings, there can be no doubt that by the materialist philosophy of Marx and Engels he meant the materialism of Engels and not the naturalism of Marx. There is no reason to suppose that he was aware of any difference. The term 'naturalism' does not occur in Plekhanov (though 'Feuerbachian humanism' does), and Lenin, who in many respects followed Plekhanov's interpretation of the teaching of Marx and Engels, consciously avoided it. In Lenin's opinion, naturalism is only an inexact description, or ineffective form, of materialism, for a naturalist is unable to withstand the onslaught of the bourgeois world-outlook unless he becomes a conscious adherent of dialectical materialism.[9] Plekhanov was one of those Marxian scholars who believed — and impressed this belief upon the world — that there was complete identity of views between Marx and Engels on all philosophical matters. As far as the conception of materialism is concerned, this meant in fact the substitution of Engels's views for those of Marx.

I. THE REJECTION OF ABSOLUTE MATERIALISM

Plekhanov accepted Engels's genetic materialism, which, in his opinion, was 'materialism in the general sense'.

> Materialism is the direct opposite of idealism. Idealism strives to explain all the phenomena of nature, all the qualities of matter, by these or those qualities of the spirit. Materialism acts in exactly the opposite way. It tries to explain psychic phenomena by these or those qualities of matter, by this or that organization of the human or, in more general terms, of the animal body. All those philosophers in the eyes of whom the prime factor is matter belong to the camp of the materialists; and all those who consider such a factor to be the spirit are idealists.

This basic distinction provides the fundamental principle of the most varied systems, and gives to the materialism of one epoch a totally different aspect from the materialism of another.[10]

Only remnants of Engels's absolute materialism are to be found in Plekhanov. They become apparent in his insistence that 'Marxism' is 'a materialist world outlook', not to be reduced to its historical and economic aspects; that the laws of dialectics reflect the regularities in nature; and that Marx and Engels were 'conscious materialists not only in the field of history but in natural science as well'.[11] As will be seen later, the main objective of these assertions was not to produce a philosophy of nature but to secure a cosmological foundation for historical materialism.

Plekhanov's reluctance to endorse absolute materialism may have been due to his awareness of the significance of Kant's critique of pure reason for all metaphysical speculations, including materialism;

in the case of Engels, who was intoxicated with the speculative enthusiasm of Hegel and felt that Hegel had risen above the pedestrian critical philosophy of Kant, such an awareness was conspicuous by its absence. Kant rejected the claim that the question as to the nature of things can ever be answered, for things are not given other than as phenomena, the knowledge of these phenomena arising from a unique relation between the cognizing subject and the cognized object. The whole system of Kant may be regarded as an attempt to abolish for ever every kind of metaphysics, including absolute materialism, that claims knowledge of things as they exist independently of our knowledge of them.

The fact that Plekhanov realized the difficulty arising from Kant's epistemological investigations is clear from the trouble he took in refuting or at least undermining their consequences for materialism.[12] Unlike Engels before him and Lenin after him,[13] Plekhanov did not consider the Hegelian axiom of the unity of thought and existence a sufficient argument against the Kantian view that though we can establish the existence of objects of some kind outside ourselves, we do not and cannot know what kind of objects they are. Plekhanov himself adopted the anthropological viewpoint of Feuerbach, who agreed with Kant that we can know nothing about things in themselves, but only as they exist for man and are given to him in experience. It would be absurd to claim knowledge of what exists quite independently of us and what, by definition, is beyond the bounds of all experience. 'The materialists never affirmed', wrote Plekhanov, 'that we know what things are in themselves, i.e. independently of their action upon us, but only maintained that these things are known to us precisely because they act upon the organs of our senses and in the very measure in which they act upon them.'[14]

Plekhanov referred approvingly to Holbach's view that

> We do not know either the essence or the true nature of matter, although by its action upon us we can judge of some of its properties. For us, matter is what acts in one way or another upon our senses.[15]

But Plekhanov did not go as far as Holbach, who came very close to John Stuart Mill's phenomenalist definition of matter. Whereas Holbach affirmed the unknowableness or non-existence of essences,[16] Plekhanov maintained that if we know some properties of the things acting upon our senses we also know their nature to a certain extent. He claimed that his assertion is in accord with the Feuerbachian principle which abolishes the counterposition of the nature of things to their properties, for the nature of things is indistinguishable from, and manifest in, their properties.[17] The distinction between appearance and the thing-in-itself leads to a scholastic labyrinth in which Kant and all who followed his example got lost.

If the distinction between appearance and the thing-in-itself is illegitimate and ultimately meaningless, the question of the unknowableness of the external world is resolved, but at the price of a retreat from the absolute materialism of Engels. Plekhanov's epistemology includes the principle of the relativity of knowledge in J. S. Mill's sense, according to which objects are nothing to us but that which affects our senses in a certain way. The epistemological conception of matter, which was firmly established by Lenin in *Materialism and Empirio-Criticism*, was first introduced by Plekhanov to neutralize the impact of Kant's critical philosophy upon materialism.

If the characteristics ascribed to the objects of the external world only signify their power of causing sensations of some kind or other, these sensations cannot and should not be conceived as similar to what excites them. This conclusion persuaded Plekhanov of the truth of critical realism in the theory of knowledge and led him to the adoption of what he called the 'theory of hieroglyphs'. According to this theory, sensations do not resemble their causes, the objects of the external world. They convey, however, their existence and the relations obtaining between their properties.[18] If we can have no notion of what exists independently of us, sensations cannot be 'copies of real things', irrespective of whether or not this constitutes a deviation from Engels's formulation of materialism, which is what Lenin accused Plekhanov of.[19]

Plekhanov thought that genetic materialism, supported by the principle of evolution, was sufficient to establish materialist philosophy as an integral and consistent world outlook. He seems to have favoured the doctrine of emergent evolution, based on the assumption that 'all the matter of which organized beings consist, possesses a certain degree of sensibility'. He denied that this hypothesis cannot be reconciled with materialism and was confident that Marx and Engels would have been interested in it had they known of it.[20]

However, the materialist world outlook must be able to explain not only the reality that surrounds man but also his activity. Plekhanov maintained that the principle underlying the explanation for the latter had already been formulated by Feuerbach, who declared that 'thinking is conditioned by being, and not being by thinking'.[21] Marx and Engels made this principle the foundation of the materialist conception of history and based their explanation of man's activity on it. Plekhanov added that the materialism of Marx and Engels was far more advanced than the materialism of Feuerbach, but that the former was elaborated in the direction indicated by the inner logic of the latter. Feuerbach's principle was closely linked with genetic materialism and derived its justification from it.[22] Plekhanov's suggestion that there was a direct connection between historical and genetic materialism dissociated the materialist conception of history from its original foundation, that is, from the naturalism of Marx, and incorporated it into Engels's metaphysical system of dialectical materialism.

2. THE TWO BASIC LAWS OF DIALECTICS

Genetic materialism is 'materialism in the general philosophical sense', and dialectical materialism, which is derived from it, constitutes a distinctive form of the materialist world outlook. It has been mentioned earlier that Plekhanov was the first to use the expression 'dialectical materialism'. He introduced it, as he explained, to differentiate sharply between dialectical materialism and metaphysical materialism, the former including, and the latter excluding, the idea of evolution.[23] The verbal distinction reflected the underlying differences and successive modifications of the conceptual frameworks. 'Holbach and Helvétius were metaphysical materialists,' wrote Plekhanov. 'They fought against metaphysical idealism. Their materialism gave way to dialectical idealism, which in its turn was overcome by dialectical materialism.'[24] It was Hegel who observed that 'the latest philosophy to appear (*die der Zeit nach letzte Philosophie*) is always the outcome of all those which have preceded it, and must include their principles'. Metaphysical materialism, dialectical idealism, and dialectical materialism could, therefore, be considered as one single philosophical trend at different stages of maturity.[25]

The term 'dialectical' fittingly qualifies 'materialism' as applied to the system of Marx because Hegel transformed dialectics into a 'most powerful weapon for the cognizance of everything which exists', and Marx made use of the idea of dialectics for the establishment of his materialist philosophy. The essential difference between modern materialism and the materialism of the eighteenth century lies in the dialectical method. F. A. Lange divided the history of materialism into two parts, before and after Kant. A more appropriate and justifiable course would be to take the philosophy of Hegel as the great divide.[26] In this respect Lenin fully agreed with Plekhanov, for Lenin believed that the best way of becoming acquainted with the dialectics of Marx was to pursue 'a systematic study of Hegel's dialectics from a materialist point of view'.[27]

Finally, according to Plekhanov, the expression 'dialectical materialism' indicated that the new materialism accepted both the principle of evolution, which is at work in all phases of change, and the principle of sudden and inevitable leaps, to which gradual change necessarily leads. In a certain sense, 'dialectical' means the same as 'evolutionary' and, consequently, Darwin's theory of the origin of species is a dialectical theory. But if an evolutionary doctrine restricts development to the process of continuous quantitative change and excludes interruption in graduality, it is no longer dialectical. 'It is a great error to think that nature or history makes no leaps.' It was one of Hegel's greatest merits to have purged the doctrine of change of mere gradualism and to have supplemented it by the conception of 'the jump from quantitative into qualitative change'.[28] Since Marx had incorporated the 'transition by dialectical leaps' into his materialist evolutionary philosophy, the proper name for it was dialectical materialism.[29]

But dialectical materialism includes more than the mere rejection of the dictum 'Natura non facit saltus'. In *The Development of the Monist View of History* Plekhanov found in Hegel three dialectical laws which he wished to incorporate into dialectical materialism, though not all in their original form. The three dialectical laws are the same as those adopted by Engels in *Anti-Dühring* and *Dialectics of Nature*, the law of the interpenetration of opposites, the law of the transition of quantity into quality, including the doctrine of leaps, and the law of the negation of the negation. Plekhanov accepted the last of these laws in a truncated form and reduced it to the first. The negation of an old quality by a new one in the process of development is the result of the operation of the law concerned with the transformation of a thing into its opposite, that is, with the contradictions inherent in all phenomena. Plekhanov also changed the order of the dialectical laws as established by Engels, for Plekhanov's first dialectical law, namely, the law of the interpenetration of opposites, is Engels's second. Lenin followed Plekhanov's, and not Engels's, order of the dialectical laws, and until the publication of Stalin's *Dialectical and Historical Materialism* this order was adopted in Soviet philosophy out of respect for Lenin.[30] It should be borne in mind, however, that the order of the laws of dialectics in Soviet philosophy was originated by Plekhanov and not by Lenin.[31]

The first law of dialectics states, 'Every phenomenon is contradictory', or 'Every phenomenon is a contradiction'. Expressed in terms of change, to which the inner polar structure of phenomena is supposed to give rise, the first law of dialectics asserts, 'Every phenomenon negates itself', that is, it 'develops out of itself the elements which, sooner or later, will put an end to its existence and will transform it into its own opposite'. The term 'contradiction' as used by Plekhanov in the formulation of the first dialectical law is not necessarily a logical term and often merely refers to the conflict of interests, to the clash of opposite forces, or to the struggle of antagonistic tendencies objectively present in a phenomenon or a complex of phenomena. For instance, Plekhanov maintained that social and economic classes are, in the non-logical sense of this expression, contradictory elements in economic and social reality and that these contradictions, inherent in the development of class societies, give rise to the struggle for existence between individuals, classes and whole societies. More generally, the polar structure of things and phenomena is responsible for the fact that by the action of antagonistic forces and tendencies, which conditions their existence, things and phenomena are inevitably transformed into their own opposites.[32]

In this formulation the first law of dialectics applies only to history and society but not to nature. But Plekhanov made it clear in his various writings that he wanted it to be extended to nature and asserted that 'every motion is a dialectical process, a living contradiction'.[33] For a materialist, wrote Plekhanov, dialectics is based on the doctrine of nature, and 'dialectical thinking' is derived from 'the dialectical properties of being'. Thus, the contradictions embodied in concepts are merely reflections, translations into the language of thought of those contradictions that are embodied in phenomena owing to the contradictory nature of their common basis, i.e. motion.[34]

The historical origins of the doctrine 'Motion is a contradiction in action' are not difficult to trace. According to Hegel, it was Zeno of Elea who had conclusively demonstrated its truth. Engels took over this Hegelian idea, presented it as if it were a solidly established scientific proposition, and tried to justify it with arguments of doubtful erudition. Finally, Plekhanov endorsed Engels's views about contradictions, and they became a canonical part of the orthodoxy.

Like Hegel, Plekhanov went back to Zeno, whom he credited with the definitive proof of the proposition that motion is an embodied contradiction, and urged the restriction of the law of non-contradiction, found to be unsatisfactory by such profound thinkers as Heraclitus, Hegel, and Marx. 'A moving body', Plekhanov argued, 'is at a particular place and at the same time it is not there', a fact, he commented, 'that even the most resolute opponents of the dialectical method cannot but accept'. For if a moving body were where it is at time t_n, and not simultaneously somewhere else, it would be, contrary to the assumption, motionless, at least at time t_n. Consequently, we would have to agree with Zeno of Elea that motion is nothing more than an illusion of the senses. In this respect Plekhanov deviated from Hegel. Whereas Hegel believed that Zeno wanted to demonstrate that motion is a contradiction, Plekhanov held that Zeno wished to prove that motion is impossible, because if it were real it would have to be a contradiction. It is now widely believed that Plekhanov's rather than Hegel's account of Zeno's intentions is the historically true account.

As there is not a single phenomenon of nature for the explanation of which we do not ultimately appeal to motion, the conclusion must be drawn that all things and phenomena of nature are a 'living contradiction'. Symbolically, we can state the principle to which Plekhanov refers in the following way

$$(x, \phi) \ (\exists \psi) : \phi x . \supset . \psi x . \sim \psi x$$

or

$$(x, \phi) \ (\exists \psi) : \phi x . \supset . \sim (\psi x \vee \sim \psi x).$$

Since the motion of matter lies at the root of all natural phenomena

— the state of motion is absolute and without exception, the state of rest being only relative — and since all motion is a contradiction, formal logic is generally inapplicable to natural events.

Like Engels, Plekhanov believed that natural phenomena belong to 'the domain of the "logic of contradiction"'. The laws of non-contradiction and of the excluded middle apply only to what is in a state of rest, but not otherwise. Just as a state of rest is a particular instance of motion, logical thinking is 'significant only within certain limits' and constitutes a particular instance of dialectical thinking, in which the law of non-contradiction and the law of the excluded middle no longer hold. While the first law of dialectics does not abolish formal logic altogether, it 'strips its laws of the absolute value', that is, it restricts its validity, subordinates it to dialectical thinking, and establishes the doctrine of logical dualism.[35]

According to Hegel, it is not only the cunning of Reason which operates in history, but also the cunning of the Notion. The cunning of the Notion reveals itself in the fact that quantity is not only capable of increase and decrease, but also of a 'sudden revulsion . . . from what is at first merely quantitative into qualitative alteration'.[36] Hegel's cunning of the Notion became Engels's law of the transition of quantity into quality and vice versa and Plekhanov's law of the inevitability of leaps in the process of development.[37]

The difference between Engels and Plekhanov is one of emphasis. Having the mechanistic conception of nature in mind above all, Engels underlined gradual accumulation and final transitions of quantitative changes into qualitative changes, alteration being thus as much a fundamental cosmic process as increase and decrease. On the other hand, Plekhanov, whose main interests were history, sociology, and politics, emphasized the fact that these 'transitions occur by leaps and cannot occur in any other manner'.[38] Both Engels and Plekhanov merely quoted from and summarized what they had read in Hegel on this matter, but they did so with different purposes in mind.

As Plekhanov repeatedly stressed, although the theory of evolution and dialectics have some points in common, they also reveal a profound and important difference. The theory of evolution is 'based on the principle that neither nature nor history proceeds in leaps and that all changes in the world take place by degrees'. Hegel had already shown that the doctrine of development thus conceived is 'unsound and ridiculous'. According to Plekhanov, Hegel 'demonstrated irrefutably' that both in nature and in human society leaps constituted just as essential a stage of evolution as gradual quantitative changes.

> Gradual quantitative changes in the given content are finally transformed into qualitative differences. The movements of its transformation are the moments of leap, of interruption in graduality.[39]

To justify the claim of the inevitability of leaps in the process of social and historical development, Plekhanov proceeded to show that the law of the gradual accumulation of small quantitative changes, which necessarily leads to a leap, describes the 'dialectical properties of being' and is a universal law applying without exception to all natural phenomena. For this purpose he repeated, as Engels had before him, Hegel's illustrations of the 'dialectical theorem'.[40] Some of these illustrations only testify to the semantical and conceptual confusion in Hegel and his followers, and others merely give instances of the alleged law, as if a law could be established and a theory verified by an accumulation of instances. Hegel could make use of this procedure for he adhered to the view, demolished by Galileo, that the laws of physics can be deduced from clear and simple intelligible principles. For Hegel it was self-evident that 'a process of becoming other . . . breaks off graduality and is qualitatively other as against the preceding Determinate Being'.[41] On this account, the particular instances of the 'transition from the quantitative into the qualitative' and of the 'jumps' had no demonstrative function for Hegel and were only intended to clarify what he had in mind. With Engels and Plekhanov the instances were not meant to illustrate but to confirm a theory or to establish a law, which is exactly what they cannot do.

Both Engels and Plekhanov intended the law of the transformation of quantity into quality, together with the doctrine of leaps, to state something more than the ontological and/or the epistemological dependence of quantitative concepts upon qualitative ones. Quantitative concepts do ultimately require a definition in ostensive terms which designate the directly experienced qualitative diversity. This statement is important and true but is hardly a law of nature. In order to express a pervasive natural regularity, the law of the transformation of quantity into quality would have to state an invariant connection between the quantitative and the qualitative change of phenomenon.

If this was the intention of Engels and Plekhanov, they did not achieve their objective. In order to accept the law of the transformation of quantity into quality as a law of nature, we would have to know whether it applies to all processes of change or only to all processes of change of a particular type. The first alternative, which some formulations of Engels, Plekhanov, and their successors strongly suggest, has to be rejected because the law would then be converted into an analytical statement, that is, its truth would be warranted by the implicit definitions of the terms 'quantity' and 'quality'.[42] Neither can we regard this principle as a tentative framework for a law or laws which we expect to discover by restricting the class of quantities and qualities involved and the admissible types of change and transformation, for this too would be incompatible with Engels's claim that his law was an empirically meaningful theoretical law.

Consequently, only the second alternative remains open, that is, that we should regard the law in question as applying to all processes of change of a certain type or as a restrictive principle that forbids certain things to happen, a narrower and more precise meaning being thus attached to the terms 'quality' and 'quantity'. To state this in the language of Popper, the Hegelian principle would have to be reformulated in such a way that instead of being a principle whose truth is manifest and whose validity is irrefutable by any conceivable event, it becomes a statement incompatible with certain possible results of observation.

The objections against this procedure are apparent. Let us assume that we are successful in discovering a statement of an invariable correlation between quantities and qualities of certain kinds. If such an invariant correlation holds, the consequences would have to be accepted that every change of quantity is a qualitative leap. For instance, the kinetic theory of matter makes use of moving solid particles and reduces the differences between the three physical states of matter to purely quantitative differences of the molecular motion and of intermolecular distances. On this assumption every quantitative change should be considered as productive of a leap. But this would show, as even Engels was ready to acknowledge, that if there are no gaps in an ordered series of quantified magnitudes 'there are no leaps in nature, precisely because nature is composed entirely of leaps'.[43] If the consequence that every quantitative change constitutes a qualitative leap is to be avoided, the occurrence of a jump would have to be fixed by a conventional decision, by giving a distinctive name to a certain arbitrarily selected change of quality. In the first case, the concept of the sudden leap would become redundant, in the second, a statement about a leap would be a metalinguistic statement, concerned with the language used and not with the extralinguistic reality.

The second objection against the suggested course is even more serious. The law of the transformation of quantity into quality, interpreted in the restrictive sense, could no longer be a universal principle, a 'general law of motion and development of nature, human society and thought'. Therefore, the Hegelian principle is either empirically meaningless or theoretically useless, that is, it does not serve the purpose for which it was designed.

3. THE ELIMINATION OF THE HEGELIAN TRIAD AND THE PERVASIVE POWER OF CONTRADICTION

According to Plekhanov, the third law of dialectics, that of the negation of the negation, 'does not at all play in Hegel's work the part which is attributed to it by people who have not the least idea of the philosophy of that thinker'.[44] That the triad does not at all constitute a 'distinguishing feature of Hegel's philosophy' is not a view with which the students of Hegel in the past and today would agree. Although it is true that the terms 'thesis', 'antithesis', and 'synthesis', generally used in the exposition of the Hegelian doctrine, do not often occur in Hegel, the triadic scheme and rhythm are constantly applied in his whole work.[45] There is much more truth in what Plekhanov says about the triadic method, namely, that it is not a method at all and that no particular succession of events can be demonstrated by making use of the principle of the negation of the negation. The question whether a particular complex of phenomena in the process of its development has created the forces that lead to its 'negation', i.e. its disappearance, cannot be answered in advance or 'proved theoretically'; it can only be seen *ex post*.[46]

However, if this is acknowledged, Hegel's triadic scheme becomes an expository device which makes for confusion rather than enlightenment in view of the multiplicity of meanings which the 'negation' is allowed to have. For 'negation' sometimes means 'negated proposition' or 'logical contradiction' or 'incompatibility', sometimes 'qualitative change' or 'emergence of a new physical characteristic', sometimes 'class conflict' or 'clash of interests', and sometimes 'stage of development in a developmental chain'.[47]   As a matter of fact, 'every kind of thing has a peculiar way of being negated', and this should really be expected, for the negation of the negation rules supreme over the barley plant, geology, the infinitesimal calculus, and many other things, all and sundry.[48]   If it is permissible to say that the butterfly negates the egg, ice negates liquid water, socialism negates capitalism, private property in land negates common land-ownership, and so on and so forth, practically every event can be regarded as a negation of one kind or another of any other event. The dialectical negation is subject to one restriction only. 'If I grind a grain of barley, or crush an insect,' Engels said, explaining what kind of negation his law excluded, 'I have carried out the first part of the action, but have made the second part impossible.' [49]   The manual *Fundamentals of Marxism–Leninism* clearly states that materialist dialectics does not concern itself with a negation which terminates the development of an object but with 'negation which involves the further development of a thing, object or phenomenon'.[50]   In other words, the triadic rhythm does not exclude anything except what would prevent the continuance of the rhythm. Thus, however, the practitioner of the triadic method need not be afraid of ever being refuted by experience. Any empirically known succession of phenomena fits the dialectical scheme and there is nothing to preclude its adaptation to the new knowledge gained. To-day, it is universally recognized that such an unrestricted adaptability reveals the presence of a fatal defect. A theory that does not take any risk of being refuted by future experience has no scientific content.[51]

According to Plekhanov, the law of the negation of the negation amounts to the statement that every phenomenon 'negates itself' and 'becomes transformed into its opposite'. Since each new phenomenon is produced by the negation of another phenomenon and is transformed in turn into its own opposite, as it were, at a higher level, it is inevitable that the 'third phase of development bears a formal resemblance to the first' and that which Lenin described as 'the apparent return to the old' occurs. The negation of the negation is not an independent principle. What is true in it is already contained in the first law of dialectics — every phenomenon is a contradiction — to which it can be reduced.[52]

Thus, the law of the interpenetration of opposites reflects the fact that every phenomenon investigated in the natural and social sciences combines properties that are diametrically opposed to one another and that it contains the forces which give birth to its opposite. The pattern of dialectical change discovered by Hegel reveals the important truth that 'every particular aggregate of phenomena in the process of its development creates out of its very self the forces that lead to its negation, i.e. its disappearance'. This principle not only implies that scientific trends, intellectual tendencies, political and economic systems, schools of thought, and styles of art give rise to their antitheses, but also that societies 'develop out of themselves, by their inherent self-activity, a force capable of destroying the old form of social relations and erecting on their ruins a new and better social edifice'.[53]

In this way Plekhanov disclosed the socio-cosmic roots of dialectical materialism in general and of the law of the interpenetration of opposites in particular, a topic to be discussed in the next section. The fitness of this law to encourage certain social attitudes and political views may leave nothing to be desired, but when it is considered as a cosmic law its cognitive value is nil. As a theory of the world, the law of the interpenetration of opposites loses whatever plausibility it may have as a descriptive historical doctrine. For if it is applied to the development of thought, that is, to the conflicting views of men who clash and struggle with each other for the acceptance of their beliefs, such development can sometimes be described, in a loose and metaphorical way of speaking, as the transformation of the disputed view into its own opposite. In such cases, however, there is no 'vital force' which creates the thesis and the antithesis; they are produced by men. Thesis and antithesis do not struggle with each other to become transformed by their inherent dynamic or the immanent necessity of events into their own opposites; the disputed and conflicting opinions are transformed in discussion, that is, by the struggle of human minds, because opinions cannot be changed in any other way. The success in the application of the law of the interpenetration of opposites — a law in name, a metaphor in substance — to ideas, theories, or social and intellectual arguments results from the fact that while we are ostensibly speaking of ideas, theories, or social and intellectual movements, we really have in mind the men who create, hold, and fight for them.

No such success can be expected if the law of the interpenetration of opposites is to apply generally, both to the world of man and to the world of nature. As a general theory of the world, the law expresses a primitive animism or anthropomorphism — a mystical form of thought, as Marx described it in *Capital* — and loses all theoretical significance. To speak of the unity and struggle of the contradictories in nature is to indulge not only in a loose and metaphorical way of describing natural phenomena but also to speak in a dangerously misleading way. This becomes clear in Plekhanov's defence of Hegel's dictum 'der Widerspruch ist das Fortleitende', contradiction leads the way forward.

There are, Plekhanov wrote, barren and fruitful contradictions. The former either result from factual errors or are errors of reasoning and sins against logic. They are barren because as long as the error remains concealed they retard the development of thought, and they disappear as soon as the error is discovered without our knowledge being thereby enriched. The fruitful contradictions push thought forward and sometimes turn out to be more fertile than the 'most harmonious theories'. This may happen when we are faced by contradictory consequences which are derived correctly from a body of views regarded as true. For instance, some accepted facts of social life lead to the conclusion that men's opinions are determined by their social environment, while other facts justify a contrary proposition, namely, that the social environment is determined by opinions. Although the thesis seems to be just as correct as the antithesis, they cannot both be true and we cannot rest satisfied until the contradiction is resolved. This is achieved if and when a new factor is discovered which determines both the development of social environment and the development of opinion. The paradox of incompatible conclusions stimulates the search for new facts and the discovery of new facts helps to resolve the paradox. Viewed from the higher vantage-point, the original propositions supplement, rather than exclude, each other ; the contradiction disappears, but it has produced an advance of knowledge. In such situations it can be said that the 'principle of contradiction does not destroy objective truth, but only leads us to it. . . . "Contradiction" appears where, and only where, there is struggle, where there is movement; and where there is movement, thought goes forward, even though by roundabout ways'. [54]

This is a striking and correct description of what might happen when a paradox is encountered and of the role which contradictions may and did play in scientific progress. There is no doubt that if a contradiction is regarded as an intellectual challenge, it may and in fact often does speed the advancement of knowledge. It should be clearly understood, however, that in such cases not the contradictions themselves are productive of progress, but our treatment of them. What produces advance is our determination to abide by the law of non-contradiction and not to relent until the paradox is resolved. As Popper said, the 'fertility of the contradictions is merely the result of our decision not to put up with them'.[55]

The reason why Plekhanov subscribed to Hegel's opinion that 'contradiction leads the way forward' was different. Contradictions are productive of progress because, generally, they themselves are a 'motive force' and a 'formative principle', that is, they originate change and motion, including the movement of thought, stimulate development, and determine the nature and direction of progress. While quoting Hegel's dictum that contradiction is the power that moves things, Bukharin wrote in a similar vein, 'there is no doubt of the correctness of this law'. Bukharin's argument was that if there was no conflict, no clash, no contradiction between opposing and colliding forces, the world would be in a condition of stable equilibrium, complete and absolute permanence. But 'the world consists of forces opposing each other' whose balance is the exception and whose actual conflict and 'internal contradiction' are the rule.[56]

The relationship between logical contradictions and 'contradictions in corporeal form' was based on the Hegelian axiom of the identity of thought and being. As Lenin put it in support of essentially the same argument, the relations of notions are reflections of the objective world, 'the dialectics of things produces the dialectics of ideas, and not vice versa'.[57] The intellectual advance arising from contradictions in thought is the reflection in the human brain of the dialectical process of motion in the external world, and this dialectical process is a 'living contradiction'. There is little doubt that Plekhanov endorsed this view in the conviction that it validates the transient nature of every existing order of things and, above all, the inevitable disintegration of every social and political system involving in its very essence its own negation. But this basic belief is expressed by the general proposition that the 'contradictions embodied in concepts' are merely 'translations into the language of thought' of the 'contradictions embodied in phenomena'. The course of ideas must be explained by the course of events, and the course of thought by the course of life. The reasons why Plekhanov and Lenin adopted this particular approach must now be examined more closely.

4. THE SOCIO-COSMIC ROOTS OF DIALECTICAL MATERIALISM

Any scientific theory must satisfy certain conditions with regard to its logical structure and its cognitive content. It should be capable of empirical validation, it should be in agreement with actual observation, and it should fulfil the requirements of comprehensiveness, consistency, and logical fertility. These conditions are not independent of one another. If a theory is not logically well constructed, we may find it difficult to establish its empirical validity. On the other hand, the most perfect logical structure of a theory does not in itself provide a sufficient guarantee that its empirical significance can be tested, unless theoretical constructs, which occur in the formulation of its laws and hypotheses, are linked with the data of observation by appropriate epistemic rules.

The requirement of logical fertility provides a good starting-point for the evaluation of the cognitive and logical worth of a theory. We speak of the logical fertility of a hypothesis or a natural law if numerous consequences can be deduced from it and can be empirically tested either directly or indirectly. The opposite of a 'logically fertile theory' is an 'inferentially hollow theory'. If somebody maintains that 'whatever happens is due to Fate', he holds an inferentially hollow theory, for his theory does not allow him to derive specific inferences as to what is or is not going to happen. A proposition from which no statements about future experiences can be derived has no factual meaning. A sentence expresses a genuine factual proposition if and only if we can derive from it, in conjunction with other either logically or factually true premisses, some observational sentences.

The laws of the interpenetration of opposites and of the transformation of quantity into quality are also instances of inferentially

hollow theories, for it is not possible to deduce determinate consequences from these laws, so that one can see, prior to empirical tests,
whether or not they entail any definite conclusions. The two dialectical laws do not fulfil this requirement any more than 'whatever
happens is due to Fate' does. They are too loosely formulated to
permit clearly logical consequences to be drawn from them and
produce the false impression that they express a genuine proposition.

The concept of logical fertility is involved in the concept of universal law. A universal law is a universal conditional statement
which can be confirmed or disconfirmed, that is, which complies
with Popper's criterion of demarcation.[58] But the condition of
testability requires that some inferences can be drawn from a
universal law prior to the inspection of the empirical data available.
Therefore, there are no genuine universal laws which are logically
sterile.[59]

The condition of logical fertility implies that a theory which
admits several different interpretations of its concepts and is compatible with any state of affairs whatsoever, that is, which is logically
over-complete (includes both p and $\sim p$ among its consequences), is
not a properly formulated theory, for it can be so modified that it
survives any refutation no matter what the facts of the case are.

Although statements upon whose standing no combination of
observation and logical inference has any bearing are unverifiable,
they are not meaningless.[60] A supporter of dialectical materialism
believes and its opponent disbelieves the laws of dialectics. Consequently, both must be able to discover some meaning in them. But
a meaningful statement, whether believed or disbelieved, still raises
the question as to its truth-value. A meaningful statement which is
not capable of being either confirmed or refuted on observational
grounds is neither true nor false, and the laws of dialectics would
seem to be such meaningful statements unverifiable with regard to
their truth-value. A theory which includes the laws of dialectics
and some verifiable statements is either true or false only in so far as
its verifiable content goes.

Whereas logically over-complete theories are not a frequent
occurrence, theories formulated in a vague language with no epistemic rules of procedure with respect to their theoretical constructs
are to be found in great abundance. In the case of such theories or
laws it is always possible to argue that some consequences may be
obtained from them and that they thus fulfil the requirement of

logical fertility. In particular, this applies to imperfect laws. A law is imperfect if it is indefinite with respect to time or hedged in by qualification.

> Consider the assertion that a boom in trade is always followed by a slump and depression. This is imprecise with respect to time for it does not tell us exactly when the latter events will follow the earlier one, nor how long each will last. Moreover, its concepts have a fringe of vagueness that makes it difficult to tell precisely when we have instances of the kinds of events mentioned.[61]

If the objection of logical sterility with respect to the laws of dialectics seems to be too severe, the objection that they are imperfect laws should be accepted without qualification. For instance, the law of the transformation of quantity into quality states that a change is bound to happen whenever a quantitative characteristic gradually increases or decreases, but we can learn nothing determinate about what is supposed to take place and when it is expected to occur. The law provides no new factual information and, in fact, it makes no difference whether we accept this law or not. It lacks any informative content and even a modicum of precision.

The proposition 'Nature proceeds in leaps' may be suggestive but has no specific content. Irrespective of whether we assert or deny it, it does not seem to entail any experiential implications or involve any difference capable of verification. Moreover, it is a factually vacuous proposition, for it refers to an unobservable process established by an extrapolation which expresses 'the inherently necessary connection between quantity and quality' and claims a dialectical, and not an empirical, relationship between the quantitative and the qualitative aspect of change. Consequently, it is extremely doubtful whether it is testable at all. First, because the concept of leap is not related to the observable traits of things and events by appropriate epistemic rules. Since the distinction between what does and does not constitute a leap is entirely vague, the line of division between them is bound to be drawn in an arbitrary manner, and the decision about the occurrence of leaps is, to a large measure, arbitrary too, being concerned with language rather than with reality. Second, the hypothesis of leaps in nature does not seem to be testable because of the loose way in which the interrelations of quantity and quality are specified, which makes it impossible for us to decide on the basis of logical considerations alone what it does and what it does not imply. But if the conjecture about leaps in nature cannot be tested, it does not lie within the limits of cognitively meaningful discourse. It is a pseudo-proposition, neither true nor false, a bogus natural law and not a law of nature. To put it differently, it is a metaphysical principle which can claim universal validity because it is consistent with any observational statements whatsoever and in this sense is independent of experience.

Therefore, the proposition 'Nature proceeds in leaps' is like a fairy-tale, invented and cherished for some reason other than the cognitive purpose. There may be some advantage in being able to consider the liquefaction of gases, the melting of metals, and social or political revolutions as different instances of one and the same law of nature, but these advantages are not relevant to what the scientist does. The scientist prefers to rely on such concepts as transformation of energy, chemical reaction, or mutation, for they fit the particular kind of facts with which he is concerned, without committing him to a metaphysical presupposition as to the manner in which nature is supposed to proceed or without implying that nature's preference for leaps can be demonstrated as a strictly universal law. The proposition 'Nature proceeds in leaps', which, according to Engels, is a principle 'as simple and clear as noon-day', has no factual content and no explanatory power; it has a hortatory but not cognitive meaning.

As the law of the transformation of quantity into quality, including the doctrine of leaps, reveals itself as a cognitively empty scheme, performing no constructive methodological function and lacking logical fertility, its elevation to the status of a fundamental law of nature requires an explanation. Although scientific theories should be accepted if and only if they are true, they are accepted not only if they can be shown to be true, but also if they can be made to serve some useful purpose, for instance, if they can be used for the construction of technical devices or for the formulation of sociological conceptions to control human behaviour, that is, to encourage a desirable and discourage an undesirable way of life.[62] The suitability for promoting certain social, political, and moral ideas, or the aptness for advocating and upholding certain ways of conduct, has provided in all periods of history a reason for the acceptance of theories. It is a sociologically well established fact that scientific theories, whether genuine or sham, recent or old, have often been used to bolster some principles of behaviour, a system of beliefs or social goals which they are supposed, rightly or wrongly, to support. In some cases these extraneous considerations only impinge upon the procedure of validation, whereas in others they can prevail over logical or factual evidence, and thus lead to the rejection of a true theory or the acceptance of a false one.

The logical analysis of the law of the transformation of quantity into quality makes it highly implausible that Plekhanov adopted it in order to promote the advance of cosmological knowledge. He accepted the assumption that leaps in nature constitute as essential a stage of evolution as gradual quantitative changes in order to establish a socio-cosmic law rather than a law of nature. A law can be called 'socio-cosmic' if its acceptance is justified on the grounds that its consequences are favourable to the realization of some definite social and political system, to the maintenance of some moral order or to the furtherance of some cherished ideal. In analogy to anthropomorphism, which ascribes human form and nature to deity, a theory which attributes social traits and regularities to the universe may be called a 'sociomorphic theory of the universe'. Sociomorphic theories are knowingly or unknowingly formulated and advanced because of their alleged fitness to support one religious creed or one moral and political doctrine rather than another.

Plekhanov made no effort to validate the doctrine of leaps. He knew from his comprehensive study of history that social and political upheavals, which are preceded by a long chain of events but which take place suddenly and, as it were, unexpectedly, are not an infrequent occurrence. The alleged universal law of nature that 'leaps are inevitable in the process of historical and social development' is meaningful and possibly true if 'leaps' mean 'revolutions'; for social and political revolutions do occur in history. As long, however, as Plekhanov considered the concurrence, sequence, and concatenation of historical events alone, revolutions and upheavals were bound to remain what they actually are, namely, contingent and unforeseeable occurrences. Only the cosmological doctrine of leaps allowed him to establish the inevitability of political revolutions by some kind of cosmic decree and natural necessity. If it is a universal law that transitions from quantitative to qualitative changes 'occur by leaps and cannot occur in any other manner', gradualists in politics of all shades and colours as well as supporters of moderation and order are wrong, for 'economic

evolution leads as sure as fate to political revolution'.[63] The implications of the socio-cosmic doctrine of leaps in nature gave to dialectics its extraordinary political significance and prompted Plekhanov's
statement that dialectics is 'the most powerful scientific weapon
bequeathed by German idealism to its successor, modern materialism'.[64]

The law of the interpenetration of opposites is clearly a socio-
cosmic law too. To affirm that the world is full of contradictions in
corporeal form implies that the law of non-contradiction has to be
rejected or restricted and that it must be replaced by or subordinated
to the law of contradiction. The law of contradiction states that for
some p the conjunction of p and $\sim p$ is true. But if 'p' and '$\sim p$' are
at once true, and a statement is true if it corresponds to what it
asserts or denies, and false otherwise, contradictory statements would
be both true and false and the difference between truth and falsehood would disappear.[65] Moreover, if 'p' and '$\sim p$' are simultaneously true, by means of a formula of propositional calculus, the
law of Duns Scotus,

$$p . \supset . \sim p \supset q,$$

we can derive from these contradictory premises the conclusion 'q',
that is, any sentence whatsoever. In particular, we can substitute
for 'q' the expression '$\sim(p . \sim p)$'. Thus the law of contradiction,
if true, is false ; therefore it is false. To ignore this consequence is to
annihilate the whole significance of thought. If at every step, to use
Engels's expression in *Anti-Dühring*, truth becomes error and error
truth, the search for truth is bound to be futile.

If in spite of these disastrous implications the law of the interpenetration of opposites is retained, its claim to universal validity
can only be supported by socio-cosmic considerations. This was
indeed the case with Plekhanov and continues to be so in the Soviet
philosophy of today.[66] A universe brimming over with strife, conflict, and contradiction offers self-evident advantages for a social and
political theory based on the concept of class antagonism and class
struggle. Moreover, the law of the interpenetration of opposites
ascribes to the universe a vital impulse or force, a kind of all-powerful
self-activity inherent in all its manifestations, which in the historical
process brings about the disintegration of the old forms of life and
their transition to a higher stage of development towards what is
deemed worthy of human endeavour. Therefore, the vital impulse

helps to bridge the gap between fact and values and reveals that what people ought to strive for is also inevitable.

The sociomorphic projection into the cosmos of certain ways of viewing social life and its problems provides the basis for presenting the universe as a normative model for man and society and the man-made laws and norms as inferences which are deduced from the cosmic order.[67]   Since a socio-cosmic theory attributes to the universe the values with which the thinker wishes it to be endowed, a socio-cosmic theory can easily be used to support definite views about the role which man should play, the course of action which he should follow and the conduct which he should adopt.   It supports the claim that the ethical, social, and political system derived from dialectical materialism is a set of genuine propositions whose validity can be determined with scientific precision, for it is actually based upon the results of science.

Dialectical materialism proves to be a sociocentric cosmology which views the universe and searches for an understanding of it by relating it to society.   In a cosmology based upon social and political thought-patterns natural events and natural regularities are conceived in analogy to the processes and regularities observed in social and political life.   The dialectical law of the interpenetration of contraries, together with the doctrine of the transition of everything into its own opposite, and the law of the transformation of quantity into quality, including the doctrine of leaps, are instances of socio-cosmic laws produced by the application of sociomorphic patterns of thought; the experiences of social life are the source from which the principles of explanation of natural events are derived.   The different relations among things are grasped under their social form, and thus the content of explanatory categories expresses the various aspects of social existence.   A sociomorphic cosmology first ascribes certain distinctively social attributes, traits, and tendencies to the universe and, having construed it as a socio-cosmic structure, derives from the order of the universe the basic characteristics of human society and the fundamental regularities of social development.   The circular course of thinking returns to its point of departure which is also its point of destination.

Although dialectical materialism only acquired a pronounced sociomorphic form in Lenin and Stalin, it was Plekhanov who initiated this development.   Plekhanov's main theoretical interest was the philosophical and methodological problems of the historical and social sciences. This dominant preoccupation is also clearly reflected in his examination of dialectical materialism ; Plekhanov often speaks of it, knowingly or unknowingly, as if it were exclusively a historical and sociological doctrine. But he was also interested in establishing a theoretical basis for political action which for him, a Marxian theorist, in order to be effective, had to conform to the laws of social and historical development. A follower of Marx takes such laws for granted, for they have been discovered by Marx. But being also a Hegelian in the sense that he put Speculative Reason over and above mere Understanding, Plekhanov must have felt that the objectivity of these laws is not fully secure unless he were able 'to deduce' them from the general laws of the universe. He could achieve this, however, only if these universal laws were expressed in socio-cosmic terms and established within a scheme of nature that puts society at its centre.

Plekhanov had a scholarly mind, but his decisive influence was in transforming dialectical materialism into a 'political cosmology' and 'cosmological politics'.[68] At any rate, it was Plekhanov who wittingly or unwittingly made the first step in this direction and pushed dialectical materialism on to this course.

VII

The Dialectical Materialism of Lenin

PLEKHANOV can justly be described as a revisionist of Engels's dialectical materialism, because he introduced some specific philosophical changes into the original doctrine. He eliminated Engels's absolute materialism, that is, the proposition 'Only matter exists', and made genetic materialism the cornerstone of the whole structure, thus preparing the ground for the rejection of the metaphysical definition of matter in favour of its epistemological definition. Furthermore, he reduced the negation of the negation to the law of the interpenetration of opposites and changed Engels's order of the two remaining laws of dialectics. This last alteration is not as insignificant as it may perhaps appear, for it intensified the conflict between dialectics and formal logic.

Practically all of Plekhanov's revisions of dialectical materialism appear again in Lenin. Lenin not only accepted his amendments to Engels, but pushed them even further, to a point which makes it possible to speak of Engels's and Lenin's dialectical materialism as two distinct doctrines, differing from each other in some important respects.

Lenin's revisions of Engels's dialectical materialism were accomplished under the guise of defending Engels's original views from misrepresentation by would-be supporters. Lenin accused the Russian Machians of having misunderstood or discarded Engels's fundamental ideas, but the whole of *Materialism and Empirio-Criticism* was an attempt to substitute a revised and amended doctrine for Engels's dialectical materialism. Lenin's technique should not have misled anybody familiar with his writings. While expounding Marx or Engels in his unmistakable way, Lenin was invariably convinced that his interpretation of their teaching was never anything but a straightforward account of their views, that anyone who took the trouble to become acquainted with the original sources ought to have seen that Lenin merely restored the true

208

doctrines of Marx and Engels in their undistorted form. As John Plamenatz so aptly put it,

> Lenin imagined himself the servant of an infallible doctrine which he alone could interpret; and so could afford to be always modest and yet always right. 'It is not I but Marx' or 'it is not I but Engels who says': these are the unseen beginnings of all his arguments: and their perpetual conclusion: 'and therefore I am right'.[1]

Although Plekhanov accused Lenin of revisionism because his voluntaristic interpretation struck 'at the roots of the philosophical, sociological, and economic doctrines of Marx and Engels',[2] this evaluation has been rejected not only in the Soviet Union, which is understandable, but also by implication in the Western world, where, as a rule, the views of Marx and Engels are interpreted in Leninist terms.

Lenin, then, not only denied any suggestion that he ever revised the general philosophical foundations of the doctrines of either Marx or Engels; indeed, according to his definition of the term, he was not a revisionist. In his view amendments to Marx and Engels constituted revisionism only when they represented a 'trend hostile to Marxism within Marxism', that is, contained implications allegedly unfavourable to the interests of the working class.[3] Although he conceded that he elaborated upon the work of Marx and Engels, to him this was not revisionism. If the social and political situation changed sharply, changes in doctrine were bound to follow in its wake. Moreover, the advance of knowledge brought new facts and new methods of inquiry and they should be utilized for the development of 'Marxism'. Marx's theory was not the last word of science but a living doctrine, and this implied that it was never 'something completed and inviolable'. When pressed hard, Lenin used to say that 'Marxist theory . . . has only laid the cornerstone of the science which socialists must further advance in all directions if they wish to keep pace with life.'[4]

I. EPISTEMOLOGICAL MATERIALISM

Lenin associated the philosophy of Marx with dialectical materialism even more closely than did Plekhanov, and succeeded in establishing their identity with each other as an obligatory tenet of Soviet philosophy. This tenet is still binding today.[5] Lenin also ascribed the introduction of the term 'dialectical materialism' to Marx and Engels, and never had any doubt that the doctrine itself was their common property.[6] He took it for granted that Marx and Engels shared all their views and thus never felt any hesitation in presenting as Marx's opinion what may be ascribed to Engels alone. It has rightly been emphasized that Lenin saw Marx exclusively through Engels's eyes.[7] Consequently, dialectical materialism has become the most fundamental part of what Lenin called the 'philosophy of Marxism', which he conceived as the sum total of the views to be found either in Marx or in Engels.[8]

Lenin accepted the thesis of genetic materialism — nature is primary and spirit secondary — and traced it back to its origin in *Ludwig Feuerbach*.[9] Whereas for Plekhanov genetic materialism expressed the most general meaning which the term 'materialism' could have, for Lenin it became its only philosophically legitimate meaning. This view of Lenin has also prevailed in Soviet philosophy to the present.[10]

Having secured the support of Engels's authority, Lenin reformulated genetic materialism in terms of the ontological priority of nature over spirit, matter over mind, body over consciousness, brain over thought, and nervous system over sensation. He also suggested that historical materialism was a particular statement of genetic materialism, for it asserted the priority of social being over social consciousness or of the development of productive forces over the development of human society.[11] Similarly, if sensation, thought, and consciousness are the product of matter, it follows that physical objects are primary and sensation is secondary, and consciousness or thought, being a function of the brain, is a reflection of the external world. Moreover, if sensation depends on matter which is organized in a definite way and matter does not depend on sensation, the proposition 'Matter is primary' is inferentially equivalent to the proposition 'Matter acting upon our sense-organ produces sensation.'[12] These spurious deductions prepared the ground for elimination of the metaphysical concept of matter and its replacement by the concept of matter defined in purely epistemological terms.

Lenin referred to Engels's absolute materialism — 'the unity of the world consists in its materiality' — as the 'most elementary proposition of materialism' but suggested that 'materiality' means simply the 'objective reality which exists outside us', for 'matter' and 'objective reality' were synonymous expressions.[13]   In other words, Lenin reduced absolute materialism to epistemological realism and, having done so, claimed that Engels never had anything else in mind.   For reasons to be considered later, Lenin asserted that the proposition 'Materialism is the recognition of the external world, that is, of the existence of things outside and independent of our mind'[14] defines the basic position of every materialism.   For the sake of brevity, this proposition will be referred to as epistemological materialism.   Lenin repeatedly advanced it throughout his *Materialism and Empirio-Criticism* and claimed it to be equivalent to genetic materialism.

Epistemological materialism is not, however, Lenin's invention. Lenin himself pointed out that he found it in *The Principles of Human Knowledge* by Berkeley, who presented this ancient doctrine in the version refurbished by Locke.[15]

According to Berkeley, the 'materialist prejudice' consists in the belief in the 'absolute existence of sensible objects in themselves, or without the mind', or simply in 'the existence of external things'.[16] To deny matter is not to deny the things we see and feel.   'Matter, or "material substance", are terms introduced by philosophers; and as used by them, they imply a sort of independency or a subsistence distinct from being perceived by a mind.'[17]   It is this definition of materialism which Lenin accepted as his own, not to refute it, as Berkeley did, but to establish it as the fundamental premiss of all materialism.

It is this sole categorical, this sole unconditional recognition of nature's existence outside the mind and perception of man that distinguishes dialectical materialism from relativist agnosticism and idealism.[18]

The sole 'property' of matter with whose recognition philosophical materialism is bound up is the property of being an objective reality, of existing outside our mind.[19]

The concept of matter . . . epistemologically implies nothing but objective reality existing independently of the human mind and reflected by it.[20]

Lenin returned over and over again to the point that his principle of materialism exceeds the standpoint of phenomenalism, as formulated by John Stuart Mill — that matter is the permanent possibility of sensation — or by Mach, for whom matter is more or less stable complexes of elements.   In contradistinction to these thinkers, Lenin emphasized that materialism discerns and recognizes beyond the phenomena a reality which is independent of the cognizing subject and transcends what is directly given in experience.   Whereas phenomenalism insists that we have no empirical evidence for the existence of permanent things and that the contrary opinion is nothing but ' a piece of gratuitous metaphysics ',[21] Lenin claimed knowledge of constant entities which are distinct from the series of their respective aspects.   On the basis of the theory of knowledge accepted in *Materialism and Empirio-Criticism*, this doctrine of Lenin is indeed untenable and confronts him with a difficulty closely resembling the predicament of Locke.   On the one hand, Locke confessed that he could not explain what matter was and, on the other, he maintained that the existence of this 'something we know not what' had to be recognized as an inescapable necessity of thought.[22]

On the basis of his own premises, Lenin could not substantiate his assertion that matter was the objective reality directly given in experience.   For if the object of perception is something of which we are exclusively aware as causing sensation in us and this, according to Lenin, is the only thing of which we are aware, our knowledge of the objects is relative to us.   Consequently, in the light of his own explanation, Lenin's position would not be distinguishable from phenomenalism.   Only if the perceived object is something more than merely a cause of sensation, only if it displays certain absolute intrinsic properties which are primary in the sense that they do not in themselves depend on the interaction between the object and subject (including his measuring and other observation apparatus), and this Lenin seems firmly to have denied, can we affirm that our knowledge of the objects is not wholly relative to ourselves.[23]   There is not the slightest doubt that Lenin rejected phenomenalism, but what he said about knowledge of external objects is exactly what a phenomenalist would maintain in justification of his point of view.

Lenin seems to have run with the hare and hunted with the hounds, for he endorsed some parts of the phenomenalist argument and at the same time claimed to be in possession of knowledge concerning the existence of material substances which the phenomenalist repudiates.   He did not succeed in refuting phenomenalism but simply confronted it with the blank statement that matter is the immediate and indisputably given reality.[24]   Faced by the choice between the mutually exclusive claims of phenomenalism and realism, he declared himself for the latter, if for sociological rather than logical or epistemological reasons.

Locke recognized the existence of matter, of which we know only 'that it is something', because without this 'support of qualities' there would be nothing in which qualities could inhere. Lenin supported Locke's belief for another reason, closely related to the philosophical developments of his own time. He went beyond phenomenalism because he understood phenomenalism, as represented by Mach or Avenarius, to imply that physical objects are constructions out of sense data, that they are literally composed of 'sensations', and that physical objects are fictitious and only sense data real. There are some passages in Mach which could possibly be interpreted this way, although it is surely incorrect to present Mach's 'theory of elements' as an idealism of some sort.[25] It is even conceivable that Lenin accused Mach of idealism to simplify the issue rather than try to give an accurate account of his views.

Lenin's hostility to phenomenalism was directed against Mach's statement that the concept of matter is redundant and that 'science suffers no loss when a "matter", which is a rigid, sterile, constant unknown Something, is replaced by a constant law '.[26] Mach maintained that his 'doctrine of elements' provided a unified monistic frame of reference which enabled us to get rid of the confusion of the dualism of mind and body and to establish a consistently empirical standpoint for natural science, one that we would not have to abandon when passing from physics to psychology or from psychology back to physics. Mach's basic aim was to make science, physics in particular, epistemologically independent of every metaphysical opinion, including materialism.[27]

Lenin's anti-phenomenalist pronouncement reflected his belief that neither Mach's positivism nor Avenarius's empirio-criticism was a suitable theoretical basis for natural science or, above all, for the performance by science of its important social function. Mach's assertion that materialism was no longer a sound foundation of scientific knowledge was unjustifiable. Lenin rightly observed that the scientists were, as a rule, inclined to adopt materialism — Mach himself complained that especially the physicists and chemists were alarmed by his revision of the traditional concept of matter — although he failed to take due notice of the fact that the 'spontaneous' materialism of the men of science was a working hypothesis rather than a philosophical creed, which is what Lenin was interested in. His concern about the materialistic foundation of science was not, however, stirred by the scientists' inclination towards it. Lenin insisted that materialism alone was compatible with natural science because he felt that the rejection of the traditional materialistic foundations of science was bound to open the door to arbitrary and wild conceptions about man and the universe, which in turn would obstruct and delay social progress toward socialism. But he could not maintain his sociologically conditioned belief in the close connection between science and materialism unless belief in the existence of matter could be made secure from doubt. That matter is primarily given in experience expressed the proposition which seemed to satisfy his quest for certainty.

Lenin sharply denied the charge that the materialist claim to an acquaintance with a reality independent of the cognizing subject necessarily accomplishes an illegitimate passage from the realm of experience to that beyond it. It is not true, he argued, that materialism is of necessity a transcendent view because it recognizes an objective source of our sensations, one independent of man.[28] There is no illegitimate passage from one fundamentally different realm to another, because there is no boundary between the appearance and the thing-in-itself nor between the thing and the image of it. Rejecting the distinction between the *Ding an sich* and its appearance, Lenin adopted the position that we can perceive things as they would be if they remained unknown, that is, as they are in themselves. He wrote that 'for idealism there is no object without a subject, while for materialism the object exists independently of the subject and is reflected more or less adequately in the subject's mind'.[29]

The conviction that we can become acquainted with entities as they are in themselves provided Lenin with his second amplified definition of matter, which states that matter is not only objectively real but also knowable owing to its power of producing sensations.

> Matter is a philosophical category designating the objective reality which is given to man by his sensation, and which is copied, photographed, and reflected by our sensations, while existing independently of them.[30]
>
> Matter is that which, acting upon our sense-organs, produces sensations.[31]
>
> The concept of matter expresses nothing more than the objective reality which is given us in sensation.[32]

Lenin's supplementary definition of matter reminds us of Holbach's definition : 'Matter is that which acts upon our senses (tout ce qui agit sur nos sens est matière)' ; it thus produces perception and ideas and reveals 'some of its properties and qualities according to the way it acts upon us'.[33] But Lenin's second supplementary definition of matter, which endows it with the power of producing sensations seems, like his first definition, to be borrowed from Berkeley rather than Holbach. Philosophers, wrote Berkeley, who believe that objects of perception have a subsistence distinct from being perceived are inclined to think that our ideas must have causes extraneous to ourselves and that they 'are only images or resemblances, imprinted by those objects on the mind'.[34] The theory which Berkeley criticized and rejected as certainly false is Locke's causal and representational theory of perception.[35] Lenin replaced Locke's broad representationism by the copy theory of perception but otherwise adopted Locke's epistemology unchanged. He maintained that objects existing independently of the mind are the cause of sensations and, on their part, sensations are the true copy or image of the objective reality.

Since Berkeley and Lenin considered materialism to be the view that matter exists independently of being perceived or experienced, they reduced materialism to epistemological realism. Lenin sometimes called the causal theory of knowledge and, in particular, the copy theory of perception, the 'materialist theory of knowledge', but more often referred to them simply as materialism.

> If you admit physical objects that are independent of my sensations and that cause sensation only by acting upon my retina . . . you are adopting the standpoint of materialism.[36]
> It is the purest materialism to say that sensations are evoked in us by real objects.[37]
> For the materialist the "factually given" is the outer world, the image of which is our sensations.[38]

Lenin repeatedly argued that to accept the copy theory of perception is to subscribe to materialism (realism), and to adopt the standpoint of materialism (realism) is to endorse the copy theory of perception ; therefore, the two should be recognized as inferentially equivalent theories. It is a general principle of all materialism that consciousness reflects being and that sensations or ideas are copies, pictures, images, or reflections of things.[39] On the other hand, if our sensations and ideas are only an image of the external world, the external world must exist independently of us; for 'the image inevitably and of necessity implies the objective reality of that which it "images"'.[40]

To say that epistemological materialism and the copy theory of perception are inferentially equivalent is an extremely strange assertion. If by epistemological materialism epistemological realism is meant, it is hard to see any compelling ground why realism should logically imply either the theory of representative perception in general or the copy theory of perception in particular. There is even less reason for making such an assertion if epistemological materialism involves the denial of the belief that the world is composed of two kinds of stuff, matter and mind. For materialism is committed to the view that there are no mental images, as the theories of representative perception suppose, which mediate between the cognizing subject and the cognized object. Consequently, materialism seems to favour epistemological monism, viz. the assertion that there are no intermediaries in cognition, that whatever we know we apprehend directly, and that the content or data or perception consist of the same elements of which the external world is composed. Epistemological monism, and not epistemological dualism, seems to imply and to be implied by materialism. Lenin's dualistic theory of knowledge is not only inconsistent with his metaphysical monism but also favours the 'bifurcation of nature', which he refuted elsewhere no less energetically than did Whitehead.

The important point to be noted in Lenin's definition of materialism is his epistemological concept of matter, to be sharply distinguished from Engels's metaphysical conception. Lenin did not ignore the fact that matter exists in time and space, that it is ever changing and in motion in conformity with the laws of nature; occasionally he referred explicitly to these properties of matter.[41] But Lenin did not make any use of these physical characteristics and defined matter in terms of the relation of sensation to its physical cause, of the cognizing subject to the cognized object, of consciousness to the external world. Matter, Lenin argued, is known to us only as that which produces, or is capable of producing, certain impressions of our senses. All that we know about matter for certain is its power to produce these effects.

Lenin's doctrine deserves the name of epistemological materialism because it makes materialism indistinguishable from epistemological realism and its validity dependent upon the copy theory of perception. Without this theory, matter, which is the sole constitutive element of reality, would transcend every possible experience and would be inaccessible to knowledge. As Kant said, we should not understand what the inward nature of matter in this sense is, even if someone were in a position to tell us.[42] But the copy theory of perception itself is not a tenable view. When more closely examined for relevance and consistency, it fails to reach its own objective — to secure the knowledge of the objects of the external world — and turns out to be not only inaccurate but also highly vulnerable to destructive criticism.[43]

2. THE REASONS FOR THE ADOPTION OF EPISTEMOLOGICAL MATERIALISM

Epistemological materialism seems to offer certain immediate advantages. It encouraged Lenin to consider all realists in the theory of knowledge as spontaneous adherents of materialism. Naïve realism, Lenin wrote, whose main premiss states that the external world exists independently of our minds, is the view of 'any healthy person who has not been an inmate of a lunatic asylum or a pupil of the idealist philosophers'.[44] Lenin's paralogism is too apparent to deserve more than passing mention. Being a materialist entails being a realist, but one can be à realist, naïve or critical, without supporting materialism.

The identification of realism with materialism enabled Lenin to accuse Avenarius, Mach, and Pearson of idealism. Since in Lenin's opinion the denial of the existence of matter entailed the denial of the existence of an objective reality, that is, of an external source of our sensations, the phenomenalists had openly or surreptitiously adopted the position of Berkeley.[45] Although Avenarius, Mach, and Pearson only asserted that in the absence of mind there would be no experience, in the sense that nobody would experience anything, they were, according to Lenin, idealists just as much as Berkeley, who believed that in the absence of mind there would be nothing to be experienced. To recognize that knowledge of the external world is relative to the mind implied that the external world is entirely dependent upon the mind. On the other hand, since 'to be a materialist' meant simply 'to recognize the existence of an external

world', materialists, contrary to the view of 'many idealists and all agnostics', were not metaphysicians. For to recognize the existence of an
objective reality outside man is not to transcend the bounds of experience, and to be a metaphysician means to transcend these bounds.[46]

Lenin did not, however, produce his new definition of materialism to exploit the shifting meaning and the changing use of the term
in spurious arguments designed to show that everybody in his right
mind was a materialist. His conception of matter was forced upon
him by the discoveries in physics and by his evaluation of these
developments. The advance of knowledge in physics made it clear
that absolute materialism was no longer a tenable standpoint and,
more generally, that materialist philosophy ran a considerable risk
in associating the concept of matter with any particular physical
theory. Matter in contemporary physics could not be defined in
terms of its ultimate particles (for the hope of discovering the irreducible particles had to be given up), nor could it be conceived
as material substance. A contemporary physicist uses the term
'matter', but to refer to material objects of macroscopic theory and
everyday life. However, there is no analogue of matter as material
substance in the theories of modern physics. 'The term "matter"
in the philosophical sense is not of direct scientific importance and
in purely scientific discussions could be dispensed with.'[47]

Lenin's main line of argument in support of his epistemological
concept of matter was as follows. A substance is supposed to be 'the
support of accidents or qualities without the mind',[48] that which has
attributes and is indestructible and permanent. While the analysis
of matter into molecules and atoms, electrons and protons, systems
of waves or systems of radiation has established the case that matter
is not a substance in the indicated sense, the dissolution of the
substantiality of matter does not abolish materialism. Only metaphysical materialism defines matter in terms of an immutable substance or immutable elements. For dialectical materialism, the
'essence' or 'substance' of a thing expresses only a given stage of
knowledge about this thing. Therefore, the mutability of scientific
knowledge about the structure of matter does not annihilate matter
nor does it refute the reality of the external world. If matter turns
out to be something relative and transient rather than absolute and
permanent, this provides only another corroboration of the truth of
dialectical materialism, which rejects the immutability and recognizes only the external changeableness of all forms of moving matter.[49]

Matter can be defined neither as an immutable substance nor as a set of properties which can be attributed to every material body. For the properties which formerly seemed to be universal and absolute, such as impenetrability, permanence, hardness, inertia, mass, and so forth, are now revealed to be either relative or ascribable only to certain states of matter. It was the discovery that some states of matter do not possess the properties traditionally associated with it that prompted Bertrand Russell to say, 'Matter has become a mere ghost', or Henry Margenau to suggest, 'Matter is no longer material.' [50] At the turn of this century the electromagnetic theory of matter and, more recently, the revolutions in theoretical physics, the relativity and quantum theories, persuaded a considerable number of eminent scientists and philosophers that modern science invalidated the materialism based upon classical physics and supported an idealistic and spiritualistic conception of nature.[51]

Lenin criticized and fought against this philosophical trend with tenacity and much common sense. He accepted the view that 'solid matter fades away' and that the traditional concept of matter becomes untenable, but he rejected the consequence allegedly deducible from these developments, namely, that matter itself turns out to be 'the creation of our mind' and that materialism can thus be dismissed as a self-contradictory doctrine. Lenin's attitude and judgment is methodologically sound. Every statement of physics is, in the final analysis, either a statement about an observation or a statement reducible to observational statements. Physics cannot, therefore, support the belief that 'mind is no longer an accidental intruder into the realm of matter' or that the universe looks 'more like a great thought than like a great machine'. When J. H. Jeans made these pronouncements, he did not make use of the descriptive function of language; he used language in an emotive way. He did not impart cosmological knowledge; he tried to convey his own cosmic mood.

The 'revolution in natural science' only convinced Lenin that the metaphysical concept of matter had become highly vulnerable and had to be abandoned, to be replaced by his own epistemological conception, defence of the 'accepted beliefs of mankind' about the external world (that is, of naïve realism), and identification of these beliefs with materialism. In general, he reasoned, the vulnerability of the metaphysical concept of matter resulted from its close association with certain particular theories of matter. When they became obsolete, and this was bound to happen sooner or later, the definition of matter based upon them became antiquated as well. On the other hand, the notion of matter conceived as a philosophical or epistemological category could never become outdated and thus was clearly superior to the metaphysical conception.[52] Whatever changes were introduced into the theory of matter, they could not affect philosophical materialism, that is, belief in the existence of the external world, which was studied by physics and natural science in general. If matter was a philosophical concept which designated objective reality, the concept of matter was immune to change, and materialism based upon such a concept was secure from destructive epistemological criticism.

3. THE INADEQUACIES OF EPISTEMOLOGICAL MATERIALISM

Unlike Plekhanov, Lenin made of matter a purely epistemological concept, not because of Kant but rather because of the development in physics. He tried to escape the difficulties arising from the 'disappearance of matter' and used against materialism by some of its opponents who were inclined to believe that the new discoveries of science favoured idealism. Lenin felt that the offensive of idealism could not be stopped unless the concept of matter were redefined. This he proceeded to do, although the gain thus obtained was rather illusory and the price he had to pay for it was extremely high. When considered closely, Lenin's definition of matter effaces the difference between materialism, on the one hand, and objective idealism, immaterialism, or phenomenalism, on the other.

His definition, in which the sole 'property' of matter is 'the property of being an objective reality, of existing outside our mind', implies that for Lenin the predicates 'exist' and 'be real' had the same meaning and that 'be material' and 'be real' were coextensive. It should be observed that the proposition 'Nothing exists but matter', equivalent to 'For all x, x exists if and only if x is matter', does not provide any criterion by which we can decide with respect to any particular value of x whether it does or does not exist, unless we know by other means what matter is and can distinguish a material object from a non-material one.

The proposition 'Nothing exists but matter' or 'Matter is all that exists' has no distinctive meaning. First, if matter is all that exists, it would be self-contradictory to specify any characteristic which distinguishes matter from what is not matter, because what is not matter does not, by definition, exist. Second, the proposition 'Nothing exists but matter' can be replaced by any other proposition of the same form and all-embracing significance, of which the proposition 'Nothing exists but mind' may provide an instance; for in these all-inclusive contexts both the concept of matter and that of mind signify the general idea of being and, consequently, denote everything and connote nothing. To put it differently, statements of all-embracing significance are without significance. This was clearly seen by Berkeley, who used it as one of his main arguments against the idea of material substance. If 'material substance' has no other meaning than that of 'being in general', the term 'matter' is used in the same sense as other men use the term 'nothing'.[53]

There is nothing distinctively materialist in Lenin's definition of matter. The best indication of this is the fact that his definition could be accepted by a Hegelian, a Platonist, or an epistemological realist, all of whom are hostile to materialism. For all of them would accept the proposition 'Nothing exists but x' — in which the values of x being coextensive and all-inclusive in their denotation would have no distinctive meaning — as well as the common-sense view of reality for which, by definition, objects exist irrespective of whether or not they are perceived. Neither Plato nor Hegel would ever say that the common-sense view of reality is false, though they would insist that it is inadequate and should not be allowed to dominate philosophical thinking. It is the proper function of philosophy to absorb the common-sense point of view and to show that its propositions, formulated in everyday discourse, cannot be sustained unless they are given quite a different meaning from that which they purport to express.

Lenin's definition of matter makes materialism indistinguishable from mentalism, idealism, or spiritualism. To say that Plato's ideas, Leibniz's monads, and Hegel's Absolute Spirit are not matter in Lenin's sense and that to pretend ignorance of this fact is simply to prevaricate, provides no answer to this objection. It is true that we may have an idea about what Lenin believed to be material, but this would not enable us to decide in each particular case what is and what is not matter. These two problems are quite different. The first requires an attentive reading of everything Lenin wrote, the second a rule by means of which the question whether 'x is real' is true or false can be resolved.

Although Lenin's definition of matter provides us with the directives concerning the use of the terms 'real' and 'material', it gives no indication how to distinguish things which are real or material from those which are not. We cannot argue that in order to gain admission to the world of real or material objects things must be able to exist without being perceived. For this criterion provides only the necessary but not the sufficient conditions for an object's being real or material. Lenin certainly would not regard a thing as a physical object unless it could exist unperceived, but it is impossible to say that nothing but physical objects satisfy this condition. That the ability to exist without being perceived is not a distinctive characteristic of material objects is clear from the fact that Plato would attribute it to ideas, Berkeley to minds, and Hegel to Absolute Spirit.

Lenin frequently said that 'sensation reveals objective truth to man' [54] and implied that if an object is capable of being perceived it satisfies the criterion of being real and material. But contrary to what Lenin assumed, the fact that in specifiable circumstances an object seems to be perceived does not necessarily imply that this object is material or that it exists at all. In advancing this criterion Lenin let himself be influenced by his phenomenalist opponent's belief that statements about physical objects are reducible to statements about sense data or that the perception of an object is a sufficient condition for the existence of the object perceived.

Since Lenin's definition of matter fails to indicate any distinctive characteristic of real or material objects, it also fails to say anything about the conditions under which 'x is real' or 'x is material' becomes a true or false statement. On the strength of what we know from Lenin's definition we are not in a position to decide whether the statements 'This table is real' or 'Centaurs are real' are true or false. The fact that from the truth or falsity of the proposition 'Centaurs are real' we can deduce the truth or the falsity of the proposition 'Centaurs are material', does not provide any help in this predicament, for, in the first place, we are unable to decide whether 'Centaurs are real' is a true or false proposition. Lenin's failure to specify the conditions which determine the truth-value of the sentences obtained from the propositional form 'x is real' or 'x is material' is a serious defect of his theory.

Lenin's supplementary definition of matter, 'Matter is the objective reality given to us in sensation', clearly distinguishes a Hegelian or a Platonist from a materialist. But there is nothing in it that a Berkeleyan idealist or a phenomenalist would not be willing to accept. Neither Berkeley nor Mach is committed to the view that there are no material or physical objects outside us, which are given to us in sensation, though both would account for this differently than would a materialist. For instance, they would say that the existence of a particular physical object is an empirical question which as such can never be conclusively verified. Neither Berkeley nor Mach would deny that the table on which I write and the lamp on the writing desk in front of me exist and that they are given to me in sensation. This objection to Lenin's definition was recognized as valid by some Marxist–Leninists in Poland.[55] They also realized another shortcoming of Lenin's supplementary definition of matter. If we say that matter is the objective reality given to us in sensation, we do not wish to contend that only what is directly given in sensation is material. However, if 'be material' is a predicate that may be used with reference to something that is not directly given in sensation, the epistemological view of materialism becomes indistinguishable from Thomist philosophy or any spiritualistic dualism.

These and similar considerations lead to the conclusion that the independence of the philosophical concept of matter from the physicist's concept of matter, as claimed and demanded by Lenin, cannot be maintained. An unambiguous answer to the question 'What is the objectivity of the external world?' depends on the further question 'What is matter?' in the physical sense of the term 'matter'. This implies, however, that Lenin's distinction between the philosophical and physical concept of matter must be abandoned and matter defined as a metatheoretical concept which signifies the set of properties inherent in all physical objects.

4. THE PRINCIPLE OF PARTISANSHIP AND THE DOGMA OF THE TWO MAIN TRENDS IN PHILOSOPHY

Despite all his protestations to the contrary, Lenin must have been aware of the fact that it is not enough to acknowledge belief in the existence of things outside our mind to endorse the viewpoint of materialism. For this reason he tried to establish a close logical link between epistemological materialism and genetic materialism, and for this reason he gave a new interpretation to Engels's genetic materialism.   Although this new interpretation is Lenin's and not Engels's, Lenin himself believed, or tried to make others believe, that his exposition faithfully reproduced Engels's views, even if expressed differently.

It will be remembered that according to Engels there are two conceptions of the relation of matter to mind.   For the materialist, matter is primary and spirit secondary, and for the idealist the reverse is the case.   Plekhanov had gone a little beyond Engels's original formulation when he conceded that, apart from materialist and idealist monism, a third standpoint is possible, that of dualism, which recognizes spirit and matter as separate and independent substances, both involved as primary factors in the constitution of the universe.[56]

Lenin ignored Plekhanov's extension of Engels's pronouncement. Instead, he transformed and sharpened the distinction of the two possible views on the relation of matter to spirit into the 'fundamental division of philosophical systems into idealism and materialism' or into the assumption of two radically different approaches to any problem of philosophy, from which, ultimately, the thesis of two and only two trends, camps, or alignments in philosophy was to emerge.[57]   If the differences of opinion concerning the problems of epistemology, methodology, and general philosophy are traced to their source, it turns out that all of them have a common origin in the struggle between materialism and idealism.

> Behind the mass of new terminological devices, behind the litter of erudite scholasticism, we invariably discern two principal alignments, two fundamental trends in the solution of philosophical problems.   Whether nature, matter, the physical, the external world be taken as primary, and mind, spirit, sensation (experience — as the widespread terminology of our time has it), the physical, etc., be regarded as secondary — that is the root question which in fact continues to divide the philosophers into two great camps.   The source of thousands upon thousands of mistakes and of the confusion reigning in this sphere is the fact that beneath the envelope of terms, definitions, scholastic devices and verbal artifices, these two fundamental trends are overlooked.[58]

The division of all schools of thought in philosophy was not merely a classification intended to establish a kind of order in the great variety of contemporary philosophical trends but reflected an essential and important trait of the social and historical situation. The antithesis of the two basic and radically different approaches to philosophy corresponded to the division of modern society into two irreconcilably hostile classes, the bourgeoisie and the proletariat, each with elements of its own culture and its own world outlook.[59] Hence, it followed immediately that there was not, and could not be, a middle course between materialism and idealism or between proletarian and bourgeois ideology. For a third ideology would have to be non-class and non-partisan, and there could be no such ideology; in a society divided by class conflicts and antagonism, all doctrines of non-class politics were sheer nonsense. The antithesis of the two basic approaches also implied that the one could not be criticized without strengthening the other; the slightest deviation from materialism harmed materialism and benefited idealism.[60] One did not need to undertake an examination of the innumerable hues of Neo-Kantianism, agnosticism, or positivism in order to declare the entire tendency of these schools of thought a step backward. They doubted, restricted, or denied the knowability of the world, they made concessions to idealism and thus opened the door to fideism, the acceptance of the existence of God, and an immortal soul. 'Idealism in philosophy' was, according to Lenin, 'a defence of a doctrine that places faith above science, or side by side with science, or in some way or another gives faith a place.' Consequently, in this respect there was little difference between Mach and the theologians.[61]

Having indicated that all differences of opinion in philosophy are connected with, or determined by, the adherence to either of the two possible philosophical parties, materialism and idealism, which result from the class division of society, Lenin proceeded to demonstrate that what he was saying had really been established by Marx and Engels. 'All Marx's philosophical utterances', wrote Lenin quoting only two of them, carefully selected for this purpose, 'revolve within these fundamental opposites [that is, idealism and materialism].' Marx excluded any intermediate position and 'moved forward along a sharply defined philosophical road'. For this reason Marx could not be taken piecemeal; he had 'either to be swallowed whole or completely rejected'.[62] The same was to be said of Engels, who constantly contrasted the materialist and idealist line 'in regard to all questions'. The demand for a consistent adherence to materialism is the dominant core in all Engels's philosophical works : 'Either materialism consistent to the end, or the falsehood and confusion of philosophical idealism — such is the formulation of the question given in every paragraph of *Anti-Dühring*.' [63]

According to Lenin, it was Marx and Engels who originated the idea of the two parties in philosophy and who were responsible for the view that adherence to materialism or idealism decided in advance the solution to practically all philosophical problems. It was they, too, who evinced the determination to keep materialism clear of any concession to idealism. Marx and Engels, Lenin wrote, were 'partisan in philosophy from start to finish'.[64] Throughout their entire careers they persistently decried the failure to comprehend the importance and significance of the struggle between the two fundamental epistemological trends. Some thinkers, Lenin commented, boasted of their non-partisanship ; others believed in their silly professorial devices and made 'the stupid claim to have "risen above" materialism and idealism, to have transcended this "obsolete" antithesis'. The fact remains, however, that philosophy was as partisan as political economy. Marx and Engels were the first to realize the impossibility of neutrality on the part of a philosopher, and they bequeathed to their successors the 'great and most precious tradition' of constant concern with the purity of materialism.[65]

5. THE REVISION OF THE LAWS OF DIALECTICS

Lenin revised not only Engels's conception of materialism but also his dialectical doctrine. It has been mentioned earlier that Plekhanov reduced the number of laws of dialectics from three to two by eliminating the law of the triad. Lenin accepted Plekhanov's reduction at the outset of his career. The development by triad 'has no connection whatever with scientific materialism' ; 'the dialectical method does not consist in triads at all' ; 'to prove anything by triads is absurd' ; and the term 'triad' itself was a remnant of the Hegelian vocabulary.[66] In *Anti-Dühring* Engels argued that Marx did not try to demonstrate anything by means of the Hegelian triads, but he also defended the negation of the negation both as an extremely general law of nature and as a fruitful method of inquiry. Lenin rejected this argument completely. He indicated that the main point in Engels's exposition of the place of the triad in Marx's thinking was to emphasize that 'the materialist must correctly and accurately depict the actual historical process', for the sole criterion of the validity of a theory was its conformity to reality. On the other hand, the 'insistence on dialectics, the selection of examples to demonstrate the correctness of the triad is nothing but a relic of the Hegelianism out of which scientific materialism has grown'.[67] Although later in Lenin's life the expression 'negation of the negation' cropped up occasionally under his pen,[68] testifying to Hegel's increasing influence upon his mind, this does not necessarily indicate his rehabilitation of the triad.

Lenin's mature views are recorded in two fragments of *Philosophical Notebooks*, entitled 'Elements of Dialectics' and 'On the Question of Dialectics'.[69] They are strongly infused with what Engels called *abstrakte und abstruse Hegelei* and do not compare favourably with the observations on the dialectical method in *What the 'Friends of the People' Are*, reference to which has just been made. In 'Elements of Dialectics' Lenin listed sixteen subjects or points of view which would have to be considered in a comprehensive study of both subjective or immanent and objective or external dialectics. The list ends with the statement,

> In brief, dialectics can be defined as the doctrine of the unity
> of opposites. This embodies the essence of dialectics, but it
> requires explanation and development.[70]

While the list contains nothing striking or new, the conception of dialectics which emerges from the content and order of Lenin's observations reveals an important shift of emphasis and a further reduction in the number of dialectical laws.

Like Plekhanov before him, Lenin attached most importance to the law of the unity of opposites, which in the fragment 'Elements of Dialectics' is clearly treated as the fundamental law and to which the others are subordinated or reduced. 'This aspect of dialectics', wrote Lenin elsewhere, 'usually receives inadequate attention : the identity of opposites is taken as the sum-total of examples and not as a law of cognition and as a law of the objective world.' Lenin mentioned both Engels and Plekhanov as being responsible for the 'inadequate attention' given to the unity of opposites.[71]

On the other hand, the law of the transformation of quantity into quality to which Engels attached the greatest significance and which Plekhanov retained, together with the doctrine of leaps, as the second law of dialectics, is mentioned by Lenin in the fragment under discussion at the very end of his list. It is presented as a particular case of the process of the transition of everything into its opposite, this process being itself a dynamic aspect of the unity and struggle of opposites. The same applies to the negation of the negation, which also appears close to the end of Lenin's list and, as Plekhanov pointed out, is not an independent principle but follows from the unity of opposites. Consequently, the whole of the objective dialectics is in fact reduced to the unity of opposites. This point is actually made and explicitly stated by Lenin in the closing remark — 'Dialectics can be defined as the doctrine of the unity of opposites' — quoted above. It is the doctrine of contradictions in corporeal form that becomes the foundation of Lenin's dialectical materialism.

Lenin's use of the term 'dialectics' points in the same direction. 'Dialectics in the proper sense', wrote Lenin, summing up in his own words the role of Hegel's immanent and external dialectics, 'is the study of contradiction in the very essence of objects.' [72] The thought that dialectics is the study of 'objective contradictions', 'mutually exclusive' or 'internally contradictory tendencies', of 'the sum and unity of opposites', of the 'unfolding of contradictory strivings' or of 'the struggle of the opposites' is a common theme of *Philosophical Notebooks*.[73] A 'dialectical contradiction', Lenin emphasized elsewhere, 'has nothing to do with a verbal and invented contradiction'; it is not produced by the human mind but comes into being as 'the contradiction of life itself'.[74] While emphasizing the importance of leaps in the process of natural development, Lenin pointed out that it is really the contradiction which generates the leap. 'What distinguishes the dialectical transition from the undialectical transition?' he asked. 'The leap. The contradiction. The interruption of gradualness. The unity (identity) of Being and not-Being.' [75] Similarly, the nodal points signify a 'unity of contradictions, when Being and not-Being, as vanishing moments (aspects), coincide for a moment, in the given moments (aspects) of the movement'.[76]

The law of the unity or identity of opposites is the only dialectical law that is discussed in the fragment 'On the Question of Dialectics'. As formulated there, it is both a 'law of cognition' and a 'law of the objective world'. In the latter capacity the law expresses 'the recognition (discovery) of the contradictory, mutually exclusive, opposite tendencies in all phenomena and processes of nature (including mind and society)'.[77] According to Lenin, its importance is based on the strange doctrine, discovered by Marx and Engels as the core of the Hegelian philosophy,[78] which recognizes in contradiction the ultimate source of change and motion. The unity of opposites, objectively present in all things and phenomena of nature, originates 'the self-movement of everything existing', 'self-movement' being defined as 'independent, spontaneous, internally-necessary movement'.[79] The unity of opposites 'alone furnishes the key to the "leaps", to the "break in continuity", to the "transformation into the opposite", to the destruction of the old and the emergence of the new'.[80] It is, therefore, the source of evolution and progress. Social development has a 'dialectical nature'; it 'proceeds in contradictions and through contradictions'.[81]

As long as things and phenomena are contradictory, we do not need any external impulse to produce change and motion; owing to their internal polar structure, change and motion are generated by things themselves. Consequently, motion, change, and development are an essential property of matter; immutability is not to be found anywhere in nature. The 'inner impulses for development' are 'imparted by the contradiction, the conflict of different forces and tendencies reacting on a given body or inside a given phenomenon or within a given society'. Things are living, mobile, becoming transformed into one another, precisely because the unity of opposites, of contradictory strivings, or of mutually exclusive tendencies is objectively present in them and makes them living, mobile, and undergoing transformation. As a result of the transformation of moving matter from one state to another and of the dialectical transitions, there are no absolute boundaries in nature. The division into opposites is the main source of evolutionary advance, of the passage of matter from a lower to a higher state, and of the emergence of novel features and structures. Change, motion, and development always dominate over rest, changelessness, and permanence, since 'the unity of opposites is . . . temporary, transitory and relative' and 'the struggle of mutually exclusive opposites is absolute'.[82] For all these reasons Lenin supported Plekhanov's view that the idea of evolution 'as formulated by Marx and Engels on the basis of Hegel's philosophy is far more comprehensive and far richer in content than the current idea of evolution' which ignores leaps, catastrophes, and revolutions and thus distorts the actual course of development in nature and society.[83] Engels, Plekhanov, and Lenin combined efforts to produce a theory of evolution in which evolutionary cosmology, emergent evolution, and Hegel's panlogism were merged into a single whole.

6. A COMPARISON OF ENGELS'S AND LENIN'S DIALECTICAL MATERIALISM

It is only to be expected and, in a certain sense, inevitable that the dialectical materialism of Engels and Lenin should differ. They formulated their respective doctrines in response to different needs. Besides, the intellectual climate had greatly changed in the period dividing *Anti-Dühring* and *Materialism and Empirio-Criticism*. What makes one wonder is not that there are differences, but the fact that they have been overlooked or ignored.

Lenin retained the genetic materialism of Engels but rejected his absolute materialism. He adopted this course to distinguish sharply between the philosophical concepts of matter which Engels did not wish to separate. Engels believed that if the concept of matter were to have scientific significance, there must be some entity or entities in physical theory which would be the analogue of matter in his sense of the word. Lenin no longer thought that this was either necessary or advisable. It was 'absolutely unpardonable' to define matter in terms of some characteristics inherent in all material objects or to equate it with some hypothetical entities which make up the universe of discourses of a physical theory. This would establish a close association between the concept of matter and such a theory and render the former dependent on the latter. At the time of radical advance in knowledge, such as the revolution in physics witnessed by Lenin at the beginning of this century, a close connection between the concept of matter and a particular physical theory armed the opponents of materialism with the argument that matter has vanished and that materialism has been refuted by science. Materialism, Lenin maintained, was not committed to any physical theory and did not recognize any property of matter except that of being an objective reality.[84]

Engels was unaware of the danger to materialism arising from the revival of the Kantian critical philosophy, of which he held a poor opinion, and considered objective idealism the main opponent of materialism. Unlike Engels, Lenin no longer needed to defend materialist philosophy against the defunct doctrine of objective idealism. But Lenin was vitally interested in protecting materialism from erosion by epistemological investigations, for he could no longer ignore the threat of Neo-Kantian and phenomenalist theories — of (epistemological) idealism and agnosticism, as he described them — to metaphysics in Kant's meaning of this term and, therefore, also to materialism. The abandonment of absolute materialism was a defensive move on Lenin's part, and the introduction of the philosophical concept of matter divorced from any physical theory was intended to make materialism immune from both the advancement of knowledge and epistemological threat.

While genetic materialism may have been the fundamental principle of materialism in a general philosophical sense, it provided materialist philosophy with no protective shield against the destructive epistemological criticism. The reassertion of epistemological realism was an appropriate answer to the criticism of materialism from the phenomenalist viewpoint, but the defence of realism in the theory of knowledge could not uphold the claims of materialism. To fail to see this, as Lenin did, was to miss the point of the phenomenalist criticism. Lenin was entirely unaware of the fact that the truth of realism does not entail the truth of materialism. The two beliefs are not entirely independent of each other, but they have to be defended on separate grounds. A statement of reasons for the acceptance of epistemological realism need not include the belief that the world is entirely material. On the other hand, a proof of the truth of materialism requires a quite different sort of evidence from that given in support of realism.

The philosophical concept of matter, which was to buttress materialism by reducing its claim, has some serious disadvantages. If the term 'matter' is used to denote everything that exists objectively, independently of being perceived, the concept of matter loses its distinctiveness, for it signifies the idea of being in general. It no longer retains any connections whatsoever with the Aristotelian material substance and becomes the inferred substratum of Locke or *substantia phenomenon* of Kant, 'a mere something' whose 'inward nature' must remain unknown for ever. Lenin's withdrawal from Engels's position may have made of materialism an impregnable fortress, but what this fortress defended was no longer clear. Here again Lenin does not seem to have been aware of the consequences of his own amendment to Engels's doctrine. Having replaced absolute materialism by epistemological materialism, Lenin thought that he could still rely on the theoretical advantages which the former but not the latter was able to provide. Consequently, he made claims which his premisses no longer logically sustained.

On the other hand, however, the philosophical concept of matter forced Lenin to enlarge the range of problems with which materialism, as he understood it, was concerned. Engels had no theory of knowledge, not even a rudimentary one, such as the copy theory of perception, though Lenin maintained that it was to be 'presented with absolute clarity' in Engels's introduction to the English edition of *Socialism: Utopian and Scientific*.[85] If the concept of matter is given a very broad meaning to designate everything that exists objectively or is real, and nothing is real unless it is independent of our mind, the question arises as to how we come to know what we claim to know, namely, objective reality existing outside the human mind. Lenin's answer was a combination of the causal theory of knowledge and the copy theory of perception. He did not realize that the first is a scientific hypothesis, philosophically irrelevant, and that the second is, in principle, unverifiable; it can never be shown to be either true or false.[86]

Lenin's epistemological materialism is hardly an improvement on Engels's absolute materialism. Its ontological implications have no cognitive significance — we can neither perceive nor say what matter in Lenin's sense is — and its epistemological assumptions fail to explain how we can claim the knowledge of objective reality which Lenin did claim to have. Since Lenin denied that knowledge of objective reality was relative to the mind, he put objective reality beyond the reach of the mind.

Some of the differences in Engels's and Lenin's conceptions of dialectics should be accounted for by the intellectually changed circumstances in which they lived and worked. The emphasis given by Engels to the law of the transformation of quantity into quality was due to his struggle against reductive materialism and the mechanistic conception of nature. Engels was anxious to establish the irreducibility of qualities to quantitative changes, the lawlike connection between the qualitative and quantitative definiteness of phenomena, and the emergence of novelty. Since he believed that the law in question secured the achievement of all these objectives, he placed it highest among the laws of dialectics.

Lenin no longer needed to struggle against reductive materialism ; the mechanistic conception of nature was being demolished by physicists and philosophers ; and the doctrine of emergent evolution could do without the law of the transformation of quantity into quality. Lenin hardly ever mentioned Engels's favourite dialectical law and, in fact, reduced it to the law of the unity and struggle of opposites. The same happened to the negation of the negation. Lenin retained the idea that the evolutionary advance preserves or reproduces the stage already passed in the ascent from lower to higher levels of development and incorporated it into the law of the unity of opposites. But the negation of the negation itself is presented as a relic of the past, or, at best, as an implication of the principle concerning the contradictory nature of reality.

Thus Engels's three laws of dialectics were reduced by Lenin to one, and the law of the unity and struggle of opposites assumed a role which it never had with Engels. It would be futile to try to explain this reduction and the importance attached by Lenin to the law of the unity and struggle of opposites by either logical or factual considerations, for none such could be found. Not much ingenuity would be required to carry out the reduction of the dialectical laws in an entirely different way. The reasons for the changes accomplished by Lenin should be sought in their socio-cosmic significance.

It can be said of Engels that he was genuinely interested in natural science and widely read in the scientific literature of his time. He was, however, always ready to recognize that at best he could claim to be no more than a dilettante or semi-initiate in matters concerning astronomy, physics, chemistry, biology, or geology. He qualified this statement by saying that despite his incompetence in matters of fact he was just as entitled as a scientist to voice his own views concerning the general assumptions of natural science, for even the professional natural scientist becomes a semi-initiate when he passes beyond his own specialty.[87]

Engels himself disclosed, however, that the general assumptions of natural science, in which he was interested, were known to him before he started his inquiry. He confessed that he undertook his studies in mathematics and natural science to convince himself in detail of what he was certain in general, namely, that the same dialectical laws of motion to which history and the development of human thought conform govern the world of nature also. The dialectical laws of motion, first discovered by Hegel, were to be stripped of their Hegelian mystic form and formulated in their 'complete simplicity and universality'.[88]   As a result of this plan Engels was engaged for many years in translating contemporary science into the language of Hegelian philosophy, only to confess in the end that this task exceeded the strength of one man.[89]

When Engels undertook this assignment, he was aware of the advantages which Hegel's dialectics could offer to a revolutionary movement.   He emphasized on several occasions that dialectical philosophy, as he understood it, dealt a death blow to the permanency of all products of human thought and action.   For dialectical philosophy nothing is final, absolute, and sacred.   'It reveals the transitory character of everything and in everything; nothing can endure before it except the uninterrupted process of becoming and of passing away, of endless ascendancy from the lower to the higher.' [90] There is also a conservative side to dialectical philosophy; it recognizes that every definite stage of social development is justified for its time and circumstances.   The conservatism of dialectical philosophy is, however, relative;   its revolutionary character, absolute.

To formulate the laws of dialectics in their 'complete simplicity and universality' was, therefore, to establish the revolution, as it were, at the very heart of the cosmos.   While the socio-cosmic character of Engels's generalizations of dialectics cannot be questioned, his interest in natural science exercised a certain moderating influence upon it.

This cannot be said of either Plekhanov or Lenin.   They were not interested in natural science and its general theoretical assumptions for their own sake, but mainly, if not exclusively, for the sake of their alleged implications with respect to the political problems with which Plekhanov and Lenin were faced.   If Plekhanov emphatically affirmed the principle of leap-like qualitative changes in nature, he did so to deduce from it the leap-like qualitative changes in social life and, as it were, to reveal the cosmic necessity of social and political revolutions.   If Lenin placed the law of the unity and struggle of opposites first and subordinated or reduced the two remaining dialectical laws to it, he did this in order to emphasize the cosmic significance of strife.   If 'everything happens through struggle' and progress is accomplished by the division into opposites, which then attain a higher unity by the destruction of old and the emergence of new forms of existence, then social life is necessarily full of contradictions, and the conflict of antagonistic classes is what determines social advance. Therefore, social progress is cosmically preordained and culminates in the inevitable victory of the revolutionary class over its conservative adversary.

It has been mentioned earlier that Engels showed a certain moderation in his generalization of the laws of dialectics into socio-cosmic laws. Engels never made any unconditional claim to truth for his doctrine and clearly rejected the view that any single individual could attain knowledge that is certain and final. Engels's genuinely evolutionary conception of nature — he preferred to refer to it as dialectical — and his theory of the relativity of knowledge are interrelated. If everything is subject to constant change and development, human knowledge must remain limited and provisional at any stage of its realization. Only an endless succession of generations can draw closer and closer to the unconditional and absolute truth.

Lenin never managed to distinguish clearly between Engels's theory of the relativity of knowledge, the thesis of phenomenalism, and the doctrine of the relativity of truth. According to Lenin, knowledge grows and expands without limit, and so there is no final truth. This does not imply that there is an 'impassable boundary between relative and absolute truth'; dialectical materialism affirms that no such boundary exists. Engels, Lenin argued, was a dialectician, and for him 'absolute truth is compounded from relative truths'. Revising Engels's view on the relativity of knowledge, Lenin claimed that human thought is capable of discovering absolute truth, compounded of relative truths, and that 'each step in the development of science adds new grains to the sum of absolute truth'. The dialectics of Marx and Engels recognizes the relativity of all our knowledge, but only in the sense that the limits and approximation to truth at any given time are historically conditioned.[91]

Lenin's socio-cosmic interpretation of the laws of dialectics was reinforced not only by his repudiation of the theory of the relativity of knowledge but also by his instrumentalist conception of philosophy and science. There is a difference between asserting p, because p is a means towards achievement of a certain cherished or valued aim, such as the invention of technical facilities, simplification of calculations, provision of predictions, or assistance in persuading people about the advisability of believing in *p*, and asserting *p*, because *p* is believed to be true. For to be interested in the truth and falsehood of our theories is to consider that the main purpose of science is to discover what actually exists in nature and to what laws nature is subject. Karl Popper called the first of these conceptions the 'instrumentalist' and the second the 'Galilean view of knowledge'. 'The instrumentalist view asserts that theories are nothing but instruments, while the Galilean view is that they are not only instruments but also — and mainly — descriptions of the world, or of certain aspects of the world.' [92] The latter conception of science is inspired by the wish to understand the world and by the belief that efforts to this effect are not in vain; although we discard our theories and replace them by others, this unceasing process of exceeding our intellectual ancestors is impressive evidence to the success of our attempts to gain an understanding of the physical world. On the other hand, the instrumentalist view of knowledge renounces the hope of ever understanding anything and sees in science nothing but an instrument devoid of theoretical or cognitive significance and true only in the sense of being operationally and technologically useful. Lenin's conception of philosophy and science is an instance of the instrumentalist view in Popper's sense. In his case, the instrumentality of science does not lie in its pragmatic significance or in the technological power which it provides but in its usefulness in guiding and influencing human attitudes and conduct.

The procedure which Lenin applied in his redefinition of matter and materialism provides an instance in point. In his endeavour to answer the questions 'What is materialism?' or 'What is matter?' Lenin was not guided by the philosopher's or scientist's interest in truth. His tactics, which he himself stated explicitly, were intended to produce a definition of matter and materialism that would be secure from change and never become dated. Lenin regarded this security as desirable and necessary, if any political and social objectives were to be achieved. He believed that people would not fight effectively for socialism and communism unless they were materialists. They could not become materialists, however, unless adherence to materialism carried a simple, clear, and invariant meaning. Philosophy had only an instrumental value; it was a means for the attainment of some superior aims.

Lenin was a 'practical thinker to the depth of his mind', one who made use of the Marxian mechanics of history to become the maker and not merely a 'midwife of revolution'. Trotsky called him 'the great engineer of history', whose whole life 'not only in politics but also in his theoretical works, in his philosophical speculations . . . was continually possessed by one and the same idea — the goal'. The goal was the seizure of power and the revolutionary conquest of the surface of the earth.[93] Lenin's whole outlook on the world and life was adapted to the requirements of revolution; he acquired knowledge, whether in agricultural economics or philosophy, for conflict and action, and he had no patience with contemplation and no use for knowledge for its own sake. In this respect the contrast between Marx and Lenin is deep and striking. The entire Marx, wrote Trotsky, is contained in the *Communist Manifesto*, in the Preface to *A Contribution to the Critique of Political Economy*, and in *Capital*.

Lenin, on the other hand, expands at once into revolutionary action. His works as a scholar mean only a preparation for action. If he had never published a single book, he would still appear in history what he now is, the leader of the proletarian revolution.[94]

Lenin's instrumentalist view of philosophy finds perhaps the clearest expression in his assertion concerning its partisan character. He boldly announced that there was no politically neutral philosophy and that non-partisanship in philosophy was impossible. In his view, this was no new development, for 'recent philosophy is as partisan as was philosophy two thousand years ago'.[95] To expect that in a society based on class division and domination philosophy may be impartial was, as Lenin put it, silly and naïve.[96] 'In a society torn by class antagonism there can never be a non-class or an above-class ideology.'[97] No thinker could escape the 'struggle of parties in philosophy', a struggle which ultimately and ideologically reflected the conflicts of the class-divided society. There was a close connection between the interests and the relative position of a social class in society, on the one hand, and the philosophical trends which it favoured, on the other. A philosopher could not and should not be free from partisanship, for his very neutrality would provide help and support to one or the other alignment of the class forces.[98] In social conditions which were characterized by class antagonism, objectivism was bound to run the risk of becoming an apology for these conditions. In such circumstances neutrality could not but be hypocritical or mendacious.

Lenin did not attempt to conceal the fact that his dialectical materialism was conceived as a weapon in the class struggle and an instrument for the achievement of victory in it. As he himself confessed, 'materialism includes partisanship, so to speak, and enjoins the direct and open adoption of the standpoint of a definite social group in any assessment of events'.[99] For Lenin knowledge was valueless if it did not assist the oppressed class in its revolutionary action. The highest merit of the Marxian doctrine was that it bound the theory and practice of this struggle for emancipation into one inseparable whole from which the revolutionaries could draw their convictions and which provided them with rules for action.[100]

7. LENIN'S POLITICAL ATHEISM

Lenin's philosophical instrumentalism helps us to understand why he attached such tremendous importance to the law of the unity and struggle of opposites. The law consists of three parts. It states the contradictory nature of all reality; it conceives all development as movement from a unity of contradictory characteristics through the division into contradictories or contraries, revealing themselves as conflict and struggle of mutually exclusive tendencies or as the transition of a thing into its opposite, to another unity of contradictory characteristics on a new and higher level; and, finally, it indicates the nature of the internal motive force of the development of matter. Development, Lenin asserted, is 'a unity of opposites, the division of a unity into mutually exclusive opposites and their reciprocal relations'.[101] All three statements included in the law of unity and struggle of opposites are socio-cosmic generalizations, but it is the last one that deserves some additional comment because of its instrumentalist significance.

According to Engels, the mechanistic conception of nature posed a false dilemma: either we are able to provide an explanation of the origin of motion and of the diversity of its forms by natural causes or we have to recognize that the universe has a creator. This dilemma can arise only if motion is reduced to change of place brought about by mechanical force. For should this be the case, then we are unable to dispense with an impulse from outside, that is, with God, unless we can explain how matter passed from an original state of equilibrium into a subsequent state of motion.

Engels himself believed that all difficulties disappear if we accept the proposition 'Motion is the mode of existence of matter.' If matter without motion is just as inconceivable as motion without matter, motion is as uncreatable and indestructible as matter itself. As has been explained earlier, this argument is not flawless. While in classical physics motion entails the existence of matter, a motionless state of matter is not inconceivable. Moreover, in the proposition 'Motion is the mode of existence of matter' the term 'motion' refers to all kinds of change. To say that motion is the mode of existence of matter is, therefore, to ascribe to matter the power of creation and thus account for the diversity of its forms as well as for the emergence of novelty. This is the principle of emergent evolution. The assertion that matter is capable of creating novelty and of producing higher and higher forms of organization has been part and parcel of dialectical materialism ever since it was first formulated by Engels. But to combine materialism with the doctrine of emergence is one thing; to say that matter is creative of novelty because a motionless state of matter is inconceivable is something quite different. While the former is a bold metaphysical assumption, arising from the belief in cosmic purpose, the latter is an invalid argument, based on an equivocation and a false assumption.

For Engels, the question concerning the existence of God was subordinated to the problem of the relation of spirit to nature or of mind to matter. The God of whom Engels spoke was the Demiurge of Plato, the clockmaker of Fontenelle, or the engineer of Newton. If materialism succeeded in showing that the world was in no need of a ruler and creator, a cosmic atheism would thus be established.

Engels spoke of the God of the philosophers, defined in terms of a set of cosmological propositions, and not the God of whom we learn from the Old and New Testament, the source of all existence, in vital relationship with his creation, and the object of worship, love, fear, and prayer. Engels would not attach much importance to the views and sentiments of such thinkers as Étienne Gilson who said, 'The fact that there is no Demiurge does not prove that there is no God.'[102] Engels endorsed Feuerbach's theory of religion which contended that religion is the projection of man's hopes and fears. The belief in God is the result of man's misery, weakness, dependence, and servitude to the elemental powers of nature and to the blind forces of society. A man who did not live in fear and oppression would have no need of God. 'All religion is nothing but the fantastic reflection in men's minds of those external forces which control their daily life, a reflection in which the terrestrial forces assume the form of super-natural forces.' [103]   Man was not created in the image of God but man created God in his own image by ascribing to God the highest attributes of the human species.   He thus inverted the true relation between man and God and transferred the attainment of the highest human potentialities from this to another world.   If man divests himself of his supreme attributes and identifies God with his essence, religion impoverishes him and strips him of his strength; he must feel empty and insignificant in comparison with the God whom he created and upon whom be bestowed everything.   To put it in Feuerbach's own words, 'To enrich God, man must become poor; that God may be all, man must be nothing.' [104]   The experience of something transcending the self and all the objects of experience can be explained without resorting to the hypothesis that there is actually a transcending object which is the cause of that experience.

For Lenin, unlike Engels, the question 'Was the world created by God or does it exist from eternity?' assumed a greater significance and a sharper form than the question as to whether nature precedes spirit or spirit nature.   As Lenin saw it, the answer to the first question determined the answer to the second, and not the other way round.   This may have been due to Lenin's dominating concern with practical, social, and political problems and to his inclination to see the universe in sociomorphic terms.   When the universe is viewed from the standpoint of society, the value of a metaphysical or theological proposition for human life and conduct becomes the decisive reason for its acceptance or rejection.   For Lenin, a meta-physical or theological proposition was important and significant if it made the desired social and political change possible.

Lenin recognized that dialectical materialism fully accepts 'the historical tradition of eighteenth-century materialism in France and of Feuerbach . . . in Germany, a materialism which is absolutely atheistic and positively hostile to all religion'.[105]   But having made this statement Lenin concentrated practically all his efforts on the thesis, prominent in Marx rather than in Engels, that in modern societies the basis of religion is primarily social.   'The deepest root of religion today is the socially downtrodden condition of the work-ing masses and their apparently complete helplessness in face of the blind forces of capitalism.' [106]   Referring to Feuerbach's philosophy of religion, Lenin wrote that 'the yoke of religion is merely a product and reflection of the economic yoke within society'.[107]   He clearly agreed with Feuerbach that God comes from 'the feeling of a want; what man is in need of . . . that is God'.[108] Religion was the ideology of helplessness and resignation which encouraged men to accept their fate.   As Marx put it, religion is an expression of misery in actual life, 'the sigh of the oppressed creature, the sentiment of a heartless world, and the soul of the soulless conditions'.[109]   Contrary to what is often said, Marx did not find in religion as such the *fons et origo malorum*;   rather he regarded religion as an expression and effect of deep-lying social evils and set out to destroy not so much religion as its source and cause.[110]

Lenin agreed not only with Marx's diagnosis but also with his remedy, deduced from Feuerbach's theory of religion.   Feuerbach's assertion that man created God in the act of imagining that God had created man, paves the way for man's emancipation from the spiritual burden of his own creation, because it discloses the fact that man's image of the highest being is man himself.   This theoretical insight gives rise to the categorical imperative to overthrow the social conditions in which man is not the highest being but a humbled, oppressed, and despised creature.   The belief in God is incompatible with political and social action which aims at the betterment of human life on earth.[111]

Lenin's atheism is social or political atheism rather than cosmological, derived from theoretical considerations.   He inherited the belief that as long as social and economic oppression is not done away with, religion dominates the minds of men and constitutes, in the hands of the exploiters, the first and foremost moral means of keeping the masses in subjection.   Religion distorts the view of the social conditions of existence, for it makes people oblivious or tolerant of social misery and injustice and persuades them to regard this evil as unavoidable, a dispensation of Providence whose wisdom should not be questioned nor its ways be mended.   The 'witchery of religion', of which Marx spoke, refers to these implications of the religious view of life and of the preoccupation with the supernatural order.

In Lenin's mind, religion was closely associated with societies founded on individual property and the exploitation of wage labour; it is economic slavery that is the true source of religion.   Therefore, in order to fight effectively the roots of modern religion one has to fight the rule of capital.[112]   'Impotence of the exploited classes in their struggle against the exploiters just as inevitably gives rise to the belief in a better life after death as impotence of the savage in his battle with nature gives rise to the belief in gods.' [113] But those burdened by want, those who work for the profit of others, do not find in religion a genuine spiritual succour and consolation. Lenin rejected the view that religion could ever contribute in any way to the well-being of men. The idea of God did not arouse social sentiments ; it lulled and blunted them, substituting a concern for the dead for an interest in the living and making people indifferent to the fate of their fellow men. 'The idea of God has never "linked the individual with society". It has always tied the oppressed classes hand and foot with faith in the divinity of the oppressors.' [114] In a society so organized that a small minority enjoys wealth and power, while the masses suffer privation, it is natural for the exploiters to sympathize with a religion that teaches the people to bear hell on earth for the sake of everlasting salvation in an alleged celestial paradise. Religions and churches and all religious organizations are only instruments of the bourgeoisie that serve to 'defend exploitation and to befuddle the working class'. [115]

Lenin endorsed the view of Paul Lafargue, Marx's son-in-law, that if it is natural for the capitalist to believe in a Providence, because it raises him to the position of wealth and opulent indolence, it is equally natural for the proletarian to consider himself as his own providence. The modern industrial class-conscious worker, wrote Lenin, leaves heaven to the priests and bourgeois bigots and, generally, casts aside all religious prejudices. 'The proletariat of today takes the side of socialism, which enlists science in the battle against the fog of religion, and frees the workers from their belief in life after death by welding them together to fight in the present for a better life on earth.' [116]

Thus, it is clear that according to Lenin one cannot truly believe in communism if one believes in the existence of God, and one cannot fight for socialism on earth if one obeys the divine laws. The two beliefs are mutually exclusive. Each of them lays a total, all-embracing claim upon man and to hold one necessitates the repudiation of the other. Therefore, every attempt to justify the idea of God, 'even the most refined and well intentioned', is, according to Lenin, 'a justification of reaction', [117] and every concession to idealism, which is a disguised form of fideism and opens the door to the belief in God, is an unpardonable philosophical sin. [118] For

Lenin, the conclusive demonstration that God did not exist took on a significance which it had never had either for Marx or for Engels.[119]

8. THE DIALECTICAL JUSTIFICATION OF COSMOLOGICAL ATHEISM

But how can the superfluity of God be conclusively demonstrated? Since the external forces dominating men's minds and lives, which are reflected in religious beliefs, may be either the forces of nature or social forces, the critique of religion can take two main forms, be either a cosmological or a political and social atheism. The two forms of atheism need not be closely associated with each other, and this was the case with Marx and Engels. Whereas Marx's atheism was social and political rather than cosmological, Engels's atheism was cosmological rather than social and political.

While the advance of natural science abolishes the cosmic basis of the belief in God, it does not do away with the social basis. Marx, Engels, and Lenin were in full agreement that mere knowledge of the social sources of religion was not enough to abolish religion. The belief in God cannot be destroyed by the provisions of the constitution, the suppressive measures of the state, by decrees and prohibitions; it must die a natural death. God will die in the minds of men when they are released from the bondage of economic conditions which they themselves have created. When people are no longer dominated by the means of production and the corresponding social relations as by an alien force, the conditions favourable to an inverted reflection of this force in religious beliefs will vanish too, for then there will no longer be anything left to reflect and invert.[120]

Consistent materialism and the critique of the cosmological sources of the idea of God provide, therefore, the main instruments for arousing people from their religious torpor. But it was inadvisable to accept, without any change, Engels's proof of the redundancy of God. Engels derived cosmological atheism from a theory of the universe and such a theory can establish only contingent truths. It is also exposed to the danger of being refuted or becoming obsolete. Lenin was fully aware of this peril and in order to avoid precisely this kind of risk he replaced absolute materialism by epistemological materialism.

Engels's procedure had to be improved upon and simplified. It is not the uncreatability and indestructibility of matter but the uncreatability and indestructibility of motion that prompts people to accept the existence of God. It was Aristotle who accomplished the conjunction of the idea of God with the notion of the prime mover and the supreme cause of the world. If whatever is in motion must be put in motion by something else ('omne quod movetur ab alio movetur', as the schoolmen rendered the Peripatetic premiss in Latin) — and this causal regress cannot go on *in infinitum*, because there would be no prime mover and, consequently, nothing would be moved — it is necessary to arrive at a prime, unmoved mover which Aristotle understood to be God. It was the identification of an external source of a spontaneous motion in the universe with God that was supposed to explain the first impulse given to matter as well as its subsequent motion.

Aristotle's natural theology exercised a powerful influence on Thomas Aquinas and, through him, on Christian theism. Aquinas gave five demonstrations for the existence of God but he regarded the proof *ex motu* as the clearest one and he preferred it to the others.[121] The Aristotelian view of the connection between cosmology and theology was later restated by Descartes to whom it seemed manifest that God himself created matter along with motion and rest and that he continued to preserve the quantity of motion which he originally imparted to the universe.[122] Locke, whose philosophy deeply affected the development of materialism, was as emphatic as Descartes about the relationship between matter, motion, and God. 'Matter . . . by its own strength cannot produce in itself so much as motion : the motion it has must also be from eternity, or else produced and added to matter by some other being more powerful than matter.'[123] In spite of Kant's penetrating analysis of the proofs of the existence of God, the Aristotelian argument *ex motu* has frequently been reproduced, in one form or another, and its distant echo can still be heard today.[124]

Aristotle's identification of the prime mover and God admitted, however, another interpretation. 'When theology assumes the existence of God who imparts movement to and remains distinct from nature', wrote Holbach, 'it only personifies the principle of mobility inherent in matter.'[125] In other words, it is the inability of science to explain the origins of motion that gives theology the chance to claim the existence of God. Conversely, as a contemporary physicist and philosopher puts it, 'if nature were self-moving, God would be supernumerary'.[126] A cosmological system which includes the principle of self-creativeness is independent of any first cause or prime mover.

In Lenin's opinion, Engels did not refute conclusively the possibility of motion being imparted to matter by an external source, that is, by God. Thus, the door leading to the acceptance of a divine principle present in the world was still left open. Engels showed only that matter and motion were in fact inseparable, that the state of rest was relative, and that motion was absolute and without exception. However, on the basis of his argument it was impossible to establish the conclusion that there was a necessary relation between matter and motion and that material objects could not be motionless because this was incompatible with the essence and laws of matter. In other words, Engels failed to provide a satisfactory solution to the problem of the origin of motion because he failed to discover its necessary ground, a self-explanatory principle which affords a sufficient reason for the existence and preservation of motion. With Hegel's help, Lenin proceeded to accomplish what Engels had left undone. He could have said in defence of his procedure that since we have a unique universe to describe,[127] the classical inductive approach to cosmology was ruled out. Every cosmological problem admits one and only one solution ; therefore, the 'logical' Hegelian method was the only suitable one.

Lenin believed that the law of the unity and struggle of opposites enabled him to attain the end which Engels had not achieved. The inherent contradictoriness of all things and phenomena is the source of all self-movement of matter and constantly generates its internal motive force and creative power. This results in evolutionary advance and in the emergence of more and more perfect forms of organized matter. The law of the unity and struggle of opposites provides conclusive demonstration that a creator and ruler of the universe, who stands outside and above nature, is superfluous. If nature is self-moving and everything in the world has an activity of its own, which takes place from within, in conformity to the law of the unity and struggle of opposites, there is no longer any need for the supernatural source of motion. Dialectical materialism establishes conclusively the proof of atheism ; the world can do without God.[128]

When we raise the question as to the existence of God we are not asking a scientific question, to which a scientific answer can be found. Holbach fully realized and exploited this fact in his polemics against natural theology. He argued that God is not an object of empirical knowledge. Therefore, we cannot have an idea of God, 'Dieu est incompréhensible'.[129]   It is indeed extremely difficult, if not altogether impossible, to make comprehensible in words something that in principle is not accessible to observation. When Lenin substituted for the question 'Does God exist?' another, 'What is the origin of motion?', which in his opinion was equivalent to the former, he was convinced that he was formulating a meaningful question and raising a scientific problem, one capable of scientific solution. Lenin was inclined to adopt this position because of the view which he held about the nature and task of scientific knowledge and which is known as methodological essentialism.[130]

Today, it is widely accepted that the aim of science is to provide a description of natural phenomena as complete and simple as possible. But an essentialist sees his task differently. He believes that science and philosophy should penetrate to the essential nature of things and reveal their hidden reality. For an essentialist, science does not consist in providing descriptions but in giving ultimate explanations. An explanation is ultimate if by its very nature it cannot be further explained and is in no need of any further explanation. Descartes's definition of matter — matter is in its essence extension — and of mind — mind is in its essence thinking substance — are essentialist definitions intended to provide ultimate explanations of any events in which either matter or mind are involved.

The term 'essentialism' fits Lenin's approach like a glove. To explain capitalism is to discover its essence, that is, the laws of its development which reveal the necessity of the disappearance of capitalism and its replacement by socialism.[131]   To answer the question 'What is motion?' is to provide the true definition of motion i.e., to give the essential characteristics of the *definiendum* from which other characteristics necessarily follow. When Lenin affirmed that the law of unity of opposites explains the origin of motion he did not mean an explanation which would consist in showing by logical inference and empirical test how the known laws operate to produce a given occurrence, but an ultimate explanation which discloses the 'true' and 'inner' essence of motion. Lenin clearly believed that hidden essences of things are accessible to human knowledge and that the 'essential nature' of motion can be discovered.

The proposition that the 'true' and 'inner' essence of motion is the unity and struggle of opposites is open to the objection that it regards natural phenomena anthropomorphically. To derive the natural phenomena of change and motion from contradiction, that is, from a logical relation, is to misrepresent each of them and to conceive their relationship in terms applicable to neither. How can an internal contradiction be an 'actual force' and a cause of motion? Contradiction is a logical relation, motion a physical process. Causal relationships and logical relations apply to objects of a different sort. If an object can be either cause or effect, it cannot be a term of a logical relation. While a proposition may contradict or entail another proposition, propositions cannot either make or fail to make something happen. An idealist like Hegel could reduce physical and causal relationships to logical categories. A materialist who considers material objects as primary and concepts as a product of man's activity, derived from the experience of material objects, is barred from following in Hegel's footsteps. The thesis that contradictions objectively present in things and phenomena are the origin of motion is inconsistent with the basic premiss of material-ism, 'Nothing but matter exists.'

Lenin spoke of the internal contradictions in the phenomena of nature as the source of their 'spontaneous' change and as that characteristic of matter which makes self-generation of motion comprehensible. He pursued this objective in order to establish a view of the universe that would do without a supernatural force or source of creative energy, one that would reveal nothing of the existence and operation of God in nature, and leave no room for natural theology. Irrespective of whether we do or do not sym-pathize with Lenin's endeavour, it should be recognized that Lenin's solution of the problem lacks adequate and scientifically satisfactory justification. A cause which is a cause of itself is a theological and metaphysical concept, comparable, as has been mentioned earlier, with Aristotle's prime mover and ultimate cause, or with God who is 'the cause of Himself'. The methods of empirical science, and of physics in particular, are not suited to the search for any ultimate and final cause such as Lenin was searching for. A physicist always has to stop somewhere in his search for causes, but he assumes the validity of unending series of causal relationships; therefore, he never accepts anything as being a cause of itself or a self-causing energy. Irrespective of whether Lenin's concept of self-generated internal motion of matter does or does not lead to certain socially desirable consequences, the concept itself lacks scientific credentials, is incompatible with the methodology of natural science and with the assumptions of naturalism and materialism.

In his search for the origin and essence of motion Lenin made use of some familiar theological conceptions, and ascribed to matter some attributes similar to those which religious thinkers have associated with the Spirit and theologians with the transcendent God. Nicolas Berdyaev said of Lenin, and Soviet philosophers in general, that they turned materialism towards 'a peculiar sort of idealism and spiritualism' and bestowed upon matter divine attributes.[132]   N. O. Lossky, himself a metaphysical and religious philosopher, spoke in the same vein.   He wrote that Lenin endowed the primary reality so richly with qualities and faculties that he no longer had any right to call it matter without doing violence to logic and traditional philosophical terminology.[133]   It is hard to disagree with this opinion. As Lenin conceived it, matter is endowed with the power of a spontaneous internal motion, capable of producing a reflection of itself, creative of novelty and purposeful in its accomplishments.   The spontaneous internal motion of matter, both a blind force and a purposeful agent, results from internal and corporeal contradictions. These contradictory characteristics and conflicting tendencies struggle with each other and give rise not only to change but also to an inevitable progress.   In conformity to its intrinsic laws, this self-moving nature produces higher and higher realms of being, each of which is subject to specific laws irreducible to the laws of the lower level of advance.   Evolution is creative: its immanent impetus is apparent in the constant ascent of the stages of development.   In general, the blind forces of nature operate with the Spencerian benevolent necessity and are productive of ever higher degrees of perfection.

Like the Stoics, and also perhaps like Spinoza, Lenin wished to be a thoroughgoing materialist, but he attributed to matter some of the characteristics of a deity.   The Stoics and Spinoza called their spiritualized universe *Deus sive Natura*, either God or Nature.   Lenin called it 'matter'.   While trying to show that nature had no need of a creator, he was driven by the logic of his speculative premises to a conclusion which identified the creator with his creation and made 'matter' substitutable for 'God'.   Without knowing it and certainly without wishing it, Lenin came close to the position whose intellectual foundations are to be found in Samuel Alexander and which is known as naturalistic theism.

Naturalistic theism shares the belief in cosmic purposes, although the purpose is realized by a kind of blind impulsion rather than by a kind of creative force. For Alexander, deity is a quality of existence beyond mind, related to mind in a way similar to that in which mind is related to life or life to matter. Deity has no distinctive characteristics but is that to which the world strives or tends ; it is not a creator of the universe, but is itself created by the entire evolutionary process. If Alexander's deity is understood to mean the emergence of higher and higher integrative levels, rising in complexity and organization, and in virtue of which the world is continually growing richer in content and more perfect in value, there is no sharp line dividing Alexander's deity and Lenin's matter.[134]

VIII

Stalin's Socio-Cosmic Conception
of the Universe

MANY academic philosophers would be loath to concede that Stalin deserves a place in the annals of contemporary philosophy. Historians of philosophical thought and, in particular, students of dialectical materialism, have no such doubts or inhibitions.[1] As a rule, they consider dialectical materialism as an indivisible whole, a single doctrine which was established by Marx and Engels and which continued to develop with their successors, particularly Lenin and Stalin. Those students of dialectical materialism who recognize a legitimate succession in the philosophical leadership of the 'Marxist' school of thought feel, of course, no hesitation in regarding Stalin as an outstanding representative of the philosophy of 'Marxism' or Marxism–Leninism, a philosopher in his own right.

Stalin's title rights to the name of philosopher are based on two publications, *Dialectical and Historical Materialism* (1938) and *Marxism and Problems of Linguistics* (1950). Those who support the conception of the doctrinal community and indivisibility of the 'philosophy of Marxism' frequently regard *Dialectical and Historical Materialism* as the most authoritative statement of this philosophy. Although they recognize that Stalin's essay is not an original work, they describe it as an intelligent summary of Lenin's views on the subject, notable for the conciseness and clarity of exposition, its common-sense language, free from confusing Hegelian terminology. Some competent Western philosophers go even further and believe that *Dialectical and Historical Materialism* provides a reliable source of information about the Marxian conception of philosophy, 'Marxist naturalism' or Marxist dialectics.[2]

One need not share these views to recognize Stalin's importance in the evolution of dialectical materialism in general and Soviet philosophy in particular. Stalin's philosophical contributions cannot be dismissed because he carried some of Lenin's interpretations of dialectical materialism to their logical conclusions. Furthermore, they cannot be ignored because of the influence which Stalin exercised on the content, manner, and development of Soviet philosophy since the late twenties, that is, for nearly thirty years. Finally, Stalin cannot be disregarded because of the social importance of his philosophical doctrine. The social importance of a philosophy should be assessed by the number of people who adhere to it and by the type of activity, the habit of thought and valuation which it originates and supports. It has rightly been observed that 'from this point of view the philosophy of dialectical materialism is easily one of the most important doctrines of our times'.[3] Although Engels was its founder, dialectical materialism owes the distinction of being a socially influential philosophy to Stalin.

It hardly needs mentioning that in the Soviet Union Stalin enjoyed the reputation of a philosophical genius as long as he was alive ; this assessment does not seem to have been radically revised after his death in 1953 and his political demotion in 1956. The appearance of *Dialectical and Historical Materialism* was hailed as an epoch-making development in Marxist–Leninist philosophy. In Stalin's lifetime Soviet and other Marxist–Leninist philosophers never ceased to shower the highest praise upon his essay, which, as it was usually put at that time, 'raised dialectical materialism to a new and higher level'. To justify its 'world-historical significance', M. B. Mitin, Stalin's court philosopher, suggested that in this essay Stalin provided a comprehensive and systematic account of the materialist dialectics which Marx had planned but never succeeded in writing, and which Engels and Lenin had failed to bring to completion in *Dialectics of Nature* and *Philosophical Notebooks* respectively.[4]

When the 'cult of personality' was denounced in 1956, Stalin lost the status of one of the 'classics of Marxism–Leninism' but *Dialectical and Historical Materialism* has continued to stand in high repute. *The Foundations of Marxist Philosophy* (*Osnovy marksistkoj filosofii*), first published in 1958, stated emphatically that *Dialectical and Historical Materialism* as well as other more specifically philosophical contributions of Stalin are a 'valuable enrichment of Marxism'. The same Soviet textbook described Stalin as an 'outstanding Marxist' who after Lenin's death continued to develop the 'philosophy of Marxism'.[5]

Whereas the importance of *Dialectical and Historical Materialism* for Soviet philosophy cannot be denied, its publication marked the moment when dialectical materialism lost even the semblance of being a philosophical school of thought. 'Dialectical materialism', wrote Stalin in the opening sentence of his essay, 'is the world outlook of the Marxist–Leninist Party.' A world outlook, explains *The Short Philosophical Dictionary* edited by Rozental' and Yudin, is a system of beliefs, concepts, and ideas concerning the world as a whole.[6] A world outlook, Rozental' and Yudin continue, has not only a theoretical and cognitive significance, but also an enormous practical importance. As it expresses the views concerning the world as a whole, it determines the relation of people to their environment and to each other, serves as a guide to action, provides the direction to their activities supporting the advance of society, and thus speeds up its progress.[7] Stalin's announcement that dialectical materialism is the world outlook of the Marxist–Leninist Party indicated that in his interpretation a cosmological and metaphysical inquiry has directly been used to justify the political programme and Party tactics in the reconstruction of society towards Communism. While Marx tried to show that the laws of social development make the fall of the bourgeoisie and the victory of the proletariat equally inevitable, Stalin set out to prove that these events are indeed inevitable because the laws of social development are derivable from and determined by the evolutionary laws of the universe. Stalin turned into a philosopher to give the Party a cosmic pat on the back.

During Stalin's lifetime his own version of dialectical materialism was often referred to as 'Marxism–Leninism–Stalinism'. This cumbersome expression was supposed to indicate that Stalin claimed the authority of both Marx and Lenin for his views which he regarded as a new contribution to 'Marxism'. Stalin said of Lenin that he expanded the doctrines of Marx and Engels and applied them to the new conditions of the struggle of the proletariat; consequently, Leninism could not be either contrasted to or separated from 'Marxism'.[8] Similarly, Stalinism neither abolished any old nor added any new propositions to the teaching of Marx and Engels, but continued faithfully in their tradition and developed it still further on the basis of the principles laid down by them. As a matter of fact, Stalin had more in common with Lenin than with either Marx or Engels whom he often quoted but rarely followed.

If Lenin saw Marx through the eyes of Engels, Stalin saw both Marx and Engels through the eyes of Lenin. The fundamental though implicit assumption of *Dialectical and Historical Materialism* that the main use of philosophy and the principal task of the philosopher is to serve the political needs of the Party comes clearly from Lenin and not from Marx and Engels. It constituted the extreme conclusion drawn from the Leninist principle that in a class-divided society and in an ideologically divided world every ideology, and ideology always includes a philosophy, expresses definite class interests. Consequently, knowledge has no intrinsic value but only an extrinsic and instrumental use as a means of social control over man's behaviour and as the leverage of far-reaching social changes brought about by the change in human beliefs about the world and social environment.

The socially and ideologically instrumental value of knowledge is not an invention of Lenin or Stalin; a philosopher of science will recognize that knowledge has an extrinsic value of which advantage has been taken, more or less consciously and for most varied purposes, at all times and places. The peculiar characteristic of Lenin's and Stalin's position is their emphasis upon the social and ideological instrumentalism of knowledge with the exclusion of its other values and, in particular, of its cognitive function, upon which both the practical and the non-practical extrinsic functions of knowledge ultimately depend. In this respect Lenin and Stalin differ not only from many philosophers outside the Soviet Union but also from Marx and Engels.

I. PHILOSOPHICAL MATERIALISM

The expression 'Marxist philosophical materialism' seems to be a term peculiar to Stalin and to Soviet philosophy in the Stalinist period.[9] It was used occasionally by Lenin to refer to what he also called the 'materialist theory of knowledge', that is, the peculiar combination of epistemological materialism, the causal theory of knowledge, and the copy theory of perception, or to any one of these doctrines separately.[10] By distinguishing philosophical materialism from dialectical materialism Lenin wished to have a term which would enable him to speak of the materiality of the phenomena of nature with the explicit exclusion of their dialectical character.[11]

Thus, dialectical materialism is a more specific conception than philosophical materialism or, as *The Short Philosophical Dictionary* puts it, philosophical materialism is a component part of dialectical materialism. The expression 'philosophical' qualified 'materialism' to underline the fact that the assumptions of materialism were formulated in terms of the philosophical instead of the scientific concept of matter and expressed propositions more certain and fundamental than those which science could ever provide. While Lenin used the term 'philosophical materialism' only rarely and defined its meaning implicitly rather than explicitly, Stalin made frequent use of it and gave it the status of a *terminus technicus*.

Stalin listed three principal features of Marxist philosophical materialism. First, philosophical materialism maintains that 'the world is by its very nature material', that is, 'the multifold phenomena of the world constitute different forms of matter in motion', and that the world develops in accordance with the laws of motion inherent in matter itself.[12] Second, philosophical materialism holds that matter is an objective reality existing outside and independent of the cognizing subject and that matter is 'the source of sensations, ideas, consciousness'. Matter is primary and consciousness is secondary, and the latter is a reflection of the former. Third, philosophical materialism asserts that there are no unknowable things in the world, but only those which are still unknown and which 'the efforts of science and practice' will make known.[13]

The three fundamental principles of philosophical materialism in Stalin's exposition are a peculiar arrangement of various beliefs and views all of which can be found either in Engels or in Lenin. The purpose of this arrangement, by no means always consistent, is not clear at first sight.

Stalin's first principal feature of philosophical materialism combines Engels's assumption of the material unity of the world, that is of materialist monism, with his absolute materialism. The thesis of materialist monism states that matter is the only reality and its development stands in no need of any outside principle, such as mind, consciousness or spirit, to account for the diversity of its forms. The monistic view that there is but one fundamental reality, matter, is reinforced by the assumption that nothing but different forms of matter in motion are real.

Engels's principles are metaphysical principles in the traditional meaning of this term ; they make assertions about being as such and these assertions clearly transcend the limitations of ordinary and scientific knowledge. The metaphysical beliefs which Stalin does not try to substantiate — they are supposed to be rigorously derived generalizations of the findings of science, and consequently, their validation remains the responsibility of science and not of philosophy — are supported by the cosmological principle of universal lawfulness. This principle states that all phenomena are determined in accordance with objective laws.

Stalin implied that the cosmological postulate of universal orderliness and conformity to law is incompatible with the existence of God. In *Philosophical Notebooks* Lenin quoted Heraclitus' views about the world being created neither by any god nor by any man. The world, Heraclitus was reported to have said, 'was, is and will be eternally living fire, regularly becoming ignited and regularly becoming extinguished'. Lenin commented on Heraclitus' statement that it was 'a very good exposition of the principles of dialectical materialism', and Stalin quoted Lenin with approval.[14] The universe does not need a creator and ruler if it is a self-contained unity in which eternally moving matter changes in conformity to laws.

Stalin justified his theological principle, there is no God, by another reference to Engels. Engels argued that there is no place for 'an extramundane creator' once the view is accepted that 'the material, sensuously perceptible world to which we ourselves belong is the only reality'.[15] Engels's assertion remains valid irrespective of whether it is given a materialistic or naturalistic interpretation. If only objects given directly or indirectly in sense experience exist and are real, and God is not such an object by definition, the existence of God cannot be asserted. This is the view to be found in the young Marx, who drew precisely this conclusion from his anthropological materialism. Once man as a natural being and nature as a reality shaped by man are recognized in his life experience, the search for an alien being, outside man and nature, becomes impossible in practice. Consequently, atheism as a denial of this unreality, is also no longer meaningful. One does not deny what cannot be affirmed.[16]

No unambiguous statement can be found in Stalin to answer the question as to whether he did or did not regard matter as material substance. In *Materialism and Empirio-Criticism* Lenin repeatedly warned his adherents that the recognition of eternally moving and changing matter should not be confused with the belief in the existence of the immutable material substratum of things which belief is incompatible with dialectical materialism. Therefore, it is fairly certain that Stalin followed in Lenin's footsteps and did not deviate from this established tenet of dialectical materialism.[17]

Stalin's second principal feature of philosophical materialism combines into a single whole Lenin's epistemological materialism — matter is an objective reality existing outside and independent of our consciousness, and Engels's genetic materialism — matter is primary and consciousness or mind is its product and reflection. It should be remembered that Lenin had joined them together, failing to distinguish materialism from realism and considering the two conceptions as inferentially equivalent. However, from the belief in the existence of an objective reality independent of the cognizing subject we cannot draw the inference that consciousness and mind emerge from matter. It is exactly this fallacious inference that is incorporated by Stalin, as a matter of course, into his second principal feature of philosophical materialism. He clearly took it for granted that epistemological realism involves genetic materialism and merged the metaphysical or cosmological thesis concerning the primacy of matter over consciousness with the ontological and epistemological assumption concerning the priority of the objects of knowledge in relation to the knowing subject.[18]

Stalin asserted that the premisses (*a*) the brain is 'matter which in its development has reached a high degree of perfection' and (*b*) the brain is the organ of thought, entail the conclusion that thought is a product of matter.[19] Stalin's description of the relationship between matter, brain, and thought has been criticized not only as an instance of confused reasoning but also as a belief shared by dialectical materialism with 'classical materialism' in general and the vulgar materialism of the nineteenth century in particular.[20] This criticism does not appear to be valid.

What Stalin did was to repeat unhesitatingly Lenin's polemical assertion, 'the brain is the organ of thought, and thought is a function of the brain', directed against Avenarius who had refuted exactly these views as misleading or false.[21] Unlike Avenarius, Lenin was not interested in the fact that the propositions 'The brain is the organ of thought' and 'Thought is a product of the brain' express relations which cannot be established by sense experience, observation, and experiment. For Lenin these statements were clearly true, because they were inferences from the true assumptions of genetic materialism. Moreover, the attribution to matter of a power productive of novelty, common to all versions of dialectical materialism, or the supposition that thought and sensation are associated with the higher forms of organic matter from which they emerged,[22] is not a thesis of vulgar materialism. Lenin did not wish to endorse the reductive fallacy of mechanistic materialism, of which, like Engels, he was no supporter, but to accomplish what he called 'the materialist elimination of the "dualism of spirit and body"'. Although Lenin and Stalin treated the subject inadequately and expressed themselves clumsily and misleadingly, the objection that they embraced vulgar materialism cannot be sustained.

Stalin closed the list of the principal features of philosophical materialism with a declaration of unbounded optimism to the effect that there were no epistemological or ontological limits to the progress of scientific knowledge. Stalin dealt with the question of the reach of science in a manner reminiscent of the philosophical disputes in the nineteenth century and unrelated to the present-day problems of the limits of knowledge. Neither in content nor formulation does Stalin's declaration differ from Engels's or Lenin's similar professions of confidence. According to Stalin, three assertions should be distinguished in the theory of knowledge of philosophical materialism, (a) 'the world and its laws are fully knowable', (b) 'the knowledge of the laws of nature . . . is authentic knowledge having the validity of objective truth', (c) 'there are no things in the world which are unknowable, but only things which are still unknown'.[23]

Although Stalin quoted Engels's 'telling refutation' of the Kantian epistemology in support of his statements, he clearly followed Lenin's rather than Engels's lead. For Lenin the unrestricted knowability of the world was a direct consequence of genetic materialism as well as of the universality of the laws of dialectics, applying equally to the external world and human thought. If reason and consciousness are products of the human brain and man himself is a product of nature, the knowledge of nature produced by the brain cannot but faithfully reflect nature. This train of reasoning is repeatedly stated and restated by Lenin in the third chapter of *Materialism and Empirio-Criticism* and succinctly summed up in *Philosophical Notebooks*, in the assertion that 'knowledge is the reflection of nature by man'.[24] For Lenin it was self-contradictory to recognize the truth of his epistemological materialism and to reject the belief in the full knowability of the world.

The question can and should be asked, however, why Stalin introduced the materialist theory of knowledge among the principal features of philosophical materialism, which is a cosmological or metaphysical doctrine. The answer seems to be that Stalin was as much inclined as Lenin to consider the copy theory of perception the only theory of knowledge compatible with materialism. To hold that matter is the objective reality existing outside our mind and to believe that our sensations are the true copy of this objective reality was, for Lenin, 'one and the same thing'.[25] Lenin accepted this equivalence in defence of materialism against epistemological criticism; Stalin adhered to Lenin's assumption on account of its alleged social and political implications.

That only the copy theory of perception is compatible with materialism is an extremely doubtful view. Even on the supposition that genetic materialism is true, it does not follow that the internal world of sensations merely reflects the external world of material objects in a passive manner without adding anything to what is given. If the epistemological dualism of the theory of representative perception, of which the copy theory is a particular case, ultimately implies psychophysical dualism, a materialist could not hold the copy theory of perception without contradiction. Furthermore, monistic materialism certainly does not imply that perception, memory, and other cognitive experiences are mirror-like images of the entities in the external world. A materialist can only gain by adherence to the view that we know material objects directly, that is, that the data of perception consist of the same realities of which the perceived objects are composed. Lenin failed to analyse all these issues. He did not succeed in providing a convincing argument in favour of the close connection between materialism and his theory of knowledge, and arbitrarily decided in advance what cannot thus be resolved.

There is no justification for the belief that materialism is factually or logically bound up with the Lockean conception which maintains that knowledge is a mere reflection resulting from the action of the environment upon the cognizing subject and engraved upon the mind which is a *tabula rasa*; there is only a historical fusion of materialism and Locke's theory of knowledge. Neither is there any reason to accept Lenin's opinion that sensation is regarded by all

science 'as an image of the external world' ; that this naïve realistic
theory of knowledge is widely, if not universally, endorsed by
scientists ; and that it has been unconsciously and instinctively taken
over from them by all sane humanity.[26]   Contrary to what Lenin
tried to show and what Stalin repeated for reasons of his own, there
is not one and only one standpoint of materialism in the theory
of knowledge.   Materialism is also compatible with a conception of
cognition which regards knowledge as the result of a process of
interaction between the subject and his natural and social environment.   Within a materialist ontology the anthropological realism
of Marx, formulated in *Economic and Philosophic Manuscripts of 1844*,
The German Ideology, and *The Theses on Feuerbach*, provides an alternative solution to this problem.

Stalin endorsed Lenin's view about the equivalence of epistemological materialism and the copy theory of perception because it
allegedly implied the existence of objective social and political truth.
He argued that if the world is fully knowable, society is fully knowable too and the study of social life becomes a science.   Therefore,
practical policies can be conclusively established as the application
of, or deductions from, the laws of the development of society.[27]
The materialist theory of knowledge makes of the Party programme,
as it were, a demonstrable faith, countenanced by the orderliness
and lawfulness of the universe.   The existence of objective social
and political truth seems in turn to support a hierarchical, techno-
cratic, and authoritarian power structure in society.

There is another reason why Stalin regarded Lenin's theory of
knowledge as one of the principal features of philosophical materialism.   In *Materialism and Empirio-Criticism* Lenin emphasized over
and over again that if knowledge does not depict objective reality,
but is a form of specifically human experience, determined both by
the external world and the cognizing subject, man becomes free to
create for himself concepts of all kinds and, in particular, the idea
of God.   'Once you deny objective reality, given us in sensation,'
warned Lenin, 'you have already lost one of your weapons against
fideism.'   On the other hand, if the world is fully knowable and
knowledge is a faithful, copy-like reflection of reality, 'beyond the
external world, with which everyone is familiar, there can be nothing'.[28]   Lenin was sure that the refutation of fideism was socially
desirable and imperative, for the exposure of religious illusions
revolutionizes thought, changes the ways of viewing the world and

the value-orientation of people, and makes them anxious to work for socialism.

Stalin, like Lenin, needed a philosophy which would induce and promote the social attitudes supposed to be favourable to the construction of socialism.   He adopted Lenin's theory of knowledge and made it one of the foundation stones of orthodoxy, since he had implicit faith in its alleged social and political implications and its instrumental value in establishing control over all fields of thought.

2. DIALECTICAL METHOD

According to the Stalinist schoolmen, the Marxist dialectical method is the second component part of dialectical materialism. In *Dialectical and Historical Materialism* Stalin dealt first with the nature of dialectics and only later proceeded to explain the nature of materialism.   This order of inquiry has puzzled some students of Soviet Marxism, for it is clearly illogical.[29] We must first know what matter is before we can discover its principal features or establish the best method for the investigation of its properties.   Stalin offered no justification of his procedure, which during his lifetime was obligatory for all, and no satisfactory explanation has been provided by anybody else either.   Since his death, the earlier and more rational arrangement — the   account   of   materialism   precedes   that   of dialectics — seems to prevail in Soviet philosophy.

It should be emphasized that for Stalin the Marxist dialectical method was a general theory of reality first and foremost and a method only by implication.   In this sense, Stalin sharply revised the views of Engels, Plekhanov, and Lenin, for whom the dialectical method has been what the term itself indicated, a method first and foremost and an ontology only by implication.   It is true, of course, that for Engels, Plekhanov, and Lenin dialectics was also a *Realdialektik* in Hegel's terminology, an immanent force inherent in all things and phenomena of nature and society; the existence and properties of this force, however, were established by inference from the alleged successful application of the dialectical rules of procedure in the investigation of nature and society.

Stalin also sharpened the distinction between the dialectical and metaphysical mode of thought and transformed them into two rival theories of reality, opposed to each other as much by their respective ontological assumptions as by their incompatible social functions. The second revision of dialectics, for which Stalin was responsible, had widespread and far-reaching implications.

Engels closely associated dialectics with a monistic and dynamic conception of nature, which was prepared by the advance of scientific knowledge in the eighteenth and nineteenth centuries, but which was due, in his opinion, above all, to Hegel. He contrasted this new conception of nature, based on what he called the 'dialectical mode of thought', with the old mechanistic conception that made use of what he referred to as the 'metaphysical mode of thought'. The latter investigated nature as the totality of things isolated from each other, also as 'fixed, rigid, given once for all', that is, unchanging and immutable. The former examined the totality of natural objects as a vast fundamentally indivisible system, all of whose parts are connected with and reciprocally act upon each other. They are all engulfed in a swiftly flowing stream of change and subjected to an irresistible process of evolution, which transforms the world as a whole and every part of it without interruption. As Engels put it, the view that the natural, historical, and intellectual world moves and transforms itself endlessly in a constant process of becoming and passing away requires a philosophy and science striving each in its particular domain for the discovery of the laws of this process of transformation.[30]

While Engels described the distinction between dialectics and metaphysics in terms of two historically different conceptions of the universe and differentiated them by what he called 'mode of thought', 'method of work', or 'habit of observing natural objects', Stalin translated the historical and methodological differences into substantive ones, expressive of the basic social conflict dividing humanity everywhere and at all times. Both dialectics and metaphysics became a general theory of reality and were conceived as mutually exclusive by their content and implications. While dialectics held that all events were interconnected and dynamic, subject to laws and progressive evolution, metaphysics rejected these assertions. According to metaphysics, events were isolated from each other and static, and nature knew neither lawfulness nor development unless it was a repetition of what had already occurred. It should be noted that dialectics and metaphysics in Stalin's sense were absolute doctrines; the concepts of which they made use admitted no difference of degree. Changeability was to be either ubiquitous or not to apply at all; everything was to be either inter-related with or completely isolated from everything else; all events were to conform to laws or be merely a matter of chance; development was to be either all-pervasive or utterly apparent. Thus, what dialectics asserted metaphysics denied, and there was nothing to mediate between their respective positions, set in every respect at opposite poles. Moreover, metaphysics and dialectics were no longer two cosmological conceptions of nature, which emerged successively in the advance of knowledge, but were considered as opposed to each other, as a Soviet textbook put it, in 'the course of the whole development of science and philosophy'. 'The history of philosophy is also the history of dialectics, the history of the struggle of dialectics with metaphysics.' [31]

Engels's distinction between dialectics and metaphysics as the two successive cosmological conceptions and modes of thought turned, in Stalin's hands, into two distinctive *Weltanschauungen*, each existentially or socially determined. What underlies Stalin's interpretation is the belief that thought is not independent, neither in its origin nor validity, of the situation peculiar to the social group in the midst of which it originates, but is bound by this situation as well as by the objectives, necessities, and other requirements of collective action. A certain point of view is adopted because it grows out of a definite social reality and favours the attainment of definite group or class purposes. Stalin asserted that the metaphysical and the dialectical *Weltanschauungen* have their respective social basis in the bourgeoisie and the proletariat and are closely associated with the political and social interests of these two classes. It is no accident, for instance, that proletarian thinkers regard the universe in terms of a system in which everything is connected with everything else in conformity to laws, and that bourgeois thinkers see nature as an agglomeration of isolated things subject only to chance. The connection between the social position of the thinker and his *Weltanschauung* follows inevitably from the determinants inherent in his situation. Moreover, a theory, a point of view, or an idea are expressions of the social and economic interests of their bearers; they are either useful or harmful to the social classes in the realization of their collective objectives and, more generally, either facilitate or hamper the progress of society.[32] Thus dialectics is essentially unacceptable in the capitalist countries, in which the ruling class considers capitalism, naturally a transient state of affairs, as a permanent order of the world, and sees in change and development its own destruction. The bourgeoisie is bound to repudiate the view that everything in the universe is in flux, and to embrace the belief that permanence and immutability are fundamental determinations of all natural phenomena.[33]

Stalin's third revision of dialectics consisted in the incorporation of some characteristics of the dialectical mode of thought into dialectics conceived as a general theory of reality. He thus introduced two new laws of dialectics which may be called the 'law of universal connections' and the 'law of universal mutability'.[34] As cosmological propositions they attribute some important characteristics to reality. Contrary to Engels, Stalin maintained that the two new laws of dialectics are not the common intellectual property of the contemporary view of nature but are recognized only by dialectical materialists and ignored or explicitly rejected by everybody else.

> Contrary to metaphysics, dialectics does not regard nature as an accidental agglomeration of things, of phenomena, unconnected with, isolated from, and independent of, each other, but as a connected and integral whole, in which things, phenomena are organically connected with, dependent on, and determined by, each other.[35]
> Contrary to metaphysics, dialectics holds that nature is not a state of rest and immobility, stagnation and immutability, but a state of continuous movement and change, of continuous renewal and development, where something is always arising and developing, and something always disintegrating and dying away.[36]

Stalin's fourth revision of dialectics concerns the number of dialectical laws. Stalin introduced two new laws and reduced Engels's three original laws to two by eliminating the law of the triad or of the negation of the negation. In Stalin's version dialectical materialism includes four dialectical laws as compared with three in Engels, and two or possibly one in Plekhanov and Lenin respectively.

Neither Plekhanov nor Lenin favoured the law of the negation of the negation and both were inclined to drop it as redundant or as a survival from the past, incompatible with scientific materialism. Stalin's rejection of the law of the triad was absolute and unconditional; he ignored it entirely and never even mentioned it. Stalin's sense of realism provided no protection against excessive philosophical simplifications but occasionally saved him from falling victim to fanciful and unrestrained speculations. The post-. Stalinist philosophy in the Soviet Union has restored the law of the negation of the negation to the original prominence given to it by Engels, for it conveys, according to *The Foundations of Marxist Philosophy*, the most general idea concerning the nature of development and progress.[37]

Of Engels's three laws of dialectics Stalin retained two, namely, the transformation of quantity into quality, including the doctrine of leaps, and the unity of opposites. In the arrangement of these two laws he followed Engels's, not Lenin's order of priority. This is not without socio-cosmic significance.[38] In Stalin's presentation, the laws of dialectics differ in their number and content from anything to be found in his predecessors. None of them had as many laws as Stalin and none formulated them as lucidly and punctiliously. The order in which he arranged his dialectical laws is peculiar to himself and reflects his didactic and political purpose.

Both of Stalin's dialectical laws proper are conceived as laws of evolution. While the law of the transformation of quantity into quality is to explain how the process of change gives rise to 'an onward and upward movement', the law of the unity of opposites is intended to account for the origin of change and motion.[39] Apart from an emphatic reassertion of the view that nature and life in all their manifestations are the product of development, the dialectical evolutionism of Stalin reveals a curious affinity to the Bergsonian criticism of modern science and contrasts the metaphysical or mechanistic concept of evolutionary change with the concept of dialectical or creative evolution.

The distinction between mechanistic and creative evolution [40] goes back to Engels and Plekhanov. Engels argued tirelessly that evolution based on the principle 'causa aequat effectum' cannot account for numerically or quantitatively new objects and for the process of growth, in which growth is nothing but the unfolding of ever-present potentialities. This conception of evolution was attributed by Engels to mechanistic philosophy which regarded everything as given once and for all and which was concerned solely with repetition, with change without novelty, and with a universe without history. Engels rejected this view of evolution and embraced a theory of change that was no longer compatible with the old maxim of causality.[41]

In Engels's doctrine of causality the principle 'causa aequat effectum' no longer holds. His doctrine of evolution allows for the emergence of entities endowed with entirely new properties and conforming to an entire set of new laws, that is, for what we would describe as the emergence of a new level of being. Thus, in Engels the law of the transformation of quantity into quality represented the groping for a law of evolutionary cosmology. It was also Engels's assumption, taken over from Hegel, that the transition from an old qualitative state to a new qualitative state and the emergence of novelty was accomplished by a 'leap' or 'jump', by a break of causal chains which enables the vital impetus of the creative force to proliferate into new forms and species. The doctrine of leaps was further elaborated and put into relief by Plekhanov, but for the benefit of revolutionary activities rather than for the purpose of explaining the passage from the inorganic to the organic world or of accounting for the mutations exhibited by living matter.

Like his predecessors, Stalin clearly rejected the thesis of the equivalence between cause and effect and adopted the law of the transformation of quantity into quality as a law of cosmological evolution, qualitative leaps being the *modus operandi* of the emergence of qualitatively richer entities and higher levels of being. Stalin regarded the process of development as the 'transition from an old qualitative state to a new qualitative state', as the 'development from the simple to the complex, from the lower to the higher', as an 'onward and upward movement'.[42] Development of this sort involves change with novelty, the emergence of a higher level of being, and what Stalin called a 'leap to a new state'. The examples of the creative development given by Stalin — 'the transition from the insentient world to the sentient world, from the kingdom of inorganic matter to the kingdom of organic life'[43] — make it clear that what he meant was the doctrine of emergent evolution.

The doctrine of emergent evolution in Engels, Lenin, and Stalin is a scheme of things which is much more determined by ideological considerations than may appear at first sight. The mechanistic conception of change with its explicit or implicit denial of the emergence of novelty could not explain the question as to the origin of the apparent diversity of natural things and left open the possibility of a supernatural source, whether Spirit or God. The maxim that there can be nothing in the effect that has not been in the cause is entirely compatible with the assumption that the cause is either higher than, or equal to, the effect. In both cases it is possible to argue that the variety of natural things requires a creator. As has been pointed out earlier, the doctrine of emergent evolution was supposed to show that a positive philosophy of nature could do without natural theology.

The doctrine of emergent evolution also enabled its supporters to justify the necessity or inevitability of social upheavals and political revolutions as preordained by the universal laws of nature. Stalin was as emphatic on this point as Plekhanov and Lenin had been. Since the passage from 'imperceptible quantitative changes to open, fundamental changes' does not occur gradually but 'rapidly and abruptly, taking the form of a leap from one state to another', the revolutionary overthrow of the old relations of production and the establishment of new productive relations is a natural and inevitable phenomenon of social progress. Progress cannot be checked, for evolution and revolution prepare the ground for each other and follow relentlessly upon each other. 'Evolution prepares for revolution and creates the ground for it; revolution consummates the process of evolution and facilitates its further activity.' [44]

However, the same socio-cosmic considerations which prompted Stalin to assume the doctrine of emergent evolution and the universality of the emergence of novelty by an abrupt leap persuaded him later to revise this view. In *Marxism and the Problem of Linguistics* Stalin put certain limitations on the doctrine of leaps as applied to social phenomena. Let us call a society in which classes have incompatible interests an 'antagonistic class society', and that in which classes have different but no longer mutually exclusive interests a 'non-antagonistic class society'. According to the revised doctrine of leaps, the 'law of transition from an old quality to a new by means of an explosion' still holds good in an antagonistic class society. In a non-antagonistic class society, however, the development of some social phenomena, whether they belong to the superstructure or should be included in the basis, does not necessarily occur by an abrupt leap. Furthermore, according to the new interpretation, some ideologically neutral elements of the superstructure, such as language and technology, are never subject to the law of development by leaps and develop gradually, without any breach of continuity. As Stalin put it, under the conditions characteristic for a non-antagonistic class society, social development may be accomplished by the gradual accumulation of the new and by the gradual disappearance of the old quality.[45] In a non-antagonistic class society social and economic development

> proceeds not by way of upheavals, but by way of gradual changes, the old not simply being abolished out of hand, but changing its nature in adaptation to the new, and retaining only its form ; while the new does not simply destroy the old, but infiltrates into it, changes its nature and its functions, without smashing its form, but utilizing it for the development of the new.[46]

Stalin's pronouncement on how the operation of the law of transformation from an old quality into a new might take on a gradual form is of no theoretical interest.[47] The true purpose of the revision is apparent. If the original doctrine of leaps were universally valid and revolution rather than evolution remained the vehicle of progressive change, Soviet society could not be spared the breach of continuity and the upheavals in its social and political advance. But Stalin no longer wished to instigate change ; he was anxious, above all, to preserve the Soviet social and political order and to protect it from change and destruction. The revision of the doctrine of leaps is significant psychologically and politically, but not theoretically, and again confirms the view that Stalin's dialectical materialism had its roots in his political outlook.

That 'internal contradictions are inherent in all things and phenomena of nature' is a principle which Stalin announced with much firmness and authority. On the other hand, his examples of internal contradictions clearly indicate that he gave the term 'contradiction' a non-technical meaning. Stalin's internal contradictions are not of a logical nature ; they are meant to refer to the polar structure in the composition of natural objects or to the absence of homogeneity. Thus, Stalin argued that internal contradictions are inherent in all things and phenomena of nature for they exhibit 'the interaction of opposed forces' and 'all have their negative and positive side, a past and a future, something dying away and something developing'.[48] Similarly, Stalin spoke of the contradictions between labour and capital, between the ruling and the colonial nations, between the financial groups in the capitalist countries and between the imperialist Powers in their struggle for the sources of raw materials.[49] Merely because correlative terms can be applied simultaneously to a material object does not imply that an internal contradiction has been disclosed in it. An object may not be homogeneous in some respect, be composed of mutually opposed parts, reveal a polar structure or opposite tendencies, and thus be subject to an inner stress. The inner stress does not involve logical contradiction and the description of the polar structure inherent in 'things and phenomena of nature' does not require the abandonment of the principle of non-contradiction.

Stalin needed the polar struggle and inner stress present in all natural objects to transform the Heraclitean and Hegelian metaphor of the struggle of opposites into a cosmological principle. He followed faithfully in Lenin's footsteps and maintained that the struggle of opposites explains the origin of motion and thus makes it possible to dispense with the Aristotelian axiom 'Whatever moves is moved by something else.' The inner stress is assumed to produce conditions in which change occurs spontaneously, that is, from within a given object and, consequently, an external efficient causation may be replaced by an intrinsic efficient causation. Things have an internal source of change and motion, an activity of their own, inherent in them. Change, motion, and development are instances of the self-movement of matter and of self-moving nature. They result from a 'disclosure of the contradictions inherent in things and phenomena' or from a '"struggle" of opposite tendencies' which operate on the basis of these contradictions and which constitute the 'internal content' of evolutionary and progressive advance.[50]

Stalin's pronouncements on the spontaneity of change and development are scraps of the doctrine of Engels and Lenin who opposed 'mechanistic causality' and laid stress on the inner, spontaneous, and self-sustaining activity of things. In the case of Engels and Lenin their return to the ideas of the Greek hylozoist philosophers concerning the self-movement of matter and the self-sufficiency of nature was prompted by their opposition to mechanistic materialism and by their concern with the claims of theology. Stalin's language and ideas on change and development are reminiscent of all these speculations but his true purpose seems to be more pedestrian and closer to the realities of political life. For Stalin, the socio-cosmic principle of the struggle of opposites was indispensable, since it entailed the inevitability of the class struggle and the inevitability of the class struggle made the policy of class domination an inexorable necessity.[51] Generally speaking, Stalin showed no interest in the laws of dialectics, which he presented as cosmological laws of the highest generality, unless their significance and specific function in the social and political sphere were directly and plainly visible.

3. STALIN AS PHILOSOPHER

Philosophy in the Socratic sense is a way of life which is characterized by devotion to truth and love of wisdom. Philosophy in a more pedestrian sense means submission to an intellectual discipline, the acceptance of logical rules and factual evidence which enables others to ask questions, raise objections, and carry further on the investigations of the subject of inquiry. A man who does not comply with these requirements is clearly not a philosopher.

That it is hardly possible to treat Stalin as a genuine philosopher according to either of these definitions is a widely accepted view outside the Soviet Union. Try as one may, it is impossible to discover in the dialectical materialism of Stalin either the originality and profundity of thought with which he is credited in the U.S.S.R., or intellectual acumen and professional competence.[52] His doctrine is an eclectic composition which freely borrows ideas, definitions, and even whole formulations from Engels and, above all, from Lenin. The fallacies taken over from his predecessors remain undisclosed and their ideas are further simplified in order to serve the requirements of social and political life. 'Marxism had, in fact, shortened the distance between politics, philosophy, and literature,' wrote Stalin's biographer. 'Stalin crudely oversimplified the Marxist view of their interconnexion, until he degraded science, history and art to the point where they became handmaidens of his politics.' [53]

Stalin's gift of lucid exposition did not save him from obvious errors and palpable absurdities, due to his unfamiliarity with the problems which he examined. Stalin had only a second-hand, sketchy knowledge both of the philosophy of Hegel and that of Feuerbach, but he did not hesitate to write on the relations between the philosophy of Hegel, Feuerbach, and Marx. He tinkered with the intricate problems of the psychology and philosophy of language and with those of the theory of knowledge in which he was not at home. He had difficulties in differentiating between the intension and extension of a term and between a word and its referent and, consequently, was inclined to consider language as a system of symbols with the power of creating, altering, or destroying the world of real objects.[54]   He discussed materialism and idealism at length without realizing the variety of meanings in which these terms are used and in which he himself actually used them.   He held firm opinions as to how history and sociology should be studied, but was a complete stranger to both.   His entire intellectual baggage was the knowledge of Lenin and of Marx and Engels in Lenin's interpretation.   Under these circumstances it is no wonder that he espoused an inconsistent system of crude metaphysics and was responsible for many primitive fallacies.

Stalin was unaware of the fact that scientific statements are something more than mere general affirmations and that the pursuit of generalities was bound to lead him to vague and illusory conclusions. Having little understanding of the philosophical problems involved, Stalin relied on mere assertions or oracular pronouncements rather than on analysis and argument.   If these assertions and pronouncements happen to be true, it is only by accident, for there is no proof of their correctness.   Since they have not been established on a sound scientific basis, they are at best plausible guesses.   Stalin did not intend to persuade others about the truth of his beliefs.   He was satisfied to state them dogmatically and to have them believed on his authority.   He simply taught what everybody ought to hold to be true.

Dialectical and Historical Materialism provides no evidence that Stalin was genuinely interested in materialist philosophy for its own sake.   What he was clearly anxious to achieve was to establish the belief that historical materialism was an inference rigorously derived from philosophical materialism and that it entailed a number of consequences all of which supported the policies of the Soviet state.   It was from this point of view that he dealt with the question of what the principal features of philosophical materialism were and what particular content should be given to the doctrine of historical materialism.   Stalin was anxious to show above all that far from being arbitrary his policies were formed in accordance with the laws of the universe and supported, as it were, by cosmic decrees.

The extreme simplification of dialectical materialism in Stalin's exposition was due to the priority given to practical and political implications over theoretical considerations.   Since dialectical materialism was the cornerstone and the foundation of the world outlook of a political mass movement, Stalin reduced it to a handful of simple beliefs which in his opinion could be understood by everybody and be used to derive rules of action and effective policies in social and political affairs. Stalin's simplifying and selective approach to the materialist tradition was also prompted by his determination to secure strict control over all manifestations of intellectual life, including natural science and philosophy, as well as over the behaviour of the people at large. He aspired towards intellectual leadership of scientists, scholars, philosophers, men of art and letters, and at the same time was anxious to replace the old philosophy — philosophy that was an exclusive preserve of a small *élite* and intellectual aristocracy — by the new one, no longer 'detached from life and alien to the people'. Zhdanov told the philosophers in 1947 that the establishment of the Party's command on the philosophical front was to arm the people with the 'consciousness of the correctness of our path and with scientifically grounded confidence in the ultimate victory of our cause'.[55]

The requirements of total control over the minds of scientists, scholars, and philosophers were reflected in various doctrinal changes but their impact is perhaps most apparent in Stalin's abandonment of Lenin's doctrine concerning the dual concept of matter. It should be remembered that Lenin distinguished between the philosophical and scientific concept of matter in order to strengthen the materialist standpoint against the criticism based on the discoveries in physics which seemed to support the tendency in modern science to describe the laws and order in the universe in the language of idealism. Stalin took no notice of this controversy and recognized only one concept of matter, namely the philosophical. The concept of matter, explained the authors of the textbook *Dialectical Materialism*, edited by G. F. Alexandrov, in their presentation of Stalin's philosophical materialism, should connote only the most general properties of objective reality and should not include any characteristics discovered in a particular form of matter in motion. Therefore, there does not and cannot exist a 'natural scientific' or 'physical' concept of matter distinct from the philosophic one.[56]

The abandonment by Stalin of Lenin's distinction was closely related to the controversy between the Deborinite and the mechanistic school of thought in Soviet philosophy, which was terminated by the formal condemnation of the mechanists and followed by a complete rout of the Deborinites by the Soviet Communist Party.[57] The original point at issue between the two groups was concerned *inter alia* with the question as to whether natural science should enjoy ideological neutrality and ideological autonomy. While the mechanists insisted that natural science should not be bound by metaphysical presuppositions, the Deborinites demanded that it should accept its philosophical and methodological principles from Marxist –Leninist philosophy. In this controversy the views of the mechanists were condemned by the temporarily victorious Deborinites, supported by the Communist Party officials, who accused the mechanists of resisting the Marxist–Leninist ideology, of deviating from Marx, Engels, and Lenin, and of undermining the proletarian dictatorship in the fatherland of socialism. Then the Deborinites were denounced and found to be guilty of a 'formalist deviation', that is, of the reluctance to recognize their subordination to the leadership of the Communist Party in matters of philosophy and ideology. As dialectical materialism is the world outlook of the Marxist–Leninist Party, the leadership of the Party is its legitimate guardian and highest authority.

The successive rout of the two schools of thought led to the establishment of a strict ideological Party supervision over both natural science and philosophy, buttressed by the principle of *partijnost'* in its most extreme interpretation. In the Stalinist period the principle of *partijnost'* was no longer restricted to the recognition of the two principal alignments in philosophy, from which Lenin deduced the demand for 'consistent adherence to materialism'. Stalin demanded 'militant partisanship' based on the understanding that 'Marxist philosophy is the most complete and decisive negation of all preceding philosophy', that it superseded all philosophical schools, and that it became 'a scientific weapon in the hands of the proletarian masses'.[58] Consequently, *partijnost'* conceived as a mere consistent adherence to materialism was no longer sufficient. *Partijnost'* meant the unconditional submission to what the party leadership declared to be true in each particular case and required the recognition of the principle that though individuals may err the Party was infallible. Stalin's principle of *partijnost'* also implied the belief in the necessary relationship between philosophical tendencies and political views, between philosophical schools and political parties. Expressed in practical terms, the Stalinist principle of *partijnost'* implied that 'every political deviation had philosophical roots, every philosophical deviation political offshoots, while philosophical orthodoxy was to be found in the correct Party line and only there'.[59] Consequently, philosophical controversies became theological rather than philosophical disputes. The point at issue was no longer the discovery of truth but the establishment of the line of division between orthodoxy and heresy. The content of orthodoxy could not be described by enumerating its accepted views; it could only be indicated by the name of an Office or an Authority with which it was entrusted or deposited.[60]

Dialectical and Historical Materialism was published after the establishment of the supremacy of the Party over natural science and philosophy, and Stalin's abandonment of the two concepts of matter should be seen in connection with this development of events. The abolition of Lenin's distinction helped in the exercise of the ideological and methodological supervision of the Party over scientists, scholars, and philosophers, and in the imposition of 'the correct line of inquiry' upon all of them. As long as it was possible to argue that the concept of matter had not only a philosophical but a scientific meaning as well, the door of escape from the Party's ideological tutelage remained open and Marxist philosophical materialism could be interpreted in various ways. According to Stalin this also meant that different political implications could be derived from the assumptions of philosophical materialism. Socialism would thus no longer be scientific in the sense that its programme of action and policies could be rigorously obtained by inference from the cosmic principles. Since the distinction between the two concepts of matter might have all these unforeseeable and undesirable consequences, it had to be eliminated altogether. As a Soviet philosopher put it, 'the notion of a dual concept of matter implies a divorcement of dialectical materialism from the living process of inquiry into nature and leads to a dissolution of the creative force and guiding role of Marxist–Leninist philosophy in gaining knowledge of the world'.[61]

The instrumentalist approach to the problems of philosophy and their revision in the light of practical and political requirements makes of *Dialectical and Historical Materialism* or *Marxism and Problems of Linguistics* a sociological and political document rather than a philosophical essay. This evaluation should surprise nobody. Stalin himself repeatedly stated that like Lenin he saw no use in theoretical thinking unless theory was able to 'serve practice'. If a theory did not help to answer questions raised by practical requirements, it was good for nothing.[62] To value a theory because it may be used as a 'guide to action' is one thing, but to believe that the

E.D.M.—T

theory is of no value except as a 'guide to action' is quite another. The latter view, which reduces the functions of knowledge to its social and political usefulness, is a particular version of the instrumentalist conception of knowledge. Stalin's instrumentalism can best be understood as part of his voluntaristic interpretation of the Marxian doctrine to be considered in the next section.

4. THE VOLUNTARISM AND INSTRUMENTALISM OF STALIN

Marx never was nor wished to be a scholar detached from reality, motivated exclusively by theoretical curiosity. In his youthful examination of Hegel's system Marx pointed out that philosophy failed to solve many of its problems precisely because their solution was a matter of real life, and philosophy saw in them purely theoretical questions.[63] Alienation and religion provided the best instances of problems of this sort. The alienation of the wage worker who sells his labour power to the capitalist entrepreneur is not merely a philosophical concept that can be used for the analysis of social relations; although alienation might be exposed by intellectual means, it will not disappear unless it is abolished by social action. In the same manner the critique of religion that shows religion to be an inverted mirror image of social reality cannot be fully successful until the social conditions reflected in religion are entirely changed, that is, until the oppressed classes are emancipated from the slavery which they endure in modern society. 'The call [to men] to abandon their illusion about their condition is a call to abandon a condition which requires illusions.' [64]

A philosophy useful in its application must grow out of actual social needs and tensions. Marx became convinced that it was the task of the philosopher to clarify the ideas of men about the social conflicts of their own day and not only to formulate a demand for their resolution but also to make this demand effective. Whenever a problem had both a theoretical and practical aspect, it was sheer intellectual hypocrisy to ignore the latter and to act as if the former constituted the sole matter worthy of consideration. It was this hypocritical pretence on the part of the Young Hegelians, who did not take account of philosophy as part of German reality, that aroused Marx's withering anger against their extravagant and abstract literary production. While Marx himself never deviated from the view that only if we know a situation can we deal with its problems, he was painfully aware of the pressure and urgency of practical considerations. He was anxious not only to enlighten men about their social conditions but also to help them conquer their poverty and misery.

Early in life, Marx made the famous statement that it was the task of the philosophers not only to interpret the world but also to change it. Marx did not make this statement in order to depreciate the importance and significance of knowledge. In his opinion there was a close and essential relationship between action and knowledge. Knowledge was a necessary condition of effective action and action was conducive to the advancement of knowledge; the will to change the world stimulates inventiveness and suggests new ways of inquiry. But the famous statement did mean that knowledge had both a cognitive purpose and a social function. Marx's admiration for Francis Bacon stemmed largely from Bacon's vision of the future when science was to become a socially revolutionary force, the foundation of action directed to the advantage of human well-being and happiness. Science, Marx argued against Proudhon, should not be reduced to 'the slender proportions of a scientific formula', that is, the instrumentalist aspect of science, apparent in its power of revolutionizing reality, should never be overlooked.[65]

In his own work, Marx accomplished what he demanded of others. In his review of *A Contribution to the Critique of Political Economy* Engels pointed out that the materialist conception of history was 'a revolutionizing discovery' which ran counter to all traditional ways of thinking in the historical sciences. But the materialist conception, Engels added, involved highly revolutionary consequences not only for theory but also for practice. 'As we pursue our materialist thesis further and apply it to the present, the perspective of a tremendous revolution, indeed, the most tremendous revolution of all time, unfolds itself before us.'[66] Marx believed that natural science penetrates into human life through its transformation of industry and social relations; even though its immediate effect may increase the dehumanization of man, the applications of natural science prepare the ultimate emancipation of humanity.

Scientific work is a social act, wrote Marx in *Economic and Philosophic Manuscripts of 1844*. He wished thereby to make a sociological statement and to emphasize that all human activity is actually, if not manifestly, social in its origin. To press this view home, he pointed out that even scientific work, which is only rarely carried out in association with others, is essentially a social act, impossible to perform outside society. But Marx's sociological statement also had some moral implications. 'When I carry out scientific work . . . I produce for society and with the consciousness of acting as a social being.' [67] Paul Lafargue, his son-in-law, remembered Marx saying that 'science could not be an egoistic pleasure' and that its first and foremost task was the application of knowledge in the service of humanity. [68]

Marx, together with Comte, supported the view that science and philosophy had a social role to play and a social obligation to carry out. However, they both recognized that before science and philosophy can serve man, man must first be known; knowledge necessarily precedes social, moral, and political change. Knowledge and practical activity have to be kept apart, for truth is to be discovered and not made by successful action. All science is based on experience, 'die Wissenschaft ist Erfahrungswissenschaft', and 'science consists in applying a rational method of investigation to the data provided by the senses'; induction, analysis, comparison, observation, and experiment are the principal forms of such a rational method. [69] To act effectively, we must be able to choose what, on the basis of evidence, is the most suitable means for achieving a desired end. But to select appropriate means is to make use of a rational method, that is, the method of science.

Marx clearly differentiated socialism as a stage in social evolution on the one hand, and as a political movement or intellectual trend on the other, from its 'real basis', his new social science which could be established only by empirical study of social facts, the comparative analysis of historical development, and the elaboration of a theoretical framework for the investigation of social systems and social change. Effective action depends on the rational choice of the most suitable and best means to desired ends. It also depends on the knowledge of the social and economic conditions under which action is to be accomplished. [70] Effective action which really succeeds in solving a practical problem is determined by the 'life situation' of the doer and by the structure of the larger society. [71] We cannot produce social change of the desired kind unless we take advantage of the new science of man which investigates the whole advance of civilization as the creation of man accomplished through his own efforts. The subordination of this power of self-creation to rational self-direction cannot succeed but on the basis of experience and knowledge which enables us to establish true conclusions about the existing situation and the rationality of means.

The alternative to the scientific mode of thought is the utopian, based on the belief that in the absence of appropriate social and economic conditions ideas alone can conquer the world by virtue of their own power. Although through no fault of their own, the utopians were supporters of the view that action can dispense with knowledge and become a guide to theory. They dealt only with the problem of the rationality of means and ignored the question of the existing situation in relation to which the rationality of means should be considered and assessed. Since they assumed that the new social situation can be created and the social organization contrived by their inventive action, the utopians produced only 'innocent and childlike fancies' or 'phantoms', that is, knowledge distorted by 'the ideological reflexes and echoes' of man's conditions in social life.[72] Marx recognized both the requirements of knowledge and those of action and did not wish to expand one at the expense of the other.

Neither Lenin nor Stalin remained faithful to this Marxian inheritance. Both were men of action, first and foremost, unappreciative of, and impatient with, the procedures by which knowledge is acquired. It is quite different, Lenin said, to be interested in 'Marxism as a theory' and to consider it 'as an answer to the question "What is to be done?", as a call to take the field against the enemy'.[73] For Lenin, and still more for Stalin, truth was to be made, not discovered. They felt that they had the power to change the whole world by their revolutionary will and activity. In order to be truly in control of the course of events, the conditions of actions have to be assessed critically, the defects of spontaneity laid bare and spontaneity itself elevated to the level of consciousness. This implied, according to Lenin, that 'the "ideologist" is worthy of the name only when he precedes the spontaneous movement, points out the road and is able ahead of all others to solve all the theoretical, political, tactical, and organizational questions which the "material elements" of the movement spontaneously encounter'.[74] Lenin and Stalin were absolutely sure that they were in possession of an important insight into the mechanism of effective social and political action which they would reveal and demonstrate by acting upon and changing the world.

Lenin and Stalin maintained by implication that the conformity of thought to reality was to be achieved in the course of changing the world and by actual mastery over it. This meant, however, that the provisionality and tentativeness of the Marxian beliefs, which in their application to practical exigencies left room for alternative possibilities of action, had to be replaced by a compelling certainty and a set of final and unconditional postulates based on one alternative to the exclusion of others. The efficiency of action not only required that the claims of alternative views be disregarded but also that doubt be suppressed and the working assumption be transformed into an absolute principle, actively supported by the whole weight of authority. When the striving after an impartial view is abandoned and the principles of action become an incontrovertible truth, they are bound to breed intolerance, repressive measures and, finally, suppression and persecution. He who dissents from what we hold to be true is only in error, but he who dissents from absolute truth provides conclusive proof of his evil and corrupted will.

For Lenin, and still more so for Stalin, the Marxian theory of history and society became an instrument which could and should be used for the purpose of intervening in the course of social events and in the historical process. As Lenin put it, the revolutionary quality 'is indeed completely and unconditionally inherent in Marxism, for this theory sets itself the task of . . . serving the proletariat as a means of ending all exploitation as quickly and easily as possible'.[75] In the celebrated introduction to *A Contribution to the Critique of Political Economy* Marx spoke of how socialism was bound to emerge from the process of social and economic development of the capitalist society, the advance towards socialism being independent of human intention, will, or active design. Stalin took the very opposite view. The old does not grow automatically into the new, the advance toward socialism is not a spontaneous process, but one dependent on deliberate action, such as the strengthening of the organs of the dictatorship of the proletariat or the intensification of the class struggle. Stalin announced that at least in the Soviet Union 'so-called objective conditions', as he put it, had practically ceased to count. 'The part played by so-called objective conditions has been reduced to a minimum ; whereas the part played by our organization and their leaders has become decisive, exceptional.' The laying down of 'the correct political line', the effectiveness of planning, the organizational and supervisory work, the quality of leadership, and human skill and determination 'decide everything'.[76]

When Marxian teaching was reduced to a set of organizational, tactical, and strategical directives of how to remake social and historical existence, its practical and instrumental aspect was bound to predominate over and finally absorb its theoretical and cognitive content. This interpretation of the Marxian doctrine will be called 'voluntarism' or the 'voluntaristic interpretation of the Marxian doctrine', for it involves the belief that the will is the inner and true nature of man and intellect is a mere tool of the will.

Expressed in more cautious terms, voluntarism asserts the primacy of the will over the intellect and over material conditions which are regarded as merely phenomenal appearance. As Schopenhauer put it, the intellect is as different from the will as the hammer from the smith. 'Will shows itself as of a nature quite different from knowledge, which only serves it for communication with the external world, but then the will follows the laws of its own nature, without taking from the intellect anything but the occasion.' [77]

Stalin was not the first to use a theory formulated for the purpose of explaining the course of events to urge and justify certain practical policies. John Dewey observed that in this respect 'Marxism' was preceded by a number of non-Marxian social philosophies which he criticized for their entirely mistaken conception of the relation between social theory and social action. In particular, according to Dewey, they made the false assumption that a social issue does not concern a choice of values to be striven for but is concerned with the discovery of ends and means determined by the constitution of human nature. Thus, the classical school of economic theory discovered that self-interest was the main human motive force and agitated for a free market economy and for the appropriate legal and political measures which were to safeguard the free market system. Similarly, utilitarianism took advantage of the principle that pleasure and pain are the main determinants of human behaviour to advocate a comprehensive plan of social reform that would secure the greatest happiness of the greatest number. Dewey believed that such theories were bound to produce both serious social ills and errors of judgment because they dealt with human motivation in 'a wholesale way', appealed to general forces, obscured the need for observation, and created an illusion of understanding where there was only a general word and a phrase.[78]

Apart from their similarity, however, the instrumentalism of Stalin and the classic school of economic theory or utilitarianism are divided by an important difference. The latter theories did not claim that their premisses and ways of viewing the world represented the total and absolute truth. While they provided a general framework for the examination of social, political, and economic events, the working assumptions derived from the theories in question were formulated tentatively as specific hypotheses which should be submitted to practical tests. In other words, they were 'piecemeal social experiments' which, unlike the experiments of large-scale or total social engineering, can be carried out without revolutionizing the whole of society.[79]

Stalin did not accept any of these restraints and limitations. Having conceived his rules of action as universally valid and applicable, he claimed to know what was the most appropriate way of dealing with any problem before he had considered it. He did not formulate specific hypotheses which could be tested practically but resorted to the sweeping measures of total engineering which involved the whole of society. Since the sociological knowledge necessary for large-scale social technology was not available and the theory did not in fact provide the guidance it was supposed to offer, the alleged 'practical deductions' from theoretical assumptions had to be made arbitrarily. Absolutism in theory leads inevitably to arbitrariness in practice, observed Comte, examining the conditions which a theory should satisfy in order that it may be suitable for practical applications.[80] Although Stalin might have claimed to act in conformity to the theory, it was he himself who determined what was or was not in conformity to the theory. Ultimately it was not the theory which determined what should be done in practical terms; the will of the leader decided what the theory should imply.

The voluntarism of Stalin should not be contrasted with the alleged fatalism of Marx, which, indeed, seems to be incompatible with his revolutionary activity and certain important parts of his doctrine. The contrast should be located at a different level and expressed in other terms than those of the antithesis between fatalism and voluntarism.

To say that Marx relied 'solely and exclusively', as Engels put it, upon the intellectual development and united action of the working class for the ultimate triumph of the ideas of *The Communist*

Manifesto,[81] is a clear misinterpretation of his views. But the opposite opinion, namely, that Marx proclaimed the absolute impotence of politics, is equally untenable.[82] Marx did not adhere to the view that political action can never bring about a decisive change in the economic and social situation. Complete abstention from political movement and the belief in the futility of all politics was the dogma of Bakunin and followers of Proudhon, and constituted a real and deep difference between Marx's ideas and anarchism.[83] Lenin did not depart from the spirit of Marxian teaching when he said that from its viewpoint 'the negation of politics' was an absurdity and that for Marx the economic and political struggle of the working class constituted a single inseparable whole.[84] Marx stated explicity that political action could under favourable circumstances alter the course of social and economic development; an instance of this was the successful struggle of the English workers to secure the passage of the Ten Hours' Bill, which brought them, in Marx's own words, 'immense physical, moral, and intellectual benefits'.[85] If Marx had not believed in the efficacy of political action, he would not have appealed to the workers to 'put their heads together, and as a class, compel the passing of a law . . . that shall prevent the very workers from selling, by voluntary contract with capital, themselves and their families into slavery and death.'[86] Politics is a rational application of force but the force itself is an economic power, as Marx pointed out in *Capital*,[87] which in certain conditions might hasten the process of transformation or shorten the transition from one mode of production into another. Marx refused to differentiate between social and political revolutions. 'Every revolution breaks up the old society, and to this extent it is social', Marx argued against Arnold Ruge. 'Every revolution overthrows the existing ruling power; to this extent it is political.'[88] More generally, social and political movements do not exclude each other, 'there is no political movement which is not at the same time social'.[89] Engels emphatically pointed out that Marx did not regard all political action as ineffective; one has only to look, Engels wrote, at *The Eighteenth Brumaire of Louis Bonaparte* and *Capital*, at the chapters dealing with the working day or the history of the bourgeoisie, to see that he did not consider political power economically impotent and political struggle futile. Why should we fight for the political dictatorship of the proletariat, Engels asked, if political power is powerless as economic force?[90]

What Marx did denounce was political action which ignored the economic and social circumstances, or did not recognize its general dependence upon economic conditions, or aimed solely at 'administrative reforms' which did not change the basic relations between capital and labour.[91]   Marx also heaped scorn and ridicule upon so-called utopian thinkers, naïve moral preachers or idealistic reformers, for believing that benevolent action could remedy the evils of capitalist society or help the underprivileged and exploited. Marx did not wish to laugh out of court every kind of political action but only that which wilfully disregarded the hard and stubborn facts of the class struggle or took no notice of the economic and social limitations inherent in every situation and restrictive of the effectiveness of action.

Marx's views concerning the efficacy and significance of political action can be described as the doctrine of the relative impotence of politics.   He attributed to politics a low degree of effectiveness, incomparably lower than that accorded either to the improvement in the productivity of the economic forces or to the changes in the system of class relationships, together with its legal and political superstructure.   'The principle of politics is the will', wrote Marx, and added, as if wishing to refute his Russian followers in the twentieth century, 'the more partial, and the more perfected, political thought becomes, the more it believes in the omnipotence of the will, the less able it is to see the natural and mental limitations on the will, the less capable it is of discovering the source of social evils.' [92]   To build a new world for themselves, men have to build on the historical accomplishment of their civilization.   They have to work to establish the material conditions of their emancipation, which are the product of a long and painful process of development, and 'no effort of mind or will can free them from this destiny'.[93]   The period of gestation and the birth-pangs can be shortened or lessened by human intervention, but they cannot be done away with by ingenuity and the exaltation of the will.

The voluntarism of Stalin did not arise from the opposition to the belief that political action was not necessary to bring about socialism but from the rejection of quite a different view.   Stalin refused to recognize the existence of economic restrictions and social limitations upon the effectiveness or relevance of action and proclaimed them to be non-existent, at least in the Soviet Union.   Thus, he also admitted by implication that everything was feasible and could be attained by skilful effort and unflagging determination. He just asserted what Marx denied, namely, the omnipotence of the will.[94] For Stalin, force was no longer the midwife — force was the mother of the new society.[95]

Stalin's determination to establish a rigorous control over social and historical processes resulted in his obsessive preoccupation with the problems of power. This preoccupation could only accentuate his disregard for ideas unless they were able to take hold of the masses and mobilize them for action. Like Lenin, Stalin was never weary of repeating Marx's dictum to the effect that the theory which gets hold of the minds of the people turns into a material force. Their frequent tributes to ideas has secured them the reputation of men of action who understood the importance of philosophy and from whom many idealist opponents of dialectical materialism could learn respect for thought.[96] In fact, the pronouncements of Lenin and Stalin meant exactly the opposite, the utter disregard of thought, which only acquired importance as a means of social control or by degenerating into the art of propaganda. Furthermore, according to Lenin's conception of the party of the proletariat, fully endorsed by Stalin, no theory can take hold of the masses without being adopted by the party, the vanguard of the working class, which in its organization and programme incarnates the class consciousness of the proletariat. By themselves, ideas are powerless. It is the party, therefore, which, in the last resort, is a history-making force and to which everything else should be subordinated.

The original Marxian theory of history and society did not require any political strategy or tactics on the part of its supporters.[97] The need for strategy and tactics arose only from the voluntaristic interpretation of the Marxian doctrine. This interpretation reduced Marxian theories to a collection of rules and techniques on how to control social processes by the application of power and, to use Stalin's expression, to change society by 'a revolution from above'.[98] This had nothing to do with the fact that Marx was no political theorist and that he had nothing to say, as Lenin was to discover, about the use of political power. For Lenin and Stalin, the Marxian theory of history was not so much a scheme of historical development but rather the consciousness of the inevitable transformation of capitalism into socialism, the determination to achieve it by whatever means might be available and as quickly as possible, and the reliance upon the class struggle as a method of solving historical and social problems.[99]   Since Marx's cognitive theory of history and society was transformed by Lenin and Stalin into a manipulative theory, political strategy and tactics became its integral part and acquired crucial importance.

Together with the recognition of the need for strategy and tactics went the increasing confidence in the effectiveness of propaganda, large-scale organization, and all forms of control over men's overt and latent behaviour as a means of solving perennial social problems. Lenin firmly adopted the assumption that without deliberately organized and correctly led action the revolution would neither come to pass nor socialism be constructed.[100]   With the interpretation of the Marxian doctrine as 'a call to take the field against the enemy', there was associated the view that it was, as Lenin put it, 'our primary and imperative practical task to establish an organization of revolutionaries capable of lending energy, stability, and continuity to the political struggle'.   Paraphrasing the well-known dictum of Archimedes, Lenin called out in *What Is To Be Done?*, 'Give us an organization of revolutionaries, and we will overturn Russia.' [101]

Stalin recognized the connection between a manipulative theory of history and society and the need for a political strategy and tactics with striking clear-sightedness at the very beginning of his rise to supreme power after Lenin's death.   'What, in the last analysis, is Leninism?', asked Stalin in *The Foundations of Leninism*.

> Leninism is Marxism of the era of imperialism and the proletarian revolution.   To be more exact, Leninism is the theory and tactics of the proletarian revolution in general, the theory and tactics of the dictatorship of the proletariat in particular.[102]

Stalin followed faithfully in Lenin's footsteps when he dismissed the importance of the 'objective conditions';   declared that the struggle and prestige of the Party, of economic and other organizations, and of their leaders 'now determine everything or nearly everything';   and announced that the responsibility for the success and failure in the construction of socialism rested 'on ourselves and on ourselves alone'.[103]

That Lenin's revolutionary Marxism did more than merely restore the revolutionary content to the Marxian theories is not a new interpretation.   Lenin's Russian opponents noticed at once that his distinctive interpretation of the Marxian doctrine, which became apparent in the columns of *Iskra* and reached its climax in *What Is To Be Done?*, was associated with a pronounced 'sectarian intolerance' on his part and with the demand for an integral dogmatic outlook on life.[104] The view that the hard core of Leninism was the voluntaristic interpretation of the Marxian doctrine and that Lenin should be held responsible for its transformation into mere rules of action should be traced back to Plekhanov. Plekhanov charged Lenin with not recognizing any limits to social action — Bukharin made the same allegation against Stalin some ten years later — and substituting the revolutionary will for the laws of history as the determinant of social and historical development.[105] Stalin attributed to Plekhanov the view that 'Leninism is the precedence of practice over theory in the sense that its main point is the translation of the Marxist theses into deeds' and, generally, that Leninism is unconcerned about theory.[106] This view of Leninism, Stalin wrote, bore no relation whatever to the truth. Lenin did not suffer from 'the disease of narrow empiricism or unprincipled practicalism' and was fully aware of the importance of theory for the proletarian movement.[107] When faced by the objection that he had been inclined to belittle the significance of the objective factors of development, Lenin was taken aback and answered, bewildered, 'How may a designer of subjective plans belittle objective development?'[108] Stalin showed as complete a lack of comprehension of what Plekhanov's criticism implied as Lenin had.

The important point to be noted in the views of Lenin and Stalin concerning the role of theory and its relationship to practice is not the rejection of every theory or the denial of its utilitarian value but the repudiation of its autonomous cognitive function. A theory, whether in science, philosophy, sociology, or politics, is nothing but an instrument of transforming nature, man, and society, a means in the hands of the Party leadership to be used for the fulfilment of the great task assigned to it by history and destiny. Both Lenin and Stalin denied, either implicitly or explicitly, that scientific knowledge in general and philosophy in particular are governed by their own standards of procedure and criteria of truth or validity. Scientific knowledge and philosophy should be regarded as a social force. They are a collective endeavour, they owe their origin to social life, and they are determined in their content by the economic and technical evolution of society; as such, they can and should be used to shape social and political development.

5. THE EQUIVOCATION OF THE CONCEPT OF CAUSE AND THE ABANDONMENT OF VOLUNTARISM

The idea of subjecting the creative power of the human mind to conscious direction and of taking advantage of it for the attainment of some all-inclusive social ends might have been suggested to Lenin and Stalin by Engels's marginal observations on how to transform social forces 'from master demons into willing servants'. Engels's reflections on knowledge which might enable man to control his natural and social environment involved an equivocal use of the concept of cause and this ambiguity greatly contributed to the adoption of the voluntaristic interpretation of the Marxian doctrine. On the other hand, the discovery of Engels's equivocation led to the abandonment of some of the extreme forms of voluntarism at a later stage.

It was Engels who defined freedom as 'the control over ourselves and over external nature, a control founded on knowledge of natural necessity'. Freedom, he explained in the same context, 'means nothing but the capacity to make decisions with knowledge of the subject'. What Engels called the 'ascent of man from the kingdom of necessity to the kingdom of freedom' consisted in the increasing knowledge of natural and social laws and in making them work towards definite ends. In this way the conditions of life are brought under man's control, the extraneous natural forces facing and dominating him as an alien blind power are mastered by him, and the natural and social causes which he sets consciously in motion have increasingly the intended effects. Man begins to conquer his destiny and in ever-growing measure to make his own history.[109]

Engels emphasized in *Anti-Dühring* and elsewhere that in spite of the diminishing influence of unforeseen effects, a colossal discrepancy between the proposed aims and the results arrived at by deliberate efforts still existed, and that the uncontrolled forces were far more powerful than those set in motion according to plan. He attributed this discrepancy, above all, to the absence of a conscious organization of social production. Since production was not regulated in accordance with a settled plan, the prevailing conditions were bound, on the one hand, to generate a predominance of unforeseen effects in the most essential activity of men, with chain reaction consequences, as we would say today, throughout society, and bound to delay the progress of natural science on the other. Engels felt that once the control over social production is established, mankind will experience an advance in all branches of its activity before which 'everything preceding it will pale into insignificance'.[110]

Whereas Engels's conception of freedom might have been the source of the voluntarism of Lenin and Stalin, Engels should only partly be blamed for their excessive claims. For Engels did emphasize the obvious point, which they tended to overlook or which they somewhat missed, that in order to make laws work towards desired ends, prior knowledge of these laws is necessary. It was, however, Engels's fault that he did not distinguish the two quite different meanings *cause* may have in the theoretical and the applied sciences, whether the natural or the social sciences, and that he was even inclined to ignore the distinction when he noticed it.[111]

We say that event A is the cause and event B the effect, if we can produce A or prevent A from happening and thus control the occurrence or non-occurrence of B. In all such cases A is the cause of B, if A is either the necessary or the sufficient condition of B. The event denoted by the term 'cause' in the first meaning is always an event which under certain conditions may be produced or prevented, directly of indirectly, by a human agency. In such cases the manipulations performed by men are a contributory factor in the occurrence of A and only upon their intervention if A occurs B necessarily follows in conformity to some natural laws. But not all events to which we refer as *causes* can be thus controlled by a human agency.

We may say that event A is the cause and event B the effect in the second meaning in which the term 'cause' may be used if and only if A is both the necessary and sufficient condition of B. In other words, A is the cause of B in the second sense if A is the invariable conditional antecedent of B; it is never the case that B takes place in the absence of A and if A happens, B happens too.

We can do nothing about the causal relationship of the second kind, for the cause is supposed to be unconditional and the effect inevitably follows it. This does not appear to be the case with the causes in the first meaning of the term which never produce their effects by themselves. Thus, our knowledge of the causal relationship between A and B might enable us to control B by producing or preventing A. But the knowledge of what is either the sufficient or the necessary condition of B does not suffice to control the occurrence of *B*, for we are not always able actually to produce or prevent *A* as we please; what is physically possible, need not be technically feasible. For both these reasons we can never be full masters of our physical and social environment. The power of mind, will, and action to create the conditions under which natural and social forces would work towards man-appointed ends is real but strictly limited.

It was only towards the end of his life that Stalin discovered the two meanings the term 'cause' may have. He belatedly conceded that there are processes in nature and society which take place independently of the will of man. Sometimes we can influence them, but this is not always the case. In many instances even the knowledge of the respective natural laws leaves us powerless. Moreover, we have first to discover the laws, 'to get to know them and master them, learn to apply them with full understanding, utilize them in the interest of society, and thus subjugate them', before we can avert or restrict their destructive effects and initiate or promote their constructive action.[112] This meant the retreat from the extreme forms of voluntarism and the recognition of its limitations. The 'laws of science' can neither be abolished nor altered nor can new ones be created. It is technically or physically impossible to produce or prevent the occurrence of all causes, to manipulate the operation of all natural laws, to improve and enforce them upon man and society at will, and to bring everything under human control. As Stalin put it, the achievements of the Soviet government resulting from the application of science to social and economic problems did not imply that the Soviet government can 'do anything' and that 'nothing is beyond it'.[113] For the voluntarist 'knowledge' means 'knowledge of adaptation to environment' and adaptation is conceived as a purposeful action intended to produce the desired kind of change in the environment. When the limitations of man's mastery over his environment were recognized, adaptation had also to be considered as adjustment to extraneous and social conditions independent of the will of man and outside his control.

Before Stalin reached this point of retreat, he pushed the doctrine of man's mastery over social environment and of his unrestricted control over nature — of which his support of the theory of the inheritance of acquired characteristics is an extreme instance — to its uppermost limits and originated what is euphemistically known as the 'period of errors and distortions'. It has frequently been observed that Stalin's policies were rooted in his determination to transform the Soviet Union into a modern industrial society as fast as possible and that, therefore, his voluntarism was nothing but a rationalization of this drive.   Whatever motives prompted Stalin to adopt the voluntaristic position, whether only to rationalize his prior decision to enter upon a definite course of action or to express his insight into the nature and activity of man, the voluntaristic outlook set a number of practical and theoretical problems.   Of these problems only those which led to significant revisions of dialectical materialism will be considered.

6. VOLUNTARISM AND THE SOCIOMORPHIC CONCEPTION OF THE UNIVERSE

The fulcrum of Stalin's manipulative theory of history was historical materialism.   For Engels, the materialist conception of history was a hypothesis or a point of view which was to be tested by accepted procedures, like any other hypothesis or point of view adopted by the historian.   For Stalin, Engels's approach to historical materialism was unsatisfactory and unacceptable.   He did not wish to establish the validity of a theory of history ; he was anxious to make use of it as an instrument for transforming social reality in conformity to a preconceived scheme.   What Stalin was in need of was a procedure that would persuade his followers of the reliability of the instrument he wished to use.   The followers were to be induced to believe that as a matter of fact 'whatever are the conditions of material life of a society such are the ideas, theories, political views, and political institutions of that society'.[114]

Lenin suggested that historical materialism is a particular case of genetic and epistemological materialism and Stalin exploited this clue to the utmost.   According to Stalin, whose views on this subject will be more closely examined in Part Three, historical materialism should be considered as conclusively established, for it can be rigorously derived from dialectical materialism.[115]   Once the truth of dialectical materialism is accepted, the materialist conception of history follows from it logically ; one cannot accept the former and reject the latter.   As dialectical materialism is a true premiss, historical materialism, the application of the principles of dialectical materialism to social phenomena, must also be true.

The derivation of the materialist conception of history from dialectical materialism provided the stepping-stone for further deductions. Already in *Anarchism or Socialism?* Stalin held that

> Marxism is not only the theory of socialism, it is an integral world outlook, a philosophical system from which Marx's proletarian socialism logically follows. This philosophical system is called 'dialectical materialism'.[116]

In *Dialectical and Historical Materialism* Stalin took up this point and tried to show in detail that his materialist philosophy entails a number of socially and politically important consequences. *Dialectical Materialism* edited by G. F. Alexandrov, the once authoritative exposition of Stalin's philosophical views, and *Fundamentals of Marxism–Leninism* edited by O. V. Kuusinen, performed the same *tour de force* and even exceeded Stalin's efforts by their systematic thoroughness and exegetic ingenuity. The Soviet textbooks demonstrated the political significance of dialectical materialism showing that it provided the basis for the prediction of the future in a scientific manner and for pursuing a scientifically grounded policy. The 'practical deductions' derived from dialectical materialism allowed the Soviet leaders to make right decisions and to resolve action dilemmas in numerous difficult situations.[117] It hardly needs mentioning that Stalin and the authors of the Soviet textbooks were able to show that dialectical materialism involved certain political and social implications because they first formulated dialectical materialism in socio-cosmic terms.

It has been pointed out earlier that in his presentation of dialectical materialism Stalin adopted a peculiar order of exposition, namely, he dealt with the principal characteristics of matter before he explained what matter was. For Stalin this order of presentation served the purpose of making it absolutely sure that matter, whatever else it might turn out to be, was endowed with characteristics which implied certain socially and politically desirable consequences and which were, therefore, important from the socio-cosmic point of view. This is no speculation, for Stalin himself showed in detail that there was an intimate connection between the four dialectical characteristics of matter, on the one hand, and the policies of the Soviet state, on the other. As Rozental' and Yudin observed, dialectical materialism was not only a set of propositions about the universe, but also the 'theoretical foundation' of the programme, strategy, and tactics of the party of the proletariat.[118]

Stalin argued that if all phenomena of nature are interdependent and constitute an integral whole,

> every social system and every special movement in history must be evaluated not from the standpoint of 'eternal justice' or some other preconceived idea . . . but from the standpoint of the conditions which gave rise to that system or that social movement and with which they are connected.[119]

What underlies Stalin's inference from the law of universal connections is the basic premiss of Hegel's evolutionary philosophy of history. Hegel taught that all successive historical systems are only transitory stages in the endless course of development of human society; that each stage is necessary and, consequently, justified for the time and conditions to which it owes its origin; and that in the face of new conditions it loses its justification, gives way to a higher stage which will also in its turn decay and perish.[120] Stalin failed, just as Hegel had, to apply this evolutionary way of viewing the historical process to his own system.

Stalin used the Hegelian premiss to establish his own version of the doctrine that everything that is real must be reasonable and just. As Stalin put it, 'everything depends on the conditions, time and place'.[121] This is the maxim of moral positivism.[122] Moral positivism holds that whatever is, is good, since everything must be judged by its own standards, appropriate to time and place; even the greatest thinkers cannot go, as Engels put it, 'beyond the limits imposed upon them by their epoch'.[123]

In Stalin's opinion the law of universal mutability entails the consequence that no social system and principle is permanent.

> Hence the capitalist system can be replaced by the socialist system, just as at one time the feudal system was replaced by the capitalist system.
> Hence, we must not base our orientation on the strata of society which are no longer developing, even though they at present constitute the predominant force, but on those strata which are developing and have a future before them, even though they at present do not constitute the predominant force.[124]

The doctrine of leaps and the principle of the unity of opposites have been filled with a socio-cosmic content by Plekhanov and Lenin, and Stalin's contribution can be reduced to stating bluntly what the other two only implied.   If the law of the transformation of quantity into quality by an abrupt change is a universal law,

> then it is clear that the revolutions made by oppressed classes are a quite natural and inevitable phenomenon.
> Hence, the transition from capitalism to socialism and the liberation of the working class from the yoke of capitalism cannot be effected by slow changes, by reforms, but only by a qualitative change of the capitalist system, by revolution.
> Hence, in order not to err in policy, one must be a revolutionary, not a reformist.[125]

Finally, the principle of the unity and struggle of opposites entails the whole doctrine of class divisions and conflicts which provide the driving force of history.   If development proceeds everywhere and always by way of the disclosure of internal contradictions, followed by the clash between opposite forces and the overcoming of the original contradiction, then it is clear that the class struggle and victory of the proletariat is a 'natural and inevitable phenomenon'.

> Hence, we must not cover up the contradictions of the capitalist system, but disclose and unravel them; we must not try to check the class struggle but carry it to its conclusion.
> Hence, in order not to err in policy, one must pursue an uncompromising proletarian class policy, not a reformist policy of harmony of the interests of the proletariat and the bourgeoisie, not a compromisers' policy of 'the growing of capitalism into Socialism'.[126]

By a socio-cosmic conception of the universe should be understood that view of the universe which attributes to it such features and regularities as could account for the superiority of a social and political order by cosmic laws rather than by the voluntary choice or decision of the policy makers.   In this sense, Stalin's dialectical materialism is a socio-cosmic conception.   Its main function is to provide the premises from which historical materialism and a number of more detailed socially and politically relevant consequences can allegedly be deduced.   Historical materialism, established as a particular case of universal regularity inherent in the nature of the universe, in turn justifies definite policies of the Party and personal decisions of its leaders 'as practical deductions' derived from the laws of development of society.   As these laws are universally valid and objectively true, their practical consequences are 'objective truths' as well. Hence, as Stalin put it, 'socialism is converted from a dream of a better future for humanity into a science'.[127]

The socio-cosmic concept of dialectical materialism helped to show, however deceitful these inferences might have been, that the policies of the Party were not arbitrary decisions of fallible individuals. The leaders of the Soviet state made their decisions by a rigorous application of the rules of logic, their policies were nothing but a deduction from scientific knowledge, and they themselves were only instruments of cosmic purpose. Since they helped to carry out the course of events determined by cosmic laws, their decisions were supported by the lawfulness and order of the universe.

Voluntarism in politics and sociomorphism in cosmology supported each other. Voluntarism strengthened the tendency to formulate dialectical materialism in sociomorphic terms, and the sociomorphic conception of dialectical materialism favoured and buttressed the voluntaristic interpretation of the Marxian doctrine. Together, they made of dialectical materialism a system of beliefs which are socially important though philosophically obscurantist. While his inadequate knowledge in philosophical matters is evident, Stalin had a perfect grasp of the social importance of philosophical ideas and was fully aware of the advantage which they can provide in effectively controlling social and political behaviour. Having been duly simplified and codified in a brief catechism, dialectical materialism, with its universal laws allegedly operating in nature as well as in human society, was turned by Stalin into a means of social manipulation and political mobilization of the masses. From a sociological point of view it was irrelevant that the ostensible political implications of the Stalinist cosmological doctrine were not logically valid. The important point was that these fancied implications were believed to have been correctly inferred and that they were widely accepted and supported. Consequently, the Stalinist version of dialectical materialism contributed to the successful imposition of definite ways of perceiving the world and to the strict enforcement of definite types of social behaviour.

On the other hand, disastrous consequences were associated with the conception of the universe from which moral positivism, the class struggle, the victory of the proletariat, the succession of the socio-economic formations, the inevitability of political revolutions, and even the vagaries of the Party internal dissensions, of its strategy and tactics, could be deduced. Stalin's exposition of dialectical materialism could not be sustained and enforced without corrupting the critical ability and intellectual integrity of its adherents. It also tended to create social myths, that is, views about social reality unsupported by, or conflicting with, ascertainable facts. These myths undermined the very assumptions which they were supposed to serve. The unintended and unforeseen consequences revealed themselves fully after Stalin's death and culminated in the denunciation of the so-called 'cult of the individual' which was followed by the rejection of Stalinism as a valid interpretation of 'Marxism'.

The reasons for this denouement are easy to comprehend. We may be inclined to search for truth only because of its usefulness. Truth is useful since we can take advantage of it for the satisfaction of practical and emotional needs. But we can use truth in this way only as long as truth and usefulness are kept distinct. Disaster is bound to overcome us, sooner or later, if we fail to respect the distinction. Our intelligence and will-power, our cunning and ruthlessness, may delay the final defeat but they cannot prevent it.

One should agree with William James that sometimes 'faith creates it own verification' and that in such cases it is 'the part of wisdom to believe what one desires'. James's rule applies to those ends whose attainment actually depends on a personal contribution of one sort or another, for in such cases faith urges and sustains a certain kind of behaviour which is a prerequisite for the realization of a desired state of affairs. The premiss 'faith creates its own verification' leads us, however, into calamity when it is extended to cover all cases and when the modes of behaviour required for the realization of ends are regarded as both the necessary and sufficient conditions for the attainment of the pursued objective. We are then driven into a magical frame of mind and into an utterly fantastic belief that it is enough to utter some prescribed words of command or to perform certain prescribed actions to secure the achievement of the desired effect.[128]

PART THREE

THE CONNECTIONS BETWEEN DIALECTICAL AND HISTORICAL MATERIALISM

IX

Marx's Philosophy of History

THE problem to be examined in Part Three concerns the relation of historical materialism to dialectical materialism, that is, whether there is a logically valid transition from the fundamental premisses of dialectical materialism to the basic hypotheses of historical materialism. This question is often answered in the affirmative, but the arguments put forward in its support involve, as a rule, the fallacy of equivocation arising from the ambiguous use of the term 'materialism'.

The belief that the materialist conception of history cannot be dissociated from the philosophy of dialectical materialism is Stalin's distinctive contribution to Soviet philosophy and ideology. Under Stalin's influence this belief was widely accepted not only by the supporters of Marxism–Leninism in and outside the Soviet Union, but also by some Western scholars.[1] Since Stalin's view on the matter will be considered in detail at a later stage, for the moment it is enough to state that it is untenable. In the technical meaning of these terms, historical materialism is neither an application of dialectical materialism nor can it be inferred therefrom; the former might be true even if the latter were false and, conversely, the latter might be true even if the former were false. There is no logically valid transition from dialectical materialism or any other form of materialism in the metaphysical sense to the materialist conception of history. Many other theories of history would be compatible with the metaphysical assumptions of materialism and could, therefore, be called historical materialism.

The rejection of Stalin's view raises the question, what reasons were given by Marx, Engels, and their followers for holding that the materialist conception of history is a true account of social and historical reality. Stalin may have been convinced that if the material world is primary and consciousness secondary the source of the spiritual life of society should be sought in the conditions of its material life.   This is not, however, as has sometimes been maintained, the 'fundamental proposition of historical materialism', and there is no sign of such a sweeping deduction either in Marx or in Engels.   Moreover, it has been established earlier that Marx cannot be considered the founder of dialectical materialism   dialectical materialism did not provide the starting-point in his formulation of the materialist conception of history.   Therefore, even if it were possible to infer historical materialism from dialectical materialism, one could not assume that Marx validated the former by deducing it from the latter.   The problem of how the materialist conception had been established before the appearance of Stalin on the scene should be examined anew for each of the major thinkers who accepted its truth.

I. TWO FORMULATIONS OF HISTORICAL MATERIALISM

Karl Korsch, who alongside Georg Lukács and N. I. Bukharin was the chief representative of the revisionist tendencies within the Marxian tradition in the inter-war period, did not believe one could attribute a philosophy of history to Marx.   In his *Marxismus und Philosophie* (1922) and later in *Karl Marx* Korsch argued that Marx never considered his new principle of social research 'as more than a new scientific approach to a strictly empirical investigation of the historical development of the modern capitalistic mode of production'.[2]   Korsch's interpretation has been taken up by some contemporary social scientists, for instance, by Georges Gurvitch and T. B. Bottomore.   In their view, Marx is, above all, a sociologist and sociology provides the basis of his whole work.[3]   If it were true to say that Marx was concerned with the elaboration of a conceptual framework adequate for the description and analysis of social systems and social change rather than with a substantive theory of history, the question of how he justified his belief in historical materialism could not arise at all.

The view that Marx regarded historical materialism solely as a methodological principle for the empirical investigation of social reality is not compatible, however, with the implications of his Preface to *A Contribution to the Critique of Political Economy*.   While in the Preface he did describe historical materialism 'as a guiding thread (*Leitfaden*) for my studies', which means that he considered it nothing more than a working hypothesis or a principle of methodological procedure, he nevertheless clearly treated it as a metaphysical theory as well. His language implies the reification of the concepts of economic base and superstructure and the transformation of their logical relation into a causal relationship of dependence and succession, the former being said to condition, to determine, to overthrow, or to change the latter.

In his celebrated Preface Marx treated history in the Hegelian fashion. He abandoned the realistic view, characteristic for his early writings such as *The Holy Family, The German Ideology*, or *The Poverty of Philosophy*, and followed the Hegelian rather than his own original approach to history. Whereas in his youth Marx maintained that 'history does nothing', for only real men can fight battles, provide proofs or propose truths, and that consequently 'history is nothing but the activity of men in pursuit of their ends', later on he seems to have forgotten his naturalistic viewpoint. History became again the ethereal reality divorced from empirical events and a 'separate entity, a metaphysical subject of which the real human individuals are only mere representatives'.[4] It was no longer made by men in pursuit of their goals but became the history of the productive forces struggling with the relations of production, producing and overthrowing the ideological superstructure, while mankind, not men, set itself only such tasks as it could solve.

Furthermore, Marx firmly rejected the suggestion that the proposition 'The mode of production of material life determines the general character of the social, political, and intellectual processes of life'[5] applied only to the bourgeois economy of the modern world. Marx had no doubt that historical materialism expresses a universal 'law of motion' of society, as universal as Darwin's theory of evolution, to which Engels often compared Marx's discovery.[6]

Marx was not only a methodologist determined to establish an empirical science of society; he also had a social philosophy, a system of general propositions concerning the nature of man and society and their relationship, as well as a general theory of historical and social causation which was clearly metaphysical. There are in Marx both a methodological and a metaphysical approach to the foundation problem of the social and historical sciences.[7]

The question as to what reasons Marx had for holding the materialist conception of history to be a true account of social reality and historical development requires different answers depending on whether his methodological or his metaphysical formulation of historical materialism is considered. It is a fallacy to maintain that there is a necessary logical connection between historical and meta-physical materialism. But the other extreme position, according to which we do not need to understand the naturalism of Marx and the philosophical materialism of Engels in order to understand their social theory, is equally indefensible.[8]

2. THE METHODOLOGICAL APPROACH TO THE PROBLEMS OF HISTORY

The methodological formula can be found in *Economic and Philosophic Manuscripts of 1844*, *The Holy Family*, *The German Ideology*, and *The Poverty of Philosophy*. It is based on the assumption that all human activity, both 'higher' and 'lower', both spiritual and bodily, can be described by means of the same naturalistic method, which applies equally to the world of nature and to the world of the mind. This assumption involves the belief that man is neither a disembodied spirit nor a body without a soul, but an inseparable unity of both. To describe man's social activity, his spiritual, cultural, and intel-lectual achievements in naturalistic terms, that is, as a natural phenomenon, we have to conceive the human individual as a social being, always living and acting in co-operation with others. The manifestations of the individual's life are in fact the manifestations of social life; the individual becomes what he is by association and interaction with other individuals. Man's spiritual, cultural, and intellectual advance is a natural process of self-creation accomplished in the course of social evolution. By acting in common with others upon his environment, man not only changes the environment but himself and his social relations with others as well. Thus he makes his own history, although he does not make it as he pleases. History is an objective, natural development, in which nothing is derived from extra-social and extra-historical factors, from an autonomous development of ideological forms, human mind, or objective spirit of which 'real', 'empirical men' are but the bearers. 'The real profane history of men' has to present them invariably 'as both the authors and the actors of their own drama'.[9]

The principle underlying the first conception of historical mat-erialism Marx called 'naturalism' or the 'assumption of empiricism', for it is not supposed to go beyond what can be observed or empirically ascertained. It is independent of one or the other form of metaphysical materialism, unless naturalism itself is regarded as a kind of materialism. To arrive at the materialist conception of history, the naturalistic assumption must be supplemented by the principle of investigating all facts of history and social life in their relation to material production.

> Men can be distinguished from animals by consciousness, by religion or anything else you like. They themselves begin to distinguish themselves from animals as soon as they begin to produce their means of subsistence, a step which is conditioned by their physical organization. By producing their means of subsistence, men are indirectly producing their actual material life. The way in which men produce their means of subsistence depends in the first place on the nature of the actual means of subsistence which they find in existence and have to reproduce. This mode of production should not be regarded simply as the reproduction of the physical existence of individuals. It is already a definite form of activity of these individuals, a definite way of expressing their life, a definite mode of life on their part. As individuals express their life, so they are. What they are, therefore, coincides with their production, both with what they produce and with how they produce. What individuals are thus depends on the material conditions determining their production.[10]

Thus, Marx arrived at the concept of the real basis of social life, which consists of definite productive forces and definite social relations established by men interacting in the production of their means of subsistence. Each generation finds the real basis in existence as something given, for it is handed down from its predecessors; each real basis conditions the life and the development of the succeeding generation, to be modified in turn by their action and passed on in its changed form. The real basis provides the starting-point to which the different forms of consciousness and ways of thinking — legal and juridical systems, class divisions, ethics, philosophy, religion, and so forth — should be related. This procedure was expected to establish the fact that the various forms of social consciousness and ideology are correlated with each other and generated in conformity with their real basis.[11]

Since the real basis is constantly modified by the cumulative action of men, and the modifications in the material production of life are reflected in the mental production as expressed in politics, law, morality, religion, or philosophy, history is the incessant movement of the expansion and decay of the means of production, the growth and dissolution of social relations, the formation and disintegration of ideas. This constant movement, the only thing permanent in its changeability, comprises also the bourgeois society, which, as Marx forcibly argued in *The Poverty of Philosophy*, was bound to disappear. Nothing is immutable, everything changes and advances. But the historical process is also thus shown to take place in conformity to laws.

> Men make their own history, but they do not make it just as they please ; they do not make it under circumstances chosen by themselves, but under circumstances directly encountered, given and transmitted from the past.[12]

The implication that history is a law-like process provides the bridge to the second formulation of historical materialism.

As long as the materialist conception of history remained closely bound up with the naturalistic conception of men and the evolutionary view of society, historical materialism was a methodological rather than a metaphysical theory of history. What clearly predominated in Marx's early investigations was the determination that theories about human behaviour and social institutions should be based on observable facts. The starting-point of such theories should be men acting 'not in some imaginary condition of fulfilment or stability, but in their actual, empirically observable process of development under determinate conditions'. Similarly, 'the connection of the social and political structure with production' must be shown 'empirically and without any mystification or speculation' in each particular case. The study of institutionalized behaviour must deal with 'determinate individuals', with men 'as they really are', and not 'as they may appear in their own or other people's imagination', that is, 'as they act, produce materially, and hence as they work under definite material limits, presuppositions and conditions, which are independent of their will'. When human behaviour and interaction are described in empirical terms, not only social institutions but also ideologies — morality, religion, or metaphysics — together with their corresponding forms of consciousness lose the appearance of having an autonomous existence and history. It is not morality, religion, or metaphysics that changes and makes progress but only men, who 'in developing their material production and their material intercourse, change, along with this their real existence, their thinking and the products of their thinking'.[13]

3. HISTORICAL MATERIALISM AS A HISTORICAL HYPOTHESIS

It is not the ontological relationship between the material base and the ideological superstructure, but the principle of evolution and the conformity of human behaviour to natural laws of coexistence and succession that are characteristic for the first formulation of the materialist conception of history. The materialist conception tries to answer the question 'how men came to behave as they do and to hold the views which they profess', the assumption being that their behaviour and ideologies correspond specifically to their material production and economic conditions of life. The materialist conception does not provide a monistic theory of social causation but tries to answer the question concerning the genesis of social and historical events or, more generally, to formulate a comprehensive hypothesis of how social evolution proceeds in conformity to natural law. Since the distinctive characteristic of this evolutionary hypothesis is the view of social evolution as a self-determined process, in which man changes himself in changing the world, the materialist conception of history in its methodological formulation is also a hypothesis of how man makes himself. It has been pointed out that this idea had its precursors in antiquity, that it was rediscovered during the Renaissance, and that it was again presented with force by Giambattista Vico, whom Marx read and commented upon, and, of course, by Hegel. But the conception of man making himself has spread only with the Marxian discovery of historical materialism and with the various social and historical metatheories influenced by Marx.[14]

If the materialist conception of history is a historical hypothesis which is to account for social evolution and to explain the genesis and momentum of social, historical, and cultural development, the reasons for holding it must be the same as in the case of any other historical hypothesis, namely, that it fits the facts of history and that it proves itself to be methodologically comprehensive and fruitful.

This is, indeed, the view which Marx held about his own evolutionary hypothesis; in his opinion, it was validated by historical and social facts. The only difference between the Marxian and the modern approach is one of terminology; in his early writings, such as *The Holy Family* and *The German Ideology*, Marx constantly referred to the empirical nature of his view of history and of the evidence that can be mustered in its support. This difference is, however, comprehensible, since Marx presented his own views in deliberate opposition to Hegel's speculative theory of history. Moreover, what Marx originally called the 'science of man' (*die Wissenschaft vom Menschen*), or the 'natural science about man' (*die natürliche Wissenschaft vom Menschen*), comprised both history and present-day social science.[15]

Marx had no doubts that he knew what kind of evidence would confirm his hypothesis and where he should look for it. In *The Communist Manifesto* he claimed that it did not require 'deep intuition to comprehend that man's ideas, views and conceptions, in one word, man's consciousness, changes with every change in the conditions of his material existence, in his social relations and in his social life'. He also maintained that the history of ideas has proven that 'intellectual production changes its character in proportion as material production is changed' and that 'the ruling ideas of each age have ever been the ideas of its ruling class'.[16] H. B. Acton suggests that the form and the vagueness of the evidence to which Marx referred in *The Communist Manifesto* and which was to corroborate his hypothesis, make it clear that for both Marx and Engels there must have been 'something obvious' about the materialist conception of history.[17] This interpretation does not seem to be right. What Marx wished to point out was only the kind of evidence that would test and establish the validity of the materialist conception. *The Communist Manifesto* merely shows that in Marx's opinion at that time this evidence was so easy to come by and so overwhelming that he did not think it worth while to collect it or to test his hypothesis by applying it to a particular historical situation. Only when in *The Class Struggles of France, 1848 to 1850* (1850) and *The Eighteenth Brumaire of Louis Bonaparte* (1852) he made his first attempt to explain some contemporary events by means of the materialist conception of history, did it become clear that the general hypothesis required additional assumptions to explain the events to which it was applied.

If Marx believed that his theory of history could be validated by testing the conclusions derived from it, as a hypothesis of natural science is tested, he was surely on the wrong track; it is clear today that no historical hypothesis can be validated in this way. Marx may have thought that he was providing evidence in support of his hypothesis by reference to history, but actually he had no confirming evidence independent of his original conjecture. He was thus bound to test the hypothesis by reference to some already interpreted historical facts, the validity of the interpretation involved being based upon the prior acceptance of the hypothesis which he wished to verify. Marx moved in a sort of vicious circle, although neither he nor Engels nor Plekhanov saw it that way or were even aware of this as a possibility; Engels and Plekhanov repeatedly referred to *The Class Struggles in France, 1848 to 1850* and *The Eighteenth Brumaire of Louis Bonaparte* as strong and reliable confirmation of the materialist conception of history. While these two brilliant studies illustrate the meaning and implications of this conception, they did not and could not provide its corroboration.

As a matter of fact, in these historical studies Marx took advantage of two assumptions which are related to, but different from, his original hypothesis, to explain the February revolution in France, the victory of the party of Order over the party of Anarchy (as the social-democratic coalition was christened by its opponents), and the successful *coup d'état* of Louis Bonaparte. These assumptions were, first, that the economic relations of a given society present themselves as group or class interests and, second, that there exists a close connection between political parties and social classes. According to these assumptions, political divisions reflect class divisions and the struggle for power is generated by the conflict of incompatible class interests. Marx abandoned the dichotomic vision of a rigidly polarized class society, familiar from *The Communist Manifesto*, and introduced a multi-divisional class system in which the expanding and advancing capitalist society was functionally divided into several, five, six, seven, or more social classes.[18]

Only the recognition of a multi-divisional class system enabled Marx to apply the explanatory principle, 'the great law of motion of history', as Engels called it, that economic development engenders class divisions and determines the conflict of class interests. Political programmes and ideas, fought over in public for their apparent content, are in fact only expressions of class interests culminating in class war, and political power is only a means to make economic interests secure. For instance, what kept the Legitimists and Orleanists apart politically was 'their material conditions of existence, two different kinds of property . . . the rivalry between capital and landed property'. As Marx wittily observed, 'it was not zeal for a definite royal house that divided them, but it was rather their divided class interests that kept the two dynasties apart'. Similarly, the revolutionary leadership assumed by some sections of the French bourgeoisie in the February revolution (1848) reflected the conflict of interests between the rising industrial bourgeoisie and finance aristocracy, between the industrial entrepreneurs on the one hand, and the bankers, financiers, railway kings, big mine-owners, and land proprietors on the other who ruled France under Louis-Philippe. With the social conditions of existence, based upon different forms of property, were correlated 'distinct and peculiarly formed sentiments, illusions, modes of thought, and views of life'. The psychology of class provided the bridge to the so-called higher ideologies. These ideologies are created by the entire class 'out of its material foundations and out of the corresponding social relations' and are applied by its ideological representatives in the formulation of the political principles, aims, and programmes which are used in the struggle for power or for the preservation of the conditions favourable to the ruling class. According to the Marxian definition, political power arises from the antagonism in civil society and is 'the organized force of one class for oppressing another'.[19] Political power protects social prerogatives and furthers economic privileges. The causal chain is thereby closed; its first link is also its last in the cycle of cause and effect.[20]

Thus, the attempt to apply the methodological formulation of the materialist conception of history to a complicated development of events revealed the multiplicity of psychological and sociological explanatory principles which would have to be explicitly formulated and added to the original conception to secure its adequacy. This unexpected result of applying the materialist conception to explain a particular set of events may have pushed Marx towards a search for a single causative force and all-embracing law which constitute the basis of the second formulation of the materialist conception of history.

4. HISTORICAL MATERIALISM AS A PHILOSOPHY OF HISTORY

Marx's social philosophy involves the idea that history and human society are in uninterrupted progressive development. Each stage is transitory, for it results from earlier developmental phases and is the starting-point of later ones by which it is bound to be replaced. Nothing can escape this constant flux. Every historically developed social form is in fluid movement, its nature is transient and its existence momentary. The Marxian theory of society and history is a reassertion of the reality and a consistent application of the principle of historical change.

While originally the materialist conception of history emphasized, above all, the evolutionary character of the state of flux, which is generated by the reciprocally modifying action of man on his environment, the second formulation underlines its conformity to law. In *Capital* the evolution of the economic formation of society is viewed as a 'process of natural history' subject to 'the natural laws of capitalist production . . . working with iron necessity towards inevitable results'. It is the ultimate aim of this work, wrote Marx in the Preface to *Capital*, 'to lay bare the economic law of motion of modern society'. The Russian reviewer of *Capital* observed that what Marx intended to do was to find 'the law of the phenomena' or, to put it differently, to reveal the invariant features of social events.[21]

This not only implies that, contrary to the belief of the utopians, men are not amenable to reason and will, but also that human behaviour and social institutions are strictly determined by laws over which men have no control. 'Marx treats the social movement', wrote the above mentioned Russian reviewer of *Capital* whom Marx quoted with approval, 'as a process of natural history, governed by laws not only independent of human will, consciousness and intelligence, but rather on the contrary, determining that will, consciousness and intelligence.'[22] For instance, under the conditions of free competition the inherent laws of capitalist production assume the shape of 'external coercive laws having power over every individual capitalist'. Little, if anything, depends on the good or ill will of the individual capitalist who merely incarnates the characteristics of the capitalist mode of production. Capital is as unmoved by the sight of physical and mental degradation, the premature death through overwork of the wage labourer, as by the plausible fall of the earth into the sun, its only consideration being the question of what increases its profits.[23]   The action of the capitalist, Marx wrote in another connection, is a mere function of capital, endowed in his person with consciousness and will.   'Fanatically bent on making value expand itself, he ruthlessly forces the human race to produce for production's sake.'   In this capacity the capitalist shares with the miser a passion for wealth as wealth.   'But that which in the miser is a mere idiosyncrasy, is in the capitalist the effect of the social mechanism, of which he is but one of the wheels.'   While the development of capitalist production makes it necessary for him to increase the proportion of constant capital, 'competition makes the immanent laws of capitalist production to be felt by each individual capitalist as external coercive laws; it compels him to keep constantly extending his capital, in order to preserve it, but extend it he cannot except by means of progressive accumulation'.   The thesis of sociological determinism, according to which in a class-divided society the individual is strictly determined in what he is and what he does by his class membership and class role, is one of the basic assumptions of the materialist conception of history in its second formulation.[24]

Therefore, men can no longer be described as both the authors and the actors of their own drama.   The drama is written and the stage is set for the play in which the actors should not be held responsible either for the allocation of parts or for their own performance;   for they are 'the personification of economic categories, embodiments of particular class relations and class interests'.   Since the reciprocal action and mutual modification between man and his environment are replaced by the strict determination of man's action by external conditions, it is no longer possible to assert that man makes his own history.   'When a society has got upon the right track for the discovery of the natural law of its movement,' Marx observed in *Capital*, 'it can neither clear by bold leaps, nor remove by legal enactments, the obstacles offered by the successive phases of its normal development.   But it can shorten and lessen the birth-pangs.'   In view of the fact that the necessity attached to the ordered march of social events abolished the power of man to change his circumstances, social evolution and advance can no longer be described as a self-generating process and remain unexplained.

In its second formulation the materialist conception of history has been transformed from a hypothesis concerning the genesis of social and historical events to a theory of historical causation, supposed to be based upon a study of historical causes and historical effects. This is the theory which explains social and historical development by the causal relationship between the economic base and the ideological superstructure, by the state of tension between the productive forces and the relations of production, by the conflict between the mode of production and property relations, or by the determination of ideological forms by the economic structure of society. The substantive materialist conception of history substitutes the law of variation and succession of historical periods for the original hypothesis of social evolution. The law of variation involves three assumptions. First, every socio-economic formation has a set of laws of its own which regulate its origin, development, and decay and which, therefore, must be *toto caelo* different from the laws of physics and chemistry. Second, the transition from one socio-economic formation to another is a necessary development, regardless of 'whether men believe or do not believe it, whether they are conscious or unconscious of it'.[25] Third, every socio-economic formation is ultimately replaced by another and higher formation, and thus a law of progress operates in social and historical development.

The second formulation of the materialist conception of history differs essentially from the first, for it is clearly a metaphysical rather than a methodological doctrine. In its capacity as a theory, historical materialism acquires an instrumental value which, as a 'guiding thread for study', it did not possess. Transformed into a theory of historical causation and social change, the materialist conception may be used as the method by means of which man can predict the future and thereby affect the course of history. No wonder, therefore, that it was the substantive, and not the methodological, formulation that was accepted by Lenin and Stalin as the basis of their voluntaristic interpretation of Marxian theories and which thus ultimately became a set of practical rules to guide the political action of the leaders of the Soviet state.

The theory of historical causation, which is the central part of the materialist conception of history in its substantive formulation, presents considerable difficulties to understanding. It does not consider the social and historical process as self-determined but explains it by the operation of reified concepts and factors external to human behaviour, either individual or collective, and human groups. In his defence of the Marxian theory against the criticism of Russian 'subjective' social philosophers Plekhanov pointed out that the relations of production are relations between men and, therefore, 'the self-development of the forms of production' is only a metaphorical way of speaking about men acting in a certain manner. Although it is clear that some of Marx's statements expressed in terms of his reified conceptual apparatus can be translated into statements about human individuals and their groups, the Marxian hypostatized language is certainly not uniformly translatable into one free from reification. Some definite relations between individuals and groups formulated in the Marxian language assume the form of relations between things and become things with definite properties. We can speak about the Fetishism of the Marxian conceptual sociological and historical framework as justifiably as Marx spoke about the Fetishism of the commodities in the capitalist mode of production. Fetishism, as Marx understood it, consists in attributing to the work of human hands and to the creations of the human mind a transcendent quality which endows it with the power of influencing and determining actual human behaviour.[26]

5. THE PROBLEMS OF THE VALIDATION OF HISTORICAL MATERIALISM

The substantive materialist conception of history is even more difficult to validate than its methodological formulation. The conceptual constructs of which it makes use, whether they are the sub- and the super-structure, the productive forces and the relations of production, are purely anlytical concepts, that is, they are distinguishable from each other in thought only, not in fact. Consequently, they have no distinct denotata in social reality which can be found separate from one another and which provide the concepts with an empirical significance. This is clear, in particular, in the instance of the productive forces, one of the component parts of what Marx called the 'social relations' or the 'material conditions of life'; according to his definition, the productive forces are the means of production together with the human skill and knowledge involved in their operation. The construct of productive forces has a connotation but no denotation; it does not designate any 'physically sensible' or 'material' object or a set of objects in the ordinary sense, as it should in accordance with Marx's implicitly, and Engels's explicitly, formulated demand.[27]   Consequently, if the propositions which state some universal relationships between the sub- and the super-structure or the productive forces and the relations of pro- duction are considered as theoretical statements, we do not know which empirically ascertainable facts would provide their confirma- tion or disconfirmation.

It is evident that criticism of the materialist conception along these lines is of modern origin and that it would not have occurred to Marx to approach the problem of validation from this point of view (although the modern supporters of the Marxian theories should be able to answer this objection).   Marx was, of course, aware that a mere assertion of logically related general propositions is not sufficient to establish a theory on a sound scientific basis. Marx repeatedly stated that unlike some social philosophers he did not invent his theory but discovered it, and this implied that his theory could be tested empirically.   The materialist conception of history faced the problem of validation as much as a contemporary theory, however different the respective views about what consti- tutes an effective validation of a scientific theory may be.

The problem of a satisfactory validation is made more complicated by the fact that the materialist conception is supposed to be a theory of social evolution (that the materialist conception provides the principles for the explanation of social evolution constitutes a common element of its two formulations).   This particular character of the materialist conception was emphatically noted by the Russian reviewer of *Capital* who, having observed that according to Marx every socio-economic formation has laws of its own,[28] continued:

> As soon as society has outlived a given period of development, and is passing over from one given stage to another, it begins to be subject also to other laws.   In a word, economic life offers us a phenomenon analogous to the history of evolution in other branches of biology.

Engels took up this suggestion and stated at the graveside of Marx that 'just as Darwin discovered the law of development of organic nature, so Marx discovered the law of development of human history'.[29]

Marx recognized that the evolution of the solar system or of life on earth or of human society is, in each case, a unique process. The socially or industrially more developed country, Marx wrote, shows the less developed the image of its own future.[30] His differentiation of the five main types of socio-economic formations, which are the necessary stages of the evolutionary process, do not contradict this fact. The concept of socio-economic formation makes it possible to investigate the similarities and dissimilarities of societies of the same type and to establish, by means of this 'criterion of recurrence',[31] the socio-economic laws which determine their structure and development. But the possibility of formulating and testing a specific set of social laws which govern the societies of a given type does not imply that we can discover and test the laws of social evolution. The numerical distinctness, the inevitable diversity of detail, and the conformity to laws characteristic for a given type of socio-economic formation should not conceal the fact that the evolutionary process as the process of transition from one economic formation of society to another remains unique. There is only one single law-like process which governs the succession of socio-economic formations and each society is bound to follow its predetermined course.

If the materialist conception of history in its second formulation is also an evolutionary hypothesis, the difficulty of validating it becomes insurmountable. We may assume that such a non-repetitive, unique process proceeds in accordance with all kinds of natural laws, established and tested by the natural and social sciences, but the statement describing this evolutionary process is bound to remain a singular historical statement. It is true that a unique historical process may be governed by a single all-embracing law. But if an observer were lucky enough to come upon this law, he would never know that he had made a true discovery. For any law, to be scientifically acceptable, has to be tested by new instances and this is impossible with respect to a process supposed to be unique and unrepeatable. 'We cannot hope to test a universal hypothesis nor to find a natural law acceptable to science if we are for ever confined to the observation of one unique process.'[32] A new, yet unrealized stage of an evolutionary process is a novelty. Although the emergence of a novelty can be announced in advance, such a forecast can turn out to be right only by a lucky guess. A novelty cannot be predicted by inference from a law which supposedly reflects the all-inclusive regularity of a unique process. On the other hand, only if we could make such a prediction successfully, would we be entitled to claim that the law was tested and confirmed. We test a theory by making predictions derived from this theory.

Marx could illustrate, but not validate, his second materialist conception of history. Thus, *Capital* provides a description of the genesis of the capitalist mode of production and the analysis of its structure and transformation, together with the laws that determine this type of economic organization. *Capital* could not and did not validate the hypothesis concerning the necessity of its replacement by a socialist formation into which the capitalist mode of production must inevitably pass over.

Marx did not, of course, share the above-explained view; he felt that he had established his evolutionary hypothesis as a universal law of history. A hypothesis may be enlightening, interesting, and fruitful without being a law; Darwin's conjecture concerning the origin of species is an instance in point. Merely because the Marxian second materialist conception of history is not a valid law of social evolution does not imply that it is not an important hypothesis.

Marx would not have been satisfied, however, with the distinction between hypotheses that are laws (for all laws are hypotheses) and hypotheses that for methodological reasons cannot raise this claim. Karl Popper suggested that Marx would not have been likely to accept this distinction because he wished to establish the coming of socialism by means of scientific prediction; since a scientific prediction is an inference from a law, the predictability of socialism presupposed a law of social evolution.[33] While Popper may rightly have seen the hidden motive of Marx's preoccupation with the evolutionary hypothesis, there is much evidence to the effect that Marx regarded this hypothesis as a genuine scientific discovery and as a law of nature securely established on an empirical basis. His reasons for believing this seem to be as follows.

Marx claimed that his own views about social evolution were superior to any others because of their conformity to the actual development of social and historical events.

> The theoretical conclusions of the Communists are in no way based on ideas or principles that have been invented, or discovered by this or that would-be universal reformer. They merely express, in general terms, actual relations springing from an existing class struggle, from a historical movement going on under our very eyes.[34]

Marx's scorn for his utopian contemporaries was inspired by their inability, as Marx said of Proudhon, to follow 'the real movement of history'.[35] The first utopians could have been excused, for as long as the productive forces were not sufficiently developed within the capitalist mode of production, the proletariat was not constituted as a class, and the struggle of the working class with the bourgeoisie did not acquire a political character, there was no indication of how the emancipation of the proletariat and the formation of a new society might be accomplished. He who saw the misery of the oppressed class could not help being utopian; in order to remedy the distress, he had to 'improvise systems and search for a regenerative science'. This was, however, no longer necessary for men like Proudhon or German 'true socialists' who remained utopians in and out of season, in spite of changed circumstances.

> As history continues, and the struggle of the proletariat takes shape more clearly, they have no further need to look for a science in their own minds; they have only to observe what is happening before their eyes, and to make themselves its vehicle of expression.[36]

When the incompatibility of the new productive forces and the capitalist mode of using them becomes apparent in the class struggle between the bourgeoisie and the proletariat, the only true and empirically valid theory of history and society is that which reflects the conflict inherent in this movement of events. Social knowledge, Marx argued, need not be 'excogitated *a priori*'; it can and should be derived 'from a critical knowledge of the historical movement which itself produces the natural conditions of emancipation'.[37] Modern socialism, wrote Engels, referring to the struggle of the two main classes of the industrial society, 'is nothing but the reflex, in thought, of this conflict in fact'.[38] Consequently, after the discovery of materialist-critical socialism, as Marx once described his own socialist theory, utopian socialism is not only a 'silly, stale, and basically reactionary doctrine, but also a false one'.[39]

Marx claimed that his fundamental laws of movement of society, the laws of the necessary relationship between the productive forces and the relations of production and between the economic foundation of society and its superstructure, were in agreement with social and historical development. The transformation of the productive forces and, more generally, of the economic foundation, can 'be determined', as Marx said, 'with the precision of natural science', that is, it is in each particular case an empirically testable state of affairs. In this sense, Marx can be said to be mainly an exponent of a theory of economic evolution and, in view of the widely ramified implications of the economic organization of society, an exponent of a theory of historical progress.[40] On the other hand, Marx clearly recognized in the Preface to *A Contribution to the Critique of Political Economy* that the relationship between the scientifically determinable economic conditions and the various elements of the ideological superstructure is not a fact to be established directly by observation. The testing of this relationship required the introduction of additional assumptions.

It was Marx's contention that the states of social consciousness, thoughts and ideas, legal, political, and other ideological forces cannot be scientifically treated unless they are investigated in their relation to the underlying economic conditions of life in which they originate This supposition may appear paradoxical and contrary to everyday observation. However, there would be no need for science at all, Marx observed, if one held fast to appearance and took it for the last word. 'It is also a paradox that the earth moves around the sun, and that water consists of two highly inflammable gases. Scientific truth is always paradox, if judged by everyday experience which catches only the delusive appearance of things.' The apparent phenomenon has to be distinguished from the concealed essence, the ostensible chaotic play of chance from the hidden conformity to law. The apparent motions of the heavenly bodies are not intelligible to anyone who is not acquainted with their real motions, motions which are not directly perceptible by the senses. 'All science would be superfluous if the forms of appearance of things coincided with their essence.'[41]

Marx accepted the ancient distinction between the delusive appearance and the true essence of things as a universally valid methodological and ontological principle, and combined it with the Kantian distinction between a phenomenal and noumenal reality in its Hegelian interpretation which denies the unknowability of the noumena. It should be remembered that Hegel countered the Kantian principle with the grand axiom, 'the magnificent absurdity', as F. A. Lange called it, of the unity of thought and existence, and announced that an unknown affirmed must be in some way known. Marx's own contribution to the views of Plato, Aristotle, Kant, and

Hegel was the identification of the essence of reality with the material world and of appearance with the world of ideas; the phenomenal world, that is, the world of ideas, was only a distorted image of the world of real, material objects. Thus, as it were, for Marx it was analytically true to say that ideas must be explained by discovering their concealed reality and their true essence, that is, the economic conditions in which they generate.[42]

Just as the real motions of the heavenly bodies have to be differentiated from the apparent ones, so the necessary tendencies underlying human behaviour and thought must be distinguished from their forms of manifestation. These necessary tendencies should not be explained on the basis of what people say about the sources of their views and the motives of their action, but 'from the existing conflict between the social productive forces and the relations of production' to be established by observation and investigation of the 'material, physically sensible conditions'.[43]

Marx claimed that although the necessary relationship between the economic conditions under which men live and their ideas is obviously not empirically observable, his hypothesis to the effect that 'men's material relations form the basis of all their relations' coincided with the 'motion of society'; while other historical interpretations had no *point d'appui* in reality, his law fitted the facts perfectly. Marx held the naïve belief, common at the time to the positivistically oriented historians and philosophers, that one and only one point of view can truly fit historical facts and that a historical hypothesis can escape the charge of being circular in its validation. Marx was unaware of the fact that since his law was supposed to be universal and all-embracing, descriptive of a unique and non-repetitive process, there could be no evidence, independent of the law, by which this theory might be confirmed or disconfirmed; for by the stipulation inherent in his point of view the only facts available are those which are interpreted and selected by means of the original assumption to be tested and which thus have to fit in with this assumption, that is, with the materialist conception of history.[44]

Marx should not be blamed for failing to see that there was no social and historical reality which, as it were, orders the facts, interprets them for us, transforms a factual series into an intelligible sequence of events, and makes us adopt one 'law of motion' rather than another; at that time the most prominent minds among historians and philosophers failed to see that history could never be a record of what 'es eigentlich gewesen war' and that the famous formula of Taine 'First collect the facts, then seek the cause' (*après la collection des faits, la recherche des causes*) could not be applied to history. Contrary to Engels's assertion,[45] there is no single red thread running through all the historical events, which one has only to follow to reach an understanding of the forward march of history. There are many such threads and we cannot accept one of them as the true one and reject the others as false. We can only evaluate them by the methodological criteria of consistency, comprehensiveness, simplicity, objectivity, and fertility.

The laws of motion of modern society looked very much like the laws found in natural science and the natural science of man was established precisely to discover laws of this sort. Once we accept the view that the whole of human history is subject to universal laws, the discovery of these laws becomes the fundamental problem of the social sciences; Turgot, Condorcet, Montesquieu, Hegel, Saint-Simon, Comte, John Stuart Mill, Marx, Spengler, and Toynbee were all seduced by this idea which turns out to be as sterile in its application as it is attractive in its general formulation. Engels managed to record for us the impression of the wide vistas which were opened to Marx and himself by the discovery of the law of human history. The materialist conception of history, Engels wrote, 'puts an end to philosophy in the realm of history. . . . It is no longer a question anywhere of inventing interconnections from out of our brains, but of discovering them in the facts.' [46] When we claim the knowledge of the law according to which a state of society produces 'with the inexorability of a law of nature' the consequent state, we are in a position to see the future in the process of formation by what is happening 'before our eyes'. If the present state of society is determined by its past, future society is determined by its present state; the law which explains contemporary history by what took place in the past allows us to foresee what the law tends to realize in our own day. Since the organization of production is fundamental for the development of all social institutions and social activities, the means of getting rid of the conflicts and evils present in contemporary society 'are not to be invented by deduction from principles, but are to be discovered in the stubborn facts of the existing system of production'.[47]

Thus, what Comte called 'scientific politics' and Engels 'scientific socialism' consists in the discovery of what 'the law of motion' tends to produce in the present state of society and in adjusting our action to the trends operating in conformity to this law. Communism as a prediction of the future state of society no longer meant, as Engels put it, 'the concoction, by means of the imagination, of an ideal society as perfect as possible, but an insight into the nature, the conditions and the consequent general aims of the struggle waged by the proletariat'.[48] Once the premiss is accepted that the law of motion of contemporary society has not been invented but simply discovered and securely established on a scientific basis, it becomes a reliable method of predicting the future and of unveiling the secrets of human destiny.

The Sociological Approach of Engels

IT is usually held to be self-evident that Marx's and Engels's views on historical materialism can be combined into a single undifferentiated whole. At the same time, there is a tendency to treat Engels's presentation of the materialist conception of history as little more than an exegetical or popular exposition of the doctrine to be found in its theoretical and complete form only in Marx. It has been pointed out earlier that owing to his admirable modesty Engels himself fostered this attitude towards his work, an attitude very widespread among students of Marxian doctrines today. This view of Engels is not altogether just or right and never less so than with respect to his part in the discovery of the materialist conception of history.

1. ENGELS'S CONTRIBUTION TO THE MATERIALIST CONCEPTION OF HISTORY

In his essay *On the History of the Communist League* (1885) Engels referred to his first stay in Manchester (1842–4) when

> it was tangibly brought home to me that the economic facts, which have so far played no role or only a contemptible one in the writing of history, are, at least in the modern world, a decisive historical force; that they form the basis of the origination of the present-day class antagonism; that these class antagonisms in the countries where they have become fully developed, thanks to large-scale industry, hence especially in England, are in their turn the basis of the formation of political parties and of party struggles, and thus of all political history.[1]

When on his way back from England to Germany Engels visited Marx in Paris in the summer of 1844, with the manuscript of *The Condition of the Working Class in England* ready for print, he and Marx discovered 'their complete agreement in all theoretical fields'. According to Engels, in his essays published in *Deutsch-Französische Jahrbücher* (1844) [2] Marx not only arrived 'at the same view' about the role played by economic facts in the modern world, but also generalized it to the effect that 'it is not the state which conditions and regulates civil society, but civil society which conditions and regulates the state'. One year later they met again in Brussels and Marx, as Engels reported, 'had already fully developed his materialist theory of history in its main features from the above mentioned basis'. What Engels described as the fully developed theory is to be found in *The Holy Family* and *The German Ideology*. From then onward 'we applied ourselves', Engels noted, 'to the detailed elaboration of the newly-won mode of outlook in the most varied directions'.[3] Engels's own account concerning the development of his ideas before 1845 is corroborated by the content of his early publication and is in agreement with Marx's testimony. In his Preface to *A Contribution to the Critique of Political Economy* and in his introduction to Engels's *Socialisme utopique et socialisme scientifique* Marx recognized the independence of Engels's ideas and his genuine contribution to scientific socialism, in particular, in his *Outlines of a Critique of Political Economy* (1844) and *The Condition of the Working Class in England*.[4]

It is clear from these accounts that only the second, the substantive formulation of the materialist conception of history, could be considered as Marx's exclusive property. The first, the methodological formulation, is the joint achievement of Marx and Engels. The independence and originality of Engels's contribution to the materialist conception of history is still preserved in his early publications and in much of what he said on the materialist conception later in life, when he provided, as is so frequently claimed, solely an exegesis of Marx's great discovery.

In *Anti-Dühring* and even more strikingly in *Socialism: Utopian and Scientific* Engels gave his views on the intellectual and social background of the materialist conception of history. On the intellectual level, the materialist conception arose from the rejection of the old materialism which 'looked upon all previous history as a crude heap of irrationality and violence'. In contradistinction to the views of the Enlightenment, nineteenth-century materialism saw in history 'the process of evolution of humanity' and aimed at discovering its laws. Engels attributed the change to the new intellectual climate brought about by the replacement of the meta-physical by the dialectical conception of nature, in Engels's original sense of the expression, to be sharply distinguished from its later application, in particular, from Stalin's use of it. The realization that we 'live not only in nature but also in society' inspired the effort to reconstruct the science of society on the same basis as the science of nature, that is, on the materialist foundation. At that time, Engels wrote, natural science made increasing use of the cate-gory of change, process, and development in its description of the world, and replaced the 'artificial interconnections' of events by the real ones discovered by observation and experiment. To be based on the evolutionary and naturalistic principle, the science of society should follow in the footsteps of natural science, do away in its own field with the 'fabricated interconnections', and try to discover the 'general laws of motion which assert themselves . . . in the history of human society'.[5] Engels's description of the pro-gramme of nineteenth-century materialism in the social and his-torical sciences strongly resembles the appeal made by the young Comte to the *savants* to elevate social physics and the art of politics to the rank of a positive science. They were to abandon the habit of considering ideas as personified abstractions and to connect facts by laws of a completely positive kind, arising from or confirmed by these facts.[6]

In Engels's view it was not, however, the revolution in the con-ception of nature which exercised a decisive influence upon the reconstruction of the science of society on a new basis; the rise of a natural science of society was bound up with certain historical events occurring at that time.

> In 1831 the first working-class rising took place in Lyons; between 1838 and 1842 the first national working-class move-ment, that of the English Chartists, reached its height. The class struggle between proletariat and bourgeoisie came to the front in the history of the most advanced countries of Europe. . . . Facts more and more strenuously gave the lie to the teachings of bourgeois economy as to the identity of the interests of capital and labour, as to the universal harmony and universal prosperity that would be the consequence of unbridled compe-tition.[7]

These facts, concluded Engels, could not be reconciled with the idealist conception of history which ignored the economic relations, the conflict of class interests, the struggle of social classes, and their role in human life.

Engels's excursion into the sociology of the materialist conception of history described in general terms his own road to its discovery. Unlike Marx, whose point of departure was the world of Hegelian abstractions, Engels based his view of history, conceived as the scene of the interplay and operation of antagonistic forces, on the observation of social developments in England and on a sociological analysis of current events. In contradistinction to Marx's investigations which made use of philosophic procedures, Engels's approach to the problems of the science of society was concrete and sociological throughout. Whenever he explained the meaning and implications of the materialist conception of history, he was inclined to emphasize its sociological aspect and formulate it in terms of social classes, the struggle and conflict of their interests rather than in terms of basis and superstructure or productive forces and relations of production. The emphasis attached to the sociological aspect of the materialist conception might have weakened somewhat during the time of Marx's ascendancy over Engels, but after Marx's death it came into its own again. Towards the end of his life, Engels increasingly concentrated on the observation and analysis of the social scene and drew his evidence in support of the materialist conception therefrom. In particular, he claimed that the industrial revolution, which, since 1848, had seized the whole of the Continent, had everywhere produced 'clarity in class relations' and so simplified the situation that 'one would have had to close one's eyes deliberately not to see in the fight of the three great classes [sc. the landed aristocracy, the bourgeoisie, and the proletariat] and in the conflict of their interests the driving force of modern history'.[8] Engels came close to the claim that in view of the ubiquity of the class struggle the materialist conception of history was self-evident and thus in no need of further validation.[9]

Engels's emphasis upon the class struggle was not only due to the fact that he discovered its function in history independently of Marx. Engels was convinced that in every historical epoch the prevailing mode of economic production, the system of exchange, and the structure of society necessarily arising therefrom, form the basis upon which is built, and from which alone can be explained, the political and intellectual history of that epoch. We cannot, however, apply this fundamental proposition of historical materialism to any social or historical situation unless we translate it into empirical language which allows us to speak of observable objects, human behaviour, social classes and their relations, that is, of the whole class system. The class system is the empirical basis of the Marxian theoretical propositions which should be regarded, therefore, as a sociological theory of the class division and class struggle. The Marxian explanatory and predictive principles concerned with the division of labour, the relations of production, the property relations or, more generally, the mode of production and of exchange, establish certain structural and dynamic properties of society, but these properties are not empirically significant unless they are attributes of the individuals of the Marxian universe of discourse, that is, of social classes.

In a simplified form the fundamental proposition of the materialist conception of history can be stated in the words, familiar from *The Communist Manifesto*, that 'the whole history of mankind, since the dissolution of primitive society, holding land in common ownership, has been a history of class struggles'. The relations into which men enter in order to produce their means of subsistence, present themselves to them, in the first place, as antagonistic or incompatible interests; these interests determine the class divisions and the ensuing struggle of the classes. If we assume generally what is quite clear in some particular cases, namely, that thoughts, ideas, legal, political, and other ideological forms are expresssions of the underlying class divisions and conflicts and that the latter are reflected, though in a distorted form, in the former, we arrive at the great law of motion of history. According to this law, which has the same significance for history as the law of the transformation of energy has for natural science, 'all historical struggles, whether they proceed in the political, religious, philosophical or some other ideological domain, are in fact only the more or less clear expression of struggles of social classes'; as Marx said, men become conscious of their economic conflicts in their ideas and beliefs and fight their conflicts out by means of these ideas and beliefs.[10]

Engels's contribution to the materialist conception of history was that he provided it with an empirical and sociological significance; he covered the bare skeleton of its abstract Marxian formulation, familiar from the Preface to *A Contribution to the Critique of Political Economy*, with the living flesh of social, historical, and cultural facts, and thus prevented the basic assumption, 'Men make their own history', from disappearing into oblivion. Without the human agent acting on the stage of history, however confused and deceived he might be about his own motives and objectives, no historiography and no philosophy of history can safeguard its profane, as Marx used to say, its realistic and common-sense character. Engels never forgot that men make their own history. While Marx was the first to state that history is nothing but the activity of men in pursuit of their various ends, later he let this insight fall into limbo and looked at men, as Karl Popper rightly says, 'as mere puppets, irresistibly pulled by economic wires'.[11] On his part, Engels never forgot that men make their own history and never treated them as symbols or the incarnation of some external force.

It is important to emphasize this contribution of Engels, for he was also inclined, particularly in Marx's lifetime, but also later when he was left alone as the guardian of the doctrine, to regard the materialist conception of history as a philosophical theory of historical causation. Engels was anxious to discover what he variously called the 'driving force' or the 'moving power' of history and was constantly searching for 'the ultimate cause', 'the determining factor', 'the ultimately decisive conditions' or *primum agens* of history.[12] Impressed by Marx's historical studies, he felt it was the historian's most important task to lay bare the course of events in their inner interconnections and to reduce this course of events to a necessary result of these interconnections; he thought that thereby history was shown to be a natural process.[13] Marx also persuaded Engels that he had discovered the economic law of motion of modern society and Engels never failed to emphasize this claim. Although historical events may appear to be subject to chance, 'history is governed by inner general laws'.[14] Engels's concern with the final cause or the ultimate decisive factor in history and his insistence on the reduction of a sequence of events to 'inner hidden laws' transformed a sociological hypothesis and a historical point of view into a speculative metaphysical doctrine, with the appearance, but not the substance, of a scientific theory.

Besides the sociological and metaphysical approaches to the fundamental proposition of historical materialism, which Engels may have considered as supporting each other, there is also a methodological interpretation to be found in Engels. Thus, in *The Housing Question* Engels defined the materialist conception of history as a procedure 'which explains all historical events and ideas, all politics, philosophy and religion, from the material, economic conditions of life of the historical period in question'.[15] As Engels said, 'to demonstrate the inner causal connection in the course of a development' is 'to trace political events back to effects of what were, in the final analysis, economic causes'.[16] That the materialist conception should be regarded by Engels both as a substantive theory and a methodological procedure, the two approaches being indistinguishably merged in the exposition of historical materialism in *Anti-Dühring*,[17] is perfectly comprehensible in view of his Hegelian apprenticeship. To apply the fundamental proposition of the materialist conception as a methodological rule is to establish the validity of this proposition as a substantive theory.

2. THE REVISION OF HISTORICAL MATERIALISM

It was the methodological rather than the metaphysical interpretation of the materialist conception of history that led to its revision by Engels in the last five years of his life. Engels assumed responsibility for himself and for Marx for the misunderstandings to which their exposition of the materialist conception gave rise and which reduced it to a monistic economic determinism. Engels's explanation of how the misunderstanding arose is plausible and convincing. We were so absorbed, he said in substance, in 'emphasizing the main principle *vis-à-vis* our adversaries' that we had neither time nor opportunity to consider in what way other factors than economic ones were involved in the process of interaction between the basis and the superstructure. The derivation of political, juridical, and other ideological notions from economic conditions became the distinctive feature of the materialist conception of history and both its supporters and adversaries concluded that the materialist conception asserted no more than that.[18] There is, indeed, very little in Marx's later writings which would suggest that he attributed a significant role to ideas, to human will and purposeful action in the course of history. As far as Engels is concerned, Eduard Bernstein correctly observed that Engels 'originally assigned to the non-economic factors considerably less influence on the evolution of society, considerably less power of modifying by their action the conditions of production' than he did later in life.[19]

If the materialist conception of history is supposed to imply economic determinism, Engels wrote over and over again, he wished to have nothing to do with it.

> According to the materialist conception of history, the ultimately determining element in history is the production and reproduction of real life. More than this neither Marx nor I have ever asserted. Hence if somebody twists this into saying that the economic element is the only determining one, he transforms that proposition into a meaningless, abstract, senseless phrase.
>
> Hanging together with this is the fatuous notion of the ideologists that because we deny an independent historical development to the various ideological spheres which play a part in history we also deny them any effect upon history . . . once a historic element has been brought into the world by other, ultimately economic causes, it reacts, can react on its environment and even on the causes that have given rise to it.[20]

Having rejected monistic economic determinism, Engels replaces it by the principle of the interaction between the sub- and superstructure and the principle of the relative independence of ideological factors. The revised materialist conception of history is thus transformed into a doctrine of a qualified economic determinism; the role of the material conditions of life in social and historical development is no longer prescriptive but only restrictive. In Engels's own terminology, the economic movement gets its way on the whole, is by far the most decisive, and asserts itself in the last resort.[21]

Engels mentioned the principle of the relative independence of ideological factors in *Ludwig Feuerbach,* where he maintained that though the realm of economic relations is decisive with respect to ideological forms or ideologies, the latter, the state, law, and religion in particular, are endowed with a relative independence and are capable of operating as causes of subsequent events.[22] It is, however, in the letters written in connection with the revision of the materialist conception of history that Engels dealt with this problem at length.

> The economic situation is the basis, but the various elements of the superstructure . . . also exercise their influence upon the course of the historical struggle and in many cases preponderate in determining their form. There is an interaction of all those elements . . .

Political, juridical, philosophical, religious, literary, artistic, etc., development is based on economic development. But all these react upon one another and also upon the economic basis. It is not that the economic condition is the cause and alone active, while everything else only has a passive effect. There is, rather, interaction on the basis of economic necessity, which ultimately always asserts itself.[23]

Engels emphasized the fact that even a genetically secondary element, such as trade or money market, which is within the direct reach of influence of the substructure, may acquire 'special laws determined by its own nature and separate phases' and follow a 'development of its own'. The relative independence with which the elements of the superstructure are endowed seems to increase in proportion to the distance from the economic base, which, therefore, least determines the pure and abstract forms of ideology. For instance, trade is less independent in some respects of the mode of production than is the power of the state or the political system, and the latter are less independent than law and the higher ideologies, such as religion and philosophy. The material mode of existence is the prime cause and determining factor in the relation between state power and economic conditions, law and production, conception of nature and economic necessity, philosophy and economic development. Nevertheless, the ideologies and ideological forms may, in virtue of their inherent relative independence, react upon the whole development of society or on the conditions and course of production and, within certain limits, modify them. While, on the whole, the economic movement gets its way, it is also influenced by ideological movements which it had established itself and endowed with relative independence.[24]

The doctrine of a qualified economic determinism still singles out one variable factor, the state of the productive forces of society, which is assumed to determine decisively all forms of social relations, the political, juridical, and moral order, and the artistic, religious, and philosophical activity. However, the charge raised against the Marxian doctrine that it isolates one single determinant which, in fact, can never operate alone and thus should never be set apart from others, no longer applies.[25] Engels refused to accept such a 'hollow abstraction' and claimed that instead of isolating one single factor producing 'an automatic effect' we should consider the whole vast social process as operating in the form of interaction in which various determinants, though of unequal force, are involved. To be a determinant is not necessarily to be genetically independent. According to Engels, when such determining factors as the political order, the system of laws, conceptions of the universe, natural science, or philosophy have once emerged, they can and do act in turn as causes. They are capable of originating new causal chains, of influencing social development, and even of modifying in some degree the economic advance, i.e. the operation of forces from which they derive. Thus, the economic movement does not act in isolation and is not a unique causal factor, but only 'the strongest, most primeval and most decisive' in a number of interacting determinants.[26]

To assume that events follow each other in conformity to laws of succession and that such sequences constitute a causal chain is (or rather used to be) a logical postulate of scientific inquiry. But the idea that all such causal chains constitute a single whole; that they are ultimately attached to one factor only, the cause of all other causes, *la grande cause, la cause universelle et permanente* of Taine; and that they are thus subject to one causal law is no longer a postulate of scientific inquiry but the expression of an extra-scientific, metaphysical principle. The revision of the materialist conception of history accomplished by Engels has done much to emancipate the materialist conception from this metaphysical principle and to replace it by a methodological postulate. Instead of prescribing what must happen, the materialist conception states restrictively what cannot take place. Thus, the materialist conception of history turned back towards the original starting-point of Marx, from which Marx himself had moved further and further away in his later years, that 'men make their own history but they do not make it just as they please'. Engels fully realized the implication of his revision. 'So it is not,' he wrote, 'as people try here and there conveniently to imagine, that the economic conditions produce an automatic effect. No. Men make their history themselves.' [27]

There was, however, one implication of the revision which Engels did not notice and which — Eduard Bernstein was again quick to observe — undermined the so-called scientific socialism in one of its important meanings. Once monistic economic determinism is abandoned, there is no other necessity in history and no methodological basis for historical prediction. If history results from a number of interacting factors, there is no single law of succession of distinct stages in social and historical development. Thus, prediction turns into prophecy, and socialism, unable to foresee the future, is no longer a science in Engels's sense.

3. ENGELS'S VIEWS ON THE VALIDATION OF HISTORICAL MATERIALISM

It has been mentioned earlier that according to some scholars there was something obvious for Marx and Engels in the materialist conception of history. It is true that in his review of *A Contribution to the Critique of Political Economy* Engels considered the proposition 'the social being of men determines their consciousness' as 'so simple that it must be self-evident to anyone who is not bemused by idealist delusions'.[28] The expression 'self-evident' must have been, however, a slip of the pen. 'Only a mass of critically sifted, completely mastered historical material', wrote Engels in the same article, can establish the validity of the materialist conception 'even in regard to a single historical example'.[29] In conformity with this view Engels announced in 1890 that 'our conception of history is above all a guide to study, not a lever for construction *à la* Hegelianism. All history must be studied afresh.'[30] The materialist conception should be validated in the same manner as any other hypothesis or point of view in history, namely, by showing that it does explain the events, fits the facts, and, generally, is a fruitful tool of research.

It is true, however, that elsewhere Engels regarded the materialist conception of history not only as a hypothesis in need of confirmation to 'be derived from history itself', but also a point of view which had been reliably verified. The confirming evidence was to be found in *The Class Struggles in France, 1848 to 1850, The Eighteenth Brumaire of Louis Bonaparte, The Peasant War in Germany*, and, above all, in *Capital* with its analysis of the laws of the capitalist mode of production, the inevitableness of capitalism at a particular stage of history, and its inexorable downfall.[31] The increasing role played in contemporary history by the class struggle which, in Engels's opinion, could be seen more and more plainly in practically every European country, must also have appeared as a strong confirmation of the materialist conception. 'In modern history at least it is . . . proved that all political struggles are class struggles, and all class struggles for emancipation, despite their necessarily political form . . . turn ultimately on the question of economic emancipation.' [32]

Moreover, it should be conceded that on certain occasions Engels went beyond the above-described evaluation and argued that Marx actually 'proved that the whole of previous history is a history of class struggles'.[33] The proof mentioned in this extraordinary claim is a clear instance of the fallacy of the *post hoc, ergo propter hoc*, often uncritically repeated since its utterance by Engels.

The fallacy might have been inspired by Marx's observation in *The German Ideology* that 'men must be in a position to live in order to be able to make history'. Since life requires 'eating and drinking, a habitation, clothing and many other things', the first act of man in history must be concerned with the production of the means of subsistence and the preservation of life. 'This is indeed a historical act,' Marx concluded, 'a fundamental condition of all history, which today, as thousands of years ago, must be accomplished every day and every hour merely in order to sustain human life.' Every child knows, Marx observed in a letter to Dr. Kugelmann, that a country which ceased to work, even for a few weeks, would die. This basic law of life cannot be abolished; one can only change the form it assumes.[34]

That in order to do anything else men must first keep alive is a view worth emphasizing only in a historical review of the evolution of human society; in such a review the insistence on a certain necessary time order in the whole range of human activity is inevitable. Engels was, of course, familiar with the idea that the material-ist conception of history could be regarded as an evolutionary hypothesis concerning the development of man and society. In *Dialectics of Nature* Engels implicitly suggested that the materialist conception could be conceived as a hypothesis of how man, the tool-maker, rose from the animal kingdom to acquire an increasing con-trol over nature and thus civilize himself.[35] This anthropological and historical approach could be used to explain how the making and using of tools resulted in the breaking up of the feudal society, the emergence and growth of the capitalist mode of production, and the transformation of the capitalist system into a new form of social life. The materialist conception would thus become a distinctive way of perceiving what happened in history and would provide a 'natural and reasonable explanation' of the rise of human civilization. As a purely evolutionary hypothesis, the materialist conception would carry its confirmation within itself; it would be entitled to demand acceptance if and so far as it could claim fruitfulness, objectivity, and a comprehensive scope of application.

This is not the use which Engels tried to make of Marx's observation. Engels used the arguments which would support an evolutionary theory of society to validate a substantive social theory, and for this purpose the time order, the temporal rhythm and the natural succession of various human activities, emphasized in *The German Ideology*, were entirely irrelevant. Engels failed to notice this and claimed that Marx discovered

> the simple fact, hitherto concealed by an overgrowth of ideology, that mankind must first of all eat, drink, have shelter and clothing, before it can pursue politics, science, art, religion, etc.; that therefore the production of the immediate material means of subsistence and consequently the degree of economic development attained by a given people or during a given epoch form the foundation upon which the state institutions, the legal conceptions, the ideas on art, and even on religion, of the people concerned have been evolved, and in the light of which they must, therefore, be explained, instead of vice versa, as had hitherto been the case.[36]

The palpable but previously totally overlooked fact, as Engels put it, that before men can fight for power, prestige, and domination, and indulge in other pursuits, they must first work to produce their means of subsistence, does not place history on 'its real basis'. The dictum 'Primum vivere deinde philosophari' does not establish the causal relationship but only a temporal succession between living and philosophizing; it expresses the fact that in every type of civilization certain activities are biologically determined by human anatomy and that certain primary needs must be satisfied to secure the survival of the individual and the group.[37] It does not establish what Marx and Engels believed to be the case, namely, that the material conditions of life determine all forms of social activity and relations, political, legal, moral, artistic, scientific, or religious. Nobody in his right senses would deny that eating and drinking, just as breathing, the sexual act, or other physiological functions, are necessary conditions of man's other activities. This does not imply that any one of these necessary conditions or even all of them taken together are the sufficient conditions, that is, the cause in the sense relevant in this context, of all other pursuits of man.   It is clearly false to assert that the temporal succession emphasized by Engels provides the explanation of all historical phenomena 'in the simplest possible way'.[38]

Finally, the Marxian way of validating the materialist conception of history is to be found in Engels.   In *Ludwig Feuerbach* Engels reached the conclusion that the motives and actions of human individuals were in relation to the total result — the ordered march of history — of secondary importance only; that the struggle of the landed aristocracy, the bourgeoisie, and the proletariat was the driving force of modern history; that the origin of these classes and the development of their struggle lay clearly and palpably in purely economic causes; and that political power served merely as a means to the furtherance of class economic interests.[39]   This hypothesis revealed the inner causal connections of events, conferred significance upon them and transformed their mere succession in time into a meaningful sequence.   Once assumed, everything confirmed it, and it spread light and understanding not only on the past, but also on the future.   The examination of the 'historico-economic succession of events' would disclose what was bound to happen.[40]   Engels clearly claimed that the materialist conception of history was a valid theory of history because it corresponds with the development of events.

4. THE RELATION OF HISTORICAL TO DIALECTICAL MATERIALISM

Although Engels may have hesitated to assert with Lenin that the materialist conception of history is no longer a hypothesis, but a scientifically proven proposition, he believed implicitly in its truth. 'After history also was subjected to materialistic treatment', Engels commented without noticing the equivocal meaning of the term 'materialistic', 'a new avenue of development has opened.'[41]   This new avenue was the possibility of inquiring into the nature and constitution of the universe as a whole, the prospect of demonstrating that the universe is uniformly material in its nature and dialectical in its constitution.

Thus, Engels started a new departure, not to be found anywhere in Marx, though it was Marx whom he named as having justified him in adventuring on the metaphysical construction. Thanks to Marx, 'idealism was driven from its last refuge, the conception of history; a materialistic treatment of history was propounded and a method found of explaining the consciousness of man by his being, instead of, as heretofore, his being by his consciousness'.[42] While Marx helped establish the material unity of the universe, comprising both the world of nature and the world of man, Engels alone extended the laws found in history to nature and conferred upon the universe as a whole ontological and dialectical uniformity.

The 'general laws of motion', which according to Engels govern the development of nature, human society, and thought, are not those discovered in the historical process by Marx but Hegel's laws of dialectics. 'I undertook the study of mathematics and natural science', Engels confessed,

> to convince myself also in details — of what in general I was not in doubt — that in nature, amid the welter of innumerable changes, the same dialectical laws of motion force their way through as those which in history govern the apparent fortuitousness of events; the same laws as those which similarly form the thread running through the history of the development of human thought and gradually rise to consciousness in the mind of man; the laws which Hegel first developed in all-embracing but mystic form, and which we made it one of our aims to strip of this mystic form and to bring clearly before the mind in their complete simplicity and universality.[43]

Engels took advantage of the materialist conception of history and of Hegel's laws of dialectics to advance a metaphysical construction which was to comprise nature, society, history, and thought.

According to Engels, genetically, dialectical materialism had its original roots in historical materialism; logically, the former is prior to the latter. However, contrary to what is so frequently asserted, neither Marx nor Engels deduced historical materialism from dialectical materialism nor did either of them suggest that this inference can or should be made. But Engels prepared the ground for the claim of the deducibility of historical materialism from dialectical materialism and thereby left to his philosophical heirs an inheritance fraught with intellectually disastrous consequences.

XI

Plekhanov's Unification of Dialectical and Historical Materialism

THAT philosophical thought is a historical phenomenon and its content subject to the restrictive conditions of its time, is one of the original ideas of Marx which were increasingly ignored by his followers, eventually to become altogether forgotten by them. In Lenin and Stalin no trace is left of the Marxian belief that history reveals something about the ontological roots, the social meaning and value of that of which it is the history. Compared with the philosophy of Bergson, Whitehead, or Dewey, with its insistence on the temporality of every existence as a constitutive attribute of being, on the one hand, and with the essentialism of Plato, Aristotle, or Husserl, who saw the chief task of knowledge in the discovery of the hidden and unchanging essence of things on the other, the present-day interpretations of the Marxian philosophy are closer to the essentialists, to Aristotle in particular, than to Marx and other philosophers of temporality. The increasing abandonment of historism (to use this word, suggested by Pieter Geyl, as the English equivalent for the German *Historismus*) by the followers of Marx is an indication of the growing subordination of historical materialism to dialectical materialism. The metaphysics of dialectical material-ism with its claim to absolute truth is incompatible with historism and its conception of philosophy as part of history and culture, caught in their movement of change.

In the case of Plekhanov, the retreat from the historicity of thought was tempered by his genuine interest in history, which clearly dominated over his other theoretical pursuits. But Plekhanov, too, was a follower of Engels rather than of Marx. In his examination of the philosophical problems of the historical sciences he was as unprepared as Engels to abandon the framework of dialectical materialism.

Plekhanov took seriously Engels's pronouncement that the materialist conception of history was a guide to study and not a lever for speculative constructions. He brought to his task a pronounced historical bent and a wide erudition ranging over fields as varied as the history of philosophy and the history of social thought, art and literary criticism, sociology and anthropology. Anyone who is familiar with Plekhanov's writings cannot fail to notice that this remarkable writer was well qualified to provide a comprehensive and detailed account of the materialist interpretation of history and to show how the materialist explanation applied to all manifestations of social life.

If Plekhanov did not fulfil the expectations which his qualifications warranted, this was largely due to the fact that in his two major works dealing with the materialist conception of history he was more concerned, as he himself admitted, with the examination and refutation of the objections to the Marxian ideas than with their systematic exposition.[1] Plekhanov was determined, above all, to discredit the view, widely accepted in Russia and also elsewhere, that the materialist conception of history was a reductive economic materialism and to show that Marx neither ignored the role of thought nor underestimated the importance of ideas and ideals in history. Plekhanov agreed with the critics of Marx that if these objections were true, the materialist interpretation should be rejected, for it would be inadequate and clearly false. He proceeded, therefore, to demonstrate that far from underestimating the role of thought and feeling in history Marx considered the explanation of man's spiritual achievements to be the most important task of social science. It was entirely wrong to present Marx as a man who saw only economic factors everywhere. On the contrary, Plekhanov declared, it was precisely Marx who made people aware of the many dimensions and levels of social reality which must be investigated if man's progress and achievements are to be adequately described and explained.

I. THE INTELLECTUAL BACKGROUND OF THE MARXIAN THEORY

Plekhanov gave two related but different interpretations of the materialist conception of history. The first, to be found in *The*

Development of the Monist View of History, presents the materialist conception as an evolutionary theory of human society. The second interpretation, set forth in *Fundamental Problems of Marxism*, is a substantive theory of history rather than an evolutionary hypothesis (though its evolutionary or dynamic aspect is constantly emphasized).

Plekhanov turned Engels's comparison of Marx to Darwin into something more than a mere laudatory figure of speech. Plekhanov compared Marx to Darwin since they both established a point of view from which the whole history of animal species and the whole history of human society and civilization could be understood.[2] The evaluation of the Marxian evolutionary hypothesis need not be postponed until the history of all periods, based on this hypothesis, is available; Marx himself could not accomplish this task just as Darwin could not write the history of all animal and vegetable species. On the other hand, the Marxian evolutionary hypothesis was not left altogether without confirmation, for *Capital* was the beginning of the study of the real history of mankind from the new point of view.[3]

The affinity between Darwin and Marx is not limited to the fact that they both tried to formulate a law of evolution; the fields to which their laws were to apply were contiguous and their principles were similar in some general aspects. The fields of application of the two hypotheses are contiguous, without the one being an extension of the other, because with the appearance of the human species further evolution ceases to be biological and becomes social. Having discovered the first implements of labour and thus acquired, as it were, new organs, man, the tool-making animal, has given quite a distinctive character to his development.

> Previously, as with all other animals, it amounted to changes in his natural organs. Since that time it has become first of all the history of the perfecting of his artificial organs, the growth of his productive forces. . . . From the point of view of the philosophy of history it is extremely important to note that from the time the artificial organs of man began to play a decisive part in his existence, his social life itself began to change, in accordance with the course of development of his productive forces.[4]

In producing their means of subsistence men not only act on nature, but also on one another and enter into definite reciprocal connections and relations, within which their action on nature and production take place. Through the social relations of production, which are transformed with the change of the productive forces and which confer upon society its peculiar and distinctive character, the material means of production determine the definite stages of social evolution.

From this point of view it can be said that Marx begins precisely where Darwin's investigation ends; there is considerable similarity in their respective approach to the solution of the problem of the origin of the animal species and of the genesis of different types of social organization. As Plekhanov put it, 'the spirit of their research is absolutely the same in both thinkers' and for this reason one can say, although chronologically this is not correct, that 'Marxism is Darwinism in its application to social science'.

> Darwin explains the origin of species not by an allegedly innate tendency to develop in the animal organism as Lamarck did, but by the adaptation of the organism to the conditions outside it; not by the nature of the organism but by the influence of external nature. Marx explains the historical development of man not by the nature of man but by the characteristics of those social relations between men which arise when social man is acting on external nature.[5]

Plekhanov believed that the Marxian evolutionary hypothesis of human society was a valid theory for two main reasons; it was confirmed by the historical and social events to which it was applied and it gave the right answer to the long-sought solution of the problem concerning the relation of man, the human individual, to his physical and social environment. That the Marxian answer was the correct one may be seen directly by reviewing the earlier unsuccessful attempts to find the solution.

According to Plekhanov, the French materialists of the eighteenth century firmly believed that in keeping with Locke's assumption, 'There are no innate principles', man and all his opinions were the product of his environment. 'L'homme est tout éducation', wrote Helvétius, using 'éducation' in the sense of the sum total of social influences. On the other hand, the French materialists were committed to the belief, incompatible with this one, that the social world was governed by opinions and that *le progrès des lumières* would bring about an inevitable social advance towards perfection. This basic inconsistency — man is the product of his environment and environment is the product of man's opinions — appeared over and over again. For instance, both Montesquieu and Sismondi argued that the political constitution is determined by the customs of the people and that the customs of the people are conditioned by the constitution under which they live. Saint-Simon recognized that ideas are conditioned by social factors and interests, but there was no doubt in his mind that philosophers rule opinion and opinion rules the world.

The inconsistency in the views of the French materialists was, however, more apparent than real. For it is certainly true that environment conditions human opinions and opinions shape the environment; they interact and are functionally related. This suggests the existence of an intervening factor, on which both the opinions and the environment ultimately depend. The search for this intervening factor constituted the main problem with which the historians and social philosophers were faced in the first half of the nineteenth century. Marx's discovery of the materialist conception of history is closely bound up with this search.[6]

The French historians of the Restoration, Guizot, Thierry, and Mignet, made a considerable step forward when they suggested that neither should the political constitutions be explained by the customs of the people nor the customs of the people by the political constitutions, but that both these factors were dependent on a third determinant, concealed behind the first two at a deeper level, namely, the property relations and the class divisions associated with them. To put it in Marxian language, the French historians discovered that the anatomy of civil society was to be sought in property relations. They were unable, however, to answer the question as to how the differences and changes in the property relations should be accounted for. The vague references to human nature provided no satisfactory explanatory principle, because no constant factor — human nature was then conceived as invariable and fixed once and for all — could account for the changes of a variable factor. Moreover, in a concealed form the explanation in terms of human nature was a return to the old vicious circle of environment being created by man and man being determined by environment.[7]

As Marx said himself in his Preface to *A Contribution to the Critique of Political Economy*, the conclusion established by the French historians of the Restoration, namely, that political constitutions are rooted in social relations which on their part are determined by the system of property, constituted the point of departure of Marx's own solution of the problem concerning the nature of the driving force and the source of social evolution. However, before Marx could arrive at his solution, the traditional view of history had first to be thoroughly revised. This revision was accomplished, according to Plekhanov, by Saint-Simon and, above all, by Hegel.

The French thinkers of the Enlightenment saw in history a chaotic tangle of fortuitous events, a record of human folly and arbitrariness, the course of which could be changed and controlled at will by human agency and reason. This was in fact a naïve idealist conception, for it assumed that reason governs or can govern the world. Hegel recognized the claim that reason governs history, but in the same sense 'as it governs the motion of the celestial bodies, i.e. in the sense of conformity to law'. In this way Hegel established the unquestionable superiority of absolute idealism over French materialism and its naïve idealist conception of history.[8]

The motions of the celestial bodies conform to law but the celestial bodies themselves are, of course, unaware of this fact. The same applies to the social relations established by human action. They are produced by individuals but are not the result of their conscious and purposeful activity; consciously and purposefully men follow their personal ends and what they actually achieve is often neither desired nor foreseen. Changes in social relations are unintended effects of human action and occur in conformity to definite laws. History and social life are a necessary process independent of man's will. It takes place in accordance with its own law, hidden from human consciousness, a law which can be discovered by philosophy only.[9]

Hegel saw in social and historical development both a necessary process and the revelation of the Absolute Idea. The Young Hegelians and Feuerbach recognized that Hegel was wrong to conceive the Absolute Idea as an objective force, in relation to which man was only something subjective, accidental and insignificant. The brothers Bauer held that it was human reason that was the active force in world history and Feuerbach perceived this force in the 'human essence' which revealed itself in man's community (*Gemeinschaft*) and unity (*Einheit*) with man and which found its proper expression in art, religion, philosophy, and science.[10] However, both the Young Hegelians and Feuerbach really left unanswered the question concerning the nature of the law to which historical and social development was supposed to conform.

Once the Absolute Idea was recognized as a figment of speculative philosophy, the question arose as to what was the vehicle of the conformity to law immanent in and manifested by development of society. This question was closely bound up with another, left over by the French historians of the Restoration. The French historians maintained that political constitutions were expressions of underlying social relations and that these relations were in turn determined by the state of property. What was, however, the cause of the property relations and their changes in the course of time? The solution of these two questions allowed Marx to go beyond the French historians, Hegel, the Young Hegelians, and Feuerbach, to formulate the materialist conception of history.

Marx's great discovery lay in seeing the error in the traditional conception of human nature; man's nature was not fixed once and for all but constantly changing as a result of social action.

> In order to exist, man must support his organism, borrowing the substances he requires from the external nature surrounding him. This borrowing presupposes a certain action of man on that external nature. But 'acting on the external world, he changes his own nature'. In these few words is contained the essence of the whole historical theory of Marx.[11]

Consequently, a scientific explanation of social and historical change is unsatisfactory unless it relates the process to be explained to man's action on external nature and his social environment. The conformity to law, manifest in society and history, reveals itself in those relations into which men enter with one another in the production of their means of subsistence. Whereas the environment is transformed through men's combined action, the altered external circumstances transform the relations binding men together. Changes in social relations, which are brought about as an indirect and unintended effect of human action, induce in turn changes in human nature. They modify the conscious activity of men and their aims of life. The materialist conception of history formulates the laws in conformity to which all these interrelated processes of change, transformation, and evolution take place.

2. HISTORICAL MATERIALISM AS A SUBSTANTIVE THEORY OF HISTORY

The materialist conception of history has many of the characteristics of an evolutionary hypothesis. But apart from being an evolutionary hypothesis, the materialist conception is also a philosophy of history. Marx viewed the succession of the economic formations of society not only as a process of natural history, but also as a development in which all tendencies work with iron necessity towards inevitable results. They realize a concealed purpose and strive towards a transcendental end, towards the establishment of a classless, socialist and, finally, communist society. Since the search for transcendental ends is a distinctive characteristic of the philosophy of history, the Marxian conception is a philosophy or a philosophical theory of history.[12]

This was also clear to Plekhanov. Although in *Fundamental Problems of Marxism* he insisted that 'the materialist explanation of history was primarily of methodological significance', he discussed and presented it mainly as a substantive theory of history.[13]

It has been mentioned earlier that Plekhanov's exposition of the materialist conception as a substantive theory of history places it at the opposite pole to a reductive materialism and a monistic economic determinism. Plekhanov emphasized that his exposition is not an interpretation but a faithful account of the views of Marx.[14] This claim, prompted by the desire to show the revisionism of Bernstein to be an accumulation of errors, is unjustifiable; Engels accepted responsibility for himself and Marx for the interpretation of the materialist conception of history in terms of reductive materialism and economic determinism. Plekhanov's exposition is very close to and inspired by the revision of historical materialism accomplished by Engels towards the end of his life. Together with the contribution of Ludwig Krzywicki, a Polish Marxian scholar,[15] Plekhanov's presentation of the materialist conception is perhaps the most enlightened and satisfactory statement of it and has remained very influential ever since its publication. It has not only been accepted by such scholars as Heinrich Cunow (the author of a standard study of the Marxian sociological and philosophical theories in the interwar period) but has also increasingly influenced Soviet Marxism.

It is one of Plekhanov's basic assertions that there is no direct relationship between the basis and the superstructure. Between the social relations of production and ideologies there are various intermediate links, such as the socio-political system or the psychology of men living in a given society. Moreover, the various ideologies are interdependent and what happens in one of them is frequently related to what happens in another rather than to some processes in the basis. These various connections and relations are ultimately determined by a definite course of economic development, that is, the basis provides only the restrictive or the necessary, but not the sufficient, conditions of what happenes in the superstructure. Plekhanov accepted the intermediate factors operative between the basis and the superstructure, the reciprocal actions and reactions exercised and suffered by the basis, the intermediate factors, and the ideologies, and the intricate web of mutual interdependence which is brought about by the interaction of social processes. Consequently, the materialist conception is monistic as far as the origin of various social phenomena is concerned. Plekhanov wrote that Marx undertook 'to trace to a universal and single source all of the acting and interacting forces of social life'.[16] However, the materialist conception is not a monistic view if it is understood to imply the reductivism of various social levels or various kinds of relationships to the level of economic relations or to economic causation respectively.

According to Plekhanov, social phenomena can be classified into five main categories or stratified in terms of five social levels. They are, the productive forces, the economic relations, the socio-political system, the psychology of the epoch, and the ideologies.[17] The nature and function of each class of social phenomena need a few explanatory remarks.

Plekhanov extended the concept of productive forces and added to the means of production and the skill of making use of these instruments a third determinant, the geographic environment. In the elaboration of the significance of geography in man's historical destiny, Plekhanov followed Hegel's view on 'the geographical foundation of history' rather than Marx's. While Marx recognized that geographical conditions set limits to social response without determining it, Hegel denied the psychological or even physiological influence of surrounding nature on man but fully accepted its determining influence upon the productive forces. Plekhanov does not seem to have noticed the important difference between the view-points of Hegel and Marx. Sometimes he appears to endorse the Marxian approach and to recognize only the restrictive role of the geographical environment,[18] and sometimes he adopted the Hegelian view that 'the properties of the geographical environment determine the development of the productive forces, which, in its turn, deter-mines the development of the economic forces, and therefore of all other social relations'.[19]

While the properties of the geographical environment determine the development of the productive forces, the productive forces determine and are determined by the development of the social relations. As soon as they have arisen, the social relations interact with the productive forces in the most varied forms and influence one another. Thus, for instance, a given state of the productive forces is the cause of a particular form of property relations, but the latter may also affect their own cause and influence its further development.[20] Plekhanov emphasized that the productive forces and the social relations of production are theoretical constructs and should not be conceived as 'motionless metaphysical essences'. They are only ways of speaking about the 'actual relationships of the men who constitute the given society in their process of produc-tion'.[21]

Plekhanov dealt with the objection, derived from the writings of Saint-Simon, that since the improvement of the implements of labour requires the inventive power of the human intellect, the intellect is the prime cause of historical progress. His refutation made use of the hypothesis of the evolutionary development of man and society and pointed out that the intellect appeared as a remote consequence of what man did with his hands, including the pro-duction of man's artificial organs, that is, the use of tools. It is the possession and use of his hands that enables man to acquire his knowledge and not the other way round. Generally speaking, 'for every given people, at every given period of its history, the further development of its productive forces is determined by their condi-tions in the period under examination'. The evolutionary argument does not leave out of account the role of the intellect in the technical and technological development, but explains its genesis and the ways and limits of its effective operation.[22]

That the socio-political relations are created by the underly-ing economic base and that these relations in turn influence the opment of society, including its 'economic movement', is, according to Plekhanov, an indisputable fact.   In his opinion, nobody who has read *The Communist Manifesto* could deny that Marx, too, accepted the functional relationship between the economic and the socio-political relations once the latter have arisen on the basis of the former.   Political institutions may influence economic life either by favouring or impeding its development.   The first possibility follows directly from the assumption that the given political system is laid down for the very purpose of promoting the expansion and improvement of the productive forces.   Plekhanov believed that the determining of economics by politics and the outdistancing of political changes by economic development account for the second possibility.[23]

The psychology or mentality of a given epoch as a category of social phenomena and analytical concept is Plekhanov's own contribution to the theoretical apparatus of the materialist conception of history.   Every stage in the development of the productive forces involves the division of men engaged in the social process of production into distinct groups, bound together by definite social bonds within and circumscribed by specific social relations of one group to another from without.   This web of social relations, corresponding to a given state of the productive forces, Plekhanov called the structure of society.

> Once the structure of society has been given, it is not difficult to understand that the character of that structure will be reflected generally in the entire psychology of men, in all their habits, manners, feelings, views, aspirations and ideals.   Habits, manners, views, aspirations and ideals will necessarily have to adapt themselves to men's way of life, to their mode of procuring their subsistence. . . . The psychology of society is always expedient in relation to its economy, always corresponds to it, is always determined by it.[24]

Plekhanov seems to have derived his concept of psychology from *The Eighteenth Brumaire of Louis Bonaparte*, where Marx spoke of the 'superstructure of distinct and peculiarly formed sentiments, illusions, modes of thought and views of life', created by each class and corresponding to its material position within society.[25]   But Plekhanov seems to have been impressed, above all, by the fruitfulness of the concept of psychology of a given epoch in aesthetics and the history of art as applied by Hippolyte Taine.   In his own studies on art and its history, Plekhanov followed Taine's method of relating the works of art to the general conditions of mind and manners as well as to the social environment, rejecting only Taine's claim that this was 'the ultimate explanation'. Even if in a given context the psychological explanation is primary, it should not be forgotten that the psychology of social classes is always a product of economic development.[26]

The psychology of the epoch can be defined as a reflection of social reality in human consciousness, a perception of the individual's position within the system of economic and social relationships, peculiar to his class location, or a view of the world in all its complexities seen in the perspective of the class to which the individual belongs and whose experiences he shares. Marx spoke of 'the material world reflected by the human mind and translated into forms of thought',[27] and Plekhanov made use of this in his concept of psychology or mentality. Psychology is man's awareness of concrete reality, the actual, physically sensible, and necessary conditions for his survival, which men acquire in their struggle for existence. No external object can, as such, get men in motion. It cannot become a conscious motive of action unless it goes through their minds and is transformed into sensations, feelings, thoughts, impulses and volitions, into 'ideal tendencies' and 'ideal powers' [28] which alone are able to release action. Psychology provides the intermediate link without which the boundary separating the two parts of nature, man and the external world, could never be crossed and, consequently, the materialist conception of history would not make sense. The peculiar function of psychology within the materialist conception of history accounts for the fact that the forthcoming changes in the state of the productive forces are first reflected in the psychology of men. As Plekhanov put it, 'slow psychological evolution precedes economic revolution'.[29]

The psychology of the epoch also provides the key to the understanding of how economy can be the foundation not only of lower ideologies and ideological forms, such as the law of property or political institutions, but also of higher ideologies, of science, philosophy or art. Psychology is this component part of the superstructure, which on the one hand is a subjective reflection of the basis, and on the other, mediates between the basis and the higher ideologies as well as providing the link in the interaction between the basis and superstructure. 'All ideologies have a common root in the psychology of the epoch to which they belong.' [30]

That Marx himself was far from the one-sidedness of economic monism is a common theme of *The Development of the Monist View of History* and *Fundamental Problems of Marxism*. Materialism did not prevent Marx from recognizing the significance of the spirit, that is, of moral, philosophical, religious, or aesthetic conceptions in history; he only wished to ascertain whence they come and to establish the law of their development.[31] The difference between historical materialism and idealism does not consist in the fact that the latter recognizes, and the former does not, the ideas and ideals as causes operating in history. The difference concerns their genesis and thus also the conditions on which their effective operation ultimately depends.[32]

A materialist denies that the intellectual and cultural development of humanity is an independent development, produced by mind or spirit, a primary and ultimate element in the constitution of the universe, determined by its own laws. No materialist would deny, however, that each ideological sphere has some specific developmental laws of its own. The laws of logic cannot be derived from the laws of physics, nor the laws of the circulation of commodities be deduced from the laws of logic. The ideologies of a particular age are often connected with the ideologies of the past, and the contemporaneous ideologies frequently influence each other. The conclusion to be drawn from these various facts is not that the ultimate cause of ideological developments should be sought in some specific laws of the human spirit but that the prevailing ideologies cannot be inferred from or discovered by the examination of the economic state of society alone. On the other hand, the dependence of the ideologies on the basis, through the psychology associated with the basis, is apparent. In order that a group of people may devote their energies to scientific and similar occupations, a certain level of prosperity is necessary. Environment does not allow all humanity to make use of its inventive capacity to an equal extent. At a given time the scope of this capacity is determined by the state of productive forces. Men co-ordinate their ideas, feelings, thoughts, according to their own particular laws but these laws 'are brought into play by external circumstances which have nothing in common with these laws'. Ideologies have a dimension that remains unaccounted for until they are related to the underlying economic realities.[33]

3. THE ROLE OF DIALECTICAL MATERIALISM IN THE VALIDATION OF HISTORICAL MATERIALISM

Plekhanov seems to have been aware of the fact that the materialist conception of history needed validation, but he also appeared to have been uncertain and confused about the ways in which it could be tested and corroborated. He felt that if the facts reported by Darwin in *The Origin of Species* were sufficient to establish the theory of biological evolution, *The Eighteenth Brumaire of Louis Bonaparte*, *The Class Struggles in France*, *1848 to 1850* and, above all, *Capital*, were sufficient to establish the Marxian theory of social evolution.[34] He stressed that the theory of Marx, like Darwin's theory of biological evolution, admits only of a partial, fragmentary, and inadequate confirmation. To the critics who complained that Marx had not given a 'theoretical substantiation of historical materialism', Plekhanov answered very rightly that only a world history written from the materialist viewpoint could provide the required verification. At present, Plekhanov explained, no such history can be written either by individual or collective effort, because the material for that purpose is not yet available; it has to be accumulated by means of systematic studies, which making use of the Marxian method would apply it to various fields of knowledge. But Plekhanov was confident that the theory of Marx would be increasingly confirmed in the course of time, for many scholars, often without realizing what they were doing, applied the materialist explanatory principles to the phenomena they studied.[35]

While Plekhanov's arguments against the critics of Marx seem to indicate that he was not entirely unaware of the difference between the confirmation of a hypothesis in natural science and of a point of view in history, at other times he appears to confuse the kind of evidence which would be required in each of these cases.[36] For instance, Plekhanov maintained that the materialist conception of history has a threefold validation. First, to recall the argument summarized earlier, the history of philosophy and the social sciences reveals that philosophers, historians, and other scholars had long searched for the solution of the problem concerning the prime cause of social change. No satisfactory answer was found until the arrival of the Marxian theory, whose correctness should be evaluated by its ability to provide the replies to previous unanswered or unanswerable questions. Second, *Capital* validates the materialist conception as much as *The Origin of Species* validates the theory of evolution. Third, to put it in Plekhanov's own words, 'the theory of Marx provides him with an astounding, previously unknown, capacity to foresee events'.[37]　Thus Plekhanov claimed that the theory of Marx has been validated, on the one hand, by satisfying the requirements of a historical interpretation, and by being shown to be a fruitful hypothesis with predictive power on the other.

In his examination of the way in which the materialist conception of history can be tested, Plekhanov went beyond the methodological viewpoint and suggested that as a substantive theory the materialist conception could be established on the basis of dialectical materialism. 'The materialist explanation of history presupposes the dialectical method of thought.'[38]　In *The Development of the Monist View of History* Plekhanov assumed the truth of dialectical materialism and appealed to the laws of dialectics, in particular to the law of the transformation of quantity into quality and to the theory of leaps, in support of his various views. He argued that the interaction between economic and political evolution, the determination of man's ideas by his environment, the development of intellectual and cultural trends or the growth of the productive forces takes place in conformity to the laws of dialectics.[39]　To the objection 'That's how Hegel used to talk', Plekhanov answered, 'That's how all nature acts'; 'the history of ideologies seems once more to demonstrate that the old "metaphysician" was not mistaken'.[40] Since the dialectics of thought is only a reflection of the dialectics of nature, the dialectics of things produces the dialectics of ideas, and not vice versa, the materialist conception of history should be considered as rooted in dialectical materialism.

This approach gains prominence in *Fundamental Problems of Marxism*. Plekhanov emphasized that historical materialism by which he understood the historical and economic aspects of the materialist world-outlook, was almost entirely the work of Marx and Engels. What their predecessors contributed to these fields was merely the preparatory work of amassing material, often valuable but neither illuminated by a single general idea nor co-ordinated by means of a comprehensive hypothesis. On this account, Plekhanov continued, the term 'Marxism' is often used not only by the general public but even by followers of Marx and Engels to signify only historical materialism. This was unjustifiable for two reasons. First, historical materialism cannot but hang in mid-air when it is divorced from its theoretical foundation. Second, Marx and Engels were conscious and consistent materialists. They followed in Feuerbach's footsteps and assumed a clear connection between their philosophical views and those in the field of history, between dialectical and historical materialism.

> It is not thinking that determines being, but being that determines thinking. That is the fundamental thought in all of Feuerbach's philosophy. Marx and Engels made that thought the foundation of the materialist explanation of history.[41]

That historical materialism is a particular case of genetic materialism is not the only assertion which Plekhanov added to the materialist conception of history and which was destined to influence its further development adversely. Plekhanov also suggested that any truly scientific view of society was bound to be ultimately based on the materialist conception of history. As he put it,

> the materialist conception of history provides the necessary prolegomena to any doctrine on human society claiming to be a science.
> This is so true that at present the study of any aspect of social life acquires scientific significance only in the measure to which it draws closer to a materialist explanation of that life.[42]

Two assumptions underlie Plekhanov's claim that the materialist conception of history is the only scientific theory of society and history. According to the first, a process is necessary if and only if it takes place in conformity to law. The second assumption stipulates that only necessary phenomena are capable of being an object of scientific investigation.[43] But to say, 'conformity to law is the necessary foundation of any scientific explanation of phenomena', is to adopt the Comtean conception of science, a fact of which Plekhanov does not seem to have been aware. Comte used to say, 'scientifique ou positif', and emphasized that no branch of knowledge can acquire a positive character unless its subject-matter conforms to an invariable law based upon the nature of things.[44] It was also Comte's view that sociology cannot become 'une science positive' unless social phenomena can be shown to be necessary, that is, take place in conformity to law. Marx accepted the Comtean precondition in his Preface to *A Contribution to the Critique of Political Economy*, when he referred to the precision of natural science with which the changes and connections of social phenomena, basic from the viewpoint of his theory, can be ascertained. Although Plekhanov was not unfaithful to Marx when he adopted the Comtean position, it is worth while to note that Plekhanov's demonstration of the scientific character of the materialist conception of history is based on the positivistic conception of science.

Historical materialism is a scientific theory of history because it enables us to study human activity, including man's conscious and purposeful action, which is necessarily perceived by the actor as free, as subject to laws and thus to examine social change from the scientific standpoint. The appearance of human aims and aspirations is a necessary effect of social processes ultimately determined by economic development and, consequently, just as subject to necessity as any other social phenomena. The changes in aims and aspirations of life adopted by men in their free activity are also caused by the changes in the social relations and take place according to definite laws. Once the circumstances in which men act are given, 'then given too, as its effect, are those human aspirations which are an inevitable factor of social development. Man's aspirations do not exclude necessity, but are themselves determined by it.' [45]

Plekhanov not only prepared the ground for the claim that historical materialism is the only scientific theory of history, but also for the argument that the failure to recognize this is due to class-determined bias and prejudice. Having discovered the laws to which social phenomena conform, the materialist conception of history is able to predict the future and to show that the present socio-economic system is bound to be radically changed.

> The philistines realize, or at least have a foreboding of this. That is why the materialist explanation of history causes them such vexation and grief; and for that reason too not a single philistine is able or willing to understand or grasp Marx's theory in all its fullness.[46]

The refusal to accept the truth of historical materialism is due to a resistance determined by class interests rather than to a genuine difference of opinion resulting from our inadequate knowledge of historical causation and social change. Class interests and prejudice encourage men to look upon the materialist conception of history as something unworthy of the attention of respectable people in general and of men of learning in particular.[47]

That there is a class-determined resistance to the acceptance of the materialist conception and a blindness to its real content, inspired by an intellectual bias, is an indisputable fact. Lenin observed that if geometrical axioms affected human interests, attempts would certainly be made to refute them. No wonder, therefore, Lenin continued, that the teaching of Marx which 'demonstrates the inevitable replacement (by virtue of economic development) of the present system by a new order . . . has had to fight for every step forward in the course of its life'.[48] Marx, Lenin wrote elsewhere, could not and did not expect impartiality from his bourgeois critics.[49] To recognize this fact, which is sociologically almost self-evident, does not imply the view that the class bias is indeed the exclusive source of the refusal to accept the materialist conception as an incontrovertible truth. Plekhanov's successors, among whom Lenin himself was prominent, did make this unwarranted inference. Plekhanov spoke of the injurious effect which class-inspired blindness must exercise on theoretical thinking. His successors did not realize that his warning could and did apply to themselves as well. The Marxian view as to the dependence of the cognitive functions upon the social class position of the thinker cannot be true with respect to some groups of people and false with respect to others.

Plekhanov considerably strengthened the link between the materialist conception of history on the one side and dialectical materialism on the other. He did so for two main reasons. He was afraid, as he himself confessed in *Fundamental Problems of Marxism*, that the abandonment of dialectical materialism would deprive the materialist conception of its theoretical foundation and thus encourage the philosophical revisionism of the whole Marxian inheritance.[50] Plekhanov was strongly opposed to any philosophical revisionism because it threatened the materialist conception of history, which he greatly admired and regarded as a sound and fruitful theory. Although Plekhanov's main interest was in the fields of the historical and social sciences, he felt — and this is the second reason why he tried to link the materialist conception of history and dialectical materialism more closely together — that the materialist conception would be weakened and found to be wanting in some respect if it were not rooted in the cosmic structure. This he tried to achieve by first conferring upon the universe certain characteristics which were determined by social and moral requirements, and then relating this sociomorphic picture of the world to the materialist conception of history and society. Having given to the universe an essentially social structure, it was not difficult for him to claim that nature, society, and history were ultimately all subject to the same laws. He could also announce that Marxian socialism was not based on ethical grounds but on historical necessity and yet was bound to realize a moral purpose.

Thus, in his views on the materialist conception of history, its validation and relation to dialectical materialism, Plekhanov was an intermediary between Marx and Engels on the one hand, and Lenin and Stalin on the other. In spite of the excellence of his exposition of the materialist conception of history, so much superior to practically everything said before and after him on this subject, Plekhanov, having originated the interpretation of the universe in socio-cosmic terms, became a precursor of Lenin and Stalin. He contributed to their crude sociomorphic views of the universe and their unrestricted voluntarism resulting from these views.

Plekhanov laid the foundation for the sociomorphic conception of the universe in order to provide historical materialism with an ostensibly incontrovertible support. The ironic aspect of this attempt is that he thereby greatly obscured the methodological issues involved and concealed his own genuine contribution to the logically sound validation of the materialist conception of history.

XII

Historical Materialism as a Guide to Action

IN view of their instrumental and utilitarian approach to knowledge in general and to sociological knowledge in particular, Lenin and Stalin initiated a sharp turning-point in the understanding of the materialist conception of history. They both believed that the main, if not sole, task of the social sciences is to acquire a body of knowledge on the basis of which individual and collective human behaviour could be controlled and social action directed towards predetermined goals.

In their view, in the Marxian *ordre de bataille* — one has to know the world in order to alter it — the first objective had been attained and what remained was, therefore, to realize the second. Notwithstanding their occasional protestations to the contrary, both Lenin and Stalin regarded the theories of Marx as an absolute truth. 'The Marxian doctrine is omnipotent because it is true', wrote Lenin, and Stalin suggested that the expressions 'un-Marxian' and 'profoundly erroneous' meant exactly the same.[1] Lenin and Stalin were as anxious to make use of the materialist conception of history as a guide to action, as Marx and Engels were to consider it only as a guide to study, that is, as we would say today, as a point of view which enables us to organize, analyse, and explain social and historical development. There is dramatic irony in the fact that Marx warned against the abuse of his theories by conceiving them as a universal *passe-partout* to all events (for even very similar events which take place in different historical conditions lead to totally different results) in a letter written to the editor of a Russian journal.[2]

To transform historical materialism into a manipulative theory of history, historical materialism itself had first to be adapted to this task, that is, its old assumptions had to be subjected to a new interpretation. These interpretative modifications involved the elimination of restrictions upon men's freedom of action ; the presentation of the materialist conception of history as a final and inviolable theory; and a new validation of the materialist conception by which it was shown to be an incontrovertible truth. Lenin was the first to see the necessity of these alterations. Lenin's interpretative modification of the theory was completed by Stalin who left no *i* undotted and no *t* uncrossed.

I. LENIN'S REVISION OF MARXIAN DETERMINISM

If the materialist conception of history was to become an instrument for the transformation of social reality to a predetermined scheme, the social and historical phenomena could not be conceived as due entirely to necessity, operating blindly like the elemental forces of nature. The recognition of the existence of a natural order and lawfulness in things and phenomena does not imply that a strict, Laplacean determinism rules supreme in nature and society. Social life may conform to law and yet not be the manifestation of irresistible laws which make one event follow another inevitably, come what may. Early in his career Lenin rightly observed that there is no incompatibility between determinism and moral responsibility, between historical necessity and the significance of individual action.

> The idea of determinism, which postulates that human acts are necessitated and rejects the absurd tale about free will, in no way destroys man's reason or conscience, or appraisal of his action. . . . Similarly, the idea of historical necessity does not in the least undermine the role of the individual in history; all history is made up of the actions of individuals, who are undoubtedly active figures. The real question that arises in appraising the social activity of an individual is: what conditions ensure the success of his actions, what guarantee is there that these actions will not remain an isolated act lost in a welter of contrary acts.[3]

If social events take place according to definite laws, the discovery of these laws provides us with a firm foundation for action. By making use of these laws, individuals can be led in the desired direction and towards the ends set in advance. This is a familiar idea, discussed by Engels and Plekhanov in their examination of the relationship between freedom and necessity. To act in conformity to law does not mean to be subject to fate or to accomplish what was bound to occur in any event. As Plekhanov explained in *The Role of the Individual in History*, conformity to law is not fatalism; it does not imply that every phenomenon occurs exactly as it had to occur. Neither does it follow from this assumption that there are no chance events, that accidents do not happen, and that talented or incompetent individuals never play a beneficial or disastrous role in history. All these things may occur under certain circumstances; only they cannot entirely alter the course of events determined by laws. There is, therefore, no contradiction in Lenin's belief that human action has efficacy and yet complies with definite laws of evolution.

Like his predecessors, Lenin strongly emphasized the similarity between Darwin and Marx. While Darwin established the mutability and succession of species, Marx revealed the mutability and succession of the socio-economic formations of society; both considered the phenomena with which they were concerned as a process of natural history, taking place in accordance with laws, independent of the will and consciousness of men. The materialist conception of history should be conceived as the study of the rise, development, and decay of socio-economic structures.[4]

Lenin's voluntaristic modification of Marxian theories goes beyond the reasonable justifiable proposition that conformity to law does not turn individuals into puppets manipulated by some immanent laws of historical inevitability. Lenin was probably psychologically incapable of submitting to the deterministic cast of Marxian thought; he was a revolutionary and Jacobin, a Blanquist, as he was described in his time, both by his temperament and frame of mind. His Jacobin proclivity made him believe more and more in the efficacy of political action and its power to modify the historical process. The urge to act eroded the Marxian historical determinism which was ultimately replaced by a revolutionary activism based on the principle of voluntarism.

As has been explained earlier, Lenin's voluntaristic interpretation of the Marxian theories should be linked with his doctrine of the induced or aroused proletarian consciousness, from which his whole organizational conception and strategy of how to dominate other men were derived. When the preoccupation with the struggle for power replaced the task of making the proletariat aware of its historic mission and of developing its revolutionary class-consciousness,[5] the alleged social or historical laws were reduced to a code of simple practical rules of action, ever adjustable to the changing circumstances and ultimately subordinated to one single precept of practical wisdom which is aptly expressed by the directive, 'Do not become a slave of the tool you employ.' [6] Throughout his life Marx fought against voluntarism, represented in his time by historical idealism, and for the acceptance of determinism which was an important component part of historical materialism. Lenin restored the old voluntarism within the Marxian tradition by substituting his own principle of activism for the Marxian principle of determinism.

The basic revision entailed others. Marx warned against the excessive concentration on political aims and activity, for it encourages the workers to see the source of bad social institutions in will alone and the means of their improvement in force. It obscures from the proletariat the roots of its misery, eclipses its social instinct and distorts its insight into the mechanism of its own emancipation.[7] For Lenin, the liberation of the working class could not be accomplished other than by the seizure of power.

Lenin's conception of the Party as the all-powerful history-making force founds its ideological expression in the doctrine which, on the one hand, attributed to the will of the revolutionary, to his determination, militancy, and passion, and, more generally, to the ideas of men, a decisive role in the course of history, and, on the other, underestimated or ignored the objective historical process, its inexorable conformity to law that sets rigid limits to rational social action. To use Plekhanov's words in his criticism of the Russian anarchists and Narodniks, Lenin did not try to understand the historical laws and to direct his revolutionary activity in accordance with them, but 'simply substituted his own conspiratorial skill for history' and laid 'new, straighter and better beaten roads for her'.[8] Lenin's doctrine could be and was supported by a skilful selection of Marx's dicta, but it is incompatible with Marx's teaching. Marx warned explicitly against the view that considered pure will or deliberate design rather than actual conditions as the 'motive power of revolution' (*das Triebrad der Revolution*). To follow this course was to substitute idealism for materialism and revolutionary phrases for revolutionary development.[9] 'A revolution', wrote Engels, 'is a purely natural phenomenon, guided more by physical laws than by the rules which in normal times determine the development of society.' Engels compared the course of revolution to a whirlpool of the inexorable natural necessity into which the participants are pulled of their own will or against it sooner or later. Revolution cannot 'be made to order, just as one makes a piece of flowered calico or a tea kettle'. When it is prematurely engineered neither practical necessity nor the instinct of self-preservation can secure its success.[10]

The rejection of the belief essential to the Marxian theory that the individual's freedom of action is narrowly restricted by his social and material environment led to the re-establishment of the pre-Marxian doctrine of society. 'Marx', wrote Lenin, 'put an end to the view of society which . . . allows of all sorts of modifications at the will of the authorities or, if you like, at the will of the government.'[11] But later in life, Lenin revived the doctrine of the omnipotent legislator and restored a wide scope to man's power of creative and directive action. Lenin followed a course of action clearly incompatible with the Marxian view which denied the possibility of an arbitrary interference with social and historical development and assumed that effective human activity is restricted within limits narrowly defined by material conditions.

2. THE INCONTROVERTIBLE TRUTH OF HISTORICAL MATERIALISM

Lenin used to point out from time to time that Marx only laid the 'foundation stone of the science which socialists must develop in all directions, if they wish to keep pace with life.'[12] This observation merely stated what common sense suggests. Lenin used it, however, to justify his own right to revise or extend the Marxian doctrines, a right which he denied to others. But more typically Leninist were the doctrinal changes which purported to be simply an exposition of what Marx or Engels really meant. Irrespective of whether Lenin pretended or sincerely believed that he was merely explicating Marx's and Engels's true meaning, in either case he was bound to present the fundamental assumptions of the Marxian doctrines as incontrovertible truths, as clear as noonday, as self-evident as one's own existence. As has been pointed out earlier, this was also one of the necessary prerequisites of transforming historical materialism into a guide to action. Guides must be fully reliable and inspire unbounded confidence if they are to discharge their function.

Lenin attributed to Marx the merit of having been the first 'to

elevate sociology to the level of science'.[13]   The scientific character
of the Marxian sociology was due to the fact that (a) Marx did not
regard society as the product of design, symbolically speaking, as a
result of a *contrat social*, and did not consider social relations as
established by men consciously and purposefully; (b) having chosen
the relations of production as primary determinants of all other
relations, Marx made certain recurrent phenomena the basis of his
system; (c) since these basic phenomena are not only recurrent but
also regular, that is, they conform to law, Marx could establish —
by generalizations and the formulation and testing of hypotheses —
a universal sociological theory; (d) the reduction of social relations
to the relations of production and of the latter to the productive
forces made a scientific sociology possible and enabled Marx to
regard the development of socio-economic formations of society as
a process of natural history.[14]

Although Marx's contribution to the establishment of sociology
as a science should not be denied, Marx was neither the first nor the
only thinker who defined the indispensable conditions for the establishment of social science; they can all be found in the young
Comte's *Système de politique positive* (1822) and also in a much improved version in the fourth volume of his *Cours de philosophie positive*.
Lenin may not have known it, and his mistake is unimportant.   The
erroneous inference which Lenin drew from his evaluation of Marx's
contribution to sociology was far more serious and fateful.   Lenin
claimed that since the appearance of *Capital*, the materialist conception of history became a materially true sociological theory,
confirmed by a 'veritable Mont Blanc of factual material'.   In
Lenin's own words, historical materialism 'ceases to be a mere
hypothesis and becomes a scientifically tested theory'; it is 'no
longer a hypothesis, but a scientifically proven proposition', not
'primarily a scientific conception of history', but 'the only scientific
conception of it'.[15]   These pronouncements have been fateful because they are without foundation; no hypothesis or theory can be
credited with the properties attributed by Lenin to the materialist
conception of history without losing its scientific character.   Furthermore, they have encouraged Lenin's followers to accept historical materialism as 'the Marxian sociology' in no need of
verification, modification, and expansion.   Finally, they have induced the belief that in its application to human affairs the materialist conception of history is as reliable and effective in producing the

intended effects as are the laws of physics or chemistry in their capacity as instruments for initiating technical and technological change.

3. THE DEDUCTION OF HISTORICAL MATERIALISM FROM GENETIC MATERIALISM

The transformation of the materialist conception of history into an
unquestionable dogma was due to practical requirements. Lenin
claimed, however, that historical materialism became a 'scientifically
proven proposition' owing to a new, meta-historical method of
validation. Plekhanov was the first to say that historical materialism
was rooted in dialectical materialism. Lenin went beyond Plekhanov's statement and announced that the materialist conception of
history was a deduction from dialectical materialism.

Although Lenin found many observations in Hegel's *The Philosophy of History* to be 'shrewd and clever', 'very good' or 'sehr
wichtig' and even discovered in Hegel 'germs of historical materialism', he was inclined to consider only the Introduction as really
important. 'Most important is the *Einleitung*,' Lenin commented,
'where there is much that is magnificent in the formulation of
the question.' It is precisely in the philosophy of history, Lenin
continued, that 'Marx and Engels made the greatest step forward'.
Compared with their achievement, even 'Hegel is obsolete and
antiquated'.[16]

> The historical materialism of Marx was a great achievement
> in scientific thinking. The chaos and arbitrariness that had
> previously reigned in views on history and politics were replaced
> by a strikingly integral and harmonious scientific theory, which
> shows how in consequence of the growth of the productive
> forces, out of one system of social life another and higher system
> develops.[17]

Lenin felt that the materialist conception of history was such a
magnificent achievement because it carried the development of
philosophic materialism to its conclusion; it extended the materialist
perception of nature to the perception of human society. While the
materialist conception of history gave an incomparable comprehensiveness to materialism, it was itself an instance of the consistency
and fruitfulness of the materialist philosophy.[18]

Lenin interpreted the principle of genetic materialism so broadly that it applied practically to any pair of correlative terms, of which one could be understood to designate a material and the other a non-material constituent of reality in some meaning of these expressions. Thus, his application of the principle of genetic materialism often hung upon a few tenuous threads of a vague analogy, entirely insufficient to support, much less establish, any valid conclusions. Lenin used, however, such analogies for deductions of far-reaching and important inferences. For instance, he claimed that 'just as material causes underlie all natural phenomena, so the development of human society is conditioned by the development of material forces, the productive forces'. [19] Similarly, 'since materialism in general explains consciousness as the outcome of being and not conversely, materialism as applied to the social life of mankind has to explain social consciousness as the outcome of social being'. On the basis of such indefinite comparisons Lenin maintained that 'the discovery of the materialist conception of history' should be more appropriately described as 'the consistent continuation and extension of materialism into the domain of social phenomena'.[20]

Lenin also established a connection between historical and dialectical materialism by means of the philosophical concept of matter and the concept of reflection. Again it is the vaguest kind of analogy that paves the way for the inference of conclusions of fundamental and wide significance which are claimed to have been established by rigorous and infallible methods.

> Consciousness in general reflects being — that is a general principle of all materialism. It is impossible not to see its direct and inseparable connection with the principle of historical materialism; social consciousness reflects social being.[21]

> Just as man's knowledge reflects nature (i.e., developing matter), which exists independently of him, so man's social knowledge (i.e., his various views and doctrines — philosophical, religious, political, and so forth) reflects the economic system of society.[22]

> Materialism in general recognizes objectively real being (matter) as independent of the consciousness, sensation, experience, etc., of humanity. Historical materialism recognizes social being as independent of the social consciousness of humanity. In both cases consciousness is only the reflection of being, at best an approximately true (adequate, perfectly exact) reflection of it.[23]

The truth of the materialist conception of history is indisputable, according to Lenin, for it is a logical consequence of the truth of the materialist conception of nature which, in turn, is firmly established by the whole development of scientific knowledge.

Thus, while it is true to say that Marx and Engels gave most of their time and attention to the materialist conception of history, this crowning achievement of their life rests upon philosophic materialism. According to Lenin, philosophic materialism is the foundation of the truth, the basis of certainty and the key to the understanding of historical materialism.[24]

4. STALIN'S CODIFICATION OF LENINIST REVISIONISM

Stalin accepted Lenin's conclusion as the basic premiss of his whole philosophy. His entire exposition of historical materialism is based upon the assumption that dialectical materialism logically implies historical materialism. This premiss is important not only for theoretical but also for practical reasons; Stalin made use of it to deduce from dialectical materialism definite basic rules of action which were to guide the Party of the proletariat in its policies and practical decisions. Stalin's belief that a logical relation of inference can be established between dialectical and historical materialism and between historical materialism and the policies of the Party constitutes his distinctive contribution to Soviet dialectical materialism, which has been preserved in Soviet philosophy to this day.[25] The questioning or rejection of Stalin's view on the logical relation between dialectical and historical materialism and the claim that the problem should be re-examined, as the position is logically unacceptable, can be found only rarely among Marxian scholars today.[26]

According to Stalin, historical materialism is an 'application' or an 'extension of the principles of philosophic materialism to the study of social life . . . to the history of society and to the practical activities of the party of the proletariat'.[27] The gist of the thesis of historical materialism — 'Whatever is man's manner of life, such is his manner of thought' — can be logically derived both from genetic materialism and epistemological materialism.

> If nature, being, the material world, is primary, and mind,
> thought, is secondary, derivative; if the material world

represents objective reality existing independently of the mind of men, while mind is a reflection of this objective reality, it follows that the material life of society, its being, is also primary, and its spiritual life is secondary, derivative, and that the material life of society is an objective reality existing independently of the will of men, while the spiritual life of society is a reflection of this objective reality, a reflection of being.

Hence, the source of formation of the spiritual life of society, the origin of social ideas, social theories, political views and political institutions, should not be sought for in the ideas, theories, views and political institutions themselves, but in the conditions of the material life of society, in social being, of which these ideas, theories, views, etc., are the reflections.[28]

Stalin's inference rests on an equivocal use of the terms essentially involved in the argument, such as the 'material world' and the 'material life of society', 'man's consciousness' or 'thought' and the 'spiritual life of society'. Stalin uses them as if they were respectively synonymous, though they have a different meaning and apply to distinct entities or designata. The material world from which mind is supposed to have emerged consists of atoms, electrons, and other sub-atomic particles; it is material in the physical sense of this term. On the other hand, the material life of society, on which its spiritual life is supposed to be based, is not material in the physical sense. It does not consist of atoms and atomic particles but of certain distinct objects, the means and instruments of production, together with the human skill of using them, and of the social relations which, being the bonds among men engaged in the process of production, are not material in the sense in which the physical world is material. Thus, what could be described metaphorically as social matter is something entirely different from physical matter, and whatever could be said with truth about the latter is not necessarily true about the former.

Should the ontological primacy of matter over mind be conclusively demonstrated, this still would not allow us to draw the conclusion that the 'material life of society' is primary and its spiritual life secondary. It is true to say, as Marx did, that men are born into a world which is not of their choosing and on which their existence greatly depends; we are bound to accept this empirical proposition irrespective of whether we are or are not materialists, for it is independent of the truth or falsehood of materialism. The

temporal priority of the material conditions of social life only establishes the fact that these conditions are necessary for the spiritual
life of society and leaves open the question as to whether they are
both necessary and sufficient. The assertion that they are sufficient
cannot possibly be established on the basis of a metaphor, nor the
ontological priority of the material conditions of social life be inferred
from their temporal priority.

Since 'social matter' is a figure of speech unrelated to what is
designated by the phrase 'physical matter', and the consciousness
of individual men is something quite different from the spiritual
life of society, the conclusion 'the spiritual life of society is a reflection
of its material life' cannot be inferred from the premiss 'consciousness is a reflection of physical reality'. What Stalin took to be the
relation of logical inference between the two assertions and what he
thought could provide a conclusive proof of the truth of historical
materialism is at best a thin analogy raising more questions that it
claims to solve. Stalin's dialectical materialism provides no axio-
matic basis in the logical sense of this term to yield the inferences
which were supposed to be deducible from it. Moreover, should the
deducibility of historical materialism from dialectical materialism
be even established, this achievement would reveal the logical fruitfulness of the latter, but, of course, would not demonstrate the truth
of the former.

While arguments based on equivocation enabled Stalin to demonstrate the truth of Lenin's dictum that the Marxian philosophy is
'cast from a single piece of steel', they are also responsible for some
internal inconsistencies in Stalin's system. His deduction of historical materialism from dialectical materialism seems to presuppose
man's passivity in relation to his environment, or, more generally,
the eighteenth-century assumption, according to which man is the
product of circumstances and upbringing. This assumption substitutes a one-sided causal dependence of man upon his environment
for the Marxian conception of interaction and mutual modification
of one by the other. Thus, the presuppositions of Stalin's deductions
seem to be incompatible with his other belief, strongly emphasized
elsewhere in *Dialectical and Historical Materialism*,[29] that men are in
a position to change their natural and social environment by the
appropriate conscious and sustained effort. In this connection
Stalin stressed the importance of social ideas and political theories
which, having arisen on the basis of given material conditions of life,

may become capable of setting into motion the broad masses of the people, of mobilizing and organizing them for creative action. Neither Lenin nor Stalin was able to extricate himself from the contradiction that on the one hand 'the highest task of humanity is to comprehend the objective logic of economic evolution' which determines the fate of man, and, on the other, that 'man makes himself'.[30]   Stalin stressed either one or the other of these maxims depending on what the social circumstances and political expediency demanded.   With the requirements of consistency he seems to have been little concerned.

There was another fatal flaw in Stalin's viewpoint concerning the relation between dialectical and historical materialism.   Up to a certain point, the socio-cosmic conception of dialectical materialism favoured the voluntaristic interpretation of the Marxian doctrine, for it helped to show, however erroneously, that the policies of the Party were not arbitrary decisions of individuals; being an application of scientific knowledge, they constituted an integral part of it.   On the other hand, however, dialectical materialism formulated in socio-cosmic terms defeated its own purpose; for no human action seems to be capable of altering the development of events, if this development is conceived as a piece of the unique cosmic pattern or an instance of how the cosmic forces, strictly determined in accordance with the universal laws, operate in nature, man and society.   The voluntaristic interpretation of the Marxian doctrine presupposes the recognition of the effectiveness of human action and of the organizing and transforming power of ideas, which dialectical materialism in the socio-cosmic interpretation tended to reduce to nothing.   Dialectical materialism formulated in socio-cosmic terms came into conflict with the requirements of practical and political action in general and of voluntarism in particular.

5. TWO VERSIONS OF HISTORICAL MATERIALISM IN STALIN

The implications of the socio-cosmic conception of dialectical materialism, unfavourable to voluntarism, were firmly rejected by Stalin as 'vulgar materialism'.   The recognition of these implications, Stalin said, would make the Party redundant and its activity superfluous.   To justify the refusal of accepting the implications of his own premises, he reformulated the original conception of the relation between social being and social consciousness and brought it into line with the views of the older Engels and Plekhanov. Historical materialism deals only with the question of 'the origin of social ideas, theories, views and political institutions, of the way they arise, of the fact that the spiritual life of society is a reflection of the conditions of its material life'. Historical materialism does not deny, however, the significance of social ideas and political institutions in history and emphasizes the important role of these factors in the life of society; such a denial would imply sinking to the level of 'vulgar materialism'.[31] That the material conditions of social life determine the origin of social ideas and theories does not imply that the latter, having been brought into being, do not reciprocally influence the former.

The second, revised version of the materialist conception of history accepts interaction rather than one-way action as the fundamental category of determination in social matters. Consequently, the superstructure, besides being a product of the material basis, may act back upon its basis, to help to maintain, modify or strengthen the very conditions from which it arose.

> The superstructure is a product of the basis, but this by no means implies that it merely reflects the basis, that it is passive, neutral, indifferent to the fate of its basis, to the fate of the classes, to the character of the system. On the contrary, having come into being, it becomes an exceedingly active force, actively assisting its basis to take shape and consolidate itself, and doing its utmost to help the new system to finish off and eliminate the old basis and the old classes.[32]

Thus, there are two different versions of historical materialism to be found in Stalin. The first, derived from dialectical materialism in its socio-cosmic formulation, seems to imply that human will is powerless and spontaneous human action is either impossible or bound to be ineffective. According to this understanding of the materialist conception, the rise of new productive forces and the change of the relations of production do not take place 'as a result of the deliberate and conscious activity of man, but spontaneously, unconsciously, independently of the will of man'.[33] Historical materialism becomes a strictly deterministic and monistic doctrine which asserts a one-sided dependence of the superstructure upon the basis and a one-way action of a single social factor over all the remaining ones. It is this version of historical materialism that Stalin considered as conclusively established, no mere conjecture or hypothesis in need of confirmation, but an instance of validated knowledge and an incontrovertible truth.

The second version of historical materialism simply states that 'whatever is man's manner of life, such is his manner of thought'; new social ideas and theories arise from and reflect the material life of society in the midst of which they appear. These new social ideas and theories 'arise precisely because they are necessary to society, because it is impossible to carry out the urgent tasks of development of the material life of society without their organizing, mobilizing and transforming action.' [34] Thus it should be recognized that new social ideas and theories are capable of reacting upon the material life of society and of creating the conditions favourable to or necessary for its further development. Instead of restricting social causation to one-sided action, the second version assumed the interaction between the basis and superstructure and did not deny the power of human will to create the new economic and social conditions. Since Stalin extolled the 'tremendous role of new social ideas, of new political institutions, of a new political power',[35] he did not run the risk of underestimating but rather of overestimating the power of will and mind in history and society.

Stalin both followed in Lenin's footsteps and revolted against the view of his predecessor in turn. He incarnated the basic contradiction in the Leninist approach which, on the one hand, conceived social development as a necessary process of natural history unfolding itself according to law, and placed the revolutionary passions and will outside the historical laws on the other. Stalin did not oscillate between these two attitudes because he was unable to solve the problem of determinism versus voluntarism; he simply refused to pay any attention to it on the theoretical level. As he saw it, the question as to whether revolutionary policy should be subordinated to the historical process or not was a practical, not a theoretical, one. At different periods of his career, Stalin assigned a greater or less decisive role to the superstructure than Lenin did for reasons which were clearly rooted in the view he took of his own part as a revolutionary leader.

Stalin resorted to the version of historical materialism which substituted the principle of activism for the principle of determinism,

the purposeful action of men for the developmental process independent of their will, whenever the materialist conception of history
was to sanction the necessity and to justify the efficacy of long-term,
extremely difficult and uncertain plans of action (such, for instance,
as the first Five-Year Plan). Since such measures were to clear
by bold leaps the obstacles offered to society by the successive
phases of its normal development, that is, to accomplish what
according to Marx was impossible of attainment, the Marxian
view of history had to be replaced by a new one, suitable for the
task at hand. The second version of historical materialism satisfied this requirement, for leaving in abeyance, as it were, the
Marxian conception 'it is the social being of men that determines
their consciousness' it was able to demonstrate that not only
the basis produces its superstructure, but also the superstructure
may bring its own basis into existence.[36] The apparent incompatibility of the new formula with the Marxian assumption was
not removed but only concealed. Marx described as Utopian the
belief in the possibility of creating a totally new world by conscious
design.

To bring its own basis into existence, the superstructure must be
controlled by an individual or a group of individuals who hold the
position of political power within it. Marx did not deny the efficacy
of political power; he claimed, however, that political power could
not be efficacious unless it operated on the basis of appropriate
economic forces and class structure. Stalin's formula ignored this
condition and transformed historical materialism into a theory of
the decisiveness of political power.[37] Instead of being dependent
upon the economic base, the political structure of society played an
independent role and determined the economic base, the alleged
source of its own efficacy. In one meaning of this phrase, the belief
that the superstructure can remake or create the basis has been the
most extreme point reached by the voluntarisitic interpretation of
the Marxian doctrine.

The first version of historical materialism helped to support
theoretically the infallibility of the Party and its leaders in whatever
they did, but otherwise it played a subordinate role. It went un-
heeded until in the closing period of his life Stalin sounded a strong
call to retreat from the previous unrestricted belief in the primacy
of will and action over material conditions.[38] While he did not
deny the power of will and action to modify the social conditions

necessary for accomplishing a major social change, he accepted the restrictions determined by an objective historical process. The power of the Party was not unlimited ; it had to respect the fact that at any given time the scope of rational and effective social action was fixed ; it could not disregard the laws of nature ; and it could not ride roughshod over the laws of social development, independent of human will. Man may discover and take advantage of the laws of nature in the interest of society, but he cannot destroy or ignore them without rendering his efforts futile.[39] Stalin encouraged the trend to shape goals and objectives with due attention to the restrictive power of external circumstances and not to expect that a whole historical stage, dividing socialism and communism, could be cleared by a bold leap.

Stalin's oscillations between the two incompatible versions of historical materialism can be considered in a twofold way. Generally speaking, there seems to exist a correlation between the perception and interpretation of the universe and the social world on the one hand, and the plans of action on the other. Moreover, a certain point of view concerning the universe and society is adopted, because it is bound up with and grows out of a certain social reality of which the planner and actor is a part. He sees primarily only those aspects of the universe, society, and history which appear to be relevant to the objectives of his purposeful action. Stalin's incompatible interpretations of the role played by the subjective factor within the materialist conception of history are sociologically comprehensible and they seem to exemplify, in a magnified form, a common human characteristic.

The fact remains, however, that at different times Stalin endorsed incompatible views of social reality and social action. Each of these views claimed to represent the only strictly scientific theory of social change and, therefore, to be the only method to effect rationally social change in the future. Yet it appears that each of these views was adopted merely because it fitted some ephemeral circumstance, satisfied some transitory requirement, or was a suitable instrument to carry out a definite task. Stalin himself explained in a moment of frankness that theory has advantages for a revolutionary movement provided that it is able to 'answer the questions raised by practice' ; otherwise it has no use.[40] In a sense, it is not the reversal of the Marxian doctrine about the relationship of men's consciousness to their social existence but the oscillations between incompatible conceptions, evaluated solely from the point of view of their momentary practical efficacy, which constitutes the most extreme form of voluntarism. In this most extreme form voluntarism no longer has any theoretical foundations and can be reduced to a single and simple rule 'stat pro ratione voluntas'.

XIII

The Concept of Scientific Socialism

THE examination of the relation of historical materialism to dialectical materialism has invalidated the view that according to Marx and Engels the former is an extension or conclusion from the latter. Only Lenin and Stalin asserted that there exists a logically valid transition from the basic assumptions of dialectical materialism to the fundamental premises of historical materialism. Since they also maintained that the advance of scientific knowledge increasingly confirms the truth of dialectical materialism, the deducibility of historical materialism from dialectical materialism transformed the materialist interpretation of history into 'the only scientific conception of history'.

The view that Marx and Engels did not consider historical materialism as a continuation of dialectical materialism may be challenged on the grounds that Marx and Engels are the founders of scientific socialism and scientific socialism is an application of the materialist conception of history to human affairs. However, Marxian socialism could not be described as scientific by its founders unless the theory, of which it is an application, were regarded by them as something more than a mere hypothesis. The socialism of Marx and Engels was scientific because they based it upon historical materialism which they established as a comprehensive scientific theory and which explained the transition of one socio-economic formation into another. Whereas historical materialism gave to the socialism of Marx and Engels its scientific character, the truth of historical materialism itself was guaranteed by the truth of dialectical materialism.[1]

To answer this objection it is necessary to trace down the history of the term and to analyse the concept of scientific socialism. Apart from the light that this task may shed on the problem at hand, it should help to expose a few more legends which tend to grow and accumulate around the name of Marx.

I. THE VICISSITUDES OF THE TERM

In spite of the widespread belief that Marx himself gave the name of scientific socialism to his doctrine,[2] this expression, as distinct from the concept, is hardly to be found in Marx at all. While Engels used it occasionally and marginally in the early seventies, he applied it as an appropriate designation of the Marxian socialism only in *Anti-Dühring*, from which he took it as the title of one of his most successful publications, *Socialism: Utopian and Scientific*. But even then Marx did not adopt Engels's use of this expression as his own.[3]

Marx appears to have conceived an intense dislike for the term 'scientific socialism' at the very beginning of his career and he did not get rid of it until the end of his life. The expression 'scientific socialism' was coined by Proudhon, and Marx may have come upon it for the first time in Proudhon.[4] 'Scientific socialism' and other similar expressions, such as '*deutsche Wissenschaft des Sozialismus*' (German science of socialism) and '*philosophische Begründung des Sozialismus*' (philosophical foundation of socialism), were introduced into German by Karl Grün in his book *Die soziale Bewegung in Frankreich und Belgien*, published in 1845 and savagely criticized by Marx in the third part of *The German Ideology*.[5] Alongside Moses Hess, Karl Grün was the best known representative of so-called true socialism (*wahrer Sozialismus*), a trend of utopian, radical social thought, inspired by French socialism, which appeared in Germany in the early forties and which itself claimed to have been based on 'science'. It was Moses Hess who first introduced both Marx and Engels to French socialism and secured the invitation of Marx to the editorial board of *Rheinische Zeitung* in 1842.

Karl Grün described the doctrine of Saint-Simon as a seed-pot containing the germs of many things, among them the first intimation of 'scientific socialism, for Saint-Simon spent his whole life in search for the new science'. While Marx acknowledged Grün's claim that Saint-Simon 'searched after a new social science and after new social laws', which were to create the conditions for the emancipation of the proletariat, he added that Saint-Simon searched for them because of the undeveloped state of the proletariat at that time which thus did not yet reveal itself as a historical force destined to transform the world. Marx saw in Saint-Simon not a pioneer of scientific socialism but a utopian, deceived by his own fantastic conceptions and his sense of superiority to all class antagonism.

Marx despised Karl Grün and attacked him pitilessly as a bombastic petty-bourgeois philistine, an indolent imitator of Louis Reybaud and Lorenz von Stein, only capable of producing a 'silly echo' of the French ideas and lost, in spite of his pride in the matchless German science, in 'the misty realm of philosophical fantasy'.[6] Marx's fierce anger and scorn for Karl Grün may have been increased by the fact that from 1844 on, 'true socialism' was gaining support among the bourgeoisie in many parts of Germany.[7]

Moreover, at that time and for a long time to come, Marx and Engels avoided being described as socialists. 'Socialist' and 'socialism' were terms introduced into the French and English language only in the 1830s, and into the German language even later, becoming firmly established in Germany owing to the success of Lorenz von Stein's book *Der Socialismus und Communismus des heutigen Frankreichs* in 1842.[8] Louis Reybaud and Lorenz von Stein were also responsible for conferring the title 'socialist', above all, on three social thinkers, Saint-Simon (and the Saint-Simonists), Charles Fourier, and Robert Owen, that is, exactly on those three social writers whom Marx later described as the 'founders of critical-utopian socialism and communism' and whose disciples were increasingly becoming, in Marx's opinion, fanatical sectarians given to the construction of castles in the air.[9] Louis Reybaud wrote in 1843 that socialism, as understood by these social writers, was the 'act of improvising irreproachable societies'. Their socialism hardly needed any refutation and was doomed to painless extinction, for no sensible person believed in the existence of a perfect social system and in a sudden transformation of man and society.[10] Marx and Engels entirely agreed with Reybaud's evaluation of utopian ideologies. A perfect society can exist only in the imagination, for all real historical societies are transitory and mere stages in the endless course of development from the lower to the higher.[11]

Having to choose between the title of socialists and communists, Marx and Engels decided to adopt the latter rather than the former. Communism, even a utopian one, was superior to socialism because, in contradistinction to the latter, it was a 'spontaneous workers' communism'.[12] Like Proudhonism, utopian and doctrinaire socialism was a 'false brother' of communism; its very name should be shunned and avoided.[13] The sharp boundary line between the two is very apparent not only in the title but also in the content of Engels's *Principles of Communism* and in *The Communist Manifesto*.

Many years after the publication of *The Communist Manifesto* Engels explained that about the middle of the nineteenth century, socialism and communism were clearly differentiated from each other. Socialists were the adherents of the various utopian systems, notably the followers of Owen in England and of Fourier in France, as well as the multifarious groups called by Engels 'social quacks' and by Marx 'socialist miracle workers', that is, those who wished to redress all sorts of social grievances by reforms alone. Socialism was at that time an essentially middle-class and respectable movement, and its protagonists and supporters were mostly intellectuals.[14] This applied equally to the French and English socialism of the forties. Engels emphasized that socialism in England in the 1840s was a bourgeois movement, 'thoroughly tame and peaceable'. It accepted the existing social order and proceeded with great consideration towards the bourgeoisie and its ruthless methods of control over the proletariat. Such socialism could never become the common creed of the working class. On the other hand, that section of the working class which rejected the idea that socialism can be achieved by peaceful means and demanded a radical reconstruction of society, for instance, the followers of Cabet in France and of Weitling in Germany and Switzerland, the League of the Just and the Workers' Educational Association, called themselves Communists.[15] It was, Engels continued, a 'crude, rough hewn, purely instinctive sort of Communism', based on the belief that equality and justice would overcome every obstacle. But it was a working-class movement and, in the public opinion, the very opposite of respectability (hence the phrase about 'a spectre' (*Gespenst*) haunting Europe, opening *The Communist Manifesto*). 'As our notion', from the very beginning, was that "the emancipation of the working class must be the act of the working class itself",' Engels wrote, 'there could be no doubt as to which of the two names [that is, socialists and communists] we must take.'[16]

Marx's use of the term 'communism' and 'socialism' did not deviate from that indicated by Engels. He declared his preference for 'communism' (and occasionally 'revolutionary socialism' or 'materialistic critical socialism') because, unlike the socialists, the first communists in France and England endorsed materialism and thus showed themselves 'more scientifically-minded' than their socialist contemporaries.[17]   Above all, they were aware of the reality of class war and were ready to abolish the property relations and the relations of production on which class war rested. 'The theory of the Communists', stated *The Communist Manifesto*, 'may be summed up in the single sentence : Abolition of private property.'[18] The phrase *Aufhebung des Privat-Eigentums* is new ; the utopian Communists spoke of the community of goods, *Gütergemeinschaft* and *communauté des biens*. Writing almost fifty years later, Engels emphasized that the definition of communism as the striving for the abolition of private property (*The Communist Manifesto*) or for the abolition of wage labour and capital (*The Class Struggles in France, 1848 to 1850*) sharply differentiated 'modern workers' socialism both from all the different shades of feudal, bourgeois, petty-bourgeois, etc., socialism as well as from the confused community of goods of utopian and spontaneous workers' Communism'. [19]

The immediate aim of communism was, according to *The Communist Manifesto*, the organization of the proletariat into a class, the overthrow of bourgeois supremacy, and the conquest of political power by the proletariat.[20]   This formulation follows and improves on the definition of communism given by Engels two years earlier.[21] Defined in terms of its political programme, communism was surely something quite different from the socialism to be found in the treatises of the contemporary socialist writers and the practice of the first socialist politicians and political leaders, like Louis Blanc, member of the Provisional Government in France after the February revolution.

In *The Class Struggles in France, 1848 to 1850* or *The Eighteenth Brumaire of Louis Bonaparte* the terms 'socialism' and 'communism' were used by Marx on the whole in keeping with Engels's distinction. It is true that in these writings the term 'socialism' glitters with many meanings, including an ironic use, calling everything that offended the interests of the party of Order or formulated the demands of the opposition, irrespective of the appropriateness of this designation, by the name of socialism.[22]   But the boundary line between 'socialism' and 'communism' was essentially clear.   On the one hand, there were 'the socialist doctrinaires of the proletariat' and 'the proletariat's real revolutionaries', on the other.   Marx related the former, writers and politicians like Alexandre Ledru-Rollin, Alphonse Lamartine, or Louis Blanc, to the founders of socialist sects, that is, probably to Fourier and Proudhon.   He described them as 'the half conservative, half revolutionary and wholly utopian reformers' and as representatives of a 'mass hovering between the bourgeoisie and the proletariat, a mass whose material interests demanded democratic institutions'.[23] 'Socialism' means here what in *The Communist Manifesto* Marx called 'petty bourgeois' and 'conservative' or 'bourgeois' socialism. 'The proletariat's real revolutionaries' were supporters of communism for which their bourgeois opponents invented the name 'Blanquism'; Louis Auguste Blanqui, together with Etienne Cabet, François Raspail, and Alexandre Martin (Albert), was the leader of the revolutionary proletariat, a section of the workers to be distinguished not only from the petty bourgeois and bourgeois socialists, but also from their working-class supporters. The socialists, in the Marxian terminology, believed in the peaceful attainment of their aims which were to be achieved by an application of a socialist system (hence their connection with the utopian socialists proper and their differentiation from communists who have 'no ready-made utopias to introduce *par decret du peuple*'). The Communists, as described by Marx, were committed to the overthrow of the social and political order prevailing in France after the February revolution, to the establishment of the class dictatorship of the proletariat, and to the abolition of class distinction.[24]

It is a fact little noted that the term 'socialism' does not even occur in *Capital*. Also Marx's correspondence in the last twenty years of his life and his *Critique of the Gotha Program* clearly indicate that while he relented somewhat, he never got rid of his dislike for the term 'socialism'.[25] When Marx achieved a wide reputation and high prestige in the international workers' movement, he conceded that in the utopias of Fourier and Owen there was also a pleasant and prepossessing aspect, 'the presentiment and imaginative expression of a new world'.[26] But he never admitted any affinity between his own views and utopian socialism, and never withdrew his evaluation of the latter as a modern mythology, a play with fancy pictures about the future, and in certain circumstances a mischievous nuisance.[27] Its representatives and supporters were deluded by pretentious moral platitudes and intoxicated by futile day-dreams about the sentimental reconciliation of contradictory class interests and the visionary elevation above the class struggle.[28] For Marx, the belief implicit in the early socialist doctrines that the co-operation and goodwill of the bourgeoisie could be enlisted for the active support of social reconstruction was pure folly.   He did not wish to have anything to do with such muddle-headed reformers and their fantastic programme for the future.

There were, however, important reasons for abolishing the sharp distinction between 'socialism' and 'communism'.   In nineteenth-century Europe, the Communards gave the term 'communism' a sinister reputation, incomparably more threatening to the workers' movement than the abuse heaped upon communism in the forties and fifties; [29] even in *The Civil War in France* one can sense Marx's concern at the efforts of the European governments to cry down the International Working Men's Association and its activity.   Although the Communards were drowned in blood by the troops under the command of the Versailles government, the victims of the massacre, and not its perpetrators, were presented to the world as responsible for unspeakable outrages and stood to pillory as a danger to civilization, order, and humanity.   Marx might not have been impressed by this repute, which he tried his best to expose, and he was certainly not sensitive to popular views about the Paris Commune; others, however, could not afford to ignore this state of affairs.   The tragic end of the Paris Commune added urgency and importance to the resolution passed at the conference of the International, held in London in September 1871, which prohibited the use of any 'sectarian names such as Positivists, Mutualists, Collectivists, and Communists'.[30]   This resolution had not much to do with the Paris Commune, but it came at an opportune time when there was public outcry and condemnation of communism.

Other developments of events also favoured the abandonment of the name 'communism' and its replacement by 'socialism'.   In the last quarter of the nineteenth century the differences of meaning between 'socialism' and 'communism' were disappearing, for socialism was increasingly purging itself of the utopian elements of the earlier socialist schools and acquiring what Marx described as the realistic outlook.[31]   On the European continent the Paris Commune was not only the 'grave of the Proudhon school of socialism', but also of other sorts of non-Marxian socialism, at least until the end of the nineteenth century.   Socialism was no longer a bourgeois but a working-class movement, more and more dominated by the doctrine of Marx, above all in Germany, but also in other countries of the continent of Europe.   In 1895 Engels could write without exaggeration of the *one* great international army of socialists 'marching irresistibly on and growing daily in number, organization, discipline, insight, and certainty of victory'.[32]

Finally, the abandonment of the term 'communism' was of vital importance to the success of the Social-Democratic movement in Imperial Germany. The change had probably been accepted not only out of necessity but also as a symbol of the changed outlook. It reflected the determination not to resort to the tactics which produced the French disaster of 1871 and implied the repudiation either of armed insurrections or of the open advocacy of violence as a means of establishing socialism by a historical short-cut. In his famous Introduction to Marx's *Class Struggles in France, 1848 to 1850* Engels himself expressed his confidence in legality, in obtaining a socialist majority by vote, and in the defeat of 'the parties of order' which would perish under conditions created by themselves.[33]

As its career in the last hundred years has amply demonstrated, 'scientific socialism' is a suggestive and, in some respect, felicitous expression, of which Engels's practical mind must have been aware. Nearly thirty years after the first onslaught upon Karl Grün, the man who took it over from Proudhon and launched it upon its meteoric career, Engels set 'German scientific socialism' against Proudhonism [34] and referred to it again approvingly in his prefatory note to the third edition of *The Peasant War in Germany* (1875). 'German scientific socialism', Engels wrote, is 'the only scientific Socialism that has ever existed',[35] and he soon began to use the once objectionable term more freely as the distinctive name of Marxian socialism. As the prefatory note to *The Peasant War in Germany* seems to indicate, 'scientific socialism' meant at first as much as 'theoretical socialism', that is, a socialist doctrine based on, or expressed in terms of, a sociological theory.

Before proceeding to the analysis of the various connotations of the concept of scientific socialism it is perhaps worth while to refer briefly to the developments which restored 'communism' to its original prominence. It was Lenin who again abandoned the terms 'socialism' and 'Social Democracy' and replaced them by 'communism'. 'The term "Social Democracy" is scientifically incorrect', Lenin argued, because 'from capitalism mankind can pass directly only to socialism', and socialism in its true sense is but a lower stage of communism.[36] Lenin urged the change of the name of the Party also for another reason, perhaps more important from his point of view. We must call ourselves a Communist Party, Lenin declared, just as Marx and Engels called themselves, to emphasize our distinctiveness from the Social Democrats, whose leaders throughout the world joined hands with the bourgeoisie.[37] What distinguishes communism from Social Democracy is the rejection by the latter of the dictatorship of the proletariat. Communism denotes a classless society but, in a more general sense, also those forms of social and political organization which emerge during the transition period from capitalism to communism. As Lenin emphasized, in this period of transition a great variety of political and social forms would appear, but their common characteristic would be the establishment of the dictatorship of the proletariat. In this sense they would all be instances of communism.[38]

2. THE THREE CONNOTATIONS OF THE CONCEPT

Although Marx seems purposely to have avoided the use of the term 'scientific socialism', he was, of course, very familiar with its concept which he himself developed. The connotation of this concept is not easy to define. Marx never did, and Engels used 'scientific socialism' in several related but distinct ways.

For Lorenz von Stein, socialism was a theory, a system, a scientific trend, even a science (*Wissenschaft*), rather than a social movement.[39] Von Stein spoke of 'die sogenannte socialistische Bewegung' (the so-called socialist movement), for there was hardly any evidence of socialism being at that time anything more than an intellectual trend initiated by middle-class writers and thinkers. Similarly, Karl Grün wrote in 1845 that 'there might be some isolated secret communist associations, but it was ridiculous to speak of a Communist Party' and Louis Reybaud spoke of the communist sects constantly quarrelling with each other.[40] This situation changed entirely during Marx's and Engels's lifetime and the socialist movement grew into strong and well-organized parties in many European countries.

Marx made a sharp and clear distinction between socialism as an emancipation movement of the proletariat and as a set of socio-logical, economic, and historical assumptions underlying the programme of the socialist movement. Numerous passages in *Anti-Dühring* clearly testify that Engels did not confuse them either.[41] To Marx, this distinction was of philosophical importance. Already in *Economic and Philosophic Manuscripts of 1844* he emphasized that history is not only what actually happens in history, but also the consciousness of the process of becoming, the comprehension of the immanent purpose of the historical world process and of its movement towards a pre-ordained goal. Communism is this immanent purpose that is realized in history and the awareness of its 'necessary pattern and dynamic principle'. It is that system towards which the whole of history has been heading and which would reverse the institutions and invert the values of the past.[42] Theoretically, we read in *The Communist Manifesto*, the communists 'have over the great mass of the proletariat the advantage of clearly understanding the line of march, the conditions, and the ultimate general results of the proletarian movement'. In other words, the communists are not carried away in an unknown direction by an elemental pressure of social events, but are always fully aware of where they are going and what their final destination is.[43]

The point which Marx was anxious to emphasize was that his theory of socialism coincided with the evolution of society. He did not invent his theory of society and history because he felt that without it a man would be lost in the fortuity of vast and complicated events or because he was moved by moral considerations, as were many other socialist doctrines reviewed in *The Communist Manifesto*. His own theory was not the invention of a reformer but the result of a generalization, based upon the observation of historical and social change 'going on under our very eyes' and upon a 'critical knowledge' of a movement inherent in social reality, which by itself was producing the material conditions of the emancipation of the working class.[44] It was rooted in and discovered from the flow of human affairs ; it was 'the theoretical expression', as Engels put it, 'of the proletarian movement'. Marxian socialism was scientific because it was in agreement with reality, reflected its momentum and explained the nature and the trend of change. Because it was scientific, Marxian socialism gave to its adherents a sense of direction and purpose. It imparted, to quote Engels again, 'to the now oppressed proletarian class a full knowledge of the conditions and of the meaning of the momentous act it is called upon to accomplish'.[45]

In order to distinguish and to clarify the various meanings in which 'scientific socialism' has been used by Marx's followers, it is important to take note of the fact that for Engels and, of course, for

Marx too, scientific socialism was one of the results of their search for the concept of social science and for an all-inclusive sociological theory.   To make a science of socialism, socialism had first to be placed upon a real basis, wrote Engels in *Anti-Dühring*.[46]   Engels understood by this real basis a theoretical social science, which, as has been mentioned earlier, Marx called the 'science of man' or the 'natural science about man', and Engels the 'science of society' (*Wissenschaft der Gesellschaft*).[47]   This theoretical social science was to be essentially historical and to combine the ideas of Hegel and Comte.   'The history of society in all its branches', wrote Engels, is coextensive with 'the totality of all sciences which occupy themselves with human things (and divine)' or, as he said elsewhere, 'the science of society' is 'the sum total of the so-called historical and philosophical sciences'.[48]   When Engels spoke of 'the sum total of the so-called historical and philosophical sciences', he seemed to have some kind of Hegelian encyclopaedia in mind which would combine and co-ordinate the science of government, jurisprudence, political economy, the historical sciences, the study of art, religion, and philosophy.   On the other hand, Marx's science of man and Engels's 'totality of all sciences which occupy themselves with human things' are close to Comte's social physics (*la physique sociale*).   Comte defined his social physics as 'the study of the collective development of the human species' whose task is to co-ordinate the social past and to determine the order which the march of civilization tends to produce.[49]   The social science as envisaged by Comte, Marx, and Engels was a study of social man, man within society, in all his manifestations, a natural history of man and a history of civilization that unfolds itself in conformity to a necessary law of evolution.

The distinction between a utopian and a scientific socialism was closely related to the search for a science of society ; for the utopians, socialism was the 'expression of absolute truth, reason and justice' and needed only to be discovered 'to conquer all the world by virtue of its own power',[50] and the scientific socialists strove to base socialism on a theoretical foundation, on the knowledge of historical and sociological laws.   The distinction under discussion goes back to the young Comte's *Système de politique positive* (1822) and even to Saint-Simon in spite of the tag 'utopian' attached to him by Marx and Engels.   Already Lorenz von Stein observed that Saint-Simon and the Saint-Simonists raised socialism to the level of a *Weltanschauung*, by which he wished to say that Saint-Simon and his followers associated the advance toward socialism with certain universal trends in the development of society. Karl Grün put it very neatly when he wrote that Saint-Simon 'searched for the organic law of human existence in order to arrange this existence in accordance with the law'. As a matter of fact, Saint-Simon said explicitly that a 'social system cannot be created'; man can only adapt himself to the necessary course of development and remove obstacles barring its march forward.[51] Comte took advantage of his law of the three stages to differentiate between the utopian approach to political problems, characteristic for the theological and metaphysical stage, and the scientific approach associated with the positive stage of the intellectual development. Utopian political thinking takes no account of the state of civilization and looks for the best possible social order irrespective of the existing circumstances; scientific thinking accepts the fact that social organization is determined by the state of civilization and that the progress of civilization is subject to invariable laws. Since the law of civilization cannot be eluded, political action can produce no durable results unless it is exerted in the same direction as the force of civilization and unless it aims at producing changes which this force necessitates.[52]

Karl Grün was not entirely wrong when he asserted that ' Saint-Simonism contained scientific socialism'. For Saint-Simonism had a theoretical foundation, however inadequate it might have been from the Marxian point of view, a set of sociological assumptions and laws whose operation was to bring socialism about. This is one of the meanings given by Engels to 'scientific socialism'. Marx could find fault with Karl Grün for many reasons, but the misapplication of the term 'scientific socialism' should not have been included among them.

In *Socialism: Utopian and Scientific* Engels described the real basis, which made of socialism a science, in terms of a *Weltanschauung*. The view of the world underlying scientific socialism is dialectic and not metaphysical, evolutionary and not static, as we would say today. With this conception of nature there was closely associated a corresponding conception of history. History was not considered as 'a crude heap of irrationality and violence', but as 'the process of evolution of humanity' which takes place in conformity to laws.[53] Socialism became a science, Engels continued, with two great discoveries, the materialist conception of history and the theory of capitalist production as the process of the appropriation of surplus-value by the capitalist.[54]   Modern scientific socialism is based on the discovery of these two important facts; they constituted, Engels wrote, 'a scientific foundation' of his own and Marx's views.[55]

Plekhanov was familiar with this neutral meaning of scientific socialism.   He emphasized that 'the founders of scientific socialism showed us in the development of the productive forces and their struggle against backward "social conditions of production" the great principle of the variation of species of social organization'.[56] Elsewhere he identified scientific socialism with the recognition of the inexorable laws of social development.   They entail the historical inevitability in the succession of the various stages through which a society has to pass in its advance and which, in Marx's words, cannot be cleared by leaps but only shortened in their passage by appropriate activity.   In the same context Plekhanov mentioned quite a different meaning of scientific socialism, closely connected with that just considered.   'For us', he wrote, 'the desirable arises from the necessary.'[57]

The neutral concept of scientific socialism can also be found in Lenin's early writings.   Marx found it impossible to content himself with utopian socialism.   'He did not confine himself to describing the existing system, to judging it and condemning it; he gave a scientific explanation of it.'   Consequently, by an objective analysis of the capitalist system, Marx was able to prove 'the necessity of its transformation into the socialist system'.[58]   But as in the case of Plekhanov, a different element is associated with this neutral concept.   'If ideals are not based on facts', Lenin observed, 'they will only remain pious wishes, with no chance of being accepted by the masses and, hence, of being realized.'[59]

The concept of scientific socialism in its neutral meaning can be found not only among Russian but also among Western followers of Marx, although almost exclusively in Germany and Austria. Eduard Bernstein distinguished between the theoretical foundation of socialism, which consists of universally valid knowledge, and the socialist programme which is related to the theoretical foundation in a similar way as is an applied science to a pure science.   In this sense, the socialist programme is capable of objective proof and rests on something stronger than a moral impulse, a mere desire or opinion.[60]   The same distinction seems to underlie August Bebel's definition of socialism, 'socialism is applied science in all avenues of human activity'.[61]

The second meaning of scientific socialism is derived from the predictive power of the Marxian theory. The sociological and historical laws, which form the theoretical foundation of socialism, constitute the basis for the predictions about the course of social evolution in the future.

Saint-Simon and Comte were the first thinkers to maintain that prediction is an important function of knowledge. 'The true, the positive knowledge consists in predicting the development of events with which one is concerned', wrote Saint-Simon, and on this account he found that history provided no adequate, positive knowledge. The historians were clearly unable to say, 'this is what will result from what had occurred, this is the order of the universe which civilization will bring about' and, generally, to deduce the future from the past. But the lack of success on the part of the historians does not prove that once the past is rightly ordered we could not discover the trends and characteristics of the social future. The predictive power of history is based on the fact that 'the future consists of the last term of a series whose first terms constitute the past'. When one studies carefully the first terms of a series it is not difficult to discover the following ones and thus to 'deduce the future from a proper observation of the past'.[62]

The young Comte adopted and developed the Saint-Simonist idea. He defined prediction as a deduction of a particular case from a universal law of succession and maintained that a determination of the future should be recognized as the proper function as much of political science and sociology as of natural science. 'It is quite in accordance with the nature of the human mind that observation of the past should reveal the future of politics as it has done in astronomy, physics, chemistry, and physiology.' [63]

In acknowledging predictability as an important criterion of knowledge Engels was clearly in debt to positivist philosophy. The materialist conception of history, wrote Engels, is of supreme significance for the socialist outlook, for it not only provides a 'natural and reasonable explanation' for what happened in the past but also serves as a basis for extrapolation and prediction of what is bound to happen in the future. Socialism became a science, for the coming of socialism could be inferred from the laws operating within a socio-economic formation and from the laws of succession of distinct socio-economic formations in the course of history.[64] Karl Kautsky emphasized that these glimpses into the future conditions of society are not mere expectations; they let us see which states of society are necessary and must come.[65]

The predictive power of the Marxian theories was emphasized by Plekhanov,[66] and, in particular, by Lenin. Marx deduced 'the inevitability of the transformation of capitalist society into socialist society wholly and exclusively from the economic law of the development of contemporary society'.[67] As Lenin put it elsewhere, the demonstration of the inevitability of socialism, resulting from the materialist conception of history, constitutes an essential part of the meaning to be attached to scientific socialism.[68]

That it is its predictive power which makes socialism scientific was also the view of many other perceptive students of Marx. According to Benedetto Croce, historical necessity is essentially associated with the Marxian theory and allowed Marx to prophesy the coming of the new era.[69] Karl Korsch derided the view as though scientific socialism were concerned with the painting of a future state of society; its basic task was to show how the socialist society would come into being as an 'outgrowth of the whole past and present history'.[70] Karl Popper agreed, in substance, with this evaluation, but stated it more incisively. Marx saw his specific mission in extricating socialism from its sentimental associations, its visionary background, and its unrealistic assumptions, and in establishing it upon the basis of scientific method and scientific prediction. The development of socialism from its utopian to its scientific stage implied that socialism 'was to be based upon a study of historical causes and historical effects, and finally upon the prophecy of its own advent'.[71]

The third meaning in which Engels used the concept of scientific socialism was concerned with the existence of class divisions and the inevitability of class struggle. According to Marx, socialism is bound to remain utopian or doctrinaire as long as it 'does away with the revolutionary struggle of the classes and its requirements by small conjurers' tricks or great sentimentality'.[72] The doctrine of class war is an indispensable component part of socialism, for otherwise, when the class struggle is pushed aside, 'nothing remains as a basis for socialism but "true love of humanity" and empty phraseology about "justice"'.[73] In the opening sentence of his *Socialism: Utopian and Scientific* Engels observed that modern socialism is, in its essence, the direct product of the recognition that society is increasingly split up into two hostile camps and rent by the class struggle between capitalists and wage-workers.[74] In the course of a further analysis Engels reached the conclusion that socialism was the 'necessary outcome of the struggle between . . . the proletariat and the bourgeoisie'. Once this view was formulated, the task of socialism was no longer

> to manufacture a system of society as perfect as possible, but to examine the historico-economic succession of events from which these classes and their antagonism had of necessity sprung, and to discover in the economic conditions thus created the means of ending the conflict.[75]

Socialism became a science with the discovery that the class divisions and antagonism were the motive force of the social development 'capable of becoming', as Lenin put it, 'the creator of a new society'.[76]

Not only the recognition of the reality of class war but also the attribution of the liberating mission to the proletariat is an essential characteristic of scientific socialism.[77] According to Marx, 'the proletariat alone is a really revolutionary class' and 'holds the future in its hands'. To ascribe to the proletariat this historic role is not to consider the proletarians as gods. The conditions of life of the proletariat drive it to revolt against the inhuman conditions of life of society as a whole, for the proletariat cannot free itself without abolishing altogether all the inhuman conditions of social life which are reflected in its own situation.[78] A class is revolutionary, Marx argued, if it 'finds the content and the material of its revolutionary activity directly in its own situation', that is, if it is able to see the measures which are directly dictated by its situation and which ought to be taken in any circumstances. Once the class acquires this ability, 'the consequences of its own deeds drive it on'.[79]

The inevitability which according to Marx compels the proletariat to assume its historic task is not, however, a natural necessity, resulting from a succession of events in conformity to law, but a dialectical inevitability, derived by the young Marx from the Hegelian logic of the negation of the negation and later preserved as an ideology of redemption.[80] Marx's belief in the liberating mission of the working class is not scientific but eschatological; it does not belong to the realm of natural regularities and there is no place for it in scientific socialism in its neutral meaning. When Eduard Bernstein appealed for a greater sense of realism, because the working men 'have the virtues and failings of the economic and social conditions under which they live, and neither these conditions nor their effects can be put aside from one day to another', his was a lonely voice and he was disowned by the orthodoxy.[81] But in the end Bernstein's view prevailed in many parts of the world not only as more realistic but also as more humane.

3. THE NATURALISTIC FALLACY AND THE SEMANTICAL CONFUSION

If the socialism of Marx were described as scientific only because of its theoretical, sociological, and historical basis (the materialist conception of history, the predictive power of this conception, and the doctrine of class struggle), the claim that Marx discovered *scientific* socialism would not be entirely out of place. His doctrine could be rightly regarded as *scientific* socialism on account of having a theoretical foundation which, as Marx and Engels maintained, rested upon experience and which showed that socialism must come in accordance with the laws of social evolution. The right way of challenging the claim of Marx's socialism being scientific would not consist in questioning the appropriateness of the term *scientific* but in testing its factual credentials, that is, the empirical validity of the theoretical foundation upon which scientific socialism is based.

This would still leave unanswered and unexplained the question as to why Marx's doctrine should be described as scientific *socialism* (unless 'socialism' is to mean only 'sociological theory', but neither Marx and Engels nor their followers ever suggested this synonymity). Socialism is not a natural event, taking place in conformity to law, like a sunrise or an eclipse of the moon ; nobody would dream of setting up a party which would strive with knowledge and sense of purpose to assist the rising of the sun or an eclipse of the moon.[82] However, such a party has been set up over and over again in different parts of the world to bring socialism about. If the advent of socialism is an inevitable event, it would be silly and absurd to say that people should exert themselves to bring it about. The silliness and absurdity of this demand are due to the fact that a certain state of affairs is considered as both necessary, come what may, and as an event to be affected by what people do or fail to do. On the other hand, if socialism is not a mere natural event that occurs in accordance with a law and if its coming may, unlike the rising of the sun or the eclipse of the moon, be promoted or impeded, speeded or delayed, by what people do or fail to do, its advent is neither strictly determined nor is it predictable, and to speak of scientific socialism is as absurd as to speak of socialist astronomy.

According to Marx's uses of this term, 'socialism' stands for one of the distinct stages in the evolution of human civilization, of which four, Asiatic, ancient, feudal, and modern bourgeois modes of production could be distinguished in the past. Socialism is the new epoch which is to follow, in conformity to the historical laws of succession, the capitalist formation, in whose womb it was born and in which it matures. But socialism also denotes the vision of a future state of society, based on equality and justice and offering to all the full and unhampered development of their human qualities and potentialities. In this latter sense, socialism is not a neutral and scientific but a value-loaded and ethical idea. If these two essentially different uses of 'socialism', the evolutionary and the moral concept of it, are not kept clearly apart, we are bound to fall victim to the fallacy of equivocation. For the failure to distinguish them confuses 'socialism' in the sense of a morally desirable ideal with socialism as the mere name of the next stage of social evolution, and leads to the conclusion that socialism, as the future state of society, is not only what has to be but also what ought to be. On the one hand, socialism is what must come in conformity to the historical and sociological laws which determine the succession of the progressive epochs in social development ; on the other, socialism is what ought to come in accordance with our sense of right and wrong.[83]

As a matter of fact, Marx did not always manage to hold the two concepts of socialism distinct. As some scholars have said, a dualism runs through the whole work of Marx, a 'dualism which consists in this, that the work aims at being a scientific inquiry and also at proving a theory laid down long before its drafting ; a formula lies at the basis of it in which the result to which the exposition should lead, is fixed beforehand.' [84] It is hardly possible to disagree with this view ; everyone who reads Marx must sense the moral impulse, the indignation with the misery, exploitation, and oppression of the workers which led him to socialism. It has rightly been pointed out over and over again that Marx's investigation of the facts of economic life was subordinate to his main purpose, which was to demonstrate that the transformation of capitalism was a necessary condition of the abolition of social evils and of the emancipation of man. The Messianic inspiration of Marx preceded the economic argument which came later to justify the original expectation. Striving for the proof of the inevitability of the revolution, Marx made of his theory a means to an end, an instrument for producing the right kind of prophecy.[85]   Marx also assumed that he established the inevitability of the transition from capitalism to socialism in conformity with his 'economic law of motion of modern society', that is, with a natural law.   Marx confused socialism in the evolutionary and neutral meaning of this term with socialism in its moral sense without being aware that judgments of value influenced his statement of fact. Marx shared this fallacy with other social thinkers of his time, with Saint-Simon and Comte in particular.   Their vision of the future interfered with their investigation of the social world, shaped the sociological and historical laws discovered in the present, and thus endowed the laws with the power of producing the envisioned future.

According to another interpretation of Marx's doctrine, the above criticism rests upon a misconception.   There is no unknowing confusion in Marx's procedure, for Marx, like Hegel, 'flatly rejected' the distinction between statements of fact and statements of value. 'Judgements of fact cannot be sharply distinguished from those of value; all one's judgements are conditioned by practical activity in a given social milieu: one's views as to what one believes to exist and what one wishes to do with it, modify each other.'[86]   It is often felt that the Marxian critique of ideologies derive its strength and power of persuasion from laying bare the impact and distortions wrought upon statements of fact by ideological, that is, by value statements.   According to the second interpretation of the Marxian position, Marx saw no error in reversing this procedure and deducing the criteria of moral evaluation or the moral principles from empirical statements about matters of fact.[87]

Irrespective of how we may judge Marx's historicist moral theory, the merger of the evolutionary and moral meanings of the term 'socialism' has been responsible for much confusion about the sense and significance of scientific socialism.   It led to an entirely erroneous belief, implicitly involved in what Marx and Engels said on the subject, that Marx was not only able to demonstrate the inevitable advent of socialism, but also to show that what ought to be also had to be.   Eduard Bernstein was the first to point out this fallacy but his discovery was greatly resented by the socialists at the time.[88]

That the rules or norms of moral conduct can never be derived from facts and that they are man-made in the sense 'that we must blame nobody but ourselves for them, neither nature, nor God', is a statement with a powerful logical argument in its favour. It is true, of course, that facts are not entirely irrelevant to the rules of conduct; a norm which would be incompatible with the laws of nature is not practicable and enforceable. Since we accept that the rule *ought* implies *can*, we cannot without contradiction blame anybody for having failed to do what he was not free to have done or for having done what he could not avoid doing. In this sense, a moral theory must have its basis in facts. Facts are not, however, decisive; they restrict our freedom of choice in adopting the rules of conduct, but do not determine it. There is no logical relation between descriptive and evaluating statements and the latter cannot be reduced to the former. We alone are responsible for the standards, by means of which we pass value judgments, compare one norm with another, and assign a variable degree of excellence to human conduct.

> The standards are not to be found in nature. Nature consists of facts and of regularities, and is in itself neither moral nor immoral. It is we who impose our standards upon nature, and who in this way introduce morals into the natural world, in spite of the fact that we are part of this world.[89]

The view about the dependence of the moral norms upon facts, which is sometimes described as moral positivism and ascribed to Marx, is the exact opposite of the above defined doctrine of the autonomy of morals.

The certainty of scientific socialism that what ought to be also had to be is a methodological misunderstanding and misapprehension, based upon the naturalistic fallacy, that is, upon the belief of the deducibility of norms and values from facts. The certainty of scientific socialism also results from the confusion of semantical categories. 'Scientific socialism' is as semantically ill-formed an expression as is 'square circle', 'socialist astronomy' or 'moral physics', whose semantical inappropriateness is recognizable at once by everybody.

4. THE REASSERTION OF UTOPIAN SOCIALISM

That socialism in the moral and evolutionary sense will coincide one day is, according to Marx, not a hope but a demonstrable truth. But no theory can demonstrate that what is inevitable is also morally desirable, for no moral decision is deducible from the knowledge of facts. We cannot help accepting as a matter of fact what is brought into existence according to a law operating through natural processes. This does not imply, however, that what has to be is thus transformed into what our moral consciousness demands. Whether we should morally accept what is inevitable remains a moral problem and its solution is our own responsibility.

It was probably a redemptive ideology that prompted Marx to transform a socialist programme, based on a scientific foundation, into scientific *socialism* which thus acquired an air of utopianism. Utopianism is an excessive moral idealism and an unjustifiable reliance upon proselytism, education, and moral persuasion as a means of accomplishing a prompt passage from strife and misery to universal well-being and harmony. But we do not escape utopianism, Eduard Bernstein observed, if we ascribe to the present what we wish to be the case in the future.[90] Marx did not hope for an instantaneous change, as the utopians did, but the difference between them was one of degree rather than of substance. His moral radicalism made him expect a complete transformation of institutions, of ideas and habits, of the patterns of interaction and of the spiritual climate, which was to take place under the impact of his evolutionary determinism. It is true to say that Marx did not justify the coming of socialism on moral grounds but on the basis of a law of social development; however, having justified the coming of socialism on the basis of his evolutionary theory, Marx claimed that the law of social development realizes moral aspirations.

Scientific socialism confuses the construction of a theory of social evolution, that is, an intellectual act, with the realization of a social ideal which requires a sustained effort of the will. Scientific socialism did not establish the belief that what the future brings is both historically inevitable and morally desirable as a demonstrable truth; it reached this conclusion by an intellectual short-cut and by an eschatological conversion of hope into certainty. Since this intellectual short-cut contributed to the accumulation of misunderstandings about the proper function of the will and the intellect in the realization of socialism, it led to the errors of voluntarism and to the reduction of the intellect to a mere tool of the will.

The concept of scientific socialism leads to the misconception that socialism as an ideal can be identified with a set of theoretical propositions which are capable of demonstration. It is easy to see that this is a misconception. Once it is defined in terms of ultimate values, socialism is inconceivable without applying both the relationship of cause and effect and the relation of aims and means in the examination of the development of events. To choose rationally the best means for the attainment of a given aim is a question of knowledge, but the decision to adopt the rationally chosen means is not dependent upon it. Generally, it can be safely assumed that where values and ideals are concerned reason cannot prevail without the participation of the will. To ignore this requirement is to attribute an undue role to reason and to err by an excess of intellectualism. Intellectualism is an error as fateful for the realization of socialism as that of voluntarism which ignores the part to be played by knowledge in its attainment.

Conclusions

IT is not easy to review in brief the main conclusions of the foregoing investigations, for Marx was not a systematic thinker, nor Engels a rigorous one, and Engels's Russian followers were bold and ingenious rather than determined to face the theoretical issues arising from the adaptation of Engels's beliefs to their own requirements. Lenin's and Stalin's knowledge of the contemporary scientific and philosophical theories, which were to be replaced by their own, was not what might justly be called comprehensive, exact, or profound. They were neither original nor competent thinkers, though they were in a certain sense successful.

The famous partnership of Marx and Engels does not comprise dialectical materialism. Moreover, there is considerable disparity between their respective philosophical positions which are not the product of a twin mind. There is no evidence, apart from what Engels said after Marx's death, that Marx was a dialectical materialist in Engels's sense. Engels was a metaphysician — he felt that he knew what the nature of the universe is and what laws the universe conforms to — and Marx was not. Marx did not claim knowledge beyond the scope of empirical inquiry and, like Kant, he believed that every claim to such knowledge must remain unfounded. While Marx evolved a naturalistic *Weltanschauung* which repudiated both materialism — the universe is all matter — and spiritualism — the universe is all mind — Engels alone was the founder of dialectical materialism. Marx and Engels were not equals either in their acquired qualifications or their innate ability and power of thought. They were thinkers of a different order and orientation. These differences become clear when they are examined in detail, for instance, when the relation of Marx and Engels to Hegelian philosophy or to positivism is investigated.

Unlike the 'Marxists' of today, neither Marx nor Engels thought that there is a logical connection between philosophic materialism and the materialist conception of history. Marx did not suggest that if materialism is true, the materialist conception of history must be true as well; he was sure about the truth of the latter but not the former, that is, he would accept the opinion that materialism may be false even if the materialist conception of history should be true. Engels indicated that dialectical and historical materialism were closely bound together, but he did not support the untenable belief that the materialist conception of history is deducible from dialectical materialism either. Marx regarded the materialist conception as an application of the principles of naturalism, and Engels considered it as a powerful argument in support of materialist metaphysics. He did not argue, however, as Lenin and Stalin did after him, that if dialectical materialism is true, historical materialism must be true too.

While it would be entirely wrong to maintain that Marx and Engels held the same views about nature, they did share very much the same views about history. The existing differences are mainly a matter of emphasis or approach. Since Marx and Engels were the co-founders of the materialist conception of history — they discovered it independently of each other at roughly the same time — the close similarity of their views on this matter should be expected.

It could be said with some justification that dialectical materialism was established by Engels by chance in response to a coincidence of events. If Eugen Dühring had never tried to capture the intellectual leadership in the German Social Democratic Party, *Anti-Dühring* would never have been written. In spite of its accidental origin, Engels established the foundations of dialectical materialism in a genuine attempt to formulate a metaphysical theory of the universe. Engels was clearly interested in only such a theory as would, in his view, reflect truly the nature and structure of the physical world. He was convinced that his metaphysical, sociological, and political beliefs were all connected and formed a coherent whole, but he did not regard the theoretical part as a mere stepping-stone to provide the best possible foundation for his practical activity. Engels believed that philosophy arose from wonder and that it was inspired by the desire to systematize our knowledge and to base it upon intelligible principles. Although the origin of dialectical materialism was more or less accidental, Engels's formulation of it was intended to serve a clearly cognitive purpose.

This cognitive purpose recedes more and more the further away we move from Engels. In Plekhanov, cosmology comes under the influence of political and social considerations. While in Plekhanov's case one could still argue that he was only guilty of a frequent error that confuses the necessity of thought in the minds of one generation of thinkers with the necessity inherent in the universe, this explanation no longer applies to Lenin's or Stalin's revisions and reformulations of dialectical materialism. In Lenin's interpretation, cosmology gives way to the picture of the universe described in socio-cosmic terms, and in Stalin's main contribution to the subject, dialectical materialism is 'political cosmology' pure and simple. The political usefulness of a socio-cosmic view of the universe turned out to be considerable. Lenin and Stalin exploited it not only for the purpose of inducing and promoting certain attitudes, desirable from the viewpoint of the Communist government, but also to justify its practical decisions and achievements. A metaphysical theory of the universe was arbitrarily transformed into an instrument for bolstering up political views and for exercising control over human behaviour. Its function was to maintain and strengthen definite social institutions, to safeguard the privileged and commanding position of one group over against the rest of society, and to support a specific form of government. This final outcome can be described as the absorption of scientific knowledge and philosophy by ideology. If we accept the partiality of all established governments towards the presentation of the results of science in one way or another, because of its alleged support to some political, social, or religious creed, the fortunes of dialectical materialism represent an extreme instance of the interdependence of politics, philosophy, and science.

Two basically different conceptions of dialectical materialism seem to emerge, the minimalistic and the maximalistic, the former represented by Engels and the latter by Lenin and Stalin, Plekhanov holding an intermediate position between the two. According to the minimalistic conception, dialectical materialism is a set of metaphysical presuppositions which were intended to provide the foundation of an empirical theory concerned with social and economic phenomena and to explain social and historical development in universal terms. The maximalistic conception presents dialectical materialism as a theory of the universe in which the laws of dialectics are raised to the status of the ultimate laws of nature, that is, laws from which all others are derived while they themselves cannot be inferred from any laws more general than themselves. Within the maximalistic conception the claim of science to being able to achieve valid knowledge is sharply reduced. Since the laws of dialectics as the ultimate laws of nature convey significance, validity, and truth upon all knowledge, derivability from, and compatibility with, these laws become the criterion of the truth and validity of knowledge.

The maximalistic conception of dialectical materialism prompted some past efforts to impose certain hypotheses and methodological principles upon the natural, social, and historical sciences and continues to support what the dialectical materialists describe as the correct line of inquiry in the running battle between metaphysical dogmas on the one hand and logical analysis of the philosophy of science on the other. The maximalistic conception tends to make of dialectical materialism a vast and indivisible system which comprehends all that we can know, explaining everything that may happen in the universe, and providing universal rules of conduct for the direction of men and society. The philosophical interpretation of knowledge is transferred to the jurisdiction of political philosophy which is the exclusive preserve of the ruling class, serving its interests and helping to maintain it in power.

It is important to realize that the maximalistic conception is not something implicit in dialectical materialism but is an interpretation of it, a deliberate change in its content and function, initiated by Lenin and completed by Stalin. It can claim the authority of neither Marx nor Engels. It never occurred to Engels that anybody, whether a dialectical materialist or not, could assume that he knew all there was to be known and that the book of human knowledge should be regarded as closed. The minimalistic conception of dialectical materialism does not claim that it provides us with a general method enabling those who master it to dictate to the scientist his line of inquiry and the kind of results he should obtain. The minimalistic conception does not enjoin him to reject a certain theory of physics, chemistry, or biology and to adopt another because the one is contrary to and the other in agreement with dialectical materialism. In the debate between the critical and the dogmatic attitudes the minimalistic conception does not take the side of the latter against the former.

The gradual retreat from the maximalistic conception, which is becoming apparent in Soviet philosophy today, should not be understood to imply the abandonment of dialectical materialism itself. Moreover, it should be observed that the relinquishing of the maximalistic conception is not due to the recognition of the unsoundness of its assumptions and the extravagance of its claims. Ideologically directed science has been unable to produce practical results, and it is this inability to produce a workable science that has led to the revision of the underlying speculative theory. As long as the maximalistic conception of dialectical materialism merely drops some of its exorbitant claims because of its practical failure, the revision does not affect the focal point at issue. Nothing short of a complete shift from the maximalistic to the minimalistic approach could justify the opinion that scientific knowledge and philosophy have managed to emancipate themselves from ideological and political interference and that dialectical materialism has regained its cognitive function.

Should this shift actually occur, it would eliminate the conflict between the dogmatic and the critical attitude. But the struggle between empiricism and metaphysics would remain. For the return to Engels's type of materialism does not imply that dialectical materialism loses the certainty of metaphysics and acquires the fluidity of science. A dialectical materialist is bound to regard his knowledge, which is doubtful and provisional, as certain, true, and final. Only if dialectical materialism were to abandon its metaphysical claims and transform itself into a methodological doctrine could it raise the claim of being a view of the world based on scientific knowledge.

Notes

PART ONE

Chapter I.   The Origins of Dialectical Materialism

1. Engels exclaimed, 'I have him on the hip now', when at the planning stage he outlined the content of *Anti-Dühring* and disclosed the tactics which he intended to follow in rewarding Dühring 'according to his just deserts'. See Engels's letter to Marx of 28 May 1876.

2. Engels, *AD*, p. 39.

3. Plekhanov, *Zu Hegel's sechzigsten Todestag* (*SAHD*), originally published in *Neue Zeit* in 1891, and Foreword to the Russian translation of Engels's *Ludwig Feuerbach* (*FNLF*), published in 1892. For the first time, Lenin used the expression 'dialectical materialism' in *What the 'Friends of the People' Are*, published in 1894.

4. As Engels himself informed us, since Marx's death his time was required for more urgent duties, that is, the publication and republication of the works and manuscripts left by Marx, above all, of the remaining volumes of *Capital*, and Engels was thus compelled to lay aside his own studies. Although he hoped that he would return to them one day, the opportunity never materialized. See Engels, *AD*, p. 19.

5. In the Special Introduction to the English edition of *Socialism: Utopian and Scientific* (*SUS*) Engels explained the political reasons why it 'became necessary to take up the gauntlet thrown down to us [sc. by Dühring], and to fight out the struggle whether we liked it or not'.

6. Engels's letter to Marx of 28 May 1876.

7. Marx's letter to F. A. Sorge of 19 October 1877.

8. Originally *Anti-Dühring* appeared in *Vorwärts*, the central organ of the united German Social Democratic Party. The first instalment was published in January 1877, and the last in July 1878, one and a half years later. As a separate book the first edition of *Anti-Dühring* appeared in 1878, the second in 1885, and the third in 1894.

9. F. Mehring, *Karl Marx*, p. 512. The scandal caused by *Anti-Dühring* within the German Social Democratic Party was not restricted to Dühring's supporters. Many people were shocked by the violence of Engels's language and the content of his attack upon the blind *Privatdozent* at Berlin University who publicly defended socialism and was persecuted by the authorities for this heinous crime. It was widely believed at that time that Dühring suffered persecution only because of his political convictions and Engels himself rose to his defence in the Preface to the second edition of *AD*. According to K. Vorländer, *Karl Marx*, pp. 251–2, this was not, however, the case. The ostensible reason why the University Senate deprived Dühring of *veniam legendi* was because of his offensive attacks on Helmholtz and

other Berlin scientists. Apparently there was no other path for the Senate to take, since at that time Dühring's alleged conceit rose to the height of a megalomaniac delusion. Whatever the true reasons responsible for Dühring's loss of his *Privatdozentur* at Berlin University were, his scholastic reputation was considerable — no lesser man than Ernst Mach spoke highly of him in *Science of Mechanics* (Preface to the first German edition) — and Engels's malice was both out of place and unjustifiable. When it came to defending Marx against his opponents, the kind, gentle, and modest Engels was quite capable of outdoing his friend in sarcasm, irony, invective, and ridicule.

10. A. Labriola, *Socialism and Philosophy*, pp. 24 and 53.

11. Lenin, 'Frederick Engels', *CW* 2, p. 25.

12. Plekhanov, *FPM*, p. 3. Lenin repeated this evaluation in 'Twenty-Fifth Anniversary of the Death of Joseph Dietzgen', *CW* 19, p. 79.

13. K. Kautsky, *Aus der Frühzeit des Marxismus*, p. 15.

14. Engels's letter to J. Bloch of 21 September 1890.

15. G. Mayer, *Friedrich Engels*, Bd. 2, p. 285. Cf. D. Riazanov, *Karl Marx and Friedrich Engels*, p. 210.

16. Engels's letter to E. Bernstein of 8 August 1882. See E. Bernstein, *Die Briefe von Friedrich Engels an Eduard Bernstein*, p. 75. The German version had the title *Die Entwicklung des Sozialismus von der Utopie zur Wissenschaft* and was first published in 1883 with the year 1882 on the cover page. It was preceded by a Polish translation which appeared in Geneva the same year as the French. The English translation was first published in 1892.

17. See, e.g., Lenin, *MEC*, pp. 19, 246; Sombart, *Der proletarische Sozialismus*, Bd. 1, pp. 122–6, 212.

18. G. A. Wetter, *DM*, p. 40. Wetter changed his view entirely in *Die Umkehrung Hegels*, pp. 28–38.

19. H. Lefebvre, *Le Matérialisme dialectique*, p. 90.

20. See, e.g., D. Joravsky, *Soviet Marxism and Natural Science*, p. 6.

21. Engels, *AD*, p. 14.

22. F. Mehring, *Karl Marx*, p. 231; G. Mayer, *Friedrich Engels*, Bd. 1, pp. 172–3, 226–7. Cf. L. Woltmann, *Der historische Materialismus*, pp. 212, 293.

23. H. Cunow, *Die Marxsche Geschichts-, Gesellschafts- und Staatstheorie*, Bd. 1, *Vorwort*.

24. M. M. Bober, *Karl Marx's Interpretation of History*, Preface.

25. K. Kautsky, *Aus der Frühzeit des Marxismus*, p. 395.

26. This qualification is important for such of Engels's publications as *Outlines of a Critique of Political Economy* (1844) and *The Condition of the Working Class in England* (1845) make it clear that Engels was at first ahead of Marx. It was Engels, says Gustav Mayer, who opened Marx's eyes to the facts of economic life.

27. K. Vorländer, *Kant und Marx*, pp. 66–67.

28. R. N. C. Hunt, *The Theory and Practice of Communism*, p. 37.

29. I. Berlin, *Karl Marx*, p. 101.

30. Engels's letter to J. P. Becker of 15 October 1884.

31. Engels's letter to F. Mehring of 14 July 1893; *LF*, p. 349 n. See also Engels's letter to E. Bernstein of 14 March 1883, and to F. A. Sorge of 15 March 1883.

32. Engels, *HCL*, pp. 311–12; *LF*, pp. 324, 349 n.; Preface to the English edition of *CWC*, p. 22; Marx, *CPE*, pp. 13–14; *Werke*, Bd. 19, p. 181.

33. See, e.g., Lenin, 'Frederick Engels', *CW* 2, p. 26; M. Eastman, *Marx and Lenin*, p. 27; G. Mayer, *Friedrich Engels*, Bd. 2, pp. 351–2.

34. S. Hook, *Towards the Understanding of Karl Marx*, p. 29. Cf. Bocheński, *SDM*, p. 22, first published in 1950, where a similar view is expressed.

35. S. Hook, *Towards the Understanding of Karl Marx*, pp. 29–33. Cf. M. Adler, *Marx als Denker*, p. 129.

36. Engels, *AD*, p. 10.

37. F. Mehring, *Karl Marx*, pp. 501, 526–8; D. Riazanov, *Karl Marx and Friedrich Engels*, pp. 205–6.

38. See, e.g., G. Mayer, *Friedrich Engels*, Bd. 2, p. 323. Mayer argued that Communism had a cosmic and metaphysical meaning for Fourier but not for Engels, who, accepting the possibility of a thermal death of the universe, was a cosmic pessimist. On this account Engels was allegedly unwilling to speculate about the constitution of the universe and to establish his historical and social theories on the foundations of a philosophy of nature.

39. Engels, *AD*, p. 14.

40. Ibid., p. 12; Engels's letter to Marx of 28 May 1876.

41. E. Bernstein, *Zur Geschichte und Theorie des Sozialismus*, p. 323.

42. L. Woltmann, *Der historische Materialismus*, p. 264.

43. Plekhanov, *FPM*, pp. 1–2.

44. G. Lichtheim, *Marxism*, p. 235.

45. G. Lukács, *Geschichte und Klassenbewusstsein*, p. 17.

46. K. Korsch, *Karl Marx*, pp. 167–71, where the main conclusions of his *Marxismus und Philosophie*, first published in 1922, are summarized.

47. S. Hook, *From Hegel to Marx*, pp. 75–76.

48. B. Russell, *Freedom versus Organization*, ch. xviii; H. Marcuse, *Reason and Revolution*, p. 314; J.-Y. Calvez, *La Pensée de Karl Marx*, pp. 374–82, 408, 416; L. Kołakowski, 'Karol Marks i klasyczna definicja prawdy', pp. 46–54; L. Landgrebe, 'Das Problem der Dialektik', pp. 50–51; I. Fetscher, 'Das Verhältnis des Marxismus zu Hegel', p. 94; J.-P. Sartre, *Critique de la raison dialectique*, tome i, p. 129; R. C. Tucker, *Philosophy and Myth in Karl Marx*, p. 183; G. Lichtheim, *Marxism*, pp. 245–6.

49. For a more detailed discussion of the distinctive characteristics of naturalism see R. W. Sellars, 'Realism, Naturalism, and Humanism', in particular p. 274, and E. Nagel, *Logic without Metaphysics*, pp. 7–9.

50. See, e.g., C. J. Ducasse, *Nature, Mind and Death*, pp. 219–22; M. Farber, *Naturalism and Subjectivism*, p. 3.

51. F. A. Hayek, *The Counter-Revolution of Science*, pp. 194, 204.

Chapter II. Marxian Naturalism

1. *MEGA* I/3, p. 160; *EPM*, p. 156.

2. L. Feuerbach, *WDLS*, p. 362. The followers of Marx, including those who had a first-hand knowledge of Feuerbach, did not understand what he

wanted to say. For instance, Plekhanov wrote that Feuerbach's anthropological viewpoint was only a methodological device, conditioned by the
circumstances of time and place, which was intended to 'bring forth a
correct view upon matter in general and its relation to the "spirit"'
(Plekhanov, *FPM*, p. 6).

3. G. Santayana, *Character and Opinion in the United States*, p. 114.

4. *Differenz der demokritischen und epikureischen Naturphilosophie*, *MEGA* 1/1/1,
p. 52. It is perhaps interesting to note that Sartre shares Marx's admiration
for Epicurus, whom he describes as 'the first man who tried to abolish
slavery within his domain' ('Matérialisme et révolution', pp. 173–4).

5. *MEGA* 1/3, pp. 34, 151–2; *EPM*, pp. 17, 144–5; *MEGA* 1/3, p. 316;
HF, pp. 186–7; Marx's letter to L. Feuerbach of 11 August 1844 (first
published in 1958 and known to the author only in Polish translation, Karol
Marks i Fryderyk Engels, *Dzieła*, tom i, pp. 640–3).

6. Engels probably followed the lead of the Young Hegelians for whom
Feuerbach's critique of religion was a paradigm of philosophical thinking
and as such completely destroyed the 'old philosophy', that is, Hegel's
speculative philosophy. It was felt that Feuerbach's critique of religion
applied equally to any dogma or abstract principle dominating the mind of
men, and hence was of universal importance. This view of Feuerbach's
philosophy is also reflected in Marx's early writings (see, e.g., *GI*, pp. 4–6;
Frühschriften, pp. 344–5) and explains the opening sentence of the *Contribution to the Critique of Hegel's Philosophy of Right*, 'For Germany the critique
(*Kritik*) of religion is essentially completed and the critique (*Kritik*) of
religion is the premiss of all critique (*Kritik*).'

7. Engels treated Feuerbach condescendingly in *Ludwig Feuerbach* and
Engels's authority tended to minimize Feuerbach's influence upon Marx in
the eyes of his followers and exponents. In this respect Plekhanov was an
exception, for he emphasized that Feuerbach 'in a considerable measure
worked out the philosophical foundation of what can be called the world-
outlook of Marx and Engels' (*FPM*, p. 5). Contemporary students of Marx
are inclined to accept Engels's testimony unquestioningly, ignore Feuerbach's philosophy, and consider the *Essence of Christianity* alone as an
important influence in Marx's philosophical development. One of the very
few exceptions to this rule is Sidney Hook's treatment of Marx's relationship
to Feuerbach in *From Hegel to Marx*. Cf. E. Thier, *Das Menschenbild des
jungen Marx*, pp. 16–17, whose author, too, is not misled by Engels's reminis-
cences in *Ludwig Feuerbach*.

8. The term 'anthropological materialism' is borrowed from German
historians of philosophy who often describe Feuerbach's doctrine as
anthropologischer Materialismus. As applied to the philosophy of Feuerbach,
'naturalism' seems to be preferable to 'materialism', for Feuerbach did not
establish matter as the principle of all that exists. It is advisable to add the
qualification *anthropological* for the following reason. Unlike pure materialists who are impressed by the insignificance of man as compared with the
whole of nature, Feuerbach gave a prominent place to man, a position
which is bound to militate against some varieties or assumptions of materialism.

9. L. Feuerbach, *The Essence of Christianity*, pp. 87, 270.

10. Ibid., pp. 91, 286.

11. Feuerbach, *VTRPH*, p. 267.

12. Feuerbach, *WDLS*, p. 362. F. A. Lange rightly observed that however close they may be, sensibility and materiality are not identical notions for Feuerbach.

13. L. Feuerbach, *The Essence of Christianity*, Preface to 2nd ed., p. xxxiv.

14. J. Locke, *An Essay Concerning Human Understanding*, book II, ch. 27, 5–10.

15. Feuerbach, *VTRPH*, p. 264; *GPHZ*, § 59, p. 344.

16. Feuerbach, *GPHZ*, § 36, p. 325.

17. Feuerbach, *WDLS*, pp. 356, 367.

18. Engels, *LF*, pp. 332–3; *AD*, p. 55. Engels's insistence that 'the "human being" is always a phantom as long as he does not have his basis in empirical man' and that the empirical man is an 'embodied individual' clearly reflects Feuerbach's conception of man. See Engels's letter to Marx of 19 November 1844 (*MEGA* III/1, p. 7).

19. Engels, *LF*, p. 337. Engels's view is very close to one of Feuerbach's aphorisms in *VTRPH*. 'Philosophy is the knowledge of what exists', Feuerbach wrote. 'The highest duty and task of philosophy is to think of things and beings and to apprehend them the way they are' (p. 254). In his interesting study *Der Begriff der Natur in der Lehre von Marx*, A. Schmidt suggested that Marx was a materialist but that 'his materialism should not be understood ontologically' (p. 22, *passim*). An anti-metaphysical materialism is a *contradictio in adiecto*, for materialism is a metaphysical doctrine. There is, however, no inconsistency in speaking of anti-metaphysical naturalism, which is one of many reasons why Marx's philosophy should be described as naturalism.

20. Engels, *LF*, p. 349.

21. Ibid., pp. 349–50.

22. Marx, *GI*, p. 37; *Frühschriften*, p. 354.

23. See, e.g., Engels's letter to F. Mehring of 14 July 1893; Marx, *GI*, p. 37; *Frühschriften*, p. 354. Historicity can be defined as that feature of the behaviour of man and, generally, living organism (*LO*) that given response R of LO at t_n, R cannot be explained unless the past behaviour of type R and other occurrences in the history of LO are included among the causes of R at t_n.

24. Engels, *LF*, p. 340.

25. While Marx, who wrote his criticism of Feuerbach's philosophy in 1845, emphasized above all its affinity with 'old materialism', F. A. Lange was impressed twenty years later by the great distance dividing Feuerbach from 'strict materialism'. See his *History of Materialism*, vol. ii, pp. 250–1.

26. Marx, *Capital*, vol. i, p. 17.

27. Ibid., p. 390.

28. Engels and some of the younger followers of Marx shared his hostility to what they sometimes referred to as 'bourgeois materialism'. Quoting from Goethe's *Dichtung und Wahrheit* where Goethe described his reaction to Holbach's *Système de la nature*, Plekhanov called the views of the French

materialists a dry, gloomy, and melancholy doctrine. They, that is, the mechanistic materialists, made it clear that 'the materialist conception of nature is still not the materialist conception of history' (*SAHD*, p. 472 ; *DMH*, p. 606). The former is of no avail in explaining historical phenomena.

29. Elsewhere Marx described Locke as 'an advocate of the new bourgeoisie in all forms' and as 'the philosopher of political economy in England, France, and Italy' (*Capital*, vol. i, p. 390). Marx probably had in mind Locke's idea of society as an aggregate of individuals each pursuing his own ends independently of the others and subordinating his action to certain rules. Marx was an outspoken opponent of this individualistic and rationalistic conception of society which might have played a useful role in economics but was disastrous for the development of social theory. Locke's conception of society was also accepted by the thinkers of the French Enlightenment. As a social philosopher Locke was not a protagonist of socialism and communism.

30. *MEGA* 1/3, pp. 306–8 ; *HF*, pp. 174–7. Rousseau was a determined opponent of the view that the individual is what education makes him and criticized it at length in *Émile*, book iv, tome 2, pp. 43 ff.

31. Marx, *MEGA* 1/3, pp. 307–8 ; *HF*, p. 176. Cf. Plekhanov, *DMH*, p. 549.

32. *MEGA* 1/3, p. 179 ; *HF*, p. 15 ; *GI*, pp. 5–6 ; *Frühschriften*, pp. 345–6.

33. *MEGA* 1/3, pp. 338–9 ; *HF*, pp. 214–15.

34. *TF* iii.

35. Marx, *GI*, p. 34 ; *Frühschriften*, p. 351.

36. Engels, *AD*, p. 16.

37. Engels, *LF*, p. 340.

38. Engels, *AD*, p. 17.

39. The materials contained in *Dialectics of Nature* were collected in preparation for accomplishing this task.

40. Marx expounded this conception in the third of his *Economic and Philosophic Manuscripts of 1844*, in *The German Ideology*, and also referred to it in the opening paragraphs of ch. vii in vol. i of *Capital*.

41. Marx, *GI*, pp. 35–37 ; *Frühschriften*, pp. 351–3.

42. *MEGA* 1/3, pp. 160–1, 171 ; *EPM*, pp. 156–7, 170. This section owes a great debt to the study of L. Kołakowski, 'Karol Marks i klasyczna definicja prawdy'. Cf. L. Landgrebe, 'Das Problem der Dialektik', pp. 52–55 ; K. Korsch, *Karl Marx*, pp. 190–1.

43. Marx, *GI*, p. 37 ; *Frühschriften*, p. 353.

44. Feuerbach, *WDLS*, p. 362 ; *GPHZ*, § 54, p. 343 ; *MEGA* 1/3, p. 160 ; *EPM*, p. 156.

45. S. Hook, *From Hegel to Marx*, p. 295.

46. *MEGA* 1/3, p. 85 ; *EPM*, p. 70. Cf. Feuerbach, *GPHZ*, § 29, p. 314 : 'Matter is the symbol of being outside thought, the substratum of reality.'

47. *Discours sur l'origine et les fondements de l'inégalité parmi les hommes*, première partie, pp. 60–61.

48. L. Feuerbach, *The Essence of Christianity*, pp. 82–83, 158.

49. Marx, *GI*, p. 19 ; *Frühschriften*, p. 357.

50. See Jordan, *PHI*, ch. 18. Sidney Hook points out that Marx only elaborated upon Feuerbach's theory of knowledge which, in turn, closely resembles that of Protagoras. See *From Hegel to Marx*, pp. 256–9. Protagoras's epistemological relativism was individualistic and that of Feuerbach and Marx was not. Moreover, in the case of Marx, it was supported by an elaborate sociological theory which makes Protagoras's and Marx's theories of knowledge entirely incomparable. To emphasize this important difference, Karl Mannheim's distinction between relativism and relationism, introduced in *Ideology and Utopia*, could be adopted. Protagoras's doctrine would provide an instance of epistemological relativism, that of Feuerbach and Marx — of epistemological relationism. For the latter position the name *perspectivism* has also been suggested. See L. von Bertalanffy, 'The Psychopathology of Scientism', p. 204.

51. *MEGA* 1/3, p. 87; *EPM*, p. 74.

52. Marx, *GI*, p. 35; *Frühschriften*, p. 351. Marx attached great importance to this view and stressed it repeatedly in *The German Ideology*, *The Poverty of Philosophy* and in his letter to P. V. Annenkov of 28 December 1846.

53. Plekhanov, *FPM*, p. 12.

54. Marx, *GI*, p. 29; *Frühschriften*, p. 368. Jean-Paul Sartre, interpreting this and other Marxian pronouncements, writes that according to this principle the specificity of the human act which transforms the world on the basis of given conditions is man's ability to go beyond this situation and to remake what has been made (*Critique de la raison dialectique*, p. 63).

55. Engels, Special Introduction to the English edition of *SUS*, pp. 92–93; *LF*, p. 336; *DN*, p. 306. Plekhanov's definition, 'dialectical materialism is the philosophy of action', seems also to reflect the original Marxian approach to the theory of knowledge. See Plekhanov, *DMH*, p. 742.

56. It should be remembered that Lenin did not know either *Economic and Philosophic Manuscripts of 1844* or *The German Ideology*.

57. The distinction between sacred and profane things in the sociological meaning of these terms is associated with Émile Durkheim. The expressions 'sacred' and 'profane' used in reference to the two types of history differentiated by Marx should not be given the Durkheimean sense but only that intended and explained by Marx himself.

58. B. Russell, *Freedom and Organization*, p. 192; 'Dewey's New Logic', p. 143. Dewey repudiated any affinity between Marx and himself by accusing Marx of the one-factor fallacy and the belief that the conditions provided by the environment are supreme. See *Freedom and Culture*, pp. 75–76. Precisely in this respect there is no difference between Marx and Dewey.

59. Marx, *MEGA* 1/3, p. 123; *EPM*, p. 111.

60. Feuerbach, *GPHZ*, § 54, p. 343.

61. Werner Sombart used the terms 'social naturalism' and 'social idealism' (*sozialer Naturalismus, sozialer Idealismus*) to designate the views of Marx and Hegel respectively, which seem, however, to be as much burdened by misleading connotations and associations as are the more familiar phrases 'the materialist' and 'the spiritualistic conception of history'. See W. Sombart, *Der proletarische Sozialismus*, Bd. 1, pp. 142, 146.

62. Marx, *MEGA* 1/3, p. 327; *HF*, p. 201.

63. Marx's letter to P. V. Annenkov of 28 December 1846. Marx might have wished also to refer to Moses Hess's *The Sacred History of Mankind* (*Die heilige Geschichte der Menschheit*), published in 1837, in which Hess called the history of mankind 'sacred' because he regarded it as a gradual revelation of the Divine Spirit. See J. Weiss, *Moses Hess: Utopian Socialist*, pp. 10–22.

64. Marx, *KHR, MEGA* 1/1/1, p. 607.

65. Marx, *GI*, pp. 22–23; *Frühschriften*, pp. 364–5.

66. Marx, *KHR, MEGA* 1/1/1, p. 608.

67. The expression 'the idealist view of history' (*die idealistische Geschichtsanschauung*) occurs in *The German Ideology*, p. 28 (*Frühschriften*, p. 368), but the other — 'the materialist conception of history' (*die materialistische Auffassung der Geschichte*) — was never used by Marx. It was Engels who applied it for the first time in his review of Marx's *A Contribution to the Critique of Political Economy*, published in *Das Volk*, a German newspaper appearing in London, in August 1859 (*MCPE*, pp. 333–4), and not in *Anti-Dühring*, as is often said. 'Historical materialism' seems to have been used for the first time by Engels in his Special Introduction to the English edition of *SUS* (1892), p. 94.

68. Marx, *GI*, pp. 39–40; *Frühschriften*, pp. 373–4.

69. Marx, *GI*, pp. 30–33, 43; *Frühschriften*, pp. 369–72, 378.

70. Marx, *GI*, pp. 6, 13; *Frühschriften*, pp. 346, 348.

71. Marx, *Capital*, vol. i, pp. 42–43, 183–4.

72. Marx, *Introduction to the Critique of Political Economy*, p. 268. Cf. *MEGA* 1/6, p. 482; *WLC*, p. 83 for an earlier formulation of the same view.

73. Marx, *GI*, pp. 7, 28–29, 38; *Frühschriften*, pp. 347, 364, 367–8; Marx's letter to P. V. Annenkov of 28 December 1846; *Capital*, vol. i, p. 80.

74. Marx, *MEGA* 1/3, p. 296; *HF*, p. 163.

75. Marx, *GI*, pp. 16–18, 26–27; *Frühschriften*, pp. 354–6, 363–4; Engels, *LF*, p. 357.

76. The expressions 'realer Grund', 'wirkliche Basis' or 'realer Boden' occur frequently in the writings of the young Marx to designate what later has become known as 'the economic base' or 'basis'. See, e.g., *Frühschriften*, pp. 368, 369. Engels took it over from Marx and used it synonymously with 'the economic structure', 'the material foundation', and similar expressions.

77. Marx's letter to P. V. Annenkov of 28 December 1846.

78. Marx, *MEGA* 1/6, pp. 179–80; *PPH*, pp. 92–93.

79. Marx, *MEGA* 1/3, pp. 87–88, 156; *EPM*, pp. 75, 151; *GI*, pp. 14–15, 28, 30; *Frühschriften*, pp. 348–9, 367–9.

80. *MEGA* 1/3, p. 371; *HF*, p. 255.

81. *MEGA* 1/3, p. 156; *EPM*, p. 151.

82. Some historians of social and philosophical thought maintain that for his concept of social evolution as the formative cause of man's distinctive characteristics Marx is directly indebted to *The Phenomenology of Mind*. See H. B. Acton, *The Illusion of the Epoch*, p. 146; A. L. Harris, 'Utopian Elements in Marx's Thought', pp. 91–92; J. Plamenatz, *Man and Society*, vol. ii, pp. 197–9. This seems to be the result, at least in some cases, of a

circulus vitiosus, namely, it is based on a prior interpretation of *The Phenomenology of Mind* in accordance with Marx's understanding of it.

83. Marx, *MEGA* 1/3, p. 305; *HF*, p. 173.

84. Marx, *GI*, pp. 16, 36; *Frühschriften*, pp. 353, 354.

85. Engels, *DN*, p. 306.

86. Marx, *MEGA* 1/3, p. 121; *EPM*, p. 109; *Early Writings*, p. 162; *Capital*, vol. i, p. 177.

87. Marx's curious linguistic habit of using the expressions 'species life', 'human species', and 'species man' when he wished to refer to social life and to social individual may have come from Saint-Simon and Comte, who saw in society *un véritable être vivant* and wanted to establish sociology as a generalized physiology. Since the expression 'la physiologie de l'espèce' was originally used to denote sociology, the term 'l'espèce humaine' acquired a sociological meaning. In *Cours* (see, e.g., iv, p. 560) Comte used the expression 'l'espèce' and 'la société' synonymously.

88. Marx, *Introduction to the Critique of Political Economy*, p. 268.

89. Marx, *GI*, p. 74; *Frühschriften*, p. 396.

90. Marx, *MEGA* 1/3, pp. 87–88, 123, 156; *EPM*, pp. 75, 111, 151; *MEGA* 1/3, pp. 307–8; *HF*, p. 176; *GI*, p. 37; *Frühschriften*, pp. 353–4.

91. Marx, *GI*, p. 19; *Frühschriften*, p. 357.

92. Marx, *GI*, pp. 49, 76; *Frühschriften*, p. 395.

93. Marx, *Introduction to the Critique of Political Economy*, pp. 265–7.

94. K. Popper, *OS*, vol. ii, p. 93.

95. *MEGA* 1/3, p. 87; *EPM*, p. 75; *MEGA* 1/6, p. 482; *WLC*, p. 83.

96. *MEGA* 1/3, p. 125; *EPM*, p. 113.

97. Marx, *GI*, pp. 20–23, 74–75; *Frühschriften*, pp. 358–61, 395–6.

98. The dispute between Marx and the supporters of individualism continues unabated. While Marx's followers consider collectivism as the only true humanism, his opponents maintain that there is an inconsistency in Marx's thought between the goal of an unfettered development of personality and the collectivistic means by which that goal is to be approached and attained. See John D. Lewis, 'The Individual and the Group in Marxist Theory', p. 56.

99. J. S. Mill, *System of Logic*, book vi, ch. vii, § 1.

100. J. S. Mill, *Auguste Comte and Positivism*, p. 84.

101. Marx, *Capital*, vol. i, p. 609.

102. Marx, *Zur Judenfrage*, *MEGA* 1/1/1, p. 595; *MEGA* 1/3, pp. 116–17; *EPM*, pp. 104–5; *TF* vi.

103. Marx rejected, therefore, the view of the eighteenth-century materialists and the nineteenth-century utopian socialists who believed that all man's sufferings are the results of his ignorance and poverty and that once these are abolished, man is bound to attain happiness.

104. Marx, *MEGA* 1/3, p. 116; *EPM*, p. 103.

105. This assumption is usually ascribed to Hegel, but when Marx adopted it there was no longer anything Hegelian about it. Comte in *Cours de philosophie positive* and John Stuart Mill in *System of Logic* stated more clearly than Hegel ever did that the peculiar characteristics of social facts are their consensus (that is, their universal interdependence) and their conformity

to the uniformities of coexistence between the states of various social phenomena. For Mill's views on the matter, see *System of Logic*, book vi. ch. ix, § 2 ; ch. x, § 2. The ideas of Comte are discussed in Ch. IV below.

106. Marx, *GI*, p. 28 ; *Frühschriften*, pp. 367–8. Cf. Plekhanov, *FPM*, p. 61.

107. Comte, *SPP*, p. 111 ; É. Durkheim, *Montesquieu and Rousseau*, pp. 13, 56–57. Lenin rightly pointed out that Marx put an end to the view that society is unrestrictively modifiable and thus 'at the will of the authorities' (*WFPA*, p. 142), but he did not realize that Marx was neither the first nor the only one to establish this important premiss.

108. Comte, *SPP*, pp. 139–46 ; *Cours*, iv, p. 243.

109. Comte, *Cours*, vi, p. 686.

110. G. Simmel, *The Web of Group Affiliations*, p. 138.

111. K. Popper, *OS*, vol. ii, pp. 102–5.

112. Engels, Special Introduction to the English edition of *SUS*, p. 94.

113. Engels's letter to C. Schmidt of 5 August 1890.

114. E. Bernstein, *Evolutionary Socialism*, p. 17 ; cf. *Zur Geschichte und Theorie des Sozialismus*, pp. 263–7, 285.

115. H. Cunow, *Die Marxsche Geschichts-, Gesellschafts- und Staatstheorie*, Bd. 2, p. 180. The same terminological preference was voiced by W. Sombart, *Deutscher Sozialismus*, p. 94, and H. B. Acton, *The Illusion of the Epoch*, p. 161.

116. Lenin, *WFPA*, p. 143.

117. Plekhanov, *DMH*, pp. 689, 720–1, 741 ; Lenin, *WFPA*, pp. 151, 161–162 ; cf. G. Gurvitch, *La Vocation actuelle de la sociologie*, tome ii, pp. 224, 225, where similar objections against the term 'economic materialism' are voiced. While Plekhanov coined the expression 'dialectical materialism' to designate the materialism of Engels in *Anti-Dühring*, he also used it occasionally in quite a different sense. Thus he described *The Holy Family* as 'the new dialectical materialism's first encounter with idealist philosophy', because in this book Marx showed that human reason, far from being the demiurge of history, is itself the product of history. See *FNLF*, p. 485 ; *DMH*, pp. 741–2. When used this way, 'dialectical materialism' means as much as the naturalistic theory of history or profane history in the terminology of the young Marx.

118. See A. Labriola, *Essays on the Materialist Conception of History*, pp. 97–99 ; B. Croce, *Historical Materialism and the Economics of Karl Marx*, pp. 8 and 26 ; E. R. A. Seligman, *The Economic Interpretation of History*, p. 146 ; E. Bernstein, *Evolutionary Socialism*, pp. 17–18 ; M. Adler, *Marxistische Probleme*, pp. 65–66 ; *Marx als Denker*, pp. 129–30 ; K. Vorländer, *Karl Marx*, pp. 178, 220 ; B. Russell, *The Practice and Theory of Bolshevism*, p. 59. In this connection it should be noted that Feuerbach, too, wondered whether his views should not be called 'realism' rather than 'materialism'. See *The Essence of Christianity*, Preface, p. xxxiv.

119. F. A. Lange, *The History of Materialism*, vol. ii, p. 240, and Bertrand Russell's introduction to that work, p. v.

120. Marx, *MEGA* 1/3, p. 152 ; *EPM*, p. 145.

121. Marx, *Capital*, vol. i, p. 372.

122. If these elements alone are considered and contrasted with a clearly idealist viewpoint, then Marx can be classified as a materialist. It was in

conformity with this use of the term that Marx wrote to Kugelmann: 'I am a materialist and Hegel is an idealist' (6 March 1868).

123. *Capital*, vol. i, pp. 513–15. Engels seemed to have come to a different conclusion when towards the end of his life he agreed that race and geography should be included in what he called 'economic relations' or 'economic factor' (see Engels's letter to H. Starkenburg of 25 January 1894). However, Engels's statement also lends itself to a different interpretation. After Engels, Plekhanov returned to the question of the relation between the geographic environment and the development of the productive forces and argued that the former determine the latter. He qualified this conclusion by adding that in the course of time the dependence of man on his geographical environment changes its nature and becomes indirect rather than direct. See Plekhanov, *DMH*, pp. 665–8, 738–40, 783–4; *FPM*, pp. 15–21. It is worth while emphasizing that Plekhanov was inclined to classify the Marxian conception of history as a 'particular case of the materialist view of history' (*DMH*, p. 784).

124. Incidentally, the fact that Montesquieu was a materialist in the indicated sense and that Marx was not, accounts perhaps for another difference between them, namely, that Montesquieu completely ignored, whereas Marx was fully aware of, social evolution. For the importance attached to physical environment tends to conceal the process whereby a society constantly changes and becomes something ever new, and favours historical explanations in terms of constant factors, such as topography, or climate, which seem to make change unreal or apparent.

125. Engels, *LF*, p. 356.

126. According to Lenin, materialism in sociology consists in recognizing the relations of production as being basic, primary, and determining all other social relations. See Lenin, *WFPA*, pp. 138–41. Lenin suggests a new meaning to be given to the term 'materialism' which, however, has no justification in the historically accepted use of this term.

127. R. N. C. Hunt, *The Theory and Practice of Communism*, p. 80.

128. Plekhanov, *The Materialist Conception of History*, p. 20.

129. The economic interpretation would not be materialistic even upon the condition that this qualification refers exclusively to its alleged ethical content, to the assumption that men are purely egoistic beings who act without any other consideration but their own interests, and who strive for a minimum of pain and a maximum of pleasure. This assumption, an egoistical interpretation of human behaviour and a hedonistic moral philosophy, is often associated or identified with materialism. It underlies Adam Smith's *Theory of Morals* and *Inquiry into the Wealth of Nations* and is described by F. A. Lange as ethical materialism (*History of Materialism*, vol. iii, pp. 233–7). It hardly needs mentioning, as H. Cunow showed in detail (*Die Marxsche Geschichts-, Gesellschafts- und Staatstheorie*, Bd. 2, p. 211), that the Marxian conception of history does not contain this assumption.

130. S. Hook, *From Hegel to Marx*, p. 275.

131. Marx, *MEGA* 1/3, p. 305; *HF*, p. 173.

132. *TF* I; Engels, *LF*, pp. 341–2. Feuerbach seemed to adhere to the antithesis between nature and culture. While nature 'gives birth to or

brings forth' its products, man makes them, that is, produces, acting according to a valued end or fostering intentionally what already exists because of
its accepted or postulated value relevance. See *The Essence of Christianity*,
p. 220. Thus, the antithesis between nature and culture reflects the irreducible difference of two classes of objects, the one composed of meaningful
objects and the other of those which just grow or come to pass and have
merely a factual existence with no inherent value relevance or meaning.
Feuerbach seems to corroborate Marx's criticism also in *VTRPH*, § 55,
p. 343.

133. Marx, *GI*, p. 30; *Frühschriften*, p. 369.

134. Engels, *LF*, pp. 338–40.

135. See Marx's letter to J. B. Schweitzer of 24 January 1865.

136. Plekhanov, *EHM*, pp. 176–80, 242–3.

137. Lenin, *PHN*, p. 276.

138. F. A. Lange, *History of Materialism*, vol. iii, p. 340.

139. Engels often spoke of the permanent impact which Hegel's resistance
against the dualism between nature and spirit as well as its outcome, the
monistic system of objective idealism, made upon Marx. Engels also
emphasized that Hegel's spiritualistic monism directly inspired Marx's
search for an equally comprehensive monistic system based on a materialistic foundation (Engels, *MCPE*, pp. 337–8, *LF*, pp. 330, 345).

After Marx, John Dewey, another Hegelian in his youth and naturalistic
thinker in maturity, recorded an immense sense of liberation imparted by
'Hegel's synthesis of subject and object, matter and spirit, the divine and
the human' and also spoke of the attraction exercised by 'Hegel's treatment
of human culture, of institutions and the arts'. The acquaintance with
Hegel left, as he put it, a permanent deposit in his thinking, in spite of the
enormous distance dividing Hegel's absolute idealism and his own naturalism and instrumentalism. See J. Dewey, 'From Absolutism to Experimentalism', pp. 19, 21.

140. The principal advances of our intelligence, Comte commented, consist mainly in fundamental extensions of previous thought (*Cours*, iv, p.
244).

141. L. Feuerbach, *The Essence of Christianity*, pp. 207, 217. Cf. Tucker,
Philosophy and Myth in Karl Marx, p. 190.

142. Marx, *Capital*, vol. i, pp. 177–8.

143. G. Santayana, *Character and Opinion in the United States*, pp. 19–20.

144. Marx, *GI*, p. 36; *Frühschriften*, pp. 351–3.

145. J. Dewey, *Logic: The Theory of Inquiry*, p. 18; E. Nagel, *Logic without
Metaphysics*, p. 11.

Chapter III. The Influence of Hegel's Philosophy

1. R. Heiss, *Die grossen Dialektiker des 19. Jahrhunderts*, pp. 324–5. Franz
Mehring, the first biographer of Marx, said that Marx started as a pupil of
Hegel, to become a Feuerbachian, but as he later moved beyond Feuerbach
he went back to Hegel (F. Mehring, *Karl Marx*, p. 127).

2. G. A. Wetter, *Die Umkehrung Hegels,* p. 5 ; R. C. Tucker, *Philosophy and Myth in Karl Marx,* p. 218. Cf. Wetter, *DM,* pp. 20–29.

3. K. Löwith, *Von Hegel zu Nietzsche,* pp. 78–84.

4. H. Marcuse, *Reason and Revolution,* pp. 251–7.

5. Engels discussed the relation of Marx to Hegel in *Anti-Dühring, Ludwig Feuerbach, Dialectics of Nature,* and in some smaller contributions, in *Karl Marx: A Contribution to the Critique of Political Economy,* in particular. Plekhanov's main contribution to this subject is the essay *Zu Hegel's sechzigsten Todestag,* first published in *Die Neue Zeit* in 1891, and Lenin's is, of course, his *Philosophical Notebooks.*

6. Engels, *DN,* p. 59. Aristotle owes the distinction of being considered an equal of Hegel to his classification of the various kinds of change (movement), to his striking analysis of genesis, and to his belief that the universal is the source and the first principle of all things. Aristotle's doctrine of the universal greatly influenced Hegel, and through Hegel, impressed Engels.

7. See, e.g., Engels, *DN,* pp. 64–66.

8. Engels, *PWG,* p. 32 ; cf. Engels's Introduction to the first German edition of *SUS, Werke,* Bd. 19, p. 188 ; Lenin, 'Frederick Engels', *CW* ii, p. 21, footnote.

9. Engels, *AD,* p. 37 ; cf. K. Korsch, *Karl Marx,* p. 61, for a later formulation of the same idea.

10. Plekhanov, *SAHD,* pp. 456, 468, 477–8 ; *FPM,* pp. 4–5.

11. Lenin, *PHN,* pp. 146–7, 160, 189–90, 311–12 ; *CW* 33, pp. 233–4. That Hegel's *Philosophy of Right* is materialistic in approach and that Hegel was the first to analyse the role of the 'material relations' in the structure of society is a fact emphasized by R. Heiss, *Die grossen Dialektiker des 19. Jahrhunderts,* pp. 180–92. Heiss went as far as to say that 'Marx only said explicitly what Hegel already recognized' (Marx nur gesagt hat was Hegel schon erkannt hat). Heiss failed to see that, unlike Marx, Hegel deduced social and economic reality from ideas and not the other way round. The fact that Hegel or, for that matter, Saint-Simon, the Saint-Simonists, Sismondi, or Proudhon, spoke of the fundamental character of the economic order in a rational organization of society did not imply that they were precursors of historical materialism. Although they recognized the importance of economic factors in social life, they differed essentially from Marx, because they regarded them as an effect rather than as a cause. Their approach to the problems of history and society and their whole way of thinking was incompatible with historical materialism.

12. Lenin, *PHN,* p. 234. Engels spoke of the Hegelian system as merely representing 'a materialism idealistically turned upside down in method and content' (*LF,* p. 336). Numerous historians of philosophy accepted Engels's observation as an incisive and true description of the relation of Marx to Hegel. It is doubtful, however, whether the substitution of the asymmetric genetic relation xRy, where x stands for matter and y for spirit or mind, for the asymmetric genetic relation yRx can best be described as turning Hegel upside down. The operation is of quite a different nature, one to which Engels's phrase does not do justice.

13. Lenin, *PHN,* pp. 196–7.

14. Lenin, *PHN*, p. 180, cf. p. 319.

15. I. Berlin, *Karl Marx*, p. 122; H. J. Laski, *Communism*, pp. 55–56.

16. R. C. Tucker, *Philosophy and Myth in Karl Marx*, p. 123.

17. Ibid., p. 98; 'The Cunning of Reason in Hegel and Marx', p. 283.

18. R. C. Tucker, 'Marxism — Is it Religion?', pp. 127–8.

19. It should be observed that the meaning of the term 'estrangement' (*Entfremdung*), which in *Economic and Philosophic Manuscripts of 1844* and *Zur Judenfrage* is a purely Hegelian, metaphysical concept, acquires a definite sociological and empirical sense in *The German Ideology*. See *MEGA* 1/3, pp. 84–86; *EPM*, pp. 71–73; *MEGA* 1/1/1, p. 603; *GI*, p. 24; *Frühschriften*, p. 362; H. Popitz, *Der entfremdete Mensch*, p. 166; and for a more detailed discussion Z. A. Jordan, 'Socialism, Alienation, and Political Power', pp. 126–32. Marx retained the empirical sociological concept of alienation in *Capital* where it reappears in a new linguistic guise and is designated by such terms as 'fetishism ','dehumanization', or 'exploitation'. See E. Kamenka, *The Ethical Foundations of Marxism*, pp. 144–5. For Hegel *Entfremdung* signified a metaphysical fact that the world of objects, originally the product of man's spiritual activity, becomes independent of man, alien and frustrating to his strivings and desires (*PHH*, pp. 27, 55). One of the main objectives of Hegel's philosophy was to show how man can reconquer the estranged reality and re-establish the lost unity of thought and reality. The alienation through productive labour is in Hegel an inevitable result of the integration of individual activities into an organized whole in a commodity-producing society in which mechanization makes the individual more and more powerless and subjugated to his labour. See, e.g., *PHR*, § 243, pp. 149–50. This metaphysical concept of *Entfremdung* is the only one of which Marx made use in *EPM*. For the Hegelian concept of alienation see H. Marcuse, *Reason and Revolution*, pp. 34–36, 78–79.

20. See, e.g., A. de Tocqueville, *Democracy in America*, pt. ii, ch. xxviii; Comte, *Cours*, iv, pp. 317 ff.; J. S. Mill, *Auguste Comte and Positivism*, pp. 94–95.

21. *MEGA* 1/3, pp. 206–7; *HF*, pp. 52–53.

22. *GI*, pp. 5–6; *Frühschriften*, pp. 344–5.

23. B. Croce, *Historical Materialism and the Economics of Karl Marx*, p. 49.

24. K. Löwith, *Von Hegel zu Nietzsche*, p. 79; G. Gurvitch, *La Vocation actuelle de la sociologie*, tome ii, p. 229. Gurvitch seems to follow Engels's definition of 'true socialism' as 'a translation of French socialist phraseology into corrupt Hegelian German' (Engels, *HCL*, p. 314).

25. W. Sombart, *Der proletarische Sozialismus*, Bd. 1, pp. 79–80. Sombart is not alone in his belief that Marx completely broke with the whole of Hegel's philosophy. See Korsch, *Karl Marx*, pp. 61–65.

26. The distinction between the young Marx, a Hegelian, and the older Marx, a thinker in his own right, was first made by Kautsky in reply to Lukács's and Korsch's revisions of the accepted interpretations of the Marxian philosophy. See I. Fetscher, 'Das Verhältnis des Marxismus zu Hegel', pp. 118–19.

27. K. Vorländer, *Karl Marx*, pp. 223–4. As Marx's letter to L. Kugelmann of 27 June 1870 seems to show, apart from the Young Hegelians,

among Hegel's depreciators Marx also included F. A. Lange, Ludwig Büchner, Eugen Dühring, and G. T. Fechner.

28. Plekhanov, *SAHD*, p. 478.

29. M. Eastman, *Marx and Lenin*, p. 190.

30. E. Bernstein, *Die Voraussetzungen des Sozialismus und die Aufgaben der Sozialdemokratie*, pp. 26, 36.

31. Plekhanov, *SAHD*, p. 477.

32. K. Kautsky, *Bernstein und das sozialdemokratische Programm*, p. 22. Bernstein's answer to Kautsky, first published in *Die Neue Zeit*, was reprinted in *Zur Geschichte und Theorie des Sozialismus*, pp. 338–66.

33. H. Cunow, *Die Marxsche Geschichts-, Gesellschafts- und Staatstheorie*, Bd. 1, pp. 245–55; Bd. 2, p. 346. M. Adler, *Marxistische Probleme*, pp. 18–19.

34. Lenin, 'The Marx–Engels Correspondence', *CW* 19, p. 554. These observations were directed against Bernstein.

35. S. Hook, *From Hegel to Marx*, pp. 15–16, 41.

36. Marx, *MEGA* 1/3, p. 294; *HF*, p. 160.

37. Marx, *KHR*, *MEGA* 1/1/1, pp. 614–15; Marx, *Early Writings*, p. 52.

38. Marx, *KHR*, *MEGA* 1/1/1, pp. 613, 615–16.

39. Hegel, *PHR*, § 244, § 303, and Addition, pp. 150, 198, 277.

40. See, e.g., A. Cornu, *The Origin of Marxian Thought*, pp. 90, 113–16.

41. Marx's letter to his father of 10 November 1837; *Frühschriften*, pp. 7, 8–9.

42. Engels, *LF*, p. 324.

43. For additional details see K. Vorländer, *Kant und Marx*, pp. 64, 308.

44. Marx, *MEGA* 1/1/1, pp. 411, 421, 432, 433.

45. Marx, *Kritik der Hegelschen Staatsphilosophie*, *MEGA* 1/1/1, p. 447.

46. The one possible exception was *Zur Kritik der Hegelschen Rechtsphilosophie. Einleitung* (1844), where Marx spoke of the German philosophy of right and of the state and, in particular, of Hegel's speculative philosophy of right, as the only German achievement that was abreast with modern times (*MEGA* 1/1/1, pp. 612–14). He stated his opposition to this 'extravagant and abstract thought about the modern state', however, abundantly and emphatically.

47. Marx, *MEGA* 1/3, pp. 257, 265, 301, 314, 345; *HF*, pp. 114, 124–5, 168, 184, 224; *GI*, p. 42; *Frühschriften*, pp. 376–7; *MEGA* 1/6, pp. 176–9; *PPH*, pp. 88–92.

48. Marx, *MEGA* 1/3, p. 262; *HF*, p. 121.

49. In his evaluation of the German intellectual scene Marx seems to have been indebted to Moses Hess's incisive analysis of Lorenz von Stein's book *Der Socialismus und Communismus des heutigen Frankreichs*, published under the title *Socialismus und Communismus* in *Einundzwanzig Bogen aus der Schweiz* (1843). Hess's review is reprinted in his *Philosophische und Sozialistische Schriften 1837–1850*.

50. Marx, 'Der leitende Artikel in Nr. 179 der *Kölnischen Zeitung*' (1842), *MEGA* 1/1/1, p. 242. 'Philosophy too', wrote Hegel, 'is its own time apprehended in thoughts. It is just as absurd to fancy that a philosophy can transcend its contemporary world as it is to fancy that an individual can overleap his own age' (*PHR*, Preface, p. 11).

51. Marx, *GI*, pp. 1–6, 18–19, 43; *Frühschriften*, pp. 341–6, 356, 377–8; *KHR*, *MEGA* 1/1/1, pp. 608, 610, 614, 616. The Marxian viewpoint was put even better by F. A. Lange in his *History of Materialism*, the first edition of which appeared shortly before the publication of *Capital*. Towards the end of the eighteenth century England and France withdrew from the theatre of metaphysical war. But England produced the industrial revolution and France the Revolution that shook Europe and, thus, both countries were devoted entirely to the tasks of real life. 'Meanwhile', Lange wrote, 'metaphysics were left to us in Germany.' Speculative fancies smothered the spirit of sound inquiry and the metaphysical *Sturm und Drang Periode*, marked by the titanic efforts of Schelling and Hegel, stimulated the ambition of philosophers 'who like Pharaohs, piled one pyramid upon another into the sky, and only forgot to base them upon *terra firma*' (*History of Materialism*, vol. ii, pp. 235–8).

52. Marx's letter to Engels of 14 January 1858.

53. G. Lukács, *Geschichte und Klassenbewusstsein*, p. 8.

54. *MEGA* 1/2 or Marx–Engels, *Werke*, Bd. 1.

55. Engels's letters to Marx of 20 January and 17 March 1845.

56. *Das Junge Deutschland* was a group of writers led by Karl Gutzkow, Theodor Mundt, and Rudolf Wienbarg.

57. In his review of Alexander Jung's *Vorlesungen über die moderne Literatur der Deutschen* (1842) Engels passed judgment not only on Young Germany, but also on his own literary youth and pointed out the direction in which he wished to go from then on. The *Deutsche Jahrbücher*, founded in 1838 and originally called the *Hallische Jahrbücher*, were published by Arnold Ruge as the organ of the Young Hegelians. They were suppressed in 1843.

58. The Freemen were by no means merely a debating society given exclusively to intellectual pursuits. They were also notorious for their buffooneries, ragging, and other exploits to *épater le bourgeois*. Marx, who at that time contributed articles to the *Rheinische Zeitung* and soon became its chief editor, first deplored their volatility and later broke with them entirely. He made no secret of the fact that in his opinion the Freemen lacked the seriousness of purpose and solid knowledge of the subjects with which they dealt in their journalistic activities, were fond of high-sounding phrases, and indulged in self-adulation. The Freemen were not the best teachers of philosophy and yet they were the only teachers Engels ever had. For the reputation of the Freemen, Marx's relation with them, and Engels's subsequent condescending attitude to *Die Freien* see F. Mehring, *Karl Marx*, pp. 44–47, and Engels's letter to Marx of 20 January 1845.

59. G. Mayer, *Friedrich Engels*, Bd. 1, pp. 14–15, 23–24, 70–72; Bd. 2, pp. 297–8, 527–9; I. Berlin, *Karl Marx*, pp. 100–1. Apart from Hegel, Engels read Schelling and during his stay in the capital attended Schelling's lectures at Berlin University. His first philosophical publication *Schelling und Offenbarung (Schelling and Revelation)* was concerned with the philosophy of Schelling whom he criticized for his 'reactionary attack on free philosophy', that is, on the philosophy of Hegel. For Engels, German idealism was Hegelian philosophy.

60. Engels, *LF*, p. 363.

61. Ibid., pp. 331, 363. When the industrial revolution started in Germany in earnest about the middle of the nineteenth century, Engels grudgingly recognized that as far as industry and commerce were concerned the German bourgeoisie was at last doing its duty but he added that politically it exhibited a 'remarkable cowardice' (*PWG*, pp. 18, 30).

62. Engels, *PWG*, p. 32.

63. Other events in Engels's life seem also to indicate that his patriotism would occasionally become transformed into the prejudice of nationalism. See G. Mayer, *Friedrich Engels*, Bd. 1, pp. 325–8.

64. Marx, *GI*, p. 4; *Frühschriften*, pp. 343–4.

65. Engels's letter to F. A. Lange of 29 March 1865. Hegel's contributions to natural science were to be found, above all, in the second part of the *Science of Logic*.

66. Engels, 'Progress of Social Reform', *Werke*, Bd. 1, p. 492.

67. See, e.g., the Preface to the first German edition of *CWC* (1845) where Engels suggested that without Hegel the first champions of German socialism and communism would not have discovered their views. Speaking of the champions of communism, Engels had Marx and himself in mind, although he might also have been referring to Moses Hess whose essay *Über die sozialistische Bewegung in Deutschland* surely inspired some of Engels's opinions in the Preface. In 1892, in the Preface to the English edition of *CWC*, Engels returned to the same subject to make the puzzling observation that his book 'exhibits everywhere the traces of the descent of modern socialism from one of its ancestors, German philosophy', meaning the philosophy of Hegel (p. 22).

68. S. Hook, *From Hegel to Marx*, p. 75.

69. Engels, *MCPE*, p. 338.

70. Engels, *DN*, p. 116.

71. Ibid., pp. 90–91, 402.

72. Ibid., pp. 84, 201, 324.

73. Engels's letter to Marx of 14 July 1858.

74. Engels's letter to Marx of 16 June 1867.

75. Engels's letter to Marx of 14 July, 1858.

76. Ibid.

77. Engels, 'Die Lage Englands: *Past and Present* by Thomas Carlyle, London 1843', *Werke*, Bd. 1, p. 550. It is amusing to observe that in the short run Engels's prophecy came true. In the second half of the nineteenth century 'Hegelianism modified by Anglo-Saxon caution' (this is H. J. Paton's expression) did become the dominant philosophical school in England and in the person of F. H. Bradley delivered a sharp attack upon the empiricist school.

78. H. Marcuse, *Reason and Revolution*, pp. 16–20.

79. Engels, *DN*, p. 273; Engels's letter to F. A. Lange of 29 March 1865. Engels rejected firmly, almost contemptuously, Lange's suggestion that Hegel lacked knowledge of science and mathematics.

80. Engels, *DN*, p. 91.

81. Engels, *LF*, p. 333.

82. Engels, *DN*, pp. 64–65.

83. Engels, *AD*, p. 18; *DN*, p. 273.

84. Engels's letter to C. Schmidt of 1 November 1891 ; J. Plamenatz, *Man and Society*, vol. ii, p. 197. Marx expressed sharply his opinion on the attempts to salvage the Hegelian philosophy by a suitable 'translation' or interpretative analysis. See *GI*, pp. 4–5 ; *Frühschriften*, p. 344.

85. Engels's letter to F. A. Lange of 29 March 1865.

86. Lenin, *PHN*, p. 141 ; cf. pp. 283–4.

87. Marx did believe that spontaneous generation is the only alternative to creation but did not derive the concept of *generatio aequivoca* from the Hegelian philosophy, as Lenin seemed to believe ; he found it as a universally known conjecture, discussed by Aristotle and revived by the biologists in the seventeenth and eighteenth centuries (C. Singer, *A Short History of Scientific Ideas*, pp. 282–7). Marx combined it with the first evolutionary ideas, particularly in geology — he called it *geogeny* — and considered it in this modernized form as a 'mighty blow' to the view of the creation of the world (*MEGA* 1/3, p. 124 ; *EPM*, p. 112).

88. *MEGA* 1/3, p. 156 ; *EPM*, p. 151. For more details and the critical discussion of these passages see Ch. II, Section 6.

89. Engels, *MCPE*, pp. 337–8 ; *LF*, pp. 330, 345.

90. Plekhanov, *SAHD*, p. 478 ; *EHM*, p. 175.

91. As a matter of fact, Marx quoted Ferguson's *Essay on the History of Civil Society* (1767) in *The Poverty of Philosophy* and *Capital*, Montesquieu's *Esprit des lois* (1748) and Vico's *Scienza nuova* (1725) in *Capital*. A German translation of *Scienza nuova* had been available since 1822.

92. Comte, *Cours*, iv, pp. 367, 369.

93. Hegel, *PHR*, § 3, Addition, § 261, Addition, pp. 16, 161. In the quoted passages Hegel recognized that he owed his 'true historical view' to Montesquieu.

94. See, e.g., H. Rickert, *Kulturwissenschaft und Naturwissenschaft*, pp. 8–10. A similar point of view was adopted by R. G. Collingwood, *The Idea of Nature*, pp. 121–32, and by the Polish Marxist–Leninist A. Schaff, *Wstęp do teorii marksizmu*, pp. 97–99, 109.

95. Cf. J. Plamenatz, *Man and Society*, vol. ii, pp. 214–15.

96. S. Hook, *From Hegel to Marx*, pp. 41–47.

97. *PHR*, § 327, Addition, p. 296.

98. Marx, *Capital*, vol. i, p. 52.

99. Marx, *GI*, p. 49 ; *Frühschriften*, p. 395. For the concept of sociological determinism in Marx see Jordan, *PHI*, pp. 133–4.

100. See Ch. II, Sections 3 and 6 above.

101. Marx, *Capital*, vol. i, p. 19 ; Marx's letter to L. Kugelmann of 27 June 1870.

102. Marx, *Capital*, vol. i, p. 20.

103. Engels, *LF*, p. 351. Engels's formulation includes the Hegelian conception of the cunning of reason, also apparent in other parts of *Ludwig Feuerbach*, which is not an integral part of, and is absent from, Marx's presuppositions of the dialectical method as distinct from those of Engels. For Hegel's definition of the cunning of reason see *EPHS*, § 209, Addition, p. 350 ; *PHH*, pp. 32–33.

104. B. Croce, *Historical Materialism and the Economics of Karl Marx*, p. 83.

105. M. Adler, *Marx als Denker*, p. 25.
106. K. Vorländer, *Karl Marx*, p. 179.
107. M. M. Bober, *Karl Marx's Interpretation of History*, p. 39.
108. S. Hook, *From Hegel to Marx*, pp. 55–56.
109. Engels, *LF*, p. 350.
110. Marx, *MEGA* 1/6, p. 175; *PPH*, p. 87. Plekhanov used the above-stated conclusion to justify the claim of the superiority of dialectics over formal logic. See Plekhanov, *FPM*, pp. 111–23; cf. Bukharin, *Historical Materialism*, p. 75; A. Schaff, 'Zasada sprzeczności w świetle logiki dialektycznej', pp. 328–53.
111. W. Sombart, *Der proletarische Sozialismus*, Bd. 1, p. 215. In *Capital* Marx refers to the 'law discovered by Hegel that merely quantitative differences beyond a certain point pass into qualitative changes' (*Capital*, vol. i, p. 309). Marx did not make use of this observation, because the way an economist might describe the fact that not every sum of money can be transformed into capital or the way a chemist might describe his findings is irrelevant to a naturalistic analysis of social activity, which would have to deal with non-quantifiable concepts.
112. See Ch. I, Section 3 above.
113. According to R. C. Tucker, Hegel means by dialectics 'the pattern or mechanism of development through inner conflict'. See *Philosophy and Myth in Karl Marx*, pp. 57–58. But while for Hegel conflict arises from the division of the Spirit against itself, for Marx conflict means what it ordinarily does, that is, 'antagonism', 'fight', and 'struggle', examples of which are the conflict of class interests or of group interests within the same class.
114. *MEGA* 1/6, p. 143; *PPH*, p. 53.
115. Hegel, *EPHS*, § 81, Addition, pp. 150–1.
116. The attribution was first made by Engels, who wrote in 1843 that communism was an inescapable result of the Neo-Hegelian philosophy and, consequently, that no opposition could stop this development of ideas ('Progress of Social Reform on the Continent', *Werke*, Bd. 1, p. 494). He repeated the same claim in 1845 and emphasized that the German champions of communism arrived at it 'by way of the Feuerbachian dissolution of Hegelian speculation' (Preface to the first German edition of *CWC*, p. 4). As has been pointed out earlier, Engels probably only reproduced the view first voiced by Moses Hess with whom he shared philosophical naïveté and an uncritical admiration for German idealism. That Marx derived his 'socialist theory' from the Hegelian negation of the negation was one of the main points in Eugen Dühring's criticism of Marx. See Engels, *AD*, pp. 178–9.
117. Marx's letter to J. Weydemeyer of 5 March 1852; Marx's letter to Engels of 27 July 1854. Cf. *Capital*, vol. i, p. 14.
118. *MCP*, p. 58. For a more detailed explanation of this fact see H. J. Laski, *Communism*, pp. 65–67.
119. H. Marcuse, *Reason and Revolution*, p. 314.
120. Marx's letter to P. V. Annenkov of 28 December 1846.
121. Marx, *KHR*, *MEGA* 1/1/1, p. 616. This is the first formulation of the famous dictum about the birth-pangs of a new society in *Capital*, vol. i, p. 10.
122. Marx, *Capital*, vol. i, p. 19.

123. A. Labriola, *Socialism and Philosophy*, p. 209.

124. Engels's letter to F. A. Lange of 29 March 1865.

125. To give one telling example, Hegel's assertion in *Philosophy of Nature* that 'there is no motion without matter, so also there is no matter without motion' (*EPHS*, § 261, Addition) is reproduced by Engels in the statement 'matter without motion is just as inconceivable as motion without matter' (*AD*, p. 86; *DN*, p. 93).

126. Engels, *MCPE*, p. 338.

127. *EPHS*, § 38, p. 78.

128. *EPHS*, § 98, Addition, p. 78.

129. *PHR*, § 2, Addition, p. 14.

130. Engels, *DN*, p. 279. Cf. Hegel, *PHM*, Preface, p. 125, where a very similar formulation can be found.

131. Engels, *LF*, p. 328.

132. S. Hook, *The Quest for Being*, pp. 222–3.

133. *EPHS*, § 79, p. 143.

134. For Hegel's views on Kant's antinomies see *EPHS*, § 48, p. 100; *SL*, vol. ii, p. 458.

135. *EPHS*, §§ 80, 119, pp. 143, 219–22; *PHM*, Preface, pp. 70, 125–6; *SL*, vol. ii, p. 67; *PHR*, Preface, p. 6.

136. *EPHS*, § 81, p. 147.

137. *EPHS*, §§ 82, 121, pp. 152, 224; *SL*, vol. i, p. 67. Incidentally, Hegel's definition of speculative philosophy became Lenin's definition of dialectics.

138. *SL*, vol. i, p. 74.

139. *SL*, vol. ii, p. 67.

140. *EPHS*, § 80, Addition, § 81, Addition, pp. 144, 146, 148.

141. *EPHS*, § 27, p. 61.

142. *EPHS*, §§ 28–32, 119, pp. 61–67, 219–22.

143. *PHM*, Preface, pp. 123–4; *SL*, vol. i, p. 64; *EPHS*, § 231, p. 369.

144. See W. T. Stace, *The Philosophy of Hegel*, pp. 98–99.

145. H. Marcuse, *Reason and Revolution*, p. 27; J. N. Findlay, *Hegel: A Re-examination*, p. 60.

146. Hegel, *PHM*, Preface, pp. 92, 102.

147. *SL*, vol. i, p. 65.

148. Ibid., p. 94.

149. Ibid., p. 97.

150. Ibid., p. 56.

151. Ibid., p. 65.

152. W. T. Stace, *The Philosophy of Hegel*, pp. 92–93.

153. *SL*, vol. i, pp. 64–65.

154. *PHR*, § 31 and Addition, pp. 34–35; cf. Hegel, *Lectures on the History of Philosophy*, vol. i, p. 264.

155. *EPHS*, § 81, Addition, pp. 148–51.

156. *SL*, vol. ii, p. 67.

157. Plekhanov, *DMH*, pp. 606, 808–10; *EPM*, pp. 177–8.

158. For instance, Marx contrasted Locke's philosophy of common sense, that is, metaphysics in Hegel's and Engels's meaning of the term, with the

'seventeenth-century metaphysics' of Descartes, Spinoza, Leibniz, and Malebranche which Marx described as the 'mere bungling of fancy and theological prejudice'. Marx also said that 'seventeenth-century metaphysics . . . was given a victorious and solid restoration in German philosophy, particularly in speculative German philosophy of the nineteenth century' and spoke of a 'metaphysical universal kingdom' founded by Hegel. Hegel's speculative philosophy was surely metaphysics in Marx's sense and had, contrary to what Hegel thought, nothing to do with 'scientific procedure in philosophy'. See *MEGA* I/3, pp. 301, 306; *HF*, pp. 168, 174.

159. Engels, *MCPE*, pp. 336–7; *LF*, pp. 351–2; Engels's letter to C. Schmid of 1 November 1891.

160. Engels, *AD*, p. 34.

161. Engels, *AD*, pp. 35–36; *DN*, pp. 284–6.

162. Engels, *AD*, p. 35; Hegel, *EPHS*, § 213, Addition, pp. 353–4.

163. Engels, *AD*, pp. 36–37.

164. Ibid., pp. 165–7; *DN*, p. 284.

165. Engels, *DN*, p. 353; cf. *AD*, p. 194.

166. Hegel, *EPHS*, § 81, p. 148.

167. Engels, *AD*, p. 185; *DN*, pp. 81, 272, 282.

168. Hegel, *EPHS*, §§ 107–11, pp. 201–6; *SL*, vol. i, pp. 357, 388–90; *PHM*, Preface, p. 68. Cf. Acton, *The Illusion of the Epoch*, pp. 81–83. Engels's example of one grain of barley which by the negation of the negation produces many grains is clearly inspired by Hegel's divagations on the flower being a refutation of the bud and the fruit a negation of the blossom.

169. Engels, *DN*, pp. 27, 83–84.

170. Hegel, *PHM*, Preface, p. 68.

171. Engels, *LF*, pp. 330–1.

Chapter IV. French Positivism and the Philosophy of Marx and Engels

1. The philosophical group in France which is misleadingly called the 'idéologues' and which flourished during the Revolution and the First Empire included such thinkers as Cabanis (1757–1808), Destutt de Tracy (1754–1836), and Volney (1757–1820). The 'idéologues' continued and systematized the ideas of Locke, Condillac, and Helvétius.

2. F. A. Hayek, *The Counter-Revolution of Science*, p. 119; F. E. Manuel, *The New World of Henri Saint-Simon*, p. 80.

3. É. Durkheim, *Socialism and Saint-Simon*, p. 104; cf. F. E. Manuel, *The New World of Henri Saint-Simon*, ch. 29, which supports Durkheim's verdict with some reservations.

4. The reader should keep in mind the fact that the six volumes of the *Cours* first appeared in the years 1830–42, and the four volumes of the *Système* in the years 1851–4.

5. Marx was not alone in his detestation of some of Comte's social and

political beliefs. John Stuart Mill, an ardent admirer of Comte, the positivist philosopher, described his programme of social and political reform as a system of spiritual and temporal despotism surpassing every precedent in history, ancient and modern. Mill's conclusion was that 'while as logicians we were nearly at one, as sociologists we could travel together no further' (*On Liberty*, pp. 19–20; *Autobiography*, p. 180). Speaking of Comte's religion of humanity and its code of religious practices, Mill said, 'others may laugh but we could rather weep at this melancholy decadence of a great intellect' (*Auguste Comte and Positivism*, p. 199). The break between Émile Littré and Comte was caused by the approval the latter accorded to Louis Bonaparte's *coup d'état* (W. M. Simon, *European Positivism in the Nineteenth Century*, p. 15), of which Mill also strongly disapproved (*Autobiography*, p. 201). Mill deeply disagreed with Comte's attacks upon what he designated with the generic name of the 'revolutionary philosophy', that is, Comte's rejection of the radical, the democratic, the liberal, the free-thinking views as alleged instances of the metaphysical mode of thought in politics. See *Auguste Comte and Positivism*, pp. 73–80.

6. See, e.g., Marx's letter to Engels of 19 March 1870; Marx's letter to L. Kugelmann of 13 December 1870. E. S. Beesly (1831–1914), professor of history at University College, London, presided at the meeting in St. Martin Hall in 1864 at which the first International was founded. Beesly was a social reformer, inspired in his activities by Comte, but not at all interested in the Comtean philosophy. What brought him and Marx together was not philosophical interests but common views on a number of public, social, and international affairs. Their association was particularly close in the period of the Franco-German War and the Paris Commune. In his letter to F. Tönnies of 24 January 1895, Engels paid warm tribute to Beesly for his defence of the International in the Press at the time of the Commune. For details concerning the relations between Marx and Beesly, see Royden Harrison, 'E. S. Beesly and Karl Marx'. The participation of the French 'positivists' in the activities of the first International is mentioned in the Marx–Engels correspondence. The resolution passed at the conference of the International held in London in September 1871, which prohibited the use of any sectarian names by the local sections and the national federal councils of the International, listed also 'positivists' among these prohibited sectarian names (J. Freymond (ed.), *La Première Internationale*, tome ii, pp. 233–4). In the above-quoted letter to F. Tönnies, Engels noted that in the middle seventies the Comtists cooled off considerably towards the labour movement.

7. Marx's letter to E. S. Beesly of 12 June 1871.

8. Marx's letter to Engels of 7 July 1866.

9. Marx's letter to Engels of 20 March 1869; Marx's letter to L. Kugelmann of 13 December 1870; *Capital*, vol. i, p. 17.

10. Engels's letter to F. Tönnies of 24 January 1895. Engels's low opinion of Comte could not have been improved by the admiration of Comte shown by Eugen Dühring. See W. M. Simon, *European Positivism in the Nineteenth Century*, pp. 251–2.

11. Engels's letter to Marx of 21 March 1869.

12. Engels, *PWG*, p. 33. Engels's admiration for the 'dazzling genius of Saint-Simon and some of his pupils' dates from the moment his interests in social and political questions were first seriously awakened. See Engels, 'Progress of Social Reform on the Continent', *Werke*, Bd. 1, pp. 482–3.

13. *MEGA* 1/6, p. 555; *MCP*, p. 59.

14. Marx, *Capital*, vol. iii, p. 591. This evaluation would put Saint-Simon in the same category as Comte ideologically. See *Capital*, vol. i, p. 332, n. 3. Marx's evaluation of Saint-Simon is irreproachable if the concept of socialism includes the recognition of a class struggle between the propertied and propertyless classes.

15. Ibid., vol. iii, p. 591 n.

16. Engels, *AD*, pp. 30, 357.

17. Ibid., p. 38.

18. Engels's letter to F. Tönnies of 24 January 1895. Engels's judgment upon the Saint-Simonists, that they buried Saint-Simon's fruitful ideas under a heap of rubbish and absurdities, is not entirely correct. The doctrine of the Saint-Simonists embodied not only a systematization but also a considerable development of Saint-Simon's views, particularly in the field of economics.

19. See, e.g., *KSF*, the entries ' Comte ' and ' Saint-Simon ' for the evaluation of these two thinkers in contemporary Soviet philosophy.

20. K. R. Popper, *OS*, vol. ii, p. 87.

21. M. Rubel, *Karl Marx*, p. 314.

22. G. Mayer, *Friedrich Engels*, Bd. 2, p. 300.

23. A. Labriola, *Essays on the Materialist Conception of History*, p. 19.

24. Idem, *Socialism and Philosophy*, p. 219.

25. Idem, *Essays on the Materialist Conception of History*, pp. 17, 19, 156.

26. K. Kelles-Krauz, *Pisma wybrane*, tom i, pp. 32–33, 43–45.

27. M. Adler, *Marx als Denker*, pp. 92–93.

28. Plekhanov, *DMH*, p. 601. Comte, Plekhanov maintained, tried to base social physics on physiology, or in modern terminology — to reduce sociology to psychology. Plekhanov was completely unaware of the fact that Comte repeatedly criticized this reduction which was advocated, for instance, by J. S. Mill. Plekhanov's error can be found reproduced uncorrected in the evaluation of Comte in *KSF* (the entry ' Comte ').

29. Plekhanov, *FNLF*, p. 534; *DMH*, pp. 574–9; Bernstein, *Die Voraussetzungen des Sozialismus und die Aufgaben der Sozialdemokratie*, p. 28.

30. See, e.g., Lenin, *MEC*, pp. 205–6; *Imperialism: The Highest Stage of Capitalism*, *CW* 22, p. 304.

31. As far as Comte is concerned see *Cours*, vi, pp. 701, 703. Cf. Ph. Frank, *Modern Science and Its Philosophy*, p. 25.

32. See, e.g., *FML*, pp. 50–53. The expressions 'second positivism' and 'third positivism' are to be found, for instance, in *KSF*. See the entry ' Positivism '.

33. Some revisionist exponents of Marx's philosophy also subscribed to the ideological critique of positivism. See K. Korsch, *Karl Marx*, pp. 17–18. The view that sociology is nothing but the ideology of contemporary bourgeois societies was the starting-point of violent attacks upon sociology

and its complete suppression in the Stalinist period. See, e.g., J. Hochfeld, 'O niektórych aspektach przeciwstawności materializmu historycznego i socjologii burźuazyjnej'; A. Schaff, 'Metoda dokumentów osobistych a społeczne badania terenowe'.

Philipp Frank completely misunderstood both the content and the ideological aspect of dialectical materialism when he suggested that it was closely related to positivism and pragmatism and that its twofold opposition to idealism and mechanistic materialism could be carried on consistently only from the viewpoint of modern positivism. See Ph. Frank, 'Logisierender Empirismus in der Philosophie der U.S.S.R.'.

34. See, e.g., P. Barth, *Die Philosophie der Geschichte als Soziologie*, p. 663; W. Sombart, *Der proletarische Sozialismus*, Bd. 1, p. 295; Wetter, *DM*, pp. 15–16.

35. J. S. Mill's letter to Alexander Bain of 15 October 1841, quoted in I. W. Mueller, *John Stuart Mill and French Thought*, p. 93. In an essay written nearly a quarter of a century later Mill described Comte as 'one of the principal thinkers of the age' (*Auguste Comte and Positivism*, p. 53).

36. It is significant that in his celebrated work *Der Socialismus und Communismus des heutigen Frankreichs*, first published in 1842, Lorenz von Stein passed over Comte in silence, although Saint-Simon and the Saint-Simonists are considered at length. Karl Grün, in a similar work published in 1845, referred to Comte once to say that Comte 'has just published a rather large work in the field of the science of government [*ein grösseres staatswissenschaftliches Werk*] under the title *Positive Philosophy*' (*Die soziale Bewegung in Frankreich und Belgien*, p. 100). To judge from the misleading content of this remark, Grün himself could not have been familiar with Comte's work.

37. D. G. Charlton, *Positivist Thought in France*, pp. 20–21; W. M. Simon, *European Positivism in the Nineteenth Century*, pp. 14, 73–75, 264.

38. Marx's letter to Engels of 25 July 1866.

39. References to Saint-Simon can also be found in *Economic and Philosophic Manuscripts of 1844* and *The Holy Family*. G. Gurvitch, *La Vocation actuelle de la sociologie*, tome ii, pp. 233–4, detected an unacknowledged quotation from Saint-Simon in Marx's *The Critique of Hegel's Philosophy of Right*.

40. *The German Ideology* conclusively establishes the fact that prior to 1845 Marx studied *Lettres d'un habitant de Genève*, Saint-Simon's famous journalistic ventures — *L'Industrie*, *L'Organisateur*, and *Catéchisme des Industriels* and *Le Nouveau Christianisme*. Marx was also familiar with the interpretation given to the doctrine of Saint-Simon by his followers, above all, by Bazard and Enfantin, in *Le Producteur* and *Le Globe*, and with the *Exposition de la doctrine de Saint-Simon* prepared by his disciples in 1829.

41. The most important second-hand sources at that time were the above-quoted books of Lorenz von Stein and Karl Grün, and *Études sur les réformateurs ou socialistes modernes* of Louis Reybaud. Marx referred to all these works in *The German Ideology*.

42. See A. Cornu, *Karl Marx et Friedrich Engels*, tome i, pp. 51–53, 67, 85–89. The name of Saint-Simon turns up repeatedly in *Die europaeische Triarchie* (1841) where Hess compares his social role in France with that of

Hegel in Germany, and in Hess's articles of 1843 (*Socialismus und Communismus* and *Philosophie der That*). The above-quoted works of Hess are reprinted in M. Hess, *Philosophische und sozialistische Schriften 1837–1850*, pp. 75–166, 197–226.

43. F. A. Hayek, *The Counter-Revolution of Science*, pp. 158–62 ; G. Gurvitch, *La Vocation actuelle de la sociologie*, tome ii, pp. 230–5.

44. *Catéchisme des Industriels* is quoted in *The German Ideology*. Comte's *Système de politique positive* of 1822 should not be confused with the four-volume work under the same title published in 1851–4. The reason for the double title is explained in F. E. Manuel, *The New World of Henri Saint-Simon*, pp. 333–7. It was this essay that enormously impressed J. S. Mill, who considered it far superior to other Saint-Simonist writings. Although he lost sight of Comte for a number of years, Mill then continued to read everything the Saint-Simonists wrote (*Autobiography*, pp. 139–41).

45. F. A. Hayek, *The Counter-Revolution of Science*, p. 193.

46. Comte, *SPP*, pp. 8–9.

47. R. von Mises, *Positivism*, p. 205.

48. P. Barth, *Die Philosophie der Geschichte als Soziologie*, p. 663.

49. H. Saint-Simon, *Mémoire sur la science de l'homme*, pp. 26–27, 246.

50. H. Saint-Simon, *L'Industrie*, p. 166; *L'Organisateur*, pp. 104, 119; cf. Durkheim, *Socialism and Saint-Simon*, pp. 100–1, 109–27.

51. H. Sait-Sinmon, *Mémoire sur la science de l'homme*, p. 182 ; cf. *Lettres d'un habitant de Genève*, *Selected Writings*, pp. 6–7.

52. H. Saint-Simon, *Le Nouveau Christianisme*, *Selected Writings*, pp. 100 ff. ; Durkheim, *Socialism and Saint-Simon*, pp. 138–9.

53. J. Plamenatz, *Man and Society*, vol. ii, p. 83. For details see Durkheim, *Socialism and Saint-Simon*, pp. 166–9, 211–22, whose exposition of the Saint-Simonist doctrine remains unsurpassed.

54. Saint-Simon used the terms 'social physiology', 'physiology of the human species' or 'science of man' to designate sociology. 'Social physics' is an expression introduced by Comte.

55. H. Saint-Simon, *Mémoire sur la science de l'homme*, p. 18.

56. Comte, *SPP*, pp. 75–76.

57. D. G. Charlton, *Positivist Thought in France*, p. 42 ; cf. F. A. Hayek, *The Counter-Revolution of Science*, p. 182. Comte did say in a youthful letter, quoted by F. A. Hayek, that he held in a supreme aversion all scientific work of which he did not see any utility, but he did not specify that it must be a practical utility. Only in his capacity of the high priest of humanity Comte showed an increasing dislike of all purely intellectual pursuits and tended to subordinate the search for truth to human use.

58. d'Alembert, *Preliminary Discourse to the Encyclopedia of Diderot*, p. 75.

59. Comte, *SPP*, p. 112 ; cf. pp. 167–8.

60. Engels, *AD*, p. 157.

61. Cf. D. G. Charlton, *Positivist Thought in France*, pp. 108–11.

62. Comte, *SPP*, pp. 109–10 ; *Cours*, iv, pp. 396, 503.

63. A more detailed definition of social dynamics is to be found only in the *Cours*, iv, pp. 310, 318, 320–1, 366. It is foreshadowed, however, by what Comte had to say about social change in *SPP*, pp. 108–14.

64. Comte, *SPP*, p. 89.
65. J. B. Bury, *The Idea of Progress*, pp. 101 ff., 136–7.
66. Marx, *Capital*, vol. i, pp. 8–10.
67. Comte, *Cours*, i, p. 54.
68. Ibid., pp. 44–46.
69. L. Lévy-Bruhl, *The Philosophy of Auguste Comte*, p. 23.
70. Marx, *KHR*, *MEGA* i/i/i, pp. 620–1.
71. Comte, *Discours préliminaire sur l'ensemble du positivisme*, p. 47.
72. Comte, *SPP*, p. 182; cf. p. 184.
73. Ibid., p. 89.
74. Ibid., pp. 93–94; *Cours*, iv, pp. 294–317, 370.
75. F. E. Manuel, *The New World of Henri Saint-Simon*, pp. 134–8.
76. Comte, *SPP*, pp. 191–2; *Cours*, i, p. 75; iv, pp. 482–9; *Discours préliminaire sur l'ensemble du positivisme*, pp. 50–51.
77. H. Saint-Simon, *De la physiologie appliquée à l'amelioration des institutions sociales*, p. 177.
78. Comte, *Discours sur l'esprit positif*, pp. 87–88.
79. Comte, *SPP*, p. 45; *Cours*, vi, p. 692. Lenin attributed to Marx the discovery that society is not a 'mechanical aggregation of individuals' (*WFPA*, p. 142), but Lenin does not seem to have read Comte.
80. Comte, *Cours*, iv, pp. 357–62, 559–60. Aristotle, too, believed that the city-state grew out of the family.
81. Comte, *Cours*, iv, pp. 539, 541.
82. Ibid., vi, p. 669.
83. Ibid., i, p. 74; iv, pp. 450–1, 483–4.
84. For this use of the term 'consensus' see J. S. Mill, *A System of Logic*, book vi, ch. ix, § 2.
85. Comte, *Cours*, iv, pp. 324, 332, 336.
86. Ibid., p. 353.
87. Comte, *SPP*, pp. 198–9; *Cours*, iv, pp. 357–62; vi, p. 777.
88. Comte's views on the relation of sociology to psychology might have been one of the reasons why Mill expressed his disappointment with the fourth volume of the *Cours*. See *Autobiography*, p. 178. Karl Popper pays tribute to Marx for his challenge of Mill's methodological psychologism in sociology (*OS*, vol. ii, p. 88), but he failed to see that this tribute should be paid to or at least shared by Comte.
89. Comte, *SPP*, pp. 191–2.
90. Comte, *Cours*, iv, pp. 487–8.
91. Comte did not say how his holistic sociological laws could be tested but pointed out how they could be falsified (in his *System of Logic*, book vi, ch. ix, § 1, Mill speaks of Comte's verification 'by deduction from the laws of human nature', but the term 'verification' is misleading in this context). If the consequences of a sociological law lead to conclusions incompatible with what we know about human behaviour, the law in question should be considered as falsified. For instance, should a sociological law state that human beings have as a rule a preponderant inclination in a good or bad direction, that reason predominates in them over their desires or that their altruistic and disinterested motives predominate over their selfishness, such

a law is clearly to be rejected (*Cours*, iv, pp. 463-7, 480-2). No such methodological provisions are to be found in Marx to guard him against the pitfalls of holistic laws.

92. Comte, *SPP*, p. 182; *Cours*, iv, pp. 450-8, 484-5; vi, pp. 781-2; L. Lévy-Bruhl, *The Philosophy of Auguste Comte*, p. 237.

93. Comte, *SPP*, pp. 74-75; *Cours*, iv, pp. 370-1.

94. Durkheim took up and elaborated this idea of Comte. See *The Division of Labour in Society*, pp. 62-63.

95. Durkheim, *The Rules of Sociological Method*, p. 29.

96. J. S. Mill, *Auguste Comte and Positivism*, pp. 52, 84, 124.

97. Comte, *Cours*, i, pp. 21-22; ii, p. 28; vi, pp. 701, 703; *Discours préliminaire sur l'ensemble du positivisme*, p. 57.

98. Engels, *DN*, pp. 307, 329; Special Introduction to the English edition of *SUS*, p. 93; *LF*, p. 336. In this respect Engels's views differed from Marx's. As will be seen later, Marx retained the distinction between the delusive appearance and the true essence of things and declared that all science would be superfluous if the appearance of things coincided with their essence.

99. Comte, *Cours*, iv, p. 298.

100. Ibid., i, p. 34; L. Lévy-Bruhl, *The Philosophy of Auguste Comte*, p. 70.

101. See Jordan, *PHI*, pp. 367-70.

102. Engels, *LF*, p. 331.

103. H. Marcuse, *Reason and Revolution*, p. 262.

104. Comte, *Cours*, i, p. 26.

105. Ibid., p. 27; vi, p. 519; Durkheim, *The Elementary Forms of the Religious Life*, p. 447.

106. Engels, *AD*, p. 41.

107. Ibid., pp. 39-40.

108. Comte, *Cours*, iv, pp. 522-3.

109. Wetter, *DM*, pp. 249-56.

110. Marx, *GI*, p. 15; *Frühschriften*, p. 350.

111. Engels, *AD*, pp. 39-40; *SUS*, p. 123. The criticized view was, as a matter of fact, the Hegelian conception of philosophy.

112. Schaff, *Narodziny i rozwój filozofii marksistowskiej*, pp. 14-24.

113. Engels, *AD*, p. 191.

114. Ibid., pp. 56-57; *LF*, p. 331.

115. Engels, *DN*, pp. 58, 279.

116. Engels, *AD*, p. 40; *LF*, p. 363; *SUS*, p. 123.

117. Engels, *AD*, p. 194; cf. *DN*, p. 353.

118. Schaff, *Narodziny i rozwój filozofii marksistowskiej*, p. 20.

119. H. Saint-Simon, *Mémoire sur la science de l'homme*, p. 18.

120. W. M. Simon, 'History for Utopia: Saint-Simon and the Idea of Progress', p. 316. *Le Nouveau Christianisme* is often interpreted as an implicit recognition by Saint-Simon that science is unable to support morals.

121. J. S. Mill, *Auguste Comte and Positivism*, p. 53.

122. D. G. Charlton, *Positivist Thought in France*, p. 55.

123. 'Scientism', as used above, designates not only the attitude of respect

for science, its achievements and method, but also and above all the belief that science alone can effectively create and support a stable and rational moral and social order. Scientism in this sense is an attitude incompatible with positivism.

124. D. G. Charlton, *Positivist Thought in France*, pp. 154–7.

125. 'Hegelian positivism' is a term introduced by F. A. Hayek, *The Counter-Revolution of Science*, p. 204, where it is used to denote a mixture of Comtean and Hegelian ideas. Wilhelm Windelband had observed that in the materialist conception of history 'motives from Hegel and from Comte cross in a peculiar manner' (*A History of Philosophy*, vol. ii, p. 655). The similarities between Hegel's and Comte's social philosophies are the subject of a recent comprehensive study by Oskar Negt, *Strukturbeziehungen zwischen den Gesellschaftslehren Comtes und Hegels*. Max Horkheimer and T. W. Adorno suggest in the preface to Negt's book that since both Hegel and Comte supported the bourgeoisie and were its defenders against the already rising social forces which were eventually to engulf it, the similarities of their views are not as puzzling as they might appear. It is more than doubtful whether this kind of explanation explains anything.

126. Comte probably had in mind Saint-Simon who played with the idea that a single principle, like the law of gravity correctly interpreted, would be sufficient to deduce all others from it. See H. Saint-Simon, *Mémoire sur la science de l'homme*, p. 303; F. E. Manuel, *The New World of Henri Saint-Simon*, pp. 117–21.

127. Comte, *Cours*, vi, pp. 703–5. It should be added, however, that Comte recognized the existence of encyclopaedic laws applying, unlike physical or astronomical laws, to all phenomena whatsoever. See *Cours*, vi, pp. 793–800, and L. Lévy-Bruhl, *The Philosophy of Auguste Comte*, pp. 99–102. These encyclopaedic laws resemble the laws of dialectics. Thus, for instance, Newton's first law of motion transformed into an encyclopaedic law explains inertia in mechanics, habits in living bodies, and the conservative inclination in human society. It is not clear what status Comte assigned to these encyclopaedic laws.

PART TWO

Chapter V. The Foundations of Engels's Dialectical Materialism

1. Engels, *LF*, pp. 335, 337. Describing the important differences between his own dialectical method and Hegel's, Marx made essentially the same distinction between materialism and idealism (*Capital*, vol. i, p. 19). The quotation from Feuerbach comes from *VTRPH*, p. 263.

2. Engels, *LF*, pp. 335–7, 350; *DN*, p. 64.

3. Some Western historians of dialectical materialism maintain that Engels's distinction between materialism and idealism is based on a confusion and misunderstanding of metaphysical, epistemological, and theo-

logical problems (Bocheński, *SDM*, pp. 70–71; Wetter, *DM*, p. 282). Their opinion is not supported by the relevant texts, although it applies to Lenin's interpretation of the passage under discussion. See Lenin, *MEC*, pp. 32, 60, 147, 260.

4. Lenin, *MEC*, p. 90. Cf. Engels, *AD*, p. 55, to which Lenin refers.

5. Engels could have assumed either that the capacity of sensation was a general property of matter, as Diderot suggested, or that mental phenomena are identical with physical phenomena. The so-called identity theory of mind could not be true unless mental and physical phenomena had the same characteristics. Neither psychology nor natural science is able to produce evidence which would provide the required confirmation of the identity hypothesis as an empirical theory. For the discussion of the identity theory in the light of knowledge available today see W. Köhler, 'The Mind–Body Problem', pp. 30–32 in particular. Engels sometimes seems to support the identity theory of mind and sometimes to criticize it in the strongest terms, declaring himself for Diderot's solution and the theory of emergence. For the latter point of view see Section 2 of this Chapter.

6. Engels, *AD*, p. 65.

7. Engels, *DN*, p. 243.

8. Marx, *MEGA* 1/3, p. 301; *HF*, p. 168.

9. The Russian Machians were particularly vocal in emphasizing the strong differences between Marx and Engels, and set Engels's crude and naïve 'dogmatic materialism' against the materialism of Marx.

10. Engels, *AD*, pp. 16–17; *DN*, pp. 57–58.

11. Aristotle, *De Caelo*, i, 275b30–276a2; Descartes, *Principia Philosophiae*, ii, ch. 23.

12. Engels, *DN*, p. 308.

13. Ibid., pp. 40–41.

14. P. Duhem, *The Aim and Structure of Physical Theory*, pp. 322–4; R. G. Collingwood, *The Idea of Nature*, pp. 40–42.

15. E. Mach, *The Analysis of Sensations*, p. 312.

16. Engels, *LF*, pp. 338, 351–2.

17. Holbach, *Système de la nature*, tome i, pp. 38–39.

18. J. B. Stallo, *The Concepts and Theories of Modern Physics*, p. 170. Stallo (1823–1900) was Engels's contemporary and his book first appeared in 1881.

19. Helvétius, *De l'esprit*, Discours i, ch. iv.

20. Engels, *DN*, p. 337. Plekhanov observed in a similar vein that to believe in the existence of a secret essence of things is harmful for the advancement of knowledge, for it hinders the study of the 'real movement of things'. By accepting the belief in essence 'we incur the danger of denying real facts for the sake of a theory which may appear to us more or less clever, but in any case is absolutely arbitrary' (*EHM*, pp. 185–6). This is a refreshingly original observation on the part of a Marxian essentialist and one striking in its modernity. Cf. K. R. Popper, *Conjectures and Refutations*, p. 107.

21. *Three Dialogues between Hylas and Philonous, The Works of George Berkeley*, vol. ii, pp. 223, 224, 260.

22. Engels, *DN*, pp. 312–13.

23. Hegel, *EPHS*, § 99, Addition; § 128, Addition, pp. 186–7, 236–7.

24. Engels, *DN*, p. 93.

25. Ibid., pp. 312–13.

26. Some physicists of today reject materialism because they believe that some sub-atomic phenomena are incompatible with a realistic theory of knowledge. See Ph. Frank, *Foundations of Physics*, pp. 54–55, and the critical analysis of this point of view in E. McMullin, 'Introduction: The Concept of Matter', pp. 28–30.

27. 'There is nothing in the world but matter in motion, and matter in motion cannot move otherwise than in space and time' (Lenin, *MEC*, p. 175). Neither Engels nor Lenin had anything to say on the subject of space and time and both were satisfied to repeat Feuerbach's views almost word for word. Where they tried to say something on their own, they talked plain nonsense. Thus, for instance, Lenin tried to show that Mach's arguments against absolute time and space amounted to 'deserting natural science for fideism' (*MEC*, p. 180).

28. Engels, *AD*, pp. 76, 86, 93; *DN*, pp. 54, 323. The principle of the uncreatability and indestructibility of matter is better known in its Latin formulation 'de nihilo nihil, in nihilum nil posse reverti' (see Kant, *Critique of Pure Reason*, pp. 212–17). This *a priori* principle, expressed in empirical terms, is known today as the principle of the conservation of matter.

29. Engels, *AD*, p. 86.

30. Engels, *DN*, p. 92.

31. Some contemporary dialectical materialists recognize this fact. See Eilstein, *Jedność materialna świata*, p. 141.

32. Engels, *AD*, pp. 84, 87; *DN*, p. 329.

33. Engels, *DN*, pp. 51–54.

34. Engels, *LF*, p. 337.

35. Engels, *LF*, p. 338; Lenin, *MEC*, p. 251.

36. The dependence of the meaning attached to the term 'matter' on the operational rules does not imply that the only legitimate problem is to agree about an unambiguous use of the term 'material object' (this seems to be the view of Ph. Frank, *Foundations of Physics*, p. 54). The linguistic problem is an important but not an autonomous issue, for its solution depends upon our knowledge of what matter is.

37. The impact of Comte's vigorous criticism of reductivism upon Engels cannot be substantiated but is plausible. As far as Comte's anti-reductivism is concerned, see Ch. IV of this study.

38. Engels, *LF*, p. 338; *DN*, p. 270.

39. É. Meyerson, *Identity and Reality*, p. 415.

40. Engels, *DN*, pp. 332–9.

41. Ibid., pp. 277, 328, 405.

42. Ibid., pp. 333–4; *AD*, pp. 95–96; *LF*, p. 338. Engels wrote these words at a time when the leading scientists in Germany and elsewhere — Kirchhoff, Helmholtz, Du Bois-Reymond, William Thomson (Lord Kelvin), and Clerk Maxwell — were emphatically announcing that the

reduction of all phenomena of nature to mechanics was the highest objective of natural science. For numerous and striking quotations see J. B. Stallo, *The Concepts and Theories of Modern Physics*, pp. 49–57, and É. Meyerson, *Identity and Reality*, ch. ii.

43. Engels's criticism of the mechanistic conception does not compare unfavourably with Mach's critical observations in *The Science of Mechanics*, ch. v, first published in 1883, or with the philosophical analysis of the mechanistic conception of the universe in Stallo's *The Concepts and Theories of Modern Physics*, first published in 1881. Stallo and Mach are, of course, greatly superior to Engels in their knowledge of natural science.

44. Engels, *DN*, p. 335.

45. In this respect, Engels, and similarly Lenin, did not depart from the views and preferences of Marx, who put the 'blooming sensuousness' of Bacon above Hobbes's 'abstract sensuousness of the geometrician' (*MEGA* 1/3, p. 305; *HF*, pp. 172–3). Whatever matter is, Bacon wrote, it must be so formed that 'all virtues, essence, action, and motion may be the natural consequence and emanation thereof' (quoted by J. B. Stallo, *The Concepts and Theories of Modern Physics*, p. 174). Lenin followed Engels's conception of matter both for temperamental and philosophical reasons. 'The very first and most familiar to us is sensation and in it there is inevitably also quality' (*PHN*, p. 319).

46. Cf. R. G. Collingwood, *The Idea of Nature*, p. 14.

47. Engels, *LF*, pp. 352–3, 363.

48. É. Gilson, *God and Philosophy*, p. 134.

49. Engels, *LF*, p. 339.

50. Engels, Special Introduction to the English edition of *SUS*, p. 92.

51. Engels, *AD*, p. 20; cf. p. 197. The corpuscular theory of matter — sometimes designated also by the expression the 'kinetic-corpuscular theory' because it tries to explain natural phenomena in terms of mass and motion — assumed that matter consisted of ultimate and invariable particles and that the forces of nature — attraction, heat, chemical, electric or magnetic energy — which acted upon these particles were also unchangeable. For the classical formulation of this axiom see Descartes, *Principia Philosophiae* ii, ch. 37. On the other hand, the dynamic theory of matter defined atoms and molecules as centres of a force which was not extraneous, impressed upon a material particle from outside, as in the corpuscular theory.

52. Engels, *AD*, p. 86; Special Introduction to the English edition of *SUS*, p. 92.

53. Quoted from John Tyndall's Presidential Address to the British Association for the Advancement of Science delivered at the meeting held in Belfast in August 1874, which became known as the 'Belfast Address'. It was published in *Nature* and reprinted in Tyndall's two-volume work *Fragments of Science* (1881). John Tyndall (1820–93) was Faraday's successor at the Royal Institution and was noted for his interest in philosophy. The Belfast Address acquired a considerable renown and provoked many rejoinders on account of its outspoken criticism of theology. Engels studied it carefully. See Engels's letter to Marx of 21 September 1874, and *DN*, pp. 268–9.

For the quotation from Marx see *MEGA* i/3, p. 304; *HF*, p. 172. Marx might have been influenced by Friedrich Schelling's conception of matter, reminiscent of that of Francis Bacon, as 'the grain of an universal seed of the universe (*das allgemeine Samenkorn des Universums*) wherein everything is wrapped up that unfolds itself in subsequent development' (F. Schelling, *Ideen zu einer Philosophie der Natur*, quoted by J. B. Stallo, *The Concepts and Theories of Modern Physics*, p. 174).

54. Engels, *AD*, p. 87; cf. É. Meyerson, *Identity and Reality*, p. 82. Modern supporters of emergent evolution continue to show as much hostility towards mechanistic theories as did Engels. See C. Lloyd Morgan, *Emergent Evolution*, p. 7. They point out that the doctrine of emergence is an alternative to the mechanistic conception not only on the ontological but also on the epistemological level. The mechanistic conception would have to be a theory of an unlimited range of validity and such a theory could hardly meet the methodological requirements which every scientific theory should satisfy. See M. Bunge, *Metascientific Queries*, p. 112.

55. M. Bunge, *Causality*, pp. 198–219.

56. 'Novelties' in the sense in which this term is used in this context mean 'entities or properties temporally or historically novel'. What is temporally novel is also *a priori* unpredictable, but *a priori* unpredictable novelties are not necessarily historically novel. Lloyd Morgan emphasized that we may speak of original novelty only when it arises on some first occasion, that is, when we think of the cosmic process as a whole. Unpredictability characterizes 'this or that bit of world process' in which some original novelty reappears as a matter of established routine (*The Emergence of Novelty*, pp. 32–40).

57. R. G. Collingwood, *The Idea of Nature*, p. 159.

58. See Ch. III, pp. 106–10. This is also apparent from Engels's Hegelian terminology. Engels spoke of the nodal lines of measure relations or qualitative leap and of the forms of motion irreducible to each other when he had the emergence and the stratification of levels in mind. See Engels, *AD*, pp. 67, 96–99.

59. See S. Alexander, *Space, Time and Deity*, vol. ii, pp. 46–47; C. Lloyd Morgan, *Emergent Evolution*, pp. 19–20; C. D. Broad, *The Mind and its Place in Nature*, ch. 2; P. E. Meehl and W. Sellars, 'The Concept of Emergence', p. 240.

60. Engels, *DN*, pp. 51–52, 278, 306–7; *LF*, p. 352.

61. Engels, *AD*, pp. 59–60; *DN*, p. 83; *LF*, p. 350.

62. Engels, *DN*, p. 84.

63. W. Sombart, *Der proletarische Sozialismus*, Bd. 1, p. 215.

64. Jean-Paul Sartre, *Critique de la raison dialectique*, tome i, p. 670. However, Sartre did not object to the application of dialectics to nature because of the inherent nonsense of this idea, nor did he exclude the possibility that the dialectics of nature was a valid metaphysical hypothesis. He objected to Engels's version of dialectical materialism — which he called 'le matérialisme dialectique du dehors' — since it distorted the anthropological content of this doctrine in its original Marxian formulation and subjected the nature of man to a principle which lies outside of himself, namely, to the uni-

versal laws of nature. See *Critique de la raison dialectique*, tome i, p. 124.

65. Engels, *DN*, p. 84.

66. Engels, *AD*, pp. 67, 173–4.

67. Ibid., p. 174.

68. Ibid.

69. See, e.g., S. Hook, *Reason, Social Myths and Democracy*, pp. 215–20, and H. B. Acton, *The Illusion of the Epoch*, pp. 80–93, where Engels's claim is examined from this point of view.

70. Engels, *AD*, pp. 174–7.

71. A primary novelty should be distinguished from a recurrent novelty, the novel occurrence being repeated on subsequent occasions.

72. That the transformation of quantity into quality explains the emergence of novelty is the view widely adopted in Soviet philosophy. See *FML*, pp. 74–76.

73. Dühring and many writers after Dühring expressed their shocked amazement at Engels's use of the term 'contradiction', which allows us to predicate it both of propositions and of things or events. (See Engels, *AD*, pp. 164–5; S. Hook, *Reason, Social Myths and Democracy*, p. 202.) There is no reason to be amazed, for we can speak, as Aristotle did, of contradictory objects at the ontological level and of contradictory statements or propositions at the linguisitic level. If the logical or metalogical (semantical) principle of non-contradiction is accepted, the existence of contradictory objects has to be rejected, and conversely. But those restricting or denying the validity of the principle of non-contradiction are perfectly free to speak of contradictory objects.

74. Plekhanov, *DMH*, p. 613.

75. Engels, *DN*, pp. 26, 271, 280; *AD*, pp. 193–4.

76. Engels, *AD*, p. 186.

77. Hegel, *SL*, vol. ii, p. 68.

78. Hegel, *EPHS*, § 81, Addition, § 98, pp. 148–51, 169–70.

79. Ibid., § 119, p. 223.

80. Hegel, *SL*, vol. ii, p. 67. Hegel believed that Zeno of Elea did not mean to deny the reality of movement, for the fact that there is movement is 'as sensuously certain as that there are elephants'. Zeno intended to show that 'the conception of movement involves a contradiction' and pointed out 'how movement must necessarily be determined'. See Hegel, *Lectures on the History of Philosophy*, vol. i, pp. 266–7.

81. Engels, *AD*, p. 166.

82. Ibid., p. 167.

83. Engels, *DN*, p. 280; *AD*, p. 168.

84. Engels, *AD*, p. 89; *DN*, pp. 271–3.

85. Hegel, *SL*, vol. ii, pp. 66–67.

86. Hegel, *EPHS*, § 119, Addition, §§ 115–18, pp. 223, 212–14.

87. Engels, *AD*, p. 165; *DN*, pp. 284–7; Hegel, *EPHS*, § 214, p. 356; *SL*, vol. ii, pp. 413–15. Lenin followed in Engels's footsteps. He commented with admiration upon the passages of the *Encyclopaedia of the Philosophical Sciences* quoted above and stated that facts described by the proposition in which 'the individual is the universal' (e.g. 'John is a man' or 'Fido is a

dog') reveal the 'materialist roots' of Hegel's 'dialectic of notion' (*PHN*, pp. 199, 361). See also Jordan, *PHI*, pp. 277–8.

88. Engels, *AD*, pp. 34–36; *DN*, p. 282.

89. Engels, *AD*, pp. 190–1. Popper has suggested that the theory of the dialectical triad should be regarded as an empirical descriptive theory comparable, for instance, with Comte's law of the three stages or with the belief that opinions are held first dogmatically, then sceptically, and finally critically (*Conjectures and Refutations*, p. 322). Such theories provide only a rough chart of intellectual history and have, therefore, little cognitive value.

90. Cf. H. B. Acton, *The Illusion of the Epoch*, p. 96; S. Hook, *Reason, Social Myths and Democracy*, pp. 213–14.

91. Engels, *DN*, p. 280; cf. p. 271; Hegel, *Lectures on the History of Philosophy*, vol. i, p. 264.

92. Engels, *LF*, p. 350; *AD*, p. 157.

93. J. S. Mill, *An Examination of Sir William Hamilton's Philosophy*, ch. ii.

94. Lenin refers to it as 'relativism, i.e., the principle of the relativity of our knowledge' (*MEC*, p. 134). Although in Lenin this is the main meaning of the phrase the 'doctrine of the relativity of knowledge', it is also used by him in the sense considered below in which it stands for the proposition that all scientific knowledge is provisional and relative. See, e.g., *MEC*, p. 137.

95. Engels, *AD*, p. 57; cf. *LF*, pp. 328, 330–1.

96. Engels, *AD*, pp. 121–2, 125, 127–8; *DN*, p. 311.

97. Engels, *LF*, p. 329.

98. See ibid., p. 338. Cf. R. G. Collingwood, *The Idea of Nature*, p. 10.

99. In *The Idea of Nature*, R. G. Collingwood differentiated the same three periods of cosmological thinking as Engels did. There is a striking agreement in the description of each period between the two writers.

100. Engels, *DN*, pp. 35, 43, 62–63; *AD*, p. 33.

101. Engels, *DN*, pp. 34–37.

102. Engels, *AD*, p. 34. Elsewhere Engels presented the metaphysical mode of thought, peculiar to natural science, as the inheritance from English empiricism. See *AD*, p. 22.

103. Engels, *DN*, pp. 37–43, 63–65; *AD*, pp. 36–37, 82–83.

104. Engels, *DN*, p. 59.

105. Wetter, *DM*, p. 318.

106. Engels, *AD*, p. 83.

107. Modern cosmology should be more or less identified with the Cartesian–Newtonian mechanistic conception of the world, in which time is the independent variable and can be given any value in the two directions of the time *continuum*, between which there seems to be no intrinsic difference. In other words, time being reversible is not an important factor in the Cartesian–Newtonian outlook. What is important is the regular behaviour of elements whose combination, impervious to time, obey invariant patterns or laws. The assumption of the mechanistic conception of the world that the 'lapse of time', as Whitehead put it, 'is an accident', gives rise to the doctrine that the universe is a running mechanism, endlessly repeating the succession of its developmental stages in an eternal cycle. This doctrine,

widely accepted in nineteenth-century cosmology, is discussed by Engels in *DN*, pp. 52–54.

108. Whitehead, *The Concept of Nature*, p. 178.

109. Engels, *DN*, pp. 35, 39; *AD*, p. 36.

110. The question as to why man should be anxious to disregard history is a fascinating sociological problem to which *The Myth of the Eternal Return* of Mircea Eliade has made a noteworthy contribution.

Chapter VI. Plekhanov's Revisions of Dialectical Materialism

1. L. Trotsky, *Lenin*, p. 52.

2. Lenin, 'On the Twenty-Fifth Anniversary of the Revolutionary Activity of G. V. Plekhanov', *CW* 5, p. 326; S. H. Baron, *Plekhanov*, pp. 142–3, and also pp. 135–7; F. Mehring, *Karl Marx*, p. 525.

3. Lenin, 'On the Significance of Militant Materialism', *CW* 33, pp. 227–8.

4. Lenin, 'Marxism and Revisionism', *CW* 15, p. 33; 'A Letter to A. M. Gorky', *CW* 13, pp. 448–9.

5. While praising Plekhanov for his philosophical and literary activity, Lenin often attacked him for his political views in which, allegedly, he often proved himself to be a philistine and a dupe of the bourgeoisie. See, for instance, 'Trade Union Neutrality', *CW* 13, p. 466 (the date of this article is practically the same as that of the just quoted letter to Gorky), and *The State and Revolution*, *CW* 25, pp. 475–6.

6. *History of the Communist Party of the Soviet Union (Bolshevik): Short Course*, pp. 11–12.

7. S. Hook, *The Hero in History*, pp. 68, 70; V. V. Zenkovsky, *History of Russian Philosophy*, vol. ii, p. 740; S. H. Baron, *Plekhanov*, pp. 287, 306–7.

8. Plekhanov, *FPM*, p. 111.

9. Lenin, *PHN*, p. 82; 'On the Significance of Militant Materialism', *CW* 33, p. 233.

10. Plekhanov, *DMH*, pp. 544–5; cf. *EHM*, pp. 3–4, 85–92. It was by reference to the definition of genetic materialism that Plekhanov criticized F. A. Lange for having refused to consider Helvétius a materialist. Lange ignored the doctrines of Helvétius whom he regarded as a 'vain and superficial' and unimportant thinker, in every way inferior to Lamettrie (*History of Materialism*, vol. ii, p. 93). There can be no doubt that Marx's interpretation of Helvétius and his place in the history of materialism, which Plekhanov adopted, is far more perceptive than Lange's scornful evaluation of him.

11. Plekhanov, *FPM*, p. 125.

12. Plekhanov, *FNLF*, pp. 510 ff., 534 ff.

13. Lenin had nothing but contempt for the theory of knowledge that abandons the naïve beliefs of mankind about the external world and indulges in critical examinations of what we do know and how we come to the knowledge which we claim to possess. The critical approach only produced 'epistemological artifices' and he had no patience with them. For this

reason Lenin admired Hegel's cavalier treatment of Kant and thought little of Plekhanov's criticism of Kantian philosophy. See *PHN*, p. 179.

14. Plekhanov, *FNLF*, p. 512.

15. Ibid., p. 152. This is a summary rather than a translation of Holbach. In the original the last sentence runs, 'Ainsi relativement à nous la matière en général est tout ce qui affecte nos sens d'une façon quelconque' (*Système de la nature*, tome i, p. 381 ; cf. tome ii, p. 95).

16. Holbach, *Système de la nature*, tome ii, pp. 60–61.

17. Plekhanov, *FNLF*, p. 513 ; cf. *EHM*, pp. 9–16. It is not by any means certain that Plekhanov rightly interpreted Feuerbach's position. Feuerbach wrote that 'matter is the symbol of being outside thought, the substratum of reality' (*GPHZ*, § 29, p. 314). Thus, in perfect agreement with his anthropological realism, he asserted both the objective reality of matter and its unknowableness. Marx seems to have adopted this view and made of it the corner stone of his naturalism. As has been pointed out earlier, Plekhanov had not the slightest idea that Marx's naturalism and Engels's materialism were quite different doctrines.

18. Plekhanov, *FNLF*, p. 536. For a detailed discussion of this point with which Plekhanov dealt on several occasions see Cackowski, *Treść poznawcza wrażeń zmysłowych*, pp. 147–67.

19. Lenin, *MEC*, pp. 232–3.

20. Plekhanov, *FPM*, pp. 29–30.

21. L. Feuerbach, *VTRPH*, p. 263. This is again a paraphrase rather than a faithful rendering of Feuerbach's original text.

22. Plekhanov, *FPM*, pp. 7, 21.

23. Plekhanov, *EHM*, pp. 10–11, 74–75.

24. Plekhanov, *DMH*, pp. 741–2 and n.

25. Hegel, *EPHS*, § 13, p. 23.

26. Plekhanov, *SAHD*, pp. 477–8 ; *EHM*, pp. 167–8.

27. Lenin, *PHN*, p. 104 ; 'On the Significance of Militant Materialism', *CW* 33, p. 233.

28. In support of this opinion Plekhanov invariably quoted certain passages from Hegel's *SL*, vol. i, pp. 388–90.

29. Plekhanov, *A New Champion of Autocracy*, pp. 413–21 ; *SAHD*, p. 480 ; *DMH*, pp. 609–10 ; *FPM*, pp. 27–31 ; *EHM*, pp. 172–5. Plekhanov's interpretation of the essential difference between mere evolution and dialectics was approvingly endorsed by Lenin (*KMX*, pp. 54–55) and, without any substantial alterations, presented again quite recently by A. Schaff, the leading Polish Marxist–Leninist philosopher. See A. Schaff, *Wstęp do teorii marksizmu*, pp. 97 ff. Both Lenin and Schaff maintained that the idea of evolution as formulated by Marx and Engels is far more comprehensive and far richer in content than the current idea of evolution.

30. Wetter, *DM*, p. 311.

31. Engels's order of the dialectical laws is to be found in *Dialectics of Nature*, which was first published in 1925 and was unknown to Plekhanov and Lenin. In *Anti-Dühring* the laws of dialectics are discussed in the same succession as that Plekhanov gave them, but Engels did not indicate that this was the order of their importance.

32. Plekhanov, *DMH*, pp. 607, 609, 631, 755.
33. Ibid., p. 607.
34. Plekhanov, *FPM*, pp. 28, 119.
35. Ibid., pp. 112–13, 115, 117–20. The doctrine of logical dualism was revived in Polish Marxism–Leninism in the 1940s. For the positive role which it played in Poland at that time see Jordan, *PHI*, p. 294.
36. Hegel, *SL*, vol. i, p. 354; *EPHS*, §§ 108, 109, pp. 202–4.
37. Plekhanov, *FPM*, p. 28.
38. Plekhanov, *A New Champion of Autocracy*, p. 418; cf. *SAHD*, p. 480; *EHM*, p. 174.
39. Plekhanov, *EHM*, pp. 174–5; *FPM*, p. 27.
40. Plekhanov, *DMH*, pp. 610–11; *FPM*, pp. 28–29, 114.
41. Hegel, *SL*, vol. i, p. 389.
42. Another reason for the rejection of the first alternative is the fact that not all magnitudes are additive. For instance, no operation of addition is defined for such magnitudes as density or elasticity.
43. Engels, *DN*, p. 358.
44. Plekhanov, *DMH*, p. 611; cf. p. 744.
45. J. N. Findlay showed in detail that the 'triplicity or triadicity does indicate something genuine about Hegel's thought'. See J. N. Findlay, *Hegel: A Re-examination*, pp. 361–73.
46. Plekhanov, *FNLF*, pp. 488–9. Engels rebuked Dühring for accusing Marx of making use of the triad as a method of proof, which did not prevent Engels from proclaiming the law of the negation 'an extremely general law of development of nature, history and thought'. Similarly, Plekhanov denied that the triad 'plays the part of an argument' and that historical materialism applies it in its investigations, but he rose to a staunch defence of the triadic rhythm when Mikhailovsky suggested that it was about time 'we ceased to believe that oats grow according to Hegel'. See Plekhanov, *DMH*, pp. 612, 623, 744. As a matter of fact, Soviet philosophers continued to believe in 1958 that 'oats grow according to Hegel' (*FML*, p. 86).
47. While constructing a polemical argument Marx once said *en passant* that 'no development that does not negate its previous forms of existence can occur in any sphere' ('Die moralisierende Kritik und die kritisierende Moral', *MEGA* 1/6, pp. 303–4). This was clearly an observation about the usage of the term 'development' and not about the process designated by this term, but Marx's observation is quoted even today in support of the view that development without negation is impossible, that is, that negation is an indispensable part of the developmental process. See *FML*, p. 84, where also the following definition of negation is to be found: 'By negation Marxist dialectics understands the law-governed replacement in the process of development of an old quality by a new one, which arises out of the old one.'
48. Engels, *AD*, p. 195.
49. Ibid. Cf. Lenin, *PHN*, p. 226.
50. *FML*, p. 84.
51. K. R. Popper, *Conjectures and Refutations*, p. 334.
52. Plekhanov, *DMH*, pp. 612–13, 631; Lenin, *PHN*, p. 222.

53. Plekhanov, *Our Differences*, pp. 155, 238; *FNLF*, p. 488; *EHM*, pp. 174–5.

54. Plekhanov, *DMH*, pp. 551–2, 717.

55. K. R. Popper, *Conjectures and Refutations*, p. 332.

56. N. Bukharin, *Historical Materialism*, pp. 73–74.

57. Lenin, *PHN*, p. 196.

58. For the concept of the criterion of demarcation see K. R. Popper, *The Logic of Scientific Discovery*, pp. 32–39.

59. For this reason laws are sometimes conceived as 'inference-tickets' and theories as sets of rules of inference in accordance with which we can link facts or which we use as devices of thought to make inferences about phenomena to be explained or predicted. For details see S. Toulmin, *The Philosophy of Science*, pp. 93–94; Milton K. Munitz, *Space, Time and Creation*, pp. 42–44. It should be clear that the predictive power which is an important evaluation criterion of the worth of theories is included in the property of logical fertility.

60. For this reinterpretation of the principle of verification see H. Mehlberg, *The Reach of Science*, pp. 35–44.

61. M. Brodbeck, 'Explanation, Prediction, and "Imperfect" Knowledge', p. 246.

62. Ph. G. Frank, 'The Variety of Reasons for the Acceptance of Scientific Theories', pp. 13–26.

63. Plekhanov, *A New Champion of Autocracy*, p. 419; cf. *DMH*, p. 688.

64. Plekhanov, *SAHD*, p. 477. That the universal dialectical law of development concerning the transformation of quantity into quality is a socio-cosmic law is revealed with a disarming frankness in contemporary Soviet philosophy. See *FML*, pp. 74–75.

65. Cf. Jordan, *PHI*, p. 264, but the argument is old. See, e.g., J. S. Mill, *An Examination of Sir William Hamilton's Philosophy*, vol. ii, p. 182.

66. See *FML*, pp. 77–78.

67. Cf. E. Topitsch, *Sozialphilosophie zwischen Ideologie und Wissenschaft*, pp. 35–36, 72–73.

68. Ph. G. Frank, 'The Present Role of Science', p. 14. It is impossible to consider here, even in a very brief way, the connection between the sociological interpretation of the validity of scientific theories, put forward by E. Topitsch and Ph. G. Frank, and the hypothesis of Durkheim that all concepts or at least all categories used in the description of the universe are collective representations and that social life is the source of logical and speculative thought. See É. Durkheim, *The Elementary Forms of the Religious Life*, pp. 431 ff.

Chapter VII. The Dialectical Materialism of Lenin

1. J. Plamenatz, *German Marxism and Russian Communism*, p. 249.

2. Lenin, 'How Plekhanov and Co. Defend Revisionism', *CW* 15, p. 281.

3. Lenin, 'Marxism and Revisionism', *CW* 15, pp. 32–33.

4. Lenin, 'Our Program', *CW* 4, p. 211; 'Review of Karl Kautsky's Book *Bernstein und das sozialdemokratische Program: Eine Antikritik*', *CW* 4, p. 196; 'Certain Features of the Historical Development of Marxism', *CW* 17, pp. 39–40, 42.

5. *FML*, p. 22.

6. See, e.g., Lenin, *MEC*, pp. 19, 246; 'The Attitude of the Workers' Party Towards Religion', *CW* 15, p. 402.

7. Bocheński, *SDM*, p. 33.

8. See, e.g., Lenin, 'Ten Questions to a Lecturer', *CW* 14, p. 15; 'The Attitude of the Workers' Party Towards Religion', *CW* 15, p. 406; 'Differences in the European Labour Movement', *CW* 16, p. 348; 'Twenty-Fifth Anniversary of the Death of Joseph Dietzgen', *CW* 19, p. 79.

9. Lenin, *MEC*, pp. 32, 75.

10. *FML*, pp. 29–31.

11. Lenin, 'Frederick Engels', *CW* 2, p. 21; *MEC*, pp. 46, 55, 90, 323, 326; *KMX*, p. 55.

12. Lenin, *MEC*, pp. 55, 90.

13. Ibid., p. 173.

14. Ibid., pp. 83, 105.

15. Ibid., p. 26; G. J. Warnock, *Berkeley*, pp. 92–97.

16. That 'matter is the same as existing externally' was also affirmed by Hegel, who traced this definition back to Leibniz. See *SL*, vol. 1, p. 203.

17. *The Principles of Human Knowledge*, § 24, § 54; *Three Dialogues between Hylas and Philonous*, *The Works of George Berkeley*, vol. ii, pp. 51, 64, 261.

18. Lenin, *MEC*, p. 262.

19. Ibid., pp. 260–1.

20. Ibid., p. 261.

21. B. Russell, *Our Knowledge of the External World*, p. 112.

22. Locke, *An Essay Concerning Human Understanding*, book ii, ch. xxiii, 1–4.

23. Cf. J. S. Mill, *An Examination of Sir William Hamilton's Philosophy*, vol. i, p. 33.

24. It is sometimes said that Lenin managed to undermine phenomenalism seriously by his criticism that it implied the denial of the well-attested fact that the world existed prior to the appearance of life (H. B. Acton, *The Illusion of the Epoch*, pp. 31 ff.). This argument is used by Lenin but it was not his own. He himself said that he found it in Feuerbach, Avenarius, J. Petzoldt, and R. Willy (*MEC*, pp. 75, 84). Lenin was very careful not to commit himself to the view that the criticism in question applied to Mach's 'doctrine of elements', since in fact it does not.

25. See, e.g., E. Mach, *The Science of Mechanics*, pp. 579, 611.

26. E. Mach, *The Analysis of Sensations*, p. 332. The law which was to replace the concept of matter was the proposition that matter is a relatively constant combination of the elements dependent on one another according to laws.

27. Cf. Ph. G. Frank, *Modern Science and Its Philosophy*, p. 76.

28. Lenin returned to this objection frequently as if he were aware of its strength and of the inadequacy of his own counter-arguments. See *MEC*,

pp. 63, 106, 116, 128, 164. Lenin seems to have believed that it was inconsistent, on the one hand, to assert that there are trees, stones, tables, or stars in the universe and, on the other, to deny that there is such a thing as matter.

29. Lenin, *MEC*, pp. 83–84. Lenin asserted that to subscribe to this view is only to agree with Feuerbach, Marx, and Engels that nature exists prior to man. Cf. Plekhanov, *FNLF*, p. 519.

30. Lenin, *MEC*, p. 130.

31. Ibid., p. 146.

32. Ibid., p. 267.

33. Holbach, *Système de la nature*, tome ii, pp. 90, 95.

34. *The Principles of Human Knowledge*, § 56, *The Works of George Berkeley*, vol. ii, pp. 64–65.

35. Locke, *An Essay Concerning Human Understanding*, book ii, ch. i; book iv, ch. ix, 1–3.

36. Lenin, *MEC*, p. 55.

37. Ibid., p. 292.

38. Ibid., pp. 111–12.

39. Ibid., pp. 42, 84, 130, 323.

40. Ibid., pp. 69–70, 253.

41. Ibid., pp. 175, 269.

42. Kant, *Critique of Pure Reason*, p. 286.

43. Jordan, *PHI*, pp. 322–40.

44. Lenin, *MEC*, pp. 45, 61, 67, 69, 74.

45. Ibid., p. 145.

46. Ibid., pp. 63, 277.

47. C. B. Mast, 'Matter and Energy in Scientific Theory', p. 595.

48. *The Principles of Human Knowledge*, § 37, *The Works of George Berkeley*, vol. ii, p. 56.

49. Lenin, *MEC*, pp. 129, 175, 261–2, 281.

50. B. Russell, *An Outline of Philosophy*, p. 304; H. Margenau, *Open Vistas*, p. 127.

51. For a survey and logical analysis of these interpretations see Ph. G. Frank, *Modern Science and Its Philosophy*, chs. 5 and 10.

52. Lenin, *MEC*, pp. 129–30, 185.

53. *The Principles of Human Knowledge*, § 17, § 80, *The Works of George Berkeley*, vol. ii, pp. 47–48, 75.

54. Lenin, *MEC*, pp. 130–1.

55. See H. Eilstein, 'Leninowskie pojęcie materii a idealizm fizyczny', pp. 184–91.

56. Plekhanov, *DMH*, p. 545. Cf. *EHM*, pp. 189–93.

57. Lenin, 'Ten Questions to a Lecturer', *CW* 14, p. 15; *MEC*, pp. 32, 147.

58. Lenin, *MEC*, pp. 335–6.

59. Lenin, 'Critical Remarks on the National Question', *CW* 20, pp. 224–6.

60. Lenin, *WIBD*, p. 384; 'The Historical Destiny of the Doctrine of Karl Marx', *CW* 18, p. 583.

61. Lenin, *MEC*, pp. 339, 344; 'Twenty-Fifth Anniversary of the Death of Joseph Dietzgen', *CW* 19, p. 80; *KMX*, p. 52.

62. Lenin, 'An Estimate of Marx by International Liberalism', *CW* 13, p. 493.

63. Lenin, *MEC*, p. 338.

64. Ibid., p. 339; cf. *KMX*, p. 52.

65. Lenin, *MEC*, pp. 336, 339, 341–2.

66. Lenin, *WFPA*, pp. 164, 183.

67. Ibid., pp. 163–4.

68. Lenin, *PHN*, pp. 222, 363.

69. Ibid., pp. 221–3, 359–63.

70. Ibid., p. 223.

71. Ibid., p. 359.

72. Ibid., pp. 253–4.

73. Ibid., pp. 97, 109, 221–2, 260.

74. Lenin, 'The Attitude of the Workers' Party Towards Religion', *CW* 15, p. 406.

75. Lenin, *PHN*, p. 284.

76. Ibid., p. 280.

77. Ibid., pp. 359–60.

78. Ibid., pp. 141, 143.

79. Ibid., p. 141.

80. Ibid., p. 360.

81. Lenin, 'Differences in the European Labour Movement', *CW* 16, p. 348.

82. Lenin, *MEC*, pp. 261–2; *PHN*, pp. 97, 109, 221, 283, 360.

83. Lenin, *KMX*, p. 54.

84. Lenin, *MEC*, pp. 129–30.

85. Ibid., p. 110. Recently, Lenin's claim has been questioned and rejected by some Marxist–Leninist scholars in Poland. See Z. Cackowski, *Treść poznawcza wrażeń zmysłowych*, part ii, ch. 1.

86. Jordan, *PHI*, pp. 326–40.

87. Engels, *AD*, p. 12.

88. Ibid., p. 17.

89. When Engels spoke of Dühring's 'lame attempt to make the Hegelian categories usable in the philosophy of reality' (*AD*, p. 85) he did not object to the attempt itself but to its inadequacy.

90. Engels, *LF*, p. 328. A similar statement by Marx, formulated in even stronger terms, is to be found in *Capital*, vol. i, p. 20.

91. Lenin, *MEC*, pp. 131–7.

92. K. R. Popper, *Conjectures and Refutations*, p. 101.

93. L. Trotsky, *The History of the Russian Revolution*, vol. iii, pp. 125–6; M. Eastman, *Marx and Lenin*, pp. 149, 256.

94. L. Trotsky, *Lenin*, p. 103. A striking and very similar portrait of Lenin is to be found in N. Berdyaev, *The Origin of Russian Communism*, pp. 114–29. That writers as different as Trotsky and Berdyaev should see Lenin in very much the same way is a persuasive evidence of the accuracy of their portraits from memory.

95. Lenin, *MEC*, p. 358.

96. Lenin, 'The Three Sources and Three Component Parts of Marxism', *CW* 19, p. 23.

97. Lenin, *WIBD*, p. 384.

98. Lenin, *MEC*, p. 344; 'On the Significance of Militant Materialism', *CW* 33, pp. 228–9.

99. Lenin, *The Economic Content of Narodism, CW* 1, p. 401.

100. Lenin, *WFPA*, pp. 327–8; 'Our Programme', *CW* 4, p. 211; 'Preface to the Russian Translation of Karl Marx's Letters to Dr. Kugelmann', *CW* 12, pp. 107–8.

101. Lenin, *PHN*, p. 360.

102. É. Gilson, *God and Philosophy*, p. 108.

103. Engels, *AD*, p. 435; cf. *LF*, pp. 360–2, and *DN*, p. 238 where the same problem is discussed on a broader social and historical basis.

104. L. Feuerbach, *The Essence of Christianity*, p. 26.

105. Lenin, 'The Attitude of the Workers' Party Towards Religion', *CW* 15, p. 402.

106. Ibid., pp. 405–6.

107. Lenin, 'Socialism and Religion', *CW* 10, p. 86.

108. L. Feuerbach, *The Essence of Christianity*, p. 73.

109. Marx, *KHR, MEGA* 1/1/1, p. 607.

110. It is true that Marx accused Christianity of defending the oppression of the proletariat (see, e.g., 'Der Kommunismus des *Rheinischen Beobachters*', *MEGA* 1/6, in particular p. 278), but such polemical sorties do not represent the main line of Marx's thinking about religion.

111. Marx, *KHR, MEGA* 1/1/1, pp. 614–15. For a more detailed analysis of the political sources of Marx's atheism see M. Reding, *Der politische Atheismus*, pp. 171–4.

112. Lenin, 'The Attitude of the Workers' Party Towards Religion', *CW* 15, p. 406.

113. Lenin, 'Socialism and Religion', *CW* 10, p. 83.

114. Lenin's letter to Maxim Gorky written in November 1913, *CW* 35, p. 129.

115. Lenin, 'Political Agitation and "The Class Point of View"', *CW* 5, p. 338; 'Socialism and Religion', *CW* 10, pp. 83–84; 'The Attitude of the Workers' Party Towards Religion', *CW* 15, p. 403. The influence of Marx's atheism upon Lenin fell on fertile ground. In *The Russian Revolution* (pp. 20 ff.) Nicolas Berdyaev pointed out that atheism in Russia has, as a rule, social motives at its source and arose from the conflict between Christian beliefs and social injustice rather than from the conflict between religious faith and scientific knowledge.

116. Lenin, 'Socialism and Religion', *CW* 10, p. 84.

117. Lenin's letter to Maxim Gorky written in November 1913, *CW* 35, p. 128.

118. Lenin, *MEC*, pp. 348, 355, 358.

119. Bocheński emphasizes a different point, namely, that the belief in God and religious faith impose restrictions upon the freedom of action with respect to one's fellow men. Lenin was a social engineer and a man of

action who wanted, above all, to change society and the course of history. Since 'God would be a dangerous rival' and an obstruction to Lenin's design, he had to be rejected and denied. See *SDM*, pp. 33, 85.

120. See, e.g., Engels, *AD*, pp. 436–7; Lenin, 'The Attitude of the Workers' Party Towards Religion', *CW* 15, pp. 403–4.

121. F. C. Copleston, *Aquinas*, p. 123.

122. Descartes, *Principia Philosophiae* ii, ch. 36.

123. Locke, *An Essay Concerning Human Understanding*, book iv, ch. x, 10–12.

124. See, e.g., the debate between Bertrand Russell and Father F. C. Copleston in B. Russell, *Why I Am Not a Christian*, in particular pp. 152–3.

125. Holbach, *Système de la nature*, tome ii, p. 94.

126. M. Bunge, *Causality*, p. 176.

127. An object is unique if and only if there is at least one and at most one entity of its kind in existence.

128. Lenin has been praised for this piece of speculative philosophy up to today even by enlightened Marxist–Leninists. See, e.g., A. Schaff, 'Zasada sprzeczności w świetle logiki dialektycznej', pp. 342, 345.

129. Holbach, *Système de la nature*, tome ii, pp. 60–61.

130. For the definitions of methodological essentialism and of ultimate explanation, see Popper, *OS*, vol. i, p. 31; *Conjectures and Refutations*, p. 105.

131. Lenin, 'The Three Sources and Three Component Parts of Marxism', *CW* 19, p. 27.

132. N. Berdyaev, *The Origin of Russian Communism*, pp. 99, 148–50. Berdyaev, who like everybody else regarded Marx as the founder of dialectical materialism, made him responsible for having 'transferred the nature of thought and spirit to matter'.

133. N. O. Lossky, *History of Russian Philosophy*, pp. 372, 376.

134. The close resemblance between naturalistic theism and certain interpretations of dialectical materialism is the subject of J. Needham's Herbert Spencer Lecture at Oxford University, 1937 (J. Needham, *Time: The Refreshing River*, pp. 233 ff.).

Chapter VIII.   Stalin's Socio-Cosmic Conception of the Universe

1. See, e.g., J. M. Bocheński, *Contemporary European Philosophy*, pp. 41–71, where Stalin is examined as a prominent representative of the philosophy of matter side by side with Bertrand Russell, logical positivists and logical empiricists, analytical philosophers and philosophers of ordinary language. The rejection of the suggestion that Stalin should be passed over in silence does not imply a favourable evaluation of Stalin as a philosopher. See Section 3 of this chapter.

2. The first of the above-mentioned evaluations of *Dialectical and Historical Materialism* can be found, e.g., in G. A. Wetter, *Die Umkehrung Hegels*, p. 43. The second is implicitly accepted by H. B. Acton in his valuable study *The Illusion of the Epoch*.

3. S. Hook, *Reason, Social Myths and Democracy*, p. 183.

4. Wetter, *DM*, p. 212.

5. Konstantinov, *GMPH*, p. 119.

6. We should distinguish between a world outlook in the wide and narrow meaning of this expression. A world outlook in the first sense contains the totality of views on man's natural and social environment, that is, it includes philosophical beliefs, social and political conceptions, moral, aesthetic, scientific and other ideas. The core of every world outlook or a world outlook in the narrower sense is the philosophical beliefs.

7. See Rozental' and Yudin, *KSF*, the entry 'Worldview'.

8. Stalin, 'Interview Given to the First American Labour Delegation' (9 September 1927), *EL*, vol. i, p. 43.

9. In Rozental' and Yudin, *KSF*, there is a separate entry 'Marxist Philosophical Materialism'.

10. See, e.g., *MEC*, pp. 41, 261.

11. Lenin may also have made the distinction in order to emphasize the fact that he regarded the philosophy of Marx as a synthesis of the materialist tradition and the philosophy of Hegel.

12. Stalin seems to have referred to Engels's consistently held view that the whole diversity of physical processes can be 'resolved into variously differentiated forms of motion of matter, passing into one another according to definite laws' (Engels, *DN*, p. 40).

13. Stalin, *DHM*, pp. 575–7.

14. Lenin, *PHN*, p. 349; Stalin, *DHM*, p. 575.

15. Engels, *LF*, p. 337.

16. Marx, *MEGA* 1/3, pp. 125–6; *EPM*, pp. 113–14.

17. See, e.g., Lenin, *MEC*, pp. 261, 262, 269, 281. In *SDM* (p. 81) Bocheński argues that both Lenin and Stalin accepted the existence of material substance. The only statement in *DHM* which seems to support Bocheński's view, 'Matter is the subject of all changes' (p. 576), is an excerpt from *HF* (p. 173). In this particular passage of *HF* Marx described Hobbes's views on matter and not his own. Stalin did not quote Marx to enlist his authority in support of the belief in the existence of material substance.

18. Stalin only followed Lenin when he assumed that these metaphysical and epistemological issues were substantially identical. See Lenin, *MEC*, p. 260.

19. Stalin, *DHM*, pp. 575–6.

20. Bocheński, *SDM*, pp. 80, 83–85.

21. Lenin, *MEC*, pp. 86–94.

22. Lenin, *MEC*, pp. 46, 47; Stalin, *DHM*, p. 572. This is the supposition which ascribes to reality a multilevel structure and holds that reality consists of irreducible domains of phenomena. Bocheński recognizes that this supposition, which he calls *kategorialer Pluralismus*, is part of Lenin's and Stalin's dialectical materialism. See *SDM*, pp. 92–93.

23. Stalin, *DHM*, pp. 576–7.

24. Lenin, *PHN*, p. 182.

25. Lenin, *MEC*, p. 130.

26. Ibid., pp. 59, 61, 65. Lenin's assertion that his copy theory of perception was widely endorsed by scientists probably referred to Heinrich Hertz's

Introduction to *The Principles of Mechanics*. Lenin described Hertz as a scientist 'who has been intimidated by the professorial hue and cry against the "metaphysics" of materialism, but who nevertheless cannot overcome his instinctive conviction of the reality of the external world' (*MEC*, p. 284). It should be emphasized that Hertz's concept of symbols ('pictures', 'images') used in scientific discourse has nothing to do with Lenin's epistemology. Hertz's '*Bild*' is not Lenin's 'image', for Hertz used it in the sense which the word 'idea' had in the old English terminology and should be translated as 'concept' or better, perhaps, 'construct'.

27. Stalin, *DHM*, p. 578.

28. Lenin, *MEC*, p. 344.

29. Bocheński, *SDM*, p. 65; Wetter, *DM*, pp. 280–1. H. Ogiermann devoted a whole book, *Materialistische Dialektik*, to this puzzling order of inquiry and its various ramifications. A possible explanation of why Stalin departed from the logical order in his presentations of the two main parts of dialectical materialism will be considered later.

30. Engels, *AD*, p. 37.

31. Stalin, *DHM*, pp. 570–3.

32. Ibid., p. 580.

33. *KSF*, the entry 'Marxist Dialectical Method'.

34. Since Stalin's death the two laws are no longer listed among the laws of dialectics. The concepts of reciprocal connections and universal mutability, like those of matter, movement, time, space, quality, and quantity, contradiction, causality, necessity and some others, are treated as categories, that is, as 'the fundamental logical notions which reflect the most general and essential relationships and relations of things and phenomena'. See *KSF*, the entry 'Categories'; Konstantinov, *GMPH*, chs. vi and vii; Wetter, *DM*, pp. 366–71.

35. Stalin, *DHM*, p. 570.

36. Ibid.

37. Even in Poland, where the Marxist–Leninist philosophers have done much to eliminate the Hegelian survivals from dialectical materialism, efforts were made to salvage the law of the triad from complete oblivion. See W. Krajewski, 'O prawie negacji negacji czyli rozwoju po spirali'.

38. In this respect nothing has been changed since Stalin's death; the way in which the dialectical laws are now ordered follows the pattern of Engels and Stalin and not that of Lenin.

39. Cf. Wetter, *DM*, p. 311.

40. See M. Bunge, *Causality*, pp. 203–17, where the history of these two conceptions of evolution is traced and analysed.

41. There is no evidence to support the view that Engels extended his criticism of the mechanistic conception of change to Darwin's theory of evolution, which, surely, did not make use of the mechanistic, but of the non-mechanistic, pattern of change. In the Stalinist period, however, this was overlooked. Darwin, his successors, and present-day philosophers were all presented as representatives and defenders of the mechanistic conception of change.

42. Stalin, *DHM*, pp. 571, 573.

43. Stalin, *DHM*, p. 572.

44. Stalin, *Anarchism or Socialism?*, *Works* i, p. 304; *DHM*, pp. 571, 574–575, 593–4.

45. Stalin, *MPL*, p. 38.

46. Stalin, *EPS*, p. 59.

47. Stalin's revision of the theory of leaps continues to be recognized in the post-Stalinist period, without reference to Stalin's name. See Konstantinov, *GMPH*, pp. 268–70. It is ironic to observe that Lenin once described the rejection of the doctrine of leaps as a clear indication of revisionism or reformism ('Differences in the European Labour Movement', *CW* 16, pp. 348–9). But as soon as Lenin achieved power he ridiculed those who did not understand that 'by "leap" the teachers of Socialism meant changes in world history, and that leaps of this kind extended over periods of ten years and even more' ('The Immediate Tasks of the Soviet Government', *CW* 27, p. 273.).

48. Stalin, *DHM*, pp. 570, 572.

49. Stalin, *Foundations of Leninism*, *Works* vi, pp. 74–75. This is the sense in which Marx, and sometimes Engels too, used the expression 'contradiction' (see, e.g., Marx, *GI*, p. 74; *Frühschriften*, p. 392; *CPE*, p. 12; Engels, *AD*, p. 392). When Marx spoke of the contradiction between the productive forces and the relations of production he referred in metaphorical form to the conflicts between classes, battles of ideas or political struggles arising in a definite state of society from the imbalance between the productive forces and the relation of production. He never thought of any real contradiction *sensu stricto*, inherent in this state of society which actually produces conflicts, battles or struggles.

50. Stalin, *DHM*, p. 573.

51. Stalin was convinced on practical grounds that the construction of socialism required an increasing and not a decreasing use of power on the part of the state (*MPL*, pp. 64–66, 70–71). 'A classless society', he told the seventeenth congress of the Soviet Communist Party (1934), 'cannot come of its own accord.' It had to be built, of course, by the efforts of all working people, but these efforts would come to naught if they were not supported by 'strengthening the organs of the dictatorship of the proletariat, by eliminating the remnants of the capitalist classes, and in battles with enemies, both internal and external' (*Works* xiii, p. 357).

52. See, e.g., Bocheński, *SDM*, pp. 37–38; H. B. Acton, *The Illusion of the Epoch*, p. 271.

53. I. Deutscher, *Stalin*, p. 365. The unfavourable evaluation of Stalin as a philosopher is not inconsistent with the opinion discussed and endorsed in the opening paragraph of this chapter that Stalin should not be banned from the annals of contemporary philosophy.

54. Cf. Leites, 'Stalin as an Intellectual', pp. 46, 49, 52.

55. A. A. Zhdanov, *On Literature, Music and Philosophy*, p. 103.

56. Wetter, *DM*, pp. 290–1.

57. The description of the defeat of the two schools in Soviet philosophy is based on D. Joravsky, *Soviet Marxism and Natural Science*, chs. 15 and 17.

58. A. A. Zhdanov, *On Literature, Music and Philosophy*, pp. 83–84.

59. D. Joravsky, *Soviet Marxism and Natural Science*, pp. 257–8.

60. For details see Z. A. Jordan, 'The Philosophical Background of Revisionism in Poland', p. 277. Orthodoxy can be defined in this context as the support given to a doctrine which serves the interests of an organization and which substitutes the loyalty to an organization for the loyalty to truth. On the other hand, heresy results from an intellectual attitude which prompts the search for what is true irrespective of its effect for the interests of an organization or for the power and prestige of those in control of this organization.

61. Quoted by Wetter, *DM*, p. 290.

62. Stalin, *Foundations of Leninism, Works* vi, p. 88.

63. Marx, *MEGA* 1/3, p. 121; *EPM*, p. 109.

64. Marx, *KHR, MEGA* 1/1/1, p. 607.

65. Marx's letter to J. B. Schweitzer of 24 January 1865.

66. Engels, *MCPE*, p. 334.

67. Marx, *MEGA* 1/3, p. 116; *EPM*, p. 104.

68. Quoted by T. B. Bottomore and M. Rubel in the introduction to Karl Marx, *Selected Writings in Sociology and Social Philosophy*, p. 14, n. 2.

69. Marx, *MEGA* 1/3, p. 304; *HF*, p. 172.

70. Cf. Engels, *AD*, pp. 392–3, 411, where Engels deals with this problem in detail.

71. Marx, *MEGA* 1/3, p. 207; *HF*, p. 53.

72. Marx–Engels, *MEGA* 1/6, p. 554; *MCP*, pp. 56–59; Engels, *AD*, pp. 364–5.

73. Lenin, *WIBD*, p. 441.

74. Lenin, 'A Talk with Defenders of Economism', *CW* 5, p. 316.

75. Lenin, *WFPA*, p. 327.

76. Stalin, 'Report to the Seventeenth Congress of the CPSU (B)', *Works* xiii, pp. 357–8, 373–4.

77. A. Schopenhauer, *The World as Will and Idea*, vol. ii, pp. 442–3; *Sämtliche Werke*, Bd. 3, p. 253.

78. J. Dewey, *Freedom and Culture*, pp. 113–18.

79. For the distinction between the two types of social engineering see Popper, *OS*, vol. i, p. 162.

80. Comte, *SPP*, p. 130.

81. Engels, Preface to the German edition of *MCP* (1890), *SW* i, p. 30.

82. This view is to be found in Popper, *OS*, vol. 2, pp. 118–20. It might be interesting to note that Marx was charged with considering political action futile by Karl Heinzen in *Deutsche Brüsseler Zeitung* in 1847, where Marx's and Engels's replies to this charge were also published. See *MEGA* 1/6, pp. 282–327.

83. Marx's letter to F. Bolte of 23 November 1871; Marx's letter to T. Cuno of 24 January 1872.

84. Lenin, 'A Protest by Russian Social Democrats', *CW* 4, pp. 175–7; 'Anarchism and Socialism', *CW* 5, pp. 327–8.

85. Marx–Engels, *MEGA* 1/6, p. 534; *MCP*, p. 41; Marx, *Inaugural Address of the Working Men's International Association*, p. 347 (this particular passage has sometimes been misread completely). Engels also commented

favourably on the Ten Hours' Bill as well as on the successes of the French, German, and English workers in Parliamentary elections and considered these developments as important stages in the emancipation of the working class. Neither Marx nor Engels did in fact endorse the doctrine of the impotence of politics. See Engels, Introduction to *CSF*, pp. 124–5; Preface to the English edition of *CWC*, pp. 31–32.

86. Marx, *Capital*, vol. i, p. 302.

87. Ibid., p. 751.

88. Marx, 'Kritische Randglossen zu dem Artikel: "Der König von Preussen und die Sozialreform. Von einem Preussen"', *MEGA* 1/3, p. 22.

89. Marx, *MEGA* 1/6, p. 228; *PPH*, p. 147. Cf. Marx's letter to F. Bolte of 23 November 1871.

90. Engels's letter to C. Schmidt of 27 October 1890.

91. Marx–Engels, *MEGA* 1/6, p. 553; *MCP*, p. 57.

92. Marx, 'Kritische Randglossen zu dem Artikel: "Der König von Preussen und die Sozialreform. Von einem Preussen"', *MEGA* 1/3, p. 16.

93. Marx, *Capital*, vol. i, p. 80; 'Die moralisierende Kritik und die kritisierende Moral. Beitrag zur deutschen Kulturgeschichte. Gegen Carl Heinzen', *MEGA* 1/6, p. 306.

94. See N. Bukharin, *Historical Materialism*, pp. 262 ff., where in the spirit of Marx he argued against Stalin that no power is unlimited and no force can transcend its own bounds and reached the conclusion that 'the alteration in the economic conditions that may be attained with the aid of the political lever is itself dependent on the previous state of the economic conditions' (pp. 264–5).

95. I. Deutscher, *Stalin*, p. 344.

96. Bocheński, *SDM*, p. 33, 112.

97. For a contrary opinion see W. Sombart, *Der proletarische Sozialismus*, Bd. 1, p. 378.

98. Stalin, *MPL*, p. 39.

99. A. G. Meyer, *Leninism*, p. 45.

100. A. G. Meyer argues that the need of strategy and tactics arose together with Lenin's loss of faith in the imminent breakdown of capitalism and in the spontaneous revolutionary development of the working classes. The seeds of Leninism should, therefore, be sought in Lenin's pessimism about the inevitable advent of socialism. See A. G. Meyer, *Leninism*, pp. 84–85.

101. Lenin, *WIBD*, pp. 446, 447.

102. Stalin, *Foundations of Leninism*, *Works* vi, p. 73.

103. Stalin, 'Report to the Seventeenth Congress of the CPSU (B)', *Works* xiii, p. 374. H. B. Mayo provides no evidence in support of his sweeping assertion in *Introduction to Marxist Theory*, p. 134, that Marx and Engels would have had no quarrel with Lenin's views about the necessity of bringing class consciousness to the working class 'from without, for they held much the same sentiments'. The point to be stressed is exactly the fundamental difference dividing Lenin from Marx in this respect.

104. Lenin, 'A Talk with Defenders of Economism', *CW* 5, pp. 313–15.

105. R. V. Daniels, 'Fate and Will in the Marxian Philosophy of History',

p. 548; S. H. Baron, *Plekhanov*, pp. 244–53, 347–8. For the references to Bukharin see note 94 above. Lenin reciprocated Plekhanov's allegations and accused him of 'hidden hypocrisy and shameful spinelessness' which compared unfavourably with the open hostility to revolution showed by its honest enemies.

106. Stalin, *Foundations of Leninism*, *Works* vi, p. 91.

107. Ibid., pp. 91, 195–6.

108. Lenin, *WIBD*, p. 393.

109. Engels, *AD*, pp. 156–7, 385–6, 390–1. Cf. Engels, *MEGA* 1/2, pp. 394–5; *Outlines of a Critique of Political Economy*, pp. 194–6.

110. Engels, *DN*, pp. 48–49.

111. See, e.g., Engels, *DN*, pp. 304–6.

112. Stalin, *EPS*, pp. 5–12.

113. Ibid., p. 13. That Stalin's acceptance of 'restraints and limitations upon action even under socialism' was due to his apprehension that otherwise Soviet planners would appear 'more responsible for chronic shortages than they really are' (Leites, 'Stalin as an Intellectual', p. 51) is a critical observation which scores a debating point rather than providing an explanation of the issues involved.

114. Stalin, *DHM*, p. 579.

115. Ibid., p. 569.

116. Stalin, *Anarchism or Socialism?*, *Works* i, p. 300.

117. Wetter, *DM*, p. 263, where *Dialectical Materialism* is quoted, and *FML*, pp. 146–7.

118. *KSF*, the entry 'Dialectical Materialism'.

119. Stalin, *DHM*, p. 573.

120. Engels, *LF*, p. 328.

121. Stalin, *DHM*, p. 574.

122. Popper, *OS*, vol. ii, p. 41.

123. Engels, *SUS*, p. 108.

124. Stalin, *DHM*, p. 574.

125. Ibid., pp. 574–5.

126. Ibid., p. 575.

127. Ibid., p. 578.

128. Jordan, *PHI*, pp. 483–5.

PART THREE

Chapter IX. Marx's Philosophy of History

1. See, e.g., Bocheński, *SDM*, p. 103; R. N. C. Hunt, *The Theory and Practice of Communism*, p. 61; J. Witt-Hansen, *Historical Materialism*, pp. 46 ff. A. L. Harris suggested that the expressions 'dialectical materialism', 'materialist conception of history', and 'economic interpretation of history' are in fact synonymous and, consequently, interchangeable. See A. L. Harris, 'The Social Philosophy of Karl Marx', p. 6.

2. K. Korsch, *Karl Marx*, p. 167.

3. G. Gurvitch, *La Vocation actuelle de la sociologie*, tome ii, p. 322 ; T. B. Bottomore and M. Rubel, *Karl Marx: Selected Writings in Sociology and Social Philosophy*, p. 23.

4. Marx, *MEGA* 1/3, pp. 250–1 ; *HF*, pp. 107, 125 ; *MEGA* 1/6, p. 197 ; *PPH*, pp. 112–13.

5. *Capital*, vol. i, p. 180 n.

6. After Marx's death Engels recognized the possibility that historical materialism might not be a hypothesis of universal validity, that it does not apply fully, for example, to primitive societies. See Engels, *The Origin of the Family, Private Property and the State*, p. 156 ; Engels's letter to C. Schmidt of 27 October 1890. Other restrictive or qualifying limitations upon the universal validity of historical materialism were formulated by K. Kautsky, *Ethik und materialistische Geschichtsauffassung*, pp. 112–17.

7. Engels recognized that the works of Marx written before and after the publication of *A Contribution to the Critique of Political Economy* in 1859 differ in some important points. He explained that in the forties Marx had not yet finished his critique of political economy and what he had then written 'contains expressions and whole sentences which from the point of view of the latter works appear unfortunate and even incorrect'. According to Engels, the earlier and the later point of view represent two stages of the intellectual development of the author, the later stage being more mature and an improvement upon the earlier one. See Engels's Introduction to *WLC*, pp. 66–67.

8. J. Plamenatz (*Man and Society*, vol. ii, p. 269) seems to favour the other extreme position which is mentioned above.

9. Marx, *MEGA* 1/6, p. 184 ; *PPH*, p. 98.

10. Marx, *GI*, p. 7 ; *Frühschriften*, p. 347.

11. Marx, *GI*, pp. 28–31 ; *Frühschriften*, pp. 367–70 ; *MEGA* 1/6, pp. 179–80 ; *PPH*, pp. 92–93.

12. Marx, *EBLB*, p. 225. Some writers infer from this statement that according to Marx man makes history and history makes man and you can choose as you please, depending on personal preference, political requirements, and the changing intellectual fashion. See Daniels, 'Fate and Will in the Marxian Philosophy of History', p. 546. Marx's statement does not carry this equivocal meaning at all.

13. Marx, *GI*, pp. 13–16 ; *Frühschriften*, pp. 347–50.

14. M. Bunge, *Causality*, p. 185.

15. Marx, *MEGA* 1/3, p. 123 ; *EPM*, p. 111.

16. *MEGA* 1/6, pp. 543–4 ; *MCP*, p. 49.

17. H. B. Acton, *The Illusion of the Epoch*, p. 143 ; cf. R. N. C. Hunt, *The Theory and Practice of Communism*, p. 75.

18. See S. Ossowski, *Class Structure in the Social Consciousness*, pp. 75–84.

19. Marx, *MEGA* 1/6, p. 227 ; *PPH*, p. 147 ; *MEGA* 1/6, p. 546 ; *MCP*, p. 51.

20. Marx, *CSF*, pp. 128–9, 216 ; *EBLB*, p. 247.

21. *Capital*, vol. i, pp. 8, 10, 17.

22. Ibid., p. 18.

23. Ibid., pp. 269–70.

24. Ibid., pp. 270, 592. For the concept of sociological determinism in Marx see Jordan, *PHI*, pp. 133–4.

25. *Capital*, vol. i, p. 18. According to Marx, all social laws vary from one formation to another. Marx criticized Malthus's law on the ground that 'every special mode of production has its own special laws of population, historically valid within its limits alone'. A law of population which would be a strictly universal statement could apply exclusively to plants and animals and only so far as man has not interfered with them. See *Capital*, vol. i, pp. 630–2. Marx's views on social laws seems to imply that in his opinion social laws can be changed by man, in a sense in which natural laws cannot be altered, and that men can initiate new regularities in human affairs by their activity functioning as antecedent conditions for subsequent developments.

26. Plekhanov, *DMH*, pp. 732–3; Marx, *Capital*, vol. i, pp. 71–72.

27. Engels, *KM*, p. 149; cf. H. B. Acton, *The Illusion of the Epoch*, pp. 160–6.

28. See note 25 above and *Capital*, vol. iii, p. 856.

29. Engels, *SGM*, p. 153; cf. Preface to the German (1883) and Preface to the English edition of *MCP*, *SW* i, pp. 24, 28.

30. Marx, *Capital*, vol. i, pp. 8–9.

31. J. Witt-Hansen, *Historical Materialism*, p. 63.

32. K. R. Popper, *The Poverty of Historicism*, pp. 108–9; cf. I. Berlin, *Karl Marx*, pp. 122–3.

33. Popper, *OS*, vol. ii, pp. 83–84.

34. *MEGA* 1/6, p. 538; *MCP*, p. 44.

35. Marx's letter to P. V. Annenkov of 28 December 1846.

36. Marx, *MEGA* 1/6, p. 191; *PPH*, p. 116; cf. *CSF*, p. 203.

37. Marx's letter to J. B. Schweitzer of 24 January 1865.

38. Engels, *SUS*, p. 126.

39. Marx's letter to F. A. Sorge of 19 October 1877.

40. Harris, 'The Social Philosophy of Karl Marx', p. 5.

41. Marx, *WPP*, p. 384; Marx's letter to L. Kugelmann of 11 July 1868; *Capital*, vol. i, p. 316; vol. iii, p. 797.

42. Cf. Popper, *OS*, vol. ii, pp. 107, 177. R. C. Tucker argues that the Marxian differentiation between the appearance and essence of social phenomena corresponds to the Hegelian distinction between the esoteric and exoteric history in which Marx substituted men of flesh and blood for Hegel's absolute spirit (R. C. Tucker, 'Marxism — Is it Religion?', pp. 125–6). The Marxian differentiation had a long philosophical tradition and to reduce it to Hegel alone would be an unjustifiable simplification.

43. Marx, *GI*, p. 13; *Frühschriften*, p. 348; *EBLB*, p. 247.

44. Cf. Popper, *OS*, vol. ii, pp. 265–9.

45. Engels's letter to H. Starkenburg of 25 January 1894.

46. Engels, *LF*, p. 363.

47. Engels, *SUS*, p. 125.

48. Engels, *HCL*, p. 312.

Chapter X.   The Sociological Approach of Engels

1. Engels, *HCL*, p. 311.
2. Engels refers to *KHR*, which, of course, should be evaluated, as Marx himself insisted in the Preface to *CPE*, together with *Kritik der Hegelschen Staatsphilosophie*.   According to Riazanov (*MEGA* 1/1/1, p. 402) the latter was written in March 1843 at the earliest, but Siegfried Landshut, the editor of Marx's *Frühschriften*, believes that this *terminus a quo* should be shifted back to 1841/2.
3. Engels, *HCL*, pp. 311–12.
4. Marx, *CPE*, p. 13; *Werke*, Bd. 19, p. 181.
5. Engels, *AD*, p. 40; *SUS*, p. 123, *LF*, pp. 340, 353.
6. Comte, *SPP*, pp. 74–76.
7. Engels, *SUS*, p. 123.   Engels's interpretation is accepted by social historians, although the revolutionary *canuts* of Lyons were craftsmen and small masters rather than proletarians in Engels's sense.   See E. J. Hobsbawm, *The Age of Revolution: 1789–1848*, pp. 150 ff.
8. Engels, *LF*, p. 356; Introduction to *CSF*, *SW* i, p. 115.
9. Cf. G. Lichtheim, *Marxism*, pp. 58–61, where the basic difference in Marx's and Engels's approach to the problems of social change is strongly emphasized.   Lichtheim seems to regard Engels's empirical and positivistic approach, however, as much inferior to Marx's Hegelian view of the historical process.
10. Engels, Preface to the third German edition of *EBLB*, *SW* i, pp. 223–224; *HQ*, p. 563.
11. Popper, *OS*, vol. ii, p. 101.
12. Engels, Special Introduction to the English edition of *SUS*, p. 94; *KM*, p. 149; *The Origin of the Family, Private Property and the State*, p. 155; Engels's letter to C. Schmidt of 5 August 1890, and J. Bloch of 21–22 September 1890.
13. Engels, Preface to the third German edition of *EBLB*, *SW* i, p. 223; Engels's letter to J. Bloch of 21–22 September 1890.
14. Engels, Preface to the third German edition of *EBLB*, pp. 223–4; *SGM*, p. 153; *LF*, p. 354; Engels's letter to J. Bloch of 21–22 September 1890.
15. Engels, *HQ*, p. 563.
16. Engels, Introduction to *CSF*, *SW* i, pp. 109–10.
17. Engels, *AD*, p. 367.
18. Engels's letter to J. Bloch of 21–22 September 1890, and to F. Mehring of 14 July 1893.   When John Plamenatz writes that Marx and Engels wanted 'to divide social activities into two main kinds, the economic and the rest, saying that the first kind determines the second' (*Man and Society*, vol. ii, p. 292), he once again ascribes to Marx and Engels a theory which Engels was so anxious to correct.
19. E. Bernstein, *Evolutionary Socialism*, p. 11.   Perhaps because of Bernstein's own revisions of the Marxian doctrine, his assertion concerning Engels's revision of the original materialist conception of history was openly

rejected as a pure invention by the representatives of 'orthodox' German Marxism. They accepted, however, the substance of Bernstein's views on the matter, that is, they accepted Engels's exposition and Bernstein's observations as Marx's own original views. See K. Kelles-Krauz, *Pisma wybrane*, tom i, pp. 110–12; Plekhanov, *FPM*, pp. 53–59; Cunow, *Die Marxsche Geschichts-, Gesellschafts- und Staatstheorie*, Bd. 2, pp. 254–60.

20. Engels's letter to J. Bloch of 21–22 September 1890, and to F. Mehring of 14 July 1893.

21. Engels's letter to J. Bloch of 21–22 September 1890 and to C. Schmidt of 27 October 1890.

22. Engels, *LF*, pp. 359, 362.

23. Engels's letter to J. Bloch of 21–22 September 1890, and to H. Starkenburg of 25 January 1894. Cf. Engels's letter to C. Schmidt of 5 August 1890.

24. Engels's letter to J. Bloch of 21–22 September 1890, to C. Schmidt of 27 October 1890, and to H. Starkenburg of 25 January 1894.

25. This charge can be found, e.g., in John Dewey, *Freedom and Culture*, p. 77, and in H. B. Acton, *The Illusion of the Epoch*, pp. 159–60.

26. Engels's letter to C. Schmidt of 27 October 1890, and to H. Starkenburg of 25 January 1894.

27. Engels's letter to H. Starkenburg of 25 January 1894.

28. Engels, *MCPE*, p. 334.

29. Ibid., p. 335.

30. Engels's letter to C. Schmidt of 5 August 1890.

31. Engels, *PWG*, p. 16; *SUS*, pp. 124–5; *LF*, pp. 362–3.

32. Engels, *LF*, p. 357.

33. Engels, *KM*, p. 149.

34. Marx, *GI*, p. 16; *Frühschriften*, p. 354; Marx's letter to L. Kugelmann of 11 July 1868.

35. Engels, *DN*, pp. 46–49.

36. Engels, *SGM*, p. 153.

37. See B. Malinowski, *A Scientific Theory of Culture*, ch. viii.

38. Engels, *KM*, p. 150.

39. Engels, *LF*, pp. 354, 356; Engels's letter to H. Starkenburg of 25 January 1894.

40. Engels, *SUS*, p. 124.

41. Engels, *LF*, p. 338.

42. Engels, *AD*, p. 41.

43. Ibid., p. 17.

Chapter XI. Plekhanov's Unification of Dialectical and Historical Materialism

1. Plekhanov, *DMH*, p. 751.

2. In spite of his great admiration for Hegel, Plekhanov did not endorse the widely accepted opinion according to which the sociological evolutionism of Marx was merely an adaptation of the Hegelian view of world history.

3. Plekhanov, *DMH*, pp. 725, 727.

4. Ibid., pp. 653–4. Plekhanov refers to *MEGA* 1/6, p. 482 (*WLC*, pp. 83–84), in support of this interpretation.

5. Plekhanov, *DMH*, p. 740.

6. Ibid., pp. 544–57.

7. Ibid., pp. 558–71.

8. Ibid., p. 632; cf. *SAHD*, p. 474. Plekhanov failed to notice that Hegel was taking advantage of Kant's definition of nature 'as the existence of things as far as it is determined according to universal law' (*Prologomena to Any Future Metaphysics*, § 14).

9. Plekhanov, *DMH*, pp. 637–8.

10. Feuerbach, *GPHZ*, §§ 55, 59, pp. 343–4.

11. Plekhanov, *DMH*, p. 652.

12. Marx was aware that the search for a transcendental end is a distinctive characteristic of the philosophy of history. Hegel's conception of history, he wrote, is constructed around the idea that 'a speculative, esoteric history' is unfolding itself within 'an empirical, exoteric history' and, consequently, 'the history of mankind becomes the history of the abstract spirit of mankind, a spirit transcending all real men (die Geschichte der Menschheit vervandelt sich in die Geschichte des abstrakten, daher dem wirklichen Menschen jenseitigen Geistes der Menschheit)' (*MEGA* 1/3, p. 257; *HF*, p. 115).

13. Plekhanov, *FPM*, p. 24.

14. Ibid., pp. 55, 56, 57.

15. For details see Jordan, *PHI*, pp. 56–58.

16. Plekhanov, *SAHD*, p. 478.

17. Plekhanov, *FPM*, p. 72.

18. Plekhanov, *DMH*, pp. 658, 739, 783–4; *FPM*, pp. 41–42.

19. Plekhanov, *FPM*, p. 34; *SAHD*, pp. 469–71; *DMH*, pp. 655–8. For Hegel's views concerning the 'geographical basis of history', see *PHH*, pp. 79 ff.

20. Plekhanov, *FPM*, pp. 36, 52.

21. Plekhanov, *DMH*, p. 760.

22. Ibid., pp. 655–6, 661.

23. Plekhanov, *FPM*, pp. 53–54; *DMH*, p. 688.

24. Plekhanov, *DMH*, p. 690; cf. *FPM*, p. 72.

25. Marx, *EBLB*, p. 247.

26. Plekhanov, *DMH*, pp. 700–2; *FPM*, pp. 60–64, 73–74; cf. Baron, *Plekhanov*, pp. 308–13.

27. *Capital*, vol. i, p. 19.

28. Engels, *LF*, p. 341.

29. Plekhanov, *DMH*, p. 694; cf. p. 691.

30. Plekhanov, *FPM*, p. 73.

31. Ibid., pp. 72–73; *DMH*, pp. 689, 720.

32. Cf. Cunow, *Die Marxsche Geschichts-, Gesellschafts- und Staatstheorie*, Bd. 2, p. 200.

33. Plekhanov, *FPM*, pp. 53–59, 72–76; *DMH*, pp. 689, 694–5, 711–12, 714.

34. Plekhanov, *DMH*, pp. 723–7.
35. Plekhanov, *FPM*, p. 80; *DMH*, p. 731.
36. Plekhanov, *DMH*, pp. 719, 726.
37. Ibid., p. 723.
38. Plekhanov, *SAHD*, p. 477.
39. Plekhanov, *DMH*, pp. 688, 708–10, 712–14; *FPM*, p. 50.
40. Plekhanov, *DMH*, pp. 689, 714.
41. Plekhanov, *FPM*, p. 21. The aphorism of Feuerbach to which Plekhanov refers is to be found in *VTRPH*, p. 263.
42. Plekhanov, *FPM*, p. 59.
43. Plekhanov, *DMH*, pp. 638, 681; *FPM*, pp. 58–59.
44. Comte, *SPP*, pp. 75, 93.
45. Plekhanov, *FPM*, p. 92; cf. *DMH*, p. 638.
46. Plekhanov, *SAHD*, p. 479.
47. Plekhanov, *FPM*, pp. 81, 84.
48. Lenin, 'Marxism and Revisionism', *CW* 15, p. 31.
49. Lenin, *WFPA*, p. 161.
50. Plekhanov, *FPM*, p. 2.

Chapter XII. Historical Materialism as a Guide to Action

1. Lenin, 'The Three Sources and Three Component Parts of Marxism', *CW* 15, p. 23; Stalin, *EPS*, p. 65.
2. Marx's letter to the editor of *Notes on the Fatherland* (*Otechestvenniye Zapiski*), written towards the end of 1877 (Marx–Engels, *Selected Correspondence*, p. 379).
3. Lenin, *WFPA*, p. 159. For the discussion of the view that human action may be both causally determined and free see M. Schlick, *Problems of Ethics*, ch. vii.
4. Lenin, *WFPA*, pp. 142, 151; *KMX*, p. 57.
5. This is Marx's own definition of the duty of the Communist Party towards the working class. See *MEGA* 1/3, p. 207; *HF*, p. 53; *MEGA* 1/6, p. 534; *MCP*, p. 41.
6. A. G. Meyer, *Leninism*, p. 85; cf. Lenin, 'Marxism and Insurrection', *CW* 26, pp. 22–27, where Lenin's purely pragmatic and technical approach to the problem of revolution is so very apparent.
7. Marx, 'Kritische Randglossen zu dem Artikel: "Der König von Preussen und die Sozialreform. Von einem Preussen"', *MEGA* 1/3, p. 20.
8. Plekhanov, *SPS*, p. 70; *OD*, p. 136.
9. Marx's statement at the meeting of the London Central Committee of the Communist League, 15 September, 1850, quoted by Marx in *Enthüllungen über den Kommunistenprozess zu Köln*, (1853), Marx and Engels, *Selected Correspondence 1846–1895*, p. 92.
10. Engels's letter to Marx of 13 February 1851; Engels, 'On Social Relations in Russia', p. 55.

11. Lenin, *WFPA*, p. 142.

12. Lenin, 'Our Programme', *CW* 4, pp. 211–12. Cf. 'Certain Features of the Historical Development of Marxism', *CW* 17, pp. 39–44, where the well-known statement about the teaching of Marx and Engels not being a dogma but a guide to action is to be found.

13. Lenin, *WFPA*, p. 140.

14. Ibid., pp. 139–41.

15. Ibid., pp. 142, 146.

16. Lenin, *PHN*, pp. 189, 307–14.

17. Lenin, 'The Three Sources and Three Component Parts of Marxism', *CW* 19, p. 25.

18. Lenin, *KMX*, pp. 55–57.

19. Lenin, 'Frederick Engels', *CW* 2, p. 21.

20. Lenin, *KMX*, pp. 55, 56.

21. Lenin, *MEC*, p. 323.

22. Lenin, 'The Three Sources and Three Component Parts of Marxism', *CW* 19, p. 25.

23. Lenin, *MEC*, p. 326.

24. Ibid., pp. 329–30.

25. *GMPH*, pp. 381, 384–5.

26. See H. Eilstein, *Jedność materialna świata*, pp. 196–7, which is a striking exception to the rule stated above.

27. Stalin, *DHM*, pp. 577–8; cf. pp. 569, 573.

28. Ibid., pp. 578–9.

29. Ibid., pp. 580–1.

30. Lenin, *MEC*, p. 325.

31. Stalin, *DHM*, pp. 580–1.

32. Stalin, *MPL*, p. 9. For the far-reaching implications of the revised version of historical materialism see Jordan, *PHI*, pp. 475–86.

33. Stalin, *DHM*, p. 592.

34. Ibid., p. 580.

35. Ibid., p. 594.

36. In *EPS*, Stalin maintained that the Soviet government successfully accomplished the construction of a socialist economy because it relied on economic laws and intelligently applied them to the task at hand (pp. 9–10). But at the time Stalin presented the issue in entirely different terms. The fundamental task of the First Five-Year Plan was not to 'shorten and lessen the birth-pangs' of the new society, but to secure its survival in a hostile world and the question was 'either perish or overtake the advanced countries economically'. Similarly, the success of the Plan was not due to its compliance with economic laws but to 'the activity and devotion, the enthusiasm and initiative of the vast masses of the workers and collective farmers', to 'the firm leadership of the Party', and to 'the colossal potentialities' of the Soviet system (Stalin, *Works* xiii, pp. 176, 218). Thus, the success of the Plan was to be explained by the competence of the leadership and its skilful use of psychological factors.

37. R. V. Daniels, 'Fate and Will in the Marxian Philosophy of History', p. 550.

38. See Wetter, *DM*, pp. 226–30, where the evidence for Stalin's 'conservative tendency' is collected and analysed.

39. Stalin, *EPS*, pp. 7–8.

40. Stalin, *Foundations of Leninism, Works* vi, p. 88.

Chapter XIII.   *The Concept of Scientific Socialism*

1. See, e.g., Rozental' and Yudin, *KSF*, the entry 'Historical Materialism'.

2. For instance, Eduard Bernstein wrote that 'the theory of society worked out by Marx and Engels . . . [was] called by them "scientific socialism"' (*Evolutionary Socialism*, p. 1).

3. Marx seemed to have used the expression 'scientific socialism' only once or twice and in French, namely in the introduction to Engels's *Socialisme utopique et socialisme scientifique*, which he wrote in 1880 and which Lafargue edited and published under his own name the same year. See Marx–Engels, *Werke*, Bd. 19, p. 181. The other occurrence of the expression is to be found in the letter to F. A. Sorge of 5 November 1880, where Marx inserts it in its French formulation (*socialisme moderne scientifique*). The expression 'scientific socialism' occurs marginally in Engels (*HQ*, pp. 554; *PWG*, p. 32) and is used in its technical sense only in *Anti-Dühring* (pp. 281, 393, 411; *Werke*, Bd. 20, pp. 189, 265, 278).

4. P.-J. Proudhon, *Qu'est-ce que la Propriété?*, p. 339.

5. K. Grün, *Die soziale Bewegung in Frankreich und Belgien*, p. 82, and *GI*, p. 143. The other expressions are taken from *MEGA* 1/6, p. 550; *MCP*, p. 55.

6. *MEGA* 1/6, pp. 549–52, 554; *MCP*, pp. 54–56, 58–59; cf. Engels, *HCL*, p. 314; *LF*, p. 333, where more than forty years later Engels spoke of 'true socialism' with a similar and undiminished contempt.

7. See Engels's unpublished article 'Die wahren Sozialisten', written at the beginning of 1847, *MEGA* 1/6, pp. 33, 73; F. Mehring, *Karl Marx*, p. 112. Later in his life Marx recognized that he overestimated the significance of 'true socialists' who represented only a local, that is, a German, movement. See Marx's letter to Engels of 15 April 1869.

8. K. Grünberg, 'Der Ursprung der Worte Sozialismus und Sozialist', pp. 500–1, 506–7; G. D. H. Cole, *A History of Socialist Thought*, vol. i, pp. 1–2, 60. 'Socialism' made its first appearance in the French language in the Saint-Simonist periodical *Le Globe* in 1832, where it was used as the opposite of 'individualism' (while in English it was just a synonym of 'Owenism' or 'Social Reform', although it was believed that Owenism favoured the 'community of property'). In Polish, the author's native tongue, the word 'socialism' was first used by the Poles who escaped to France and England after the collapse of the Insurrection of 1830. In English, French, and Polish the word was the same but the concept was very different.

9. *MEGA* 1/6, pp. 553–5; *MCP*, pp. 58–60. According to G. D. H. Cole,

the term 'utopian socialists' was apparently first used by J. Blanqui in his *History of Political Economy* (1839), which was well known to Marx (he quoted it repeatedly in *Theories of Surplus-Value*). But Blanqui probably had it from L. Reybaud, who published three comprehensive studies, namely, 'Les Saint Simoniens', 'Charles Fourier', and 'Robert Owen' in the *Revue des Deux Mondes* of 1836–8. These three studies appeared in book form under the title *Les Socialistes modernes* in 1840.

10. L. Reybaud, *Études sur les réformateurs ou socialistes modernes*, tome ii, pp. 45–46.

11. Engels, *LF*, p. 328.

12. Engels, Preface to the 1888 English edition of *MCP*, *SW* i, p. 27; Introduction to *CSF*, *SW* i, p. 112.

13. Marx's letter to J. Weydemeyer of 1 February 1859.

14. This is true of the Saint-Simonists and also of the French Socialists and Utopian Communists. The leading 'Communists' in the 1848 revolution in France, Louis Blanc, Louis Auguste Blanqui, Étienne Cabet, François Raspail, were all middle-class professional men and intellectuals, and only Alexandre Martin (Albert) was a worker. See also Engels, Preface to the first German edition of *CWC*, p. 3.

15. The open educational society, associated with the secret *League of the Just*, founded by the German craftsmen in London in 1840, called itself *The Communist Workers' Educational Association* (*Kommunistischer Arbeiterbildungsverein*).

16. Engels, *CWC*, pp. 271–3; Preface to the 1888 English edition of *MCP*, *SW* i, p. 27. Cf. Preface to the 1890 German edition of *MCP*, *SW* i, pp. 30–31; *HCL*, pp. 309–11. In this connection it should be remembered that the original title of *The Communist Manifesto* was *The Manifesto of the Communist Party*. Its purpose was to present to the world the views and aims of a party that was no longer a conspiratorial secret society and, although numerically weak, was a working-class international movement dedicated to the realization of a revolutionary reconstruction of society. Engels's views about the differences between communism and socialism and about their respective reputation in the 1840s are confirmed by what Lorenz von Stein or Louis Reybaud, for instance, have to say about communism. See *Der Socialismus und Communismus des heutigen Frankreichs*, pp. 439, 502–12; *Études sur les réformateurs ou socialistes modernes*, tome ii, ch. ii (first published in 1843).

17. *MEGA* i/3, p. 308; *HF*, p. 177; *CSF*, p. 203.

18. *MEGA* i/6, p. 539; *MCP*, p. 45. Cf. *MEGA* i/3, p. 114; *EPM*, p. 102; *CSF*, p. 157. Nearly twenty-five years later the same definition of communism was given by Marx in *CWF*, p. 474.

19. Engels, Preface to *CSF*, *SW* i, p. 112. The definition of communism to be found in *The Communist Manifesto* was first formulated by Engels in *Grundsätze des Kommunismus* (*Principles of Communism*). See *MEGA* i/6, p. 511.

20. *MEGA* i/6, p. 538; *MCP*, p. 44.

21. 'I defined the objects of the Communists in this way: (1) To achieve the interests of the proletariat in opposition to those of the bourgeoisie; (2) To do this through the abolition of private property and its

replacement by community of goods; (3) To recognize no means of carrying out these objects other than a democratic revolution by force' (Engels's letter to the Communist Correspondence Committee, Letter No. 3, Paris, 23 October, 1846; quoted in Marx–Engels, *Selected Correspondence 1846–1895*, p. 2).

22. Marx, *CSF*, p. 202; *EBLB*, pp. 260–1.

23. Marx, *CSF*, pp. 176–7.

24. Ibid., p. 203.

25. See, in particular, Marx's letter to F. A. Sorge of 5 November 1880, and to F. Domela-Nieuwenhuis of 22 February 1881. Also Engels expressed his preference for the term 'communism' over 'socialism' as late as 1887 (Preface to the American edition of *CWC*, p. 15), that is, at the time when socialism changed entirely (as compared with utopian socialism of the past) and was clearly recognized as a revolutionary class-movement. In answer to the inquiries whether Kautsky should replace the word 'communism' for 'socialism' in the title of the book *Geschichte des Sozialismus* which Kautsky was writing with Bernstein, Engels answered that the word 'communism' was not 'generally suitable' (*allgemein passend*). 'Communism' had a narrower range of application than 'socialism' and its meaning was no longer self-explanatory since it had been little used in the past thirty years. While Engels accepted the fact that the usage of the words in question changed, his personal linguistic preference seemed to remain unaltered. See Kautsky's letter to Engels of 7 February, and Engels's reply of 13 February 1894, in Kautsky, *Friedrich Engels' Briefwechsel mit Karl Kautsky*, pp. 399–401.

26. Marx's letter to L. Kugelmann of 9 October 1866.

27. Marx's attitude to 'utopian communism', to the communist conspiratorial groups of the early 1840s, was more sympathetic but ultimately differed little from his opinion on utopian socialism. The first communist sects consisted, as a rule, of the followers of Auguste Blanqui. They believed that the established governments could be overthrown by a surprise attack carried out by a group of resolute revolutionaries — 'Blanquism', wrote Sorel, 'is, in essence, nothing more than the revolt of the poor conducted by a Revolutionary Staff' (*La Décomposition du marxisme*, p. 45) — and that once this was accomplished Communism could be introduced at once. The members of the communist sects came from the artisans and highly skilled workers, but they did not ascribe any definite role to the working class as the architect of the communist revolution. For instance, Weitling did not recognize any role of an organized working-class movement and this was one of the important causes of his quarrels and final break with Marx who greatly admired him originally. See K. Marx, 'Kritische Randglossen zu dem Artikel: "Der König von Preussen und die Sozialreform. Von einem Preussen"', *MEGA* 1/3, p. 18.

28. Marx, *CSF*, p. 138; Marx's letter to P. V. Annenkov of 28 December 1846, to L. Kugelmann of 9 October 1866, and to F. A. Sorge of 19 October 1877.

29. The sharp attacks upon communism at that time are mentioned by Marx in his letter to Engels of 27 July 1854.

30. J. Freymond (ed.), *La Première Internationale*, tome ii, pp. 233–4; F. Mehring, *Karl Marx*, p. 473.

31. Marx, *Critique of the Gotha Program*, p. 23; cf. Engels's letter to A. Bebel of 18–28 March 1875.

32. Engels, Preface to *CSF*, *SW* i, pp. 115–6.

33. G. Lichtheim, *Marxism*, p. 230. Both Marx and Engels intensely disliked the term 'Social Democracy'. See Engels's letter to Marx of 16 November 1864, and Marx's letter to Engels of 18 November 1864. According to Marx's definition, 'Social Democracy' meant an alliance of bourgeois democrats and the workers under the banner of reformist socialism. See *CSF*, pp. 175–7, 202.

34. Engels, *HQ*, p. 544.

35. Engels, *PWG*, p. 32. Engels attributed to the 'sense of theory', notable as much in German philosophy as in the German workers and their leaders, the achievements and advance of German socialism, and to the indifference towards all theory the 'crawling progress' of the English working-class movement. As a matter of fact, Engels felt that among other Western European nations, the English, the French, the Belgians, the Spaniards, and the Italians, only the Germans were capable of becoming scientific socialists. This opinion was shared by Marx, who wrote, 'it must be admitted that the German proletariat is the theoretician of the European proletariat as the English is its national economist and the French proletariat its politician' ('Kritische Randglossen zu dem Artikel: "Der König von Preussen und die Sozialreform. Von einem Preussen"', *MEGA* i/3, p. 18).

36. Lenin, 'The Tasks of the Proletariat in Our Revolution', *CW* 24, pp. 84–85.

37. Lenin, 'The Tasks of the Proletariat in the Present Revolution', *CW* 24, p. 24.

38. Lenin, *The State and Revolution*, *CW* 25, pp. 411–13.

39. L. von Stein, *Der Socialismus und Communismus des heutigen Frankreichs*, pp. 203–15.

40. K. Grün, *Die soziale Bewegung in Frankreich und Belgien*, p. 335; L. Reybaud, *Études sur les réformateurs ou socialistes modernes*, tome ii, pp. 113–16.

41. Engels, *AD*, pp. 32, 43, 393.

42. *MEGA* i/3, pp. 114, 126; *EPM*, pp. 102, 114.

43. *MEGA* i/6, p. 538; *MCP*, p. 44. The importance attached by Marx to 'the ultimate aim of socialism' explains the indignation aroused by Bernstein's famous proposition, 'To me . . . the ultimate aim of socialism is nothing but the movement is everything.'

44. *MEGA* i/6, p. 538; *MCP*, p. 44; Marx's letter to J. B. Schweitzer of 24 January 1865.

45. Engels, *AD*, p. 393.

46. Ibid., p. 32.

47. Marx seems to have taken up the German equivalent of Saint-Simon's term 'la science de l'homme', which occurs, for instance, in the title of the *Mémoire sur la science de l'homme* (1813). Karl Grün's expression 'die menschliche Wissenschaft' (the human science) is clearly Saint-Simonist in its origin. Engels probably adopted the term 'Wissenschaft der

Gesellschaft' from Lorenz von Stein, who used it frequently in his book *Der Socialismus und Communismus des heutigen Frankreichs*. The Comtean term 'la physique sociale' (social physics) and 'la physiologie de l'espèce' (the physiology of the species) are not to be found either in Marx or in Engels, which might indicate their dislike of the reductive materialism suggested by the French expressions.

48. Engels, *LF*, pp. 340, 353.

49. Comte, *SPP*, pp. 182, 194.

50. Engels, *AD*, p. 31.

51. H. Saint-Simon, *L'Industrie*, p. 166; L. von Stein, *Der Socialismus und Communismus des heutigen Frankreichs*, pp. 228, 283–4; K. Grün, *Die soziale Bewegung in Frankreich und Belgien*, p. 86; W. M. Simon, 'History for Utopia : Saint-Simon and the Idea of Progress', pp. 319–20. An incisive criticism of Saint-Simon's views from the utopian standpoint is to be found in Plekhanov, *DHM*, pp. 574–9, 588–99. Plekhanov points out both the similarities and the differences between Marx and Saint-Simon.

52. Comte, *SPP*, pp. 89–93, 109–10, 112.

53. Engels, *SUS*, p. 123.

54. Ibid., p. 125.

55. Engels, *KM*, p. 152, cf. 149, 151; *HCL*, p. 312.

56. Plekhanov, *SPS*, p. 76. The quoted passage follows directly the comparison of Marx's achievement in the social sciences with that of Darwin in biology.

57. Plekhanov, *OD*, p. 146.

58. Lenin, *WFPA*, pp. 157–8.

59. Lenin, *The Economic Content of Narodism*, *CW* 1, p. 417.

60. E. Bernstein, *Evolutionary Socialism*, pp. 1–3.

61. Quoted by W. Sombart, *Der proletarische Sozialismus*, Bd. 1, p. 227.

62. H. Saint-Simon, *Mémoire sur la science de l'homme*, p. 182; W. M. Simon, 'History for Utopia : Saint-Simon and the Idea of Progress', pp. 318–19.

63. Comte, *SPP*, pp. 167–8.

64. Engels, *SUS*, pp. 124–5; *KM*, pp. 150–1.

65. K. Kautsky, *Ethik und materialistische Geschichtsauffassung*, p. 144.

66. Plekhanov, *DMH*, p. 723.

67. Lenin, *KMX*, p. 71.

68. Lenin, *WIBD*, p. 353.

69. B. Croce, *History: Its Theory and Practice*, p. 267.

70. K. Korsch, *Karl Marx*, pp. 49–51.

71. Popper, *OS*, vol. ii, pp. 83–84.

72. Marx, *CSF*, p. 203.

73. Marx's and Engels's letter to A. Bebel, W. Liebknecht, W. Bracke, and others of 17–18 September 1879.

74. Engels, *SUS*, p. 107.

75. Ibid., p. 124.

76. Lenin, 'The Three Sources and Three Component Parts of Marxism', *CW* 19, p. 27. In connection with this particular meaning of 'scientific socialism' see R. C. Tucker, 'The Cunning of Reason in Hegel and Marx', pp. 290–1; G. D. H. Cole, *The Meaning of Marxism*, pp. 106–7.

77. Plekhanov, *SAHD*, p. 472; Lenin, *WIBD*, pp. 519–20.

78. *MEGA* 1/3, pp. 206–7; *HF*, pp. 52–53; *MEGA* 1/6, p. 227; *PPH*, p. 146; *MEGA* 1/6, p. 533; *MCP*, pp. 41–42.

79. Marx, *CSF*, p. 136. A revolutionary class may not, however, attain the necessary level of knowledge about its position in the social world and, being potentially a revolutionary class, still remains incapable of accomplishing its own revolution. In *CSF* Marx tried to show that this was what actually happened in France. At the time the French proletariat was still unequal to its revolutionary task.

80. See *MEGA* 1/3, p. 126; *EPM*, p. 126. Cf. *KHR*, *MEGA* 1/1/1, pp. 617–18.

81. E. Bernstein, *Evolutionary Socialism*, p. 219.

82. W. Sombart, *Der proletarische Sozialismus*, Bd. 1, p. 315; R. Stammler, 'Materialistische Geschichtsauffassung', *Handwörterbuch der Staatswissenschaften*, Bd. vi, p. 533.

83. A similar jump from a statement of fact to an ethical claim is to be found in Comte. See D. G. Charlton, *Positivist Thought in France*, p. 45.

84. E. Bernstein, *Evolutionary Socialism*, pp. 209–10.

85. Cf. A. L. Harris, 'Utopian Elements in Marx's Thought', p. 79; J. L. Talmon, *Political Messianism*, p. 205; R. Heiss, *Die grossen Dialektiker des 19. Jahrhunderts*, p. 387.

86. I. Berlin, *Karl Marx*, p. 140; cf. R. C. Tucker, 'The Cunning of Reason in Hegel and Marx', p. 277; R. Heiss, *Die grossen Dialektiker des 19. Jahrhunderts*, p. 40. That valuation is a constitutive rather than a restrictive factor in the knowledge of social facts in general, and of human activity in particular, and that in this kind of knowledge observation and value judgment are inextricably bound up, is a basic assumption of what in the Russian philosophy of the nineteenth century was called the 'subjective method'. See V. V. Zenkovsky, *History of Russian Philosophy*, vol. i, p. 369. When Plekhanov and Lenin subjected the subjective method to a severe criticism in their polemics against Mikhailovsky, they were attacking Mikhailovsky's personalism and not his rejection of the dualism of facts and norms. In the latter respect, there was no difference between Mikhailovsky and his critics.

87. The political consequences of this belief, culminating in the 'logical inevitability of revisionism', are analysed in Z. A. Jordan, 'Philosophical Background of Revisionism in Poland', pp. 263–9.

88. E. Bernstein, *Die Voraussetzungen des Sozialismus und die Aufgaben der Sozialdemokratie*, last chapter, and *Wie ist wissenschaftlicher Sozialismus möglich?* Karl Kautsky both accepted and denied the existence of the fallacy. 'The materialist conception of history', he wrote, 'has taught us that we should deduce our social aims exclusively from our knowledge of the given material conditions.' On the other hand, Kautsky maintained that socialists cannot do without a moral ideal in their fight against the exploitation and class oppression and added that 'this ideal has nothing to do with scientific socialism' (*Ethik und materialistische Geschichtsauffassung*, pp. 140–1).

89. Popper, *OS*, vol. ii, p. 61.

90. E. Bernstein, *Evolutionary Socialism*, p. 219.

Bibliography

THIS bibliography contains only works and articles cited in the text and footnotes. The following conventions are adopted.

A date in parentheses succeeding the date of a work in English or in a foreign language is the date of its first publication.

A date in parentheses succeeding the date of a foreign work translated into English is the date of its original translation.

The letter *P* following an entry means that the work listed in the bibliography is a Paperback.

Acton, H. B. *The Illusion of the Epoch: Marxism–Leninism as a Philosophical Creed*. London, 1955.

Adler, M. *Marxistische Probleme. Beiträge zur Theorie der materialistischen Geschichtsauffassung und Dialektik*, Dritte Auflage. Stuttgart, 1919.

— *Marx als Denker*, Zweite Auflage. Wien, 1921.

d'Alembert, J. *Preliminary Discourse to the Encyclopedia of Diderot* (The Library of Liberal Arts), trans. R. N. Schwab and W. E. Rex. New York, 1963.

Alexander, S. *Space, Time and Deity*, vols. i–ii. New York, 1950 (1920). Reissued, with a Foreword by Dorothy Emmet, 1966.

Baron, S. H. *Plekhanov: The Father of Russian Marxism*. Stanford, 1963.

Barth, P. *Die Philosophie der Geschichte als Soziologie*, Dritte Auflage. Leipzig, 1922.

Berdyaev, N. *The Russian Revolution, P*. Ann Arbor, 1961 (1931).

— *The Origin of Russian Communism, P*, trans. R. M. French. Ann Arbor, 1962 (1937).

Berkeley, G. *The Works of George Berkeley*, ed. A. A. Luce and T. E. Jessop, vol. ii. London–Edinburgh, 1949.

Berlin, I. *Karl Marx: His Life and Environment*, 2nd ed. London, 1948.

Bernstein, E. *Die Voraussetzungen des Sozialismus und die Aufgaben der Sozialdemokratie*. Stuttgart, 1899.

— *Zur Geschichte und Theorie des Sozialismus. Gesammelte Abhandlungen*. Berlin–Bern, 1901.

— *Wie ist wissenschaftlicher Sozialismus möglich?* Berlin, 1901.

— *Die Briefe von Friedrich Engels an Eduard Bernstein*. Berlin, 1925.

— *Evolutionary Socialism: A Criticism and Affirmation, P*, trans. E. C. Harvey. New York, 1961 (1909).

Bertalanffy, L. von. 'The Psychopathology of Scientism', in H. Schoeck and J. W. Wiggins (eds.), *Scientism and Values*, New York, 1960.

Bober, M. M. *Karl Marx's Interpretation of History*. Cambridge, Mass., 1927.

Bocheński, I. M. *Der sowjetrussische dialektische Materialismus*, Zweite Auflage. München, 1956.

460   Bibliography

Bocheński, I. M. *Contemporary European Philosophy*, trans. D. Nicholl and K. Aschenbrenner. Berkeley and Los Angeles, 1956.
Bottomore, T. B., *see* Marx, K. *Early Writings*.
— and Rubel, M., *see* Marx, K. *Selected Writings in Sociology and Social Philosophy*.
Broad, C. D. *The Mind and its Place in Nature*. London, 1937 (1925).
Brodbeck, M. 'Explanation, Prediction and "Imperfect" Knowledge', in H. Feigl and G. Maxwell (eds.), *Minnesota Studies in the Philosophy of Science*, iii, 231–72. Minneapolis, 1962.
Bukharin, N. I. *Historical Materialism: A System of Sociology*. New York, 1928 (1925).
Bunge, M. *Causality: The Place of the Causal Principle in Modern Science*. Cambridge, Mass., 1959.
— *Metascientific Queries*. Springfield, Ill., 1959.
Bury, J. B. *The Idea of Progress*, P. New York, 1955 (1920).
Cackowski, Z. *Treść poznawcza wrażeń zmysłowych (The Cognitive Content of Sensations)*. Warszawa, 1962.
Calvez, J.-Y. *La Pensée de Karl Marx*. Paris, 1956.
Charlton, D. G. *Positivist Thought in France During the Second Empire 1852–1870*. Oxford, 1959.
Cole, G. D. H. *A History of Socialist Thought*, vol. i. London, 1962 (1953).
— *The Meaning of Marxism*, P. Ann Arbor, 1964 (1948).
Collingwood, R. G. *The Idea of Nature*. Oxford, 1945.
Comte, A. *Système de politique positive* (also known as *Plan des travaux scientifiques nécessaires pour réorganiser la société*), in *Œuvres de Saint-Simon et d'Enfantin*, xxxviiie vol. Paris, 1875 (1822).
— *Cours de philosophie positive*, tomes i–vi. Paris, 1852 (1830–42).
— *Discours sur l'esprit positif*. Paris, 1909 (1844).
— *Discours préliminaire sur l'ensemble du positivisme*, in *Système de politique positive*, tome i. Paris, 1851.
Copleston, F. C. *Aquinas*. The Pelican Philosophy Series, 1955.
Cornu, A. *The Origin of Marxian Thought*. Springfield, Ill., 1957.
— *Karl Marx et Friedrich Engels*, tomes 1–3. Paris, 1955–62.
Croce, B. *Historical Materialism and the Economics of Karl Marx*. London, 1922.
— *History: Its Theory and Practice*, P, trans. D. Ainslie. New York, 1960 (1920).
Cunow, H. *Die Marxsche Geschichts-, Gesellschafts- und Staatstheorie*, Bde. 1–2. Berlin, 1923.
Daniels, R. V. 'Fate and Will in the Marxian Philosophy of History', *Journal of the History of Ideas*, xxi (1960), 538–52.
Descartes, R. *Principia Philosophiae. Œuvres de Descartes*, publiées par C. Adam et P. Tannery, tome viii. Paris, 1905 (1644).
Deutscher, I. *Stalin: A Political Biography*, P. London, 1961 (1949).
Dewey, J. 'From Absolutism to Experimentalism', in G. P. Adams and W. P. Montague (eds.), *Contemporary American Philosophy: Personal Statements*, ii, 13–27. New York, 1930.
— *Logic: The Theory of Inquiry*. New York, 1938.
— *Freedom and Culture*, P. New York, 1963 (1931).
Ducasse, C. J. *Nature, Mind, and Death*. La Salle, 1951.

Duhem, P.   *The Aim and Structure of Physical Theory, P,* trans. P. P. Wiener. New York, 1962 (1954).

Durkheim, É.   *The Elementary Forms of the Religious Life,* trans. J. W. Swain. London, 1957 (1915).

— *The Rules of Sociological Method,* trans. S. A. Solovay and J. H. Mueller. Glencoe, Ill., 1958 (1938).

— *Socialism and Saint-Simon,* trans. C. Sattler. London, 1959.

— *Montesquieu and Rousseau: Forerunners of Sociology,* trans. R. Manheim. Ann Arbor, 1960.

— *The Division of Labor in Society,* trans. G. Simpson. Glencoe, Ill., 1960 (1933).

Eastman, M.   *Marx and Lenin: The Science of Revolution.* New York, 1927.

Eilstein, H.   'Leninowskie pojęcie materii a idealizm fizyczny' (Lenin's Concept of Matter and Idealism in Physics), *Myśl Filozoficzna,* 4/10 (1953), 183–221.

— (ed.), *Jedność materialna świata (Material Unity of the World).* Warszawa, 1961.

Eliade, M.   *The Myth of the Eternal Return,* trans. W. R. Trask. New York, 1954.

Engels, F.   *Outlines of a Critique of Political Economy,* in K. Marx, *Economic and Philosophic Manuscripts of 1844,* 175–209.

— *The Condition of the Working Class in England,* in Marx and Engels, *On Britain,* 35–336.*

— Preface to the first German edition of *The Condition of the Working Class in England,* in K. Marx and F. Engels, *On Britain,* 3–5.

— *Karl Marx: A Contribution to the Critique of Political Economy, SW* i, 332–41.

— *Marx's Capital, SW* i, 419–25.

— *The Peasant War in Germany.* Moscow, 1956.

— *The Housing Question, SW* i, pp. 495–574.

— *On Authority, SW* i, 575–8.

— *On Social Relations in Russia, SW* ii, 46–56.

— *Anti-Dühring: Herrn Eugen Dühring's Revolution in Science.* Moscow, 1959.

— *Socialism: Utopian and Scientific, SW* ii, 107–42.

— *Speech at the Graveside of Karl Marx, SW* ii, 153–4.

— *Karl Marx, SW* ii, 143–52.

— *The Origin of the Family, Private Property and the State, SW* ii, 155–296.

— *On the History of the Communist League, SW* ii, 306–23.

— *Ludwig Feuerbach and the End of Classical German Philosophy, SW* ii, 324–64.

— Preface to the American edition of *The Condition of the Working Class in England,* in K. Marx and F. Engels, *On Britain,* 6–16.

— Preface to the English edition of *The Condition of the Working Class in England,* in K. Marx and F. Engels, *On Britain,* 17–33.

— Special Introduction to the English edition of *Socialism: Utopian and Scientific, SW* ii, 86–106.

* The German edition of this work, published in 1845, had the title *Die Lage der arbeitenden Klasse in England.* Both the American and English editions, published in 1887 and 1892 respectively, were entitled *The Condition of the Working Class in England in 1844.*

Engels, F.   *Dialectics of Nature.*   Moscow, 1954 (1925).

Farber, M.   *Naturalism and Subjectivism.*   Springfield, Ill., 1959.

Fetscher, I.   'Das Verhältnis des Marxismus zu Hegel', *Marxismusstudien*, Dritte Folge, 1960, 66–169.

Feuerbach, L.   *Sämtliche Werke*, Bde. i–x.   Leipzig, 1846–66.

— *Vorläufige Thesen zur Reform der Philosophie*, Bd. ii.

— *Grundsätze der Philosophie der Zukunft*, Bd. ii.

— *Wider dem Dualismus von Leib und Seele, Fleisch und Geist*, Bd. ii.

— *Das Wesen des Christenthums*, Bd. vi.

— *The Essence of Christianity*, P, trans. George Eliot.   New York, 1957 (1854).

Findlay, J. N.   *Hegel: A Re-examination*, P.   New York, 1962 (1958).

Fourier, J.-B.   *Théorie analytique de la chaleur*, Nouvelle Édition.   Breslau, 1883 (1822).

Frank, Ph. G.   'Logisierender Empirismus in der Philosophie der U.S.S.R.'. *Actes du Congrès International de Philosophie Scientifique, Sorbonne, Paris*, 1935, tome 8.   Paris, 1936.

— *Foundations of Physics.*   International Encyclopedia of Unified Science, vol. 1, no. 7.   Chicago, 1946.

— 'Present Role of Science'.   *Atti del XII Congresso Internazionale di Filosofia.*   Firenze, 1958.

— *Modern Science and its Philosophy*, P.   New York, 1961 (1941).

— 'The Variety of Reasons for the Acceptance of Scientific Theories', in Ph. G. Frank (ed.), *The Validation of Scientific Theories*, P.   New York, 1961 (1954), 13–126.

Freymond, J. (ed.).   *La Première Internationale*, tomes i–ii.   Genève, 1962.

Gilson, É.   *God and Philosophy*, P.   New Haven, 1959 (1941).

Gray, A.   *The Socialist Tradition: Moses to Lenin.*   London, 1947.

Grün, K.   *Die soziale Bewegung in Frankreich und Belgien, Briefe und Studien.* Darmstadt, 1845.

Grünberg, K.   'Der Ursprung der Worte Sozialismus und Sozialist', *Zeitschrift für Sozialwissenschaft*, ix (1906), 495–508.

Gurvitch, G.   *La Vocation actuelle de la sociologie*, tomes i–ii.   Paris, 1963.

Harris, A. L.   'The Social Philosophy of Karl Marx', *Ethics*, lviii (1947–8, no. 3, part ii), 1–42.

— 'Utopian Elements in Marx's Thought', *Ethics*, lx (1949–50), 79–99.

Harrison, R.   'E. S. Beesly and Karl Marx', *International Review of Social History*, iv (1959), 22–58.

Hayek, F. A.   *The Counter-Revolution of Science: Studies on the Abuse of Reason.* Glencoe, Ill., 1952.

Hegel, G. W. F.   *Sämtliche Werke.*   Hersg. von Georg Lasson.

— *Phänomenologie des Geistes*, Bd. 2.   Leipzig, 1928.

— *Wissenschaft der Logik*, Bde. 3–4.   Leipzig, 1923.

— *Enzyclopädie der philosophischen Wissenschaften*, Bd. 5.   Leipzig, 1930.

— *Grundlinien der Philosophie des Rechts*, Bd. 6.   Leipzig, 1930.

— *Die Philosophie der Weltgeschichte. Allgemeine Einleitung*, Bd. 8.   Leipzig, 1920.

— *The Phenomenology of Mind*, trans. J. B. Baillie.   London, 1961 (1931).

Hegel, G. W. F. *Science of Logic*, vols. 1–2, trans. W. H. Johnston and L. G. Struthers. London, 1951 (1929).
— *The Encyclopedia of the Philosophical Sciences* (first part), trans. W. Wallace. London, 1959 (1892).
— *The Philosophy of Right*, trans. T. M. Knox. Oxford, 1962 (1942).
— *The Philosophy of History*, P, trans. J. Sibree. New York, 1956 (1899).
— *Lectures on the History of Philosophy*, vols. i–iii., trans E. S. Haldane. London, 1955 (1892).
Heiss, R. *Die grossen Dialektiker des 19. Jahrhunderts. Hegel, Kierkegaard, Marx.* Köln–Berlin, 1963.
Helvétius, C. *De L'esprit. Œuvres d'Helvétius*, Nouvelle Édition, tomes 1–2. Paris, 1795 (1758).
Hertz, H. *The Principles of Mechanics*, P, trans. D. E. Jones and J. T. Walley. New York, 1956 (1899).
Hess, M. *Philosophische und sozialistische Schriften 1837–1850. Eine Auswahl.* Hersg. von A. Cornu und W. Monke. Berlin, 1961.
History of the Communist Party of the Soviet Union (Bolsheviks): Short Course. Moscow, 1943.
History of the Communist Party of the Soviet Union. Moscow, 1960.
Hobsbawm, E. J. *The Age of Revolution: 1789–1848*, P. New York, 1964 (1962).
Hochfeld, J. 'O niektórych aspektach przeciwstawności materializmu historycznego i socjologii burżuazyjnej' (Some Aspects of the Antagonism between Historical Materialism and Bourgeois Sociology), *Myśl Filozoficzna*, 1–2 (1951), 106–54.
Holbach, Le Baron de. *Système de la nature ou des lois du monde physique et du monde morale*, tomes i–ii. Paris, 1821 (1770).
Hook, S. *Towards the Understanding of Karl Marx: A Revolutionary Interpretation.* New York, 1933.
— *From Hegel to Marx: Studies in the Intellectual Development of Karl Marx*, P. Ann Arbor, 1962 (1936).
— *The Hero in History: A Study in Limitations and Possibility.* London, 1945 (1943).
— *Reason, Social Myths and Democracy.* New York, 1950 (1940).
— *The Quest for Being and Other Studies in Naturalism and Humanism.* New York, *s.a.*
Hunt, R. N. C. *The Theory and Practice of Communism.* Pelican Books, 1963 (1950).
Joravsky, D. *Soviet Marxism and Natural Science 1917–1932.* London, 1961.
Jordan, Z. A. *Philosophy and Ideology: The Development of Philosophy and Marxism–Leninism in Poland since the Second World War.* Dordrecht, 1963.
— 'The Philosophical Background of Revisionism in Poland', in W. J. Stankiewicz (ed.), *Political Thought Since World War II: Critical and Interpretative Essays*, 250–88. New York, 1964.
— 'Socialism, Alienation, and Political Power', *Survey*, 1966, no. 60, 119–133.
Kamenka, E. *The Ethical Foundations of Marxism.* London, 1963.

Kant, I. *Critique of Pure Reason*, trans. N. Kemp Smith. London, 1958. (1929).

Kautsky, K. *Bernstein und das sozialdemokratische Programm. Eine Antikritik.* Stuttgart, 1899.

— *Ethik und materialistische Geschichtsauffassung.* Stuttgart, 1906.

— *Aus der Frühzeit des Marxismus. Engels Briefwechsel mit Kautsky.* Prag. 1935.

— *Friedrich Engels' Briefwechsel mit Karl Kautsky.* Wien, 1955.

Kelles-Krauz, K. *Pisma wybrane* (Selected Works), T. i–ii. Warszawa, 1962.

Kłósak, K. *Materializm dialektyczny. Studia krytyczne* (Dialectical Materialism. A Critical Study). Kraków, 1948.

Köhler, W. 'The Mind–Body Problem', in S. Hook (ed.), *Dimensions of Mind: A Symposium*, 15–32, P. New York, 1961 (1960).

Kołakowski, L. 'Karol Marks i klasyczna definicja prawdy' (Karl Marx and the Classical Definition of Truth), *Studia Filozoficzne*, 2/11 (1959), 43–67.

Konstantinov, F. V. *et al. Grundlagen der marxistischen Philosophie* (German translation of *Osnovy marksistkoj filosofii*, The Foundations of Marxist Philosophy). Berlin, 1961.

Korsch, K. *Marxismus und Philosophie.* Leipzig, 1922.

— *Karl Marx.* New York, 1963 (1938).

Krajewski, W. 'O prawie negacji negacji czyli rozwoju po spirali' (The Law of the Negation of the Negation and the Spiral Development), *Myśl Filozoficzna*, 5–6/19–20 (1955), 191–218.

Kuhn, H. 'Dialectic in History', *Journal of the History of Ideas*, x (1949), 14–29.

Kuusinen, O. V. *et al. Fundamentals of Marxism–Leninism* (2nd rev. ed.). Moscow, 1963.

Labriola, A. *Essays on the Materialistic Conception of History*, trans. C. H. Kerr. Chicago, 1904.

— *Socialism and Philosophy*, trans. E. Unterman. Chicago, 1934.

Landgrebe, L. 'Das Problem der Dialektik', *Marxismusstudien*, Dritte Folge, 1960, 1–65.

Lange, F. A. *The History of Materialism and Criticism of its Present Importance*, 3 vols. in one, trans. E. C. Thomas. London, 1957 (1925).

Laski, H. J. *Communism.* London, 1930.

— *Communist Manifesto: Socialist Landmark.* London, 1961 (1948).

Lefebvre, H. *Le Matérialisme dialectique* (4e ed.). Paris, 1957.

Leites, N. 'Stalin as an Intellectual', *World Politics*, vi (1953–4), 45–66.

Lenin, V. I. *Collected Works.* Moscow, 1960 ff.

— *What the 'Friends of the People' Are, CW* 1.

— *What Is To Be Done?, CW* 5.

— *Materialism and Empirio-Criticism, CW* 14.

— *The Three Sources and Three Component Parts of Marxism, CW* 19.

— *Karl Marx: A Brief Biographical Sketch with an Exposition of Marxism, CW* 21.

— *Philosophical Notebooks, CW* 38.

— *The Essentials of Lenin*, in 2 vols. London, 1947.

— *Imperialism: The Highest Stage of Capitalism, CW* 22.

Lenin, V. I.   *The State and Revolution. The Marxist Doctrine of the State and the Tasks of the Proletariat in the Revolution, CW* 25.
— *Marx–Engels–Marxism.* Moscow, 1951.
Lévy-Bruhl, L.   *The Philosophy of Auguste Comte,* trans. K. de Beaumont-Klein. New York, 1903.
Lewes, G. H.   *Problems of Life and Mind,* vols. 1–2. London, 1874–5.
Lewis, J. D.   'The Individual and the Group in Marxist Theory', *Ethics,* xlvii (1936–7), 45–56.
Lichtheim, G.   *Marxism: An Historical and Critical Study.* London, 1961.
Locke, J.   *An Essay Concerning Human Understanding,* ed. A. S. Pringle-Pattison. Oxford, 1924 (1690).
Lossky, N. O.   *History of Russian Philosophy.* London, 1952.
Löwith, K.   *Von Hegel zu Nietzsche. Der revolutionäre Bruch im Denken des neunzehnten Jahrhunderts.* Stuttgart, 1953.
Lukács, G.   *Geschichte und Klassenbewusstsein. Studien über marxistische Dialektik.* Berlin, 1923.
Mach, E.   *The Analysis of Sensations, P,* trans. C. M. Williams, rev. S. Waterlow. New York, 1959 (1897).
— *The Science of Mechanics, P,* trans. T. J. McCormack. La Salle, 1960 (1893).
Malinowski, B.   *A Scientific Theory of Culture and Other Essays, P.* New York, 1960 (1944).
Mannheim, K.   *Ideology and Utopia: An Introduction to the Sociology of Knowledge,* trans. L. Wirth and E. Shils. London, 1946 (1936).
Manuel, F. E.   *The New World of Henri Saint-Simon, P.* Notre Dame, 1963 (1956).
Marcuse, H.   *Reason and Revolution: Hegel and the Rise of Social Theory* (2nd ed.). New York, 1954.
Margenau, H.   *Open Vistas: Philosophical Perspectives of Modern Science.* New Haven, 1961.
Marx, K.   *Kritik der Hegelschen Staatsphilosophie, MEGA* i/i/i, 401–553.
— *Zur Kritik der Hegelschen Rechtsphilosophie. Einleitung, MEGA* i/i/i, 607–621.
— *Die Frühschriften.* Stuttgart, 1953.
— *Early Writings.* London, 1963.
— *Economic and Philosophic Manuscripts of 1844.* Moscow, s.a.
— *Theses on Feuerbach, SW* ii, 365–7.
— *Selected Writings in Sociology and Social Philosophy.* London, 1961.
— *The Poverty of Philosophy.* London, 1941.
— *Wage Labour and Capital, SW* i, 74–97.
— *The Class Struggles in France, 1848 to 1850, SW* i, 128–220.
— *The Eighteenth Brumaire of Louis Bonaparte, SW* i, 221–311.
— *A Contribution to the Critique of Political Economy.* Calcutta, s.a.
— *Introduction to the Critique of Political Economy,* in *A Contribution to the Critique of Political Economy,* 265–312.
— *Inaugural Address of the Working Men's International Association, SW* i, 342–349.
— *Wages, Price and Profit, SW* i, 361–405.

Marx, K. _Capital_, vols. i–iii. Moscow, 1957–9.
— _Theories of Surplus-Value_, part i. Moscow, _s.a._
— _The Civil War in France_, SW i, 441–94.
— _Critique of the Gotha Program_, SW ii, 13–34.
Marx, K.–Engels, F. _Historisch-kritische Gesamtausgabe, Werke/Schriften/ Briefe._ Hersg. von D. Rjazanov. Frankfurt a.M.; 1927 ff.
—— _Dzieła_ (Works), T. i–v. Warszawa, 1960–2.
—— _Werke_, Berlin, 1958 ff.
—— _Selected Correspondence 1846–1895._ New York, 1942.
—— _Selected Correspondence._ Moscow, _s.a._
—— _Selected Works_ (in 2 vols.). Moscow, 1951.
—— _On Britain._ Moscow, 1953.
—— _The German Ideology_, parts i and iii. London, 1940.
—— _The Holy Family or Critique of Critical Critique._ Moscow, 1956.
—— _Manifesto of the Communist Party_, SW i, 32–61.
—— _Address of the Central Committee to the Communist League_, SW i, 98–108.
Mast, C. B. 'Matter and Energy in Scientific Theory', in E. McMullin (ed.), _The Concept of Matter_, 585–95. Notre Dame, 1963.
Mayer, G. _Friedrich Engels. Eine Biographie_, Bde. 1–2. Haag, 1934.
Mayo, H. B. _Introduction to Marxist Theory, P._ New York, 1960.
McMullin, E. 'Introduction: The Concept of Matter', in E. McMullin (ed.), _The Concept of Matter_, 1–41. Notre Dame, 1963.
Meehl, P. E. and Sellars, W. 'The Concept of Emergence', in H. Feigl and M. Scriven (eds.), _Minnesota Studies in the Philosophy of Science_, i, 239–52. Minneapolis, 1956.
Mehlberg, H. _The Reach of Science._ Toronto, 1958.
Mehring, F. _Karl Marx: The Story of His Life_, trans. E. Fitzgerald. London, 1948.
Meyer, A. G. _Leninism, P._ New York, 1962 (1957).
— _Marxism: The Unity of Theory and Practice, P._ Ann Arbor, 1963 (1954).
Meyerson, É. _Identity and Reality, P_, trans. K. Loewenberg. New York, 1962 (1930).
Mill, J. S. _An Examination of Sir William Hamilton's Philosophy_, 2 vols. in one. New York, 1884 (1865).
— _A System of Logic._ London, 1886 (1843).
— _On Liberty. Representative Government. The Subjection of Women._ The World's Classics clxx. London, 1940 (1859, 1861, 1869.)
— _Autobiography_, The World's Classics ccxii. London, 1940 (1873).
— _Auguste Comte and Positivism, P._ Ann Arbor, 1961 (1865).
Mises, R. von. _Positivism: A Study in Human Understanding_, trans. J. Bernstein and R. G. Newton. New York, 1956 (1951).
Morgan, C. Lloyd. _Emergent Evolution._ London, 1923.
— _The Emergence of Novelty._ London, 1933.
Mueller, I. W. _John Stuart Mill and French Thought._ Urbana, Ill., 1956.
Munitz, M. K. _Space, Time and Creation: Philosophical Aspects of Scientific Cosmology, P._ New York, 1961 (1957).
Nagel, E. _Logic without Metaphysics._ Glencoe, Ill., 1956.

Needham, J. *Time: The Refreshing River.* London, 1943.

Negt, O. *Strukturbeziehungen zwischen den Gesellschaftslehren Comtes und Hegels.* Frankfurt a.M., 1964.

Ogiermann, H. *Materialistische Dialektik. Ein Diskussionsbeitrag.* München, 1958.

Ossowski, S. *Class Structure in the Social Consciousness,* trans. S. Patterson. New York, 1963.

Plamenatz, J. *German Marxism and Russian Communism.* London, 1954.

— *Man and Society: A Critical Examination of Some Important Social and Political Theories from Machiavelli to Marx,* vols. i–ii. London, 1963.

Plekhanov, G. *Selected Philosophical Works,* trans. R. Dixon, vol. i. Moscow, *s.a.*

— *Socialism and the Political Struggle, SPW* i, 57–121.

— *Our Differences, SPW* i, 122–399.

— *A New Champion of Autocracy, SPW* i, 411–50.

— *For the Sixtieth Anniversary of Hegel's Death. SPW* i, 455–83.

— Foreword to the first edition and Plekhanov's *Notes* to Engels's book *Ludwig Feuerbach and the End of Classical German Philosophy. SPW* i, 484–541.

— *The Development of the Monist View of History,* trans. A. Rothstein. *SPW* i, 542–872.

— *Fundamental Problems of Marxism.* London, *s.a.*

— *Essays in the History of Materialism,* trans. R. Fox. London, 1934.

— *The Materialist Conception of History.* New York, 1940.

— 'The Role of the Individual in History', in P. Gardiner (ed.), *Theories of History,* 139–166. Glencoe, Ill., 1962.

Popitz, H. *Der entfremdete Mensch. Zeitkritik und Geschichtsphilosophie des jungen Marx.* Basel, 1953.

Popper, K. R. *The Poverty of Historicism.* London, 1957.

— *The Logic of Scientific Discovery.* London, 1959.

— *The Open Society and Its Enemies.* Vols. i–ii, *P* (4th edn.). New York, 1963 (1945).

— *Conjectures and Refutations: The Growth of Scientific Knowledge.* London, 1963.

Proudhon, P.-J. *Qu'est-ce que la Propriété? Œuvres complètes de P.-J. Proudhon.* Paris, 1926.

Reding, M. *Der politische Atheismus.* Graz, 1957.

Reybaud, L. *Études sur les réformateurs ou socialistes modernes,* tomes i–ii. Paris, 1856 (1843).

Riazanov, D. *Karl Marx and Friedrich Engels.* London, *s.a.*

Rickert, H. *Kulturwissenschaft und Naturwissenschaft.* Tübingen, 1926.

Rousseau, J.-J. *Discours sur l'origin et les fondements de l'inégalité parmi les hommes.* Cambridge, 1944 (1750).

— *Émile ou de l'éducation,* tomes i–ii. Paris, Classiques Flammarion (1762).

Rozental', M. M., and Yudin, P. *Krótki słownik filozoficzny* (Polish trans. of *Kratky filosofsky slovar,* The Short Philosophical Dictionary (4th edn.), Moscow, 1955). Warszawa, 1955.

Rubel, M. *Karl Marx: Essai de biographie intellectuelle.* Paris, 1957.

Russell, B. *Our Knowledge of the External World.* London, 1926 (1914).
— 'Dewey's New Logic', in P. A. Schilpp (ed.), *The Philosophy of John Dewey*, 137–56. New York, 1951.
— *Why I Am Not a Christian and Other Essays on Religion and Related Subjects.* London, 1957.
— *An Outline of Philosophy.* London, 1961 (1927).
— *The Theory and Practice of Bolshevism*, P. London, 1962 (1920).
— *Freedom versus Organization 1814–1914*, P. New York, 1962 (1934).
Saint-Simon, H. *Œuvres de Saint-Simon et d'Enfantin*, 47 vols. Paris, 1865–1878.
— *L'Industrie ou discussions politiques, morales et philosophiques*, xviiie vol.
— *L'Organisateur*, xxe vol.
— *Le Nouveau Christianisme*, xxiiie vol.
— *De la physiologie appliquée à l'amélioration des institutions sociales*, xxxixe vol.
— *Catéchisme des Industriels*, xxxviie–xxxixe vols.
— *Mémoire sur la science de l'homme*, xle vol.
— *Selected Writings*, trans. F. M. H. Markham. Oxford, 1952.
Santayana, G. *Character and Opinion in the United States*, P. New York, 1956 (1920).
Sartre, J.-P. 'Matérialisme et révolution', *Situation, III*, 135–225. Paris, 1949.
— *Critique de la raison dialectique*, tome i. Paris, 1960.
Schaff, A. 'Zasada sprzeczności w świetle logiki dialektycznej' (The Principle of Non-Contradiction in the Light of Dialectical Logic), *Myśl Współczesna*, 3–4 (1946), 328–53.
— *Wstęp do teorii marksizmu* (Introduction to the Marxist Theory). Warszawa, 1948.
— *Narodziny i rozwój filozofii marksistowskiej* (The Origin and Development of the Marxist Philosophy). Warszawa, 1950.
— 'Metoda dokumentów osobistych a społeczne badania terenowe' (Personal Document Method and Social Field Studies), *Myśl Filozoficzna*, 3/5 (1952), 221–59.
Schlick, M. *Problems of Ethics*, P. trans. D. Rynin. New York, 1962 (1939).
Schmidt, A. *Der Begriff der Natur in der Lehre von Marx.* Frankfurt a.M., 1962.
Schopenhauer, A. *Die Welt als Wille und Vorstellung. Sämtliche Werke*, Bd. 3, Leipzig, 1938 (1819).
— *The World as Will and Idea*, trans. R. B. Haldane and J. Kemp, vol. ii. London, 1896.
Seligman, E. R. A. *The Economic Interpretation of History*, 2nd ed. New York, 1934 (1907).
Sellars, R. W. 'Realism, Naturalism, and Humanism', in G. P. Adams and W. P. Montague (eds.), *Contemporary American Philosophy: Personal Statements*, vol. ii, 261–85. New York, 1930.
Simmel, G. *Conflict* and *The Web of Group Affiliation*, trans. K. H. Wolff and R. Bendix. Glencoe, Ill., 1955.
Simon, W. M. 'History for Utopia: Saint-Simon and the Idea of Progress', *Journal of the History of Ideas*, xvii (1956), 311–31.

Simon, W. M. *European Positivism in the Nineteenth Century: An Essay in Intellectual History.* Ithaca, N.Y., 1963.
Singer, C. *A Short History of Scientific Ideas to 1900, P.* London, 1962 (1959).
Sombart, W. *Der proletarische Sozialismus ('Marxismus'),* Bd. 1. Jena, 1924.
— *Deutscher Sozialismus.* Berlin, 1934.
Sorel, G. *La Décomposition du marxisme.* Paris, 1908.
Stace, W. T. *The Philosophy of Hegel: A Systematic Exposition, P.* New York, 1955 (1923).
Stalin, J. *Works,* vols. i–xiii. Moscow, 1954 ff.
— 'Interview Given to the First American Labour Delegation' (9 September, 1927), *EL* i, 39–44.
— *Problems of Leninism.* Moscow, 1947.
— *Dialectical and Historical Materialism,* in *Problems of Leninism,* 569–95.
— *Marxism and Problems of Linguistics.* Moscow, 1954.
— *Economic Problems of Socialism in the USSR.* Moscow, 1952.
Stallo, J. B. *The Concepts and Theories of Modern Physics.* Cambridge, Mass. 1960 (1881).
Stammler, R. 'Materialistische Geschichtsauffassung', in *Handwörterbuch der Staatswissenschaften,* Bd. 6, Vierte Auflage.
Stein, L. von. *Der Socialismus und Communismus des heutigen Frankreichs. Ein Beitrag zur Zeitgeschichte.* Zweite umgearbeitete Ausgabe. Leipzig, 1848.
Talmon, J. L. *Political Messianism: The Romantic Phase.* New York, 1960.
Thier, E. *Das Menschenbild des jungen Marx.* Göttingen, 1957.
de Tocqueville, A. *Democracy in America,* The World's Classics 496, trans. H. Reeve. London, 1946 (1835–40).
Topitsch, E. *Sozialphilosophie zwischen Ideologie und Wissenschaft.* Neuwied, 1961.
— *Vom Ursprung und Ende der Metaphysik: Eine Studie zur Weltanschauungskritik.* Wien, 1958.
Toulmin, S. *The Philosophy of Science: An Introduction.* London, 1953.
Trotsky, L. *The History of the Russian Revolution,* vol. iii. New York, 1932.
— *Lenin, P.* New York, 1962 (1925).
Tucker, R. C. 'The Cunning of Reason in Hegel and Marx', *The Review of Politics,* xviii (1956), 269–95.
— 'Marxism — Is it Religion?', *Ethics,* lxviii (1957–8), 125–130.
— *Philosophy and Myth in Karl Marx, P.* Cambridge, 1961.
Tyndall, J. *Fragments of Science,* vols. 1–2. London, 1889 (1881).
Vorländer, K. *Kant und Marx. Ein Beitrag zur Philosophie des Sozialismus,* Zweite Auflage. Tübingen, 1926.
— *Karl Marx. Sein Leben und Sein Werk.* Leipzig, 1928.
Warnock, G. J. *Berkeley.* The Pelican Philosophy Series, 1953.
Weiss, J. *Moses Hess: Utopian Socialist.* Detroit, 1960.
Wetter, G. A. *Dialectical Materialism: A Historical and Systematic Survey of Philosophy in the Soviet Union,* trans. P. Heath. London, 1958.
— *Die Umkehrung Hegels: Grundzüge und Ursprünge der Sowjetphilosophie.* Köln, 1963.
Whitehead, A. N. *The Concept of Nature.* Cambridge, 1920.

Windelband, W.   *A History of Philosophy*, P, trans. J. H. Tufts, vols. i–ii. New York, 1958 (1901).

Witt-Hansen, J.   *Historical Materialism.   The Method, the Theories, Book One.* Copenhagen, 1960.

Woltmann, L.   *Der historische Materialismus.   Darstellung und Kritik der marxistischen Weltanschauung.*   Düsseldorf, 1900.

Zenkovsky, V. V.   *History of Russian Philosophy*, trans. G. L. Kline, vols. i–ii.   New York, 1953.

Zhdanov, A. A.   *On Literature, Music and Philosophy.*   London, 1950.

Index of Names

As a rule, no references to the works of Hegel, Saint-Simon, Comte, Marx, Engels, Plekhanov, and Lenin, cited in the notes, are included in the Index. Notes references are listed only when they involve a substantive point.

471

Index of Subjects

PRINTED BY R. & R. CLARK, LTD. EDINBURGH